HUMAN MOTOR ACTIONS
BERNSTEIN REASSESSED

ADVANCES
IN
PSYCHOLOGY
17

Editors

G. E. STELMACH

P. A. VROON

NORTH-HOLLAND
AMSTERDAM • NEW YORK • OXFORD

HUMAN MOTOR ACTIONS
BERNSTEIN REASSESSED

Edited by

H. T. A. WHITING
Department of Psychology
Interfaculty of Human Movement Science and Education
The Free University
Amsterdam, The Netherlands

NORTH-HOLLAND
AMSTERDAM • NEW YORK • OXFORD • TOKYO

ISBN: 0 444 86813 5

First edition: 1984
Second printing: 1986

Publishers:
ELSEVIER SCIENCE PUBLISHERS B.V.
P.O. Box 1991
1000 BZ Amsterdam
The Netherlands

Sole distributors for the U.S.A. and Canada:
ELSEVIER SCIENCE PUBLISHING COMPANY, INC.
52 Vanderbilt Avenue
New York, N.Y. 10017
U.S.A.

Library of Congress Cataloging in Publication Data
Main entry under title:

Human motor actions.

    (Advances in psychology ; 17)
    Includes text of The coordination and regulation of
movements, by N. Bernstein.
    Bibliography: p.
    Includes indexes.
    1. Human mechanics--Addresses, essays, lectures.
2. Bernshteĭn, Nikolaĭ Aleksandrovich, 1896-1966.
Coordination and regulation of movements. I. Whiting,
H. T. A. (Harold Thomas Anthony), 1929-   .
II. Bernshteĭn, Nikolaĭ Aleksandrovich, 1896-1966.
Coordination and regulation of movements. 1984.
III. Series: Advances in psychology (Amsterdam,
Netherlands) ; 17.
QP303.H86 1984   612'.76   83-20523
ISBN 0-444-86813-5

PRINTED IN THE NETHERLANDS

FOREWORD

This book comprises six sections. <u>Each</u> section provides two sources of information:

a) a reproduction of <u>one</u> of the six chapters from the original English-language text:

Bernstein, N. The Co-ordination and Regulation of Movements.

Oxford: Pergamon, 1967.

b) Two <u>original</u> chapters provided by scientists from an international forum.

The sequence:

Bernstein chapter (without post script - e.g. CHAPTER I);

original contribution chapter (with post script - e.g. *CHAPTER Ia*);

original contribution chapter (with post script - e.g. *CHAPTER Ib*) is

maintained throughout each section.

The nature of the original contributions is elaborated upon in the Preface.

Apart from the correction of spelling faults, where they arise, the six chapters of Bernstein are reproduced verbatim from the original text. This means that throughout the book two different systems of referencing are used (some of the references from Bernstein also being incomplete). It was thought however better not to magnify any errors which may have arisen as a result of translation from the original German or Russian language. To help the reader further to obtain access to original sources, the complete list of references from the Bernstein book is reproduced at the end of the text.

CONTENTS

PREFACE

In 1967, Pergamon Press Ltd. (Oxford, England) published a seminal text:

The coordination and regulation of movements

which comprised a collection of the more important publications - written
between 1934 and 1962 - of the eminent Russian physiologist Nicholas Bernstein.
Unfortunately Bernstein died shortly before the appearance of that publication
but his immense influence on what he called 'the science of human movements'
lives on both through his own publications and those of his students and
devotees. The extent of his influence is reflected in the fact that it would
be unusual - even to this day - to find any important publication on movement
control and organization which did not make reference to this, the best known
English translation of his work (see for example: Arbib, 1981; Fitch & Turvey,
1978; Gallistel, 1980; Magill, 1983; Pribram, 1971; Shaw & Bransford, 1977;
Stelmach, 1976; Stelmach & Requin, 1980; Wadman, 1979).

In spite of this fact, 'The coordination and regulation of movements'
has, for the last five years, been out of print and there were no plans by
the original publishers to reprint.

It is not intended here to debate the reasons for and against such a
decision except to say that it was undoubtedly contributed to by a <u>feeling</u>
that the literature was somewhat 'dated'. However, in the light of the frequency
of its citation, it is not at all clear to what extent this label is either
meaningful or justified and in how far the position reached by Bernstein
needs to be challenged and/or modified. This interesting and important
question together with the fact that many students and scholars find it
difficult to gain access to the 1967 text, prompted the decision not only to
re-publish the original articles but, in addition, to include an evaluation
and elaboration by some of the scholars who have distinguished themselves
in the field of human movement study.

It is interesting to note that in his 1957 paper 'Some emergent problems
of the regulation of motor acts', Bernstein refers to the fact that 'during
periods of scientific quarrying, glimpses of the new ideas and general
forecasts may now be noted in the work of the older classical physiologists'
- thus recognising his indebtedness to his predecessors. In turn, in the

present text, a similar indebtedness to Bernstein is recognized for, as Reed
in his reaction to Chapter II clearly indicates, Bernstein (in this chapter)
not only produced glimpses of what today are often considered to be new ideas,
but also produced provocative analyses of 'some of the most contested issues
of contemporary movement science'. Amongst such issues would figure 'distributed
brain function', 'mass-spring models', 'phase relations in action', 'functional
hierarchies of the nervous system' and 'the role of sensory processes in motor
control'. This is only to confirm Luria's (in his introduction to Bernstein's
1967 book) contention that Bernstein 'was a man who had the remarkable gift
of penetrating into the future'.

Although generally labelled a physiologist it is clear from the breadth
and scope of his ideas that such pigeon-holing is a reflection more of his
formal training than of his conceptualization. In the papers that follow in
the present text, there are hints of the biologist, the psychologist, the
mathematician and the philosopher. It is indeed humbling to recognize so many
talents in one man. This makes not only the selection of the contributors to
this text that more difficult but also makes their task that much more complex.
It was with these considerations in mind that a team of contributors was put
together. Fortunately, to a man, they were enthusiastic about the proposal.
While one or two of the original team were unable, for personal reasons, to
complete their assignments there were fortunately others of similar stature
able to take their places.

The assignment for the contributor was twofold:
1.   To give a general evaluation of the chapter assigned to them,
2.   To indicate the way in which more recent research and thinking
      has led to the need either for a reconsideration of the ideas
      presented by Bernstein or the way in which this thinking needs to
      be extended and/or modified.

In general, contributors were asked to restrict the extent of their
contribution to a similar number of words as appeared in the chapter assigned
to them. Deviations in this respect reflect the individual wishes of the
contributors.

It was never the intention that the final text should comprise a
critique of Bernstein but that it should rather be prospective in nature.
In his chapter on the Biodynamics of Locomotion, Bernstein distinguishes

between the <u>prospective</u> approach of his own workers and the <u>retrospective</u>
approach of Fischer in the following way:

> Fischer's approach was essentially <u>retrospective</u>, that
> is, he was mainly motivated by a desire to order
> critically the basic information available on the
> mechanics of the act of walking which had been gathered
> up to his time. Our approach may be termed <u>prospective</u>
> as we were not particularly concerned with which details
> might be found to be reliable and which false in the
> work of the older authors, but attempted to provide
> a more reliable and comprehensive <u>descriptive</u> basis
> for a subsequent broad extension of investigation
> into the genesis and pathology of locomotion.

It was in this spirit, while not confining themselves to the locomotive act,
that contributors were asked to work. The extent to which they have fulfilled
their assignment is left to the reader. As editor I express my gratitude to
all the contributors for their enthusiasm and commitment. A special word of
thanks is due to Peter Greene and Curtis Boylls who had the very difficult
assignment of writing the introduction based, not only on the papers of
Bernstein but, also on the work of the other contributors.

Finally, I would like to express my gratitude to Pergamon Press for
allowing reproduction of the original text of Bernstein, to North-Holland
Publishing Co. for undertaking the publication of the present text and to
George Stelmach and Peter Vroon (editors) for allowing the text to form a
part of the series 'Advances in Psychology'. The mammoth task of typing
this very lengthy manuscript fell to my secretary Irma Reijnhout. Her skill
in this respect is attested to by the quality of the manuscript - for her
contribution I am indebted.

H.T.A. Whiting
Amsterdam, The Netherlands
July, 1983

REFERENCES

Arbib, M.A., 1981, Perceptual structures and distributed motor control. In, V.B. Brooks (Ed.), Handbook of Physiology. Maryland: The American Physiological Society.

Fitch, H.L. & M.T. Turvey, 1978. On the control of activity: Some remarks from an ecological point of view. In, D.M. Landers and R.W. Christina (Eds.), Psychology of motor behavior and sport 1977. Champaign, Ill.: Human Kinetics Publishers.

Gallistel, G.R., 1980. The organisation of action - A new synthesis. Hillsdale, N.J.: Lawrence Erlbaum Associates.

Magill, R.A., 1983. Memory and control of action. Amsterdam: North-Holland.

Pribram, K.H., 1981. Languages of the brain. New Jersey: Prentice-Hall.

Shaw, R. & J. Bransford (Eds.), 1977. Perceiving, acting and knowing. Hillsdale, N.J.: Lawrence Erlbaum Associates.

Stelmach, G.E., 1976. Motor control: Issues and trends. New York: Academic Press.

Stelmach, G.E. & J. Requin (Eds.), 1980. Tutorials in motor behavior. Amsterdam: North-Holland Publishing Company.

Wadman, W.J., 1979. Control mechanisms of fast goal-directed arm movements. Unpublished Ph.D. thesis, Faculty of Mathematics and Physics, University of Utrecht, The Netherlands.

CONTRIBUTORS

Agarwal, G.C.
Department of Industrial and Systems Engineering
University of Illinois at Chicago, P.O. Box 4348
Chicago, Illinois 60680, U.S.A.

Arbib, M.A.
Department of Computer and Information Science
University of Massachusetts
Amherst, U.S.A.

Beekman, G.J.
Department of Psychology
Interfaculty of Human Movement Science and Education
The Free University, Amsterdam
The Netherlands

Bernstein, N.
Deceased (1966)

Bonnet, M.
Department of Experimental Psychobiology
Institute of Neurophysiology and Psychophysiology
National Center for Scientific Research
Marseille, France

Boylls, C.C.
RER and D Center (153)
VA Medical Centre 3801 Miranda
Palo Alto, California 94304
U.S.A.

Gottlieb, G.L.
Department of Physiology
Rush University College of Medicine
Chicago, Illinois 60612
U.S.A.

Greene, P.H.
Department of Computer Science
Lewis College of Sciences and Letters
Illinois Institute of Technology
Chicago, Illinois 60616, U.S.A.

Hinton, G.E.

Computer Science Department
Carnegie-Mellon University
Pittsburgh, Pennsylvania 15213
U.S.A.

Kugler, P.N.

The Crump Institute for Medical Engineering
University of California
Los Angeles, California, 90024
U.S.A.

Pickenhain, L.

Holzhaüserstrasse 8
DDR-7027
Leipzig
Deutsche Demokratische Republik

Pribram, K.H.

Department of Psychology and of Psychiatry
and Behavioral Sciences, Stanford University
Stanford, California 94305
U.S.A.

Reed, E.S.

Institute for Independent Social Journalism
New York, N.Y. 10011
U.S.A.

Requin, J.

Department of Experimental Psychobiology
Institute of Neurophysiology and Psychophysiology
of CNRS
Marseille, France

Rozendal, R.H.

Department of Functional Anatomy
Interfaculty of Human Movement Science
and Education
The Free University, Amsterdam
The Netherlands

Semjen, A.

Department of Experimental Psychobiology
Institute of Neurophysiology and Psychophysiology
of CNRS
Marseille, France

Sharafat, A.   Neuropsychology Laboratories
                      Departments of Psychology and of Psychiatry and the
                      Behavioral Sciences, Stanford University,
                      Stanford 94305
                      U.S.A.

Trevarthen, C.   Department of Psychology
                      University of Edinburgh
                      Edinburgh EH8 9JZ, Scotland

Turvey, M.T.   Department of Psychology
                      The College of Liberal Arts and Sciences
                      The University of Connecticut 06268
                      Storrs, Connecticut, U.S.A.

Whiting, H.T.A.   Department of Psychology
                      Interfaculty of Human Movement Science
                      and Education,
                      The Free University, Amsterdam
                      The Netherlands

Wilberg, R.B.   School of Physical Education
                      University of Alberta
                      Edmonton, Alberta
                      Canada

Woltring, H.J.   Biomechanics Consultant
                      Craeyenbergh 42
                      NL-6611 AV Overasselt
                      The Netherlands

ACKNOWLEDGEMENTS

The editor and publishers wish to express their appreciation at being granted permission to reproduce figures, tables and/or text from the following publications:

Pergamon Press Ltd., Oxford England:
    The complete text of: Bernstein, N. The Co-ordination and regulation of movements.
and,
    Fig. 4 from: Yamashita, T. & Katoh, R. Moving pattern of point application of vertical resultant force during level walking. Journal of Biomechanics, 1976, 9, 95.

S. Karger AG, Basel:
    Fig. 2a from: New possibilities for human motion studies by real-time light spot position measurement. Biotelemetry, 1973, 1, 132-146.

Williams and Wilkins Co., Baltimore:
    Figs. 1.6, 1.12 and 3.1 from: Inman, V.T., Ralston, H.J. & Todd, F. Human walking, 1981.
and,
    the Journal of Bone & Joint Surgery (who hold the copyright) for figure 1.12 reproduced in that text.

Plenum Publishing Corporation and the authors:
    Fig. 6 from: Herman, R.M., Grillner, S., Stein, P.S.G. & Stuart, D.G. Neural control of locomotion, In, Human solutions for locomotion, 1976.

Elsevier Biomedical Press and the authors:
    Figs. 1 & 2 from: Grillner, S., Halbertsma, J., Nilsson, J. & Thorstensson, A. The adaptation to speed in human locomotion. Brain Research, 1979, 165, 177 & 179.

Springer-Verlag, Heidelberg and the authors:

Fig. 6 from: Zarrugh, M.Y., Todd, T.N. & Ralston, H.J. Optimization of energy expenditure during level walking. European Journal of Applied Psychology, 1974, 33, 301.

The Zoological Society of London and the author:

Fig. 7 from: R. McN. Alexander. Optimum walking techniques for quadrapeds and bipeds. Journal of Zoology (London), 1980, 192, 97-117.

The American Physiological Society and the author:

Fig. 3 and Table 1 from: Winter, D.A. A new definition of mechanical work done in human movement. Journal of Applied Physiology, 1979, 46, 82.

The editor and publishers also express their thanks to A.J. Verkerke (University of Technology, Twente, The Netherlands) for the measurement of certain foot reaction forces during walking and the provision of recordings of such forces which were utilised by Rozendal in reaction to Chapter III of Bernstein (Fig. 1b, p. 270 - this text).

INTRODUCTION

BERNSTEIN'S SIGNIFICANCE TODAY

C.C. Boylls, Jr., P.H. Greene

N.A. Bernstein, dead now for nearly twenty years, remains a difficult figure for many Western scientists to confront. He is often the center of an uncomfortable mythology, the predictable fate of individuals who, like Socrates, become known more through their students' accounts and accomplishments, than via their own presence. Certainly the language barrier can be blamed for some of Bernstein's remoteness. Even at this writing, the classic monograph, On the Construction of Movements (5), for which Bernstein was awarded a State price in 1947 (10), remains untranslated. However, we also have little doubt that the ill-informed prejudice of past years compromised both the development and the evaluation of Bernstein's achievements. Only one year after Bernstein received his prize, the Lysenko clique began its regency over Soviet biological science (50). Bernstein began to be "subjected to unworthy and unfounded 'criticism'..." which materially interfered with his research program (10). The early Soviet attitude toward cybernetics was also not conducive to Bernstein's thinking during much of this time (Arbib, this volume). Both in the Soviet Union and in the West, a paucity of conceptual tools for studying structure at the task level of description fostered a tendency to dismiss reports of the Soviet accomplishments, as each of us (PHG and CCB) discovered in the 1960's and early 1970's when we discussed the work of Bernstein and his colleagues (and the constructive role of the CNS in sensorimotor activities in general) with Western neuroscientists (3, 23, 24, 25, 26).

There consequently is reason, as Requin and co-workers (this volume) observe, for some to feel "guilty" about not having taken stock of Bernstein's output sooner (not to mention that of his successors). There has been room for a Bernstein "cult" to play upon such uneasiness. We feel that our task here, therefore, must in part be to demythologize Bernstein. But having done that, we believe that the result will be to leave his legacy unspent - a valuable inheritance worthy of the most responsible and diligent scientific stewardship.

Essential Bernstein: The Realization of Controllability and Observability
in Motor Tasks

In his introduction to the first English publication of the present
collection, Bernstein stressed that his was the study of motor tasks –
activities which feature not only motor performances, but also the setting
and realization of behaviorally significant goals through planning and
problem-solving. Although Bernstein clearly prided himself on the ability
of his experimental methods to examine such tasks in great detail (sometimes
amplifying error in the process (Rozendal, this volume), he also required
that such minutiae be brought back to the understanding of complete tasks
using "the widest possible synthetic grasp of experimental evidence". We
would point out that as part of this "synthetic grasp", Bernstein was quite
prepared to exploit the full scope of longitudinal, clinical, and
rehabilitative studies in a framework scarcely attempted even now.

Bernstein's emphasis upon motor tasks led him naturally to consider
both the efferent initiation of motor activity and its resulting afferential
or sensory consequences. In metaphors such as the "peripheral synapse"
(Chapter III, this volume), he forcefully argued that afferent and efferent
signals merely mediate communication between concurrent biomechanical and
neurophysiological processes that unwind in time during the course of a
motor act. This formulation of a neuro-biomechanical dynamics for a given
motor task is implicit in the taxonomic mathematics of Chapter II (this
volume). Had Bernstein left his description of task dynamics at this stage,
then his views would not have differed much from the closed-system notions
of Sechenov years earlier, or the advocates of homeostatic control (Arbib,
this volume). However, Bernstein left his task-dynamical systems open to
external "forcing functions" and parameterizations (or "tuning") supplied
by outside agencies – most notably, the resources of the CNS – and in doing
so, asked and answered questions that comprise (we believe) the essence
of his philosophy:

The first such question has become famous as the "degrees of freedom"
problem (e.g.,   71). Oftentimes this is posed in the context of the many
hundreds of muscles the nervous system is to control, and how nice it would
be if the brain had mechanisms for handling such muscles as global units with
"simple" control signals (70). Bernstein, however, originally expressed the
issue as the straightforward consequence of determining the integration
constants for the solution of the dynamical equations of motion (Chapter II,

this volume). He implied that the CNS would have to take cognizance of such constants (most likely in the form of initial conditions on the neuro-biomechanical state) in order both to calculate motor commands and to achieve predictable outcomes from their issuance. In other words, the absence of this information would render the skeletomotor system "uncontrollable"; and sensory feedback would have to be arranged minimally to make the system state "observable". With the abundance of sensory information reaching the CNS, one might consider that problem trivial. But Bernstein pointed out (Chapter II, this volume) that the mapping between, say, muscular contractile states and skeletal dynamics is not always unique (differing contractile patterns lead to the same mechanical result, and vice versa). To the extent that motor commands constitute feedback to preserve a pre-established set point, we should expect (59) them to be correlated, not with movements, but with disturbances. But Bernstein's problem surely arises in specifying efferent commands to establish conditions close to the desired set points in the first place. In the present chapters, Bernstein returns to these issues repeatedly in a variety of guises, perhaps because in his era the relationship between CNS activity and motor outcomes was thought to be determinate (Rozendal, this volume). To us it seems rather apparent that Bernstein's concern with the degrees-of-freedom problem is very much bound up in the avoidance of the uncertain, the unpredictable, and the equivocal in synthesizing motor tasks. Other interpretations (see below) came later.

Bernstein's classic solution to the degrees-of-freedom problem was to achieve both skeletomotor controllability and observability by means of constraint. In principle, this idea followed directly from his pursuit of functional relationships describing the dynamics of motor tasks in the interaction of peripheral and central agencies. The intent of constraint is to render these dynamics tractable both to observation and control. In practice, of course, the entire study of "simplifying constraints" - either biomechanical or neural - has now developed such a vitality of its own (to be dealt with shortly) that it is difficult to separate Bernstein's original notions from what has followed. We can safely say (see Chapters II and III) that Bernstein posited agencies in the CNS whose task is to establish a known dynamical regime within which particular motor tasks can be conducted. This regime is to be established in advance of the delivery of any commands for explicit movement, and is chosen "to guarantee optimal selection of conductivity" allowing delivery to the periphery of "the right impulse at the right moment" (Chapter III). Furthermore, these dynamics are to take

advantage of such biomechanical phenomena as reaction torques, and they are
to minimize the number of equivocal degrees of freedom. As to the CNS
faculties which are to effect the necessary constraints among skeletomuscular
system states, Bernstein has little to say, except that they "must operate
through quite different paths and employ quite different innervational
processes" than those used by explicit descending control signals (Chapter
III). We shall discuss the accuracy of these insights below.

In other portions of his work, Bernstein may have been considering the
further ramifications of motor activities given known dynamics by means of
active constraints. Thus, he developed at length (Requin, et al., this
volume) the notion that the brain utilizes a model of the future sensory
consequences of action in elaborating motor activity, an idea not altogether
foreign to portions of Williams James, "ideomotor" mechanism for movement
(28). He also considered the so-called "topological" representations of a
motor task, whereby invariant relationships among the elements of a task are
encoded. Both of these ideas are clearly related to the concept of a stored
recipe or function that defines a family of dynamical "flows" of the
sensorimotor state during the elaboration of a task in time. Bernstein indeed
is quite explicit at times in arguing that the complete time course of a
motor act is neurally represented as a manipulable whole (see Chapter II),
although he remains vague on mechanism. It is noteworthy that, although
present-day theorists tend to presume that hierarchical organization permits
the supervisory level to operate with less complexity than lower levels, in
Bernstein's hierarchy it appears that higher levels are at least as complex
as lower.

Bernstein is also typically associated with hierarchical theories of
motor coordination (e.g., 35). The externalized control variables and
"tunings" of his task-dynamical functions, which could be supplied by higher
levels of a motor hierarchy, lend themselves readily to that interpretation.
Bernstein often postulates (Chapters II, IV) "a series of hierarchical levels,
each of them, inevitably, having a degree of qualitative independence".
However, beyond the positing of constraint mechanisms and accounting for the
"automatization" of certain motor tasks (Chapter III; 35), it remained for
others to exploit hierarchical motor control architectures to the fullest,
as we shall presently describe.

Extensions, Modifications, and Criticisms

As we have described above, Bernstein's conception of motor task
realization is founded on the achievement of a known neuro-biomechanical
dynamics by means of a hierarchically organized system of constraints that
ameliorate the degrees-of-freedom problem. Each element of this philosophy
has undergone evaluation and development since its first prescription,
certain elements much more than others. We scarcely can deal with every such
offshoot here; but there certainly are particular trends and ramifications
that bear watching, in our opinion, as we hope now to illustrate:

(1) The status of the 'degrees of freedom' problem

So-called "endpoint" control" has handily finessed Bernstein's original
concerns about the nervous system's requirements for knowledge of the
skeletomotor state prior to the issuance of motor commands. As is well known,
this development can be traced to Feldman's utilization of the "controllable
spring" metaphor for muscle parameterization (4), which originally assigned
to the nervous system the role of positioning muscle force-length
characteristics along the length dimension, thereby storing potential energy
in the musculature. Release of this energy, via the relaxation of the
musculature to equilibrium "endpoints" governed by the balance of all static
forces, could then account for the carrying out of motor tasks independently
of initial conditions. The theory has been augmented by demonstrations that
descending spinal pathways could indeed effect the necessary endpoint
adjustments (18) and that ratios of antagonistic muscular activity could
encode movement endpoints (41). Most recently, propositions about "impedance"
or "compliance" control (33, 49) have generalized the endpoint strategy to
include the dynamics of endpoint achievement through parametric manipulations
of joint stiffness, damping, etc. (see also 17).

Bernstein, who seemed to identify the elasticity of muscle as yet another
source of dynamical uncertainty in movement programming (as in the elastically-
powered ski pole described in Chapter IV of the present volume), might
conceivably have viewed these notions as examples of "the older physiology
of rest and equilibrium" (Chapter V, present volume) that lacked the dynamics
of directed development which he favored (Chapter VI). However, it seems
likely that the theory of impedance or endpoint control will soon be recast
in terms of potential functions (with endpoints identifiable as the extrema
of such functions to be "sought", gradient-fashion, by the state of the
skeletomotor system). The realization of this formulation will then lead, we

predict, to instances where potential functions are permitted to admit system
states into their algebraic structure, thus preparing us for the "discovery"
of the bifurcations and catastrophes that may model more closely the
unidirectional, branching task-dynamics which Bernstein envisioned.

But would such developments replace Bernstein's original concerns about
the problems introduced by degrees-of-freedom in the skeletomotor system?
In one sense, the answer is "yes", since considerations of optimum effector
configurations taken within the framework of impedance control have identified
rationales for the apparently "redundant" presence of muscle that often
disturbed Bernstein. Thus, for example, it can be proved that two-joint
muscles are required in addition to one-joint muscles to program the directions
of maximum overall stiffness or free movement of a limb (33); a four-bar
linkage of near-isometric, multijoint "muscles" proves useful in minimizing
the energy utilization of legged vehicles (69, 73).

In another sense, Bernstein would probably have felt more comfortable
with experimental demonstrations that humans do sometimes attend to both
initial and in-progress conditions in the programming and retention of
motor tasks (47, 9), and that many elements of even simple task performances
are inexplicable in the simple context of endpoint control (68,72). Moreover,
as we now will see, one need only to survey recent work on skeletomotor
constraints to witness the continued relevance of the degrees-of-freedom
issue:

(2) The status of constrained skeletomotor dynamics

In the mid-1960's, as Bernstein's ideas began to be explored by a newer
generation of Soviet investigators, remarkable multijoint "synergisms" were
found to characterize the covariation of joint trajectories in a number of
basic motor tasks (e.g., postural maintenance (32); movement of wrist and
elbow (37)). While subsequent investigations have uncovered many more
instances of "neurally constrained" movement dynamics (e.g., 11, 12, 14, 39,
40, 51), they also have allowed a more systematic grouping of such constraints
according to their likely methods of implementation:

Constraints mediated by structured efference: Among students of motor
control, can there be any who have not yet heard of "muscle linkages" (7),
"synergies" (21, 20), motor "oscillators" (76), "pattern" (65) and "function"
(27) generators, and other members of the class of "coordinative structures"
(34, 71)? All these constructs describe ways in which efferent signals
correlated in space and/or time (i.e., as either an outflow vector or temporal
sequence thereof) can be employed task-specifically to constrain the actions

of groups of muscles. And to one extent or another, they all owe something
to Bernstein's dictum that ongoing movement "responds as a whole to changes
in each small part, such changes being particularly prominent in phases and
details sometimes considerably distant both spatially and temporally from
those initially encountered" (Chapter II, this volume). Each construct
additionally effects that "chunking" of the control effort (74) ostensibly
required for the hierarchical organization of task execution (described
further below).

   Constraints mediated by structured afference: Sherrington suspected
(64) and Gellhorn proved (44, 45) that the musculature assigned to particular
spinal reflexes often share in a common pool of afferent signals. In a
trivial sense, therefore, the spatial structuring of this afference applies
the constraint which creates reflexive muscular groupings. Recently, however,
the infant "motor psychophysics" that has been applied to reveal the
invariant properties of the efferent neural constraints described above has
recreated interest in an older idea about afference. Following Gibson's
postulates of "direct perception" (see (43) for details), one could propose
that the physical structure of sensory inputs (as manifested, for example,
in Euclidean visual or auditory space) can become mirrored in constraints
placed on motor outputs. An operational example of this notion may be found
in the (untenable!) mechanism proposed years ago by Pitts and McCulloch
(58) for constraining the eyeball to aim at the physical centroid of a
retinal image. We doubt that so immediate a correlation will often obtain
between sensory and motor constraints. However, the translation process
between the two (dealt with more fully later) may certainly rely upon an
appreciation of sensory structure in the form, for example, of standard
"reference orientations" of body parts (30, 67).

   Constraints mediated by structured performance criteria: The idea that
motor activity might be constrained by certain performance or "cost"
guidelines has probably occurred to almost every scholar of the subject; and
it was certainly the approach taken by Gelfand, Tsetlin, and colleagues in
their initial attempts to formalize mathematically Bernstein's constrained
dynamics (22). This work posited the existence not only of cost functionals
of the skeletomotor state, but also of mechanisms for "searching" such
functionals for their extrema. A functional could be associated with each
motor task category; and searching (which required manipulation of the motor
state) produce task execution almost as a byproduct, with dynamics constrained
both by the search method (e.g., steepest descent) and the topology of the

cost function. This seemingly roundabout formulation of dynamical constraints led to some rather strange experimental demonstrations of "searching" in both humans (1, 2, 38) and animals (77) that today look very curious indeed. However, if potential function theory and its associated gradient "searches" are used to describe neuro-biomechanical dynamics as we suggested earlier, then we may well see the resurrection of some of the earlier theoretical (and experimental?) approaches. Of course, performance criteria have also been applied in quite other ways to the understanding of motor programming, and we shall have occasion to consider certain of the results in the next section.

(3) The status of hierarchical control

Perhaps no element of Bernstein's thinking has had more impact than the hypothesis that predictable motor task dynamics result from control signals delivered to a pre-orchestrated interaction among hierarchically arranged centers of the CNS (see above). This proposition was initially applied in detail to the putative relationship between spinal and supraspinal circuitry (21, 60) and provided the rationale for numerous experimental investigations of spinal reflex "pretuning" in advance of movement (see (36) for review). It was only logical for attention then to be focussed upon the nature of the descending commands reaching these interacting spinal centers. The well-known sequence of studies on locomotion, scratching, and other spinal "automatisms" in animals resulted (54, 65). Recently, however, at least four aspects of the "traditional" Bernsteinian hierarchy have come under closer scrutiny:

Defining borders between hierarchical levels: In their "principle of least interaction", Gelfand and colleagues (21) argued that the cooperating processes of the motor task hierarchy ought to be arranged to promote maximum functional autonomy at each level, and a minimal necessity for communication among levels. This proposition accords with the release of complex behavior through a paucity of "command neurons" of the sort described for animal locomotion (29) and even complex human performances (61). Nevertheless, Bernstein himself also advanced a vague "principle of equal simplicity" (Chapter II, this volume) which appears to call for a distribution of hierarchical responsibilities based upon the partitioning of motor "task space" into regions that correspond to the (parameterized) actions of a single hierarchical level - see also the "equivalence classes" of motor function generators described by one of us (27). While such a partitioning rule also preserves the autonomy of hierarchical levels, it places no strictures on the complexity of communication between them. In that regard, then, it is interesting that recent attempts to compute optimal motor control strategies constrained either by cost functions (42) or by both cost functions and the assumption of "muscle linkages" (52) have discovered boundaries in the control space where saltatory changes in control strategy are required as a function of skeletomotor system state. Might the control regions so partitioned be construed as the domains of different hierarchical centers?

Communication among hierarchical levels: It is easy to conceive of what sorts of signals might percolate down a motor task hierarchy to the periphery; but until lately, there has been little consideration of what any returning reports might look like beyond the raw data of peripheral receptors. One worry that comes to mind is how to get different levels to understand each others' "language" while still preserving the autonomy of levels. This problem is currently being recast in terms of the "reconciliation of coordinate systems" (8). Thus, for example, the optimal spatial response axes of the semicircular canals and those of visually-driven climbing fibers do not quite coincide in the rabbit (66). But each provides information in its own "coordinates" about rotations the animal experiences (and this even ignores the differing temporal dynamics of the two systems!). How are these separate communications to be integrated into a single experience (or visuovestibular response)? One can raise similar questions about how one leg of a spinal frog is able to reach discrete areas on other legs (19), or how vestibular information is reinterpreted to account for voluntary inclinations of the head (53). Answers ranging from complex tensorial transformations (56) to the simple construction of a "transform table" in short-term memory have been directed at this problem; but we likely remain ignorant of many of the relevant phenomena. In any event, such considerations require a substantially broader view of the constraints on communication among cooperating motormanagement processes than heretofore has been the case.

The serial versus parallel activation of hierarchical levels: Hinton (this volume) proposes that we see the work of differing motor hierarchical levels primarily as the algebraic sum of their efforts. The levels work in parallel, and no level is truly out of communication with the periphery. Clearly there are many instances in which this view is quite accurate - as typified in vestibular influences on locomotion (46), optokinetic reactions (13), and eye-head coordination (6; but see 63). Still, a number of studies suggest that certain elements of human reaction-time movement are prescribed serially in time (e.g. limb selection and gross coordination versus the

explicit timing of muscle activity; (48, 62, 75)), with each such stage
depending upon the proper completion of its antecedent.

The validity of hierarchies: Despite the support given hierachies in
the preceding discussion, it may well be possible that we sometimes invoke
these artifices in lieu of more fastidious scrutiny of motor control processes
(discarding, as it were, the attention to detail and experimental confirmation
that Bernstein himself advocated). Thus, for example, Gurfinkel and his
colleagues established experimentally that the threshold of short-latency
ankle stretch reflexes was lowered during free standing relative to their
excitability in seated subjects (16). The observation fits conveniently with
a hierarchical view that allows such reflexes to "free higher centers" from
the details of equilibrium maintenance. However, these investigators then
found that not only did stretch responses not occur during the sway periods
of free standing (i.e., when the hierarchy would have them act (31)), but
that those reflexes became even more active when subjects stood with support
(i.e., when the reflexes would apparently be "unnecessary" (15)). Gurfinkel
et al. were finally drawn to the conclusion that perhaps free standing is a
task that higher hierarchical centers would like to accomplish on their own,
using the global information available to them, and without the meddling of
low-level reflex systems operating with partial information (15). Similarly,
we wonder if faculties such as spinal locomotor pattern generators exist
primarily to support hierarchical control - or instead, to "bootstrap" basic
movement patterns into a young, developing CNS that knows neither much about
movement programming, nor about the meaning of the sensory data that results
from program execution.

Conclusions

This brief survey of ours may only have compounded the history of Western
neglect of Bernstein by overlooking in turn many facets of motor task control
that his work has touched upon. We scarcely have dealt with the broad issue
of performance feedback, where observations of the necessity for integrated
trajectory measures (57) and of the correlation of efference with peripheral
disturbances (59) are very much in the spirit of Bernstein's early
observations. We have avoided completely any questions concerning the role of
experience in, say, the acquisition of neural constraints - even though
Bernstein's successors have also produced provocative results in this area
(e.g., 55). We have not considered the ontogeny of posture or locomotion.

We have only hinted at how geometrical and physical considerations can
minimize the task of intervention by higher levels of the nervous system.
But we do hope that the positive outcome of this exercise has been to
reinforce one rationale for the republication of the present reports: That
Bernstein's ideas remain a renewable resource for all attempts to understand
the physiology of human activity; and that, as was once said of the senior
programming language ALGOL, Bernstein's contributions continue to be a
significant advance over many of their successors!

REFERENCES

1. Aizerman, M.A. & Andreeva, E.A. Simple search mechanism for control of skeletal muscles. Automat. Rem. Control, 1968, 29, 452-463.

2. Andreeva, E.A., Turakhanov, K.A., Khutorskaya, O.E. & Chernov, V.I. Connection between joint tremor and the joint angle control process. Automat. Rem. Control, 1969, 30, 1988-1993.

3. Arbib, M.A., Boylls, C.C. & Dev, P. Neural models of spatial perception and the control of movement. In, W.D. Keidel (Ed.), Cybernetics and Bionics. Munich: Oldenbourgh, 1974.

4. Asatryan, D.G. & Feldman, A.G. Functional tuning of nervous system with control of movement or maintenance of a steady procedure. I. Mechanographic analysis of the work of the joint on execution of a postural task. Biophysics, 1965, 10, 925-935.

5. Bernstein, N.A. On the Construction of Movements (In Russian). Moscow: Medgiz, 1947.

6. Bizzi, E., Kalil, R.E. & Tagliasco, V. Eye-head coordination in monkeys: Evidence for centrally patterned organization. Science, 1971, 173, 452-454.

7. Boylls, C.C. A theory of cerebellar function with applications to locomotion. II. The relation of anterior lobe climbing fiber function to locomotor behavior in the cat. COINS Technical Report 76-1, Department of Computer & Information Sciences. University of Massachusetts, Amherst, 1976.

8. Boylls, C.C. Climbing fibers and the spatial reference frame for motor coordination. In, M.A. Arbib (Ed.), Proceedings of the Workshop on Visuomotor Coordination in Frog and Toad: Models and Experiments, COINS Technical Report 82-16, Computer and Information Science. University of Massachusetts, Amherst, MA, 1982.

9. Capaday, C. & Cooke, J.D. The effects of muscle vibration on the attainment of intended final position during voluntary human arm movements. Experimental Brain Research, 1981, 42, 228-230.

10. Chkhaidze, L.V. Scientific legacy of N.A. Bernstein. Biophysics, 1967, 12, 203-205.

11. Cohen, L. Interaction between limbs during bimanual voluntary activity. Brain, 1970, 93, 259-272.

12. Cohen, L. Synchronous bimanual movements performed by homologous and non-homologous muscles. Perceptual and Motor Skills, 1971, 32, 639-644.

13. Collewijn, H. The Oculomotor System of the Rabbit and Its Elasticity. New York: Springer-Verlag, 1981.

14. Elner, A.N. Possibilities of correcting the urgent voluntary movements and the associated postural activity of human muscles. Biophysics, 1973, 18, 966-971.

15. Elner, A.M., Gurfinkel, V.S., Lipshits, M.I., Mamasakhlisov, G.V. & Popov, K.E. Facilitation of stretch reflex by additional support during quiet stance. Agressologie, 1976, 17, 15-20.

16. Elner, A.M., Popov, K.E. & Gurfinkel, V.S. Changes in stretch-reflex system concerned with the control of postural activity of human muscles. Agressologie, 1972, 13, 19-24.

17. Feldman, A.G. & Latash, M.L. Interaction of afferent and efferent signals underlying joint position sense: Empirical and theoretical approaches. Journal of Motor Behavior, 1982, 14, 174-193.

18. Feldman, A.G. & Orlovsky, G.N. The influence of different descending systems on the tonic stretch reflex in the cat. Experimental Neurology, 1972, 37, 481-494.

19. Fukson, O.I., Berkinblit, M.B. & Feldman, A.G. The spinal frog takes into account the scheme of its body during the wiping reflex. Science, 1980, 209, 1261-1263.

20. Ganor, I., Golani, I. Coordination and integration in the hindleg step cycle of the rat: kinematic synergies. Brain Research, 1980, 195, 57-67.

21. Gelfand, I.M., Gurfinkel, V.S., Tsetlin, M.L. & Shik, M.L. Some problems in the analysis of movements. In, I.M. Gelfand, V.S. Gurfinkel, S.V. Fromin and M.L. Tsetlin (Eds.), Models of the Structural-Functional Organization of Certain Biological Systems (translated by C.R. Beard). Cambridge, MA: MIT Press, 1971.

22. Gelfand, I.M. & Tsetlin, M.L. Mathematical modeling of mechanisms of the central nervous system. In, I.M. Gelfand, V.S. Gurfinkel, S.V. Fomin and M.L. Tsetlin (Eds.), Models of the Structural-Functional Organization of Certain Biological Systems (translated by C.R. Beard). Cambridge, MA: MIT Press, 1971.

23. Greene, P.H. An approach to computers that perceive, learn, and reason. Proceedings of the Western Joint Computer Conference, San Francisco, 1959, 181-186.

24. Greene, P.H. New problems in adaptive control. In, J.T. Tou and R.H. Wilcox (Eds.), Computer and Information Sciences. Washington: Spartan Press, 1964.

25. Greene, P.H. Models for perception and action. Proceedings of the First
    Annual Princeton Symposium on Information Sciences and Systems,
    Electrical Engineering Department, Princeton University, 1967, 245-
    253.

26. Greene, P.H. Seeking mathematical models for skilled actions. In,
    D. Bootzin and H.C. Muffley (Eds.), Biomechanics (Proceedings of the
    First Rock Island Arsenal Biomechanics Symposium, 1967. New York:
    Plenum Press, 1969.

27. Greene, P.H. Strategies for Heterarchical Control. I. A style for
    controlling complex systems. II. Theoretical exploration of a style
    of control. Technical Reports 77-7 and 77-8, Computer Science
    Department, Illinois Institute of Technology, 1975.

28. Greenwald, A.G. Sensory feedback mechanisms in performance control:
    with special reference to the ideo-motor mechanism. Psychological
    Review, 1970, 77, 73-99.

29. Grillner, S. & Shik, M.L. On the descending control of the lumbosacral
    spinal cord from the mesencephalic locomotor region. Acta Physiologica
    Scandinavica, 1973, 87, 320-333.

30. Gross, Y., Webb, R. & Melzack, R. Central and peripheral contributions
    to localization of body parts: Evidence for a central body schema.
    Experimental Neurology, 1974, 44, 346-362.

31. Gurfinkel, V.S. Muscle afferentation and postural control in man.
    Agressologie, 1973, 14, 1-8.

32. Gurfinkel, V.S., Kots, Y.M., Paltsev, Y.I. & Feldman, A.G. The
    compensation of respiratory disturbances of the erect posture of man
    as an example of the organization of interarticular interactions.
    In, I.M. Gelfand, V.S. Gurfinkel, S.V. Fomin and M.L. Tsetlin (Eds.),
    Models of the Structural-Functional Organization of Certain
    Biological Systems. Cambridge, MA: MIT Press, 1971.

33. Hogan, N. Mechanical impedance control in assistive devices and
    manipulators. In, M. Brady, J.M. Hollerbach, T.L. Johnson and T.
    Lozano-Pérez (Eds.), Robot Motion: Planning and Control. Cambridge,
    MA: MIT Press, 1982.

34. Kelso, J.A.S., Southard, D.L. & Goodman, D. On the nature of human
    interlimb coordination. Science, 1979, 203, 1029-1031.

35. Kohout, L.J. Representation of functional hierarchies of movement in the
    brain. International Journal of Man-Machine Studies, 1976, 8, 699-
    709.

36. Kots, Y.M. The Organization of Voluntary Movement. New York: Plenum Press, 1977.

37. Kots, Y.M. & Syrovegin, A.V. Fixed set of variants of interaction of the muscles of two joints used in the execution of simple voluntary movements. Biophysics, 1966, 11, 1212-1219.

38. Krinsky, V.I. & Shik, M.L. Single model motor task. Biophysics, 1964, 9, 661-666.

39. Kulagin, A.S. & Shik, M.L. Interaction of symmetrical limbs during controlled locomotion. Biophysics, 1970, 15, 171-178.

40. Lacquaniti, F. & Soechting, J.F. Coordination of arm and wrist motion during a reaching task. Journal of Neurosciences, 1982, 2, 399-408.

41. Lestienne, F., Polit, A. & Bizzi, E. Functional organization of the motor process underlying the transition from movement to posture. Brain Research, 1981, 230, 121-131.

42. Levine, W.S., Christodoulou, M. & Zajac, F.E. On propeling a rod to a maximum vertical or horizontal distance. Automatica, 1983, 19, 321-324.

43. Lishman, J.R. Vision and the optic flow field. Nature, 1981, 293, 263-264.

44. Loofbourrow, G.N. & Gellhorn, E. Proprioceptively induced reflex patterns. American Journal of Physiology, 1948, 154, 433-438.

45. Loofbourrow, G.N. & Gellhorn, E. Proprioceptive modification of reflex patterns. Journal of Neurophysiology, 1949, 12, 435-446.

46. Lundberg, A. & Phillips, C.G.T. Graham Brown's film on locomotion in the decerebrate cat. Journal of Physiology (London), 1973, 231, 90P-91P.

47. Marteniuk, R.G., Shields, K.W. & Campbell, S. Amplitude, position, timing and velocity as cues in reproduction of movement. Perception and Motor Skills, 1972, 35, 51-58.

48. Marteniuk, R.G. & MacKenzie, C.L. A preliminary theory of two-hand co-ordinated control. In, G.E. Stelmach and J. Requin (Eds.), Tutorials in Motor Behavior. Amsterdam: Elsevier/North-Holland, 1980.

49. Mason, M. Compliance. In, M. Brady, J.M. Hollerbach, T.L. Johnson and T. Lozano-Pérez (Eds.), Robot Motion: Planning and Control. Cambridge, MA: MIT Press, 1982.

50. Medvedev, Z.A. The Rise and Fall of T.D. Lysenko. Garden City, NY: Doubleday, 1971.

51. Nashner, L.M. Fixed patterns of rapid postural responses among leg
    muscles during stance. Experimental Brain Research, 1977, 30, 13-24.

52. Nashner, L.M. & McCollum, G. The organization of human postural
    movements: A conceptual basis and experimental approach. Brain and
    Behavioral Sciences, 1983 (to appear).

53. Nashner, L.M. & Wolfson, P. Influence of head position and proprioceptive
    cues on short latency postural reflexes evoked by galvanic stimulation
    of the human labyrinth. Brain Research, 1974, 67, 255-268.

54. Orlovsky, G.N. & Shik, M.L. Control of locomotion: a neurophysiological
    analysis of the cat locomotor system. In, R. Porter (Ed.),
    Neurophysiology II, International Review of Physiology, 1976, 10,
    281-317.

55. Paltsev, Y.I. Functional reorganization of the interaction of the spinal
    structure in connection with the execution of voluntary movement.
    Biophysics, 1967, 12, 313-322.

56. Pellionisz, A. & Llinas, R. Tensorial approach to the geometry of brain
    function: Cerebellar coordination via a metric tensor. Neuroscience,
    1980, 5, 1125-1136.

57. Pew, R.W. Levels of analysis in motor control. Brain Research, 1974, 71,
    393-400.

58. Pitts, W.H. & McCulloch, W.S. How we know universals: The perception
    of auditory and visual forms. Bulletin of Mathematical Biophysics,
    1947, 9, 127-147.

59. Powers, W.T. The nature of robots. Byte, 1979, 4, no. 6, 132-144, no. 7,
    134-152, no. 8, 94-116, no. 9, 96-112.

60. Pyatestsky-Shapiro, I.I. & Shik, M.L. Spinal regulation of movement.
    Biophysics, 1964, 9, 525-530.

61. Rosenbaum, D.A. Selective adaptation of 'command neurons' in the human
    motor system. Neuropsychologia, 1977, 15, 81-91.

62. Rosenbaum, D.A. Human movement initiation: Specification of arm,
    direction, and extent. Journal of Experimental Psychology, 1980, 109,
    444-474.

63. Roucoux, A. & Crommelinck, M. Eye and head fixation movements: Their
    coordination and control. In, G.E. Stelmach and J. Requin (Eds.),
    Tutorials in Motor Behavior. Amsterdam: Elsevier/North-Holland, 1980.

64. Sherrington, C.S. Flexion-reflex of the limb, crossed extension-reflex,
    and reflex stepping and standing. Journal of Physiology (London),
    1910, 40, 28-121.

65. Shik, M.L. & Orlovskii, G.N. Neurophysiology of locomotor automatism. Physiological Review, 1976, 56, 465-501.

66. Simpson, J.I., Graf, W. & Leonard, C. The coordinate system of visual climbing fibers to the flocculus. In, A. Fuchs and W. Becker (Eds.), Progress in Oculomotor Research. Amsterdam: Elsevier/North-Holland, 1981.

67. Soechting, J.F. Does position sense at the elbow reflect a sense of elbow joint angle or one of limb orientation? Brain Research, 1982, 248, 392-395.

68. Soechting, J.F. & Lacquaniti, F. Invariant characteristics of a pointing movement in man. Journal of Neuroscience, 1981, 1, 710-720.

69. Song, S.M., Vohnout, V.J., Waldron, K.J. & Kinzel, G.L. Computer-aided design of a leg for an energy-efficient walking machine. Proceedings of the 7th Applied Mechanisms Conference (Kansas City, MO), 1981. (To appear in Mechanism and Machine Theory).

70. Tomovic, R. & Bellman, R. A systems approach to muscle control. Mathematical Biosciences, 1970, 8, 265-277.

71. Turvey, M.T., Fitch, H.L. & Tuller, B. The Bernstein perspective: I. The problems of degrees of freedom and contex-conditioned variability. In, J.A.S. Kelso (Ed.), Human Motor Behavior: An Introduction. Hillsdale, NJ: Lawrence Erlbaum Associates, 1982.

72. Viviani, P. & Terzuolo, C. Trajectory determines movement dynamics. Neuroscience, 1982, 7, 431-437.

73. Waldron, K.L. & Kinzel, G.L. The relationship between actuator geometry and mechanical efficiency in robots. Proceedings of the 4th CISM-IFTOMM Symposium on Theory and Practice of Robots and Manipulators (Zaborow, Poland), 1981. (Elsevier, to appear).

74. Welford, A.T. On the sequencing of action. Brain Research, 1974, 71, 381-392.

75. Wing, A.M. Timing and co-ordination of repetitive bimanual movements. Quarterly Journal of Experimental Psychology, 1982, 34A, 339-348.

76. Yamanishi, J., Kawato, M. & Suzuki, R. Two coupled oscillators as a model for the coordinated finger tapping by both hands. Biological Cybernetics, 1980, 37, 219-225.

77. Zakharova, L.M. & Litvintsev, A.I. Search activity of muscle enclosed by artificial feedback loop. Automat. Rem. Control, 1966, 27, 1942-1950.

SECTION 1

CHAPTER 1

THE TECHNIQUES OF THE STUDY OF MOVEMENTS

N. Bernstein

(Published in *Textbook of the Physiology of Work* , edited by G. Conradi,
V. Farfel and A. Slonim, Moscow, 1934)

1.   THE CINEMATOGRAPHIC STUDY OF MOVEMENTS

Human movements have long been of great interest to investigators.
Attempts have been made to observe and measure them for a considerable time.
In the beginning of the 19th century the brothers Weber (76) carried out an
extensive study of walking, employing the primitive observational techniques
of their period - measuring lines and diopters. However, the rapid sequential
patterns of human movements would have made precise observation unattainable
if special opportunities had not arisen; these opportunities could be
realized by the experimenter only with the development of instantaneous
photography in the sixties of the 19th century. It was at just this time
that energetic attempts to decipher the physiological mechanisms of human
motor skills were begun; the end of the 19th century is marked in our field
by such outstanding studies as those of Muybridge in the United States,
Marey in France, and Braune and Fischer in Germany. The methodological
innovations of the first two authors form the basis of later developments in
cinematography; the last two authors laid the foundations of rigorously
scientific quantitative investigation of movements with the help of photography.

It is not necessary in our own time to prove the value of cinematography
as a technique for the study of movements; it provides an opportunity to
record and to fix the rapidly interchanging phases of live movements in
order to subsequently analyse them with any required degree of accuracy.
Figure 1 presents a series of successive phases of fast running by a human
being, taken by synchronizing two cameras from separate view points. These
photographs were taken by Muybridge in 1887 and are evidence of the high
technical level attained by this forefather of cinematography.

It can be seen in Fig. 1 that the right leg later assumes the position
which was earlier occupied by the left leg in the sixth frame; there is a
correspondence, for example, between frames 1 and 7, 2 and 8, and so on. In

this way a single step is spread out over 6 frames. This corresponds, in
the given series, to a frequency of 24 frames per sec; during this period
of time the subject could accomplish 4 single steps. For comparison we may
observe that in contemporary cinematography the standard frequencies are
16 frames per sec for silent films, and 24 frames per sec for films with a
sound track. At the present time high-speed cameras have shutter speeds of
160, 400 and even 1500 frames per sec. A single step of Muybridge's run
would be broken down by these later cameras (Zeiss system) into 375 separate
frames.

It may be easily be imagined what occurs if motion-picture films exposed
in high-speed processes are projected through conventional cinematographic
equipment. Four hundred frames taken by a high-speed camera in 1 sec may be
run through a projector which operates at 16 frames per sec over the period
400/16 = 25 sec; consequently, we may examine on the screen events
photographed in the course of a single second. The time is increased, as it
were, by a factor of 25; the term 'time magnification' which has been
applied to high-speed cameras can be justified in this way. Events which
take place quickly in nature can be made many times slower, permitting
leisurely examination of all their temporal details. Bernstein and Dement'ev
(17) have constructed a special motion-picture projector allowing smooth
projection on a screen at a frequency of 4-5 images per sec, that is, one-
third or one-fourth as fast as the normal projection rate. This technique
allows an increase in the augmentational effect of time magnification and
it is possible, for example, to examine the high-speed camera photographs
referred to above with a time augmentation of 400/4 = 100 times.

2.   CYCLOGRAPHY- THE PLANAR PROJECTION OF MOVEMENTS

Marey introduced another method which, after numerous improvements of
his basic idea, has come to occupy an unconditionally predominant place in
the study of movement. Separate, independent cinematographic exposures
illustrate every phase of a movement excellently but they do not give a
direct representation of the interrelations between successive phases. In
the photographs in Fig. 1 there are positions but not movements. It cannot
be seen from them in what direction or with what velocity any given joint
of the body is moving at the moment when a single exposure is made. These
elements of a movement, its direction and velocity, are clearly visible by
projection of the film on a screen but they can still only be observed by
the naked eye and not by means of measuring instruments. Cine-film reproduces

the movement in its entirety, but fixes in a form convenient for scientific measurement merely positions and isolated phases. Marey's idea consisted in recording on the photograph all the dynamic changes in the phases of the movement.

In order to achieve this, Marey isolated from the rest of the subject's body narrow strips on the long axes of the limbs and made them luminous while keeping the rest of the subject's body black so as not to record on the photographic emulsion (Fig. 2). He then photographed the subject, in this clothing, many times on a single plate in the course of making a movement (Fig. 3). As a result multiple images were obtained - chronophotography - providing a perfect opportunity to measure the directions and velocities of movements of particular points of the body. Braune and Fischer improved this technique by replacing Marey's tapes with Geisler tubes which provided intermittent light at intervals of 26 per sec. A photograph of walking taken by Braune and Fischer is given in Fig. 4.

Marey's school (Bulle, Gastine) replaced the tapes by points; in order to do this they fixed miniature incandescent bulbs to the points of the body under investigation. This alteration in technique, as adopted by American (Gilbreth, Townsend) and German (Thun) investigators, was termed cyclography. The Moscow School of Biometrics developed the cyclographic technique to a high degree in comparison with the forms in which it was employed in the West; for this reason the most useful approach will be to describe the current status of cyclography in terms of the studies carried out by this school. A typical cyclogram of walking is given in Fig. 5.

Small electric bulbs (Fig. 6) are fixed at the points of the subject's body that are to be photographed. If necessary, flashlight bulbs may be used for the light (Fig. 6(c)), but tiny gas-filled bulbs (Fig. 6(b)) with a spiral filament, as prepared by F. Wolf in Berlin for Bernstein's project, are more suitable and provide ideal point representations because their filaments are only 1 mm in length. The bulbs are most frequently fixed over the centres of joints. The current (at a potential of 3-5 V) is led to the bulbs through thin flex from a belt worn by the subject; it is led to the latter through thin six-stand flex-a 'tail'-20-80m long, and thus not interfering with any movements, even running, which is connected to the experimenter's distribution board. It is also possible to supply the bulbs from dry batteries worn by the subject, but then they cannot be controlled from a distance, and it is often very important.

A cyclogram of uncomplicated movements (e.g. walking or running) is

recorded on a fixed plate in a standard camera. If the subject carries out
a movement in front of the camera with bulbs lit when the lens is uncovered,
the displacement of each bulb will be represented on the photograph by a
single continuous curve. In order to break down the image of the movement
into distinct successive phases - to obtain a chronogram - the exposure is
made through a rapidly rotating shutter (an interrupter, Fig. 7) which covers
the lens for very brief periods at equal intervals some tens or hundred times
a second. When the lens shutter is open the light from all the bulbs falls
simultaneously on the plate and then is immediately blocked out when the lens
is again covered. For this reason all the dots (Fig. 5) into which the
rotating shutter breaks the different traces of the bulb trajectories
correspond closely to each other in time. If points from adjacent trajectories
which correspond to each other in time are joined by straight lines, schemata
of successive positions of the movement are obtained which are exactly similar
to the chronophotographs of Marey and Fischer (Fig. 8; see also Fig. 27(a)).
With the help of a rotating shutter it is easy to obtain frequencies of up
to 600 per sec, i.e. higher than are given by Debri's high-speed camera; it
is difficult to operate faster than this frequency as the points of the
trajectory then begin to merge into each other. We will not touch here on
auxiliary techniques employed for more reliable identification of
corresponding points of merging trajectories.

Exact measurement of the frequencies given by the rotating shutter is
essential for the quantitative study of movements. A siren device employed
by the Moscow school is very useful in this respect, the technique being
based on determination of the frequency of a tone emitted by a siren located
on the shutter and rotating with it. This device, with a series of auxiliary
devices, permits accuracy within a fraction of one per cent in the
determination of frequencies. Mukhin's technique, employing the characteristics
of neon bulbs, is even more accurate. Bernstein's measuring device, called a
strobometer, is constructed on this principle and consists of an accurately
calibrated electromagnetic tuning-fork, a low frequency amplifier and a neon
bulb. Oscillations of the tuning-fork are amplified and control the neon bulb
which goes on and off in synchrony with the oscillations. The bulb illuminates
a small circle of concentric asterisks fixed on the axis of the rotating
shutter. If the rotation speed is regulated with a rheostat so that the
asterisk intermittently illuminated by the neon bulb appears to be motionless,
the speed wil be exactly syncronous with the oscillations of the tuning-fork.
It is possible to calibrate it within some thousandths of one per cent with

this apparatus. The advantage of Mukhin's method over the siren lies in the
fact that several rotating shutters may be very accurately synchronized so
as to work together, that is to say, the movement may be studied from
different angles with several cameras. The action of the shutter may be
rendered even more accurate if a frequency stabilizer with a Lacour wheel is
coupled to the drive motor. The low frequency source for these stabilizers
may be obtained from a sound-frequency oscillatory circuit with a subsequent
stage of amplification.

Cyclography, in the form just described, is a poor device for the
investigation of cyclical overlapping movements – to which category the
majority of industrial processes belong: in movements of this type the images
of the trajectories of the bulbs on a stationary plate appear as overlapping
undifferentiable tangles. In order to overcome this inadequacy in cyclography
Bernstein introduced kymocyclography (12), i.e. cyclographical exposures on
slowly and evenly moving photographic film. The traces of rapid repetitive
movements are resolved on the film by this technique into wave-like curves
(Fig. 9) which are always easy to decipher. Taking the movement of the film
into consideration (this can be done by means of very simple devices) and
excluding it in calculations the observer can arrive at just as accurate
and reliable data on the duration of movements from the curves obtained on
the film as is available for the simplest movements from standard cyclograms.

3.   STEROSCOPIC RECORDING OF MOVEMENTS

Both cyclography and kymocyclography give, in the applications described
above, only the planar projection of the movement photographed. In order to
examine movements in depth one must turn to complex observations. The
displacement of any object in space, in other words changes in all three
spatial coordinates of an object, must be recorded by observation from no
fewer than two different points of view. Braune and Fischer photographed
walking from 4 points simultaneously with separate independent cameras.
Nowadays many investigators rely chiefly on stereoscopic cameras, i.e.
cameras with two lenses with parallel optical axes. It is, however, easy to
show that the accuracy of determination of the coordinate of depth is greater,
the further apart are the two points of observation, in our case of both
stereoscopic lenses. In standard stereoscopic cameras the lenses are 6.5 cm
apart and the accuracy of measurement of the coordinate of depth is very low.
It is necessary to separate the stereoscopic lenses a greater distance of
the order of tens of centimetres. This separation results in gross differences

in the fields of view of both cameras with parallel optical axes of the
lenses. For this reason it is more convenient to photograph the movements
with two cameras, and with the optical axes of the lenses convergent rather
than parallel. This type of apparatus was employed by Drill (36). For
synchrony this author set the shutters of two cameras placed at some distance
from each other on the same long axis. The Moscow biomechanic school selected
another technique which is incomparably more accurate and convenient. The
mirror method developed by the author (16, 18) allows one to obtain two
distinct points of view with a single camera and thus only a single rotating
shutter.

For this purpose a large plane mirror is placed in the field of view of
a camera at a given angle to its optical axis. The mirror is set so that the
moving object to be studied is visible twice in the field of vision of the
camera, (a) directly and (b) reflected in the mirror (Fig. 10). The mirror
replaces the second, distant point of view. If, for example, it is placed at
an angle of 45° to the main optical axis of the objective, then the accuracy
obtained is equivalent to the accuracy for convergent photographs with two
cameras separated by twice the distance of the camera from the mirror.
Strictly speaking, the accuracy of the photograph with the mirror is still
higher as here we need not worry about either the perfect matching of two
lenses or the careful alignment of their two main axes which is of decisive
importance for photography with two convergent cameras.

Material obtained with the help of mirror kymocyclography is in a class
of its own in comparison with the accuracy which may be obtained by means of
other existing techniques of recording movements. Kymocyclography allows one
to obtain several hundred phases of a moment in a second, while measurement
of the time intervals between successive phases may be carried out with the
help of a strobometer with an accuracy of within one millionth of a second.
Skilfully, taken mirror kymocyclograms also give excellent spatial accuracy,
to within not less than 1 mm on any of three mirror coordinates. However,
the most important advantage of the technique just described in the most
general terms lies in the ease with which the material obtained in this way
can be subjected to quantitative analysis and to mechanical interpretation.
Photographic registration of movements is in no way the final aim of
investigation but merely its raw data, and thus permits an approach to the
real goal of investigation - physiological and biomechanical analysis of the
processes of movement.

Methods of Analysis of the Cyclogram. To decipher a cyclogram it is necessary in the first place to measure the photograph of the movement which we have obtained. It is exceedingly difficult to measure the positions of the cyclographic points directly on the photographic plate or film; moreover, such a process would in this case be very inaccurate. Fischer measured his negatives under a special microscope which is also inconvenient and insufficiently accurate because of the small field of view of the lens. The Moscow biomechanicians employ for this purpose a process of photographic measurement suggested by Lavrentiev. Cyclographical or kymocyclographical negatives are greatly enlarged, and during this process a millimetre or even a half-millimetre grid is transferred to the paper by the same photographic process. Then it is easy to calculate the coordinates of all cyclographical points with a high degree of accuracy (Fig. 11). These coordinates are the basic raw material to obtain which all the techniques that have been described above are necessary, and from the analysis of which it is now possible to extract the maximum available amount of information about the process of the movement which has been photographed. The inadequacy of the cinematographic method lies in the facts that it is considerably more difficult to obtain these coordinates from a moving-picture film and that the degree of accuracy which can be attained is much lower.

All the cyclographical devices and procedures which have been described in this chapter have perforce been treated very briefly and superficially. The reader who wishes to acquaint himself more thoroughly with cyclogram-metrical processes may refer to Refs. 12, 16 and 18.

First of all it is necessary to establish from the coordinates obtained the successive positions in space occupied by the joints of the body from moment to moment during the time over which the cyclographical exposure was made (see Figs. 22 and 23(a)). Once a graph of these successive positions has been obtained, it is easy to measure the angles of articulation, repeating the process for all variations with their gradual changes. The coordinate data obtained from mirror kymocyclograms allow one to obtain all required projections of the successive stages of the movement under observation: to 'see' it from behind, from the side and from above. This type of observation gives information about the whole extent or range of movements, the amplitudes of movements of particular points of the body, the limits of the changes of the angles of articulation, the distribution of the trajectories of the movements in relation to surrounding objects and the forms of these trajectories. The value and the practical importance of information of this type does not require further emphasis.

Changes in one of the coordinates of movements in time may be
represented in the form of a curve. Such a curve describes with particular
clarity the characteristic peculiarities of movements, their differences
from other similar movements, symptoms of fatigue which appear in them, and
so forth. These features are expressed more clearly in curves of changes in
velocity of the movements which may also be obtained by very simple methods
from data on the coordinates of movements. Curves of the angular velocities
of the movements of joints may also be obtained with the help of simple
techniques.

Analysis of the forces which produce a given movement is of great and
sometimes decisive importance. The first steps towards the description of
these forces by means of chronophotograms were made by Braune and Fischer
who indicated the way in which calculations of this type might be made. It
is impossible to obtain direct data on these forces from chronophotographs
or cyclograms. However, from these, and especially from the velocity curves
which have just been mentioned, it is possible to obtain information on the
acceleration of one or another point of the body. The dynamic forces are
calculated by multiplication of the accelerations by the masses of the parts
of the body undergoing acceleration. As will be apparent from the subsequent
discussion, analysis of the forces producing movements and juxtaposition
of these force data with data about the movements produced by operation of
these forces gives a clear insight into the biomechanical and physiological
characteristics of the processes of movement. The reader will see this for
himself from the examples to be presented later.

4. MASSES AND CENTRES OF GRAVITY OF THE LIMBS OF THE HUMAN BODY

It is clear from the preceding discussion that it is possible to
describe the work done by the skeletal musculature only if we have precise
knowledge of the masses of the limbs of the human body and of the locations
of their centres of gravity. Until recently this aspect of the problem was
one of the most obscure in anatomy, and it is only now that an extensive
investigation carried out by the author of this paper and his colleagues
has in some degree begun to illuminate the problem of distribution of mass.

Two investigations of the problem indicated above are available in the
literature; these are studies by Harless and by Braune and Fischer. These
investigators employed the technique of dissection of frozen cadavers,
following which the separate limbs were weighed and their centres of gravity
determined by one of the methods of elementary mechanics. The number of

cadavers used was extremely small; Braune and Fischer used 3 or 5 (the authors statements are contradictory), and the number used by Harless is unknown. The cadavers were those of adult males; there is no indication of their ages or physiques. The figures obtained from both studies are mean values without any indication of variation, and they differ significantly from each other (Tables 1 and 2).

It is already clear from the data presented here in brief that the material is inadequate. It is impossible to determine the most important facts of all - in what way these figures may be applied to a given individual and in what ways they may vary for persons of different sex, ag

TABLE 1. RELATIVE MASSES OF THE LIMBS
(MASS OF THE ENTIRE BODY = 1)

	Fischer	Harless
Head	0.0706	0.0712
Upper arm	0.0336	0.0324
Forearm	0.0228	0.0181
Hand	0.0084	0.0084
Thigh	0.1156	0.1118
Lower leg	0.0527	0.0439
Foot	0.0179	0.0183
Trunk	0.4270	0.4630

TABLE 2. THE DISTANCES OF THE CENTRES
OF GRAVITY OF THE LIMBS FROM
THE PROXIMAL JOINT (LENGTH OF
LIMB = 1)

	Fischer	Harless
Thigh	0.44	0.467
Lower leg	0.42	0.36
Upper arm	0.47	0.485
Forearm	0.42	0.44

and body structure. Finally, they beg the most important question of all –
to what extent the relationships that hold true for cadavers are
characteristic of live subjects.

  The primary obstacle to experimental analysis of all these questions
has until recently been the complete absence of methods which would permit
the necessary measurements to be made on living subjects. It appeared to be
an impossible business to weigh a living human being, as it were, piecemeal.
It was only after the author of this paper together with O. Salzgeber and
P. Pavlenko solved experimentally the auxiliary problems which were most
important for this purpose that it was possible to proceed to the study of
the weights and the centres of gravity of the limbs of living subjects by
employing the ideas of Scheidt and Hebestreit. It is impossible to present
in this chapter even a brief account of the complicated and delicate method
employed by the author and his colleagues for measurements of his type. It
can only be said that the problem is ultimately related to the planimetric
measurements of the volumes and volume moments of the limbs of the body and
to the weighing of the subject in numerous carefully determined controlled
positions on special twin-support scales (see Fig. 12). From analyses of the
figures obtained in this way and by comparison with data obtained from the
most accurate microscopic examination of photographic plates of the
positions assumed during the weighing, data on the locations of the centres
of gravity of the limbs and on their masses could be obtained.

  An analysis was undertaken of material obtained from 152 subjects of
both sexes with an age range of 10-75 years. This study did not include
investigation of the locations of the centres of gravity of head, hands or
feet such as were determined by Braune and Fischer; rather, we investigated
the locations of the centres of gravity of the upper arm, forearm, thigh
and lower leg and the masses of all the major limbs of the body. The
locations of the centres of gravity of the trunk and of the body as a whole
were also included in the program of investigation.

  I append below some of the data from the results we have obtained.

  The mean values of the radii of the centres of gravity of the long
limbs appeared to be much closer to those obtained by Fischer than to those
by Harless (I term as the radius of the centre of gravity the distance from
the centre of gravity to the centre of the proximal joint with the length
of the limb taken as a unit). We may recall that Fischer's material was
obtained on 3-5 subjects, while our material provides information on about
150 persons; because of this the reliability of the present data is many

times greater than that of the old figures. I append a list of the means we
obtained for comparison with those obtained by Fischer (Table 3).

TABLE 3. THE RADII OF THE CENTRE OF GRAVITY

	From our data		According to Fischer
	Mean value	Mean square deviation	
Thigh	0.3880	± 0.0332	0.44
Lower leg	0.4175	± 0.0224	0.42
Upper arm	0.4746	± 0.0338	0.47
Forearm	0.4145	± 0.0309	0.42

In the material as a whole, therefore, only in the case of the thigh
does a significant difference from the position determined by Fischer occur,
but the second column of figures in Table 3 is of much greater importance
indicating that the spread of the data, in other words the variation, is
considerable. If we take the mean square deviation as a measure of the
variation, it appears that the overwhelming majority of cases fall between
the following limits.

Thigh	0.3548 - 0.4212
Lower leg	0.3951 - 0.4399
Upper arm	0.4408 - 0.5084
Forearm	0.3836 - 0.4454

These variations are comparatively insignificant. The deviations found

TABLE 4. RADII OF THE CENTRES OF GRAVITY OF THE LIMBS (IN MEN AND WOMEN)

	Men		Women	
	Mean value	Variations due to the mean square deviation	Mean value	Variations due to the mean square deviation
Thigh	0.3857	0.3543-0.4171	0.3888	0.3534-0.4242
Lower leg	0.4140	0.3942-0.4318	0.4226	0.3983-0.4469
Upper arm	0.4657	0.4394-0.4920	0.4840	0.4484-0.5196
Forearm	0.4124	0.3850-0.4398	0.4174	0.3835-0.4513

with sex of subject, contrary to expectation, do not significantly affect
the values of the radii obtained as Table 4 shows.

In the first place, it is apparent from this list that sex differences
have very little effect on the radii of the centres of gravity. Generally
speaking, the radii are slightly longer in women, that is, the centres of
gravity lie closer to the middle of the limb and in the case of the upper
arm they sometimes lie even lower which is almost never observed in men.
In the second place, the indication in the first table of the great variation
of the radii as encountered in practice is confirmed. Even if Fischer's
figures, for example, those for the upper arm, closely coincide with our
mean values (0.47 and 0.4746), it is possible to employ them in calculations,
given the probability that for the overwhelming majority of subjects the
values of the radius for the upper arm may vary in men between 0.44-0.49,
and in women between 0.45-0.52. Figure 13 provides a picture of how the
distribution of the values of radii of the forearm appear for men and women.

There are only two possible paths to choose in order to analyse this
chaos of variations. Either we may resign ourselves to measuring with the
complex techniques we have developed every new subject with whom we deal
– or we may attempt to find such anthropometric and structural
correspondencies (correlations) as will enable us to determine with
sufficient accuracy the probable radii of our subjects on the basis of their
general habitus and anthropometric data. It was this latter which we set as
the objective of our investigations.

If we now turn to the masses of the limbs of the body, we may say that
in this respect the data of Fischer and Harless were even more unreliable.
The massive sample of material we examined gives an entirely different
picture *, even if we consider only the mean values obtained quite
independently of any variation (Table 5).

The following interesting circumstances may be observed from Table 5.
In the first place Fischer greatly overestimated figures for all the
extremities of the limbs except the feet. In fact, the masses of all these
extremities of the limbs are much smaller than is represented by these
figures, which have been for 40 years the only data available on the question
of the distribution of masses in the human body. In the second place, we
here observe significant and characteristic differences between the sexes.
The column giving the ratio of the mean masses illustrates these differences

---

* The figures given here are only preliminary and after final revision
  may undergo small changes.

TABLE 5. RELATIVE MASSES OF THE LIMBS (MASS OF THE BODY AS A WHOLE = 1)

	Our Data				Mass according to Fischer
	Men	Women	General mean	Ratio M/W	
Thigh	0.12213	0.12815	0.12485	0.948	0.1158
Lower leg	0.04655	0.04845	0.04731	0.961	0.0527
Foot	0.01458	0.01295	0.01313	1.126	0.0179
Upper arm	0.02655	0.02600	0.02632	1.021	0.0336
Forearm	0.01818	0.01820	0.01819	1.000	0.0228
Hand	0.00703	0.00550	0.00642	1.279	0.0084

most clearly. Male thighs are significantly lighter than female thighs and lower legs and upper arms are almost the same for men and women (it should not be forgotten that in all these cases we are discussing relative masses, that is to say masses estimated with the total body weight taken as the unit); but distal portions of the limbs in men are significantly heavier than those of women. Both for the legs and for the arms the ratio M/W shows an increase from the proximal to the distal end of the limbs becoming particularly significant for the feet (13 per cent) and for the hands (28 per cent). It is also necessary to determine variation in the relative masses of human limbs. So as not to enter into complications we give only a general table which illustrates this considerable variation (Table 6).

TABLE 6. THE VARIANCE OF THE RELATIVE MASSES OF THE LIMBS (THE VALUES ARE GIVEN IN HUNDRED-THOUSANDTHS OF THE WEIGHT OF THE WHOLE BODY AND IN PERCENTAGES OF THE MEAN MASS OF THE LIMB)

	Men		Women		General figure	
Foot	± 1620	± 13.3%	± 1190	± 9.2%	± 1480	± 11.8%
Lower leg	507	10.9%	389	8.0%	469	9.9%
Thigh	126	8.6%	105	8.1%	142	10.2%
Upper arm	312	11.8%	344	13.2%	322	12.2%
Forearm	184	10.1%	169	9.3%	177	9.7%
Hand	84	11.9%	98	17.8%	117	18.2%

The variation both in the radii and in the relative masses is least for the lower legs, feet and forearms; the masses of the thighs, upper arms and in particular of the hands display greatest variance.

The Centre of Gravity of the Entire Body and of the System as a Whole. If the masses and the positions of the centres of gravity of all the separate limbs of the body are known, the problem of discovering the centre of gravity of the whole body or of any particular system (for example, that of the whole arm or of the whole leg) presents no difficulty whatever. This possibility is of inestimable importance for the physiology of movements because it opens the way to the dynamic analysis of the movements of the whole body and of its sub-systems and also allows us to study the statics of the body and, as has been explained above, the loads on any given group of muscles.

Fig. 1. Instantaneous photographs of running taken by Muybridge in the 1880's at the dawn of instantaneous photography. The time interval between successive frames is $1/24$ sec.

Fig. 2. One of Marey's subjects in a black costume with white tape.

Fig. 3. Chronophotograph of walking taken by Marey. Movement is
from left to right. The frequency is about 20 exposures
per sec.

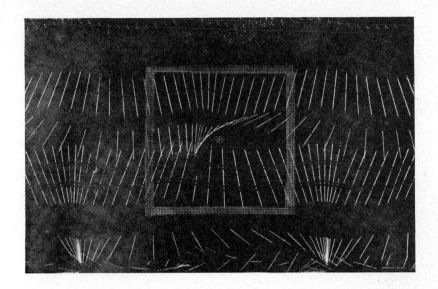

Fig. 4. Chronophotograph of walking taken by Braune and Fischer. Right side of the body; movement is from left to right. The square in the centre of the picture is a superimposed scale. Frequency – 26 exposures per sec.

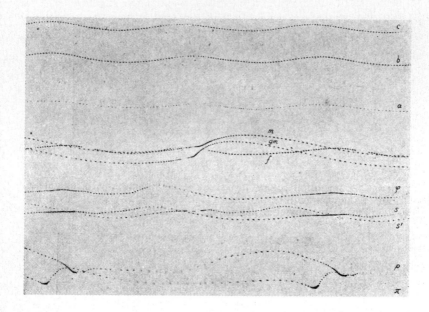

Fig. 5. Cyclogram of walking (Bernstein and Popova). Left side of
the body; movement is from right to left. Trajectories from
top to bottom: c, centre of gravity of the head; b, shoulder
joint of the left arm; a, elbow joint of the left arm; m,
radial side of the wrist joint of the left hand; gm, centre
of gravity of the wrist; f, hip joint of the left leg, ϕ,
a point on the longitudinal axis of the left thigh; s, knee
joint of the left leg; s', knee joint of the right leg, p,
ankle joint of the left leg; π, a point near the end of the
foot. Frequency - 90 exposures per sec.

Fig. 6. Bulbs used for cyclography, placed on a millimetre grid
so that their dimensions may be gauged. (Left) a Wolf
socket; (centre) a Wolf-Bernstein bulb; (right) for
comparison, the type of bulb commonly used in pocket
flashlights.

Fig. 7. Camera with rotating shutter, equipped with a siren so
that its velocity of rotation may be estimated. In a later
system used by the author the rotating shutter is semi-
transparent; this provides faint lines on the cyclogram,
uniting successive points on the same trajectory.

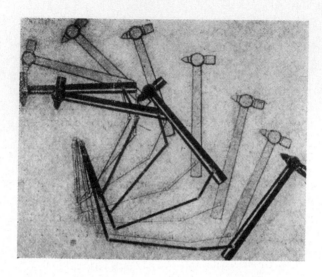

Fig. 8. Successive positions of the right hand and a hammer during
        correct striking with a chisel. The time interval between
        each phase shown is $^1/_{15}$ sec. The sketch was made from a
        cyclogram.

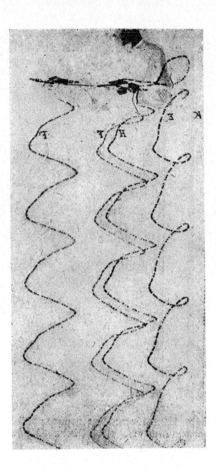

Fig. 9. A kymocyclogram of filing. The figure of the subject is
       visible at the top of the illustration, with a standard
       cyclogram of a single cycle of the movement of filing.
       This can be seen to be quite unanalysable. Below is
       a series of curves of the same movement, separated by
       being photographed on a moving film. *K*, a control bulb;
       E, the elbow joint; *H*, the radial side of the wrist joint;
       F, the fingers of the right hand; *F'*, the fingers of the
       left hand. Frequency - 73 frames per sec (1923).

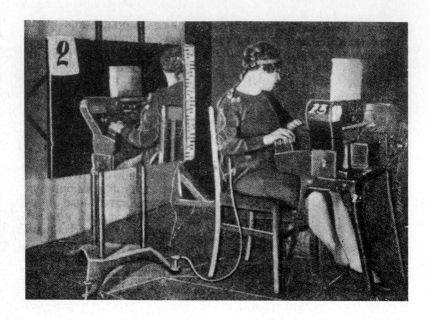

Fig. 10. Apparatus for mirror kymocyclography. The subject is operating a Powers perforator. On the left we have a mirror with a scale and the serial number (1929).

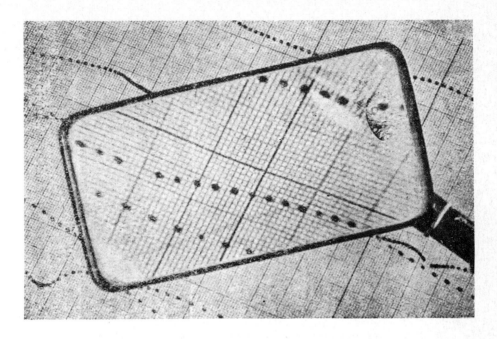

Fig. 11. A section of a photograph on a measuring grid and the means by which it is studied through a lens.

Fig. 12. An experiment on the determination of masses and the
         centre of gravity of the limbs by Bernstein's method.
         The subject lies in a predetermined position on a
         platform supported at two points, the placement of the
         head and the lower extremities being determined by
         upright boards. At the end the platform is fixed upon
         a fulcrum, at the lower extremity it is supported by one
         of the pans of accurate scales. The assistant balances
         the static moment of a given position of the scales, the
         position being photographed at the same instant on a
         predetermined scale.

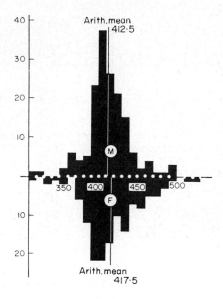

Fig. 13. Distribution of the values for the radii of the centres
of gravity of the forearm from data obtained by the
author and his colleagues. Above: the limits for men;
below: those for women. The values of relative radii
are plotted along the abscissa. The number of cases
observed is plotted along the ordinate.

REFERENCES

12. Bernstein, N.A. Die kymocyclographische Methode der Bewegungs-Untersuchung.
    Handbuch der Biologischen Arbeitsmethoden, Vol. 5, Pt. 5a, Abderhalden,
    1927.

16. Bernstein, N.A. Analyse der Körperbewegungen und Stellungen im Raum
    mittels Spiegel-Stereoaufnahmen. Arbeitsphysiologie, 1930, 3, 3.

17. Bernstein, N.A. & Dement'ev, E. Ein Zeit-Okular zu der Zeitlupe.
    Arbeitsphysiologie, 1933, 6, 4.

18. Bernstein, N.A., Mogilanskaia, Z. & Popova, T. Technics of Motion-Study
    (in Russian), Moscow, 1934.

36. Drill, R. Chronocyclographische Arbeitsstudien-Nagel-Einschlagen.
    Psychophysiologische Arbeit, Riga, 1930.

76. Weber, W. & Weber, E. Mechanik der menschlichen Gehwerkzeuge (1836),
    Berlin, 1894.

CHAPTER Ia
THE UNIT OF ANALYSIS

R.B. Wilberg

The technique of recording movement in 'real-time' as a series of linked
events were initiated by several investigators, but was most completely
developed by Bernstein over a period of approximately 30 years. Some of the
recording techniques are equipment specific, but on the whole tend to measure
the time-course of a particular movement as opposed to its simple result.
Depending upon the particular effect desired, the results can be: the temporal
record of the movement of a specific joint or angle; a composite of many such
chronologically and sequentially related points; or a derivative as in the
case of certain accelerative functions taken through time. These direct
measures enabled Bernstein and others to view the time-course of a movement
in its entirety and to examine its production from both an absolute and a
relative basis. From these initial observations Bernstein developed a view of
movement as important as it was unique in the study of voluntary, overt,
guided behavior. The importance of his works to our present knowledge will be
examined in later chapters, but suffice to say that his observations are still
relevant today.

Since Bernstein's demise, several advances in both measurement and
experimental procedure have taken place. The development of commercially
available computer software packages of mathematical and statistical programs,
has meant that virtually every investigator has access to very powerful
analytic tools. As a consequence, much of Bernstein's original work has been
surpassed, particularly by the biomechanists. However, a much more fundamental
change has taken place in the study of movement. The manipulating of
experimental factors has extended our knowledge far beyond the horizon that
Bernstein sought. The bases of this expansion are many, but they are tightly
bound to the rise of cognitive psychology. Of particular interest is the
emphasis that is placed upon the theories of memory and decision-making that
underlie our present view of performance. Movement cannot be meaningfully

studied without taking cognizance of the task the subject is attempting to
to perform. As a result, a substantial amount of information regarding
movement has arisen from the comparison of movement behavior under varying
experimental conditions. Often the crux of the experiment involves making
inference from comparative results - thereby turning the dependent variable
into a 'secondary' indicator of an unobservable underlying phenomenon. Both
the biomechanical and the experimental developments are examined more fully
in the remaining paragraphs.

BIOMECHANICAL DEVELOPMENTS

    The natural evolution of Bernstein's approach to direct measurement
has resulted in a sophistication of measurement technique that was neither
technically feasible nor economically possible at an earlier time. The most
recent advances in the measurement of skilled performance have arisen from
the study of the biomechanical aspects of movements. Those interested in
biomechanics for example have been responsible for several cinematographical,
mathematical, and mechanical engineering applications to the study of
movement. These advances have had their basis in Bernstein's original work
and should be considered as extensions rather than original contributions.
    Plagenhoef (1968) and McLaughlin, Lardner and Dillman (1977) assessed
the minematic and kinetic parameters of human movement from a two dimensional
or planar viewpoint. Further investigations by Miller and Petak (1973) and
Shapiro (1976) have assisted in the development of cinematographic techniques
to calculate three dimensional coordinate data relative to such kinematic
features as the centre of mass displacement and the absolute angular
displacement-time history of a given movement. This new method is known as
'the direct linear transformation' (Walton, 1979; Miller, Shapiro & McLaughlin,
1980). Variations of Newtonian and Lagrangian equations of motion have also
been advanced to describe movement paths through three dimensions, following
the establishment of angular displacement-time data relative to their
specified axes when defined in space.
    A recent parallel development has been the adaptation of spline functions
to describe the path of movements arising from experimentally-produced data.
The functions result in fitted curves that can more accurately follow a
movement's path than do those arising from the more commonly used interpolated
polynomials (Gerald, 1973). Although the spline functions tend to smooth the

data during the curve-fitting process, a more versatile smoothing procedure
has arisen from the development of digital filters. Such filters can be set
to 'pass' frequencies of a certain range while rejecting and/or attenuating
others. This selectivity allows the researcher an opportunity to remove
unwanted noise from the experimental data, so that the desired signal can
be seen more clearly (Winter, 1979; Zernicke, Caldwell & Roberts, 1966).

These most recent developments indicate a trend away from the simple
recording and measurement of the time course of a movement to a position
where the movements can be described in terms of mechanical and/or
mathematical statements. Although these attempts to model the movements of
limbs and bodies are still in their infancy, they do mark a change in
emphasis from one of mere analysis to one of projection and simulation. For
example, a number of procedural developments have occurred which allows the
experimenter to define the total position of a body and its posture within
an inertial frame of reference for a specific environment. Predicted movement
paths then become probability statements with the attendant confidence limits
providing a basis for prediction success (Reynolds & Hubbard, 1980).
Extensions of this approach to computer modelling of movement is not only
likely, but obvious. Some initial work by Hinton (1981) elucidating movement
behavior based upon an alternate solution to Bernstein's 'degrees of freedom'
concept, shows how powerful that tool can be to the understanding of movement.

PSYCHOLOGICAL DEVELOPMENTS

The significance of the change from simply recording and measuring
movements to the act of modelling and simulating those same movements should
not go unnoticed. These differences in approach, parallel to a large extent,
the two different traditional approaches to experimental psychology, namely
functionalism (associationists) and structuralism (cognitivists). The
differences between the two approaches are most apparent in the unit of
analysis which the experimenter adopts. Studies which attempt to measure and
define simple movements in isolation, e.g. Bernstein (1967), Bizzi, Polit
and Morasso (1976), Houk (1979) and Hoffer and Andreassen (1981) focus upon
the control factors which come into play when the movement is initiated.
Unravelling the integrative processes that occur between the conscious
initiation of a movement and the actual occurrence of that movement is of
prime interest. The problem with such an approach is that it is difficult if

not impossible to obtain a <u>functional equivalent</u> between the phenomena noted
when such movements are made in isolation, than when they are made as part
of a larger integrated movement pattern. Clearly the behavior of emitting
a simple response is not always functionally the same, and it suggests that
the functional significance of a simple response is dependent upon the way
in which the behavioral output is patterned or organized. For example, in
certain instances the simple movement of the head to left or right may
constitute an independent functional unit, but when combined with eye
movements and postural adaptations it becomes integrated into the well known
'observing response' - an entirely different functional unit. The neck
movements in both instances may arise from the same anatomical and neurological
bases but they could only be considered equal in the fact that each one is
a conscious act. This view suggests that a given movement can be considered
as a functional unit in one context and not in another, and secondly that a
functional unit may not be just a simple response but may indeed involve a
very complex and structured behavior.

The functionalist and structuralist approaches may address issues and
problems specific to their viewpoints as well as problems in common. The
measurement of observable and unobservable phenomena is an issue of concern
to both of these traditional approaches. Nowhere is this issue more clearly
defined than in the recent work on the behavioral patterning, segmentation
and organizational sequencing of movements in a list. It may be helpful at
this point to examine some studies in which the unit of analysis was of
paramount importance in the complete examination of a subject's performance.

In this first experiment by Restle and Burnside (1972) the effects of
list repetition are inter-related to the organization apparent in the
behavioral output. Previous work by Restle (1970, 1972) and Restle and
Brown (1970) had shown that subjects tended to group serial movement list
items into sub-units. Although Restle did not develop a measure of behavioral
patterning such as did Tulving (1962, 1964), he was able to demonstrate that
more errors were made by subjects when transiting between sub-groups than
were made within such units. Restle and Burnside (1972) required subjects
to track the stimulus as it moved from one location to another in a continuous
sequence. A serial pattern learning paradigm was used and Restle and Burnside
(1972) found that subjects tended to break the total list into sub-groups that
had the characteristic of a 'run' (abc) or (cba), 'trill' (aba) or (bab), or
'repetition' (aaa). This tendency to form sub-units increased as the number
of repetitions increased and led Restle and Burnside to the conclusion that

the new functioning unit of analysis was no longer a single movement, but
one composed of a number of such movements. These results are certainly in
agreement with the Handel and Todd (1981) finding that, when left to their
own devices, subjects will segment undifferentiated lists in a variety of
ways.

In general, those who support a functionalist point of view would not
have interpreted the data this way. The functionalists (associationism) would
have focussed on the increase in the number of remembered items as a result
of trials with each correct item being considered as the functional unit.
Any patterning that may have resulted would be viewed as a by-product of an
increase in the strength of the invariant units, i.e., the individual
movements. The structuralists' viewpoint, on the other hand, would focus on
the degree of clustering (sub-group consistency) that took place as a
function of trials. That is, it would focus on the emergence of new behavioral
patterns. In this sense the increase in the number of movements remembered
would be viewed as a by-product of the emergence of new patterns, the true
functional unit.

Bernstein's approach to both the measurement of movement and its
experimental methodology, follows almost completely the functionalist
viewpoint. Although Bernstein eventually came to the conclusion that very
little of movement behavior could be described by the measurement and
observation of single movements, his research methodology and measurements
did not by itself provide such evidence.

The unit of analysis in the Restle and Burnside study was aimed at the
relationship of movements within and between sub-groups, and could be derived
from experimentally-produced data. In the following class of experiments the
unit of analysis is manipulated by the experimenter; usually by provisionally
varying the level of the independent variable. As Pachalla (1974) observed,
much of the structuralist (cognitive) research is carried out by making
inferences about unobservable mental events, and by studying the subsequent
behavioral results that follow as a consequence. The reaction time score is
perhaps the most widely used measure of such unobservable activity, with
variations in latency being primarily due to changes in the amount,
difficulty, or complexity of the information processing task demands.

Cognitivists such as Sternberg (1969) have used reaction time data to
support their hypothesis that the search through memory for an encoded probe
character is a sequential process with each comparison between the probe item
and the to-be-remembered list items being equated to a single mental operation.

The reaction time latency should then reflect the number of mental operations (list length) being required of a subject. The reaction time score is then a function of a sequential pair-wise comparison process and as such can be set by the experimenter in different experimental conditions. From a structuralist's (cognitivist's) viewpoint the unit of analysis is not the simple latency that accrues from different experimental conditions, but is rather the item-to-item sequential pair-wise comparison.

Because the associationist viewpoint would not recognize memory in the sense that the cognitivists view it, the increase in latency as a function of list length would not be interpreted in the same way. Variations in reaction time latencies would be construed to arise from differences in associative strength or perhaps stimulus-response compatibility. While both the structuralists and functionalists would view the mechanisms underlying the reaction time latencies as being unobservable, the associationist's view would be essentially atheoretical.

The measurement techniques used by Bernstein were quite capable of producing reaction time data in terms of 'lag' time and that such system response times could monotonically vary as a function of practice, task difficulty and/or task complexity. Bernstein however, does not appear to have varied his subjects' behavior in order to determine the part played by decision making and memory in the production and control of movement. While it is quite clear that Bernstein did not study memory per se, it is nonetheless true that a contemporary view of movement demands an understanding of the control feature that guide the intended movement, and the cognitive aspects that first generated, then initiated it.

REFERENCES

Bernstein, N. The co-ordination and regulation of movements. Oxford:
   Pergamon Press, 1967.

Bizzi, E., Polit, D. & Morasso, P. Mechanisms underlying achievement of
   final head position. Journal of Neurophysiology, 1976, 39, 435-444.

Gerald, C.F. Applied Numerical Analysis. Don Mills: Addison-Wesley
   Publishers, 1973.

Handel, S. & Todd, P. Segmentation of sequential patterns. Journal of
   Experimental Psychology: Human Perception and Performance, 1981, 7,
   41-55.

Hoffer, J.D. & Andreassen, S. Limitations in the servo-regulation of
   soleus muscle stiffness in premammillary cats. In, A. Taylor and A.
   Prochazko (Eds.), Muscle receptors and movements. London, Macmillan,
   1981.

Houk, J.C. Regulation of stiffness by skeletalmotor reflexes. Annual Review
   Physiology, 1979, 41, 99-114.

Hinton, G. Movement stimulation demonstration program using independent
   joint vector procedures as a basis for target capture. Presented to:
   The Motor Skills Exchange Conference MRC, Applied Psychology Unit,
   Cambridge, England, 1981.

McLaughlin, T.M., Dillman, C.J. & Lardner, T.J. Biomechanical analysis
   with cubic spline functions. Research Quarterly, 1972, 48, 570-582.

Miller, D.I. & Petak, K. Kinesiology III, Washington, D.C.: A.A.H.P.E.R.,
   1973.

Miller, N.R., Shapiro, R. & McLaughlin, T.M. A technique for obtaining
   special kinematic parameters of segments of biomechanics systems from
   cinematographic data. Journal of Biomechanics, 1980, 13, 535-547.

Plagenhoef, S. Computer program for obtaining kinetic data of human
   movement. Journal of Biomechanics, 1968, 1, 221-234.

Restle, F. Theory of serial pattern learning. Psychological Review, 1970,
   77, 481-495.

Restle, F. Serial patterns: The role of phrasing. Journal of Experimental
   Psychology, 1972, 92, 385-390.

Restle, F. & Brown, E.R. Serial pattern learning. Journal of Experimental
   Psychology, 1970, 83, 120-125.

Restle, F. & Burnside, B.L. Tracking of serial patterns. Journal of
   Experimental Psychology, 1972, 95, 229-307.

Reynolds, H.M. & Hubbard, R.P. Anatomical frames of reference and biomechanics. Human Factors, 1980, 22, 171-176.

Shapiro, R. The direct linear transformation method for three-dimensional cinematography. Research Quarterly, 1976, 49, 197-205.

Sternberg, S. Memory scanning: mental processes revealed by reaction time experiments. American Scientist, 1969, 57, 421-457.

Tulving, E. Subjective organization in free recall of "unrelated" words. Psychological Review, 1962, 69, 344-354.

Tulving, E. Intratrial and intertrial retention: notes towards a theory of free recall verbal learning. Psychological Review, 1964, 71, 219-237.

Walton, J.S. Close-range cine-photogrammetry: a generalized technique for quantifying gross human motion. Ph.D. Thesis, Pennsylvania State University, Pennsylvania, 1979.

Winter, D.D. Biomechanics of Movement. Toronto: John Wiley and Sons, 1979.

Zernicke, R.F., Caldwell, G. & Roberts, E.M. Fitting biomechanics data with cubic spline functions. Research Quarterly, 1976, 47, 9-19.

CHAPTER Ib

ON METHODOLOGY IN THE STUDY OF HUMAN MOVEMENT

H.J. Woltring

1. Introduction

The dichotomy between material content and methodology in any field of scientific endeavour is artificial in the sense that neither can justify itself in isolation: without an external purpose, methodology is sterile and a potential, 'academic' waste of effort, while facts worthy of the qualification 'scientific' can only be obtained through a proper, generally acknowledged methodology. This does not imply that speculation and intuition do not deserve a place in science, as is borne out by the existence of academic journals such as *Speculation in Science and Technology*[*].

Yet, there is a tendency that methodology is relegated to a secondary position, with the risk that incorrect procedures remain unrecognized. In other instances, methodology and material results are reported separately, in that order, and here the risk exists that the earlier publication is taken for granted. It is, therefore, appropriate, that the editors chose Bernstein's *Techniques for the Study of Movement*, originally published in 1934, as the first chapter of the 1967 book, and it is intriguing that the editors of a German translation of a selection from his work adopted a somewhat different view (Bernstein, 1975, p. 15),

> The works of Bernstein and his collaborators which appeared
> in the years 1927 through 1936 in German periodicals and
> in Abderhalden's *Handbuch der biologischen Arbeitsmethoden*
> could only give a very incomplete and therefore single-
> minded impression of the creations and ideas of this
> important Soviet scientist. Through these, the German
> reader was given the impression that this work was merely
> concerned with a continuation of the old movement research
> line which is more or less characterized by the names of
> B. and E. Weber, Muybridge, Marey, Braune and Fischer. It

---

[*] *Speculation in Science and Technology*. An International Journal Devoted to Speculative Papers in the Physical, Mathematical, Biological, Medical, and Engineering Sciences. Elsevier Sequoia, ISSN 0155-7785.

> was merely the methodology which appeared more perfected
> through kymocyclography, cyclogrammetry, and the spatial
> data acquisition through mirror registration, while bio-
> mechanical data processing was rendered more accurate
> and simple.

They went on to state that "the important and general results of

investigations during many years on biomechanical fundamentals (cf. the

chapter on Biodynamics of Locomotion)" did not become known in Germany. On

the other hand, Gurfinkel (Moscow) wrote in the introduction to the same

book (Bernstein, 1975, p. 10),

> Important steps were undertaken in order to improve the
> technique of movement registration and the methods for
> the evaluation of experimental results. Spurred by
> Nikolai Alexandrovitch, the cyclographic technique was
> rendered highly perfect and a cyclographic mirror method
> was developed allowing spatial movement registration. For
> cyclically repetitive movements whose trajectories would
> superimpose themselves upon each other, also the methods
> for cyclogramme evaluation were further developed, and
> nomogrammes were constructed rendering the calculations
> more simple. This total complex of methodological and
> technical procedures enabling a 'microscopy of movement'
> was given the designation 'cyclogrammetry'. A detailed
> presentation of this material is contained in the monograph
> 'Techniques for the Investigation of Movement' which
> appeared in 1934 under the redaction of N.A. Bernstein.

In his chapter on Biodynamics of Locomotion (p.178), Bernstein himself

states

> All these circumstances determined the third and, in
> principle, the most important aspect of our approach
> to the study of locomotion. We refused to theorize about
> our object or investigation in advance by forcing it to
> fit one or other analog in the field of general mechanics.
> We regarded the locomotion process as a living *morphological
> object* of inexhaustible complexity and set as our primary
> task the necessity of observing and describing it as
> closely as possible.

It is from this point of view that Bernstein's work is subject to both

praise and criticism. His achievement in measuring a considerably larger

amount of movement data than Braune & Fischer[*], with a temporal resolution

ranging from 60 to 190 frames per second constitutes a significant

improvement with respect to his predecessors, and he was right to criticise

---

[*] Condensed translations of two key publications Braune & Fischer (1889) and
Fischer (1906) are available as Braune et al. (1963).

them for their *a priori*, subjective smoothing of displacement data, sampled at only 26 Hz. Moreover, he was far ahead of his time in conducting sensitivity studies on the stochastic measurement errors affecting his estimates for velocities and accelerations (Bernstein, 1936). On the other hand, he failed to relate these sensitivity studies to his data on the Biodynamics of Locomotion, and he did not realise – like many investigators who followed him, even up to the present day – that the finite difference algorithm adopted for estimating velocities and accelerations was quite unsuitable in view of its deviation from a true low-pass differentiating filter in which signal and noise properties of the observed data are *both* taken into account. This point will be discussed more fully in a later part of this commentary.

Furthermore, in rejecting the earlier investigators' approaches to model the leg as a pendulum, or the foot as a class I or II lever, he did not acknowledge that his own approach to the estimation of centre of gravity forces, joint forces, and joint moments was based on another, more general mechanical model, namely the rigid body for which a theoretical structure was readily available even in his day. As far as this author is aware, the non-rigid character of the soft tissues in the body segments was hardly mentioned by Bernstein, and the occurrence of local landmark movements caused by skin shifts with respect to the underlying skeletal structure not at all.

Considering Bernstein's views, it seems reasonable to conclude that he was influenced by the traditional empiricist interpretation of the ethology of the research process. Medawar (1963, 1967, 1969) gives a lucid account of the empiricists' view that scientific research is an *inductive* process starting with "simple, unbiased, unprejudiced, naïve, or innocent observation", out of which an orderly theory will somehow emerge. In his opinion, scientific discovery or the formulation of a scientific idea on the one hand, and demonstration or proof on the other, are two essentially different notions. In this positivist, *hypothetico-deductive* view of the research process, hypotheses may be obtained in any fashion available to their proponent, for subsequent, rigorous testing in the deductive phase. It is in this latter phase, that a well-founded, generally acknowledged methodology is essential, particularly in applied fields drawing on a number of parent disciplines.

The iterative character of the research process is a natural consequence of this *Popper*ian view of science: each finding evokes new

hypotheses to be scrutinized in turn by appropriate methodology, and any
theory or interpretation remains on probation until rejected in later
research. In this sense, Bernstein's work may be characterized as an
inductive attempt to collect human movement data in as unbiased a fashion
as possible, using the most general biomechanical model currently available,
in order to allow the formulation of hypotheses with minimal prejudice.

It might be argued that methodology is the most 'dated' aspect of
Bernstein's work in view of current availability of automatic data
acquisition and processing technology; however, few investigators have taken
the trouble to attempt to measure human kinematics at the same degree of
accuracy. It is, therefore, in honour of Bernstein, that the following
sections of this commentary present a synopsis of developments in kinematic
data acquisition and processing, mass distribution parameter estimation,
and kinetic modelling. Suitable introductory texts in this field are those
by Miller & Nelson (1973), Grieve et al. (1975), and Winter (1979).

In this commentary, the data *acquisition* orientation of chapter I is
transcended. However, biomechanics suffers, as so many experimental sciences
do, from a lack of sufficiently direct measurement facilities. The
investigator measures what he can, and bridges the gap to what he desires
to know by *modelling*. Data acquisition and modelling thus become complementary,
and should be treated as such. By consequence, measurement methodology and
'biomechanical fundamentals' should be viewed in a wholistic manner, when
assessing the reliability of the data acquisition and processing chain:
estimated forces, moments, and energies are affected by both aspects.

2. Techniques for biokinematic data acquisition

Cinematography and Stroboscopic Photography. It is perhaps appropriate
that Bernstein's photographic and cinematographic methodology is commented
on by someone who was originally concerned with *avoiding* these as a data
acquisition tool! Although cinematography (henceforth to include stroboscopic,
multiple-exposure photography) is the perfect means for recording time-
fleeting movements, conversion of these records into a quantitative,
processable form is notoriously laborious and error-prone. Therefore, the
perseverance of Bernstein's group and of his predecessors in digitizing
large amounts of movement data is to be commended. Besides, even today, the
large variety of electrogoniometric, ultrasonic, and optoelectronic methods
for automatic acquisition, identification, and digitization of kinematic
data have not obviated the need for cinematography in certain movement

studies. Particularly in sports (Marhold, 1979) and in ethology (Lehner, 1979), where affixing measurement devices or artificial landmarks for increased observability may be tantamount to destroying essential parts of the movement process, high-speed cinematography remains a unique approach, recently complemented by high-speed video recording technology (e.g., Terauds, 1981). In biomechanical impact research, requirements concerning spatio-temporal resolution have caused that cinematography has been retained as the major technique for kinematic registration.

In sports biomechanics, digitization of kinematic data is still largely done by hand. On the other hand, in the case of impact studies in car crash research it is usually possible to affix special landmarks to dummies, cadavers, animals, or volunteers, and this facilitates automatic identification and digitization of the points of interest in individual film frames, when used in conjunction with current pattern recognition techniques (e.g., Aten; 1975; Niederer et al., 1981; MacKay et al., 1982).

In his 3-D studies, Bernstein used mirrors to obtain multiple views from different vantage points on a single film, thus avoiding the problem of synchronizing multiple cameras which today still arises in high-speed cinematography. However, the disadvantages of this method are that mirror planarity errors and, in the case of back-coating, refractive errors may assume significance.

As an alternative to mirror approaches, the work of Baum (1980, 1983) on anaglyph *Motography* qualifies him as a worthy successor to Bernstein. Here, the use of carefully chosen optical filters and light sources in the visible, infrared, and ultraviolet ranges allows simultaneous registration of cyclographic trajectories and instantaneous movement snapshots on a single photograph. When flashing light bulbs are used as landmarks, approximate velocity information is made available, and 3-D perception is possible by means of anaglyph spectacles (red/green glasses). Quantification of these data remains a problem, and the major utility of this approach is in making direct, qualitative judgments.

Electrogoniometry. Most contemporary methods for non-cinematographic/photographic acquisition of biokinematic data rely on electrogoniometry, ultrasound, or various optoelectronic methods, which were not used by Bernstein, or - it would seem - available to him. More recently, electro-goniometry has been used extensively for joint or body segment kinematics monitoring (Lamoreux, 1971, 1978; Chao, 1980; Zarrugh & Radcliffe, 1979).

Typically, potentiometric linkage systems are affixed to body segments on
either side of a joint, and the potentiometer rotations are registered
electronically. Remote measurements have also been carried out in this fashion,
using strings or rubber bands attached between the subject and an external
transducer. The advantages of these systems are their low cost and easy
application; disadvantages include the load imposed on the subject and (in
the case of potentiometric linkages) the limitation to relative joint movement
measurement. Absolute body segment measurement, as required when dynamic
analysis is to be performed, is not possible in this way, and other methods
are required if full estimation of joint or segment forces, moments, and
energies is contemplated.

Ultrasound. One 'wireless' approach for biokinematic measurement has
been based on the Doppler-effect. Whenever a sound source emits a continuous
wave of frequency f_s, the frequency f_v perceived by a receiver depends on
the velocities of the sound source and receiver with respect to the medium
through which the sound is propagated. In the case of a stationary receiver
and moving sound source, e.g., an external microphone and an ultrasonic
emitter attached to the wrist of a sportsman, the wrist velocity component
v_s towards or away from the microphone will be

$$v_s = c \; \frac{f_r - f_s}{f_r} \tag{1}$$

where c is the velocity of sound in the medium (in air, c = 343 m/s at 20° C).
The frequency change can be measured by techniques similar to those used in
conventional UHF/FM receivers. In an ergonomics context, this approach was
used by Nadler (1955) and by Nadler & Goldman (1959) who derived 3-D
velocities, translations, and accelerations by further signal processing.
Hennig & Nicol (1976) reported a multichannel system based on ultrasonic
emitters in the 25-40 kHz range, and stated that errors on the order of 0.5%
may be expected as a result of turbulence and variations in temperature and
humidity of the air. Furthermore, reflections from neighbouring surfaces may
cause errors by interfering with the 'direct sight' waves.

An alternative technique is based on pulsed ultrasound. Here, long
microphonic 'bars' detect the travel time of the sound resulting from the
generation of an electric spark between two adjacent contacts. Originally
designed for manual image digitization purposes, such systems have been used
for direct measurement of 3-D wrist kinematics *in vivo* (Brumbaugh et al., 1982).

Opto-electronics. With the emergence of video technology, many attempts have been made to adapt standard closed-circuit TV equipment for biokinematic data acquisition (Furnée, 1967; Jarrett, 1976; Whittle, 1982; Taylor et al., 1982). Typically, retro-reflective landmarks affixed to the subject are stroboscopically illuminated by light sources close to the observing cameras. The light is reflected back along the line of sight, irrespective of the landmark attitudes, and special circuitry detects the circumference of the landmark images. Images blur is prevented because of the short, stroboscopic flash synchronous with the image scanning rate. From the circumference measurements, the horizontal and vertical coordinates of the landmark images' centroids are calculated with a much higher resolution than the basic scanning resolution of the video system (Taylor et al. (1982) claimed a figure of 1:2000 per image axis). Temporal resolution is essentially limited by standard video conventions, namely 50 fps in Europe, and 60 fps in North-America.

Such TV systems only allow the measurement of x-y coordinates, not the identification of landmarks (e.g., wrist, elbow, hip, knee). For the latter purpose, some form of interactive *pattern recognition* is required. In the commercial VICON[†] system, this is achieved by means of extrapolative prediction, for each camera independently, in partial interaction with an operator at a graphics terminal. In the GALATHEA system (MacKay et al., 1982), identification is further facilitated by correlating unidentified landmarks in a particular view with comtemporaneous observations which have already been identified in different views.

TV systems suffer from low resolution in time, since the standard line-by-line scanning norm causes most time to be spent on deciding where the landmark images are *not* located. By means of a 'random-access' approach, the landmark prediction algorithm described above for non-real-time identification may be use, on-line, for the definition of a suitable search area. Image dissector tubes and solid-state arrays are currently used for real-time tracking of single and multiple targets, usually in a military context, and such technology may be straightforwardly adapted for biomechanical purposes.

Macellari (1983) has described a video system for 3-D measurement of up to 8 infra-red light emitting diodes (IR LEDs). This CoSTEL* system consists of a spatial arrangement of three linear, 2048-elements charge-coupled

---

[†] VICON (VIdeo CONverter for Biomechanics). Trademark of *Oxford Dynamics Ltd*, ABINGDON, Oxon, United Kingdom.

[*] CoSTEL (Co-ordinate Spaziali mediante Transduttori Elettrici Lineari). An Italian acronym for "spatial coordinates by linear electrical transducer".

photodiode arrays in combination with cylindrical lenses. As is the case in
the SELSPOT system discussed below, the LEDs are operated in *time-division
multiplex*, at a sampling time of approximately 100 μs per LED. By means of a
spatial averaging technique, an image resolution of 1:4000 is attained.

     A completely different class of sensing systems does not require scanning
of an image area at all. Here, the incident light distribution is directly
converted into position-dependent signals (cf. Woltring, 1974). An example
which has led to actual biokinematic equipment is based on the *lateral
photoeffect* (cf. Woltring, 1975) - see Fig. 1. In this approach, the image
of an external light source is focused onto the surface of a special photo-
detector having lateral contacts on both faces. When properly connected, the
generated photocurrent divides itself between the two contacts per face of
the detector, each of the currents being a linear function of either the x-
or y-coordinate of the incident light distribution's centroid. These currents
can be processed to compensate for signal light intensity (which varies with
distance), and for background light influences (Woltring & Marsolais, 1980).

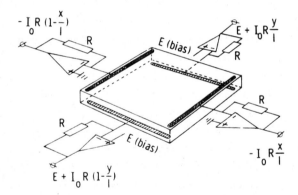

Fig. 1. Dual-axis, duo-lateral photodiode for 2-D, linear position
        detection of the centroid of an incident light distribution
        (from Woltring, 1974, 1975).

A multi-landmark system based on this principle was originally developed by
Lindholm (1974), and has since been made available as a commercial, multi-
camera system SELSPOT[+] (cf. Woltring & Marsolais, 1980). Recently, a
substantially improved version SELSPOT-II has become available with a

---

[+] SELSPOT (SElective Light SPOT recognition). Trademark of *SELCOM Selective
     Electronic Company AB*, PARTILLE, Gothenburgh, Sweden.

spatial resolution of 1:4096 per image axis (i.e., 12 bits), 100 μs sampling time per landmark (the system uses IR LEDs which are operated in time-division multiplex), and improved compensation both for background light interference and observed intensity variations caused by landmark orientation and distance changes. Intensity dependence may be compensated by means of a feedback system controlling the light power of the LEDs, although at the expense of increasing the sampling time per LED by a factor equal to the number of cameras in operation.

A fundamental problem with the lateral photoeffect is its sensitivity to reflections. Whenever false images occur on account of reflection of the IR LEDs' light at neighbouring surfaces (ground, walls, ceiling, adjacent body segments), the integrating character of the lateral detector will cause substantial and irreversible errors. Furthermore, the system uses *active* landmarks, with concomitant encumbrance to the subject, and the possibility of crosstalk to any neighbouring EMG-wires unless all cables are carefully shielded. On the other hand, major advantages of the system are its real-time characteristics, the automatic identification of multiple landmarks, and its high spatio-temporal resolution in comparison to TV approaches (unless the number of time-multiplexed landmarks becomes inordinately high). These features allow its use in real-time situations, such as in biofeedback paradigms; furthermore, if clinical use puts high emphasis on short turn-around times, the system is superior to TV-approaches. However, further data processing is also time consuming, for any data acquisition system.

Another approach is based on scanning mirrors. Güth et al. (1973) and Heinrichs (1974) reported a method in which a V-shaped light image is projected onto a rotating mirror. The mirror sweeps the reflected image through space, and the legs of the V repeatedly hit small photodiodes affixed as landmarks to the subject's body. The times at which a photocurrent pulse occurs are converted into 2-D direction information, with a claimed resolution of better than 1 mm at 8 m distance, and 40 Hz sampling frequency. More recently, a commercial system CODA-3*, based on similar principles, has been announced. Unlike its predecessor (Mitchelson, 1975), it uses three rotating mirrors, two of which rotate about a vertical axis, with a stereobasis of 1 m between the rotation axes, the remaining one rotating about a horizontal axis at a position halfway between the other two mirrors. An l-shaped light image

---

* CODA-3 (Cartesian Optoelectronic Digital Anthropometer). Trademark of *Movement Techniques Ltd*, BARROW-UPON-SOAR, Leicestershire, United Kingdom.

is projected onto the three mirrors by means of fibre-optics, and the subject
wears retro-reflecting, *coloured* prisms. The times at which the light is
reflected back to the mirrors is read out, and converted *on-line* into 3-D,
cartesian coordinates. Identification is brought about by the distinct colours
of the prism landmarks. At the present time, the basic resolution per mirror
is reported to be 1:16000, over an angle of 40°, and at a scanning frequency
of 600 Hz. For the given stereobase, the resolution (in mm) at a distance Z
(in m) from the scanner is quoted as 0.1 Z for the transverse and vertical
axes, and as 0.1 Z² for the longitudinal axis, at a field width (in m) of
0.8 Z - 1. Low-pass filtering will improve these figures, e.g., by a factor
of $\sqrt{12}$ at 50 Hz. Currently, the number of landmarks which can be simultaneously
accommodated is 8, but an increase to 12 - 16 is to be expected.

     All these optoelectronic systems are complementary in terms of active/
passive character and number of landmarks, spatio-temporal resolution, real-
time properties, and subject encumbrance; none is superior to the others in
all respects, and the choice between them depends on the individual application.

     Accelerometry. As discussed in the section on data processing, displacement
measurements tend to be unreliable if velocities and accelerations are to be
derived from them, because of the amplification of high-frequency noise due
to, e.g., quantization and electronic signal processing. For this reason,
direct measurement of accelerations has been preferred by various investigators
especially in impact studies (Morris, 1973; Becker & Williams, 1975; Padgoankar
et al., 1975; Voloshin & Wosk, 1982). As with aerospace navigation methodology,
these data may be integrated to yield velocities and displacements, both
translational and rotational (Mital & King, 1979). Unfortunately, integration
of measured data results in amplification of low-frequency errors (drift), and
much effort in the area of aerospace navigation has been directed to the
optimal combination of displacement, direction, and distance measurements with
direct measurements of velocities and accelerations. Recently, such methods
have begun to appear on the biomechanical scene (Seemann & Lustick, 1981), as
discussed in the next section.

3. Biokinematic Data Processing

     As a prerequisite to the estimation of movement kinetics (forces and
moments in body segment and joints), and movement energies and power, a
substantial amount of calibration and kinematic data processing is required.
As discussed in the preceding section, the measurement of 3-D human movement

through projective imagery involves the calibration of a multi-camera or
camera-mirror configuration, the estimation of individual landmark positions
in a laboratory-defined coordinate system, position and attitude estimation
of body segments marked with at least three non-collinear landmarks having
known coordinates with respect to local, body-fixed coordinate systems, and
the estimation of translational and rotational velocities and accelerations.
The term *estimation* is used here in the statistical sense: all measurements
relating to the movement process are susceptible to error, and an important
issue is the effect which these errors may have on calculated positions,
attitudes, velocities, accelerations, energies, forces and moments.

All components in the signal processing chain involve a certain amount
of implicit or explicit *modelling* of the real world (with concomitant modeling
errors), and definition or calibration of certain model parameter values.
Unlike contemporary system identification methodology (e.g., Eykhoff, 1974),
biomechanics suffers to a considerable extent from the use of insufficiently
validated models, particularly where the underlying assumptions are concerned.
Thus, cameras are assumed distortion-free, optical axes in stereo configurations
to intersect at exactly 90°, and simple, intuitively appealing algorithms are
used without criticism. It is the purpose of this section to evaluate
Bernstein's data processing work in this light, with special reference to the
work he published in 1930, 1935 and 1936, and to outline more appropriate
methodology which has been developed in a number of parent disciplines during
the past 30 years.

Bernstein's Photogrammetry. Bernstein's papers in the German literature
contain a wealth of methodological considerations and should be digested by
anyone who intends to do experimental work in movement analysis. Amongst other
things, he analyzed the influence of observation distance Z_p (see Fig. 2) and
stereo base b on position reconstruction, utilizing planar triangulation for
the conventional case of parallel stereophotogrammetry, and with specified
resolution of the image data. For given camera field angles, the stereometric
'overlap' between the cameras for an acceptable ratio of depth-to-parallel
resolution, $\sigma_Z/\sigma_X \leq 2Z_p/b$, was found to be a serious limitation, and Bernstein
developed his mirror-method in order to improve in this respect. Also the
mirror-camera configuration was extensively analyzed in terms of image error
influence. Furthermore, in order to minimize the influence of systematic lens
distortion errors, he advocated using the same lens for observing the movement
and for projecting movement data onto a digitizing table.

In Bernstein's day, automatic equipment for processing his large amount

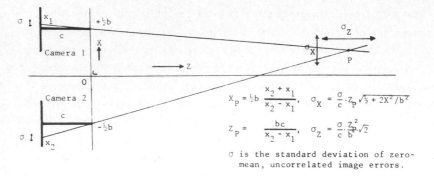

$$X_p = \tfrac{1}{2}b \, \frac{x_2 + x_1}{x_2 - x_1}, \quad \sigma_X = \frac{\sigma}{c} \cdot Z_p \sqrt{\tfrac{1}{3} + 2X^2/b^2}$$

$$Z_p = \frac{bc}{x_2 - x_1}, \quad \sigma_Z = \frac{\sigma}{c} \cdot \frac{Z_p^2}{b} \cdot \sqrt{2}$$

σ is the standard deviation of zero-mean, uncorrelated image errors.

Fig. 2. Error propagation in the normal, stereophotogrammetric case.

of measurements did not yet exist, and his group devoted considerable effort to the design of *nomogrammes* for the graphic conversion of image data - scaled to a reference plane in object space - into 3-D coordinates. For constructing these nomogrammes, certain configurational constraints had to be met, and certain parameters had to be quantified by calibration. In particular, the camera had to be level, and the mirror vertical; these requirements were verified by means of a spirit level and a plumb line. Furthermore, the distance F between the camera and the mirror, along the camera's optical axis, and the angle α (see Fig. 3) were required. Contrary to the situation in conventional geodetic surveying, Bernstein found that direct angle measurement was insufficiently accurate in his close-range situation, and he resorted to an indirect approach in which F and α were calculated from measured distances between the camera lens, mirror vertices, and a vertical yardstick somewhere in the observation field, in combination with image data on these targets.

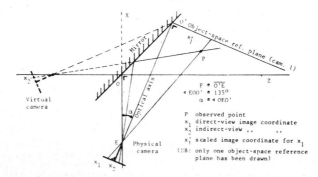

Fig. 3. Geometry of Bernstein's mirror photogrammetry.

In Bernstein's work, the cameras and mirrors were assumed to be free of distortion; similar assumptions have been entertained by many recent biomechanicians.

Contemporary Photogrammetry. Unverified assumptions on model appropriateness are largely avoided in contemporary photogrammetry (e.g., Ghosh, 1979; Slama, 1980), and more general camera configurations and image error models are used. An essential notion in this context is that of *redundancy* or *overdeterminacy*, i.e. the use of more measurements than is minimally required, in order to improve on the accuracy of estimated variables and parameters by means of some form of averaging. Bernstein was apparently not aware of the advantages of redundant measurement, although another explanation might be that he ruled this out on account of the already overwhelming amount of work required for processing nonredundant data. For example, the horizontal X-Z coordinates in Fig. 3 are exactly determined by the real and virtual, horizontal image coordinates, but the vertical coordinate Y is overdetermined in that both the real and virtual, vertical image data yield estimates for the Y-coordinate, for prior estimated X- and Z-coordinates. Bernstein did acknowledge that the discrepancy between these Y-estimates could be used as an accuracy measure, but did not mention the possibility of calculating some weighted average as an improved estimate.

In contemporary analytical photogrammetry, camera calibration and 3-D target position reconstruction are often treated in a dualistic or in a simultaneous manner. A highly popular approach in biomechanics today is the one based on the *Direct Linear Transformation*, or DLT, originally developed by Karara and his associates (cf. Miller et al., 1980) which accommodates all forms of linear image distortion, and which allows virtually arbitrary camera positioning with respect to a given laboratory coordinate system. The relation between an object point P, with object coordinates $\underline{X}_P \triangleq (X_P, Y_P, Z_P)'$, and the corresponding image point p, with image coordinates $\underline{x}_p \triangleq (x_p, y_p)'$ is described by the bilinear ratio

$$x_p = (a_1 X_P + a_2 Y_P + a_3 Z_P + a_4) \, / \, D$$
$$y_p = (a_5 X_P + a_6 Y_P + a_7 Z_P + a_8) \, / \, D \tag{1}$$
$$\text{where} \qquad D = (a_9 X_P + a_{10} Y_P + a_{11} Z_P + 1\ )$$

For a given 3-D distribution of at least 6 *control points* having known coordinates $\underline{X}_{Pi}$, and corresponding measured image coordinates $\underline{x}_{pi}$, the DLT parameters $\underline{a} \triangleq (a_1 \ldots a_{11})'$ may be determined in a statistically optimal fashion, for a given measurement error model. Conversely, for given parameter vectors $\underline{a}_j$, the coordinates $\underline{X}_P$ of some unknown point P may be determined from image coordinates $\underline{x}_{pj}$ in at least two cameras (j= 1,2).

Particularly in the study of locomotion, the construction, maintenance, and (trans)portability of a sufficiently large and stable, 3-D calibration object is rather problematic. One should note in this context that the calibration distribution should encompass the full observation volume, in order to minimize the influence of extrapolation errors. Recent developments in photogrammetry have resulted in procedures which avoid the need for a precisely known 3-D calibration distribution. The most general of these is called *Analytical Selfcalibration*. Here, a stationary 2-D or 3-D distribution of targets with unknown coordinates is observed by a camera with stable but unknown internal parameters (e.g., focal length), while held in different *attitudes*, and possibly in different positions, and both the unknown targets and the unknown camera parameters are recovered. In this approach, it is merely necessary to define a coordinate system and a yardstick, e.g., by defining one target to be the origin of object space, a second target to be at a certain position on the X-axis, and a third target, non-collinear with the other two, to have Z=O. For each individual 'frame', i.e., the set of image coordinates for the camera in a specific attitude and position, determinacy does not obtain, but the combination of at least three different attitudes yields a unique, highly overdetermined solution. Since the positions of the targets are usually the eventually required quantities, the name "selfcalibration" has been adopted for this approach.

Such calibration and reconstruction procedures impose limited constraints on the equipment being used in that only *stability* of the complete configuration is required. In cinematography, this may be a problem on account of mechanical vibration and sprocket tolerances in the film transport mechanism, but opto-electronic systems generally meet this requirement. On the negative side, the complexity of some of the more advanced photogrammetric methods has deterred many non-photogrammetrists from exploring this field, despite the availability of comprehensive software packages.

A number of investigators in biomechanics have opted for solutions intermediate to the DLT and Analytical Selfcalibration. Woltring (1980) has described a procedure using a known, *planar* distribution, to be held at various different and numerically unknown attitudes throughout the observation field, for complete calibration of internal and external camera parameters. Dapena et al. (1982) used a distribution of known linear 'yardsticks' placed at unknown positions throughout the field, while estimating internal camera parameters in a separate method.

The reconstruction of landmark positions in these procedures follows similar lines. Ideally, iterative adjustment calculus is used to find those spatial coordinates for which a statistically motivated costfunction on image residuals (i.e., discrepancies between observed image data and predictions following from estimated 3-D positions) is minimized. A slightly biased solution is the one which optimizes in terms of object-space distances, i.e., that particular and usually unique point for which a (weighted) sum of squared distances to direction lines emanating from the cameras is minimized. For given camera positions $\underline{P}_{c_i}$ and observed direction lines $\underline{S}_i$ (both expressed in terms of a laboratory-defined coordinate system), the ODLE-solution (for *Object-Distance Least-squares Error*) becomes

$$\hat{\underline{X}} = \left(\sum_i Q_i \right)^{-1} \cdot Q_i \underline{P}_{-c_i}, \quad \text{where } Q_i \triangleq I - \underline{S}_i \underline{S}_i' \, / \, \underline{S}_i' \underline{S}_i \tag{2}$$

Rigid-Body Kinematics. The estimation of individual point coordinates is merely an intermediate phase in kinematic calculus. For complete movement analysis, translations and rotations of body segments are sought; these may be evaluated once global and local landmark coordinates are known (e.g., Spoor & Veldpaus, 1980). Alternatively, these variables may be evaluated directly from observed image coordinates by means of iterative adjustment calculus, even when not all landmarks are completely observed so as to allow their individual reconstruction (Miller et al., 1980; Woltring, 1982).

The calculation of these kinematic variables is quite costly, and this presumably deterred Bernstein from carrying out a complete 3-D analysis involving at least 3 non-collinear landmarks per body segment. Instead, he limited himself to landmarks close to the joint 'centres' per body segment, thus rendering axial rotation unobservable, for each segment. For normal locomotion studies, or as one phase in the iterative conception of research, this simplification was quite viable; only recently has axial rotation been deemed important in the study of pathological gait in such fields as neurology and orthopaedics. Besides, the precision with which axial rotation can be determined is a linear function of the distance of a third landmark to the axis defined by the joint landmarks, and this has given rise to practical difficulties in the case of typically oblong arm and leg segments.

Two other important issues are, first, the validity of the rigid-body concept which underlies these kinematic models, and secondly, the definition of local coordinate systems, since no two body segments are exactly equal. These questions will be addressed more fully in the section on body segment

description and parameter estimation. On the kinematic level, deviations
from the rigid-body model such as may be caused by skin shifts can be
ascertained from the intermarker distances calculated from reconstructed
point positions; these discrepancies can then be used to adjust the local
landmark coordinates.

  Derivative Estimation. As apparent from Newton's laws, velocities and
accelerations are required input data for dynamic modelling and data
processing. The optimal estimation of these derivatives seems to be a
perpetual bone of contention in experiment biomechanics. There would appear
to exist two reasons for this situation. First, *stochastic* and *deterministic*
errors are confounded, and secondly, the Shannon sampling theorem is taken
to be a *sufficiency* criterion instead of a *necessary condition*. Furthermore,
certain intuitively appealing, 'simple' algorithms for derivative estimation
are taken at face value, without proper analysis.

  As regards the first point, it is often argued - as Bernstein did in
criticizing the need for Braune & Fischer's 50 μm resolution in estimating
landmark coordinates - that the large discrepancies found in the case of
redundant measurement do not warrant such high resolutions. However, suppose
that all measurements are affected by the *same* constant error, differences
calculated from these data as used in derivative estimation will be error-
free. By analogy, low-frequency errors such as those due to skin shifts
during movement will have comparatively little influence on the estimation
of velocities and accelerations. On the other hand, uncorrelated, wide-band
errors have a considerable influence, since differentiation in the time
domain is equivalent to multiplying the frequency spectrum by the frequency,
thus emphasizing higher frequencies in the data. Quantization errors tend
to belong to this class, and Bernstein actually investigated their influence
on his derivative estimators.

  As regards the second point, the sampling theorem (formulated since
Bernstein's day) prescribes that a signal should be sampled at a rate which
is at least twice the largest signal frequency contained in the data. Since
physically realizable signals are not strictly band-limited (cf. Slepian,
1976), and always affected by some wide-band noise, one should sample at a
frequency which is at least twice as large as the cross-over frequency
beyond which the noise level is dominant. In this way, frequency 'aliasing',
i.e., the occurrence of stroboscopic effects, is minimized. On the other
hand, the sampling theorem does not say anything about the utility of sampling

at much higher frequenceis. If the signal is disturbed by wide-band (i.e., largely uncorrelated) noise, it can be advantageous to sample at a much higher frequency, and then pass the data through a suitable low-pass filter. In this way, the influence of noise is reduced by averaging. For a strictly band-limited signal (bandwidth $\omega_B \triangleq 2\pi f_B$), sampling interval τ, and additive white noise with standard deviation σ, Lanshammar (1981, 1982) has shown that an ideal low-pass estimator for the k-th derivative (or for the signal proper, with k=0) has output noise with standard deviation

$$\sigma_k = \sigma\sqrt{\tau}.\omega_B^{2k+\frac{1}{2}}/\{\pi(2k+1)\}^{\frac{1}{2}}, \ k = 0,1,2,\ \ldots \tag{3}$$

This ideal estimator is perfect up to the frequency ω_B, and a perfect attenuator for higher frequencies.

The model (3) is ideal in three respects: (i) no signal is strictly band-limited, (ii) noise cannot be perfectly white, and (iii) a filter cannot have a perfect discontinuity in its frequency response. However, the ideal filter may be approximated arbitrarily closely. From (3) one can see that increasing the sampling frequency, i.e., decreasing τ, will result in smaller values of σ_k. In fact, the term $\sigma\sqrt{\tau}$ demonstrates the utility of defining a combined *spatio-temporal resolution criterion* in addition to the sampling theorem requirement. On the other hand, the white-noise assumption underlying (3) may be significantly violated if τ is chosen too small when quantization noise is the dominant error source: in this case, adjacent samples may remain within the same quantization interval, and thus contain perfectly correlated errors.

The availability of a spatio-temporal resolution criterion allows the evaluation of different measuring systems such as the various optoelectronic systems discussed in section 1 of this chapter. In order to render a comparison valid, stereometric configurations must be defined in such a fashion that the different systems, with their different viewing angles, encompass the same field of view. For example, Braune & Fischer used equipment with $\sigma = 50$ μm and $\tau^{-1} = 26$ Hz, which was definitely superior to Bernstein's in terms of the $\sigma\sqrt{\tau}$ criterion, but they failed to process their data properly for derivative estimation, as demonstrated by Bernstein (1935). In view of Bernstein's claim that sampling frequencies higher than 26 Hz were necessary for the detection of minor but stable 10 Hz signals in his locomotion data, it is of interest to compare the signal and noise transmission properties of his derivative estimators with the ideal case (3). In one experiment, he

reported a sampling frequency of 90 Hz, and a measurement accuracy of ±0.5mm.
If the quantization noise is assumed to be uncorrelated (i.e., 'white'), and
uniformly distributed throughout the quantization interval, its standard
deviation may be calculated as $1/\sqrt{12}$ mm. Substitution of these values into
(3) yields σ_1 = 4.94 mm/s and σ_2 = 0.24 m/s² for ideal, single and double
differentiators up to 10 Hz, and perfect attenuators beyond this frequency.
Now, Bernstein (1935) used the following estimators for the first and second
derivatives,

$$\hat{v}_i = (x_{i+2} - x_{i-2})/4\tau, \quad \hat{a}_i = (\hat{v}_{i+2} - \hat{v}_{i-2})/4\tau \qquad (4)$$

where i is the sample index. The noise output from these estimators, again
assuming white noise with $\sigma = 1/\sqrt{12}$ mm, can be calculated as $\sigma_1' = \sigma\sqrt{2}/4\tau$ =
9.19 mm/s and $\sigma_2' = \sigma\sqrt{6}/(4\tau)^2$ = 0.358 m/s², respectively; these figures are
considerably higher than those for the ideal differentiators. Furthermore,
Bernstein's estimators appear to be significantly *biased* when analyzed in
terms of their frequency response. From (4), it may be shown that the
transfer function of Bernstein's differentiator for $\hat{v}_i$ is $j.\sin(2\omega\tau)/(2\tau)$,
whereas the ideal characteristic is $j\omega$, with $j \triangleq \sqrt{-1}$. The ratio $H_1(\omega\tau)$ of
these functions, and its square $H_2(\omega\tau)$ for the double differentiator are

$$H_1(\omega\tau) = \mathrm{sinc}(2\omega\tau) \triangleq \sin(2\omega\tau)/(2\omega\tau), \quad H_2(\omega\tau) = \{\mathrm{sinc}(2\omega\tau)\}^2 \qquad (5)$$

and these approach unity for the limiting case $\omega\tau \to 0$. However, at higher
frequencies, considerable attenuation occurs as shown in Fig. 4 for the
double differentiator. For the above numerical values, H_1= 0.71 and H_2 =
0.5. Thus, the signal-to-noise ratio (SNR) of Bernstein's acceleration
estimator is worse by a factor $q_2 \triangleq H_2.\sigma_2/\sigma_2'$= 0.334, in comparison with the
SNR of the ideal low-pass differentiator. As discussed in the section on
kinetic data processing, this fact is relevant when assessing the significance
of some of Bernstein's force estimates. The bias in (4) explains in part
Bernstein's criticism of Braune & Fischer's 26 Hz frame rate. As Bernstein
(1935) demonstrated by means of Fourier analysis, the investigation of
higher harmonics is facilitated when dealing with accelerations and forces,
since higher harmonics are amplified by a larger amount during differentiation.
Using τ^{-1}= 26 Hz and f_B= 10 Hz, the low-pass gain H_2 in (5) becomes 0.042,
i.e., smaller by a factor of 11.8 than that obtained for τ^{-1}= 90 Hz. On the
other hand, Braune & Fischer attained a resolution of 50 μm, which was better by

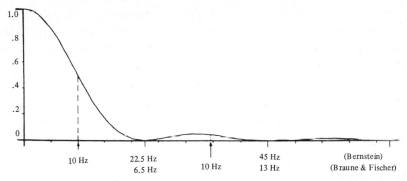

Fig. 4. Low-pass characteristic $H_2(\omega\tau)$ in Bernstein's acceleration estimator.

a factor of 10 than Bernstein's, thereby producing an actual SNR proportional to H_2/σ_2' of about the same magnitude. This explains why Bernstein (1935), having processed some of the raw data provided by Braune & Fischer, found harmonics similar to those in his own data!

Since Bernstein's day, considerable progress has taken place in the domain of digital signal processing, and a number of efficient algorithms have been described which afford suitable balancing of passband and stopband transfer characteristics (see, for example, Oppenheim & Schafer (1975), and especially Rabiner & Gold (1975)). One of the rare applications in biomechanics is that of Lesh et al. (1979). Other variable approaches include the optimal regularization method of Andersson & Bloomfield (1974), introduced into biomechanics by Hatze (1981b), and the use of spline functions (Soudan & Dierckx, 1979; Wood & Jennings, 1979). Spline functions are more general than the preceding algorithms since they do not require equidistant time intervals; as a result, they combine the techniques of low-pass filtering, derivative estimation, and interpolation in the case of temporary data loss due to shadowing effects between a landmark and an observing camera.

For all these algorithms, information on signal and noise properties is required. To some extent, this distinction is semantic insofar it may be the investigator's purpose to decide what is signal, and what is 'noise'. However, technical limitations, particularly those imposed by the spatio-temporal resolution criterion, are often dominant, and this justifies the use of an effective cross-over frequency, beyond which a flat frequency spectrum is deemed to be mainly due to measurement artefacts.

In summary, the selection of a proper data acquisition *and* processing

chain is essential for reliable estimation of numerical derivatives. Of
course, Bernstein can hardly be blamed for not fulfilling this desideratum,
since most of the theory underlying the criticism of his derivative
estimation was developed after his time, and he did attempt some comparisons
with more elaborate filtering algorithms. For example, the finite difference
(4) was shown to be the slope at x_i of a parabola fitted to the points
x_{i-2}, x_i, x_{i+2}, and Bernstein did look into improvements on the *displacement*
level when higher order polynomials were fitted. However, he did not compare
the error levels in the slopes of these functions, and merely looked at the
errors for his finite difference model (4). Presumably, he choose the ±2
increment in (4) after finding that the use of adjacent samples resulted in
excessively noisy derivatives. Furthermore, the noise terms in adjacent
acceleration estimates $\hat{a}_i$ and $\hat{a}_{i+2}$ are strongly correlated ($\rho = -0.67$). By
interspersing uncorrelated estimates derived from odd and even samples, it
is possible that the data would have appeared less noisy.

State-Space Modelling. In most data processing approaches discussed
hitherto, the various stages of landmark position reconstruction, rigid-
body calculus, derivative estimation, and so on, were treated as independent,
sequential operations. For more or less ideal data, this approach is quite
efficient, but experimental data are unfortunately by no means ideal. In
particular, the temporary loss of sight of moving landmarks and the non-
rigid nature of the body segments cause considerable problems. Thus,
rotations and translations may become *unidentifiable*, or - in the case of
redundant measurements - residual error changes caused by the combination
of skin shift and reappearence of a landmark may entail sudden, apparent
acceleration peaks. This will be discussed more fully in the section on
kinetic data processing.

Recent developments in engineering system identification and state/
parameter estimation, particularly in control engineering and aero-space
navigation, have resulted in comprehensive models and algorithms for the
simultaneous estimation of relevant variables and parameters from whatever
measurements are available. Typically, a statistically motivated *state-
space* description of the dynamic process under study is provided, for
instance, in terms of positions, rotations, and velocities. These *state
variables* are viewed as stochastic quantities which propagate themselves
according to a given set of dynamic or kinematic equations, and they are
corrected by any incoming measurement in accordance with the statistics of

the measurement and process models. In this way, it becomes possible to
carry out, at the same time, the estimation of rigid-body kinematics and
its derivatives, the interpolation for lost data, and the correction for
discrepancies between the rigid-body model and the real body segment under
study.

When using state-space models, the measurement system may observe
different entities such as directions and accelerations which are then
merged in a statistically optimal fashion. This is one of the most common
situations in aero-space navigation, and recent work in crash biomechanics
has been along similar lines (Seemann & Lustick, 1981). In this way, the
limitations of each data source are corrected by the complementary data
source: accelerations errors entail low-frequency errors in velocities and
displacements obtained via integration, whereas velocities and accelerations
obtained via differentiation of noisy displacement data suffer from high-
frequency errors.

Recommended texts in this field are those by Eykhoff (1974), Gelb
(1974), Maybeck (1979), and various AGARD publications. It is to be expected
that system identification methods will find increased use in biomechanics
(cf. Hatze, 1980a), in view of their succesful application in other fields
of engineering and medicine (cf. Bekey & Beneken, 1978; Murray-Smith, 1982).

4. Kinetic Data Acquisition and Body Segment Description

Once the kinematic data processing phase has been completed, the
kinetics (forces, moments) of the movement process may be investigated. For
this purpose, the mass distributions of the body segments must be known in
relation to local segment-defined coordinate systems. Furthermore, explicit
force and moment measurements are necessary in the case of *closed kinematic
chains*, e.g., during the double stance phase of locomotion when strong
'circulating' forces may exist within a closed chain of body segments and
the environment; such forces cannot be determined from the kinematics of
the movement, or from stationary posture.

Bernstein confined himself to the investigation of those inertial and
gravitational forces and moments which are identifiable from kinematic
measurements. Bernstein appears to have been particularly interested in the
high-frequency microstructure of the movement process, and in its significance
for the underlying movement control processes. By contrast, some investigators
in recent years have neglected the inertial components, by estimating total
joint forces and moments 'from the ground up', starting from force plate

measurements and assuming that the masses of the legs may be neglected.
Since these investigations are usually for orthopaedic purposes, with
special interest in maximum joint loadings during slow pathological gait,
the neglect of inertial effects in the legs may be acceptable, particularly
in most of the stance phase where the forces are largest, and the
accelerations smallest. Furthermore, the assumption of negligibly small
inertial effects renders the data acquisition and processing phases much
simpler, and this is an attractive feature for routine clinical purposes.
On the other hand, the alternating character of maximum and minimum loading
may eventually prove to be a much more relevant factor in mechanical stress
and fatigue analysis of components of the locomotor system. In addition, the
occurrence of co-contractions between flexing and extending muscles over a
joint causes much higher joint loadings than can be identified from kinematic
and kinetic measurements. This point will be discussed in a later section.

From the 'prospective' point of view, model simplifications should be
minimal, and the aim should be to analyze all kinetic components of human
movement. In the following sections, the use of force plates and the
acquisition of body segment parameters for the comprehensive analysis of
movement kinetics is discussed.

Force Plates. Simple force plates for ground reaction force measurement
were already known in Bernstein's time (Amar, 1916), and it is unclear why
Bernstein did not use, or even refer to these measurement tools. Today,
force plates of various sizes, based on piezo-electric transducers or
strain-gauges, are commercially available. Typically, they provide force and
moment information integrated over their surfaces (cf. the integrating
nature of the lateral photoeffect detector depicted in Fig. 1), that is,
vertical and horizontal force components, vertical moment, and mean point
of impact. Some disagreement exists as to the need for high sampling
frequencies in the case of impact transients, such as heel- and toe-strike
during gait, since the recorded peaks might be caused by mechanical
resonance ('ringing'). Furthermore, the mounting of force plates requires
proper damping of vibrations from other sources. The possibility to place
multiple force plates in different positions with respect to each other is
useful when it comes to accommodating different gait patterns, e.g.,
childrens' versus adults', or normal versus 'scissors' gait where one foot
is placed partly in front of the other.

When conducting comprehensive movement studies using both kinematic and kinetic measurements, careful calibration of, and synchronization between the data sources is necessary. Thus, the force plate coordinate system must be known with respect to the kinematic coordinate system, and the integrity of the data collection system must be verified. Some of the kinematic data acquisition systems described in section 1 of this chapter incorporate the possibility of synchronized data collection from other sources.

Body Segment Description. It is particularly in the quantitative description of body segments that the intimate relation between mathematical modelling, data acquisition, and data processing becomes obvious. In all kinematic and kinetic analyses, modelling of the human body as a linked system of rigid bodies is perhaps one of the crudest approximations to reality. Bernstein (1936) recognized the limitations of the rigid-body model when reproducing Fischer's data on the proximal and distal, relative distances (0.44 and 0.56, respectively) for the 'by no means rigid' trunk, in addition to the data in Table 2 of Chapter I. For lack of better information, he nevertheless used these parameters to estimate body segment forces and total centre of gravity forces from landmarks observed at the hips and shoulders (Bernstein, 1935). However, he demonstrated that the influence of random errors in his acceleration data on the force estimates was much stronger than the non-rigid nature of the body segments.

Since Bernstein carried out his investigations, considerable attention has been paid to quantitative anthropometry, particularly in sports, aero-space, and crash biomechanics where high accelerations do not allow the neglect of inertial effects (see, e.g., Miller & Nelson (1973), Chandler et al. (1975), and Herron et al. (1976) which give an adequate account of the literature). Hay's biomechanical bibliography (1981) contains about 10 pages on anthropometry, and only 4 on data smoothing and general mathematical modelling! Current methods for body segment anthropometry include volume determination by immersion, biostereometrics, and tomography, under the assumption of certain mass densities for the estimation of inertial properties. Furthermore, a variety of dynamic system identification methods are used for estimating inertial properties from observed kinematics, e.g., the swing time of a freely swinging leg modelled as a pendulum. More recently, inconsistencies in estimated kinematics and kinetics have been used for the correction of mass distribution parameters (Vaughan et al., 1982).

Comprehensive mathematical models have been presented by Hanavan (1964)

and, more recently, by Hatze (1980b). Hatze's 17-segment model of the human
body requires 242 measurements to be taken on the subject, and this renders
his model impractical for routine use. However, the availability of such
comprehensive models will allow systematic evaluation of those measurements
and parameters which may be neglected in the estimation of total movement
dynamics.

As discussed in the next section of this chapter, considerable
attention is currently being given to the *redundancy* or *indeterminacy* problem
in biomechanics. Mass distribution parameters, kinematic measurements, and
reaction force measurements with the environment only provide total,
external forces and moments, not the contributions of individual muscles,
ligaments, and other components of the musculoskeletal system. For the
latter, *internal* forces, a number of models are currently being developed,
and these require information on muscle and ligament attachment points,
ligament stiffnesses, and geometry of the articulating surfaces. Originally,
this information was mostly inferred from anatomical textbooks, but more
recently, Röntgen measurements and anthropometric scaling procedures have
been used (Brand et al., 1982).

5. Kinetic Modelling and Data Processing

Under the rigid-body assumption, the kinetics and energetics of the
movement are comparatively simple as explained in the 'Technical Note' of
Hardt & Mann (1980). If each segment is viewed as a free body, with forces
and moments acting at its proximal and distal ends (apart from gravity
forces which work at its centre of gravity), the following force and moment
balance equations based on Newtson's second law apply,

$$\underline{F}_{cg} = m \cdot \underline{\ddot{x}}_{cg} = \underline{F}_1 + \underline{F}_2 + m \cdot \underline{g}$$
$$\underline{M}_{cg} = I_{cg} \cdot \underline{\alpha}_{cg} = \underline{M}_1 + \underline{M}_2 + \underline{r}_1 * \underline{F}_1 + \underline{r}_2 * \underline{F}_2 \tag{6}$$

with

$\underline{F}_{cg}$ the total force acting on the segment's c.o.g.

$\underline{M}_{cg}$ the total moment acting at the segment's c.o.g.

m   the mass of the segment

I_{cg} the inertia matrix of the body at the c.o.g.

$\underline{x}_{cg}$ the position of the segment's c.o.g.

$\underline{\ddot{x}}_{cg}$ the acceleration of the segment's c.o.g.

$\underline{g}$ gravity acceleration vector (g= 9.81 m/s²)

$\underline{\alpha}_{cg}$ the angular acceleration of the segment

$\underline{F}_1, \underline{F}_2$ distal and proximal external forces acting on the segment

$\underline{M}_1$, $\underline{M}_2$ distal and proximal external moments acting on the segment

$\underline{r}_1$, $\underline{r}_2$ the moment arms of the proximal and distal forces with respect to the segment's c.o.g.

where all quantities are expressed with respect to a common, inertial coordinate system (NB: the inertia matrix I_{cg} is a function of the segment's attitude). Starting from the distal end of a segment with known $\underline{F}_1$ and $\underline{M}_1$ (these are zero in the case of a freely swinging extremity, or otherwise given by a force-place measurement), the proximal values $\underline{F}_2$ and $\underline{M}_2$ follow from (6), for given kinematics and mass distribution parameters. By virtue of Newton's third law (action = reaction), the distal forces and moments of an adjacent segment are equal to the estimated proximal forces, albeit with opposite sign. Thus, all segments may be processed sequentially in the case of open kinematic chains or closed chains with explicit kinetic measurements.

The vector and matrix products in the moment equation of (6) indicate the limited validity of separate analyses in the frontal and sagittal planes, since the moments acting in a given plane may be affected by force components acting outside that plane. Complete, 3-D models for kinetic analysis (e.g., Hatze, 1980a) have recently become available, so it will now be possible to verify the sagittal analyses of Bernstein and many later investigators. In particular, the lateral 'swing' at the hip level in ordinary gait by means of which weight is transferred to the stance leg, is a significant source of extrasagittal kinetics (cf. Bresler & Frankel, 1950).

Bernstein's model and results. Bernstein (1936) regarded the complete 3-D calculation of the product $I_{cg} \cdot \underline{\alpha}_{cg}$ as "one of the most tiring and complicated calculations of applied mathematics", and went on to simplify his model, by neglecting axial rotation in the oblong body segments, and by modelling the mass distribution of the segments in terms of two point masses, one on each side of the segment's c.o.g., at 3/10 of the segment's length. In this way, he was able to separate sagittal from extra-sagittal components, and could confine himself to planar, sagittal analysis with one observing camera per body side.

Adopting these simplifications, Bernstein estimated segment forces and total body forces during locomotion, with particular emphasis on the micro-structure of his curves, and it is here that serious doubt exists as to the significance of his results. In the sagittal analysis, the position of a segment's c.o.g. is derived as a linear function of the landmark positions

at the segment ends, using Fischers' data (cf. Table 2, Chapter I) as
weight factors. Total body c.o.g. forces were subsequently calculated as a
weighted sum of individual segment c.o.g. forces, using Fischer's relative
masses (Table 1, Chapter I) as weight factors. Mathematically, this results
in a formula of the form

$$\underline{F}_{body} = \sum_{i=1}^{20} w_i \ddot{\underline{x}}_i M/g \tag{7}$$

where $\ddot{\underline{x}}_i$ are the estimated landmark accelerations, w_i the weight factors
calculated from Fischer's tables, M the total mass of the subject, g the
gravitational acceleration, and $\underline{F}_{body}$ the total body force expressed in kgf.
Now, if the $\ddot{\underline{x}}_i$ are disturbed with additive, uncorrelated measurement noise,
with standard deviation σ_2', the standard deviation of the components in $\underline{F}_{body}$
follows as

$$\sigma_{\underline{F}} = wM\sigma_2'/g, \quad \text{with } w \triangleq \left(\sum_{i=1}^{20} w_i^2 \right)^{\frac{1}{2}} \tag{8}$$

According to Fischer's tables and the other data in Bernstein (1935), w= 0.33.
Using M= 70 kg and $\sigma_2' = 0.358$ m/s², as derived in the section on kinematic
data processing, we find $\sigma_{\underline{F}} = 0.8$ kgf. Considering the amplitudes of the
various peaks in, for example, the horizontal components of whole-body c.o.g.
forces (Fig. 22, Chapter III), one might well question Bernstein's elaborate
account of the minute details in his curves. As pointed out above, if he had
better differentiating algorithms at his disposal, his signal-to-noise ratio
might have been better by a factor not larger than 3.

    This criticism is even more serious in view of the fact that Bernstein
(1935) used an additional landmark at approximately the c.o.g. of the thigh.
Whenever the freely swinging hand of the subject obscured the hip landmark,
he relied on this additional landmark to recover the hip's position, by
formally extrapolating from it and from the knee landmark. Not only does
this increase $\sigma_{\underline{F}}$ to 1 kgf if one hip landmark is obscured, and to 1.2 kgf
if both are simultaneously obscured (it is assumed that the additional
landmark was halfway between the hip and knee landmarks), but residual error
changes, due to skin movement, in the transition from one model to the other
may also have caused sudden, apparent acceleration peaks. This effect is
most likely to occur in the case of γ^ζ peaks in Fig. 22 and the γ peaks of
Fig. 23 (Chapter III; cf. Bernstein, Fig. 11 & 12, Expt. 331).

Unfortunately, it is unclear from Bernstein's description whether he allowed for the possible occurrence of such artefacts.

Comparison with later research. During the 1940-s and early 1950-s, a long series of investigations on normal and prosthetic gait was conducted in the Biomechanics Laboratory of the University of California at Berkeley (Anonymous, 1947; Inman et al., 1981). A frame rate τ^{-1} = 30 Hz was used, and a digitization error of 10^{-4} inch was attained, corresponding to a quantization noise standard deviation σ= 21 μm in object space (assuming that image blur was negligibly small, and that the digitizing operator was perfectly capable of locating the centroid of a landmark image). Numerical derivatives were estimated from finite differences of *adjacent* samples, a procedure which results in a low-pass transfer function $H_2(\omega\tau) = \text{sinc}^2(\omega\tau)$. Using f_B= 10 Hz as was done in the case of Bernstein's data above, this yields H_2 = 0.171, σ_2'= 0.046 m/s^2, and H_2/σ_2'= 3.69 s^2/m, as compared to Bernstein's H_2= 0.5, σ_2'= 0.358 m/s^2, and H_2/σ_2'= 1.40 s^2/m. Thus, the SNR of the Californian acceleration estimates for a 10 Hz bandwidth was better than Bernstein's by a factor of 3.69/1.40 = 2.64. For a 5 Hz bandwidth, this factor increases to 6.28, and it is gratifying to see that most of the acceleration curves published by the California group show quite significant waves in the 5 - 10 Hz range, e.g., in the horizontal components at the ankle, knee, greater trochanter, and iliac crest. Thus, there is some basis for Bernstein's conclusion that "characteris and stable dynamic waves (oscillations)" with a frequency of 10 Hz occur during normal locomotion.

In direct contrast to these conclusions are those of Winter (1982), who claims that human movement at normal walking speed contains no significant frequencies beyond 5 or 6 Hz, and that there is no need to sample at frequencies beyond those of the standard 24 fps cine camera or 30 Hz TV system. He bases these conclusions on his earlier finding that virtually no signal power is contained in the *displacement* data beyond the sixth harmonic of the stride frequency. However, double differentiation of ideal, noisefree measurements may be expected to show quite a different picture, and this may not have revealed itself to Winter since the noise level of his equipment was considerably higher than the noise level of the equipment used by Bernstein or the California group (cf. Winter, 1983). In fact, most contemporary research on the biomechanics of locomotion seems to suffer from much lower spatio-temporal resolution than was achieved by the German, Russian, and Californian investigators, and a suitable research topic would

be to repeat some of the old experiments with contemporary, high resolution
equipment in combination with proper forms of low-pass derivative estimation.
The accelerometric findings of Wosk & Voloshin (1981) concerning the
presence of a major frequency component in the 25 - 35 Hz range at the *head*,
during normal locomotion, are quite striking in this context.

    Contemporary neuromusculoskeletal models. The free-body model (6) may
be generalized to more complicated systems if anatomical information on
muscles, ligaments, and joint surface shapes is included. The most important,
mechanical models are based on the Lagrangian and Newton-Euler methods
(Hemami et al., 1975). The Lagrange method is based on the difference between
total kinetic and potential energy, expressed in terms of generalized,
independent coordinates and their time derivatives, and allows direct
calculation of active (external) forces and moments. The Newton-Euler method
is directly based on Newton's laws, and leads to equations similar to those
in (6); it admits interdependencies between coordinates, and allows the
calculation of both active and reactive *constraint* forces and moments. An
advantage of the Lagrange method is its smaller number of equations. On the
other hand, the Newton-Euler equations have a simpler structure, with less
changes being required when the model is changed, e.g., in the transition
from single to double stance in locomotion. In recent years, the advantages
of both approaches have been combined by Wittenburg (1977) in a method based
on d'Alembert's principle of virtual work. Hatze (1981c) and Hatze & Venter
(1981) used similar methods in their comprehensive models for analysis and
synthesis of human movement.

    An important topic in current *bio*mechanics is the study of the
indeterminacy problem. Many muscles and ligaments cross a single joint, and
various muscles cross multiple joints. By consequence, the kinematic/kinetic
analysis of a mechanistic rigid-body model does not reveal the distribution
of forces over all anatomical components. A customary hypothesis is that the
redundancy in the neuromusculoskeletal system serves as a safeguard, so
that the organism may redistribute its activity over different elements in
order to compensate for fatigue and damage, such compensatory effects being
hardly or not at all observable on the kinematic level, if only for
aesthetic reasons. If compensatory effects involve multiple joints, e.g.,
when transferring load from a painful joint to another, this can be revealed
by kinetic analysis (Winter, 1981b; Brown et al., 1981), but if they are limited
to a single joint, other measurement techniques are required, e.g., for
assessing the relative contributions of ligaments and muscles in joint

stabilization. Such measurements may be non-invasive as in the case of surface-EMG, which can indicate the contributions of individual muscles (Hof & van den Berg, 1981), or invasive, as when strain gauges are used in ligaments or artificial joints. Naturally, the use of invasive methods is constrained to animal or volunteer work, or to those clinical situations where surgery is indicated for medical reasons.

Because of these constraints, much research has gone into further modelling. Various engineering models for optimal force distribution based on minimal energy or equal force density across muscles have been used. However, these techniques were used because they happened to be available, rather than because there were sound reasons for believing in the physiological rationale of their optimization criteria; cf. Crowninshield (1978), Hardt (1978), Chao & An (1978), Hatze (1980a), and Brand et al. (1982). Hatze (1980a, 1981a) has been one of the few to model the neural innervation process in complex human movement.

6. Trends and Speculations

One of Bernstein's criticism of his predecessors concerned the limited amount of data on which they based their conclusions. Bernstein (1935) reported that 120 out of 800 cyclographic photographs were analyzed by his group, corresponding to more than 500 single steps, and about 400,000 digitized coordinates. In contrast, Braune & Fischer only analyzed 3 out of 12 cyclographic photographs, corresponding to about 5000 digitized coordinates. After processing the measurements with his chosen biomechanical model, Bernstein attempted to recognize a pattern in the estimated forces and moments, particularly in their microstructure. It is in this sense that Bernstein's work constitutes a unification of two major trends in contemporary studies of human movement, locomotion in particular. One of these is the use of 'simple', direct measurements (electrogoniometry, force plates, EMG) in statistical, empirical studies on large numbers of subjects (Donath, 1978; Chao et al., 1980). The other is the inclusion of more 'complex' measurements (3-D kinematics, mass distribution parameters) with the object of carrying out deterministic, biomechanical analyses on a small number of subjects (Winter, 1981; Brown et al., 1981). In view of the indeterminacy issue, both approaches seem too limited: the 'simple' features used in the former approach are insufficiently discriminative, while the limited amount of data in the latter do not allow generalization to the population at large. Ideally, both approaches would be combined through the development of both deterministic, biomechanical models, and statistical, empirical pattern recognition procedures with suitable data base management. For the latter purpose, current developments in interactive pattern recognition (Gelsema, 1980) are promising.

In orthopaedics and physiotherapy, the investigation of functional load distributions within and between joints is an important, long-term issue. In particular, orthopaedic implant failure and irradiation of arthritis to other joints requires longitudinal studies on the kinetic level, over large numbers of patients. Once an estimation of *in-vivo* loading during functional activity has been made, the study of dynamic stress distributions within the bones and in the interface between bones and prostheses becomes feasible. Until now, stress analysis of biomechanical structures has been predominantly static and *in vitro*, using standard software packages developed in the domain of structural mechanics (Huiskes & Chao, 1983).

Other issues in orthopaedics include those of critical timing for surgery, pre/postoperative assessment, and even diagnostics - which is the most elusive of all applications. In particular the identification of pathological and compensatory effects on the kinetic level may render bio-mechanical analysis of human movement an efficient clinical tool. The notorious pathologies following professional athlete achievements may also be investigated in this way, and hopefully prevented.

In applications of a psycho-motor nature (rehabilitation, sports training), biomechanical analysis can provide essential information about causes and consequences in the generation of movement patterns, both as regards optimization in the direction of a given norm ('normal' gait, peak sports performance), and comparison of alternative norms (structural limitations in a damaged body, different high-performance sport styles); here again, the biomechanically oriented *feature extraction* should be followed by a suitable pattern recognition policy.

At the present time, rehabilitation of specific muscle groups through biofeedback methods is performed via EMG or kinematic measurements. Neither data source provides unequivocal information about the effective contribution by the muscle group under investigation, because of co-contractions, compensatory effects, and limited validity of dynamic EMG-to-force transformation models. It is surmised that kinetic models either by themselves or in combination with EMG data will provide a reliable information source.

Practical problems in all these applications include the large amount of developmental and computer processing effort required. Fortunately, both measurement equipment and suitable software packages are available. The validation of biomechanical models is an important aspect, in view of the healthy distrust on the part of clinicians of 'black-box' models of biological reality. However, collaboration between medical and engineering participants will allow the inclusion of anatomical information, and thereby change the model into a 'gray box' (Murray-Smith, 1982). Validation or refutation will follow from the explorative use of these models on large numbers of subjects, i.e., in the pattern recognition phase. In this fashion, the hypothetico-deductive conception of the research process outlined in the introduction to this chapter on Bernstein's methodology will find its proper realization.

7. Acknowledgements

The author is indebted to dr. L. Lamoreux and Mr. F. Todd for providing him with a copy of Bernstein (1935) which has been essential for assessing the reliability of Bernstein's data processing methodology. Furthermore, he wishes to thank dr. A. Cappozzo, dr. R. Huiskes, dr. M.O. Jarrett, ir. F.M. Maarse, dr. G. Richardson and dr. M.W. Whittle for their critical review and suggestions on earlier drafts of the manuscript. Finally, he would like to thank prof. dr. H.T.A. Whiting for the opportunity to write this chapter, and for his linguistic comments.

REFERENCES

Amar, J. Trottoir dynamographique. Compt. Rend. Acad. des Sci., 1916, 163,
    130-132.

Anonymous. Fundamental studies of human locomotion and other information
    relating to design of artificial limbs. Subcontractor's Report to the
    Committee on Artificial Limbs, National Research Council. Prosthetic
    Devices Research Project, College of Engineering, University of
    California, Berkely. Serial No., CAL 5, 2 volumes, 1947.

Anderssen, R.S. & Bloomfield, P. Numerical differentiation procedures for
    non-exact data. Numerical Mathematics, 1974, 22, 157-182.

Aten, D.R. Automatic analysis of automobile impact evaluation. In, G.G.
    Manuella, R.A. Wilson and L.W. Roberts (Eds.), Effective utilization of
    photographic and optical technology to the problems of automotive safety,
    emission, and fuel economy. Proc. S.P.I.E., 1975, 57.

Baum, E. Motografie I. Bremerhaven: Wirtschaftsverlag N.W., 1980.

Baum, E. Motografie II. Bremerhaven: Wirtschaftsverlag N.W., 1983.

Becker, E. & Williams, G. An experimentally validated three-dimensional
    inertial tracking package for application in biodynamic research. In,
    Proc. 19th STAPP conference, S.A.E. paper 751173. Society of Automobile
    Engineers, U.S.A., 1975.

Bekey, G.A. & Beneken, J.E.W. Identification of biological systems: a
    survey. Automatica, 1978, 14, 41-47.

Bernstein, N.A. Untersuchung der Körperbewegungen im Raum mittels Spiegel-
    verfahren (Investigation of body movements in space by means of mirror
    methods). Arbeitsphysiologie, 1930, 3, 179-206.

Bernstein, N.A., Popova, T.S. & Mogiljanskaja, Z.V. Technika izučenija
    dviženij (Technique for the investigation of movements). Moscow, 1934.

Bernstein, N.A. (Ed.), Issledovania po biodinamike lokomocij (Research in
    biodynamics of locomotion). Vol. 1: Biodinamika chod'by normal'nogo
    vzroslogo mužčiny (Biodynamics of walking of normal and adult man).
    Moscow and Leningrad, 1935, NB: A condensed translation of this book was
    prepared for the California project by B. Bresler, 1947; this translation
    was used for the present reaction to Chapter I.

Bernstein, N.A. Die kymocyclographische Methode der Bewegungsuntersuchung
    (The kymocyclographic method for movement research). In, E. Abderhalden
    (Ed.), Handbuch der biologischen Arbeitsmethoden (Handbook of biological
    experimental methods). Volume 5, Part 5A. Berlin and Vienna: Urban and
    Schwartzenberg, 1936.

Bernstein, N.A. Bewegungsphysiologie (Movement Physiology). Edited by L. Pickenhain and G. Schnabel. Leipzig: Barth, 1975.

Brand, R.A., Crowninshield, R.D., Wittstock, C.E., Pedersen, D.R., Clark, C.R. & van Krieken, F.M. ASME Journal of Biomechanical Engineering, 1982, 104, 304-310.

Braune, W. et al. Human mechanics - four monographs abridged. AMRL-TDR-63-123, Wright-Patterson Air Force Base, Ohio. Acquisition number AD 600 618, National Technical Information Service, U.S. Department of Commerce, Springfield (VA), 1963.

Braune, W. & Fischer, O. Ueber den Schwerpunkt des menschlichen Körpers, mit Rücksicht auf die Ausrüstung des deutschen Infanteristen (The center of gravity of the human body as related to the equipment of the german infantry). Abh. der math. -phys. Classe der k. Sachs. Gesellsch. der Wissensch., 1889, 26, 561-672.

Bresler, B. & Frankel, J.P. The forces and moments in the leg during level walking. Transactions of the ASME, 1950, 72, 27-36.

Brown, T.R.M., Paul, J.P., Kelley, I.G. & Hamblen, D.L. Biomechanical assessment of patients treated by joint surgery. Journal of Biomedical Engineering, 1981, 3, 297-304.

Brumbaugh, R.B., Crowninshield, R.D., Blair, W.F. & Andrews, J.F. An in-vivo study of normal wrist kinematics. ASME Journal of Biomechanical Engineering, 1982, 104, 177-181.

Chandler, R.F., Clauser, C.E., McConville, J.T., Reynolds, H.M. & Young, J.W. Investigation of inertial properties of the human body. DOT HS-801 430, AMRL/AMD, Wright-Patterson Air Force Base, Ohio, 1975.

Chao, E.Y.S. Justification of triaxial goniometer for the measurement of joint rotation. Journal of Biomechanics, 1980, 13, 989-1006.

Chao, E.Y. & An, K.N. Graphical interpretation of the redundant problem in Biomechanics. ASME Journal of Biomechanical Engineering, 1978, 100, 159-167.

Chao, E.Y., Laughman, R.K. & Stauffer, R.N. Biomechanical gait evaluation of pre- and postoperative total knee replacement patients. Archives of Orthopaedic Traumatic Surgery, 1980, 97, 309-317.

Crowninshield, R.D. Use of optimization techniques to predict muscle forces. ASME Journal of Biomechanical Engineering, 1978, 100, 88-92.

Dapena, J., Hartman, E.A. & Miller, J.A. Three-dimensional cinematography with control object of unknown shape. Journal of Biomechanics, 1981, 15, 11-19.

Donath, M. Human gait pattern recognition for evaluation, diagnosis, and control. PhD-thesis, Department of Mechanical Engineering, M.I.T., Cambridge (MA), 1978.

Eykhoff, P. System identification - parameter and state estimation. New York: Wiley, 1974.

Fischer, O. Theoretische Grundlagen für eine Mechanik der lebenden Körper mit speziellen Anwendungen auf den Menschen, sowie auf einige Bewegungs-Vorgänge an Maschinen (Theoretical fundamentals for a mechanics of living bodies, with special applications to man, as well as to some processes of motion in machines). Leipzig and Berlin: Teubner, 1906.

Furnée, E.H. Hybrid instrumentation in prosthetics research. Digest 7th International Conference on Medical and Biological Engineering. Stockholm, 1967.

Gelb, A. (Ed.), Applied optimal estimation. Cambridge (MA): The MIT Press, 1974.

Gelsema, E.S. ISAPAHAN: an interactive system for pattern analysis: structure and application. In, E.S. Gelsema and L.N. Kanal (Eds.), Pattern recognition in practice. Amsterdam: North-Holland, 1980.

Ghosh, S.K. Analytical Photogrammetry. New York: Pergamon, 1979.

Grieve, D.W., Miller, D., Mitchelson, D., Paul, J. & Smith, A.J. Techniques for the analysis of human movement. London: Lepus Books, 1975.

Güth, V., Abbink, F. & Heinrichs, W. Eine Methode zur chronozyklographischen Bewegungsaufzeichnung mit einem Prozessrechner (A method for chrono-cyclographic movement registration by means of a process computer). Int. Z. Angew. Physiol. 1973, 31, 151-162.

Hanavan, E.P. A mathematical model of the human body. AMRL-TR-64-102, Wright-Patterson Air Force Base, Ohio, 1964.

Hardt, D.E. Determining muscle forces in the leg during normal human walking - an application and evaluation of optimization methods. ASME Journal of Biomechanical Engineering, 1978, 100, 72-78.

Hardt, D.E. & Mann, R.W. A five body - three dimensional analysis of walking. Journal of Biomechanics, 1980, 13, 455-457.

Hatze, H. Neuromusculoskeletal control systems modelling - a critical survey of recent developments. IEEE Transactions on Automatic Control, 1980(a), AC-25, 375-385.

Hatze, H. A mathematical model for the computational determination of parameter values of anthropomorphic segments. Journal of Biomechanics, 1980(b), 13, 833-843.

Hatze, H. Myocybernetic control models of skeletal muscle - characteristics and applications. Pretoria: The University of South Africa Press, 1981(a).

Hatze, H. The use of optimally regularized Fourier series for estimating higher order derivatives of noisy biomechanical data. Journal of Biomechanics, 1981(b), 14, 13-18.

Hatze, H. A comprehensive model for human motion simulation and its applications to the take-off phase in the long jump. Journal of Biomechanics, 1981(c), 14, 135-142.

Hatze, H. & Venter, A. Practical activation and retention of locomotion constraints in neuromusculoskeletal system models. Journal of Biomechanics, 1981, 14, 873-877.

Hay, J.G. A bibliography of biomechanics literature (4th ed.). Department of Physical Education, University of Iowa, 1981.

Heinrichs, W. Eine digitale Zeitmesseinrichtung hoher Auflösung zur Weiterentwicklung der chronocyclographischen Bewegungsaufnahme mit Prozessrechner (A digital timer of high resolution for the continued development of chronocyclographic movement registration by means of process computers). European Journal of Applied Physiology, 1974, 32, 227-238.

Hemami, H., Jaswa, V.C. & McGhee, R.B. Some alternative formulations of manipulator dynamics for computer simulation studies. Proceedings of the 13th Allerton Conference on Circuit and System Theory, University of Illinois, 1975.

Hennig, E.M. & Nicol, K. Velocity measurement without contact on body surface points by means of the acoustical Doppler effect. In, P.V. Komi (Ed.), Biomechanics V-B. Baltimore: University Park Press, 1976.

Herron, R.E., Cuzzi, J.R. & Hugg, J. Mass distribution of the human body using biostereometrics. AMRL-TR-75-18, Texas Institute for Rehabilitation and Research, Houston (TX), 1976.

Hof, A.L. & van den Berg, Jw. EMG to force processing: I-IV. Journal of Biomechanics, 1981, 14, 747-792.

Huiskes, R. Design, fixation and stress analysis of hip implants. In, Hastings & Ducheyne (Eds.), CRC Series "Structure-property Relationships in Biomaterials", Vol. IV, "Interaction between Musculoskeletal Tissues and Orthopaedic Devices" (in print), 1983.

Huiskes, R. & Chao, E.Y.S. A survey of finite element analysis in orthopaedic biomechanics: the first decade. Journal of Biomechanics, 1983, 16 (in print).

Inman, V.T., Ralston, H.J. & Todd, F. Human Walking. Baltimore: Williams
    and Wilkins, 1981.

Jarrett, M.O. A television/computer system for human locomotion analysis.
    PhD-thesis, Bioengineering Unit, University of Strathclyde, Glasgow,
    Scotland, 1976.

Lamoreux, L.W. Kinematic measurements in the study of human walking. Bulletin
    of Prosthetics Research, 1971, 10-15, 3-84.

Lamoreux, L.W. Electrogoniometry as a tool for clinical gait evaluation.
    Proceedings of the fifth Annual Conference on Systems and Devices for
    the Disabled, 1978.

Lanshammar, H. Precision limits on derivatives obtained from measurement
    data. In, A. Morecki, K. Fidelius, K. Kedzior and A. Wit (Eds.),
    Biomechanics VII-A. Baltimore: University Park Press, 1981.

Lanshammar, H. On precision limits for derivatives numerically calculated
    from noisy data. Journal of Biomechanics, 1982, 15, 459-470.

Lehner, P.N. Handbook of ethological methods. New York: Garland STPM Press,
    1979.

Lesh, M.D., Mansour, J.M. & Simon, S.R. A gait analysis subsystem for
    smoothing and differentiation of human motion data. ASME Journal of
    Biomechanical Engineering, 1979, 101, 205-212.

Lindholm, L.E. An opto-electronic system for remote on-line movement
    monitoring. In, C.A. Morehouse and R.C. Nelson (Eds.), Biomechanics IV.
    Baltimore: University Park Press, 1974.

Macellari, V. CoSTEL: a computer peripheral remote sensing device for 3-
    dimensional monitoring of human motion. Medical and Biological Engineering
    and Computing, 1983, 21, 311-318.

MacKay, S.A., Sayre, R.E. & Potel, M.J. 3D Galathea: entry of three-
    dimensional moving points from multiple perspective views. Computer
    Graphics, 1982, 16, 213-222.

Marhold, G. (Ed.), Biomechanische Untersuchungsmethoden im Sport (Biomechanical
    research methods in sport). Berlin: DDR Wissenschaftlicher Rat beim
    Statssekretariat für Körperkultur und Sport, 1979.

Maybeck, R.S. Stochastic models, estimation, and control - Vol. I. New York:
    Academic Press, 1979.

Medawar, P.B. Is the scientific paper a fraud? The Listener, 1963, 70,
    377-378.

Medawar, P.B. The art of the soluble. London: Methuen, 1967.

Medawar, P.B. Induction and intuition in scientific thought. Memoirs of the American Philosophical Society, Vol. 75. London: Methuen, 1969.

Miller, D.I. & Nelson, R.C. Biomechanics of sport. Philadelphia: Lea and Febiger, 1973.

Miller, N.R., Shapiro, R. & McLaughlin, T.M. A technique for obtaining spatial kinematic parameters of segments of biomechanical systems from cinematographic data. Journal of Biomechanics, 1980, 13, 535-547.

Mital, N.K. & King, A.I. Computation of rigid-body rotation in three-dimensional space from body-fixed linear acceleration measurements. ASME Journal of Applied Mechanics, 1979, 46, 925-930.

Mitchelson, D. Recording of movement without photography. In, D.W. Grieve, D. Miller, D. Mitchelson, J. Paul and A.J. Smith. Techniques for the analysis of human movement. London: Lepus Books, 1975.

Morris, J.R.W. Accelerometry - a technique for the measurement of human body movement. Journal of Biomechanics, 1973, 6, 729-736.

Murray-Smith, D.J. System identification and parameter estimation techniques in the modelling of biological systems: a review. In, J.P. Paul, M.M. Jordan, M.W. Ferguson-Pell and B.J. Andrews (Eds.), Computing in medicine. Proceedings of a seminar held at the Bioengineering Unit, University of Strathclyde. Glasgow: MacMillan Press, 1982.

Nadler, G. Motion and time study. New York: McGraw-Hill, 1955.

Nadler, G. & Goldman, J. The UNOPAR. Journal of Industrial Engineering, 1959, 9, 58-65.

Niederer, P., Mesqui, F. & Schlumpf, M. Automated motion analysis of simulated pedestrian impacts with the aid of digital high speed film processing. Department of Medical Physics, Institute of Technology and University of Zürich, Switzerland, 1981.

Oppenheim, R.W. & Schafer, R.W. Digital signal processing. Englewood Cliffs (NJ): Prentice-Hall, 1975.

Padgaonkar, A.J., Krieger, K.W. & King, A.I. Measurement of angular acceleration of a rigid body using linear accelerometers. ASME Journal of Applied Mechanics, 1975, 552-556.

Paul, J.P., Jordan, M.M., Ferguson-Pell, M.W. & Andrews, B.J. (Eds.), Computing in medicine. Proceedings of a seminar held at the Bioengineering Unit, University of Strathclyde. Glasgow: MacMillan Press, 1982.

Rabiner, L.R. & Gold, B. Theory and application of digital signal processing. Englewood Cliffs (NJ): Prentice-Hall, 1975.

Seemann, M.R. & Lustick, L.S. Combination of accelerometer and photographically derived kinematic variables defining three-dimensional rigid-body motion. In, J. Terauds, (Ed.), Second International Symposium of Biomechanics, Cinematography and High Speed Photography. Proceedings of the SPIE, 1981, 291.

Slama, C.C. (Ed.), Manual of Photogrammetry (4th ed.). Falls Church (VA): American Society of Photogrammetry, 1980.

Slepian, D. On bandwidth. Proceedings of the IEEE, 1976, 64, 292-300.

Soudan, K. & Dierckx, P. Calculation of derivatives and Fourier coefficients of human motion data, while using spline functions. Journal of Biomechanics, 1979, 12, 21-26.

Spoor, C.W. & Veldpaus, F.E. Rigid body motion calculated from spatial co-ordinates of markers. Journal of Biomechanics, 1980, 13, 391-393.

Taylor, K.D., Mottier, F.M., Simmons, D.W., Cohen, W., Pavlak, Jr. R., Cornell, D.P. & Hankins, G.B. An automated motion measurement system for clinical gait analysis. Journal of Biomechanics, 1982, 15, 505-516.

Terauds, J. (Ed.), Second International Symposium of Biomechanics cinematography and high-speed photography. Proceedings of the SPIE, 1981, 291.

Vaughan, C.L., Andrews, J.G. & Hay, J.G. Selection of body segment parameters by optimization methods. Journal of Biomechanical Engineering, 1982, 104, 38-44.

Voloshin, A. & Wosk, J. An in vivo study of low back pain and shock absorption in the human locomotor system. Journal of Biomechanics, 1982, 15, 21-27.

Whittle, M.W. Calibration and performance of a 3-dimensional television system for kinematic analysis. Journal of Biomechanics, 1982, 15, 185-196.

Winter, D.A. Biomechanics of human movement. New York: Wiley, 1981(a).

Winter, D.A., 1981b. Biomechanics in the rehabilitation of human movement. In, H. Matsui and K. Kobayashi (Eds.), Biomechanics VIII-A. International Series on Biomechanics, Vol. 4A. Champaign (I11): Human Kinetics Publishers, 1983.

Winter, D.A. Camera speeds for normal and pathological gait. Medical and Biological Engineering and Computing, 1982, 20, 408-412.

Winter, D.A. Moments of force and mechanical power in jogging. Journal of Biomechanics, 1983, 16, 91-97.

Wittenburg, J. Dynamics of systems of rigid bodies. Stuttgart: Teubner, 1977.

Woltring, H.J. New possibilities for human motion studies by real-time light spot position measurement. Biotelemetry, 1974, 1, 132-146.

Woltring, H.J. Single- and dual-axis, lateral photodetectors of rectangular shape. IEEE Transactions on Electron Devices ED-22, 1975, 581-590 and 1101.

Woltring, H.J. Planar control in multi-camera calibration for 3-D gait studies. Journal of Biomechanics, 1980, 13, 39-48.

Woltring, H.J. Estimation and precision of 3-D kinematics by analytical photogrammetry. In, J.P. Paul, M.M. Jordan, M.W. Ferguson-Pell and B.J. Andrews (Eds.), Computing in medicine. Proceedings of a seminar held at the Bioengineering Unit, University of Strathclyde. Glasgow: MacMillan Press, 1982.

Woltring, H.J. & Marsolais, E.B. Optoelectronic gait measurement in two- and three-dimensional space. Bulletin of Prosthetics Research, 1980, 17, 46-52 (BPR 10-34, Fall 1981).

Wood, G.A. & Jennings, L.S. On the use of spline functions for data smoothing. Journal of Biomechanics, 1979, 12, 477-479.

Wosk, J. & Voloshin, A. Wave attenuation in skeletons of young healthy persons. Journal of Biomechanics, 1981, 14, 261-268.

Zarrugh, M.Y. & Radcliffe, C.W. Computer generation of human gait kinematics. Journal of Biomechanics, 1979, 12, 99-112.

SECTION 2

CHAPTER II

THE PROBLEM OF THE INTERRELATION OF CO-ORDINATION AND LOCALIZATION

N. Bernstein

(Published in *Arch. biol. Sci.*, 38, 1935)

1.   THE BASIC DIFFERENTIAL EQUATION OF MOVEMENTS

The relationship between movements and the innervational impulses which evoke them is extremely complex and is, moreover, by no means univocal. I have already undertaken an analysis of this relationship in a series of previous studies (8, 9, 14, 15) and for this reason I shall present here only a short summary of such statements as may be regarded as firmly established at the present time. The main object of this summary is to serve as an introduction to a further discussion.

The degree of tension of a muscle is a function, in the first place, of its innervational (tetanic and tonic) condition E, and, in the second place, of its length at a given instant and of the velocity with which this length changes over time. In an intact organism the length of a muscle is in its turn a function of the angle of articulation α; for this reason we may write that the momentum of a muscle with respect to the joint is

$$F = F\left(E,\ \alpha,\ \frac{d\alpha}{dt}\right).\tag{1}$$

On the other hand, we may assert that the angular acceleration of a limb controlled by a given muscle is directly proportional to the momentum of the muscle F and inversely proportional to the moment of inertia of the limb I. In this way

$$\frac{d^2\alpha}{dt^2} = \frac{F}{I}.\tag{2}$$

If there are other sources of force than the muscle operating on the limb, the situation is a little more complicated. Let us limit ourselves for simplicity to only one external force, namely gravity. In the simplest case which we have just described, where we are considering the movement of a single limb segment in relation to a second fixed one, the momentum due to gravity G is, like the momentum of the muscle, a function of the angle of articulation

$$G = G(\alpha). \tag{1a}$$

The angular acceleration of the limb segment under the influence of both momenta together is expressed by the equation

$$\frac{d^2\alpha}{dt^2} = \frac{F + G}{I}$$

If we introduce into this equation expressions (1) and (1a) for F and G, we obtain a relation of the following form:

$$I \frac{d^2\alpha}{dt^2} = F\left(E, \alpha, \frac{d\alpha}{dt}\right) + G(\alpha). \tag{3}$$

This is the fundamental equation for the movement of a single limb in a gravitational field under the influence of a single muscle where the level of innervation is E. In cases where the moving system consists not of one but of several limb segments and where we are obliged to take into consideration the activity of several muscles, eqn. (3) becomes extremely complicated, not only quantitatively but also qualitatively as considerations of the mechanical effect of one muscle upon others also enter into the problem and the moment of inertia of the system becomes a variable term. However, in spite of the fact that the complications which arise in this case are so great that equations of type (3) cannot always be written even in the most general form, the physiological aspects of the problem differ only slightly, and the complications essentially involve only the mathematical and mechanical aspects of movement. For this reason in the present context we may limit ourselves only to the consideration of the most simple equation (3).

The basic equation is a differential equation of the second order which may be integrated if the functions F and G are known. Solutions of an equation of this type, that is to say, the determination of the movement which will take place in each given case, will be different depending on the so-called initial conditions of integration: that is, the initial position of the limb segment determined by the angle α_0 and on its initial angular velocity $d\alpha_0/dt$. By altering these initial conditions in various ways we may obtain very different effects of movement from one and the same governing law (3), i.e. for the same functions F and G.

It must first of all be noted that eqn. (3) directly bears on the cyclical character of the relation between the momentum of the muscle F and the position of the limb α. The limb segment changes its position as a result

of the operation upon it of the momentum of effort F and this momentum in
its turn changes because of the changes in the angle α. A cyclical chain of
cause and effect operates in this way.

This chain would be ideally cyclical if the momentum (eqn. (1))
depended solely on α and $d\alpha/dt$, that is, if the movement were completely
passive (for example, the falling of the arm). But, as in eqns. (1) and (3)
given in this report, the value of F also depends on the degree of excitation
of the muscle E, which appears most clearly from the areas lying outside
the circle which we have just described. It is apparent that there are two
possibilities here; either the degree of excitation E depends wholly or
partly on the values of α and of $d\alpha/dt$, or it is quite independent of them
and is solely a function of time t.

The choice between the two possibilities indicated here is clearly of
great physiological significance as may be revealed with sufficient clarity
only by further discussion in this chapter. At the moment I shall only
indicate some of the consequences of each of the hypotheses we have raised.

If the degree of excitation E is simply a function of position and
velocity and not a function of time, then eqn. (3) will take the form of a
classic differential equation,

$$ I \; \frac{d^2\alpha}{dt^2} \; = \; F \left[E \left(\alpha, \; \frac{d\alpha}{dt} \right), \; \alpha, \; \frac{d\alpha}{dt} \right] \; + \; G(\alpha), \qquad (3a) $$

the partial integrals of which depend only on the initial conditions. In
this case, consequently, a movement must occur if the required initial
conditions are fulfilled (from without), and once having begun it must
proceed with the same uninterruptable regularity with which a s ring will
oscillate if displaced to a precisely determined initial position and then
released. It is clear that this hypothesis does not correspond to
physiological reality and in effect completely ignores the role of the
central nervous system.

On the other hand, it may be supposed that the degree of excitation E
is a value which changes with time and depends entirely on a predetermined
sequence of impulses from the central nervous system without any relation
to the local conditions operating in the system of the moving limb being
studied. If, as in the hypotheses formulated above for the elastic
oscillation of a string, the muscle can be compared to some sort of
independent spring or rubber band, then in the second hypothesis it may be
represented as a sort of solenoid which attracts its core solely in relation

to the potential of the current which is supplied to the coil from an
external source. The law of the variation in this current must be
represented in the system of eqn. (3) as a function of time; in fact,
whatever may be the real causes of these changes, the changes themselves
are presented to system (3) in a completely finished and independent form
as quite unalterable data. Equation (3) in this case takes on the form

$$I\ \frac{d^2\alpha}{dt^2}\ =\ F\left[E(t),\ \alpha,\ \frac{d\alpha}{dt}\right]\ +\ G(\alpha),\qquad\qquad (3b)$$

which does not permit of any concrete solution.

It is important here to draw attention to the following. In spite of
the fact that the degree of excitation E, as has been hypothesized, is
independent of α and of $d\alpha/dt$, the momentum of the muscle F is dependent on
them as before. Meanwhile, as we have shown above, the operation of this
momentum, that is, the entire picture of the course of a movement, will
vary with the initial conditions which in no way enter into the expression
for the degree of excitation E and consequently do not in any way affect
the course of its changes in time. It follows from this that the general
results of interactions from eqn. (3b) cannot be foreseen or regulated in
advance because the changes in excitation will be involved in the interplay
of forces and dependencies which can in no way alter the further course of
these changes following a fully independent law. Movements which are
regulated according to the law (3b) will necessarily be ataxic.

And so we are left with the hypothesis that the excitation of a muscle
E must be both a function of time and a function of position and velocity,
and must be described in eqn. (3) in the form

$$I\ \frac{d^2\alpha}{dt^2}\ =\ F\left[E\left(t,\ \alpha,\ \frac{d\alpha}{dt}\right),\ \alpha,\ \frac{d\alpha}{dt}\right]\ +\ G(\alpha).\qquad\qquad (3c)$$

This purely analytical deduction of the functional structure of muscle
excitation permits of exceptionally simple translation into physiological
terms. The dependence of the variable E on time, proceeding from the
absurdity of the opposite hypothesis (3a), underlies the necessity for the
changes in excitation which are directly effected by the activity of the
motor areas of the central nervous sytem. The dependence of the excitation
on the position of the limb α and its angular velocity $d\alpha/dt$ is the
proprioceptive reflex so well known in physiology. It necessarily follows
from the preceding analysis that both position and velocity directly and
independently influence the changes in the degree of excitation of the

muscles, and in reality both these effects have been subjected to precise physiological investigation.

Turning to clinical evidence we may say that (3a) is the equation of movement for an extremity in a case of central paralysis and that (3b) represents the equation of movement in a case of proprioceptive ataxia.

In this way we have stated in the basic equations of movement a superposition of two cyclical connections of different orders and related to different topics. The first cyclical connection is the mutual interaction of the position α and the momentum F, and exists purely mechanically as has been pointed out above. The second connection constructed on the first one, is a similar interaction between the position α (and also of the velocity) and the degree of excitation E; this connection is effected by means of systems of reflexes and is related to the activity of the central nervous system.

The principal significance of the general conclusions examined above may easily be deduced. The customary older representation implicitly accepted and, until the present, retained by many physiologists and clinicians, describes the skeletal link as being completely passive under the control of the central impulses and as being unequivocally subservient to these impulses. In this scheme the central impulse a always produces movement A, and impulse b always produces movement B, from which it is easy to proceed to a representation of the motor area of the cortex as a distribution panel with push-buttons. However, eqn. (3b) indicates that one and the same impulse $E(t)$ (ignoring the periphery) may produce completely different effects because of the interplay of external forces and because of variations in the initial conditions. Equation (3c) shows, on the other hand, that a determinate effect is possible for a movement only in a case where the central impulse E is very different under different conditions, being a function of the positions and the velocities of the limbs and operating very differently in the differential equation with various initial conditions. Parodying the well known tag on nature we may say that *motus parendo vincitur* (movement is conquered by obedience).

It must be pointed out, finally, that the external force field does not consist of the force of gravity $G(\alpha)$ alone and it may even occur that this latter expression does not enter at all into the basic equation in such a simple form. Because it necessarily affects the position and the velocity of a system, and because in the norm these latter affect the changes in E, we may say that the *parendo* of the central impulses must sometimes go to

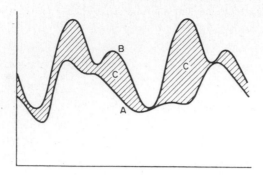

Fig. 14. A semi-schematic representation of the course of a single
central impulse during a rhythmical movement. *A*, the non-
rhythmical curve of changes in external forces; *B*, the
summed rhythmical result; *C* (Hatched area), an impulse
bridging the gap between the curve *A* and the result *B*.

great lengths. It is obliged to adapt to all internal and external forces
operating in the system while forces which do not directly depend on the
operation of the impulse *E* may frequently play a decisive part in the
general balance of forces affecting movement. In such cases (Fig. 14), if
for a given movement the required changes of forces at the joint are
represented by the curve *B* and the resultant forces in the external field
are represented by the curve *A*, then the central nervous system will be
obliged to provide only the additional fraction *C* so that the sequence of
impulses cannot maintain even a remote correspondence to the contours of
curve *B* and frequently even less correspondence with this curve than to the
changes in the external field *A*. These supplementary compensatory impulses
sometimes appear in an indirect way from cyclogrametric observation.

And so, not to enter into details discussed in the studies mentioned
above, it may be said that:

(a) a unequivocal relationship between impulses and movements does
not and cannot exist;

(b) the relation between impulses and movement is the further removed
'from unequivocality the more complex is the kinematic chain operating in
the movement under consideration;

(c) movements are possible only under conditions of the most accurate
and uninterrupted agreement - *unforeseen in advance* - between the central
impulses and the events occurring at the periphery, and are frequently

quantitatively less dependent on these central impulses than on the external
force field.

2.   THE INTEGRITY AND STRUCTURAL COMPLEXITY OF LIVE MOVEMENTS

In the treasury of experimental physiology there are vast collections
of experimental observations and facts characterizing the course of single
impulses or of the more simple patterns of impulses. There are most detailed
studies of all aspects of excitation, inhibition, *parabiosis*, *chronaxie*, and
so on, for a single nerve pathway. However, we have up to the present only
two major advances along the lines of investigation of the total or systemic
operation of impulses: Sherrington's principle of reciprocity and A.
Ukhtomskii's principle of dominance. But even these groups of data are very
far removed from the areas we touch upon - the problems of the study of
structures of movements as integral formations.

It is, however, precisely this integration of movements that is the
most important feature implied by 'motor co-ordination'. The fact of this
integration may be investigated in many experimental situations and
significant connections and correlations are observed in all these cases
between the various components of the integrated processes. The simplest and
most easily observed phenomenon in this category is the appearance of gradual
and smooth redistribution of tensions in muscular masses, which is particularly
clearly expressed in cases of phylogenetically ancient or highly automatized
movements. A muscle never enters into a complete movement as an isolated
element. Neither the active raising of tension nor the concomitant (reciprocal)
inhibition in antagonistic[*] subgroups is, in the norm, concentrated in a
single anatomical muscular entity; rather, there is a gradual and even flow
from one system to others. I shall suggest a short experiment; stretch the
arm out anterolaterally and describe a great circle with the hand as shown
in Fig. 15, and then find out by means of anatomical analysis how the change
in muscular innervation and the process of inhibition of the antagonists are
accomplished during this movement. Exactly the same process of gradual

---

[*] The concept of antagonism may be applied unconditionally only to cases of
muscles operating on joints with a single axis and, further, to those which
cross only this one joint. The number of muscles of this type is extremely
small; in the skeletal extremities we find as examples of this type only
m. brachii and internus, m. pronator quadratus, the short position of m.
triceps brachii and m. vastus femoris. All other muscles may be only
functionally antagonistic in a single situation and in quite different
relationships in other situations.

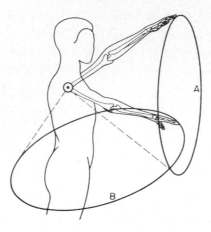

Fig. 15. Circular movements made with the arm extended in various
positions are accomplished by completely different
innervational schemes for trajectories of the same type.

transfer of innervation may be clearly observed in any plastic movements;
with more accurate means of registration this may be observed as a general
phenomenon.

The integration discussed above is even more clearly demonstrated in
the analysis of automatic rhythmical movements by the appearance of
extremely marked reciprocities in the interrelationships of the components.
I have described examples of such reciprocity in other studies (9, 19); I
shall here merely refer to the fact that in rhythmical work with a hammer
the direction of the trajectory of the elbow (forwards or to the side) gives
a close correlation with such phenomena apparently far removed from the
elbow as the relationship of the maximal velocities of the head of the
hammer in the movements of raising and striking, the angle of inclination
of the hammer to the horizontal in raising, the relationship between the
length of the trajectories of the hammer and of the wrist, and so on. It
seems to me that the effects of changes in tempo and the whole construction
of a movement are relevant here, as I have discussed in other studies (14,
19) on striking piano keys and on locomotion. A movement never responds to
detailed changes by a change in its detail; it responds as a whole to
changes in each small part, such changes being particularly prominent in
phases and details sometimes considerably distant both spatially and
temporally from those initially encountered.

Finally, it is necessary to comment on a fact to which I have drawn attention in a number of places (14, 15, 19, 21); that the course of rhythmical live movements may be presented in the form of rapidly converging trigonometric series. I have been able to demonstrate that a diversity of rhythmical human movements (walking, striking with a hammer, filing, piano-playing, etc.) may be interpreted to an accuracy of within a few millimetres in the form of a sum of three or four harmonic oscillations, the so-called Fourier trigonometrical sums:

$$r = A_0 + A_1 \sin \frac{2\pi}{T} (t + \theta^1) + A_2 \sin \frac{4\pi}{T} (t + \theta^2)$$

$$+ A_3 \sin \frac{6\pi}{T} (t + \theta^3) + \ldots \tag{4}$$

The rapidity of convergence of these sums may be seen from the numerical examples of Table 7.

TABLE 7.

Walking	Absolute amplitudes				Relative amplitudes ($A_1 = 100\%$)		
	A_1 cm	A_2 cm	A_3 cm	A_4 cm	$A_2\%$	$A_3\%$	$A_4\%$
Longitudinal displacement of the point of the foot	38.50	9.09	0.80	0.67	23.6	2.08	1.74
Longitudinal displacement of the centre of gravity of the whole arm	7.60	0.81	0.15	0.07	10.65	1.98	0.92
Longitudinal displacement of the center of gravity of the whole leg	14.47	1.22	0.49	0.22	8.42	3.39	1.52

The fact that such an interpretation is possible is of great importance to the question under discussion. If one complete cycle of a movement lasts for 1 sec, and in this case may be represented with an accuracy of within 1-3 mm as the sum of three sinusoids, this means that all the details of this movement must have been organized with the required degree of accuracy a full second beforehand. Further, its period being known, the sinusoid is determined by two parameters, that is, it can be determined from two points.

The sum of four sinusoids may thus be theoretically determined from eight points; in other words, it is possible to reconstruct from a small section of a movement of the type which we have represented, to within a fraction of one per cent in the form of the sum of four sinusoids, the entire movement as a whole with the same order of accuracy. This experimental fact is evidence in its most cogent form of the organizational interaction and mutual reciprocity of rhythmical movements in time while the mutual interdependence between the elements of the movement which I studied (of striking with a hammer) suggests a similar interaction in terms of spatial components.

If the external expression of co-ordinational activity provides a picture of such a high degree of reciprocity and interrelatedness, then, on the other hand, its anatomical structure in terms of our present knowledge also displays a picture of no less highly organized complexity. The extreme variety of clinical studies of damage to the motor area suggests that a large number of different subordinate and variously interacting systems co-operate in order to make possible a movement in its entirety. The spinal system alone contains up to five independent centrifugal pathways (pyramidal, rubrospinal, vestibulospinal and two tectospinal pathways). In the cortical region we have a very large number of centres which in one way or another appear (most often from pathological evidence) to be necessary components in a complete movement. All attempts to describe their activity in the norm are necessarily limited at the present time to very general statements and hypothetical descriptions, but there is no doubt whatever of their synthetic activity. For example, the attempts of Bianchi, Brown, Dupré, Foerster (44), Goldstein, Gurevitch, Homberger, Jacob, Lashley, Lewy (52), Magnus (55), v. Monakow (59), and many other investigators to describe in one way or another the functional interactions of various parts of the cortex must be mentioned here with recognition of the great service these authors have rendered to the physiology of movement[*]. A brief summary of what these authors have uncovered in areas directly bearing on the objectives of this report would be approximately as follows. An impulse reaching the terminal plates in a muscle

---

[*] Bianchi, *The Mechanism of the Brain*, etc., Edinburgh, 1922; T.G. Brown, *J. Physiol.* 10, 103; Dupré, *Revue neurol.* 1909, p. 1073, 1910, No. 13; K. Goldstein, *Deutsche Ztschr. Nervenheilk.* 70, P, p. 7; M. Gurevitch, *Ztschr. ges. Neurol. Psych.* 93, 1924; *Ibid.* 108, 1927; Homberger, *Ztschr. ges. Neurol. Psych.* 85, and *Arch. f. Psychiatrie* 69; Jacob, *Ztschr. ges. Neurol. Psych.* 89; K.S. Lashley, *Brain* 41, 255; *et al.*

from the centrifugal fibre of the last neuron is the resultant of a whole
series of separate central impulses which reach the synapses of the anterior
horn by different pathways. Among these latter we must recognize the
significant innervational independence of pyramidal impulses (the cortico-
spinal tract) and the combined impulses from the striopallidal groups of
nuclei (c. striatum-gl. pallidus-nucleus ruber-tr. rubro spinalis) which
are found in close co-operation with centres whose functional relationships
are less apparent (substantia nigra, Dark-schewitsch's nucleus, corpus
Luysi, and so on). Centripetal proprioceptive impulses give rise to
answering effector impulses from the cerebellum and from other many stations
related to the spinal cord through the quadrigeminal system. Finally, the
decisive role in the production of a movement must be referred not to a
centrifugal but to a central-informational system (an older physiology
would have termed this 'commissural-associative') interplaying along the
lines of the frontal pontocereballar pathways. It would be possible to list
the general characteristics of the functional peculiarities of each of these
anatomical stations (often the details given by different authors are
contradictory), but this is not my aim at present. It is important here to
point out a single peculiarity which is common to all these characteristics
and which has been stated as an undisputed fact for the last 20 years.

All the clinical observations noted above, as well as those of many
other authors, agree on the position (quite foreign to the ideas of
physiologists of the last century) that these central nervous subsystems
have one and the same object of excitation at the periphery - the same
muscles and most probably the same peripheral conducting pathways. The
idiosyncracies and differences in the operations of the pyramidal,
striopallidal, cerebellar and other systems lie not in differences and
peculiarities in the peripheral objectives on which they operate but solely
in differences in the forms of influence exercised on these objectives. The
pallidum is concerned with the same musculature as is the brain cortex; it
is not the objective but the manner of excitation which is specific. None
of the data from contemporary physiological investigations contradicts the
reliability of the fact that, for example, both flexion and extension in
any single-axis joint can be achieved through both pyramidal and the
striopallidal systems; both these systems may and do give the effect of
reciprocity. In 'gross pathology' this is carried out separately and in the
healthy norm both systems in some way co-operate in a rhythmical process.
As accounts of the way in which this co-operation may be effected we have

in the literature many observations, impressions, and deliberations which
are often quite persuasive and in many cases not contradictory. What is
common to all these descriptions is not in general important; what is
important, with the object of a formal examination of material, is the
general tendency found in all of them – the recognition of the common
presence in all cases of the qualitatively peculiar operation of central
subsystems on one and the same peripheral objects.

Closely related to these considerations is the currently established
picture of the multiplicity of projections of peripheral organs in the
central nervous system. Along the lines of the exceptionally detailed
knowledge of cortical projection of the motor periphery, which was already
under investigation in the 19th century, and which has been worked out in
very great detail in our time (Fig. 16), we are now obliged to hypothesize
localized projections of the same periphery both on the globus pallidus
and on the cerebelli vermis. It is immaterial to our purpose in what way
this multiplicity has occurred as a result of phylogenetic stratification
and superimposition. In the human being, it is presented to us as given
data, a given problem, and our task lies in the search for non-contradictory
explanations of the mechanisms of a multistaged functioning of this sort.

If we attempt an examination from the point of view of such
multiplicity of the equations for elementary movements (3c) which we have
deduced above, we necessarily arrive at the following. A nerve impulse E,
which, as appears on close examination of peripheral processes, is not
related in a univocal way to its consequence – a movement – and is therefore
restricted to the most precise concordance between its evolution and the
proprioceptive input for α and $d\alpha/dt$, is at the same time the sum of (or is
in some other form of linked equivalence to) a series of impulses which have
very different points of origin in the brain. Each of these impulses arises
in a separate area in the brain that is distinct from other centres. Each of
these centres has its particular interrelationships with other centres in
the brain, its own conducting pathways, a particular degree of relationship
with and form of connections to the receptors, and, finally, as clinical
practice in nervous disorders shows, its own mode of operation in time and its
own particular means of interaction. The difficulty of co-ordinating all
these facts is very great indeed as I shall attempt to demonstrate. If the
impulse E were to follow the pattern in eqn. (3b), that is to say if it had
the form $E(t)$, it would not in principle be difficult to represent a series
of independent sources (a very high degree of agreement between them being

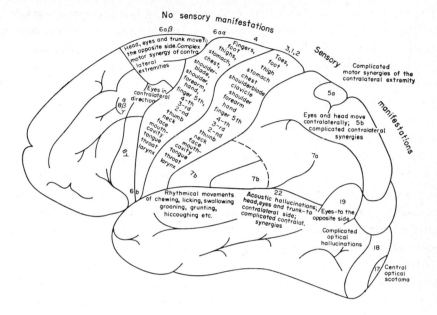

Fig. 16. Summary of data given by O. Foerster on results of
stimulation of various points of the human cortical
hemisphere (1926).

implied) which would ultimately unite in a single common path of a motor
nerve and transmit the result of their common action $E(t)$ through it to the
end plate. In exactly the same way it would not be difficult to conceive of
the possibility of multiple action of impulses in a case where the actual
form was (3c), that is, $E(t, \alpha, d\alpha/dt)$, if each of the separate impulses
had its own particular object of excitation at the periphery (in the form,
for example, of a particular muscle which was controlled by it alone). If
we suppose, for example, that control of a flexor group at a joint is
concentrated in the centre A and control of the extensor group of the same
joint in centre B while the proprioceptive connections secure the possibility
of either centre being able to react to α and to $d\alpha/dt$, then the mechanism
in this case would be merely quantitatively and not qualitatively difficult
to comprehend. The actual situation – that is, a system of impulses without
unequivocal correspondence to the movement, and controlled by proprioception,
being sent to the object from a number of sources – is one which does not
permit us any simple escape from the question. The sole (apparent) possibility
of explanation for a structure of this type lies in referring the proprioceptive

"perception" to only one of the effector centres of the brain, for example,
to the cerebellum, and supposing that the other effectors function purely
according to type $E(t)$. The mathematical expression of such a structure
might be regarded in the following way: the summed impulse E is made up of
a series of centrel impulses E_1, E_2, E_3,...

$$E\left(t, \alpha, \frac{d\alpha}{dt}\right) = E_1(t) + E_2(t) + \ldots + E_n\left(\alpha, \frac{d\alpha}{dt}\right). \qquad (5)$$

However, this combination appears to be unacceptable for a number of
reasons. In the first place, we have no guarantee whatever that E is the
sum of E_1, E_2, ..., E_n, and not some other function of them such as would
considerably alter the case and complicate for the co-ordination centre E_n
the possibility of suppressing the "blind" impulses E_1, E_2 with precisely
proportinal additions. In the second place, the centripetal impulses are
directed in the spinal cord not through one channel, but through a large
number of channels, and reach by direct pathways at least two central nuclei,
cerebellar and thalamic, attaining a further series of areas by indirect
pathways; but the problem lies precisely in the interpretation of the
possibility of proprioceptive multiplicity. To visualize this is about as
difficult as to imagine the movement of a two-seater bicycle each seat of
which is equipped with its own separate set of handle-bars. It is clear
that the presence of two effector centres responding to proprioceptive
input requires the closest possible co-ordination between them. I would deny
neither the possibility that such connections may exist nor that they exist
in fact. My aim in the first two sections of this chapter is merely to
indicate the great difficulties which confront functional explanations of the
co-ordination of movements. It is already apparent that eqn. (3c) is quite
different from our usual, qualitatively simple models of the interaction
between the centre and the periphery; when, however, we are obliged to
confront their complex interaction as a result of the mutual activity of
entire systems of organs which, anatomically and clinically, display varying
degrees of independence, then the resulting great structural complexity
becomes more obvious still. Yet this is fruitful, since a failure to realize
the difficulty of a problem frequently defers the moment of its solution.

3.   THE INTERRELATIONSHIP BETWEEN CO-ORDINATION AND LOCALIZATION

     The discussion in the preceding sections has already largely revealed
the close connection between problems of co-ordination and localization. It

is clear from all that has been said above that no nuance of a single
impulse $\left[E(t)\right]$ can serve as an explanation of even the simplest case of
repeated accomplishment of automatizing movements, and still less as an
explanation of the involved complexity of natural movements carried out by
many muscles, each of which involves control from many centres. To digress:
at the beginning from the indubitable presence of functional "inter-
departmental" connections between brain centres which organize these latter
into hierarchical order (*Über- und Unterordnung*), the following innervational
scheme for effector impulses will be obtained (Fig. 17). It is clear that
co-ordination is determined not so much by differences in the effect of each
of the impulses Aa, Ab, ..., Ba, Bb... taken separately, but also by the
systematic modes of their common operation and joint effect. The term co-

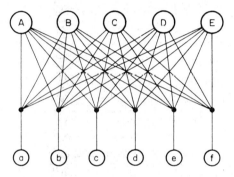

Fig. 17. The multiplicity of efferent pathways for the control
of six muscles a, b, c, d, e, f, by five effector centres
A, B, C, D, E, gives, even in this intentionally simplified
case, a complex structural scheme of innervation.

ordination hints at the common actions of separate elements. The solution
to the problem of co-ordination lies not in analysis of the tonal and
expressive resources of a single instrument in an orchestra but in the
technical construction of the score and in the mastery of the conductor.

The basic guiding thesis for investigations of co-ordination must for
this reason be formulated in the following way. Co-ordination is an activity
which guanrantees that a movement shall have the homogeneity, integration
and structural unity which has been described above. This activity is
principally based not on particular processes in individual neurons, but on
the determinate *organization* of their common activity. This organization
must necessarily be reflected in the anatomical plan in the form of

localization.

This seems to me to be an extremely expedient way of formulating the
question. On the one hand, organization and the forms in which it exists
must inevitably be represented in the structural forms of localization. In
the same way as we may derive from an examination of a diagram of an
electrical circuit some idea as to the nature of its function, so data of
the localization-anatomical type may serve at least as circumstantial
evidence in the consideration of the new experimental problems I have put
forward - *the structural physiology* of movement. On the other hand, such a
structural analysis of movements should aid considerably in critical
evaluation of existing and future conceptualizations of the type and
structure of cerebral localization. It is impossible to visualize a situation
in which localizational structure would be found to contradict structural
organization.

A pertinent point must be made here. One must not in any way confuse
localization with topography. Topography is the geography of the brain, the
study of the spatial distribution of its functionally existing points.
Localization is the structural plan of anatomical interrelationships between
these functional points. If we shuffle in Fig. 17 the positions of the centres
A, B, C, D and E, this will change the entire topographical picture, but will
not alter their localizational structure. The distribution (topography) of
the elements in a diagram of a receiving set are completely different in the
diagram from the topography of these elements in an actual apparatus
constructed from this diagram. On the other hand, for one and the same
topography completely different schemes are possible.

Figure 18 makes the latter clear in regard to circuit-diagrams which
are extremely convenient for illustrating our problems; diagrams (a) and
(b) in this figure have exactly the same structure for different topographies,
schemes (b) and (c) have the same topography but different structures. The
problem which obsessed our physiological forefathers, that of the inversion
of the retinal image, and in particular whether this inversion is transmitted
in exactly the same way to the cortex, and if so, how it is compensated,
appears to us now to be childishly simple-minded. We still remember how some
of their contemporaries hypothesized, to explain the matter, that the soul
was located in the brain with its feet uppermost, without however determining
more precisely whether souls have feet. Nowadays we hypothesize with great
facility much more complex transpositions of elements in the representation
of the retina on the cortex without experiencing structural difficulties from

this fact; indeed, in a central telephone station, for example, we do not have to worry whether the commutator links for subscribers from the northern and southern parts of a town are located respectively at the northern and southern ends of the switchboard. However, this old question permits of new

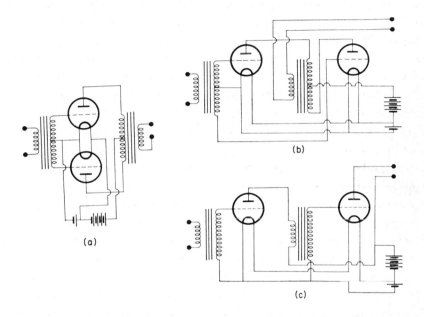

Fig. 18. Three diagrams for two-tube audio-frequency amplifiers. Diagrams (a) and (b) (a single-cascade push-pull block) are identical in all details; that of (c) (a double-cascade amplifier with transformers) is very different in principle from the other systems.

and less childish formulations; are there, nevertheless, limits to this type of transposition? And if such limits exist, what are the borders which separate transpositions that do not change structure from transpositions which inevitably destroy structure? An analysis of the problem when framed in this way shows us first of all that different structural schemes may show different degrees of tolerance to transpositions, but this aspect of the problem will be developed a little later.

Thus, in the problem of localization what is important for our purpose is not precisely where in the cortex one or another peripheral object or function is reflected, but *what* is represented, and *how*; and what are the distinguishing characteristics of those objects represented in the cortical hemispheres and in subcortical centres. Topographical problems are for the

most part clearly unrelated to the analysis of the co-ordinational structure
of movements, while the problems of localization are of paramount and
principal significance.

This significance may be very well explained from the example of the
old conception of localization which has already been mentioned in Section 1.
This conception would answer perfectly to reality if every central impulse
unconditionally governed a single determinate movement, that is, if there
existed a one-to-one correspondence between impulses and movements. In this
case the effector impulses would be able to operate purely as a function of
time $E(t)$, giving always one and the same effect independently of what
occurred at the periphery; the push-button control-board model of the cortex,
similar in plan to an organ keyboard, would be suggested in the types of
explanation we employed. But, on the contrary, this type of one-to-one
correspondence does not exist and the cerebral motor area organizes responses
by deftly adjusting and balancing between resultant external forces and the
manifestations of inertia, constantly reacting to proprioceptive signals and
simultaneously integrating impulses from separate central subsystems, so
that ten successive repetitions of the same movement demand ten successive
impulses all different from each other; and the presence in the cortex of
localizational equipment of the Hitzig or Foerster type begins to seem a
very dubious interpretation. I would like to recall here the failure in 1923
of the invention of "a symphony of whistles". An attempt to convert steam
whistles into a musical instrument with an organ keyboard failed because any
given whistle could not be relied upon to sound the same on every occasion,
and its pitch would vary with the pressure of steam, with the number of
whistles sounded simultaneously, with the degree to which the steam-channel
was clear, and so on, so that it was impossible to obtain a one-to-one
correspondence between the keyboard, on one hand, and the frequencies of the
tones obtained, on the other.

It is understood that a statement of complexity, of "impractivality"
from our point of view, is not in any sense a decisive argument for the
acceptance or rejection of any physiological hypothesis. There is no reason
to suppose that physiological structure should be maximally rotational from
our technico-social anthropomorphic point of view. The localizational
structure of the cortex according to Foerster's scheme (Fig. 16) does not
directly contradict eqn. (3c) with its proprioceptive cycle and lack of simple
one-to-one relationships; it only makes the problem of functioning of its
cell centres extremely difficult. The decisive argument against the theory

of direct representation of muscular systems on the cortex comes from quite
another, perhaps unexpected, direction. I present this argument in its most
general formulation below; here I shall employ only one of its partial
modifications as applied to a particular case.

Let us suppose that the cells of the gyrus centralis are in reality
the effector centre for the muscles. Let us further suppose that the activity
of these cells must be (as is inevitable in the given hypothesis) sharply
different from instant to instant on the multiple repetition of a given
movement, in relation to changes in the external force field and
proprioceptive signals. If we suppose for clarity that we may represent
each excited effector cell in the cortex as lighting up like an electric
bulb at the moment when its impulse is transmitted to the periphery, then
under such an arrangement the effecting of every movement will be visible
to us on the surface of the cortex as a zig-zag discharge. The absence of
one-to-one correspondence and all the considerations which have been
described above as consequences of eqn. (3c) will be obvious in this case
because on every repetition of a given movement the zig-zag discharge will
be visibly different. Now suppose that this repetitive movement is an
automatized act, the realization of a habit of movement, in other words, a
conditioned motor reflex. From the discussion above it follows as an
inescapable deduction that the conditioned reflex of movement operates each
time through a new zig-zag - through new cells; in other words, we arrive
at the conclusion that the hypothesis of cellular localization of muscles
necessarily leads to a denial of cellular localization of conditioned
reflexes. One of the two chess pieces must here be taken, and it is here a
very pertinent question which of the two the old-fashioned localizationalist
would rather sacrifice.

I do not for a moment imagine that I can overthrow the old localizational
concept at a single blow, but it is not possible to disguise the fact that
it is already threatened in very serious ways. The experiments of Bethe
(30) and of Trendelenburg on the extirpation of cortical tissue in monkeys
has indicated the possibility of far reaching compensations and, moreover,
the extensive investigations carried out by Lashley, experimenting on rats
and observing the appearance of compensation and of the re-establishment of
conditioned reflexes for the most varied and topographically different sites
of extirpation, and very persuasive evidence in favour of a radical re-
examination of the old conceptions. Lashley could not discover any clear
relationship between the topographical loci of the areas he destroyed and

the degree to which the conditioned reflexes could be re-established; he found, on the contrary, that there is a strong correlation between the time required for re-establishment and the quantity of brain substance removed, without reference to its locus. These results cause him to favour the theory that there is no cortico-cellular individuality of operation, in which, it seems to me, he is quite mistaken. His data are extremely dangerous for the old localizational theory, but they far from disprove the possibility of any form of localization in general terms.

Lashley's error sets off very well the opposite error made by Gall in his time. Nobody now believes that phrenology was doomed to failure because the very principle of cortical localization was found to be defective. Nobody ascribes its downfall to the fact that Gall did not localize avarice or ambition to areas in which they were located in reality. Gall's theory was essentially faulty not because of the topography he assigned but because of the principles of selection underlying those categories for which he thought that he could find discrete localizations in the cortex. The categories suggested by Fritsch, Hitzig, Foerster, and others appeared to be more physiological and nearer to reality than Gall's fantasies, which were impregnated with the moral rationalism of the 18th century, and appeared, as it were, to be the next approximations to the discovery of reality. The evidence which has accumulated against these Foersterian categories up to the present time must inevitably lead to their abandonment, but this does not yet threaten the fall of the principle of localization in general. It should be recalled that immediately after the abandonment of phrenology the idea of localization also appeared for a long while to be compromised until it gradually became appararent that it was possible that the baby had been thrown out with the bath water. Now, again, after the development and establishment of the understanding of conditioned reflexes, to deny the structural anatomically engraved specificity of the brain would amount to an affirmation that its nature is absolutely beyond knowledge.

Our experimental aim at present lies in the correct formulation of categories which are really represented in the brain centres. The key to this search for the true categories clearly must lie in structural analysis: of the recepter moment, as it appears in experiments with conditioned reflexes; and of the effector moment, as it appears in the co-ordination of movements.

4. ECPHORIA OF THE ENGRAMS OF MOVEMENT

So far I have touched in this report only on those phenomena which point to the momentary, extensively structured nature of the co-ordination of movements. It appeared important to me to demonstrate that a movement could not be understood in terms of some nuance in operation of a single impulse, but that it is the result of the simultaneous co-operative operation of whole systems of impulses, while the structure of this system - its structural schema - is important for the understanding of the result. It is only a short step from this to the central argument in this report, that the innervation and localization of this structure is in reality not only not contradictory to the observable structure of the movements of the organism but is necessarily an exact representation of the latter. To proceed further it is now necessary to attend to another side of the phenomenon, that is, its duration in time. It is necessary to elucidate experimentally whether a simple parallelism exists between the duration in time of a series of system-related impulses or whether there also exists on the co-ordinational time axis the same mutual structural interdependence as has been described above for every separate moment of force.

This formulation of the question may be clarified by the following illustration. In order to achieve a given co-ordination at a given moment, we have Schema I (for example that illustrated in Fig. 18). Is it possible to regard all co-ordinations over all possible durations of time as un-interrupted functionings of Schema I, or do they exist, and may be regarded as a sequence of changes of Schema I to some other schema, qualitatively different from it (Schema II, and then to Schema III, Schema IV, and so on), while the law of the transition between the schemas and their order of transition, in its turn, has its own determinate structural features? Our factual data on this problem are so far extremely scanty but some observations may still be made.

Firstly, we must turn to the facts described above of the homogeneity of a movement and its unity in terms of the interrelations of its parts in space and in time. Having established our model for a rhythmical movement in the form of a three-four term trigonometric series of the type of eqn. (4), it is possible to prove beyond doubt that this homogeneity also exists in time, and that this particular homogeneity is indeed not peripheral or mechanical but certainly originates in the operation of the central nervous system. This demonstrates that there exist in the central nervous system exact formulae of movement (*Bewegungsformeln*) or their engrams, and that these

formulae or engrams contain in some form of brain trace the whole process
of the movement in its entire course in time. We may affirm that at the
moment when the movement began there was already in existence in the central
nervous system a whole collection of engrams which were necessary for the
movement to be carried on to its conclusion. The existence of such engrams
is proved, however, by the very fact of the existence of habits of movements
and of automatized movements.

A problem of considerable structural significance now arises. Let us
suppose that to a given co-ordinated movement there correspond, in the
brain n engrams by means of which it is ensured that the movement will take
place with successive ecphoria in a determinate time sequence and with
determinate tempo and rhythm. All these n engrams exist in the central nervous
system at any given moment as the habit of movement exists, but they exist
in a hidden, latent form. How are we to explain the facts that, firstly,
they do not all undergo ecphoria simultaneously but in sequence, secondly,
they do not lose their order of ecphoria, and thirdly, they observe
determinate time intervals between ecphoria (tempo) and quantitative
relationships in their duration (rhythm)? There are here two basic
possibilities, two "temporal structures"; either (a) each successive ecphoria
of the engram (or perhaps a proprioceptive signal of its effect at the
periphery) serves as an ecphorator for the next engram in order; or (b) the
mechanism for ecphoria, the ecphorator, lies outside the engrams themselves
and directs their order by a hierarchic principle of *Überordnung*. The first
hypothesis may be called the "chain" hypothesis, the second the "comb"
hypothesis (Fig. 19).

Very weighty considerations may be found to support both these
hypotheses. The chain hypothesis brings to the fore proprioceptive moment,
and in this connection it explains independently and satisfactorily the
observation of tempo and rhythm referring them to a regular synchrony with
events occurring at the periphery. Because, on this hypothesis, the stimulus
for the arousal of each successive ecphoria is the existence of the preceding
one, it is possible to explain both the maintenance of an order of succession
and the impossibility of separate links being left out of a succession of
ecphoria in this way. Finally, the hypothesis recommends itself by its
simplicity, and by the fact that it is unnecessary to postulate any particular
structure for the ecphorator.

The arguments in favour of the comb hypothesis are no less cogent. The
presence in the C.N.S. of "the plan of a movement", the homogeneity of its

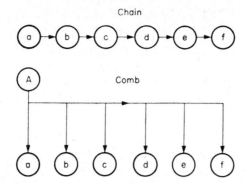

Fig. 19. Two theoretically possible schemes for successive ecphoria of motor engrams a, b, c, d, e and f.

formula and the homogeneity of the movement itself and of its course from beginning to end does not answer to the hypothesis that a movement is fractioned in this way, or that there is no guiding principle of succession among elements of the chain type other than events at the periphery. We do not see in this case any sign of a guiding principle unifying the whole. Further, if we recall the facts discussed above which indicate that the central impulses merely adjust to, and compensate for, the external force field so that the pattern of the impulses over time may have very little in common with the picture of the movement, the comb hypothesis finds a new and important reinforcement. At the same time, a glance at Fig. 14 shows that the central impulse C, which is represented by a hatched area (and is entirely unlike the summed rhythmical equilibrium B which is finally achieved because of the presence of external disturbing forces A), shows a succession of elements which in no case resemble each other. The possibility of obtaining the homogeneity and regularity of B on every repetition, agreeing at the periphery with the law expressed in eqn. (4), necessarily requires the existence in the C.N.S. of some type of guiding engram which encompasses the entire law of succession of B. If a guiding engram of this type exists (we may refer to it as the motor image of a movement) it must have a dual nature; it must contain within itself, in some way uniquely and simultaneously existing like an embryo in an egg or track on a gramophone record, the entire scheme of the movement as it is expanded in time. It must also guarantee the order and the rhythm of the realization of this scheme; that is to say the gramophone record mentioned above must have some sort of motor to turn it. To pursue this metaphor, what I have called the gramophone record is the directing engram, and what I have compared to a gramophone motor is the ecphorator[*].

Both of the hypotheses which we have examined are completely bound up with the structure of the peripheral impulse which we have deduced above in terms of eqn. (3c), that is, its dependence on the form $E(t, \alpha, d\alpha/dt)$, but they only illuminate this dependence in different ways. On the chain hypothesis the critical agents which determine the development of the process are the dependence of E on α and $d\alpha/dt$, that is, their proprioceptive relationships, while the temporal moment of the relationship to t is determined in this case only by the tempo and by the maintenance of each individual element of the chain a, b, c (Fig. 19). In the comb hypothesis, on the other hand, the dominant relationship is $E(t)$, that is, the independent initiative and the regulating activity of the C.N.S., and proprioceptive effects merely play the role of correctors to the general whole.

It must not be forgotten that the hypothesis of the necessity for an effector mechanism which is distinct from the engrams themselves and is in some sense dominant over them, is not necessarily related to the comb hypothesis but is necessary in equal degree for both hypotheses. Whatever we may ascribe to the regulating engram in the comb hypothesis and to the elementary engrams a, b, c, ..., in the chain hypothesis they are all alike bound to contain in latent form the impulse E in dependence not only on α and $d\alpha/dt$ but also on t. It makes no difference whether the central mechanism of tempo – this "gramophone motor" - is related in its action to the duration of the physico-chemical intercellular reactions or to some other physiological rhythms;[**] they must in any case exist as some functions which differ from the collection of engrams which they activate, because real time cannot be incorporated in the latter. A decision between alternatives in favour of one or other of

---

[*] It is interesting to note here that the question which I have raised of the ecphoria of movements in a chain system or a comb system is a repetition in new terms in the area of the physiology of movement of the ancient psychological dispute of association (Bleuler, Adler) versus action (Berze) in the manner in which psychological processes are carried on. The chain model corresponds to the concept put forward by the associationists and the comb model is very similar to Berze's hypothesis. I am in no sense a partisan of the latter opinion in view of its deeply idealistic basis (the psychology of voluntarism), but I cannot deny that the attacks made on the opinions of pure associationists were extremely opportune.

[**] For example, the velocity of the dispersion of waves of excitation through the C.N.S., time phenomena related to the interference of these waves, rhythmical heart activity, etc.

these two hypotheses, or perhaps in favour of some other more complex
organizational synthesis which incorporates both of them, is a topic for
further investigation. At present is is important for us to discover what,
in principle, is implied in the actual manner in which the problem is framed.

What is important is that the motor image of a movement (that has been
termed by neurologists "the program of a movement", *Bewegungsformel*, *Be-*
wegungsgestalt, and so forth) must necessarily exist in the C.N.S. in the
form of an engram. This directional engram does not merely exist on the comb
hypothesis; indeed, the same fact of successive "stamped-in" connections
between elementary engrams a, b, c, d, e, ..., in the chain hypothesis is
also the engram in the other scheme, only in this case it is represented by
an arrow rather than by a circle; this is the engram that determines the
law of systematic succession of ecphoria and that consequently controls it.
This motor image corresponds to the real, factual form of the movement, that
is, *to the curve B* in Fig. 14, and in no way to the curve of the impulse C;
it is indeed true that its presence makes it possible to control the course
of the impulse C so that, as a result, a smooth performance of the movement
habit B is achieved. Therefore it is necessary that there should exist in
the supreme nervous organ an exact representation of what will later occur
at the periphery; meanwhile, the unfolding of the activity in the field in
the intervening operational stages and the realization of the impulse C
(which by the argument given above is accordingly dissimilar to the
peripheral effect), must therefore also be dissimilar to the contents of
the controlling engrams. We may use the following metaphor: it is as if an
order sent by the higher centre is coded before its transmission to the
periphery so that it is completely unrecognizable and is there again
automatically deciphered. In Section 3 above I have said that the possibility
of a habit of movement, of the establishment of a conditioned motor reflex,
necessarily implies its unitary localization in the central areas, and that
a unity of this type cannot be related to the theory of the representations
of muscles in the higher centres of the cortex. The considerations which have
just been raised once again confirm this theses, on this occasion from the
point of view of the time structure of movements; that level of the C.N.S.
in which the centrifugal impulse C is formulated and in which we might
consequently expect to find a representation of the muscular system is not
the supreme level of the C.N.S., but is in fact that level at which the
elementary engrams a, b, c, ..., etc., of the comb hypothesis are located.
Between the mechanism represented by the comb hypothesis and the mechanism

involved in the case of muscular representation we are obliged to insert
another process of the coding of the image of the movement and its
presentation in the form C. In the terms of our equation this coding
process is the transformation of the relationship $E(t)$ in the pure form
prevalent in the higher level into a full dependence of the form $E(t, \alpha,$
$d\alpha/dt)$; that is, the adaptation of the impulse to proprioception[*].

In this way, the analysis of the course of a movement in time again
brings us to a recognition of the structural complexity of an act of movement,
and consequently also of the complexity of its representation in terms of
localization. Here, also, the recognition of the necessity for the existence
of directional engrams and mechanisms of ecphoria demands that we postulate
a series of hierarchical levels, each of them, inevitably, having a degree
of qualitative independence.

5.   TOPOLOGY AND METRICS OF MOVEMENTS. THE MOTOR FIELD[**]

If we now turn from the temporal moment to the spatial it will be
necessary to touch on two considerations: the distinction between the metric
and topological properties of physiological space, and the peculiarities of
the motor field of the central nervous system. Because of their fundamental
importance these two points should really be the objects of separate reports.

------

[*]
  The formation and development of new habits of movement, that is, the
  engraphy of conditioned reflexes of movement, also appears to be a
  structurally complex process in the light of the analysis undertaken in
  this report. It is in fact the case that new directional engrams with
  their spatio-temporal details must be built up in the C.N.S.; however,
  those auxiliary proprioceptive mechanisms which I have just described as
  "coding" the impulse, and which provide the higher engram with the
  possibility of an actual detailed existence, must also be built up. The
  fact that the habit of movement is not engraphed in those centres in
  which the muscles are localizationally represented is at once demonstrated
  by the fact that an acquired habit may exist while incorporating very
  different muscles in various combinations. When a child learns to write
  he can only form large letters, but a literate adult can form either large
  or small letters with equal facility and write either straight ahead or
  sideway, etc. Apparently the motor directional engrams are developed,
  generally speaking, later than the auxiliary coding mechanisms and
  correspond to a higher degree of mastery in the acquisition of a habit.

[**]
  The term "topology" as used here does not coincide exactly with the strict
  mathematical definition. For lack of a more adequate expression I have
  adopted this term for the whole of the _qualitative_ characteristics of
  space configurations and of the form of movements in contrast to the
  quantitative, metric ones. The more detailed definition of what is meant
  here under the term topology will be understood from the text.

I will for this reason discuss them only as much as is necessary to develop my basic thesis.

In any geometrical representation we may make a distinction between topology and metrics. By the topology of a geometrical object I mean the totality of its qualitative peculiarities without reference to its magnitude, form, any distortion in its reproduction, etc. As topological properties of a linear figure, for example, we may discuss whether it is open or closed, whether the lines composing it intersect with each other as in a figure eight or whether they do not intersect as in the case of a circle and so on. Besides these properties, in the determination of which quantitative considerations are irrelevant, we may also consider such topological properties as incorporate the concept of number, not, however, including the concept of measure. Among these properties we may refer, for example, to that of quadrangularity, membership in the group of five-pointed stars, and so on. I shall arbitrarily describe this group of properties as topological properties of the first order while the former may be considered zero order properties. All figures in the upper row in Fig. 20 belong to one and the same topological class of figures of the first order (being, however, completely dissimilar in metric relations); they are indeed identical in respect to the numbers which characterize them. All of them have five angles or points, all of them display five intersections of the lines composing them, and so on. No. 6 in this illustration belongs to another class of the

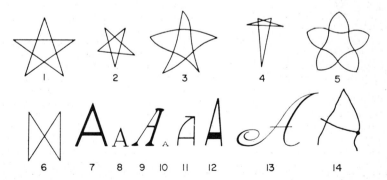

Fig. 20. 1–5, topological class of five-pointed stars; 6, topological
class of figure-eights with four angles; 7–14, topological
class of letters *A*.

same order containing four angles and one intersection, but it is located,
as are the first five figures, in the class of zero order, being as they are
a closed figure with intersecting lines. In order to illustrate characteristic
properties of the first order with an example with which we are all familiar
I shall point out that every printed letter is a separate topological class
of the first order, while to the single class of letter *A* there belong
letter *A*'s of all dimensions, scripts, outlines, embellishments, etc. (see
7-14 in Fig. 20), though we ignore certain additional details of purely
calligraphic significance. The chalk figures for the game of "hopscotch",
which appear in great numbers on our pavements every spring, are also all
representatives of one and the same topological class of the first order
for each equivalent representation of the game, and in this respect the
scale of the figure or the age and skill of the draughtsman do not matter.
The habitual scheme on which a given child draws a house or a face is also
usually a determinate topological class and nothing more.

   After this general introduction we may turn from geometry to psychophysiology. If we draw the attention of a psychologist or a teacher to our
collection of letter *A*'s in Fig. 20, he will immediately remark that the
whole set displays a common characteristic in terms of its essential sign,
that is to say without circumlocution, that the topological characteristics
of a figure are of paramount psychologico-pedagogical importance in comparison
with properties of a metrical sort. Our psychologist or teacher will be quite
right, because the recognition of the letter *A* does not require the presence
of any metrical properties and is, on the contrary, entirely dependent on
the presence of determinate topological cues. This great affinity between the
process of recognition and topology, which has also been noted and studied
for some considerable time by adherents of Gestalt psychology, is certainly
a psychophysiological phenomenon and may even be of general biological
significance, but in any case it cannot be deduced from purely geometrical
considerations. The biological characteristic of the predominance of
topological categories over metric ones may be pursued in a multiplicity of
examples. A maple leaf differs from a birch leaf in respect to topological
properties of the first order, while at the same time all maple leaves
belong to one and the same topological class in spite of all the thoroughly
investigated biometric variation between separate specimens. The structure
of the brain and the disposition of the main convolutions of the cortex
again provide an example of an object having the same topology for all possible
metrical variations. It is possible to say with certainty that in the area of

biological morphology those cases in which metrics is of importance together with topology (for example, the lens of the eye) are rare exceptions[*]. This overwhelming importance of topology in the case of living objects should be attentively compared, for example, with the morphology of crystals where the essential relationships are all metric ones.

A whole series of biologically important morphological signs must unquestionably be referred to topology, although they cannot be numbered either in the zero or in the first order. Every child will naturally distinguish between a cat and a dog; the distinction is certainly not made on the basis of anatomical considerations such as the comparative structure of the claws and the teeth, on which topic he may be fully ignorant, but on the general appearance - on a certain *je ne sais quoi* - that indubitably appears to be a topological category. However, the difference between the appearance of a cat and a dog cannot be related to topological signs of the first order. It is likely that some higher orders which await future analysis are operating here.

Insufficient attention has so far been given to the fact that the movements of live organisms, to no less a degree than their perceptions, are determined by topological categories. This is illustrated with great clarity by the example of drawing, perhaps because this type of movement leaves a record which may be conveniently studied. It is easy for everyone to draw a five-pointed star, but we can say with certainty that this picture is made by using only topological and not metric relationships. As proof on this I suggest the experiment of drawing ten such stars in succession and comparing the pictures. I doubt if it is at all possible to make a metrically perfect copy of a similar object without the help of a compass and a ruler, that is, the human motor system cannot attain any high degree of metric proficiency, but it can be said that our motor system is very sensitive to topological distinctions of higher orders than one and zero. It is sufficient, for example, to draw attention to *handwriting*. I pointed out above that the letter *A* belongs to a single topological class of the first order no matter how or by whom it is written. Besides this, all letter *A*'s written in my hand are similar to each other and are simultaneously different from letter *A*'s written by second and third persons. The similarity between my *A*'s is far from metrical, but is topological; the differences between my *A*'s and those written by other hands must in the same way be related to topological

---

[*] It may never cross the mind of an anatomist or a topographical anatomist that all his life he considers only various topological categories - a new variation of Molière's M. Jourdain!

differences involving higher orders than the first. The topological
propensities in our perception seize upon what may be regarded as common
features within the limits of a given handwriting - once again in a form
which it is not easy to subject to analysis in terms of impressions - a *je
ne sais quoi*, the analysis of which is not yet practicable for us because
of our lack of acquaintance at present with whatever may constitute higher
topological orders and what properties we must ascribe to them.

Such of our movements as do not leave a trace upon paper have drawn
less attention to themselves in the manner indicated. Parallel with the
knowledge on handwriting there exist structurally similar bodies of knowledge
on gait, touch in music and accent of voice, although the analysis of these
phenomena has not been carried very far. One thing may, however, be already
affirmed with certainty; all attempts to draw distinctions of this type in
terms of quantitative metrical signs (as can be done, for example, with
pitch) are doomed to failure in advance. It is here necessary to make new
discoveries in qualitative geometry, but consideration of the perspectives
which are now unfolding in this direction would be for us at present too
far from our main goal.

A circumstance of great and immediate interest in the structural
analysis of movements is the fact that topological peculiarities in visual
perception display marked similarities to some signs of idiosyncrasies in
the topology of motor organization. So, for example, the category of
dimension is equally indifferent to visual perception and to movement. I
find it equally easy to recognize a triangle, a star or a letter whether it
is presented to me in a large or in a small form. The same indifference to
the absolute dimensions of a geometrical object was demonstrated in dogs by
Pavlov and in rats by Lashley. In precisely the same way I find it equally
easy to draw a star or write a word large or small, and to do this on a
piece of paper or on a classroom blackboard. It would be interesting to
make a study of the quantitative relationship between the variation in these
drawings and their size; but we may say in any case that, whatever the size,
they retain their topological properties not only of the first but also of
higher orders; so, for example, all the characteristics of handwriting which
are peculiar to a given person when writing on paper are also apparent in
writing on a blackboard, although, in a word, the entire muscular structure
of the movement is absolutely different in the two cases.

Visual perception, however, shows great sensitivity to such concomitantly
metric cues as symmetry, a category that is at the same time completely

ignored by the motor system. On the other hand, the metrical category of
extensity is, without doubt, of greater importance to the motor than to the
visual receptors because the estimation of dimension in perception (for
example, visually) is always ultimately based on deep-seated kinaesthetic
associations related to the field of sensitivity of the receptor. The
perceptual and motor systems are to all appearances equally indifferent to
the category of position in space (right, left, above, below), which is of
exceptional interest for the structural analysis of localization. In fact a
figure which may be placed in the most diverse portions of the visual field
is recognized with equal facility as being the same*; in the same way the
process of carrying out an habitual action, for example, writing a word or
playing over a passage which one has learnt by heart on the piano, is carried
out with approximately the same facility and with the same degree of accuracy
independently of the position of the hand or of the register on the piano.
It is interesting that the purely metrical abilities of the kinaesthetic
apparatus (for example the estimation of length or of distance) are
characterized by gross differences in various zones of the spatial field.

Both perceptual recognition and motor reproduction are extremely
sensitive to the orientation of a figure in space. The identification of a
triangle after it has been rotated 180° is incomparably more difficult than
the identification of triangles of different size with the same orientation.
In just the same way it is extremely difficult to draw figures upside down
with a pencil.

---

* I consider this fact to be an extremely clear illustration of the structural
complexity of every conditioned reflex, even what is apparently the most
simple one. In presenting a conditioning stimulus visually to a dog neither
the head, and still less the eyeballs, are in any way immobilized and for
this reason the visual stimulus may fall on the most various points of the
retina, and consequently on different points of the first visual centre.
If the visual stimulus is, for example, a triangle, on each presentation
of this stimulus to the animal's retina a whole series of sensory elements
are excited, and here, every time the animal turns its head and eyes this
series is either wholly or partially different. The appearance of a single
reaction in all these cases proves, it would seem, that the engram for a
given conditioned reflex is not located at those points (the primary
visual centre) on which the separate lines and points are represented but
at some structurally higher centre, the connection of which to the former
is very similar to that which has earlier been described in the case of
the successive levels of the centres of movement. Here we find an example
of the same fact which was employed above (section 3, p. 29) as proof of
the impossibility of localization of the muscles and of conditioned
reflexes in one and the same centre.

It is an important fact that in a very large percentage of cases
children draw the mirror images of letters, that is to say they change
about the right and left sides although they never turn the letter upside
down. Another fact is also interesting (being indicative of some sort of
structural hierarchy); children never either read or write an entire word
from right to left, they only do this separately and successively for
individual letters of the world. It is clear that in both these cases there
must exist different mechanisms which cannot be compared to each other.

These analogies and differences may be pursued to great lengths: a
study of these and others promises to be extremely fruitful. At present,
however, it is necessary only to summarize all that has been said above
about the topological properties of perception and movements.

First of all, it may be stated that the totality of the topological and
metrical characteristics of the relations between movements and external
space can be generalized under the term *motor field*, analogous with the
concept of the visual field recognized by psychologists. An immediate task

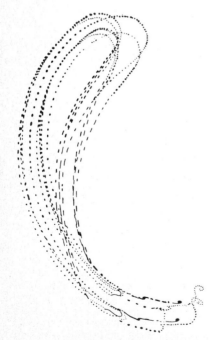

of physiology is to analyse the properties
of this motor field. The preceding
statements permit us to assert that the
physiological motor field is as widely
different from objective external space
as is the visual field. Its typical
differences from theoretical Euclidian
space consist, first of all, in an obvious
preference of the motor field for
topological categories as compared with
metric ones, in the presence of some
evident tropisms, or tendencies toward
certain directions, in the absence of
bilateral symmetry (which is peculiar to
the visual field), and so on. The predominance of topology is revealed also
in the fact that straight lines and
their distinction from curved ones are
not proper to the motor field (in this
it differs from the visual), nor are
stable, identical lines. In biomechanics
this is manifested in that successive

Fig. 21. Cyclogram of a series
of successive poorly
automatized movements
taken on the same
plate.

movements of cyclical nature never exactly repeat themselves (Fig. 21). The co-ordinational net of the motor field must be regarded, in distinction to a net in Euclidian geometry, firstly as non-rectilinear, and secondly as oscillating like a cobweb in the wind. Its "oscillation" does not, however, in every case proceed so far as to destroy topological relationships either of zero order (for example the category "between") or of the first and perhaps of even higher orders.

Some of the properties of the motor field which we have now disentangled are of great interest for the theory of localization. Firstly, there is the deeply seated inherent indifference of the motor control centre to the scale and position of the movement effected, as we have discussed above. It is clear that each of the variations of a movement (for example, drawing a circle large or small, directly in front of oneself or to one side, on a horizontal piece of paper or on a vertical blackboard, etc.) demands a quite different muscular formula; and even more than this, involves a completely different set of muscles in the action. The almost equal facility and accuracy with which all these variations can be performed is evidence for the fact that they are ultimately determined by one and the same higher directional engram in relation to which dimensions and position play a secondary role. These engrams, which determine the muscle structure of each of the concrete variations, clearly lie still lower than those described in section 4 and in particular in the area C of Fig. 14, whereas the engrams of dimension and spatial position may already be referred to area B. We must conclude from this that the higher engram, which may be called the engram of a given topological class, is already structurally extremely far removed (and because of this also probably localizationally very distant) from any resemblance whatever to the joint-muscle schemata; it is extremely geometrical, representing a very abstract motor image of space. This makes us suppose – for the time being merely as an hypothesis though it forces itself upon us very strongly – that the localizational areas of these higher-order motor engrams have also the same topological regulation as is found in external space or in the motor field (and that in any case the pattern is by no means that which maintains in the joint-muscle apparatus). In other words there is considerable reason to suppose that in the higher motor centres of the brain (it is very probable that these are in the cortical hemispheres) the localizational pattern is none other than some form of projection of external space in the form present for the subject in the motor field. This projection, from all that has been said above, must be congruent with external space, but

only topologically and in no sense metrically. All danger of considering the
possibility of compensation for the inversion of projection at the retina
(section 3) and many other possibilities of the same sort are completely
avoided by these considerations. It seems to me that although it is not now
possible to specify the ways in which such a topological representation of
space in the central nervous system may be achieved, this is only a question
of time for physiology. It is only necessary to reiterate that the
topological properties of the projection of space in the C.N.S. may prove to
be very strange and unexpected; we must not expect to find in the cortex
some sort of photograph of space, even an extremely deformed one. Still, the
hypothesis that there exist in the higher levels of the C.N.S. projections
of space, and not projections of joints and muscles, seems to me to be at
present more probable than any other.

6.   THE PRINCIPLE OF "EQUAL SIMPLICITY"

It is now time to give a general formulation of an heuristic principle
which I have already presented in a partial modification in section 3 above,
and to examine its application in terms of a few examples. I shall call it
the *principle of equal simplicity*.

I begin with non-physiological examples. I have three devices with which
it is possible to draw a circle; a circular template, a compass and an
ellipsograph. A circle of the same radius as the template may be drawn as
easily with the template as with the compass; a circle may also be drawn
with the ellipsograph, as it is a particular case of an ellipse, but it will
be a little more complicated to do this than with either the template or the
compass. If we have a circle of some other radius the template immediately
becomes useless. The compass draws circles of all radii with equal facility.
A given actual ellipsograph may only describe a circle of a single determinate
radius, and for this reason it is eliminated together with the template. If
we wish to draw an ellipse we may do this using the ellipsograph with exactly
the same difficulty, no more or less than we had in drawing the circle, but
both the compass and the template are useless.

In this example we are considering a set of curves of the second order
which differ (a) in radius and (b) in eccentricity. One of our instruments,
the template, gives us with great simplicity one curve and no others. The
second instrument gives us equally easily all variations in radius, but
only a single eccentricity, zero, peculiar to a circle. The third instrument
gives us with equal ease - although in absolute terms the process is slightly

more complicated than in the case of the compass - all eccentricities, but only one radius. A circle of the same radius as the template may be drawn by means of all three instruments but the functional relationship between their simplicity and the possible variations in all three cases are quite different. The type of this functional relationship is determined with great accuracy by the scheme of construction of the instrument.

In mathematical language the preceding example may be presented in the following way. We designate the degree of simplicity (for example the speed with which the task can be completed, or unity divided by the time of completion, etc.) by S, the radius of the circle by r and the eccentricity by e. Then, for all our devices,

$$S = F(r, e). \tag{6}$$

For the template of radius r we have:

$$F(r, e) = 0; \qquad F(R, O) \neq 0. \tag{6a}$$

For the compass:

$$F(r, e)_{e \neq o} = 0; \qquad F(r, 0) = \text{const} \ddagger 0. \tag{6b}$$

For the ellipsograph:

$$F(r, e)_{r \neq R} \qquad F(R, e) = \text{const} \neq 0. \tag{6c}$$

Equations (6b) and (6c) may be represented by a line; eqn. (6a) is the point of intersection of the lines (6b) and (6c).

Examples are possible in which the degree of simplicity does not change abruptly from zero to some final value as in the preceding case, but changes from one value to another with a certain regular continuity. So, for example, in multiplying numbers with Odner's calculating machine the degree of simplicity (or the speed of the work) decreases in parallel with an increase in the number of multiplication signs and with the number of units involved with each of these signs. At the same time the degree of simplicity is invariable with respect to the number of digits multiplied. In the Millioner calculating machine the degree of simplicity is invariable in respect to the number of digits in the multipliers and depends only on the number of multiplication signs. Finally, on a slide rule the degree of simplicity is almost invariable with respect to both components involved.

In all these cases we encounter the same fact, that different structural schemes may carry out the same set of operations but the differences in their structures are always accompanied by differences *in the form of the function*

S. We may say with certainty that the more marked are the changes in S in
the transition from one element of the set to another adjacent to it, the
smaller is the degree of the adaptation to this transition possible with the
structural peculiarities of the system in question. On the other hand, for
any given system there are "lines of equal simplicity", that is, those
transitions from one element of the set of possible tasks to another which
do not result in any change in the simplicity of manipulation, corresponding
to transitions which are most closely related to the structural scheme of
the device.

We arrive from this case to the following formulation of the principle
of equal simplicity: for every system which is capable of undertaking a set
of different elementary processes of a given range, the lines of equal
simplicity correspond to those directions in this range along which movement
does not involve any change either in the structural principles or in the
principles of operation of the system. Instead of the expression "simplicity"
which does not have any concrete association we may insert a whole series of
parallel expressions in relation to the case under investigation: the
expressions of speed of completion, degree of accuracy, degree of variance
and so on. For a general formulation I have selected the term simplicity as
being the most general in spite of its lack of concrete associations.

We may extract an heuristically valuable principle from the discussion
above. If we are concerned with any given system, the structure of which is
unknown to us but whose operation we may observe under a variety of conditions,
then by a comparison of the changes *in the variable S* (speed, accuracy,
variation, etc.) encountered as a function of each of the variables in the
conditions, we may come to determinate conclusions as to the structure of
the system which are unattainable by direct means.

Let us imagine, for example, that we are invited to see a film without
having any idea of how cinematography works. We may suppose that we are
attending it in a puppet theatre (as our grandfathers might have). We are
astonished by the wealth and variety of the material we are shown, exceeding
by far all that could be met with in these days, but we still have an
indisputable right to consider that we are watching only marionettes which
have been greatly improved in principle. It is true that in a puppet theatre
we never, for example, saw the sea; but then (says grandfather) it is obvious
that here they have only an extremely cunning mechanical imitation of the sea.
In the old puppet theatre figures could not be made to diminish as they grew
more distant, as this occurs in the cinema, but once again it is possible to

consider this as a new achievement of the technology of the marionette
theatre. All this, although extremely difficult, is possible. It is, however,
very easy to show that we are not in a puppet theatre and to do this precisely
with the help of the principle of equal simplicity. It is sufficient, for
this purpose, to select two objects which are sharply different in their
difficulty of representation in the puppet theatre, for example, a rotating
wheel and a stormy sea, and without reference to cinematic technique (let
us suppose that its technical structure is inaccessible to us) to turn to
the studio's accountant and ask how much it would cost to obtain representations
of both these objects on the screen for one minute. As soon as we discover
that a strip of 20 m of film costs about the same for either object (or, to
put it more accurately, that the cost of the film is related to some other
arbitrary factors and in no way to the mechanical properties of the objects
on the screen), the hypothesis of a puppet theatre collapses. In general, a
skilful interview with an accountant may give many positive technical details
– we may recall that it was in just this way that Mendeleev discovered the
secret of an important French explosive.

For the puppet theatre all is possible (at least potentially) that is
possible to the cinema. But the "all" is, in principle, unattainable with
the same degree of simplicity as operates in the cinema. We encounter the
same interrelationships between the gramophone and such talking machines as
were experimented with a hundred years ago by von Kempelin, for example. The
whole structural nature of the gramophone lies in the fact that the sounds
to be reproduced make no difference to it, whereas von Kempelin would have
been obliged to construct a new mechanical gullet for each new pitch. A
rural deacon in L. Andreev's story was brought into an extremely amusing
collision with the principle of equal simplicity as applied to the gramophone
when he could not conceive how the gramophone could reproduce with equal
ease both a music-hall song and the voice of the Son of Man. The principle
described proves to be extremely fruitful in its application to the structural
analysis of the function of the central nervous system, both in its receptor
and in its effector aspects. In section 2 I used a circular movement of the
extended arm of the type shown in Fig. 15 as an example of the smooth redistribution of muscle pull. We may return to consideration of the same
movement from a new point of view. If a circle is described with the arm
directly to the front, then directly out to one side and then about some
intermediate axis, both the muscle and the innervational schemes of the three
movements will be sharply different. However, all three movements are

subjectively very much alike in terms of difficulty and objectively they
display approximately the same amount of accuracy and of variation. This
allows us to conclude with a high degree of probability that the structure
of the central complex which governs the production of a given series of
movements is much more closely related to spatial form than to muscle scheme,
because all three variations of the circular movement which we have attempted
lie on lines of equal simplicity in regard to the properties of the movement
and the properties of their forms, but not the properties of the muscular
schemes. This conclusion may be made more clear from the following example,
which I have thoroughly analysed in another study (23). In order to carry
out with precision any given automatized movement, for example, cursive
writing, the positions and the means of fixation in the intermediate links
of the arm are almost completely indifferent. I write with the same
handwriting and with almost equal ease when I rest my forearm on a table-top
and when my arm supports its own weight, as well as in a variety of
positions. All these variants are sharply different from the point of view
of muscle structure and if it were assumed that the object of the working
out of a habit of movement were one of these structures we would be obliged
to suppose that the others would lie completely outside the range of this
habit, that is to say, on a quite different level of simplicity. The fact of
identical simplicity and the retention of the characteristics of the habit
is immediate evidence that the habit of writing is not a habit of the muscle
scheme and consequently that the traces in the C.N.S. which govern these
habits are closely related to the topology of handwriting and considerably
removed from joints and muscles. All these, and many similar examples, must
be experimentally analysed both qualitatively and quantitatively and each
such analysis allows us to arrive at new basic conclusions as to the structure
of the activity of the motor centres of the C.N.S.

An extremely interesting example of the application of the principle of
equal simplicity may be taken from the psychology of perception which is, at
the moment, far more developed than the structural physiology of movement.
This example refers to a theory of hearing. A whole series of hypotheses
have been put forward in order to explain the mechanism operating in the inner
ear and allowing us to discriminate sounds (Hemholtz, Ewald, Hering, Gray)
among which the most popular at the moment is Helmholtz's hypothesis. On
this hypothesis each of the numerous fibres of the basilar membrane is supposed
to act as elastic string tuned to a particular frequency. When this particular
frequency operates on the organ of Corti and the basilar membrane the given

fibre goes into a condition of resonant oscillation and mechanically stimulates the auditory receptors attached to it. In this way each of the sensitive endings of the acoustic nerve are stimulated only by a single sound frequency and the recognition of the frequency in the C.N.S. is achieved by the same process which effects the perception of tactile local signs (*Lokalzeichen*). Complex sounds or harmonics are analysed in this way which explains the recognition of pitch and the discrimination of chords.

Many serious psychological objections have been raised against this hypothesis. Additions and corrections were soon made. Helmholtz himself was not able to explain in these terms the perception of consonance and dissonance for which he was obliged to hypothesize the presence of a separate system perceiving beat (*Schwebungen*). There have been numerous later additions and emendations (F. Alt, A. Gray, L. Hermann Waetzmann, Budd-Feldafing, W. Köhler, G. Revesz, F. Brentano, and others), and the very fact of their necessity has cast serious doubt on Helmholtz's hypothesis. It is very probable that should a new hypothesis appear which adequately explains all the requisite phenomena and is at the same time simpler, it would be preferred to the older hypothesis on the principle that the true explanation is the simpler one[*] (although there is nothing objective in this guarantee). However, no hypothesis of this type has so far appeared. Meanwhile, there are serious objections to Helmholtz's hypothesis independent of its simplicity or complexity. It is only necessary for this purpose to show (and there are in the literature an enormous number of experimental and clinical facts pointing in this direction) that the lines of equal simplicity are distributed in an essentially different way for the function of auditory perception and for a resonant harp. So as not to encumber this report I shall limit myself to two points.

We are making a comparison between a system whose functional operation is unknown to us, the apparatus of auditory perception and a known physical model - a set of resonators which for the sake of vividness I have called a

---

[*] This conviction may very easily be false. Contemporary physics provides various examples of this. The theories of de Broglie, Einstein, Heisenberg, Schrödinger or Dirac are far more complicated than the concepts which they have supplanted. To set up simplicity as a criterion of reliability would be to affirm in principle that the categories of logic and psychology dominate the categories of objective reality and determine them, and we have no authority for apriorities of this type.

resonant harp. For this latter structure the simplest of all operations
is the determination of the absolute frequency of a tone; this follows from
its very structure. The determination of the relationship between the
frequencies of the components, and is for this reason more complicated.
However, the statistics of musical pedagogy (J. v. Kries, O. Abraham, G.
Revesz) show that the possession of absolute pitch is a very rare occurrence
while a majority of people have relative pitch. In other words, for the
organ of hearing relative determinations of intervals are easier than those
of absolute tones.

On the other hand, a pure musical tone is simpler in its acoustic
structure than the sounds of the human voice - vowels with their numerous
formants, and consonants with their characteristic phonation. For a
resonating harp these can be recognized in no other way than by their analysis
into simple components and only after the determination of these components;
consequently, on this model the discrimination of speech sounds is more
complicated than the discrimination of pure tones and is based entirely on
the latter process. As far as the human organ of hearing is concerned, *many*
people have musical (relative) discrimination while *all* understand and
perceive speech. Very striking cases of tone deafness have been described
(L. Alt, W. Köhler). Köhler's patient not only did not understand what was
meant by a melody, but was even unable to distinguish between a low and a
high tone, while he could distinguish all shades of speech and accent very
well, indeed, imitating provincial accents quite well in telling anecdotes
(such persons have no physical defects of hearing). We again find an inversion
of the levels of difficulty with respect to the resonator apparatus which we
have hypothesized.

It is clear from both comparisons that the organ of hearing gives an
essentially different gradation of simplicity than that of the hypothesized
resonator mechanism - a gradation amounting in some examples to a direct
transposition of the order of difficulty. It is this circumstance which is
critically dangerous for Helmholtz's hypothesis, independently of its
simplicity or complexity.

The discussion in section 3 of the example of the lack of correspondence
between the theory of muscle localization in the cortex and the idea of the
localization of conditioned reflexes is clearly a particular case of the
use of the principle which has here been described in full. Further experiments
and observations on changes in the accuracy of movements in their different
variations and for corresponding changes in the irradiation of a habit of

movement may disclose for us a whole series of structural regularities in the motor field, and the motor functions of the brain in their entirety – regularities which cannot be foreseen at present. Only one thing may already be foreseen with certainty. Every new discovery in the field of co-ordinational structure will at the same time be a new discovery along the lines of localizational structure; and on that day when we understand the one we shall be able to say that we understand the other.

Symbols Used in this Chapter

I. SPATIAL COORDINATES

x longitudinal (sagittal) coordinate.

y vertical coordinate.

z transversal coordinate.

For x, positive direction is forward.

For y, positive direction is upward.

For z, positive direction is to the left.

II. SYMBOLS FOR PARTS OF THE BODY

Initial letter	Limb		Centre of gravity of the limb segment	Proximal joint of limb segment
	Latin term	English term		
c	caput	Head	gc	–
b	brachium	Upper arm	gb	b shoulder joint
a	antebrachium	Fore arm	ga	a elbow joint
m	manus	Hand	gm	m wrist joint
t	truncus	Trunk	gt	–
f	femur	Thigh	gf	f hip joint
s	sura	Shin	gs	s knee joint
p	pes	Foot	gp	p ankle joint
H	homo	The whole body	gH	–

III. TERMS FOR THE CENTRES OF GRAVITY OF SYSTEMS (EXAMPLES)

The centre of gravity for the system (shin + foot) $g(sp)$.

The centre of gravity for the system (whole + leg) $g(fsp)$, etc.

Other points along the long axes of the limbs are indicated by Greek letters corresponding to the initial letters of the Latin term for the limb. For example:

φ a point on the longitudinal axis of the thigh (f).

π a point at the end of the foot (p).

IV. SYMBOLS FOR THE MECHANICAL FUNCTIONS OF MOVEMENT

S displacement (along a line described by real coordinates).

V velocity.

W acceleration.

F force.

M moment of force.

The symbols for joints or centres of gravity of a limb segment are attached to these letters as subscripts. Symbols for coordinates are given in parentheses. For example:

$S_a(y)$	the vertical component of the path followed by the elbow joint.
$V_s(x)$	the sagittal component of the velocity of the knee joint.
$W_\pi(z)$	the transversal component of the acceleration of the end of the foot.
$F_{gs}(y)$	the vertical component of the force at the centre of gravity of the shin.
$F_g(fsp)(x)$	the longitudinal component of force at the centre of gravity of the whole leg system.
M_f	the moment of force at the hip joint.

ADDENDA

1. A point on the facial plane of the head in the region of the upper edge of the aural helix is projected upon the centre of gravity of the head in profile photographs, and is provisionally termed the semi-centre of gravity on these photographs, and is designated by $gc/2$.

2. The angles mentioned in this handbook are designated as follows:

α the angle of the longitudinal axis of the thigh to the horizontal, directed forwards.

β the angle of the longitudinal axis of the shin to the horizontal, directed forwards.

φ the angle between the longitudinal axes of the thigh and shin.

REFERENCES

8. Bernstein, N.A. Studies of the biomechanics of the stroke by means of photo-registration, Research of the Central Institute of Labour, Moscow 1 (in Russian), 1923.

9. Bernstein, N.A. A biomechanical norm for the stroke. Research of the Central Institute of Labour, Moscow 1,2 (in Russian), 1924.

14. Bernstein, N.A. & Popova, T.S. Untersuchung der Biodynamik des Klavieranschlags. Arbeitsphysiologie, 1929, 1, 5.

15. Bernstein, N.A. Clinical Ways of Modern Biomechanics. Collection of papers of the Institute for Medical Improvement, Kazan, 1929.

19. Bernstein, N.A. et al. Studies of the Biodynamics of Locomotions (Normal Gait, Load and Fatigue). Institute of Experimental Medicine, Moscow (in Russian), 1935.

21. Bernstein, N.A. et al. Studies of the Biodynamics of Walking, Running and jumping (in Russian), Moscow, 1940.

23. Bernstein, N.A. On the Construction of Movements. Monograph (in Russian), Moscow, 1947.

30. Bethe, A. & Fischer, R. Die Plastizität der Nervensysteme. Handbuch der normale und pathologische Physiologie, 1927, 10.

44. Foerster, O. Die Physiologie und Pathologie der Koordination. Zbl. f. die ges. Neurol. Psychiatrie 41, 11-12.

52. Lewy, F. Die Lehre vom Tonus und der Bewegung. Berlin, 1923.

55. Magnus, R. Die Körperstellung. Berlin, 1924.

59. Monacow, C. Die Localisation im Grosshirn. Wiesbaden, 1914.

CHAPTER IIa
FREQUENCY ENCODING IN MOTOR SYSTEMS

K.H. Pribram, A. Sharafat, G.J. Beekman

THE ISSUES

Introduction

There is considerable reason to suppose that in the higher
motor centers of the brain (it is very probable that these
are in the cortical hemispheres) the localization pattern
is none other than some form of projection of external space
in the form present for the subject in the motor field. This
projection, from all that has been said above, must be
congruent with external space, but only topologically and in
no sense metrically. All danger of considering the possibility
of compensation for the inversion of projection at the retina
... and many other possibilities of the same sort are completely
avoided by these considerations. It seems to me that although
it is not now possible to specify the ways in which such a
topological representation of space in the central nervous
system may be achieved, this is only a question of time for
physiology. It is only necessary to reiterate that the
topological properties of the projection of space in the C.N.S.
may prove to be very strange and unexpected; we must not
expect to find in the cortex some sort of photographic space,
even an extremely deformed one. Still, the hypothesis that
there exist in the higher levels of the C.N.S. projections of
space, and not projections of joints and muscles, seems to me
to be at present more probable than any other (Bernstein, p. 109).

With these insights Bernstein set the problem which neurophysiologists
must address if they are to relate the anatomical organization of the central
motor mechanism to the organization of behavior. Neuroanatomists have
demonstrated a somatotopic representation of muscles onto the cerebral cortex.
But as Bernstein points out it is the topological representation of external
space, not of projections of joints and muscles, that is needed if patterns
of behavioral acts, the consequence of movements, and not just patterns of
movements per se are to be explained. Bernstein, in his experiments, used

Fourier analysis to specify the topology of such behavioral actions and his specifications were sufficiently accurate to allow prediction of the patterns of continuing action.

The experiments reported here were undertaken to test the hypothesis that the Fourier approach might also be as useful in analyzing the physiology of single neurons in the motor mechanism as it was for analyzing patterns of behavioral actions. Support for such an approach comes from its success when applied to the analyses of the functions of the sensory systems. These analyses are reviewed in some detail in order to provide a background of expectations and of problems faced using this approach.

The Fourier Approach to the Sensory Systems:

The first suggestion that brain processing might involve a Fourier analysis was made a century ago for the auditory system by Ohm (1843), the same Ohm who formulated Ohm's Law of Electricity. This suggestion was adopted by Herman v. Helmholtz (1863) who performed a series of experiments which led to the place theory of hearing - essentially a view of the cochlea as a piano keyboard, whose keys, when struck by acoustic waves, would iniate nerve impulses to the brain where resonant neurons were activated. This view was modified in this century by George v. Bekesy (1959). His experiments showed the cochlea and peripheral neurosensory mechanism to operate more like a stringed instrument which is sensitive to the superposition of acoustic wave forms. This work led to the discovery that the initial stages of auditory processing can be described in terms of a Fourier transform of the acoustic input (Evans, 1974).

Bekesy went on to make a large-scale model of the cochlea composed of a row of five vibrators (1959). When the model was placed on the forearm and the phase of the vibrators adjusted manually, the phenomenal perception was that of a point source of stimulation which could be moved up and down the arm. When two such model "cochleas" were applied, one to each forearm, the point source appeared at first to jump alternately from one forearm to the other, and then suddenly to stabilize in the space between the two arms. The stimulus was "projected" away from the stimulating source and the receptive surface into the external world, much as sound is projected into the environment away from the source in audio speakers of a high fidelity system.

Both macro- and microelectrode studies performed in my laboratory have shown that multiple simultaneous vibratory stimulations of the skin also

evoke only unitary responses in cortex (Dewson, 1964; Lynch, 1971). Just as
in perception, the cortical electrical response does not reflect the actual
physical dimensions of the stimulus. Bekesy noted that sensory inhibition,
due to lateral inhibition in dendritic networks, might be the responsible
agent in the transformations.

Evidence is therefore at hand to indicate that the input to the ear and
skin becomes transformed into neural patterns that can be described by sets
of convolutional integrals of the type that Gabor (1969) has suggested as
stages in achieving a fully developed Fourier holographic process.

The manner in which such a stepwise process occurs is best worked out
for the visual system. Recordings from units in the optic nerve (Rodieck,
1965) demonstrated that the moving retina decomposes the image produced by
the lens of the eye into a "Mexican hat" organization which can be described
as convolving retinal organization with sensory input. A second step in the
process occurs at the lateral geniculate nucleus where each geniculate cell
acts as a peephole "viewing" a part of the retinal mosaic. This is because
each geniculate cell has converging upon it some 10,000 optic nerve fibres
originating in the ganglion cells of the retina. The receptive field of the
geniculate neuron is composed of a center surrounded by concentric rings of
receptivity, each consecutive ring of sharply diminishing intensity and of
a sign opposite to that of its neighbors (Hammond, 1972).

At the cortex the transformation into the Fourier domain becomes complete.
Beginning with the work of Campbell and Robson (1968), Pollen, Lee and Taylor
(1971), Maffei and Fiorentini (1973), and Glezer, Ivanoff and Tserhback
(1973), investigators using gratings as stimuli (e.g. Schiller, Finlay &
Volman, 1976; DeValis, Albrecht & Thorall, 1978; Movshon, Thompson &
Tollhurst, 1978; Pribram, Lassonde & Ptito, 1981) have repeatedly confirmed
that the cells in visual cortex are selectively tuned to a limited band width
of spatial frequency of approximately an octave (1/2 to 1-1/2 octaves).
Ordinarily the term frequency implies a temporal dimension, but the spatial
frequency (or wave number) of a grating reflects the width and spacings of
the bars making up the grating. When such widths and spacing are narrow the
spatial frequency is high; when widths and spacing are broad the spatial
frequency is low[*].

---

[*] The temporal dimension can be evoked by successively scanning across the
grating (as, for instance, by walking across the path of illumination of
a projection of a slide of such a grating). Conversion to the temporal
dimension is, however, not necessary. The grating is a filter whose
characteristics can be expressed either in the spatial or temporal
dimension, or both.

These findings do not, however, mean that the visual system performs
a global Fourier transform on the input to the retine (see also Julesz and
Caelli, 1979). The spread function, as such transformations are called, does
not encompass the entire retina: rather it is limited to the receptive field
of a retinal ganglion cell. Similarly at the cortex encoding is restricted
to the receptive field of the cortical neuron.

This patchy organization of the Fourier domain (Robson, 1975) does not
impair its functional characteristics. The technique of patching or stripping
together Fourier transformed images has been utilized in radioastronomy by
Bracewell (1965) to cover expanses which cannot be viewed with any single
telescopic exposure. The technique has been further developed by Ross (see
Leith, 1976) to produce a hologram by which three dimensional moving images
are constructed when the inverse transform is effected. Movement is produced
when spatially adjacent Fourier encoded strips, which capture slightly
different images are scanned (temporally) as, for instance, when frames of
a motion picture are used as the image base for the Fourier transformation.

The Place of the Fourier Transform
in Modelling the Cortical Microstructure:

The hybrid nature of cortical organization serves as a warning that any
simply conceived "global-Fourier-transform-of input-into-cortical-organization"
is untenable. Furthermore, the multiple selectivities of cortical cells in
the visual (Spinelli, Pribram & Bridgeman, 1970; Spinelli, Starr & Barrett,
1968; Morell, 1972) auditory (e.g. Evans, 1974) and somatosensorymotor (e.g.
Bach-y-Rita, 1972) projection areas clearly indicate that such cells serve
as nodes in neural networks in which the Fourier transform is only one, albeit
an important, process. E. Roy John speaks of "hyperneurons" constituted of the
distributed system of graded potentials he records from the brains of problem-
solving animals, while Edelman (1974) has proposed a degenerative group model,
also based on an essentially random connectivity.

Thus, several attempts have been made to characterize mathematically
such cortical networks in terms of their essential properties. Modifications
of the Fourier model have been proposed. For instance, Longuet-Higgins (see
Willshaw, Bunewman & Longuet-Higgins, 1969) derived an associative-net model
from a Fourier transform base and Leon Cooper (1973) has developed this model
into a self-organizing distributed net whose mathematical description contains
as a special case the Fourier transform hologram. Barlow (1981; Sakitt &

Barlow, 1982) and Marcelja (1980; Kulikowski, Marcelja & Bishop, 1982) have presented evidence which makes them invoke the Gabor function in which the spatial interrelations among cortical neurons serve, via lateral inhibition, to constrain the frequency domain by placing Gaussian envelopes upon the spatial frequency responses inherent within each receptive field. This model and those of Julesz (1971), Uttal (1978), Borsellino & Poggio (1973), Poggio & Torre (1981), and, in my laboratory, Sutter (1976) relate the Fourier and other continuous function domains to the statistical. Thus, for instance, Uttal emphasizes spatial autocorrelation functions while Poggio and Sutter rely on Wiener polynomial expansions. In addition, Poggio treats the dendritic potential microstructure in terms of the Volterra solution of wave guide equations. His carefully worked out proposal includes a stage of Fourier analysis and another in which the Laplace transform occurs. Marr, Poggio and Whitman Richards (Marr, 1976a, b; Marr & Poggio, 1977; Richards, 1977; Richards & Polit, 1974) have developed a model based on repetitive convolving of Laplacians with a Gaussian distribution in terms of a zero crossing theorem. Cortical organizations have also been described in terms of Lie groups by Hoffman (1970), vector matrices by Stuart, Takahashi and Umezawa (1978), and tensor matrices by Finkelstein (1976). These modifications have attained sufficient richness and precision to allow comparisons the descriptions of processing in distributed systems in cerebellum and cerebrum. Pellionisz and Llinas (1978) have elegantly reviewed the evidence which indicates that cerebellar cortical processing operates as a distributed tensor matrix system. Further, they have invoked Taylor expansions to describe the convergence of Purkinje cell operations onto the dentate nucleus. Cerebellar cortical computations are time limited because of the 50 msec inhibitory sweep generated by the basket cells which wipes out prior computations thus leaving the cortex available for another round - much as in a computational buffer. Taylor expansions are ideal descriptors of such processes. By contrast, the basal ganglia-cortical interaction is constituted of a cyclic resonant loop (Purpura, 1976; Denny-Brown, 1976) in which oscillations, limit cycles and Fourier operators, are more likely to describe functional relationships.

On looking over these various proposals one finds one overriding issue which needs further inquiry: To what extent can brain systems be treated with linear (and reversible) equations and to what extent must nonlinearities be introduced to explain the available data? Good evidence is at hand that at least some properties of the primary sensory systems (as discussed above) are within broad limits essentially linear in their overall operations. The

research conducted in my laboratory and reported here addresses this issue
within the context of Fourier theory with respect to the primary motor
systems (see also Granit, 1970).

Encoding in the Motor Systems:

The direction of this inquiry was derived directly from the experiments
performed by Bernstein (1967). Bernstein clad people in black leotards with
white spots over their joints, had them perform relatively complex repetitive
acts such as running over rough terrain, hammering nails, writing, etc., and
took cinematographs of their behavior. The cinematographic record showed
continuous fluctuating lines - the representations of the white spots indicating
the varying locations of the joints. Fourier analysis made it possible to
predict the location of any next point on the line from the fluctuations of
location of previous points on that line.

To understand, at the physiological level, how Bernstein accomplished
this computation, we need to examine in some detail the functions of various
levels of the motor system. Essentially, muscle contraction can be analyzed
into two different modes: an isotonic mode in which tone, i.e. tension does
not change but the motor unit shortens; and an isometric mode during which
no change occurs in motor unit length while tone increases. Muscle spindles
sense changes in length; Golgi tendon receptors are sensitive to changes in
muscle tension.

There is evidence that to some extent length and tension are controlled
by separate neural systems. Changes in length, as measured by the velocity
of change in position, is dramatically influenced by cooling the dentate
nucleus of the cerebellum (Brooks, Horvath, Atkin, Kozlovskaya & Uno, 1969;
Kozlovskaya, Uno, Atkin & Brooks, 1970). Also experiments by Rushworth (as
reported by Stark, 1968) have shown that when spindles are blocked by
procaine, "the so-called cerebellar syndrome of hypotonia, asthenia, ataxia,
overshooting, rebound, dysmetria, and postural drift" was produced.

As would be expected on the basis of the cerebellar input to the cerebral
cortex, responses of some of the cells in the monkey motor cortex - which
receive the output from the dentate nucleus via the thalamus - have been shown
to correlate with the speed of motion of a tracking task (Humphrey, Schmidt
& Thompson, 1970). However, recordings made from other cells in the sensorimotor cortex, especially those which give rise to the pyramidal tract do not
show any such relationship to velocity of movement (Evarts, 1966).

The question arises as to which motor structures are involved in
controlling muscle tension and changes in muscle tension. Clinical and
experimental evidence suggests that the basal ganglia are especially involved
in regulating postural bias (Kornhuber, 1971, 1974) and the tonic changes in
bias due to slow muscle contractions called ramp functions (DeLong, 1971,
1972, 1974). Such biases maintain the normal relatively tremorless steady
state of muscle tension. When the functions of basal ganglia cells are
disturbed by disease, tremors at rest and other steady-state changes such as
cogwheel rigidity result.

There is a convergence of cerebellar and basal ganglia functions onto
the neurons in the motor cortex from which the pyramidal tract originates.
Evarts (1966, 1967, 1968, 1969) has studied the functions of these neurons in
great detail. In his experiments the monkey grasped a rod which could be moved
in a 30° arc. To obtain a reward the monkey had to complete the movement through
that arc and return by a flexion and extension of the wrist and forearm within
a limited time. Electromyograms, displacement of the rod and the muscle tension
caused by resistance to the load were measured. The pyramidal electrical
activity produced by this manipulation did not reflect the displacement nor
the velocity of the rod, but rather directly reflected the magnitude of the
load. When additional loads were imposed the responses of the pyramidal neurons
increased proportionately. Most of the cells responsed irrespective of the
direction of movement; however, most cells were more responsive to flexion
than to extension (though some showed the opposite responsivity) irrespective
of load. The results also showed that load per se was not the only or even the
main critical variable represented by the response of the pyramidal neurons.
The typical response was an increase in firing at the onset of a loaded motion
or when a load was <u>changed</u>. After a short interval the firing pattern always
resumes a steady state, which varies in proportion to the weight of the load.

A Vector Space: Force as Defined by Load

The interpretation of these results has been that the pyramidal neurons
encode "force". Force is ordinarily defined to vary as a function of the
acceleration of a mass. Thus, in physiology, force has been conceived as the
product or resultant of the organism's metric motor activity: "Force can be
looked upon as the body's basic output quantity: velocity is thus the single
integral of this and displacement the double integral" (Bates, 1947). But if
one takes displacement as basic to a measure of acceleration (a spatial

derivative), Evarts' (1966, 1967, 1968, 1969) failure to obtain responses to
displacement argues against the interpretation that force is being represented.
Rather as Evarts and Houk (1967, 1981) have pointed out muscle tension, not
change in length, must be thought of as the generator of force. In such a
view muscle tension is conceived as the equivalent of mass. Hoffer (1982)
has suggested that changes in tension are represented as a function of their
mechanical impedance which reflects their elasticity and viscosity. Just as
it is not mass but the accelleration of mass which defines force, it is not
tension per se but changes in tension measured as its derivative and even
its second derivative - acceleration in changes of muscle tension - which
produce the best correlation with the responses of pyramidal neurons. Thus,
differentiation of muscle tension, i.e. changes in tension with respect to
time, become the corrollary of "force".

More operationally, force is represented in terms of load and changes
in load. Load adjusting mechanisms are well known in the sensory domain -
e.g. in vision the mechanism of retinal adaptation (see Dowling, 1967) and
in audition the mechanism mediated by the olivocochlear system (see Dewson,
1968). In the motor mechanism that function has been ascribed, as we shall
see below, to the gamma system of muscle spindle control (Matthews, 1964).

Changes in load are reflected either as changes in tension (force) or
in the length of motor-units or both. One way to determine whether these load
changes will result in a compensatory change in the innervation of motor-
units is to look at the ratio of change in muscle force to muscle length[*],
which has been labelled stiffness (e.g. Houk, 1981). A change in this ratio,
dependent as it is on the elasticity and viscosity of the muscle, therefore
defines the fluency of control. We will make this clear through the following
derivations.

The direction and magnitude of compensatory changes in motor-unit
innervation will be determined by the balance between changes in muscle length,
registered by muscle spindle afferents and changes in muscle force, registered
by tendon organ afferents. Summarized in the following equation this means:

---

[*] Relationship between muscle and motor-unit: The basic unit of activation
is the motor-unit, being one alpha or gamma motoneuron with its connecting
muscle fibrers. Muscle spindles and Golgi tendon organs register changes
in length and tension (or force) of individual motor-units. However, force-
length relationships are recorded from whole muscles. These gross recordings
should be thought of as representing the integrals of force and of length
provided by some group of individual motoneurons.

$$\Delta e = g_s \Delta x - g_t \Delta f \tag{1}$$

where Δe represents the compensatory change in motor-unit innervation, the parameters g_s and g_t the gains or sensitivities of respectively muscle spindle and Golgi tendon organ receptors, while x and f stand for muscle length and muscle force.

Consider next the ideal case in which there would be no need for a compensatory change in motor-unit innervation, i.e. $\Delta e - 0$, solving for Δf gives:

$$\Delta f_i = (g_s/g_t) \cdot \Delta x \tag{2}$$

in which the subscript i indicates this is an ideal change in muscle force, not resulting in a compensatory change in motor-unit innervation. Usually changes in muscle force are not ideal and made up of mechanically and neurally mediated components:

$$\Delta f_i = K \Delta x + A \Delta e \tag{3}$$

where K represents the mechanical stiffness of a muscle, or the slope of the force-length relationship is muscles and A is an activation factor converting a compensatory change in motor-unit innervation into a neurally mediated component of force change.

Again, assuming there is no need for a compensatory change in motor-unit innervation, i.e. $\Delta e = 0$, substitution in equation (3) yields:

$$\Delta f_m = K \Delta x \tag{4}$$

where the subscript m indicates the purely mechanical nature of his response. Looking back upon equations (1) to (4), we see that the postulated $\Delta e = 0$ will occur only if the change in mechanical force Δf_m equals the ideal force-change Δf_i. Comparison of equations (2) and (4) indicates that this condition is met, if:

$$K = g_s/g_t \tag{5}$$

Next assuming $\Delta e = 0$ for equation (1) we find:

$$g_s/g_l = \Delta f/\Delta x \tag{6}$$

When there is no need for a compensatory change in motor-unit innervation, the mechanical muscle stiffness K equals the ratio of change in muscle force to muscle length which in turn equals the ratio of receptor properties g_s/g_t.

This means that fluency as determined by ongoing innervation of motor-units, leading to a change in stiffness, is determined by the ratio of change of the sensitivities of muscle spindles to Golgi tendon organs.

The equality between the ratio of change of muscle force to muscle length and the ratio of receptor properties g_s/g_t is especially important when one considers how the central nervous system encodes placement or displacement of limbs. When the central nervous system encodes either of these it will want to do so without the need for any change in motor-unit innervation compensatory to the encoded placement or displacement. This can be accomplished fluently by encoding the changes in stiffness, i.e. changes in the ratio of change of muscle force to muscle length $\Delta f/\Delta x$, since this ratio is equal to g_s/g_t the ratio of the sensitivities of muscle spindles to Golgi tendon organs. We will call either of these ratios the reference ratio. The evidence is that the CNS encodes reference ratios in the following manner.

At the spinal cord, the activity recorded from e.g. alpha motorneurons is cyclic and can be thought of as constituting a central pattern generator (Grillner, 1975; 1981). These oscillatory rhythmic activities are brought under cortical control by way of pyramidal and extra pyramidal pathways to produce a motor-program (Schmidt, 1980). This motor-program operates in such a way, that to move a limb segment from one position to the next terminal position it encodes just the terminal position as the equilibrium point between tensions of agonist and antagonist muscle groups (Asatryan & Feldman, 1965; Bizzi et al., 1976, 1978, 1979; Schmidt & McGown, 1980). When more than one limb segment is involved the motor-program must also encode the timing or phase-relationships among different limb segments or different limbs in order to specify new equilibrium points for each joint (Schmidt, 1980).

Each equilibrium point is determined by the intersections of force-length relationships between agonist and antagonist muscle groups (see e.g. Schmidt, 1980, Fig. 1 & 2). It is, therefore, easy to infer that these equilibrium points actually are equal to the mechanical stiffness K of the muscle groups and are, by means of equations (5) and (6), equal to the reference ratio g_s/g_t and $\Delta f/\Delta x$. However, the organism does not encode a reference ratio once and stop, but continuously encodes new reference ratios. Fluency is thus a measure of the alteration of a current reference ratio g_s/g_t to a new reference ratio g_s/g_t.

In the reference ratio, the g_t, which is the sensitivity of the Golgi tendon organs, is fixed and very high (see e.g. Houk et al., 1967; Jami et al., 1976; Stuart et al., 1972). By contrast the sensitivity of the muscle spindles g_s is variable. Dynamic gamma or fusimotor-axons greatly sensitize the primary endings of the muscle spindle to dynamic stimuli, while the static fusimotor-axons greatly sensitize both primary and secondary endings to static stimuli (Matthews, 1981). It is thus by means of gamma motoneuron innervation, changing the sensitivity of muscle spindles, that new reference ratios are reached.

As already noted, motor-programs are generated when the cyclical activities of the spinal central pattern generators are brought under cortical control. This implies a higher order encoding of the g_s/g_t or $\Delta f/\Delta x$ ratio. Therefore change in muscle tension, which is the corollary of Δf, the change in force, would be expected to provide the best correlation with pyramidal neuron responses. Changes in muscle length Δx as well as changes in g_s the sensitivity of muscle spindles, would then be expected to operate within the fixed value of g_t and influenced soley by the descending pathways projecting onto the gamma motor-neurons.

Conceived in this fashion, the failure to find cortical units responsive to spatial position, in Evarts' (1966, 1967, 1968, 1969) experiments reflects a bias to viewing the motor-cortex in terms of a representation of changes in muscle length rather than in terms of a vector-space constituted of reference ratios which are primarily determined by changes in muscle tension. This vector space of reference ratios reflects, as we have seen, the sensitivities of muscle spindles operating within the matrix of sensitivities of Golgi tendon organs.

To relate the ideal muscle stiffness ratios g_s/g_t to Bernstein's Fourier analysis of joint motion, we observe that for a body in simple harmonic motion (motion under the influence of an elastic restoring force in absence of friction), the restoring force is a function of displacement according to Hooke's law: $F = -kx$, where x is the displacement from the equilibrium position and k is the stiffness, a constant dependent on the elastic properties of the material. From Newton's second law, we have for a body of mass m

$$F = -k\,x = m\,d^2\,x/dt^2,$$

a differential equation for the displacement, x, whose solution is the elementary harmonic

$$x(t) = x(o)\,\exp\left[i\,(k/m)^{1/2}t\right],$$

where x(o) is the initial placement; x(t) is the displacement after time t, and exp denotes the exponential function whose real coordinate is the cosine and the imaginary coordinate is the sine of the product of angular frequency

(k/m) times time. Thus by adjusting the stiffness setting $k = g_s/g_t$, the
motor system controls the frequency of joint motion to an equilibrium point
dependent on the external load m.

There is further evidence that resection of the motor cortex impairs
the sensitivity to changes in load which define the fluency of behavioral
acts, the consequences of movements, rather than movements per se (Pribram,
Kruger, Robinson & Berman, 1956). The results of these experiments showed that
in addition to encoding the anatomical spatial arrangement of muscles (e.g.
Chang, Ruch & Ward, 1947; Woolsey, 1952) and the physiological patterns of
movements (Phillips, 1966) the motor systems must also encode the topological
arrangement of the space in which actions, the consequences of movements,
take shape (Pribram, 1971). In short, the motor cortex is truly a sensory
cortex for action in that it receives multimodal input (e.g. Malis, Pribram
& Kruger, 1953; Albe-Fessard & Liebeskind, 1966; Welt, Aschoff, Kameda &
Brooks, 1967) via the dorsal thalamus which is a sensory way station. Thus
it is feasible for this part of the motor mechanism to furnish the vector
space coordinates (an "image") for an action to be achieved.

The current study was undertaken to furnish more direct evidence that
the cells of the motor cortex encode such coordinates defined by the
consequences of muscular contractions and to provide a plausible mechanism
as to how this is achieved. The relationship between an image and a motor
program is detailed in Plans and the Structure of Behavior (1960).
Essentially, the motor program is an operation which effects congruance
between input and image.

As detailed above, there is thus the possibility that the motor cortex
shares this ability to Fourier-analyze and predict locations of joints with
respect to some externally constrained vector space - i.e., a task - as in
Bernstein's experiment. Within such a vector space, fluency in control over
a rhythmic central pattern generator by a motor program which must simultaneously,
compute several equilibrium points related to one another by phase differences,
is readily accomplished in the frequency domain. By contrast, such computations
would be extremely tedious if not entirely impossible if ordinary Newtonian
mechanical dimensions such as changes in length per se were encoded.

Thus, in a series of experiments we explored the possibility that the
response characteristics of cells in the motor systems of the brain (such as
the basal ganglia) might reflect changes in muscle activity in Fourier or
related frequency terms. Further, the question was posed as to whether the
cells of the cortex are so tuned as to provide a representation of the

equilibrium points which specify the matrix of locations within which action takes place.

METHODS

Surgical Procedure

Six cats weighing from 3 to 5 kilograms were used. Each animal was anesthetized initially with an intramuscular injection of equal parts of Ketamin and Rompun (20 mg/kg) and placed in a stereotaxic frame. During the operation, anesthesia was maintained using Fluothane. A midline incision was made and the skin and temporal muscle reflected laterally to expose the dorsal surface of the skull. Two openings of 10 mm in diameter were trephined with stereotaxic coordinates so that an electrode passing through the center of one opening vertically would intersect the desired section. The coordinates for caudate nucleus were A15, L5, and H4-8; and for sensorimotor cortex were A27, L5, and H10-12. The approximate coordinates for the center of the opening over the caudate nucleus were A15, L5, and over the sensorimotor cortex were A27, L5. A block with two nuts was fixed to the skull on the midline and posterior to both openings. This was used to restrain the head during recording. The dura was left intact and a stainless steel chamber was held vertically over each opening and secured with a dental acrylic cement. Non-penetrating holes were made on the surface of the skull, and on half a dozen of these holes small screws were installed to made the bond between the cement and skull stronger. Prior to the application of cement the surface of the skull was cleaned thoroughly with dental cavity primer. The skin was closed with surgical clips anterior and posterior to the chambers-block-acrylic assembly. The chambers were filled with Elastomer. After the operation 300,000 units of antibiotic (Bicillin) was administered intramuscularly.

Animal Restraint and Recording Apparatus

The animal was placed on a half section of a 7" diameter PVC tube with openings for legs and padded with foam for one hour every day until he became familiar with the environment. After one week of posoperative recovery the animal was lightly Ketaminized (15 mg/kg) and placed on the restraint device with his head fixed to the stereotaxic device via two bolts to the block with

two nuts on it. During the length of the recording the animal was kept lightly
Ketaminized by intramuscular injections when it seemed necessary (see Figure
1).

Fig. 1. Schematic diagram of restraining device for the cat while
        recording.

Epoxylite coated tungsten electrodes made by Fredrick Haer & Co. were
used. They were 7.5 cm long and the diameter of tungsten was 0.010". The
diameter of exposed tip was 15μ, the length of exposed tip was 50μ and tested
impedance was 12± 2Mμ. The Elastomer was removed from the chambers and one
electrode was lowered vertically until its tip touched the dura. Then the
chamber was filled with Bacto-Agar solution. After this solution settled the
electrode was pushed through the dura using hydraulic drive (Trent H. Wells,
Jr. Mechanical Developments Co.) until the tip of the electrode reached the
desired area.

Movement Apparatus

Movements were generated by a DC motor. The shaft of the motor was
coupled to a 360° continuous potentiometer. The other side shaft of the
potentiometer was coupled to a mechanical sine wave generator which decomposed

a rotary movement to its vertical and horizontal components. Thus a constant speed rotary movement would be decomposed into a vertical and a horizontal sinusoidal movement. The frequency of movement was changed by changing the DC voltage applied to the motor. A load cell (Interface model 50-B) was connected between the moving section of the vertical element and the paw holder to measure the tension/load on the paw holder.

Data Collection

The extracellular activity was picked up by the microelectrode. It was amplified by a very low noise, very low bias current and high impedance preamplifier with a gain of 1000. The output of this preamplifier was then amplified (gain between 1 and 10), high passed filtered (f_o = 300Hz) and passed through a window discriminator which gave a pulse of fixed duration (1 msec) whenever the input exceeded a certain voltage.

The experiment started with a control period (C) when there was no movement. Following this control period there was a movement period where the right front paw was moved passively up and down sinusoidally. This was followed by another control period and the sequence repeated so that immediately before and after each movement period there were control periods. Each movement period was distinguished from the others by the DC voltage applied to the motor during that period. The voltages were 10, 15, 20, 25, 30, 35, 40, 45 and 50 volts corresponding to 0.27, 0.49, 0.71, 0.93, 1.11, 1.33, 1.48, 1.60 and 1.74 Hz. The sequence of these voltages was sometimes randomized to see if any significant change would occur. The control and movement periods were equal to 25.6 seconds, which we call a frame. Analog data (the outputs of the potentiometer and the load cell) were sampled at a 40 Hz sampling rate. Thus there were 1024 points per analog data channel per frame. The digital data (the output of the window discriminator) indicating neuron activity was recorded by counting the number of pulses between sampling instances (25 msec) using the interrupt system of the AR-11 system on the PDP-11/34A computer. Before starting to record from one cell, enough care was used to ensure that the cell would remain normally active during the whole recording period, and moreover, would have a reasonably high signal-to-noise ratio. The level of window discriminator was set according to the cell "height" for each individual cell and was untouched during the recording period for that cell. If during the recording period the cell became abnormal, the program was aborted and a new cell was "fished".

Anatomical Verification of Electrode Placements

When good recordings could no longer be obtained, the cats were given
an overdose of barbituate intraperitoneally and perfused intracardially with
normal saline solution followed by 10% formalin containing potassium
ferrocyanide. The brains were blocked in the stereotaxic plane, removed from
the skull and placed in formalin. Later they were removed to 20% alcohol.
Frozen section were cur at 50μ saving every fourth section. These were mounted
and stained with thionine.

All subcortical electrode tracts were found to traverse the head of the
caudate nucleus. Two of the cortical placements were found to be post-cruciate;
all others were pre-cruciate. The post-cruciate placements accounted for 9
recordings of narrowly tuned cells while the pre-cruciate placements accounted
for 26.

RESULTS AND DISCUSSION

Frequency:

Three hundred and six cells from six cats were recorded and analyzed.
Of these 144 cells were recorded from caudate nucleus and the remaining 162
from sensorimotor cortex. As can be seen in Figure 2, a sizeable number of
cells in both caudate nucleus and sensorimotor cortex are selectively
responsive to only a limited range of the frequencies with which the forelimb
is moved. The response can be either in the form of increasing or decreasing
the average spontaneous spike activity when a movement with a certain
frequency occurs. Thirty-three out of 144 cells (approximately 23%) in the
caudate nucleus and 35 out of 162 cells (approximately 22%) in the sensorimotor cortex were narrowly tuned to a specific band. Narrowly tuned is
defined to be cell whose maximum or minimum activity at a certain frequency
is at least 25% higher (lower) than the average baseline activity which
remains relatively steady over the entire range of frequencies. Further,
narrowly tuned cells are defined as responding only with a band width limited
to less than 1/2 octave.

In examining the movement frequency tuning curves of cells, we find a
wide range of maxima (minima). This range in tuning would be necessary if
one were to build a system of band pass movement frequency filters which

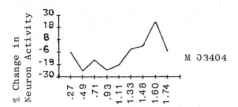

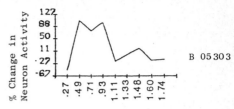

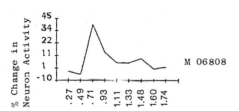

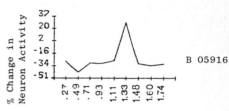

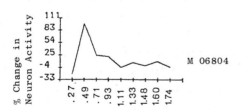

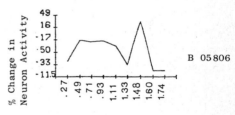

Fig. 2. Frequency tuning curves for narrowly tuned cells. The frequency
of the mechanical sine wave generated by the motor is represented
on the x axis; the % change in response over baseline is
represented on the y axis. The six letter/digit alphanumeric
code at the righthand side of the tuning curve gives the
following information.

$$M \quad 1 \quad 6 \quad 2 \quad 1 \quad 2$$

Recording site: Cat nr.   Cell number for this site
B: Basal Ganglia
M: Sensorimotor Cortex

covered the whole range of frequencies. In support of such a filter model
is the finding that all the remaining cells were not selective to a single
frequency band, but rather showed maxima (minima) within several frequency
bands.

Of 35 narrowly tuned cells in the sensorimotor cortex, 18 (11%) of the
total of 162 cells, showed inhibitory responses to their tuned frequencies,
that is, they acted like a notch filter (Figure 3). Most of these (16) and
those which showed biphasic responses were obtained from placements which
were shown post-mortem to be located in the post-cruciate gyrus. Only eight
out of 44 or 5.5% of the total of 144 cells in the caudate nucleus showed
similar behavior.

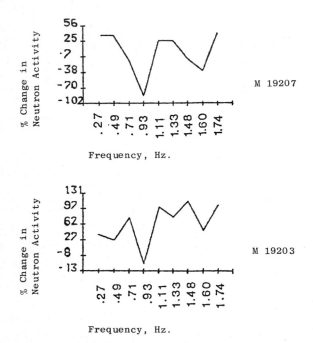

Fig. 3. Frequency tuning curves for narrowly tuned "notch filter"
        type cells.

The primary thrust of the experiment thus proved fruitful. There can
be no question that some cells in the caudate nucleus and some cells in the
sensorimotor cortex of the cat responded selectively to only a limited range

of movement frequencies. The number of such cells compares favorably with the number of cells in the visual system which are classified as having simple or complex properties (Hubel & Wiesel, 1959; Spinelli, Pribram & Bridgeman, 1970), properties which have been shown to be related to the spatial frequency of visual patterns (Schiller, Finlay & Volman, 1976; DeValois, Albrecht & Thorall, 1978; Pribram, Lassonde & Ptito, 1981). In the visual cortex approximately 10-12% of cells are frequency specific, tuned to a range of 1/2 to 1-1/2 octaves; in the sensorimotor cortex approximately 20-22% of cells are tuned to a 1/2 octave band width of the frequency with which a forearm moves.

Although it is clear that some cells in the motor system "resonate" to movements at certain frequencies, the results presented so far do not indicate 1) whether these resonances are spurious in the sense that other variables conjoin to produce the effect, or 2) whether these resonances reflect the encoding of frequency per se as would be demanded by the model of a set of band pass filters for movement which was suggested above. In order to initiate the search for variables other than frequency to which these cells might be responsive three likely candidates were chosen: velocity, tension and position. The results of observations on these variables follow.

Velocity and Tension:

In order to test whether the frequency tuned cells were responsive to other variables, the neuronal activity of narrowly tuned cells was plotted against position in the cycle of movement, velocity of movement within cycles of various frequencies and the tension at different frequencies. As can be seen in Figure 4, the minimal increase in activity when velocity or tension are plotted is spread over all frequencies and fairly broadly within each frequency (especially at the higher frequencies). Since velocity and tension vary as a function of frequency, the nonspecificity of even this minimal increase in activity indicates that the cells were not responding to these variables. To make this clear, picture the velocity of movement when the frequency of the cycle is low: velocity is also low, the forelimb moves slowly. Now we increase the frequency of the movement cycle: velocity is now high, the muscles of the forelimb are contracting and lengthening rapidly. If velocity (or acceleration) were being encoded by these cells this would be reflected in a region of selective increase in their activity which would be localized within each frequency and the location of the increased activity would move in a systematic fashion across the various cycle frequencies. This

a)

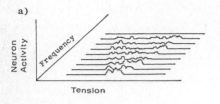

Tension

b)

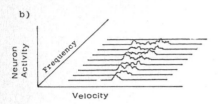

Velocity

c)
c)

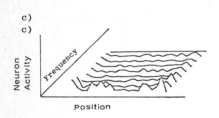

Position

d)

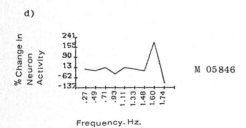

M 05846

a)

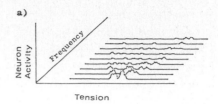

Tension

b)

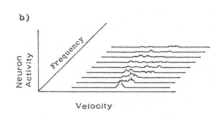

Velocity

c)
c)

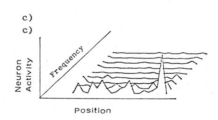

Position

d)

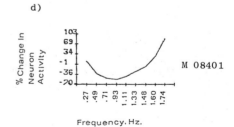

M 08401

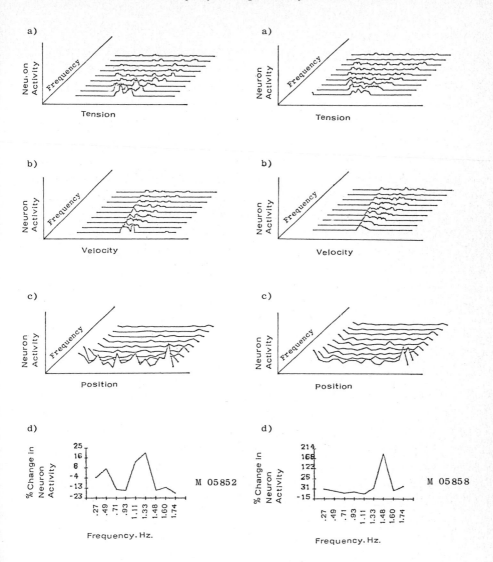

Fig. 4. Characteristics of some narrowly tuned cells:

    a. Neuron activity versus tension (measured by the load cell) for each frequency.
    b. Neuron activity versus velocity for each frequency.
    c. Neuron activity versus position for each frequency.
    d. Tuning curves for narrowly tuned cells.

behavior was not observed.

The same argument applies to tension. Response to tension and change
in tension should be reflected in a localized increase in cell activity
which systematically moves across the various cycle frequencies. This
phenomenon was not detected. These frequency selective cells are insensitive
to velocity and tension passively imposed on the muscles of the forelimb.
This result appears to differ from results obtained by others (Brooks,
Horvath, Atkin & Kozlovskaya, 1969; Evarts, 1968) who have found velocity
and tension sensitive cells in the motor system. However, in their experiments
active rather than passive movement was involved. Furthermore, in the current
experiments no search was made for cells that selectively encode velocity
or tension, although the non-narrowly tuned cells of the current sample were
subjected to the same procedure and no velocity or tension specificity was
found. The purpose of this part of the experiment was thus accomplished: it
has been established that the frequency selectivity which was observed for
this population of cells is not an artifact of their selective sensitivity
to velocity and/or tension.

Position in the Movement Cycle:

By contrast, as can be seen in Figure 4, narrowly tuned cells in the
sensorimotor cortex show sensitivity to the position of the forelimb in the
movement cycle. This sensitivity occurs almost always at the ends of the
cycle of movement where the maximum phase shift is taking place. But it must
be emphasized that these cells are not sensitive to phase shift (or change
in direction) per se since the increase in the cell's activity does not occur
at all cycle frequencies. Rather, these cortical cells encode phase shift,
i.e. position in the cycle, for a particular frequency band. This supports
the hypothesis that these cells are indeed encoding frequency per se since
at the encoded frequency phase shift is also responded to.

The encoding of phase shift was found to be a property primarily of
cortical cells. Only one cell of the total population of those recorded in
the caudate nucleus was found to encode position in the cycle and that cell
was not maximally responsive to the ends of the cycle where the maximum phase
shift occurs. Once again, this result is reminiscent of results in the visual
system where cortical cells but not those below cortex show a selectivity to
the orientation in space of a pattern. The results of the current experiments
can be similarly expressed: below cortex the cells encode the frequency of

movement regardless of phase; at the cortex, shift in phase - i.e. in the orientation of the movement at a certain frequency - is an additional consideration.

CONCLUSION

These experiments were undertaken to find out whether some cells in the motor system behave in a manner similar to some cells in the auditory system and in the visual system. Recall that in the introduction evidence was reviewed which suggested that a frequency analytic approach to sensory function in the nervous system has proved rewarding. Furthermore, evidence was reviewed that a similar frequency analytic approach to the motor behavior in the intact organism had been equally effective. It therefore seemed reasonable to apply this approach to an analysis of the motor systems of the brain. Thus the question was directly posed as to whether there are cells in the motor system which respond selectively within a range of frequencies of a cyclic up-down passive movement of a forelimb. The results of the experiment showed that a 20% portion of a total of 306 cells sampled are tuned (i.e. increase or decrease their activity at least 25% over baseline spontaneous activity) to a narrow (1/2 octave) band of the range of cycle frequencies.

Tuning could be due to a spurious convergence of factors relating to the basic properties of muscle as discussed in the introduction: metric displacement and tonicity or stiffness. An examination was therefore undertaken of variables related to these basic properties, variables such as velocity, change in velocity (acceleration), as well as tension, and change in tension. These factors in isolation were found not to account for the frequency selective effects. This does not mean that other cells in the motor system are not selectively sensitive to velocity and changes in tension. But is does mean that the frequency selectivity of the cells described is dependent on some higher order computation of the metric and tonic resultants imposed on the foreleg musculature by the external load.

The other variable investigated was position in the cycle of movement. Position is encoded by cortical cells (but not by caudate nucleus cells), but only at the site of phase shift and only for a particular frequency. This result supports the hypothesis that the cortical cells are in fact frequency selective in that any sensitivity to phase shift presupposes an encoding of phase and therefore of frequency. Furthermore, the fact that the cortical cells

respond to position suggests that they are directly involved in the computation
of the vector space coordinates within which actions are achieved.

There is thus no question that an approach to analysis of the functions
of the motor system in frequency terms is useful not only in studying the
overall behavior of the organism as initiated by Bernstein but also in
studying the <u>neural</u> motor mechanism. That some such an approach is required is
amply documented in a review of the field, initiated by R.B. Stein in an
article entitled "What muscle variable(s) does the nervous system control
in limb movements?" which became available in the December issue (Vol. 5,
No. 4) of <u>The Behavioral and Brain Sciences</u> just as our chapter was being
sent to press. In the peer commentary the following statements appeared:

Discussing servo assistance in the regulation of muscle contraction
by way of their afferents, Granit (1982) points out that an "error has no
existence in midair" and that thus "an error detector can act sensibly only
if it is related to the purpose of the movement in which it operates. ...
Clearly the concept of error is tied to the concept of goal. More often than
not, the nervous structure incorporating the goal will be cortical".

Masao Ito (1982) takes this argument a step further: "...There is no
straightforward extrapolation from elementary reflexes to complex movements
such as postural adjustment, locomotion, skilled hand and finger movements,
or speech. An idea diametrically opposed to the Sherringtonian view may be
that the CNS is basically a multivariable control system handling a set of
parameters, and that only in an extreme condition, in which all parameters
but one are fixed, does it appear to have a reflex for that single parameter".
He adds that "Perhaps we have difficulty in understanding the mechanism of
motor control because we still know little about the structure of the CNS
as a multivariable control system, about how the operation of the system is
organized toward a certain superordinate goal above the level of the various
parameters, each of which may be related only partially to the goal".

Partridge (1982) discusses the requirements which such a superordinate
organization must meet: "Motor control, like operations of other mechanical
systems has been treated in terms of force, velocity, position, and
mechanical impedance. It is almost never described in other equally valid
coordinate systems from mechanics, those with dimensions such as momentum,
power, work, kinetic energy, potential energy, etc. (e.g. Brooks, 1981). In
favor of such an alternative coordinate systems is the constancy, over a
wide range of velocities, of the relationship between neural drive and power
output from muscle. Similarly, neural drive adjusts the ratio of energy

absorption with muscle stretch also independent of stretching velocity
(Partridge & Benton, 1981). Yet these alternative coordinate systems are
almost as limited for describing motor control as the elementary Newtonian
descriptions. Encouraging these forms is the unrecognized assumption that
evolution must have chosen to operate in one of the coordinate systems from
a mechanics text while ignoring the infinte variety of other equivalent
systems. Evidence from the study of receptor responses indicates that, at
least at the input level, mechanical information is carried in a non-Newtonian
frame of reference (Partridge, 1978)".

Partridge (1982) goes on to suggest that the only way that such a frame
of reference can be properly "described as a single variable using conventional
dimensions is by choosing for that variable the magnitude of a vector
represented nonlinearly within those dimensions". In those coordinates the
orientation of the vector depends more on load than on neural activity". Thus,
"The neural representation of the problem requires conversion into a neural
representation of the solution by a single set of transformation rules - a
difficult enough problem without the necessity of transforming the signals
into arbitrary intermediate coordinate systems".

Stark (1982) addresses the problem of what those transformation rules
might be. He points out, as does Stein in the target article, that servo
control theories as initially proposed by Merton and embellished by reference
to alpha-gamma coactivation, have their limitations. His experiments have
led him to embrace sampled-data control theory in which "the actuator
intermittently moves the plant in an open-loop mode, alternating with a
closed-loop mode of control". Ashby (1960) and Pribram (1971) have suggested
that open-loop, feedforward operations of this sort coordinate the operations
of several closed loop servos by virtue of the parallel processing configuration
of neural control. Such a configuration demands the establishment of optimization
criteria to operate its control-signal structure, just as the simpler servo
loops demand goals in order to determine what might constitute an error. Stark
notes that "Recent studies in robotics suggest that control of hand movement,
for example, is apparently much simpler in the three dimensional visual-motor
world than in the complex kinematic joint-angle, muscle-force, and muscle-length
world. This is particularly true because the multidimensional interactions
among changing interrelations with varying loads and the corresponding
calculations become overwhelming, even for a good sized computer".

Terzuolo and Soechting (1982) come to a similar conclusion in reviewing
their own work: "Perhaps if one were ...to concentrate on the rules which

govern the organization of different types of movements, the nature of the
control process would begin to unfold. Indeed, both the organization and
control of movement are aspects of the same problem, which can only be
addressed by examining the global properties of the system during tasks with
specific constraints and under physiological conditions".

What these global processes, these constraints which are best described
in terms of the visuomotor spatial world might be is the topic addressed by
Stelmach and Diggles (1982). These investigators point out that the most
convincing evidence for the shortcomings of attempting to understand the
motor control process by reductionist techniques which isolate motor units
or groups of units from each other, is the evidence provided by motor
equivalence. They note that, for example, "individuals retain the same unique
style of writing with a pen and paper or with chalk and board (Stelmach &
Diggles, 1982)". Transfer functions must describe progressive hierarchies
of control which become distributed among "collections of neurons that may
interact to achieve the desired goal". Stelmach and Diggles do not specify
what these transfer functions might be but suggest that "The mechanisms which
provide input to these distributed control systems are neural maps. They are
viewed as control surfaces from which the spatial-temporal patterns for
movement may be derived. Neural maps are used as control surfaces, with the
map providing information about the topographical relationship one item shares
with several others. Thus information from one item will provide relative
information about other items, suggesting a certain economy in storage and
a basis for cooperative computation. It is then plausible that a layered
motor controller exists in which position of input on the control surface,
determined by the 'center of gravity' of an array of activation points,
encodes the target to which musculature will be directed. In this manner each
activation point contributes to target determination, and responsibility for
the course of movement is distributed among these points".

Stelmach and Diggles' (1982) control surfaces, their neural maps, have
identical properties to the "Images of Achievement" which were suggested to
be constructed by the operations of the motor cortex by Pribram (1971).
Further, the proposal was made that such maps of Images with distributed
properties resulted from the operation of transfer functions which transformed
the Newtonian dimensions based in space/time coordinates into phase operations
in the frequency domain. Such transformations are known as spread functions
since they distribute information across a surface. The proposal was derived
from the work of Bernstein, much as reviewed in the introduction to this

chapter.

A similar approach is taken by Kelso and Saltzman (1982) who, though they make important additional points, fail to come to grips with the nature of the transfer functions by which any control system has to operate. Nonetheless, their contribution is an important one: they affirm the spontaneous oscillatory aspects of neuronal functioning which demand more than feedback regulation and homeostasis. Emphasizing the mass-spring model of muscle-joint operation with its controllable equilibrium length, they discuss the homeokinetic and equifinal properties of such systems. In such systems "control is dynamically effected by means of coupled ensembles of limit cycle oscillatory processes. Limit cycles represent the only temporal stability for non-conservative, non-linear systems... Limit cycles are manifestations of thermodynamic engines and quantize <u>action</u> (formally the product of energy and time; Iberall, 1978) at every level of the system".

Kelso and Saltzman (1982) indicate that "For spectrally distributed limit cycle regimes to be observed and for new spatiotemporal organizations to emerge, certain necessary conditions must exist. Among these are the presence of many interacting degrees of freedom, nonlinearities, a relatively constant source of potential energy, and the requirement that the energy be dissipated. Given such conditions, and subject to critical scaling values, constraints emerge that are capable of mashalling the free variables into coherent functions". Kelso and Saltzman propose that the problem of motor control "might be attacked more effectively by seeking out a single set of physical principles that can apply at all levels, rather than by positing different units at all levels".

We believe that the results of our experiment as reported in this chapter show that we met "the certain necessary conditions" for "spectrally distributed limit cycles to be observed". We also believe that it is the transfer functions which transform the variables operating in Newtonian mechanics into those operating in the frequency domain, which are the "single set of physical principles" which allow neural control systems to operate as they do. The fact that such transfer functions are spread functions, and that the overwhelming conclusion of the analyses reviewed in the article in <u>The Brain and Behavioral Sciences</u> is that control is a function of distributed variables in distributed systems, additionally supports this conclusion.

Nonetheless, the results regarding the motor systems of the brain presented here are but a beginning. The question remains as to whether the frequency transform shown to operate at the forebrain level is linear. In order to show that the Fourier or any other linear process is involved in motor behavior and the motor functions of the brain, the requirement of superposition must be met. Thus, the interactive effect of two cyclic sinusoidal frequencies of motion of the forelimb need to be tested.

Furthermore, all of the experiments run in this series used passive movement. Much movement is active and the question remains unanswered as to whether the frequency approach is directly relevant to active movement. The results of the current experiments do indicate, however, that the frequency approach can yield useful results in understanding the coordinate matrix which passive movements (and posture, temporary equilibrium positions of phase shift) provide to form the context within which active movements are undertaken.

ACKNOWLEDGEMENTS

We wish to thank Bruce Quinn for his excellent help in carrying out the experiments and Jeffrey Evans for astute commentary in developing the manuscript. The research was carried out with funds from the EST foundation. The senior author is supported by research career award nr. 4 K06 MH 15214-21.

REFERENCES

Albe-Fessard, D. & Liebeskind, J. Origins des Messages Somatosensitifs Activant les Cellules du Cortex Moteur Chez le Singe. Experimental Brain Research, 1966, 1, 127-146.

Ashby, W.R. Design for a Brain: The Origin of Adaptive Behavior. New York: John Wiley & Sons, Inc., 1960, 2nd. Edition.

Asratyan, D.G. & Feldman, A.G. Functional tuning of the nervous system with control of movement or maintenance of a steady posture. 1. Mechanographic analysis of the work of the joint on execution of a postural task. Biophysics, 1965, 10, 925-935.

Bach-y-Rita, P. Brain Mechanism in Sensory Substitution. New York: Academic Press, 1972.

Barlow, H.B. Critical Limiting Factors in the Design of the Eye and Visual Cortex.

Bates, J.A.V. Some Characteristics of Human Operator. In Proceedings at the Convention on Automatic Regulars and Servo-Mechanisms. Journal of Inst. of Elect. Engrs., 1947, 94, Part IIa, No. 2, 298-304.

Bekesy, G.V. Synchronism of Neural Discharges and Their Demultiplication in Pitch Perception on the Skin and in Hearing. Journal of Acoustical Society of America, 1959, 31, 338-349.

Bernstein, N. The Co-ordination and Regulation of Movements. New York: McGraw-Hill, 1965.

Bizzi, E., Dev, P., Morasso, P. & Polit, A. Effect of load disturbance during centrally initiated movements. Journal of Neurophysiology, 1978, 41, 542-556.

Bizzi, E., Polit, A. & Morasso, P. Mechanisms underlying achievement of final head position. Journal of Neurophysiology, 1976, 39, 435-444.

Borsellino, A. & Poggio, T. Convolution and Correlation Algebras. Kybernetik, 1973, 13, 113-122.

Brooks, V.B. (Ed.), Motor Control. The Nervous System. Vol. 2. In: Handbook of Physiology. Bethesda, MD: American Physiological Society, 1981.

Brooks, V.B., Horvath, F., Atkin, A., Kozlovskaya, I. & Uno, M. Reversible Changes in Voluntary Movement During Cooling of Sub-cerebellar Nucleus. Fed. Proc., 1969, 28, 396.

Campbell, F.W. & Robson, J.G. Application of Fourier Analysis to the Visibility of Gratings. Journal of Physiology, 1968, 197, 551-565.

Chang, H.T., Ruch, T.C. & Ward. Jr., A.A. Topographical Representation of
    Muscles in Motor Cortex of Monkeys. Journal of Neurophysiology, 1967,
    10, 39-56.

Cooper, L.N. A Possible Organization of Animal Memory and Learning. In,
    F. Lindquist and S. Lindquist (Eds.), Proceedings of the Nobel Symposium
    on Collective Properties of Physical System. New York: Academic Press,
    1973.

DeLong, M.R. Activity of Pallidal Neurons During Movement. Journal of
    Neurophysiology, 1971, 34, 3, 414-427.

DeLong, M.R. Activity of Basal Ganglia Neurons During Movement. Brain
    Research, 1972, 40, 127-135.

DeLong, M.R. Motor Functions of the Basal Ganglia Single Unit Activity
    During Movement. In, F.O. Schmitt and F.G. Worden (Eds.), The
    Neurosciences: Third Study Program. Cambridge, MA: The MIT Press, 1974.

Denny-Brown, D. & Yamagisawa, N. The Role of the Basal Ganglia in the
    Initiation of Movement. In, M.D. Yahr (Ed.), The Basal Ganglia.
    Research Publication of the Association for Research in Nervous and
    Mental Diseases, 1976, 55.

DeValois, R.L., Albrecht, D.G. & Thorall, L.G. Spatial Tuning of LGN
    and Cortical Cells in Monkey Visual System. In, H. Spekreijse and L.H.
    van der Tweel (Eds.), Spatial Contrast. Amsterdam: North-Holland, 1977.

DeValois, R.L., Albrecht, D.G. & Thorall, L.G. Cortical Cells: Bar and
    Edge Detectors, or Spatial Frequency Filters? In, S.J. Cool and E.L.
    Smith (Eds.), Frontiers of Visual Science. New York: Springer-Verlag,
    1978.

Dewson, J.H. III Cortical Responses to Patterns of Two-Point Cutaneous
    Stimulation. Journal of Comparative and Physiological Psychology, 1964,
    58, 387-389.

Dewson, J.H. III Efferent Olivocochlear Bundle: Some Relationships to
    Stimulus Discrimination in Noise. Journal of Neurophysiology, 1968, 31,
    122-130.

Dowling, J.E. Site of Visual Adaptation. Science, 1967, 155, 273.

Edelman, G.M. & Mountcastle, V.B. The Mindful Brain. Cambridge, Mass:
    The MIT Press, 1978.

Evans, E.F. Neural Processes for the Detection of Acoustic Patterns and
    for Sound Localization. In, F.O. Schmitt and F.G. Worden (Eds.),
    The Neurosciences: Third Study Program. Cambridge, MA: The MIT Press,
    1974.

Evarts, E.V. Pyramidal Tract Activity Associated with a Conditioned Hand
   Movement in the Monkey. Journal of Neurophysiology, 1966, 29, 1011-
   1027.

Evarts, E.V. Representation of Movement and Muscles by Pyramidal Tract
   Neurons of the Precentral Motor Cortex. In, M.D. Yahr and D. Purpura
   (Eds.), Neurophysiological Bases of Normal and Abnormal Activities.
   New York: Raven Press, 1967.

Evarts, E.V. Relation of Pyramidal Tract Activity by Force Exerted During
   Voluntary Movement. Journal of Neurophysiology, 1968, 31, 14-27.

Evarts, E.V. Activity of Pyramidal Tract Neurons During Postural Fixation.
   Journal of Neurophysiology, 1969, 32, 375-385.

Finkelstein, D. Classical and Quantum Probability and Set Theory. In,
   Harper and Hooke (Eds.), Foundations of Probability Theory, Statistical
   Inference and Statistical Theories of Science, Vol. III. Dordrecht-
   Holland: D. Reidel, 1976.

Gabor, D. Information Processing with Coherent Light. Optica. Acta, 1969,
   16, 519-533.

Glezer, V.D., Ivanoff, V.D. & Tscherbach, T.A. Investigation of Complex
   and Hypercomplex Receptive Fields of Visual Cortex of the Cat as Spatial
   Filters. Vision Research, 1973, 13, 1875-1904.

Granit, R. Multiple roles of muscular afferents. The Behavioral and Brain
   Sciences, 1982, 5 (4), 547.

Grillner, S. Locomotion in Vertebrates: Central Mechanisms and Reflex
   Interaction. Physiological Reviews, 1975, 55, 247-304.

Grillner, S. Control of Locomotion in Bipeds, Tetrapods and Fish. In, V.B.
   Brooks (Ed.), Handbook of Physiology, Section 1: The Nervous System.
   Vol. II. Motor Control. Bethesda, MD: American Physiological Society,
   1981.

Hammond, P. Spatial Organization of Receptive Fields of LGN Neurons.
   Journal of Physiology, 1972, 222, 53-54.

Helmholtz, H. Lehre von den Tonempfindungen. Braunschweig: Vieweg, 1863.

Hoffer, J.A. Central Control and Reflex Regulation of Mechanical Impedence:
   The Basis for a Unified Motor-Control Scheme. The Behavioral and Brain
   Sciences, 1982, 5, 548-549.

Hoffman, W.C. Higher Visual Perception as Prolongation of the Basic Lie
   Transformation Group. Mathematical Biosciences, 1970, 6, 437-471.

Houk, J.C. & Henneman, E. Responses of Golgi Tendon Organs to the Active
   Contractions of the Soleus Muscle of the Cat. Journal of Neurophysiology,
   1967, 30, 466-481.

Houk, J.C. & Rymer, W.Z. Neural control of muscle length and tension. In, V.B. Brooks (Eds.), Motor Control. Bethesda, MD: American Physiological Society Handbook of Physiology, 1981.

Hubel, D.H. & Wiesel, T.N. Receptive Fields of Single Neurons in the Cat's Striate Cortex. Journal of Physiology, 1959, 148, 574-591.

Humphrey, D.R., Schmidt, E.B. & Thompson, W.D. Predicting Measures of Motor Performance from Multiple Cortical Spike Trains. Science, 1970, 170, 758-762.

Iberall, A.S. A Field and Circuit Thermodynamics for Integrative Physiology. 3. Keeping the Books - A General Experimental Method. American Journal of Physiology/Regulatory, Integrative, and Comparative Physiology, 1978, 3, R85-R97.

Ito, M. The CNS as a multivariable control system. The Behavioral and Brain Sciences, 1982, 5(4), 552-553.

Jami, L. & Petit, J. Heterogeneity of motor neurons activating single Golgi tendon organs in cat leg muscles. Experimental Brain Research, 1976, 24, 485-493.

Julesz, B. Foundations of Cyclopean Perception. Chicago: University of Chicago Press, 1971.

Julesz, B. & Caelli, T. On the Limits of Fourier Decomposition in Visual Texture Perception. Perception, 1979, 8, 69-73.

Kelso, J.A.S. & Saltzman, E.L. Motor control: Which themes do we orchestrate? The Behavioral and Brain Sciences, 1982, 5(4), 554-557.

Kornhuber, H.H. Motor Functions of Cerebellum and Basal Ganglia: The Cerebellocortical Saccadic (Ballistic) Clock, the Cerebellonuclear Hold Regulator, and the Basal Ganglia Ramp (Voluntary Speed Smooth Movement) Generator. Kybernetik, 1971, 8, 157-162.

Kornhuber, H.H. Cerebral Cortex, Cerebellum and Basal Ganglia: An Introduction to their Motor Functions. In, F.O. Schmitt and F.G. Worden (Eds.), The Neurosciences: Third Study Program. Cambridge, MA: The MIT Press, 1974.

Kozlovskaya, I., Uno, M. Atkins, A. & Brooks, V.B. Performance of a Step-Tracking Task by Monkeys. Commun. Behav. Biol., 1972, 5, 153-156.

Kulikowski, J.J., Marcelja, S. & Bishop, P.O. Theory of Spatial Position and Spatial Frequency Relations in the Receptive Fields of Simple Cells in the Visual Cortex. Biological Cybernetics, 1982, 43, 187-198.

Leith, E.N. White-Light Holograms. Scientific American, 1976, 235, No. 4, 80.

Lynch, J.C. A Single Unit Analysis of Contour Enhancement in the Somesthetic System of the Cat. Ph.D. Dissertation, Neurological Sciences, Stanford University, May, 1981.

Maffei, L. & Fiorentini, A. The Visual Cortex as a Spatial Frequency Analyzer. Vision Research, 1973, 13, 1255-1267.

Malis, L.I., Pribram, K.H. & Kruger, L. Action Potential in "Motor" Cortex Evoked by Peripheral Nerve Stimulation. Journal of Neurophysiology, 1953, 16, 161-167.

Marcelja, S. Mathematical Description of the Responses of Simple Cortical Cells. Journal of the Optical Society of America, 1980, 70, No. 11, 1297-1300.

Marr, D. Analyzing Natural Images: A Computational Theory of Texture Vision. Cold Spring Harbor Symposium Quantitative Biology, 1976a, 40, 647-662.

Marr, D. Early Processing of Visual Information. Philosophical Transactions of the Royal Society B. 1976b, 275, 483-524.

Marr, D. & Poggio, T. From Understanding Computation to Understanding Neural Circuitry. Neuroscience Research Program Bulletin, 1977, 15, 470-488.

Matthews, P.B.C. Muscle Spindles and Their Motor Control. Physiolog. Review, 1964, 44, 219-288.

Matthews, P.B.C. Muscle Spindles: Their Messages and their Fusimotor Supply. In, V.B. Brooks (Ed.), Handbook of Physiology. Bethesda, MD: American Physiological Society, 1981.

Miller, G.A., Galanter, E. & Pribram, K.H. Plans and the Structure of Behavior. New York: Henry Holt and Co., 1960.

Morell, F. Visual System's View of Acoustic Space. Nature, 1972, 238, 44-46.

Movshon, J.A., Thompson, I.D. & Tolhurst, D.J. Receptive Field Organization of Complex Cells in the Cat's Striate Cortex. Journal of Physiology, 1978, 283, 79.

Ohm, G.S. Uber Die Definition Des Tones, Nebst Daran Geknupfter Theorie Der Sirene Und Ahnlicher Tonbildener Vorrichtungen. Ann. Physik. Chem., 1943, 59, 513-565.

Partridge, L.D. Methods in the Study of Proprioception. In, B.N. Feinberg and D.G. Fleming (Eds.), Handbook of Engineering in Biology and Medicine. West Palm Beach: CRC Press, 1978, 211-255.

Partridge, L.D. How was movement controlled before Newton. The Behavioral and Brain Sciences, 1982, 5(4), 561.

Partridge, L.D. & Benton, L.A. Muscle the motor. In, V.B. Brooks (Ed.), Handbook of Physiology. Bethesda, MD: American Physiological Society, 1981.

Pellionisz, A. & Llinas, R. Brain Modeling by Tensor Network Theory in
    Computer Simulation. The Cerebellum: Distributed Processor for Predictive
    Coordination. Neuroscience, 1979, 14, 323-348.

Philips, C.G. Changing Concepts of the Precentral Motor Area. In, J.C.
    Eccles (Eds.), Brain and Conscious Experience. New York: Springer-Verlag,
    1966.

Polit, A. & Bizzi, E. Characteristics of Motor Programs Underlying Arm
    Movements in Monkeys. Journal of Neurophysiology, 1979, 42, 183-194.

Poggio, T. & Torre, V. A New Approach to Synaptic Interactions. In, H.
    Palm (Ed.), Approaches in Complex Systems. Berlin: Springer-Verlag, 1981.

Pollen, D.A., Lee, J.R. & Taylor, J.H. How Does the Striate Cortex Begin
    the Reconstruction of the Visual World. Science, 1971, 137, 74-77.

Pribram, K.H. Languages of the Brain: Experimental Paradoxes and Principles
    in Neuropsychology. Englewood Cliffs, New Jersey: Prentice-Hall, 1971;
    New York: Brandon House, Inc., 1982 (5th printing).

Pribram, K.H., Kruger, L., Robinson, R. & Berman, A.J. The Effects of
    Precentral Lesions on the Behavior of Monkeys. Yale Journal of Biology
    and Medicine, 1956, 28, 428-443.

Pribram, K.H., Lassonde, M.C. & Ptito, M. Intracerebral Influences on the
    Microstructure of Receptive Fields of Cat Visual Cortex. Experimental
    Brain Research, 1981, 43, 131-144.

Purpura, D. Physiological Organization of the Basal Ganglia. In, M.D. Yahr
    (Ed.), The Basal Ganglia. Research Publication of the Association for
    Research in Nervous and Mental Diseases. Raven Press, 1976.

Richards, W. Stereopsis with and without Monocular Cues. Vision Research,
    1977, 17, 967-969.

Richards, W. & Pelit, A. Texture Matching. Kybernetik, 1974, 16, 155-162.

Robson, J.G. Receptive Fields, Neural Representation of the Spatial and
    Intensive Attributes of the Visual Image. In, E.C. Carterette (Ed.),
    Handbook of Perception, Vol. V: Seeing. New York: Academic Press, 1975.

Rodieck, R.W. Quantitative Analysis of Cat Retinal Ganglion Cell Response
    to Visual Stimuli. Vision Research, 1965, 5, 581-601.

Sakitt, B. & Barlow, H.B. A Model for the Economical Encoding of the
    Visual Image in Cerebral Cortex. Biological Cybernetics, 1982, 43, 97-108.

Schiller, P.H., Finlay, B.L. & Volman, S.F. Quantitative Studies of Single
    Cell Properties in Monkey Striate Cortex. Journal of Neurophysiology,
    1976, 39, 228-1374.

Schmidt, R.A. Past and Future Issues in Motor Programming. Research Quarterly
    for Exercise and Sports, 1980, 51, 122-140.

Schmidt, R.A. & McGowan, C. Terminal accuracy of unexpectedly loaded rapid movements: Evidence for a mass-spring mechanism in programming. Journal of Motor Behavior, 1980, 12, 149-161.

Spinelli, D.N., Pribram, K.H. & Bridgeman, B. Visual Receptive Field Organization of Single Units in the Visual Cortex of Monkey. International Journal of Neuroscience, 1970, 1, 67-74.

Spinelli, D.N., Starr, A. & Barrett, T.W. Auditory Specificity in Unit Recordings from Cat's Visual Cortex. Experimental Neurology, 1968, 22, 75-84.

Stark, L. Neurological Control Systems: Studies in Bioengineering. New York: Plenum Press, 1968.

Stark, L. Neurological ballistic movements: Sampled data or intermittent open loop control. The Behavioral and Brain Sciences, 1982, 5(4), 564-566.

Stein, R.B. What muscle variable(s) does the nervous system control in limb movements? The Behavioral and Brain Sciences, 1982, 5(4), 535-577.

Stelmach, G.E. & Diggles, V.A. Motor equivalence and distributed control: Evidence for nonspecific muscle commands. The Behavioral and Brain Sciences, 1982, 5(4), 566-567.

Stuart, D.G., Mosher, C.G., Gerlach, R.L. & Ranking, R.M. Mechanical Arrangement and Transducing Properties of Golgi Tendon Organs. Experimental Brain Research, 1972, 14, 274-292.

Stuart, C.I.J.M., Takahashi, Y. & Umezawa, H. On the Stability and Non-local Properties of Memory. Journal of Theoretical Biology, 1978, 71, 605-618.

Sutter, E. A Revised Conception of Visual Receptive Fields Based on Pseudo-Random Spatio Temporal Pattern Stimuli. In, P.Z. Marmarelis and G.D. McCann (Eds.), Proceedings First Symposium on Testing and Identification of Nonlinear Systems. Pasadena, CA: California Institute of Technology, 1976.

Terzuolo, C., Soechting, J.F. & Dufresne, J.R. Operational Characteristics of Reflex Response to Changes in Muscle Length During Different Motor Tasks and their Functional Utility. In, Brain Mechanisms of Perceptual Awareness and Purposeful Behavior, IBRO Monograph Series, Vol. 8. New York: Raven Press, 1981.

Terzuolo, C.A. & Soechting, J.F. Reductionism cannot answer questions of movement control. The Behavioral and Brain Sciences, 1982, 5(4), 567-568.

Uttal, W.R. The Psychobiology of Mind. Hillsdale, New Jersey: Lawrence Erlbaum Associates, 1978.

Welt, C., Aschoff, J.C., Kameda, K. & Brooks, V.B. Intracortical Organization
    of Cat's Motor Sensory Cortex. In, M.D. Yahr and D.P. Purpura (Eds.),
    Neurophysiological Basis of Normal and Abnormal Motor Activities. New
    York: Raven Press, 1967.
Willshaw, D.J., Buneman, O.P. & Longuet-Higgins, H.C. Nonholographic
    Associative Memory. Nature, 1969, 222, 960-962.
Woolsey, C.N. Patterns of Localization in Sensory and Motor Areas of the
    Cerebral Cortex. In, Biological and Mental Disease. New York: Paul B.
    Hober, Inc., 1952.

Human Motor Actions – Bernstein Reassessed
H.T.A. Whiting (editor)
© Elsevier Science Publishers B.V. (North-Holland), 1984

CHAPTER IIb

FROM ACTION GESTALTS TO DIRECT ACTION

E.S. Reed

INTRODUCTION

If he had published nothing else but "The problem of the interactions
of coordination and localization" Nikolai Bernstein would still be one of the
most important students of bodily movement in recent history. Although he
discussed in detail only two problems and emphasized the simplified case of
coordinating a single limb-joint system, a science, like a movement "never
responds to detailed changes by a change in its detail; it responds as a
whole to changes in each part" (p. 84). The general outlines of the theory
of action have been affected profoundly by Bernstein's important detailed
insights.

It is both surprising and humbling to read this essay - written half a
century ago - and find in it still-provocative analyses of some of the most
contested issues of contemporary movement science. Bernstein anticipated (and
often improved upon!) recent discussions of distributed brain function, the
articular system as a "mass-spring" of sorts, the centrality of phase relations
to understanding bodily coordination, the importance of understanding the
functional hierarchies of the nervous system, the fundamental role of "sensory"
processes in "motor" control, the importance of dealing with bodily movements
and postures as a whole, not merely with motions of sections of the body.

The various detailed contributions made by Bernstein in this chapter are
brought together by his principle of the "lines of equal simplicity" (p. 112).
This principle still has important implications for both theorists and
researchers today. In the first part of this response I will use this
principle to highlight Bernstein's own achievements. In the second part I
will show how the lines of equal simplicity principle can help to deepen and
extend Bernstein's own ideas.

BERNSTEIN'S ACHIEVEMENTS

The Principle of Lines of Equal Simplicity

"Our experimental aim at present", Bernstein wrote, "lies in the correct
formulation of categories which are really represented in the brain centers"
(p. 96). Our goal still is to discover the proper taxonomy of action: what
movement tasks are really of the same kind, and what kinds of actions are
truly different? As simple-minded as this sounds it is tremendously important
experimentally and theoretically. A line of equal simplicity is revealed when
a "transition from one element of the set of possible tasks to another" has
a negligible effect on performance (p. 112). "Simplicity" here is used as a
general term, meant to cover such empirical variables as "speed of completion,
degree of accuracy, degree of variance and so on" - in short, empirical
measures of a movement's intrinsic structure and function (p. 112). For
example, it is equally simple for most of us to write at various scales with
the same (preferred or non-preferred) hand, although these tasks involve
totally different sets of muscles. However, it is not equally simple for
most of us to write with our non-preferred as opposed to our preferred hand.
This is not some absolute simplicity (cf. Bernstein's note at p. 115) but an
empirical one. It is likely, judging from some of my own informal observations,
that the phasing and timing of writing movements varies negligibly with
changes in either scale or lateralization, whereas the accuracy and variance
of the traces will vary with lateralization far more than with scale changes.

At the beginning of this chapter (pp. 77 - 81), Bernstein uses a
logical argument, based on classical mechanics, to show that animal movements
are neither passive responses to environmental influences or to commands from
the brain. Following this, Bernstein uses his principle of equal simplicity
to show how properly to classify and describe movements without assuming that
individual muscles are commanded to act or called into play by reflexes. The
argument is straightforward and widely accepted by modern researchers (who
often, however, try to avoid its implications): if the brain controls
movements by means of controlling the particular muscles involved in them,
then transfer experiments in which new muscles and nerve centers are involved
in achieving previously learned effects should prove difficult. As Bernstein
notes (p. 96), Lashley's (1929) experiments show that considerable
compensation is possible. The experiments (unknown to Bernstein) of Gibson

(Gibson, Jack & Raffel, 1932; Gibson & Hudson, 1935) and Wickens (1938)
directly confirm this hypothesis: learned movement patterns (in these
experiments, conditioned reflexes) transfer easily to alternate muscle
groups. Unlike Lashley, however, Bernstein did not use this point to argue
against localization; on the contrary, he used it to help explain what it is
that is controlled in action (p. 93).

What is Specified by "Motor Commands"?

If specific muscles are controlled by specific brain centers, then
learned functional movements (conditioned responses or more complex actions)
which are equally simple when transferred to two or more muscle groups cannot
be so specifically controlled. "The hypothesis of cellular localization of
muscles necessarily leads to a denial of cellular localization of conditioned
reflexes" (p. 95) and any other higher movement functions. With some caution,
Bernstein uses this ingenious argument to move outside of the sterile
localizationist debate into the far more important issue of what functions
must be controlled if coordination is to be achieved. Anticipating modern
theories of "distributed control" (Arbib, 1981) and neural redundancy
(Diamond, 1979) by five decades, Bernstein raised the problem of sensorimotor
integration as follows. Stimulation at the periphery before and during movement
is carried to diverse regions of the CNS (Merzenich & Kaas, 1980); sensory,
motor and association cortical regions are all multiply interconnected,
embodying redundant representations of the periphery (Asanuma, 1981; Diamond,
1979; Masterton & Berkley, 1974). Therefore, "we are obliged to confront
(coordination) as a result of the mutual activity of entire systems or organs
which, anatomically and clinically, display varying degrees of independence"
(p. 90). This seems bewilderingly complex to those who - like all classical
and many modern motor theorists - think of actions as comprised of specific
muscle movements caused by specific motor commands.

Once again, Bernstein applies his principle of lines of equal simplicity:
it would be incredibly complex to control each and every individual muscle of
a body and keep up to date on their proprioceptive inputs as well (Turvey,
Shaw & Mace, 1978). But the task of the nervous system is not to produce
specific commands to achieve specific movements, because "a determinate
effect is possible for a movement only where the central impulse is very
different under different conditions" (p. 81). Taken separately, the idea
of diverse innervation patterns producing specific movements or diverse

neural centers with variable involvement coordinating into specific actions
seems complex and confusing. Taken together, these concepts support each
other, and begin to offer a fruitful new way of looking at the functional
principles of the motor system.

In this chapter Bernstein did not take his concept of mutual or
distributed control farther then a critique of "keyboard" theories of brain
localization. In the end, he himself appealed to the concept of a "motor
engram" which embodied an "image of achievement" - the intended movement
pattern. Although he was certainly aware that no motor engram alone could
determine a specific movement pattern (not without the cooperation of other
brain centers and a properly integrated proprioceptive system - see p. 101)
Bernstein nevertheless wrote of this motor image or engram as though it were
a new kind of motor keyboard - as if motor commands were not commands to
muscles, but something closer to motor gestalts. The historical comparison
with gestalt theory is extremely close, and worth some consideration.

Bernstein's Gestalt Theory of Movement

This chapter played the same historical role in the theory of motor
control as Wolfgang Köhler's pathbreaking "On unnoticed sensations and errors
of judgment" (Köhler, 1913, 1971) did in the theory of sense perception.
Somewhat oversimplified, Köhler's argument was that the specific effects of
sensory stimulation could not give rise to determinate perceptions. Köhler
showed that, if sensory inputs have constant effects, then actual perceptions
cannot be based on sensory input alone (e.g., the perceptual effects, the
perceived color, of a specific optical wavelength vary depending on the
surrounding wavelengths) or one must give up the idea of sensory constancy
altogether. (That this argument is strictly analogous to Bernstein's is
demonstrated by the latter's critique of Helmholtz's resonant harp theory of
hearing. Bernstein uses this critique to illustrate his principle of lines
of equal simplicity and in so doing recreates Köhler's argument against
Helmholtz). To explain perception one thus has to resort to (often ad hoc)
hypotheses about non-sensory "cognitive" processes which correct and adjust
the sensory input.

Bernstein argued that if motor processes cannot determine specific
movements, then one must appeal to non-motor (proprioceptive or cognitive)
processes to explain action, or abandon the hypothesis that central commands
have univocal peripheral effects. As mentioned above, Bernstein explicitly

states this as the dilemma for localizationists: either muscle movements are univocally commanded and more complex movements are not, or vice versa, but not both (p. 95). It is for this reason that Bernstein invented the gestalt-like concept of a motor engram of the "image of achievement" which he thought of as a central determinant of specific complex movements (p. 100).

Like Köhler, Bernstein developed a form of neural isomorphism theory. Speaking of the motor engram he wrote, "it is necessary that there should exist in the supreme nervous organ an exact representation of what will later occur in the periphery" (p. 101). Such a representation would be able to give rise to determinate commands for specific movements, although at the cost of having to encode a practically limitless amount of environmental and peripheral contingencies. There is no evidence that such specific representations do exist, and Bernstein's own arguments about the non-univocality of central commands for muscles calls the very possibility of such engrams for the muscular details of complex movements into question. Bernstein's theory here is limited in a way quite analogous to Köhler's - both fail to recognize that perceiving/acting is not a relation between the bodily periphery and the CNS, but an inter-relation of an animate organism (with both sensory and motor processes) and its surroundings. (Bernstein and Köhler also failed to realize that it is environmental information that is specific to perception and action, not internal representations, but the arguments to demonstrate this cannot be developed in this small space - see Gibson, 1966, chaps. 2 & 4; 1979, section II; Reed & Jones, 1982, chaps. 4.6 and 4.7).

Just as Köhler realized that specific properties of sensory processes cannot be the basis of perception, so Bernstein realized that the specific properties of motor processes could not be the basis of action. Yet neither of these thinkers were able to extend their insights by re-thinking the concepts of sensory and motor processes to take into account the implications of their arguments. Both these writers assumed that if particular sensory/motor processes did not lead to specific perceptions/actions, then perhaps multiple sensory/motor processes - such as a motor engram - could fit the bill. Bernstein, far more than Köhler, acknowledged the need to rethink the whole sensori-motor concept, but on the fundamental issue of whether action/perception is based on efference/afference both Bernstein and Köhler failed to reject incorrect orthodoxy.

Are there "Motor Commands"?

Bernstein's own arguments can be used against his own position in this
instance. If a "central command" has no univocal peripheral effect, then it
is not a "command" but a variable factor or influence. (Similarly, because
proprioceptive "signals" have no univocal central effects, they are not
"signals" as Bernstein claims). Furthermore, a combination of these variable
factors is still a variable factor - not leading to a specific action -
unless those factors which underlie invariant results are also included.
Yet, as Bernstein himself proves in this chapter, any specific action is in
part determined by the environmental field of forces, initial conditions of
the movement, and perceptual factors. A "motor engram" that does not include
these factors cannot yield invariant results - as Bernstein himself later
argued (see p. 445). It has been found, to mention a single example, that
the illusory perception of bodily support or non-support results in postural
adjustments similar to those engendered by actual support or non-support
(Nashner & Cordo, 1981).

The goal of research on action should be to explain how specific kinds
of actions are determined. By accepting that such entities as 'motor commands"
existed, Bernstein in 1935 placed many crucial factors in the process of
coordination outside of what he would have called action, locating these
factors in the environment or in the perceptual process. Later on, when he
began to replace the concept of the motor engram and the motor command alike
with the "motor problem" (p. 344, p. 445) Bernstein began to rectify this
mistake. In his later work, Bernstein began to see than the implication of
this early essay was not that one should replace muscle localizationalism
with a gestalt theory of movement, but that one should abandon altogether
the idea that within the motor system proper there are "commands" in the
sense of patterns of efference that specify peripheral results. This difference
is of the greatest theoretical significance. I have chosen to characterize
this distinction between the earlier and later Bernstein as the difference
between a theory of indirect action on the environment and a theory of direct
action.

TOWARDS DIRECT ACTION

Bernstein's great insights in this chapter show how powerful his principle

of lines of equal simplicity was in revealing new and fruitful ways of
understanding bodily movement. Yet, as I have stressed above, Bernstein's
conclusions left unresolved a number of problems which forced him and other
students of action to extend and modify his early ideas. Most importantly,
Bernstein began to replace the motor engram concept with a more functionally
defined concept of the "motor problem". Elsewhere I have argued that this
insight needs to be deepened into a full-fledged account of actions as
specific to biologically evolved functions of an animal in its environment
(Reed, 1982; in press). I haven't the space here to argue this case in full,
so I will instead merely explain the significance of this transition from an
indirect to a direct theory of action, without attempting to justify a theory
of direct action.

According to David Hume (1779, 1948, p. 186) "no animal can move
immediately anything but the members of its own body". As William James
(1890, II, p. 480) puts it, "the only _direct_ outward effects of our will are
our bodily movements". This assumption should be called the theory of indirect
action, because it holds that we act on our environment only indirectly, by
causing our bodies to move. This theory, which goes back at least to
Descartes' Passions of the Soul (1649; see Lawrence, 1972, chaps. 2 & 3;
Reed, 1982b), underlies most of our thinking about action. Bernstein's
arguments showing the impossibility of univocal peripheral results of central
"commands" should have led him to reject this entire approach, but even he
did not see this implication in 1935, and he only saw it dimly as late as in
the 1960s.

Animals act, I would argue, by changing the relations between themselves
and their surroundings. These changes are effected by bodily movements and
postures, but we do not ordinarily move our bodies in a specific way and thus
cause the desired change. On the contrary, we cause the specific desired
change by whatever movements and postures are needed to get the job done
(see Reid, 1785/1969, p. 50). The specificity of the action lies in the
meaningful changes wrought, not in the pattern of the movements made. This
theory, by contrast to the above, should be called the theory of direct
action on the environment.

Most theorists have seen some merit to thinking of actions both as
bodily movements and as their external effects. This has led to a number of
variations on the idea that actions are bodily movements _plus_ something else
– learned habits, volition, goals, and so on. This something else is supposed
to ensure that specific movement patterns also have specific desired

environmental effects. In his essay of 1935 Bernstein favored the idea that
actions were movements caused by motor engrams embodying images of achievement
- and even in his work of the 1950s and 1960s he still maintained something
like the concept of a mental goal as causing movements and thereby creating
specific acts (the "sollwert").

Yet if an action is a specific way of altering an animal's relation with
its environment, then what makes it just that action is the precise change
effected, not the mechanisms or motions leading to the change. Nothing about
the causes of a movement can make it bear a specific function - except that
it fulfils the desired goal or purpose. The lack of morphological stereotypy
of natural movements has been amply demonstrated time and again (so much so
that many ethologists treat "fixed action patterns" as - at best - statistical
distributions of a varying pattern).

The mistake made here by Bernstein is to reason as follows: when an
animal exhibits a definite movement habit, then all the determinants of that
habit must exist in the CNS "in a hidden, latent form" (p. 98). A potential,
the ability to act in a determinate way, is thus turned into an actuality
(a latent engram) and the actuality is claimed to cause all instantiations of
the potential. (This mistaken argument concerning action has been subjected
to a book-length critique by Lawrence, 1972). This is a muddle into which all
existing theories of indirect action seems to lead. The solution requires
abandoning the assumption that the brain causes the body to move and that
actions are the environmental consequences of such movements.

The determinants of a specific action (any specific environmental
accomplishment of an animal) are a complex relation of the forces in the
environment surrounding the body and the initial physical and biological
conditions of the animal. Moreover, if animals have access to perceptual
information specifying their relations with their surroundings, and if they
can use that information to regulate their posture and movement, then one
can explain action without any appeal to "commands" causing specific effects.
On this view, perceptual information serves to establish ranges of tolerable
variation for the action system. For example, Lee and his colleagues (Lee,
Lishman & Thomson, 1982; Lee & Reddish, 1982; Lee & Thomson, 1982) have shown that
optical information specifying the time it will take an observer to contact
an environmental surface is used by animals and humans to regulate the pace
of their locomotion. Because optical information is not in the nervous system
(but in an external energy field) it cannot issue any commands at all to the
neuromuscular system (which would not respond invariantly to the same influences

at different times anyway). However, the availability of such information allows active observers to regulate relevant parameters of their behavior (e.g., force output, rhythm, timing) according to the specific demands of a situation.

The theory of direct action is still in its infancy and relies on a number of hypotheses that require further testing. Gibson's theory of ecological information as specific to an animal's environmental situation (Gibson, 1979, Section II) still needs further development. Lee's hypothesis that information parameters can constrain movements has been tested only for a small number of cases. The simple-sounding idea of treating action as an animal's means of directly affecting its surroundings needs to be developed through experimentation on functional parameters of movement - an area consipicuously under-researched at present. Here Bernstein's lines of equal simplicity principle will be very fruitful: we need to design experiments that test whether actions are indeed functionally specific - whether it is more "simple" for animals to accomplish the same movement or to accomplish the same environmental effect. For example, Forster's (1982) studies of jumping spider predation suggest that the pattern of each pounce is adjusted to the "ballistics" of each case, and Olive's (1980, p. 1134) work showed that the attack mode chosen is specific to the size, shape, and behavior of the prey. These spiders apparently do not jump in order to predate, they predate by jumping.

CONCLUSION

Bernstein's great contribution to movement science in this chapter was to use his principle of lines of equal simplicity to raise profound questions about what action is, and how it is controlled and coordinated. If I have argued here that we must go even farther than Bernstein in reconceptualizing action, it is only because his own principles can still be developed in fruitful ways. When Bernstein wrote this chapter - and to some degree this is still the case - action was conceived as the passive response of the body to environmental stimuli or to central commands. It is only because of Bernstein's insights that we now realize that animal movements and postures are cooperative phenomena, resulting from an active interlocking of forces and processes throughout the nervous system, the bodily periphery, and the environment as well. Current research on the coordination of complex movements, on phase relations in action, on complex actions as the result of abstract "schemata" or "images", on the intricate sensori-motor integration of the spinal segments and higher centers, on the redundancy of cortical sensori-motor representation, on the central anticipation and "tuning" 'of peripheral motor processes - all this important work was prefigured in this chapter from 50 years ago.

Less obviously present in this essay, but nevertheless visible dimly, is the idea of direct action - of action as being the means whereby animals change how they relate to their surroundings, not how the CNS causes the limbs to move. Bernstein used his lines of equal simplicity argument to disprove the classical idea that central commands cause specific peripheral movements. I have argued that this same principle refutes even the idea that what is commanded are specific complex peripheral movements. The very idea of a "motor command" is called into question by Bernstein's principle. Action systems would seem to function not merely by outflow, or even by outflow as modified by feedback, but via a circular process of adjustment in which parameters of information set constraints on action. If this information is specific to the animal's situation, then the action so constrained will also be specific and appropriate, despite the lack of outflowing commands or inflowing signals. The division of labor in the nervous system is not between receptive (sensory systems and effective motor systems, but between information-seeking perceptual systems (themselves involving both afferent and efferent processes) and environmental-adjustment seeking action systems (involving both efferent and afferent processes as well). To come to understand how such action systems work we can do no better than to follow Bernstein in experimentally seeking the functional properties of purposeful action in the environment.

REFERENCES

Arbib, M. Perceptual structures and distributed motor control. In, V. Brooks
    (Ed.), Handbook of Physiology, Section 1: The Nervous system, Vol. II,
    Part 2, Motor Control. Bethesda, MD: American Physiological Society, 1981.

Asanuma, H. The functional role of sensory inputs to the motor cortex.
    Progress in Neurobiology, 1981, 16, 241-262.

Diamond, I. The subdivisions of Neocortex: A proposal to revise the
    traditional view of sensory, motor, and association areas. Progress
    in Psychobiology, 1979, 8, 1-43.

Forster, L. Vision and prey-eating strategies in jumping spiders. American
    Scientist, 1982, 70, 165-175.

Gibson, J. The senses considered as perceptual systems. Boston: Hougton-
    Mifflin, 1966.

Gibson, J. The ecological approach to visual perception. Boston: Hougton-
    Mifflin, 1979.

Gibson, J. & Hudson, L. Bilateral transfer of the conditioned knee-jerk.
    Journal of Experimental Psychology, 1935, 18, 774-783.

Gibson, J., Jack, E. & Raffel, G. Bilateral transfer of the conditioned
    response in the human subject. Journal of Experimental Psychology, 1932,
    15, 416-421.

Hume, D. Dialogues concerning natural religion. Edition prepared by N.K.
    Smith, Indianapolis: Bobbs-Merril, 1948 (First published: 1979).

James, W. The principles of psychology. New York: Holt, 1890.

Köhler, W. (On unnoticed sensations and errors of judgment). Zeitschrift
    Für Psychologie. Reprinted in M. Henle (Ed.), Selected papers of
    W. Köhler. New York: Liveright, 1971.

Lashley, K. Brain mechanisms and intelligence. Chicago: University of
    Chicago Press, 1929.

Lawrence, R. Motive and intention. Evanston: Northwestern, 1972.

Lee, D., Lishman, R. & Thomson, J. Regulation of gate in the long jump.
    Journal of Experimental Psychology: Human Perception and Performance,
    1982, 8, 448-549.

Lee, D. & Reddish, P. Plummeting Gannets: A paradigm of ecological optics.
    Nature, 1982, 293, 293-294.

Lee, D. & Thomson, W. Vision in action: The control of locomotion. In,
    D. Ingle, Mo. Goodale and R. Mansfield (Eds.), Analysis of visual
    behavior. Cambridge: MIT Press, 1982.

Masterton, R. & Berkley, M. Brain function: Changing ideas on the role of
    sensory, motor and association cortex. Annual Review of Psychology,
    1974, 25, 277-312.

Merzenich, M. & Kaas, J. Principles of organization of sensory-perceptual
    systems in mammals. Progress in Psychobiology and Physiological Psychology,
    1980, 9, 1-42.

Nashner, L. & Cordo, P. Relation of automatic postural responses and
    reaction-time voluntary movements of human leg muscles. Experimental
    Brain Research, 1981, 43, 395-405.

Olive, C. Foraging specializations in orb-weaving spiders. Ecology, 1980,
    61, 1133-1144.

Reed, E. An outline of a theory of action systems. Journal of Motor
    Behavior, 1982, 14, 98-134.

Reed, E. An ecological approach to the evolution of learning. In, T.
    Johnston and A. Pietrawicz (Eds.), Issues in the ecological study of
    learning. Hillsdale, N.J.: Erlbaum, in press.

Reed, E. The corporeal ideas hypothesis and the origin of scientific
    psychology. Review of Metaphysics, 1982b, 35, 731-752.

Reed, E. & Jones, R. (Eds.), Reasons for realism: Selected essays of James
    Gibson. Hillsdale, N.J.: Erlbaum, 1982.

Reid, T. Essays on the active powers of the human mind. Cambridge: MIT
    Press, 1969 (First published, 1785).

Turvey, M., Shaw, R. & Mace, W. Issues in the theory of action. In, J.
    Requin (Ed.), Attention and performance (Vol. 7). Hillsdale, N.J.:
    Erlbaum, 1978.

Wickens, D. The transference of conditional excitation and inhibition
    from one muscle group to the antagonistic group. Journal of Experimental
    Psychology, 1938, 22, 101-123.

SECTION 3

CHAPTER III

BIODYNAMICS OF LOCOMOTION

N. Bernstein

(Published in *Studies of the Biodynamics of Walking, Running and Jumping*
by the author and co-workers. Researches of the Centr. Scientific Inst. of
Physical Culture, Moscow, 1940)

1.   SOURCE MATERIAL, POINTS OF DEPARTURE, TECHNIQUES

On beginning the cyclogrametric investigation of locomotion in 1926,
we set ourselves a very restricted and practical aim: the investigation of
force phenomena at the centre of gravity of the whole body in walking and
running in order to deduce dynamic coefficients for use in the design of
footbridges[*].

In subsequent years we came to the conclusion that locomotion could
also provide very extensive and interesting material for investigations
from the physiological point of view.

The advantages of locomotion considered as an object for investigation
of the processes of movement are essentially as follows.

Firstly, locomotor movements, in particular walking, are amongst the
most highly automatized of movements. The most rigid succession of all
details is followed from cycle to cycle and these details are extremely
repetitive for each particular subject. This allows one to fix one's
attention and to adopt constant criteria for the discrimination of the
random from the regular.

Secondly, locomotor movements display an extremely widespread synergy
incorporating the whole musculature and the entire moving skeleton and

---

[*] The principal result of this research was the finding that the amplitude
of vertical dynamic forces at the centre of gravity of the body in walking,
in other words, the amplitude of vertical reactions of the supporting
surface is proportional to the square of the step frequency: $A = \pm P.Qn^2$,
where P is the static weight, n the number of single steps per sec. $Q = 0.095$
± 0.005 for normal gait. In the case of carrying a load (up to 120 kg) on
the back the value of Q rises to 0.100-0.110. Running is characterized by
the inequality $A > P$; in fast running the maximal values of vertical
dynamic force can reach more than $3P$. The longitudinal components of force
in walking and running depend on the length of the step, and we could not
find simple expressions for them.

bringing into play a large number of areas and conduction pathways of the central nervous system. We may therefore expect in them the most clear-cut reflection of the interaction of central and peripheral processes, with a great abundance of detail characteristics of the process of movement in general.

Thirdly, locomotor movements have generality. Their selection as an object of investigation assures the investigator of a large number of subjects who have all mastered, for example, the act of walking incomparably better and more completely than any of their individual professional skills. The beginning and the development of locomotion in normal subjects is achieved with no less regularity and orderliness than is found in morphological development and the development of tissues and organs. This generality and regularity guarantees material for broad comparisons and opens the way to a study of the ontogeny of movements, their growth, establishment, development and involutional disintegration.

Fourthly, locomotor acts belong to the category of extremely ancient movements. They are phylogenetically older than the cortical hemispheres and have undoubtedly affected the development of the central nervous system in the same manner as have the distance receptors mentioned by Sherrington; for example, some clinicians have recently assumed a direct connection between the development of the corpus Luysiand the transition from quadripedal locomotion to the erect posture. This antiquity assures for the investigator the existence of deep organic connections between locomotor processes and the most varied structural levels of the central nervous system and allows us to hope that we shall observe in the very course of the locomotor act traces of these different levels and of successive phylogenetic stratification.

Fifthly, and finally, locomotion presents an unusually stable and typical structure. This could not be assumed in advance; but it had already become apparent to us by 1934 that all the basic details of normal walking may be found in all normal adult subjects without exception, and that individual differences between subjects depend neither on differences in the structure of the locomotor act nor on the assembly of details encountered in it, but occur only in the rhythms and amplitudes of the ratios between these details. This result allowed us to build up a detailed nomenclature for the structural elements of the locomotor act[*], incorporating many dozens

---

[*] *See Investigations into the Biodynamics of Locomotion*, Vol.I,Ch.III,1935.

of stable phenomena which were invariably characteristic for each adult normal subject. The material collected by us (21) showed that the stability and generality of the structure of the locomotor act is even more widespread than we could then suppose, and that its roots may be clearly followed in early ontogeny and phylogeny in qualitative changes of locomotion, such as running or marching, and finally in a number of pathological disturbances. This will be discussed later.

All these circumstances-automatization, degree of synergy, generality, ancientness- and their staibility of character make locomotor processes extremely favourable objects for investigations in the general physiology of movements.

In order to make clear in what lies the main interest in movement as a physiological topic we may recall the general features of its structure.†

The movements of an organism from the mechanical point of view arise because of changes in the conditions of equilibrium in the force field encompassing the animal's organ of movement.

In the case of spontaneous movement equilibrium is destroyed because of redistribution of tensions in the animal's muscles, within the organ of movement itself or outside it. Once the movement of an organ has begun changing both its position in relation to external forces (the force of gravity is foremost) and the degree of tension of the muscles connected to this organ, the relationships between the forces in the surrounding field continue to change until they approach to, or move still further away from, a state of equilibrium. During this process changes in muscle tension bring about a movement and the movement affects the condition of the muscles by shortening or stretching them causing further changes in their tension. We call the reciprocal connection which we have described here *the peripheral cycle of interaction*.

A mathematical analysis of similar relationships between forces (of the muscles) and movements (of the organs) shows that this form of interaction *does not presuppose a one-to-one correspondence between force and movement*, that is, that one and the same sequence of changes in forces may produce different movements on successive repetitions. This absence of one-to-one correspondence is due to the fact that the biomechanical relationships between forces and movements may be expressed in the form of a differential equation of no lower than the second order, demanding among the conditions of its solution no fewer than two values independent of the equation itself.

---

† The thorough analysis here has relationships with our report The problem of the interrelation of co-ordination and localization (Ch.II,p.15).

These independent constants of integration (the original position of the organ, its initial velocity, the condition of the force field as a whole, etc.) may change from moment to moment, resulting in completely different effects from the same initial innervation.

Adequate co-ordination and a correspondence of the movement to the animal's intention are only possible under conditions in which the central nervous system constantly receives information as to the state of these independent parameters of integration and adapts its effector impulses in an exact relationship to changes in the latter. This flow of information primarily involves the proprioceptive system and provides a second ring of reciprocal connections - in our terminology *the central cycle of interaction*.

In this cycle the effector impulses change the tensions in the muscles so as to bring about acceleration of the limbs and of the system, the acceleration results in changes in positions and velocities, and the latter, like the changes in muscle tension, give rise to *proprioceptive signals*. These signals affect the course of the effector impulses introducing necessary corrections and allowing the central effector apparatus to adapt itself with *plasticity* to changing conditions at the periphery.

In this way the connection between movements and the activity of the nervous system is at once very close and very complex.

The cyclogrametric method of investigation of movements here provides invaluable opportunities for the investigator. It permits the complex registration of the movements of a whole organ or even of the whole body, giving a picture of changes on a space-time grid of coordinates for any required number of points of the body simultaneously. It allows us to pursue this description in terms of very brief time intervals by the use of shutter frequencies of the order of 150-200 per sec and higher. And what is still more important, it allows us to obtain accurate quantitative data from these pictures.

As has been said, the central nervous effector impulses do not immediately reveal themselves in a movement. The concept in elementary textbooks that excitation of the *flexor* muscles results in flexion and that stimulation of the *extensor* muscles results in extension of the joints which they control, was seen to be erroneous even when the cyclogrametric study of movement was first begun. What is incomparably more essential and more frequently encountered is the connection between the active onset of muscular contraction (produced by the effector impulse) and the *acceleration of* the moving organ connected to the muscle. This connection was known to Fischer (43), thoroughly investigated for simple objects by Wagner (75), and taken

as a starting point by our investigational group. For cases where this form
of connection is applicable the cyclogrametric method gives all the data
necessary for investigation, as by this means we may investigate simply, and
with a high degree of accuracy, the acceleration of the movement of any given
portions of the body in which we are interested. In cases of this type the
curves of acceleration may give a very reliable picture of the course of
effector impulses to the extremities on their final common pathway.

In more complex and general cases, where there are large-amplitude
movements of complex kinematic linkages (for example, a whole arm or a whole
leg), the acceleration of particular points may be quite unrelated to the
course of the muscular contractions involved. We are here obliged to turn to
another form of mathematical description - the *resultant moments of forces*
in joints, which can be obtained in the same way from experimental material
by cyclogrametric methods of analysis. These force momenta, the method of
calculation of which was first developed by us in 1928, are values which are
almost directly proportional to the resultant of contractions of all the
muscles around a given joint. For this reason the curves of the changes in
muscular force momenta in one joint or another provide us with a picture
which is extremely close to the real characteristics of the course of
effector impulses in every distinct neuromuscular biomechanical group.

It is now possible to turn to locomotion, in particular to walking. The
analysis of the muscle momenta in the joints of the leg in walking shows
beyond doubt that the curves of muscle force momenta in walking in the
majority of their details are *very close to the curves of the longitudinal*
component of the dynamic forces at the centres of gravity of the limb
segments and systems(i.e. for the component in the direction of the sagittal
axis of the body, from back to front, which we have designated by the symbol
X). The dynamic forces which we calculated on the basis of the linear
acceleration of points by Fischer's method are much more easily obtained from
cyclogrametric material and are numerically more reliable than muscle
momenta. The close correspondence between both forces and muscle momenta in
the act of walking can be explained mainly by the fact that the actions of the
force momenta are always directed perpendicularly to the longitudinal axes
of the limbs. In walking, the deviation of the limbs of the leg from the
vertical is not great; that is to say, lines perpendicular to them deviate
only slightly from the direction of the longitudinal coordinate axis X. It
follows from this that the curves of the longitudinally acting forces in the
leg during walking give quite a reliable *qualitative* picture of the course

of the neuromuscular effector impulses. The curves of the *acceleration* of
centres of joints observed in walking, in their turn, show very close and
regular correspondence to the curves of dynamic forces at the centres of
gravity of the limbs. This allows us, proceeding with critical circumspection
and constantly taking technical precautions, to come to conclusions as to
the course of neuromuscular impulses during walking, not only from the
curves of longitudinally acting dynamical forces, but also from their closest
derivatives - the curves of acceleration for these same elements. The analysis
of the material presented by us (21) has been carried out in this way, in
cases where the calculation of dynamic forces was not possible without
information on the masses of the limb segments and the locations of their
centres of gravity. For running, in which we observe considerable and sharp
deviations of the limb segments from their vertical axes, it was not possible
to proceed with an analysis based only on the accelerations, or even, without
special critical techniques, on dynamic forces, and here the conclusions of
the whole work are based entirely on the calculation of the curves of the
momenta.

It will appear below how complex and varied are the inter-relationships
in various dynamic situations in walking, between the effector impulses,
their most direct reflections - the force momenta - and their more distant
functions - forces and accelerations - and how many characteristic signs
may be recognized in these types of connection which already allow us to
reach conclusions as to the central nervous origin and character of these
and other impulses. It is important here to make another point. *The*
structural elements of the dynamics of a locomotor act may certainly be
deciphered by means of more or less complex mathematical and physiological
alphabets which permit the revealing through them of underlying central
nervous processes.

In the 1890's, in the epoch of the brillant flowering of studies by
Marey, Braune and Fischer, it was not expected that so much would come out
of a study of movement. Marey was chiefly enthusiastic about his new
processes of recording, by the possibilities of halting the fleeting moment
and examining, by this means, what could not be seen by means of the naked
eye. Braune and Fischer were concerned, on the other hand, with correcting
the observations which had accumulated in preceding years and drawing
parallels between them and the more accurate material which they had
collected, and, on the other end, with solving some problems in the field of
the theoretical mechanics of movements, regarding the leg in terms of levers,

pendulums and the other accessories of general theoretical mechanics.

The main advances of our experimental group from those of Braune and Fischer must be briefly stated[*]. We sharply increased the shutter frequences we employed (from 26 exposures per sec, as used by Braune and Fischer, to 60-190 exposures per sec); we increased by many times the quantity of material we employed, we simplified, mechanized and verified our methods of investigation. All this allowed us to study movements in incomparably greater detail than was possible for Braune and Fischer and to obtain highly reliable data because we had more methods of verifying our experimental material and, in particular, because we used a great amount of experimental material, while Braune and Fischer were obliged to restrict themselves to three experiments on a single subject. In close connection with these differences are also the basic differences between our and Fischer's points of view.

Firstly, Fischer's approach was essentially *retrospective*, that is, he was mainly motivated by a desire to order critically the basic information available on the mechanics of the act of walking which had been gathered up to his time. Our approach may be termed *prospective*, as we were not particularly concerned with which details might be found to be reliable and which false in the work of the older authors, but attempted to provide a more reliable and comprehensive *descriptive* basis for a subsequent broad extension of investigation into the genesis and pathology of locomotion. The main object of our investigations into locomotion from the first was to provide for future work as detailed a standard of average normal locomotion as possible, which might then be compared with whatever material might be accumulated in the future.

Secondly, Fischer was interested in the course of walking in the most general and basic terms. Therefore he ignored the details, referring a whole series of details on his photographs to errors of measurement[**]. Fischer supposed *a priori* that the act of walking must display a high degree of mathematical simplicity and dynamic regularity. Apparently for this reason he was satisfied with his very low shutter frequencies. Even those irregularities in the curves which could be retained on the coarse 'sieve'

---

[*]For a more detailed discussion of this, see *Investigations in the Biodynamics of Locomotion*, Vol. I, p. 30, Moscow, 1935.

[**]See *Investigations in the Biodynamics of Locomotion*, p. 11, 1935.

that resulted from his low frequencies - and which, as our investigations
revealed, are indicative of most important biodynamic processes - were
smoothed out by Fischer and declared non-existent.

We, in contradistinction to this, gave most careful attention to these
details - which on our high-accuracy, high-frequency sieve were retained
much more clearly. If Fischer had *a priori* been sure that the movement of
walking is maximally smooth and simple, then we, on the other hand, being
aware of what complex synergy is involved in walking, expected from the
very first to encounter a process of a degree of complexity which had been
completely unrecognized beforehand, and which was in every case certainly
impregnated with live micro- and macroscopic details, just as is living
organic tissue. Our expectations in these respects were fulfilled in the
highest degree. 'The biodynamic tissue' of live movements - of locomotion -
appeared to be full of an enormous number of regular and stable details. In
the course of one complete cycle of movement - one double step - each of the
moving organs appeared to participate in a complex melody of scores of
dynamic waves which followed each other with precision and regularity.
Amongst these there were large and powerful waves, for example, the waves of
the forward and backward thrusts which would have been visible even through
Fischer's weak 'telescope' if he had not smoothed them out of the curves
together with the 'dust-spots' and waves of the second order and, finally,
the smallest objects which are located at the very limit of the resolution
power of our present technology. The transition between stars of the first
magnitude and the faintest visible objects is such a gradual transition,
that without any doubt a multitude of stable particulars in locomotor
processes are still invisible to us; there is considerable reason to suppose
that it is precisely these ultratelescopic objects - these still unresolvable
details of biomechanical tissue - that will seem the most interesting in the
future.

All these circumstances determined the third and, in principle, the
most important aspect of our approach to the study of locomotion. We refused
to theorize about our object of investigation in advance by forcing it to
fit one or other analog in the field of general mechanics. We regarded the
locomotor process as a living *morphological object* of inexhaustible
complexity and set as our primary task the necessity of observing and
describing it as closely as possible.

As early as 1928 (15), I put forward in general terms the concept that
the movements of a living organism could be regarded as morphological

objects. That they do not exist as homogeneous wholes at every moment but develop in time, that in their essence they incorporate time coordinates (in ways different from tissues and organs, for example), and that they are in no way dissimilar to objects in the morphological field of investigation. On the contrary, the concept that movements are in many respects similar to organs (existing, as do organs, in a system of space-time coordinates (x, y, z, t)) appears to be extremely fruitful, particularly when the discussion concerns such stable and general forms of movement as locomotion.

The basic vital properties which exist in the movements of living beings clearly confirm their close analogy to anatomical organs or tissues. Firstly, a live movement *reacts* and secondly it regularly *evolves and involutes**.

I noted and described the former of these properties as early as 1924 (8, 9). Studying the biodynamics of movements involved in cutting with a chisel I was able to show that it is impossible to alter selectively any one given detail in this movement without affecting others. If, for example, the trajectory of the elbow is slightly altered, the form of the trajectory of the hammer is also unavoidably changed, as are the relationships between the velocity of the swing and the impact, and between the velocities of the wrist and of the hammer head, and a whole series of other nuances of the movement.

In subsequent years it was possible to establish from material obtained on walking that the reactivity of movements is extremely selective. Movements react to changes in one single detail with changes in a whole series of others which are sometimes very far removed from the former both in space and in time, and leave untouched such elements as are closely adjacent to the first detail, almost merged with it. In this way *movements are not chains of details but structures which are differentiated into details*; they are structurally whole, simultaneously exhibiting a high degree of differentiation of elements and differing in the particular forms of the relationships between these elements. This justified the analogy

---

*The reactivity of the live structure of movements cannot be simply mechanically related to the reactivity of live organic tissues which take part in the given movement. The discussion does not concern the point that movement is a basic substrate – this would be completely false – but that the forms of the reaction of the material substrates of movement, which determine by their existence the course of a living movement, have quite particular qualitative characteristics.

which I made earlier between the characteristics of living movements and tissues, calling them both biodynamic tissues.

A second property of the movements of a living being has been established for a long time - they develop and involute. However, the problems of the ways in which they develop, and the stages they pass through in this process, etc., have been very little investigated. We will give some account below of the most important results obtained in this direction.

2. THE BASIC STRUCTURAL COMPONENTS OF THE LOCOMOTOR ACT

We shall discuss in general terms the basic biodynamic characteristics of the process of walking (19). These must serve as points of departure for further analysis.

The movement of walking consists, for each leg, in alternation of periods of *support* and *swing-through*. The swing phases are of shorter duration than the periods of support (for running the pattern is inverted), for which reason there are intervals during which one leg has not yet completed and the other has already begun its support phase. We call these intervals periods of *double support*.

The dynamics of the legs in their interactions with the supporting surface have their most clear-cut reflection in the behaviour of the centre of gravity of the whole body. In fact the forces which operate during walking at the centre of gravity of the whole body are equal in magnitude and opposite in direction to the forces which are applied to the supporting

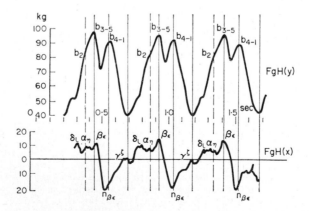

Fig. 22. Curves of forces at the centre of gravity of the whole body during normal walking. Above: vertical components. Below: horizontal components.

surface by the supporting leg or legs. By the principle of the equality of
action and reaction, these forces in the legs are, in their run, equal and
opposite to the support reaction, that is, the reaction of forces in the
surface supporting the body of the walker. For this reason the curve of the
dynamic forces at the centre of gravity of the whole body is exactly the
same as the curve of the support reaction, that is, the curve of the
interaction between the lower extremities and the supporting surface.

Graphs of dynamic forces at the centre of gravity of the whole body
(Fig. 22) are among the types of evidence which may be quite easily
obtained from live movements by the cyclogrametric method. These graphs
incorporate a series of clear-cut and reliably stable elements which are
evident in all normal human subjects without exception. The vertical
component of stresses in the centre of gravity of the body as a whole
$F_{gH}(y)$ displays to high peaks, h and v, which we have termed the backward
and forward thrusts (h-*Hinterstoss*, v-*Vorderstoss*). The rear thrust is
delivered by the leg, standing behind at the beginning of the period of
double support; the front thrust is delivered towards the end of this period,
about 100-200 msec later by the front leg. In this way every period of
double support in walking begins with a rear thrust (with one leg) and ends
with a front thrust (with the other leg). The support period for each leg
begins with its front thrust and ends with the rear thrust. The entire
sequence of events is clearly represented in Fig. 23.

Shortly before the rear thrust the leg that is behind delivers another
vertical thrust of varying magnitude – the auxiliary thrust h'. The middle

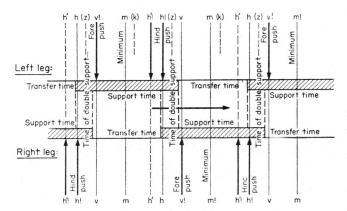

Fig. 23. Diagram of alternation of principal thrust forces in
normal walking (the figure is corrected by data obtained
from recent studies by O. Saltzgeber).

of the single support time - that moment when the swinging foot moves past the supporting foot - corresponds to the principal minimum m of the vertical component $F_{gH}(y)$. At that moment the pressure of the foot on the supporting surface is significantly less than the static weight of the walking subject, whereas, at the moments of the two principal thrusts h and v, it is significantly greater than this weight.

The longitudinal components of the forces at the centre of gravity of the whole body $F_{gH}(x)$ (Fig. 22) are significantly less constant than the vertical components in form, though not in the dynamic elements which they incorporate. These latter always appear in a strict sequential order varying only in their magnitudes and in the nuances of their rhythmical interrelationships. The most significant in amplitude are the direct (that is, forward-directed) thrust β_{ε} which occurs almost simultaneously with the rear thrust h, and the reverse (directed to the rear) thrust $n_{\beta\varepsilon}$ which appears a little before the front thrust v. If we examine both components in their entirety, that is, if we consider the forces at the centre of gravity as a vector, then the alternation in the waves which has been described will be visible in this way: The rear thrust manifests itself at the centre of gravity as a vector directed forwards and upwards which displays a small oscillation forward (β_{ε}) immediately after its maximum (h); the front thrust is a vector directed upwards and backwards ($n_{\beta\varepsilon}$) which deviates slightly further forward at the moment of its maximum (v).

The intermediate stable elements of the curve of the longitudinal components γ_{ζ}, δ_{ι}, χ, α_{η}, are of great value in the co-ordination of the movements of the legs and determine all the details of these movements, but their relation to the movements of the centre of gravity of the whole body is not at present very clear. The wave α_{η} occurs close in time to the auxiliary thrust h'.

The curves of the dynamic forces at the centre of gravity of the segments of the leg and at the centre of gravity of the whole leg may be considered as indicators of the locomotor structure on one side of the body. While the curves of forces at the centre of gravity of the whole body F_{gH} show the periodicity of a single step and reflect in equal measure the dynamics, now of one, and now of the other side of the body (this is the reason for the two-letter symbols which I have given to elements of the longitudinal components), the curves for the segments in the leg display periodicity over a double step. As examples in the present brief discussion of the curves of focus for the legs we may consider the force vector for the thigh (F_{gf}) which is shown in Fig. 24 as curves for the vertical $F_{gf}(y)$ and longitudinal $F_{gf}(x)$ components. This vector is the richest of all the force-vectors in the legs in structural details, for which reason we draw attention to it. The vector for the thigh is, for two reasons, in a particularly favourable position to allow a large number of biodynamic structural details to appear in it. Firstly, the thigh is located at the centre between the 'shin-foot' system at one end and the trunk at the other so that it is simultaneously affected by the operation of both systems and is an arena for the interplay of reactions of support and of forces which originate in the trunk and the contralateral leg. Secondly, its moment of inertia in relation to the hip joint is significantly less than the moments of other distal segments relative to this joint, i.e. the lower leg and foot; for this reason the thigh reacts more sensitively to all the nuances and shifts in the thrust impulses communicated to the leg by the hip musculature.

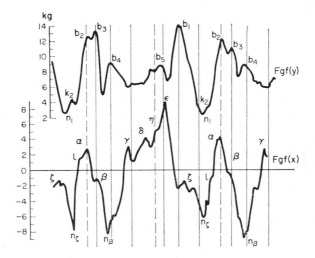

Fig. 24. Force curves at the centre of gravity of the thigh in normal walking. Above: vertical components. Below: horizontal components.

The vertical component of forces at the centre of gravity of the thigh $F_{gf}(y)$ (Fig. 24) is made up of an alternation of high groups of peaks with the raised plateau of the support period, and the deep troughs (n) of the transfer period. The group of peaks after the swing period minimum includes the peaks b_2, b_3, and b_4 if we do not consider the small irregular wave k_2 at the very bottom of the trough n. The peak b_2 coincides in time with the

auxiliary thrust h' and is apparently caused by it. The peak b_3 is an echo
of the rear thrust h of the opposite leg, that is, it directly precedes the
beginning of support by the given leg. The peak b_4 , which is always much
lower than both the previous peaks, is the effect of the operation of the
front thrust by the given leg. The powerful wave of this thrust is transmitted
through the thigh, and the small peak b_4 is a part of this thrust deposited
into the curve of the thigh itself.

The support plateau is terminated by the poorly differentiated low
group b_5 (sometimes b_5-b_5') reproducing the thrusts h' and h on the given
side in the same order as b_4 reproduces the front thrust. There then follows
the high wave b_1 - the reflection of the front thrust on the opposite side -
after which comes the swingphase minimum n_1 .
And so the vertical component of the forces F_{gf} incorporates the main waves
b_2, b_3, b_1 corresponding to the main thrusts on the opposite side and the
lower peaks b_4 and b_5 corresponding to the same thrusts on the given side.
All these elements are stable in normal adult subjects and are repeated in
the same order in the curves for the action of forces in the shin and the
leg as a whole. Except for these force elements, nothing stable and
characteristic is observed in the curve $F_{gf}(y)$ and $F_{g(fsp)}(y)$.

In this way the vertical components of forces in the leg during walking
basically incorporate only elements which reflect the struggle of the moving
organism as a whole with the force of gravity: the after-effects of its
supporting thrusts and the reflections of thrusts on the opposite side. This
completely agrees with what has been said above in section 1; the manifestation
of local muscular activity in walking must be observed mainly in the forces
visible in the curves of the longitudinal components, while in the vertical
components we find only very remote and generalized phenomena directly
related to the integral dynamics of the centre of gravity of the whole body.

For all these reasons it seems that the most comprehensive and
interesting neurodynamic material available to us must be the *curves for the*
longitudinal components in the legs, and this expectation is fully verified.
We may recall the nomenclature which we have adopted for the longitudinal
components of forces.

The most distinct direct (inclined forward) force waves of the curve
$F_{gb}(x)$ have been indicated by the first letter of the greek alphabet in
their sequential order: α, β, γ, δ, ε, ζ. We have designated the reverse
waves by the symbol n with the addition of an index to indicate the prior
direct wave, for example, n_ε is the reverse wave immediately following the

direct wave ε, and so on.

This nomenclature could not be retained in such a simple and schematic way. New smaller waves and previously unnoticed details, etc., are constantly being observed. For this reason we now regard the entire nomenclature we have given as only a series of proper names and we do not seak greater rationality in them than may be found in geographical or astrophysical terms.

The support period of the legs (see Fig. 24) commences with the very marked reverse wave n_{β}. This wave occurs immediately before the front thrust of the given leg and essentially represents the braking effect of the planting of the foot on the supporting surface. In the curve for the forces at the centre of gravity of the body at this moment we observe the appearance of the reverse wave $n_{\beta\varepsilon}$.

During the course of the support period itself there is a gradual stepwise rise in the curve $F_{gf}(x)$. It displays a small rise close to the zero level, γ (between $v!$ and $m!$), a direct wave δ of moderate amplitude height, another higher region with poor relief η (close to h') and, finally, a large direct peak ε at the moment of the rear thrust on the same side.

The gradual jagged rise γ-δ-η corresponds to the steady increase of the horizontal velocity of the thigh, particularly its distal end; that is, it reflects the increase in the activity of the supporting leg pressing on the ground. The wave ε, the last and distinct direct peak of the curve $F_{gf}(x)$, occupies precisely the same dominant position in the curves for the shin and foot, and sharply falls after the rear thrust. From this point on, that is to say, from the beginning of the swing period on, the forces in the thigh display a course which is quantitatively different from those at the centres of gravity of the whole leg and its lower segments, but there nevertheless remain the same structural elements common to all moving organs, which are only disposed differently in relation to the axis of the abscissa (Fig. 25).

The direct element of the curve $F_{gf}(x)$ following immediately after ε is the jagged region ζ located between the front thrust v and the minimum m for the opposite leg. In the curve for the centre of gravity of the whole leg this region is located a little above the zero level (in the direct waves), whereas in the curve for the thigh it lies below zero (in the reverse waves). It is preceded in the curve $F_{gf}(x)$ by the reverse wave n_{ε}

---

*The exclamation mark is used to designate the main thrusts on the same (ipsilateral) side of the body.

and terminates in another reverse wave n_ε. The reason for the different
disposition of the region ζ in different curves is explained below; at
present it need only be said that the reverse waves n_ε and n_ζ represent the
braking effect, which begins at this point, on the forward velocity of the
leg (and of the knee joint) which is accompanied by increases in the
longitudinal velocities of the foot and the shin. The muscle forces in the
hip and knee joints during the period represented by the region ζ are
extensory (Fig. 25) so that the braking of the thigh is reactively provoked
by peripherally operative forces.

Following n_ζ in the curve $F_{gf}(x)$ there appears a high and compact
group of waves, the summit of which constitutes the wave α. This direct
wave only exists in the thigh; for the shin and the foot we have at this
point the reverse wave n_α. At that moment there are also reverse waves in
the curves of the force moments at the hip and knee joints (Fig. 29). In
this way the wave α for the thigh is not a resultant of muscle action, but
is reactively produced by the periphery in the same way as is the braking
effect on the knee in area ζ which has been noted above. The wave α and its
functional pair n_α correspond closely in time with the supplementary thrust
in the opposite leg h'.

Almost merging with α in the curve for the thigh we find the trace of
a sharp peak β (the phase h in the opposite leg), in which, however, all
the signs indicate quite another process than that at α. Firstly, this
rise is observed in the form of a direct peak in all curves for the leg
while there is no trace whatever of α in the curves for the shin and the
foot. Secondly, as will be shown below, the whole history of the development
of this peak β is radically different than that for α. By these means we
ascertain that it is related to its neighbour not functionally, but as 'an
optical pair'[*].

This, in its most general features, is the framework of the structure
of the longitudinal forces in normal adult walking. We may deduce from the
inventory of the primary properties of the force impulses, which determine
the stepping movements of the leg in walking given above, that these are
certainly not limited to one simple pair of impulses, a forward impulse and
a backward impulse, for each double step. Examples of such reciprocal
impulses might be, for instance, ε and n_β which operate practically

---

[*] *Translators note*: The distinction made in astronomy between physical and
                        optical pairs in the case of double stars.

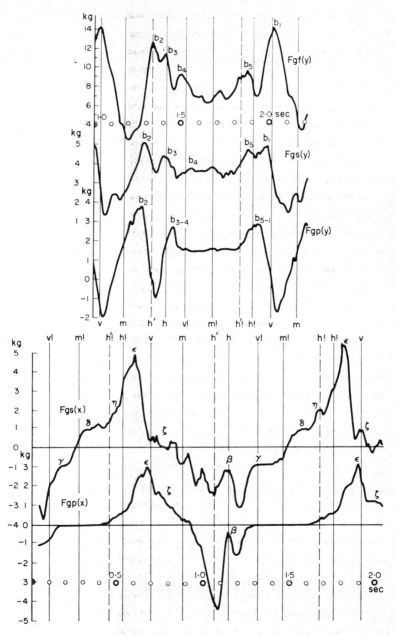

Fig. 25. Curves of thrust forces at the centres of gravity of the
limbs of the leg in normal walking. Above: vertical components
of the thigh, shin and foot. Below: longitudinal components
for the shin and foot.

simultaneously in both legs in opposite directions to one another. The facts
of the matter make evident that this most simple pair will not in any way
exhaust the data. The multiplicity of elements interacting regularly with
one another and making up a complex and idiosyncratic rhythm of alternation
gives to the dynamics of each separate step a radically different physiognomy
from that which may be observed in the simple stepping reflex in a
decerebrate preparation. All these elements are strikingly constant and
general, they occur in precisely the same unchanging sequence in all the
longitudinal force curves for all the elements of the leg and the trunk in
normal walking, they retain this constancy of structure in all normal
subjects and they remain the same even in a whole series of central nervous
system disorders. Further these very structural elements, in this precise
sequence, are retained in a form of locomotion as qualitatively different
from walking as running; and gross peripheral disturbances of structure,
such as amputation, are necessary before they are lost to any significant
degree. All this indicates that the structural elements of muscle action
which have been described above are not in any way accidental, they are of
essential co-ordinational significance for the locomotor act and that to all
appearances they must consequently have a peculiar genesis, history and
basis in the central nervous system or elsewhere. The confirmation of all
these suppositions is the basis for the material discussed in this work (21);
in subsequent sections we shall examine the facts which relate to these
topics.

3. THE GENESIS OF THE BIODYNAMICAL STRUCTURE OF THE LOCOMOTOR ACT

The first fact revealed to us by our study of the ontogenesis of
walking and running in the child was that *biodynamic structures live and
develop*.

All the numerous elements which were briefly described in the preceding
sections, and which were there irrefutably shown to participate in the co-
ordinational formulation of an act of locomotion, are absent from the walk
of a child which has just started to walk by himself. Considering the
longitudinal acceleration curves of the child, in the first day of
independent walking only the direct wave ε is present in the leg as a whole;
the reverse wave n_α in the foot is accompanied by its functional pair α in
the thigh; and the region for the hip joint is, as we see, entirely
different from the adult ζ. There are no traces of β, γ, δ, η, θ, or ι.

This picture is retained during the whole of the 1st year of walking, that
is to say, until nearly the 2nd year of life.

In other words, in the whole of the muscular-dynamic inventory of the
child in the first months of the development of his walk we may observe
only one pair of independent muscle impulses ε and n_α,[*] the identical
simplest reciprocal pair which we have described in the previous sections
and which were believed by physiologists of the last century to explain the
entire muscular dynamics of walking in adults. The other two waves which
are observed in this early stage of ontogenesis have essentially a peripheral
origin; namely, the purely reactive-mechanical α which arises in the thigh
as a reaction to the active muscle stress n_α, and the reactive pair $\zeta - n_\varepsilon$
for which the same is true. The impulses ε and n_α develop first, and
initially there are no others. I should term this level of development the
innervationally primitive stage.

The following elements of the biodynamic curves develop much later:
within 2 years of birth the infant has, besides the curves mentioned above,
the waves γ and η in the thigh and signs of the beginning of the development
of β in the knee and the ankle joint. These new elements are not yet clear-
cut, and where, for example, tempo is increased, they have a tendency to
disappear.

The whole inventory of dynamic waves develops very slowly, being
complete by about the 5th year. The separate elements very gradually change
over from the group of those which are not constantly encountered, and which
are not observed in every step (γ) to the category of those which are
constant for slow tempos, and finally to the category of unconditionally
constant signs. The development of the adult forms of the structural
elements is also completed slowly, and, for example, even by the 4th year
the 'childish' ζ has not fully given place to the adult version.

In the first place, all this is evidence that the gradual appearance
and consolidation of new structural elements is not in any way related to
the elaboration of elementary co-ordination and equilibrium in walking. By
the age of 3 or 4 the child is not only able to walk without difficulty,
but can also run, hop on one leg, pedal a tricycle, etc. This means that
the mechanisms of co-ordination for all types of locomotor movements and
for the maintenance of equilibrium have been thoroughly elaborated for some
time, whereas the inventory of the dynamic impulses for normal walking is

---

[*]Not n_β as β still does not exist.

still far from complete. A little later on we shall see that the nervous
mechanisms of elementary co-ordination and the maintenance of equilibrium
are illuminated in quite another way by the curves obtained for children.
The basic structural elements which we have just been discussing clearly
have some other significance and are related to finer details of motor
co-ordination.

The development of the structural elements of walking is completed in
a manner which is far from direct. On the contrary, during ontogenesis a
whole series of redundant signs which are not peculiar to adults appear, to
disappear again at adolescence. These childish elements appear very early
among the vertical components. By the 1st year of independent walking, while
the child has only b_1 and b_3 among the whole range of adult components,
there are also apparent, alternating with them, the 'infantile' waves k_1
and k_2. The second of these may also survive in adulthood in the form of a
step k at the bottom of the wave b_2, although the homology of both these
forms has not yet been rigorously proved; k_1 certainly disappears by the
age of 7 appearing again only in cases of amputation in the transverse
components of the forces $F(z)$. The infantile mechanical-reactive wave ζ in
the thigh appears, as we have seen, very early and is maintained during the
course of the entire 1st year of walking. It then falls away like a milk-
tooth; the adult innervationally reactive form of ζ develops in its place
only in the 4th-5th years of life.

An extremely interesting overemphasis of structural details occurs in
the period of development between 5-8 years. During this period all
possible variations of θ, η and ι often occur with very large dimensions;
the vertical infantile thrusts k_1 and k_2 also attain very significant
dimensions as do the horizontal details γ and ι which are still bound in
synchrony to them. This overabundance energetically involutes between 8 and
10 years, but even by the age of 10 the process of formation of the adult
structure has not been entirely completed.

In the course of the development of the biodynamic structure of walking
there also appear qualitative deviations of another type which cast light
upon the gradual mastery of the mechanisms of co-ordination and equilibrium.
In the very first days of independent walking the vertical components of
forces at the centre of gravity of the head of the infant already appear to
be completely ordered and invariable from step to step, although primitive
in form - only the waves b_1 and b_3 may be discerned in them. Meanwhile, the
movements of the head (the curves $S_c(y)$ are extremely chaotic, uneven and

involved. Towards the age of 2 the curves of the vertical forces for the head are gradually enriched by new waves and in extremely close connection with these the curves of *movements* $S_c(y)$ become increasingly more simple and stable. We may relate this to the fact that in various children we observe less intervariance in the curves of forces and accelerations of their heads than in the extremely diverse and individual curves of displacements.

An explanation of these phenomena follows directly from the basic conditions of the structure of movement which were discussed above. The given curve of changes in muscle forces (and it follows, in the simplest cases, of acceleration) cannot alone entirely determine the resulting movements as dependent parameters of integration[*].

The effect of these independent parameters is stabilized in the normal development of the central nervous system by the proprioceptive apparatus; this signalling compels the motor areas of the central nervous system to adapt the form of their effector impulses. If the proprioceptive impulses are interrupted, as occurs, for example, in the classic case of tabes, we

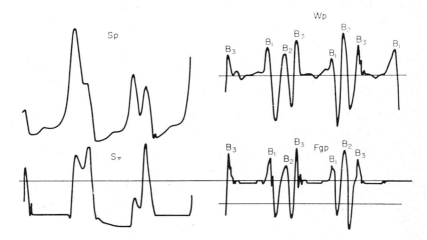

Fig. 26(a). Left side: vertical translations of the ankle and the toe end. Right side: vertical accelerations of the ankle joint and vertical efforts in the foot during two consecutive paces in walking of a patient with tabetical ataxia. It can be seen clearly that a moderate variability of accelerations and efforts in consecutive cycles of movement of a tabetic patient can result in strikingly different forms of translation curves in the same cycles.

---

[*] Mathematically and not in a Sherringtonian sense.

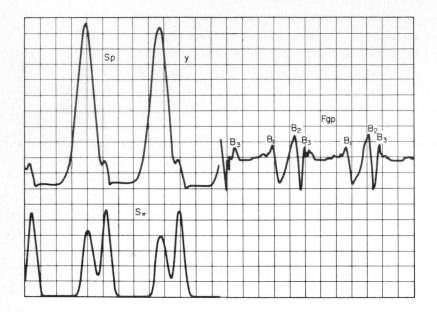

Fig. 26(b). Left side: vertical translations of the ankle and the
toe end. Right side: vertical efforts in the foot during
two consecutive paces in walking of a normal subject.
The curve of efforts shows only a slightly lesser
variability of cycles in comparison with those of the
preceding figure, while the translation curves are
absolutely identical from pace to pace.

obtain as a result extremely regular and constant successive cycles of
forces F and *accelerations W* with completely disordered and dissimilar cycles
of *displacements S*. We have material on tabes among our unpublished data
which provides very clear examples of this type (Fig. 26). We may deduce
from this that the principal and most general symptom of disturbances in
proprioceptor signalling (proprioceptive ataxia) is the *disturbance in
successive cycles of the constancy of S* with (sometimes marked) retention
of *constancy of F and W*.

In small children we are dealing, naturally, not with disorders in
proprioceptive signalling, but only with the slow and gradual appearance of
the mechanisms of adequate response to this signalling. In cases where this
mechanism has not yet been built up we may observe the ataxic symptom which
we have described - the regularity of W and chaotic disorder of S. In this
stage of ontogenesis the spontaneous effector impulses are consequently
already developed (W is in order) while the innervational-reactive impulses
do not operate in conjunction with them.

In locomotion of children there are a whole series of phenomena of this sort which are clearly observable at first, and later grow feinter and feinter. In children who have only just begun to walk there is as a rule no constant correspondence between dynamic phases and the positions of the body. Their phases, appearing in successive steps as the phase of one and the same force waves, are quite unlike each other. For adults, on the other hand, there is an exact repetition of positions in simultaneous dynamic instants (see Fig. 27(a)). Further, for some dynamic waves, for example ζ, the connection between positions and phases is extremely stable and is not even destroyed by very gross changes in gait. The absence of a similar correspondency in small children is naturally an indication of the same relationships seen in the chaotic forms of the S curves; the absence of correct response to proprioception.

In slightly later stages of childhood development when the most elementary mechanisms of locomotor co-ordination have already been mastered, the same symptom of inadequate mastery of proprioceptive signalling appears in a feinter and partly transformed aspect. The situation is the same in the case of the ζ wave, which, when all is considered, is one of the most complex and enigmatic of all the co-ordinational waves. T. Popova observed that the height of the ζ wave in children between the ages of $1\frac{1}{2}$ and 3 years is in very close correspondence with the length of the stride and that apparently the inadequate participation in one or another separate step of the main ε impulses is compensated, so that a step may be correctly made by the incorporation of the ζ wave. In some cases, ζ in this context considerably overshadows the basic ε impulses and in this pattern of walking waves appear which vary considerably in magnitude from step to step. This observation discloses a connection between proprioception and the effector system, but now in a new scheme. Because of the inadequacy of the motor responses, which are not yet proportionally related to the amount and the exact graduations of the force ε (the auxiliary waves δ and $\eta!$ are undeveloped), unequal steps are obtained for constant values of ζ, while for steps of constant length variations in ζ are necessary. In the adult norm it is both the case that ζ are of constant value and that steps are of constant length; this means that even *before the completion* of the main impulse ε an exact regulation of the direct longitudinal forces on the basis of propriosignalling is necessary in carying out steps of constant metric proportions. This preparatory regulation has not yet been developed in the child and it depends on subsequent compensation including the *termination* of the impulse ε. The proprioceptive

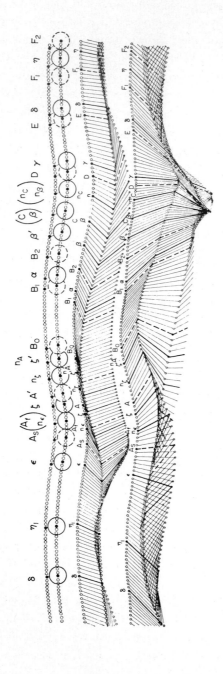

Fig. 27(a). Successive positions of the right side of T. Ladoumeg's body, taken at a frequency of 187/sec in experiment No. 731. Heavy lines mark phases of the movement corresponding to characteristic dynamic phenomena. Continuous heavy lines indicate longitudinal dynamic elements. Heavy dotted lined indicate vertical elements.

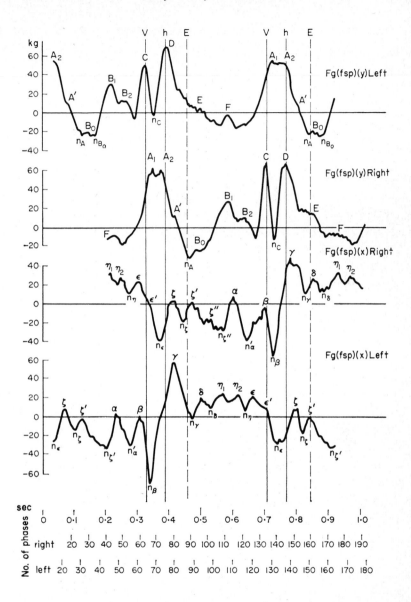

Fig. 27(b). Forces at the centres of gravity of Ladoumeg's right
and left legs. Standard terminology.

activity is still inadequate to allow metric *planning* of movements but is
capable (in distinction to the very earliest stages) of introducing metric
correctives.

The evolution of the locomotor act involves nearly the whole of
childhood and extends almost to the beginning of puberty. The last stage
through which it must pass, which begins to be observable only after the
age of 5, and which disappears only after the age of 10, is the conversion
of an undifferentiated collection of biodynamic elements into a determinate
structure. All the structural elements of walking have developed by the 5th
year and, as has been said above, are still encumbered by a whole collection
of infantile peaks and hillocks for the next few years. However, at the
beginning of this stage of development all the 'teeth' in the curves, both
the 'adult teeth' and the 'milk teeth' although they are already located in
the correct sequential order, have not yet as a whole adopted the *form* which
is characteristic of the adult curve. This form is finally apparent when
regular and constant proportions are established between the elements of the
curve, when the smaller 'half-tone' elements merge and are effaced, and the
larger elements emerge into dominant positions. It is only then that the last
and highest stage of development of co-ordination is completed: the
displacements (S) become regular and of equal lengths, and here neither curves
of forces (F), nor accelerations (W), necessarily vary in order to compensate
for irregularities (as it were, *post factum*, in proprioception), so that it
is possible to maintain a unity of movements without violating the unity of
the force curves (as a result of proprioception *ante factum*).

A similar picture may be observed in the *running* of children. In giving
an account of the adult run, we have been able to show that running considered
as a *neurodynamic* structure displays many incontestable signs of similarity
to walking. This relationship is clearly marked in an analysis in depth of
running, and is in sharp contrast to running regarded as a *biomechanical*
structure in which respect it is in many ways exactly opposite to walking.
The problem of moving the body through space is solved in almost directly
opposite ways in running and walking and a whole series of features of the
structure of innervational processes undergoes basic changes in running in
comparison with walking, notwithstanding the incontestable common genesis
of both processes in the nervous system. This common origin may be studied
and proved with the greatest clarity in the context of the evolution of
running in children, where we clearly observe the common operation of
locomotor structure as well as the gradual course of their biomechanical and

neurodynamic *divergencies*.

In the very earliest phases of development of locomotion (in the 2nd year of life) it is impossible to observe clear differences between running and walking in the child. His run is quite free of the most characteristic sign of a true run - the interval of flight - and is only very slightly different from walking. Only a few dynamic elements similar to those encountered in true running appear at the proximal ends of the legs while the distal ends still present the picture characteristic of walking. All these changes are concentrated in the *support period* in the structure of which all the first signs of divergences are incorporated.

Very gradually, during the 2nd and 3rd years of life, parallel with the mastery of new elements in the curves for walking, we find the development of divergencies in the running curves. The front and rear thrusts of the supporting leg (C and D in Fig. 28(a)) are shifted nearer in time as compared with those observed in the walk of a given child; the longitudinal force waves γ and δ develop in place of the older primary wave ε which is reduced in running and changes its position from the support group γ-δ-η to the transfer group ζ-α; we also observe the first traces of *flight*. It is an interesting fact that the curves of the vertical dynamic components diverge earlier than the curves of the longitudinal components (Fig. 28(b)). If we remember that the former are closely concerned with the integral dynamics of the organism and with its biodynamic activity in its struggle with the force of gravity, whereas the latter mainly reflect the internal more intimate structure of the force impulses in the given extremity, an explanation of this phenomenon may be attempted. It seems to me that the delay in the appearance of divergency in the case of the longitudinal curves in comparison with the vertical is a sign that the reorganization of the movement begins with its biomechanics, that is to say, with the *peripheral parts* of the process (the reorganization of the support interval, the organization of the phase of flight, etc.); this biomechanical reorganization sets new problems for the central nervous system, to which it gradually adapts, mirroring that adaptation in subsequent changes in the longitudinal dynamic curves. This secondary character of *central divergency* is also very marked in another phenomenon which will be discussed a little later, that is, in the diminution of the amplitude of the longitudinal force curves in the qualitative development of running with increasing age.

Though it was necessary in the first stages of the development of running to use care in determining differences from walking, in subsequent

Fig. 28(a). Schemes for positions of the body during phases of the step. n_A downward push in the thigh of the rear leg; C, thrust to the rear by the rear leg; m, limit of raising of the knee to the rear; D, thrust to the rear; E, the last dynamic element of the support period.

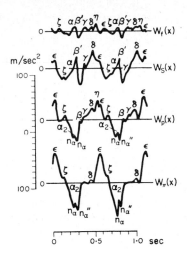

Fig. 28(b). Longitudinal acceleration of the hip (f), knee (s), and ankle (p) joints and of the point of the foot (π) during walking of a child ages 3 years and 5 months. (T.P.; experiment No. 963). The support period is indicated by horizontal lines at the bottom of the graph.

stages (from 2 to 5 years) the basic properties of running are quite incontrovertibly apparent. In this age group the organization of the *transfer period* in running has already begun (firstly the latter half of transfer, then the former). In particular, during this stage of development dynamic novelties appear in the transfer period and, curiously, the overwhelming majority of them appear at the *proximal* points of the lower limbs, while the distal points do not display noticeable signs of divergency for some time. From 2 to 5 years the longitudinal curves for the thigh already display the typical structure of the running swing-phase period in its entirety, while the curves for the foot are still not differentiated from those obtained for walking, even in respect to the support interval.

This prevalent course of evolution and of divergency from above to below, from proximal to distal points, leads to an interesting physiological generalization. It is very improbable indeed that the nerve dynamics of the distal musculature are so sharply different (by a whole year of development) from the dynamics of the proximal muscles. It is much more probable that there is another explanation here. The proximal ends of the legs (for example the hip joints) are surrounded by far more massive muscles than are the distal ends (the feet), while at the same time the moments of inertia of the former are much less than the moments of inertia for the latter. For this

reason the muscles of the hip can move the upper sections of the limbs much
more easily than the foot, since to move the foot they must oppose the
inertia of the entire leg from top to bottom. There is also the fact that
the (relative) velocities are higher as a rule for distal than for proximal
parts, so that the kinetic energies of the former are higher and it is more
difficult to overcome them. The distal parts play roles reminiscent of heavy
flywheels in relation to the legs as a whole.

It follows that the nerve effector impulse at any given strength of its
operation appears far more easily in the proximal curve and is mirrored
there in the form of observable dynamic waves, because it does not have to
overcome all the inertial resistance of the distal system. In order to be
perceptible in this latter system, the effector impulse either must be very
strong or must coincide exactly with the moment when conditions in the
distal system are particularly favourable for its appearance. It is still
to say what these particularly favourable conditions are, and here a wide
field of investigation is opened. It is possible that we have here simply a
convenient position of the extremities which offers the muscles the most
favourable biomechanical conditions of operation; it is possible that this
most opportune moment is a critical moment in the velocity of the limb when
the inertial resistance is least perceptible; finally, it may be the case
that it is at this moment that the degree of excitability of the muscle
apparatus is most receptive because of some favourable concurrence of
proprioceptive signals (this latter hypothesis may be successfully tested
by electrophysiological techniques). In one way or another the control of
the distal parts demands a greater deftness, a higher degree of
co-ordinational technique in respect to the skill of selecting the optimal
moment to give just the right impulse at just the right time. If this
moment is lost, even by a fraction of a second (it must never be forgotten
that all processes in running are measured in terms of hundredths and
thousandths of a second), then the impulse will fail to penetrate; that is to
say, it will not produce any noticeable effect at the periphery.

We must stress here that we are not discussing small co-ordinated
movements of the distal sections such as finger movements, but global general
displacements of distal portions of the body of the extrapyramidal type. The
dynamics of these latter depend, in the last analysis, on the same hip muscles
which control the dynamics of the proximal portions of the legs; the distal
dynamics become, however, richly differentiated in biodynamic detail, not
when these details are incorporated in the effector impulse and are first

reflected in the dynamics of the pliant proximal points, but only when *functional integration of the receptors and effectors* is achieved and when the effector side of the nervous system learns to seize the fleeting moments of functional conductivity.

The reliability of this explanation is well illustrated by observations on the world-famous runner, Jules Ladoumeg. In his case, the dynamic curves of the distal limbs reach their maximum degree of resolution, far exceeding the degree of resolution observable in the curves of other runners; and, further, in his case this degree of resolution was accompanied by a particularly rich set of modulations of forces in the distal limbs corresponding to extremely accurate control of external, biodynamic processes. In the complicated multijointed pendulum, by which the leg may be represented in biodynamic terms, the dynamic interactions of the limbs, the play of reactive forces, the complex oscillations of the links, etc., are extremely varied and abundant; the fact that they are kept in the background in the case of this great runner, but have at the same time such abundant reflections in the dynamic curves, is evidence of the extremely delicate degree of adaptation to proprioceptive signalling achieved by Ladoumeg's neuromotor apparatus. It is precisely this adaptability which allows him a high degree of differentiation and control over the active dynamics of his distal limbs; in his case this is accompanied by a considerable degree of quantitative economy of force.

We may also cite in favour of this explanation an observation made by T. Popova. For a given value of the velocity in running in various children, such of them as have at the time of observation a more differentiated biodynamic structure give as a rule smaller amplitudes of acceleration, that is to say, a smaller range of dynamic forces. In order to arrive at the same final result the child with the qualitatively less differentiated dynamic picture must expend more energy. This can only mean one thing: that a higher degree of resolution of the distal force curves is a sign that the system is learning to seize the moments of least resistance or, to put the matter another way, to utilize the whole rich play of external forces and possibly also the entire physiological (involuntary) gamma reciprocals and other more complex reactive processes at the muscle periphery.

The further development of running in children after the age of 5 closely repeats that for walking and I shall not dwell on it at present.

An analysis of changes in walking in old persons undertaken by

P. Spielberg[*] has reinforced the data discussed above on the *development* of
the structure of the locomotor act with interesting data on its *involution*.
Spielberg distinguishes three involutional stages in the walking of old
people. In the first of these stages some decrease in the normal activity
of the structural mechanisms of walking can already be discerned, but this
decrease is effectively compensated for by the involvement of the higher
psychic functions in the realization of the act of walking: consciousness,
voluntary attention, and so on. In the second stage of involution this
alerting of consciousness gives way to a heightened degree of fussiness,
hyperproduction of movements, hasty and short steps, etc. The inventory of
the dynamic structural elements becomes poorer; the vertical wave b_2 for
the foot gradually diminishes and then disappears (in early childhood this
wave develops, on the other hand, last of all), then the peak of the
longitudinal component β undergoes attrition. The reactive wave α is
retained longer. In the third stage we observe gross dissolution of the
structure of movement. The force curves become small in amplitude and
impoverished in terms of their components. They lose element after element.
Meanwhile, the equality between successive steps disappears and irregularity
begins with alternation of relatively large and small steps and deeper signs
of disco-ordination (disorder of the forms of the S curves). To this picture
of decay we may also add P. Spielberg's observation of the disintegration
of normal unitary co-ordination. The synergy existing in normal walking
between the action of the arms and legs is destroyed, the movements of the
arms become arrhythmical and the amplitude of these movements gradually
diminishes to zero, after which the arms are stretched our rigidly slightly
in front of the body - as if in constant readiness to support the body in
case of falling. The vertical amplitude at points of the feet is still
perceptible, but amplitudes for the upper portions of the body rapidly
decline to zero, destroying the normal proportion between movements of the
upper and lower portions of the body. In extreme senescence a man eventually
has force curves which are as devoid of peaks as his jaws are of teeth.
Among the force curves there survive only the earliest reciprocal elements
ε and n_a (not counting α) and some vestiges at times of ζ, and at times of
γ or η. The dying of the structure is clearly marked in this material[**].

---

[*]   This study was undertaken at the Laboratory of Physiology of Movement
      of the All-Union Institute of Experimental Medicine.
[**] In recent times, extensive and interesting studies of senile gait have
      been published by R. Drillis (81).

In this way the ontogenetic material has shown us beyond all doubt that the biodynamic structure of walking emerges, passes through a series of regular stages of development, and then regularly involutes in senescence. Most important in principle is the fact that this development is related to extremely determinate *qualitative* changes in the structure itself. In respect to its *morphology*, this structure passes in early ontogenesis through: (a) a reciprocal innervationally primitive stage; (b) a stage of gradual development of morphological elements; (c) a stage of abundant proliferation of these elements; and (d) a stage of inverse development of infantile elements and the final organization of complete and proportional forms.

In their relations to *motor co-ordination* the biodynamic structures of walking pass through a series of qualitatively different stages of development in exactly the same way.

(1) At the beginning we encounter the signs of general hypofunction of proprioceptive co-ordination. There is no correspondence between positions and dynamic phases; there is no unity of S for the existing adjustment between W and F; there is no similarity of S for various children.

(2) Later the child passes through a stage of development of proprioceptor co-ordination *post factum* (compensation by means of secondary co-ordination) and only significantly later on develops:

(3) Co-ordination *ante factum*, or more accurately, *in facto* (adjustment or primary co-ordination).

It is perfectly natural to compare these sequences in morphological and functional development. This comparison may give as a key with which to decipher the meaning of particular morphological phenomena.

We may first suppose that the initial ontogenetically earliest (and clearly also phylogenetically the most ancient) impulses ε and the infantile n_a are *spontaneous preproprioceptive impulses*. They represent the original and most ancient framework of movements, their rhythmic and dynamic basis. All the waves developing later, which are brought forth during the period of the development of compensatory co-ordination, are already indubitably effector responses to proprioceptive signals; we have termed these waves *innervationally reactive*. Among these waves we have, for example, ζ and β. The connections between the positions of a moving organ and its velocity must be biodynamically characteristic for these waves.

Finally, the appearance of forms and of concrete proportionalities in

the dynamic curves is deeply involved with the development of compensatory
co-ordination, that is, with the activity of those highly organized
apparatuses of the central nervous system which ensure the completion of the
entirety of a projected movement, the definition and accuracy of movements,
etc.

And so we have established at least three forms of elements among the
component waves of the biodynamic structure which differ from each other in
essential ways: (1) *spontaneously innervated*, the earliest and most primary
(ε and n_a); (2) *reactively innervated* (γ, ζ, β); and (3) *mechanically
reactive* which do not have as their basis either innervational impulses or
changes in muscular activity, but which arise entirely at the periphery as
a result of the complex collision of internal and external forces in the
kinematic linkage of the extremities. Amongst these mechanically reactive
waves we may place α, which will be discussed further, and a whole series of
other smaller waves.

4.   A SKETCH OF THE QUALITATIVE ANALYSIS OF THE BIODYNAMIC ELEMENTS OF THE LOCOMOTOR ACT

In the 'constellations' of biodynamic elements which we have observed
and studied, the degree of visibility and clarity of the individual
elements and the degree of investigational interest they possess, are not
always coincident. This has been the case in regard to astronomical
constellations, where very often objects of the first magnitude, the 'alpha'
of the constellations, have considerably less scientific interest than some
quite faintly discernible phenomena such as 'delta' of Cepheus, which not so
long ago was epochmaking in astrophysics. However, the large and bright
objects are always noticed first and they provide the investigator with an
impetus towards the examination of their fainter fellows.

This also occurred in the present study in the case of the first
magnitude star of the α wave. At present this wave is of considerably less
interest to us than such weak and nebulous objects as the ζ group in walking,
or the A' and $n_{B}2$ waves in running, but it originally guided our
investigational group towards the study of waves in general. For this reason
it deserves a short general characterization.

The tension of the flexor musculature at the knee results in the bending
of the lower leg and foot backwards *relative to the knee*, though the
movement in space of the knee itself and of the thigh with it, is not
predetermined by this. According to the basic principles of biomechanics the

musculature at the knee cannot displace the centre of gravity of the leg as a whole either forwards or backwards, but only along the straight line joining it to the hip joint, that is to say, in walking, only upwards or downwards. For this reason the isolated operation of the musculature at the knee moving the lower leg and the foot backwards inevitably moves the thigh forwards in compensation. The same *forward* displacement of the thigh is effected even in a case where it is itself pulled gently *backwards* by the action of the hip musculature, especially because this latter must surmount significantly higher moments of inertia than the musculature at the knee.

In this way the result may be that, should the moment of flexion in the hip muscles be not much greater than the moment of flexion at the knee,

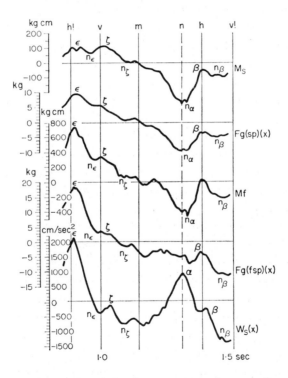

Fig. 29. Curves for the muscle force moments in normal walking compared with curves for the forces and accelerations of the limbs of the legs. From top to bottom: 1, the force moments in the knee joints; 2, the longitudinal components of acceleration at the centre of gravity of the shin-foot system; 3, the force moments in the hip joints; 4, the longitudinal components of the forces at the centre of gravity of the leg as a whole; 5, the longitudinal components of acceleration at the knee joint.

there occurs only a very slight backward displacement of the centre of
gravity of the leg as a whole, whereas the momentum at the knee can effect
considerable flexion of the more compliant shin-and-foot system relative to
the knee. As a result the thigh will be displaced *forward* in spite of the
fact that the hip muscles are pulling it backwards. If it were not for this
pull the thigh would be displaced even further forward; for it not to be
moved forward at all it would be necessary for the flexing force of the hip
muscles to reach a significantly higher level. So towards the end of the
swing period, forces which operate *forward* arise in the thigh in spite of
the fact that the whole of the surrounding musculature, both at the knee
and at the hip joints, is pulling *backwards* at that moment (Fig. 29). This
constitutes the force wave α which we term *reactive-mechanical* for the quite
logical reason that it arises in opposition to the muscle forces at a given
moment, entirely as a result of the peripheral interplay of action and
reaction in the complex kinematic linkage of the leg.

It is clear that if the knee joint were to be immobilized in any way
the wave α would rapidly disappear.

This is confirmed in fact. In *Handbuch der normalen und pathologischen
Physiologie*[*] is cited a cyclogrametric of the forms of the curves for the
longitudinal velocities of the knees in the walk of a subject with strained
ligaments at the knee joints. Because of pain in the joints this patient
walked carefully avoiding flexing his knee joints (antalgic walking) and as
a result there is no sign of the α wave in the curve obtained for his knee
(this wave forms a second smaller prominence in the normal velocity curve
for the knee (see Fig. 29, on left). We have also tested this position
experimentally. A healthy subject had his knee joints splinted and bandaged,
and as a result the α wave entirely disappeared from the curves or was at
least very much reduced. The latter fact may be explained by some 'leakage'
of the flexibility of the knee as a result of the bandages not having been
tied tightly enough. It is interesting that under all these conditions the
β wave which, in normal walking, almost merges with the α wave, and is
difficult to distinguish from it with the naked eye on normal curves for the
thigh, becomes completely isolated, and begins to tower above the remnants

---

[*] W. Steinhausen, Mechanik des menschlichen Körpers, *Hdb.d.norm.u.path.
Physiol.*, Vol.15, part 1, p. 215, from my papers in the handbook *Problems
of the Dynamics of Bridges*, edn. 63, p. 67, Moscow. See also Ref. 15.

of the α wave. All this gives final and conclusive proof that α is a reactive-mechanical curve. We found an opportunity to put this problem to experimental verification, which now leaves no doubt in the matter. † A subject with a very short above-knee amputation had an artificial limb which replaced the lower section of the thigh, the knee joint and the shin and foot. It was possible to lock the knee joint or to give it some passive flexibility restricted on both sides by elastic buffers. When this subject walked with the knee joint locked, as can be seen in the cyclograms, the curves of movement do not show the smallest trace of α; when, however, the lock was left open, the artificial limb immediately began to reproduce the phenomenon of α in walking (Fig. 30). It would be difficult to prove more completely the essentially mechanical nature of this phenomenon[*].

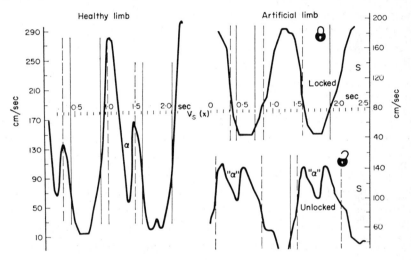

Fig. 30. Appearance of force and reactive wave α at the knee hinge of a prosthesis after unlocking of the hinge (from a study by O. Saltzgeber carried out at the Central Institute for Study of the Disabled).

We must at once admit that it appears, on the basis of our most recent observations, that the α phenomenon is not entirely *mechanically reactive*. Some accessory phenomena of an innervationally reactive type begin to be apparent in this wave. The appearance of α in running is not limited to the

---

[†] A study by the Candidate for Medical Science, O. Salzgeber, carried out in the central Institute for Study of the Disabled, N.K.S.O.

[*] The flexing force of the knee muscles necessary for the appearance of the α phenomenon is replaced in this case by the force of the springs in the knee joint of the artificial limb.

single simultaneous pair of waves n_α-α, but gives rise to an entire chain
of successive waves. This might be expected as, in life, no phenomenon is
exhaustively described by any single explanation.

It is possible to count very many mechanically reactive waves in
locomotion and there certainly exist even more mechanically reactive
components which are part of phenomena of another type. Among mechanically
reactive waves we may enumerate, for example, the childhood ζ which is an
echo of the force n_ζ (the beginning of the main reverse wave n_α); the waves
n_α and n_ϕ of the Prussian goose-step, and so on. We may include among
mechanically reactive components the lowering of the ζ area in the thigh as
compared with the centre of gravity of the whole leg in normal walking,
indicating the effect of reverse reaction in the thigh as a result of the
tension ζ of the extensor muscles of the knee. We may also refer to this
category the passive maximum flexion of the knee in running, which occurs
in spite of the quite considerable and long-lasting tension of its extensor
muscles. By thoroughly studying one representative of such a family we may
now quite easily establish its position in the same family of less distinct
objects. It is only necessary to formulate common characteristics by which
these may be recognized.

The basic indication of mechanically reactive waves is the presence, in
the curves expressing linear force or acceleration of a limb, of any waves
which are absent in the corresponding moments in the curves of muscle
momenta of the nearest proximal joints. This most essential sign answers the
question of the mechanically reactive nature of a wave at once and without
further argument. To employ here another of the terms popular with
morphologists, the curves of momenta are the best reagents for the
recognition of elements of this type.

The second indication is less rigorous and less general, but is
nevertheless more conveniently used in the majority of cases, as the
'momentum reagent' is very time-consuming and therefore expensive. The
condition is that the mechanically reactive wave always arises as an offshoot
of another active wave, making itself felt in one of the intermediate limb
segments. From the explanation of the α wave given above it is apparent that
the mechanically reactive wave arises because it is impossible for the
internal muscles of a system to displace the centre of gravity of the system.
Because of this, if the internal muscles communicate an acceleration to a
single link in one direction, another link will undergo compensatory
acceleration in the opposite direction in a mechanically reactive manner.

The second indication mentioned above follows from this: if, in two adjacent limbs of a freely moving system (for example, in the swing of a leg), there exist two simultaneous waves in opposite directions, it is almost always the case that these are a mechanically reactive pair and that one of the elements represents a reaction of the recoil type.

It goes without saying that a very careful analysis of the surrounding phenomena is necessary here in order to recognize which of the two waves of a pair is active and which is reactive, and whether it is possible to regard the phenomenon as being entirely mechanically reactive or whether innervational components are incorporated in it.

The meaning of this analysis is quite clear. It is only after eliminating from the picture of a movement such components as are imposed upon it from the periphery that it is possible to say that it really reflects the internal processes of innervation. Braune and Fischer, in their time, thought that it was possible to go about the matter in the opposite, synthetic way by setting determinate dynamic conditions and attempting to resolve the manner in which the complex, many-linked pendulum of a limb must move under these conditions. The problem is completely unresolvable mathematically if approached in this way because of its extreme difficulty. We have chosen the other approach, which is much easier, and which is in any event always possible. We take the evidence of real live movements which are already established and integrated by nature, and we then gradually free them of all their external mechanical components, that is always possible by analytical methods. After this preparation only the central innervational core of a movement remains and this is appropriate for further purely physiological investigation to reveal how, and in what way, the discrete events occur.

At present we stand only at the very beginning of this study. Much time has been spent on the development of techniques and not a little on the formulation of the questions. Nevertheless, some observations, still difficult to systematize, have already begun to accummulate in directions that reveal the nature of biodynamic elements. Some of these observations I summarize here.

If the curves for the forces in various limbs of the body are examined together, in terms of the same somponent, then it is at once strikingly obvious that whole series of these elements are common to all limbs. In all the curves for a given moment there occurs, with a greater or lesser degree of synchrony, a distinct direct wave (maximum wave) or a reverse wave (minimum wave). In other cases this generality is not apparent, and sometimes the maximum wave of one limb or system corresponds more or less in time with the minimum wave of another limb or system. We designate waves of the first type as *univocal* (i.e. single-signed), and waves of the second type as *contravocal* (i.e. opposite-signed). Exceptions are almost unknown to the rule that the *point of the body on one side of which the waves are univocal, and after passage through which they become contravocal, incorporates the active dynamic source of these waves*. If at any given moment all points of the leg located below the knee display greater or lesser synchrony at the maxima of their force curves, while, above the knee, instead of the maximum there appears a minimum in the curves of the same components, this signifies that the dynamic cause of all the waves which have been examined lies in the musculature about the knee. We see an expression of this law both in the case of the reactive pair $n_a-\alpha$ described above and in the case $n_\varepsilon-\zeta$ in the walking of children.

It follows from this observation that if any given wave can be followed in the same form through the entire length of a given limb, the source of arousal of this wave is located outside this limb. In this way we may be sure that the sources of the b_1, b_3, b_4, b_5 waves of the main vertical thrusts in walking lie outside the leg, since they appear as univocal waves in all the force curves of the leg. Moreover, as these waves are univocal for both sides of the body they cannot be referred to the hip musculature of one leg - yet another proof of their high degree of integration.

The same cannot be said of the b_2 wave in the thigh (see Fig. 24), which we see to be in almost exact synchrony with the trough (minimum) n_2 in the curve for the vertical forces in the shin and foot. The change of signs takes place in the region of the knee, which means that the musculature of the knee is somehow involved in the appearance of this pair b_2-n_2 (it can hardly be involved on its own because the case is complicated by the absence of a strict synchrony between b_2 for the thigh and n_2 for the shin and foot).

Clearly, most longitudinal waves in the swing period (other than α) arise outside the leg; in the curves for running it is possible to follow the univocality of the majority of these waves over an interval approximately from δ to ζ with particular clarity. At the same time the origin of these waves is clearly established by the circumstance that the waves simultaneous with them in the other leg are opposite in sign to the former (see Fig. 27(b)); this means that the source of the force lies in the hip musculature - in the region joining one leg to the other.

There are signs which allow us to specify, in many cases, not only the muscular region where a given element appears but also its deeper innervational properties. We are obliged to consider a number of cases (running, marching, etc.) where the force wave rises and falls in strict parallellism with changes in the angle of articulation; the more strongly, for example, the hip joint is extended, the more intensive becomes the flexion moment in this joint. The maximum of the angular displacement and the maximum of the force or of the moment become almost absolutely synchronous, or the maximum of the force lags by a few milliseconds in relation to the maximum angular displacement. This relationship leaves no doubt of the fact that the given wave is a reflex produced by the extension of a muscle group; a reflex of the myotatic or Eigenreflex type, etc. Similar phenomena are also regularly encountered in running (the n_A wave), in the goose-step (n_2), and in stepping tot three-part time (n_1). Apparently these occur only under conditions of very considerable angular displacement of the limbs from their mean positions.

There are waves which display very little relationship to the degree of angular displacement, but a very close correspondency to position. As we have already said above, in general the majority of dynamic phases in normal healthy walking are very closely related to the specific positions in which they occur. This is an indication that proprioceptive elements are involved in all of them. Some waves are, however, more easily separated from their usual positions by changes in the type of locomotion than are others. So, for example, we may be sure that in the various forms of marching the ζ wave is so indissolubly linked with the positions normal to it in walking that even the usual order of succession of waves is destroyed. Usually, in normal walking ζ begins after the reflection of the front thrust b_1, but at the precise moment when the leg reaches the ζ position. The b_1 wave is displaced by the conditions of the change in gait, but the ζ wave is not.

In running, a wave which corresponds to ζ in all respects begins, however, at another position of the leg than in walking. It is possible that we are not justified in calling this a ζ wave and it is also possible that it is simply the case that there are in general no positions in running that resemble the ζ position for walking, so that the entire kinematics of the transfer of the leg are completely different in the two cases.

This question as to the extent to which it is permissible to apply to one or another wave the symbol of a wave which has already been investigated in the context of quite another form of locomotion leads on to a very

important general question: to what degree are waves which we have
designated by the same symbols in various forms of locomotion really
homologous and not simply analogous?

This question has been analysed by us primarily in relation to three
groups of objects: in walking of children, running and military marching.
In all these cases we have come to the conclusion that among the dynamic
waves of various forms of locomotion we undoubtedly encounter analogies
which have only an external mechanical relationship with each other and
gross differences in their nature (for example, the n_2 wave in the Prussian
goose-step and the n_1 wave in the triple-time step); however, it is usually
not difficult to distinguish these from true homologs. In general, all the
data on the course of the development of movements, and a careful analysis
of qualitative variations, indicate that the waves to which we have given
a single name in all these types of locomotion are real genetic homologs in
the overwhelming majority of cases. Nevertheless, the question, for example,
of the nature of the integral waves of the vertical components is still
sufficiently complicated for us not to be able to establish any homology
between running and walking, so that we have given the vertical curve for
running a separate nomenclature.

Important material for the determination of internal similarity of
different waves may be obtained by observing the chronology of these waves.
We have only just begun an analysis of components of this type, but it is
necessary to say a few words on the topic at this point. If we study the
waves of the curves of various points of the limbs it appears that waves
which are absolutely synchronous at all points of the limbs do exist (for
example, ε' or n_{B2} in running), but only as extremely rare exceptions. Any
given wave usually runs along the limb from top to bottom, or from bottom
to top; some waves pass through these stages faster than others. The classic
central spontaneous waves ε and n_α move along the leg from top to bottom –
from the centre to the periphery. Waves which are reactive thrusts from
external forces spread from the point of application of these forces, for
example, the supporting front thrust C in running. It is still difficult
to say whether this is absolutely correct.

It is interesting that for a number of waves which have been studied
the velocity of the passage along the limb is close to the velocity of
passage of a nerve impulse along a neuron. This raises a series of very
interesting problems which will definitely form topics of investigations
in the immediate future.

5. CONCLUSIONS TOWARDS THE STUDY OF MOTOR CO-ORDINATION

It is necessary as a general summary of this chapter to say a few words indicating in what respect the material published here will offer new points of departure for the understanding of motor co-ordination.

The understanding of motor co-ordination, like many other scientific goals, has been achieved by a negative method – through observation of the phenomena of lack of co-ordination – and has been only gradually enriched by the accumulation of observations on pathological movement. Like all knowledge acquired by negative means it has constantly suffered, and suffers at present, from the absence of accurate determinations.

Knowledge about the processes of co-ordination is not obtained deductively from knowledge of the effector process. Until the present, while the moving periphery has been regarded as an exact somatic projection of the central effector apparatus, reproducing in the form of movements with particular exactitude and simplicity all those chains of effector impulses which operate in it, there has seemed no need for any special physiological organization in the form of co-ordination. If the centre transmits a regular and efficient chain of effector impulses to the periphery, it will appear at the periphery in the form of equally regular and efficient movements; if the chain of central effector impulses is irregularly and inefficiently organized, its peripheral projection will also be an irregular and badly organized movement. But in both cases the movements will be *co-ordinated*, that is, they will accurately reflect what is contained in the central impulse. Both of them will be accurately fulfilled (reflected) at the motor periphery, in exactly the same way as a grand piano reflects with equal accuracy the playing of a good or a bad pianist.

Knowledge of co-ordination ought to be applied to the explanation of the effector process only from the moment when it becomes clear that the motor periphery does not have such rigid mechanical connections with the centre as were taken for granted in the preceding examples. *Movements are not completely determined by effector processes*.

But, if it is inadequate to send to the periphery any completed effector impulse in this way, and it is still necessary to attend to the periphery to ensure that it has obeyed by being moved in the required direction, there must exist together with the initial effector system more or less complicated auxiliary systems which ensure constant and complete *control* of the periphery by the centre. The deeper the functional gap with the absence of univocality

between the centre and the periphery, the more complex and unstable is the
real relationship between impulses and movements; the greater (in
mathematical language) are the number of degrees of freedom of the motor
periphery relative to the central effector, the more complex and delicate
must be the organizational control to which we have referred. This
organizational control is motor co-ordination.

In this context the idea of co-ordination is in the closest relationship
to the idea of *functional non-univocality* of the connections between the
motor centre and the periphery, between impulses and effects. The more our
knowledge of the forms and types of these univocalities increases, the deeper
becomes our understanding of the co-ordination of movements.

At present a whole series of sources of this indeterminacy are known.
In the first place we must recall the *anatomical* sources described earlier.
The fact of the presence of a large number of degrees of freedom of movement
at the joints, and more so in the complex kinematic chains found in the
make-up of the organism, provides very many conditions for indeterminacy.
Among these we may count the impossibility of the existence of fixed
anatomical antagonists at many joints; the variation in the function of one
and the same muscle group at a multiaxial joint in relation to the disposition
of the limb segments; the multiplicity of action of muscles, first described
by Fischer, where they act on more than a single joint, and so forth. Amongst
anatomical sources we must also mention the fact of multiplicity of innervation
of the skeletal muscles, resulting in their convergent motor dependence on a
whole series of conduction pathways both in the central and in the autonomic
nervous systems.

Next there are a number of sources of indeterminancy of *a mechanical*
order such as we attempted to investigate in experimental terms. Among basic
facts of principal significance in this respect we must include, first, the
fact described above of a closed dependence between muscle tensions and
movements - a fact establishing the presence of indeterminancy in strictly
mathematical expressions and directly pointing to the necessity for at least
two conditions of integration independent of the primary effector impulse.

The second principal fact in this group is the existence of a high
degree of mechanical complexity in the multisegmental kinematic chains (of
the limbs and, in particular, of the body as a whole) which conditions the
great abundance of all sorts of reactive forces and moments in these chains
and makes them extremely capricious and uncertain instruments for the
fulfilment of movements. We should note here that the mathematical theory

of pendulums with many links is extremely complicated and leads to solutions
only for a few particular cases, and that so far we have been quite unable
to employ multilinked kinematic chains in which more than a single degree of
freedom is used at one time in contemporary technology.

The third group of sources of indeterminacy has begun to be described
only during the last 10 or 20 years as new data have been obtained. This is
the *physiological* group. In this group we must include all such data as
give evidence of selective relationships between the motor periphery and
effector impulses reaching it. If in previous years the pathway followed by
the effector impulse from the giant pyramidal area of the cortex to the
myoneural plates appeared to be (functionally) continuous and uninterrupted,
now the matter must be considered in a new light. The selective and
integrational character of the function of the synapses at the anterior horns
has already been explained by Sherrington. The principle of isochronism of
Lapicque may serve as a possible explanation of these phenomena. The
observations of Adrian's school on the spinal transforms of rhythms when
compared with the abundant material on lability and parabiosis emphasize
still more the physiologically active nature of the latter synapses. The
selective character of myoneural transmission has been demonstrated by
Lapicque and has also been elucidated in an original way in the studies of
Paul Weiss. The active filtering role of the motor periphery in respect to
the impulses that reach it appears to hold true for all these data, as does
the fundamental dependence of this activity not on the central relationships
but on the afferentational field.

All these many sources of indeterminacy lead to the same end result;
which is that the *motor effect of a central impulse cannot be decided at the
centre* but is decided entirely at the periphery: at the last spinal and
myoneural synapse, at the muscle, in the mechanical and anatomical changes
of forces in the limb being moved, etc. It is thus obvious that the decisive
role in the achievement of motor control must be played by *afferentation* and
that it is this which determines the physiological conductivity of the
peripheral synapses and which guides the brain centres in terms of the
mechanical and physiological conditions of the motor apparatus. The central
effectors achieve co-ordination of movements only by plastically reacting to
the totality of the signals from the afferent field, adapting the impulses
transmitted to the situation that actually obtains at the periphery.

Co-ordination is therefore a type of complex sensory motor reflex
beginning with afferent input and ending with an exactly adequate central

answer. The afferentational input part of this reflex is, however, itself a form of reaction of the periphery of the body to the beginning of course of a movement. We observe in this phenomenon a sort of inverted reflex where the effector pathway acts as the exciting arc and the afferent nerve pathway acts as the reacting arc. The point of closure of this reflex arc appears here as the functional connection between motor impulses and the resulting movements, i.e. the same area of physiological indeterminacy which was discussed above. For this reason this functional area deserves a metaphorical description as a peripheral synapse.

Because this is so we may guess that the structure of the co-ordinational reflex differs considerably in principle from the sensory reflexes known to us from other areas; the co-ordinational reflex is not an arc *but a closed circle with functional synapses at both ends of the arcs*. In this reflex the centripetal impulses as in all other reflexes are transformed above into centrifugal ones, but the centrifugal impulses going out to the periphery are there rapidly converted into new centripetal impulses.

Like very other form of nervous activity which is structured to meet particular situations, motor co-ordination develops slowly as a result of experiment and exercise. Since co-ordination is, as we have established, a means of overcoming peripheral indeterminacy, it is clear that the basic difficulties for co-ordination consist precisely in the extreme abundance of degrees of freedom, with which the centre is not at first in a position to deal. And, in reality, we observe as a rule that improvement in co-ordination is achieved by utilizing all possible roundabout methods in order to reduce the number of degrees of freedom at the periphery to a minimum. When someone who is a novice at a sport, at playing a musical instrument or at an industrial process first attempts to master the new co-ordination, he is rigidly, spastically fixed and holds the limb involved, or even his whole body, in such a way as to reduce the number of kinematic degrees of freedom which he is required to control. Invertebrate organisms have in their make-up a form of co-ordinational surrogate in mechanisms of muscular locking (*Sperrung*) which by physiological means eliminate such degrees of freedom as are unnecessary at any given moment. But we must add that all lower forms of vertebrates (up to birds inclusively), for which the striatum still predominates over the cortical hemispheres, possess analogous auxiliary muscular mechanisms and employ them widely. Lizards, snakes, many brooding birds (eagles, parrots, etc.) are as rigid as statues in the intervals between voluntary movements. Reptiles show particularly clearly a statue-like

stiffening of the body as soon as successive voluntary movements cease. If a
lizard turns head to tail its body and limbs are motionless as sculpture.
Mammals, apparently in healthy condition, find similar locking completely
superfluous, and return to it only in cases of diseased hyperfunction of the
extrapyramidal system (catalepsia, catatonia, hypertonic symptom complexes
in encephalitis). In the norm there is no rest in mammals and in human beings,
and outside of deep sleep there is no similar immobility; careful observation
of standing or sitting human beings, dogs or cats give evidence of this.
Even the set immobility of a cat or a tiger is quite unlike the immobile
period in a reptile (or a spider) - it is sufficient to watch its tail.

Artificial tetanic elimination of superfluous degrees of freedom which
is observed in the form of tenseness and constraint gradually gives way during
the course of training to complete freedom. Having mastered the first degree
of freedom the organism increasingly raises its ban on further degrees of
freedom. Where there has been a high degree of expensive tetanic fixation,
now there comes a greater economy of movement and a diminution of fatigue.
Here two successive stages of release may be observed. The first degree
corresponds to the lifting of all restrictions, that is, to the incorporation
of all possible degrees of freedom. They no longer interfere with the
movements of the organism but introduce complicating reactive phenomena,
additional oscillatory frequencies, and so on. The organism has learnt to
extinguish them, not prophylactically (by eliminating the given degree of
freedom as a whole), but in an innervationally reactive way (by means of
single dynamic impulses). The second, highest stage of co-ordinational
freedom corresponds to a degree of co-ordination at which the organism is
not only unafraid of reactive phenomena in a system with many degrees of
freedom, but is able to structure its movements so as to *utilize entirely
the reactive phenomena* which arise. Our material allowed us to examine a
great many such cases, both in great masters of movement and in advanced
students of movement.

Apparently this second stage corresponds to that described by sportsmen
and music teacher as 'relaxing', a phenomenon which they instinctively feel
but which they do not know how to describe. The economical effect of the
transition to this stage is apparent; not only is there evidence here of
minimal use of physio-reactive-innervational impulses, but it is also the
case that all those mechanical-reactive forces in the complicated link
systems, which, in the best cases, occurred without damage at the previous
level of co-ordination, are used in a positive sense. This second

co-ordination level is a biological control of highest perfection which
explains the great wealth of kinematic utility of the degrees of freedom in
the higher mammals - evidence that a level of co-ordination is possible at
which this wealth is of immediate use.

It is much more difficult to determine the means by which the organism
so far overcomes the internal physiological indeterminacy of the periphery;
it is, however, perhaps possible to make a few suggestions at this point.

All that has been said above on the initial suppression and later use
of the multiplicity of degrees of freedom may be put in the following way.
The movable limbs of the organism always do respond in the same manner to
the impulse which is transmitted through the muscles. The secret of
co-ordination lies not only in not wasting superfluous force on extinguishing
reactive phenomena but, on the contrary, in employing the latter in such a
way as to employ active muscle forces only in the capacity of complementary
forces. In this case the same movement (in the final analysis) demands less
expenditure of active force. It is possible to express this (by means of an
analogy with simpler, but similar, electrical phenomena) in the form of a
statement that in the second case the reactive resistance of the moving
system to the neuromuscular impulses is less than in the former, or, which
amounts to the same thing, that its reactive conductivity is higher in the
second case than it is in the first. A higher degree of co-ordination secures
a higher reactive conductivity to muscle force impulses at the periphery.
We must note that, because this heightening of conductivity is entirely
achieved by employing the *dynamic* transitory phenomena, such high conductivity
cannot be a stable or constant value. The mastery of co-ordination must
consist in the ability to give *the necessary impulse at the necessary moment*,
seizing the fleeting phases of higher conductivity of force and avoiding
those phases during which this conductivity falls to low values.

It is quite in order to draw an analogy here between the examples of
reactive-mechanical conductivity which we have studied and those phenomena
of changes in synaptic conductivity, mentioned above, which have been
explained by neurophysiology in recent years. Observations both by Lapicque
and by P. Weiss indicate that the effector impulse *may arrive but not pass
through*. It is obvious that at this level also the most effective impulse
will be that which arrives at a synapse at the moment of its attainment of
a level of highest conductivity, or that which is, by its nature, most
adequate to meet the conditions of conductivity (lability) at the final
synapse (which from the point of view of the result amounts to the same

thing). It follows that in this case also co-ordination will consist in the ability to order events so that the effector impulses will encounter conditions of the greatest physiological conductivity at the periphery and will not collide with phases of physiological refractoriness which would doom them to ineffectuality.

The role of co-ordination at this level must therefore consist in the *preparatory organization of the motor periphery in order to guarantee optimal selection of conductivity*. This opinion is extremely unusual but necessarily proceeds from the facts. As the effector impulse cannot in principle bring about by itself a co-ordination without being entirely dependent on afferent processes, we must not regard this impulse as somehow precisely differentiated - as there is no biological basis for this. There is no possibility that accurate *effector* differentiation can be developing here because, as has been shown above, the peripheral indeterminacy demands different effector connections for each successive repetition of a given movement. Co-ordination at the level described lies basically not in the character and the accuracy of a tetanic effector impulse but in the accuracy of some sort of preparatory (not tetanic) effector impulses *which organize and prepare the periphery* for the reception of the right impulse at the right moment. The co-ordinational process does not enter into the composition of the tetanic impulse, or follow immediately after it; it goes *before*, clearing and organizing the path for it, and therefore must operate through quite different paths and employ quite different innervational processes.

What may be the path along which the co-ordinational process reaches this given level and what are the non-tetanic effector channels which it employs we may at the moment only guess. Nevertheless, it is possible to put forward a few hypotheses in this area.

Firstly, there is no doubt that the co-ordination is certainly not organized independently at the periphery alone and that the preparation of the periphery for the selective transmission of 'the right impulse at the right time' discussed above is, to a very considerable degree, centrally determined (in Lapicque's order of 'sub-ordination' in its broader sense) by means of a proprioceptive reflex cycle. The co-ordinational process on the level described is obviously not a tetanic process, but it undoubtedly incorporates both receptor and effector components.

We find it very tempting to draw upon the concepts of *tonus* to explain the phenomenon described here.

The physiological data available on tonus has considerably extended the

initial ideas on this topic which incorporated first only the idea of a
condition of elasticity of the muscle fibres. Without any more accurate
determinations tonus, in the vocabulary of physiologists, began gradually
to cover a very wide range of facts beginning with decerebrate rigidity and
extending to Magnus and de Klein's tonus which has already been understood
as a very generalized state of the motor periphery of preparation (in
particular of the musculature of the neck and body) for the accomplishment
of positions or movements.

The older, static concept of tonus as physiological elasticity constricted
and retarded the understanding of these phenomena. It seems that there is at
present evidence enough to decide upon a judgement, perhaps preliminary, and
to say the following about tonus:

(a) Tonus as an ongoing physiological adaptation and organization of
the periphery is *not a condition of elasticity but a condition of readiness.*

(b) Tonus is not merely a condition of the muscles but of the entire
neuromuscular apparatus, including at least the final spinal synapse and the
final common pathway.

(c) Tonus, from this point of view, is related to co-ordination as a
state is to an action or as a precondition is to an effect.

If taken as working hypotheses these suppositions allow us to explain
much more.

Firstly, one is struck by the fact (which was not considered before,
but which after these hypotheses are made becomes quite obvious) that not a
single case of pathological co-ordination is known in which there is not at
the same time a pathology of tonus, and that not a single central nervous
apparatus is known which is related to one of these functions without being
related to the other. The cerebellum has for some time been known as an
apparatus which is of decisive importance for co-ordination, and it is also
the most important effector for tonus. The same is true of the pallidum and
the nucleus ruber. Disorders of the vestibular apparatus lead to functional
lack of co-ordination and to destruction of tonus. Section of the posterior
spinal tracts results simultaneously in ataxia and atomia; both of these
are the basic motor symptoms of tabes. Experimental deafferentation rapidly
results in the disappearance of co-ordination and the disappearance of tonus.
The number of examples of this type could easily be extended *ad infinitum.*

Secondly, we now see the significance of the flexible and reactive tonic
reactions studied by the school of Magnus, which were, however, studied
because of inadequacies of techniques, mostly in the static supporting organs

of the body - the neck and trunk. It is clear that these systemic reflexes
of high degrees of plasticity are decisive co-ordinational prerequisites to
movement or positions and that their physiological purpose is not limited to
the communication of a necessary and simultaneous rigidity to the trunk of
the body but incorporates the entire preparatory reaction of the periphery
to the conditions of the external (static and dynamic) field of forces.

Thirdly, tonus and those centrally directed mechanisms which regulate
the conductivity of the distal synapses is very clearly explained by the
circumstance that the anatomical substrate both of Rademacher's tonical
phenomena and of Lapicque's subordination phenomena are one and the same -
that is, the lower stage of the extrapyramidal system and the nucleus ruber
group. Section of the brain stem at this level gives a picture of a
disorganization of sub-ordination - of the return of muscular chronaxie to
its constitutional value. It also leads to a picture of decerebrate rigidity,
that is to say a picture of set, non-reactive spread of tonus, with marked
appearance of flexion in some cases and extension in others. This
correspondence is certainly not accidental and allows us to discuss the
position of the anatomical substrate of the co-ordinational layer, referring
it to the nucleus ruber group and to the paleocerebellum functionally
related to it.

The innervational paths for the control of tonus in our model would be
the rubrospinal and the vestibulospinal tracts for the tonomotor effects,
and the sympathetic tract for tonotropic impulses.

REFERENCES

8. Bernstein, N.A. Studies of the biomechanics of the stroke by means of
    photo-registration, Research of the Central Institute of Labour,
    Moscow 1 (in Russian), 1923.

9. Bernstein, N.A. A biomechanical norm for the stroke. Research of the
    Central Institute of Labour, Moscow 1,2 (in Russian), 1924.

15. Bernstein, N.A. Clinical Ways of Modern Biomechanics. Collection of
    papers of the Institute for Medical Improvement, Kazan, 1929.

19. Bernstein, N.A. et al. Studies of the Biodynamics of Locomotions (Normal
    Gait, Load and Fatigue). Institute of Experimental Medicine, Moscow
    (in Russian), 1935.

21. Bernstein, N.A. et al. Studies of the Biodynamics of Walking, Running
    and Jumping (in Russian), Moscow, 1940.

43. Fischer, O. Methodik der speziellen Bewegungslehre. Handbuch der
    physiologischen Methodik, Vol. 2, Pt. 1. Leipzig: Tigerstedt, 1911.

75. Wagner, R. Probleme und Beispiele biologischer Regelung. Stuttgart:
    Thieme, 1954.

81. Drillis, R. The influence of ageing on the kinematics of gait, Geriatric
    Amputee, Publication 919, National Academy of Science, National
    Research Council, U.S.A.

Human Motor Actions – Bernstein Reassessed
H.T.A. Whiting (editor)
© Elsevier Science Publishers B.V. (North-Holland), 1984

CHAPTER IIIa
HOW CONTROL OF MOVEMENT DEVELOPS

C. Trevarthen

Bernstein's study of walking and running beautifully exemplifies his
method of research. The observations are restricted to bipedal locomotion on
a level surface in a straight line. Nevertheless the principles Bernstein
elucidates would apply not only to other less regular paths and ways of
getting about, but to gymnastics in which the whole body is thrown through
the air and to arm movements displacing or intercepting objects while the
body is standing or seated. Most importantly, his account of changes in
locomotion during development from infancy, and of its involution in
senescence, help clarify his general theory of the interactions between the
cerebral centres (neural structures) and the periphery (motor and mechanical
structures and sense organs); that is, between what he calls the central and
peripheral 'synapses' or 'cycles of interaction'. This assists appreciation
of what is involved in the perfection of mature coordinated movements.

The central principle of Bernstein's method is accurate measurement, in
time and in space, of the displacements of joints and body segments. His
measurements by the cyclogrametric method were much more precise than those
of any of his predecessors or contemporaries. Physical and mathematical
analysis of forces and moments about joints and at centres of mass of body
segments are then carried out to tease apart the causes of movement. From
such a rich description Bernstein derived, already in the late '20s, an
entirely new picture of motor control in which the interplay of cerebral,
corporal and environmental factors could be appreciated as never before. In
his subsequent writings, he states and restates the laws of movement he
discovered, using locomotion as his example with such intuitive brilliance
that one experiences a discovery of a general insight into the brain's creative
role in governing the interplay of forces in the concealed world of living
body mechanics. Thus Bernstein built a genuine psychology of movement on
physiological foundations, with far reaching implications for the psychology
of cognition, motivation, learning and intention. Bernstein's findings on the

control of human locomotion may be extended to gain a richer and more productive view on how objects and events are conceived. I believe they also provide an important insight into inherent mechanisms of human communication.

The following synopsis of Bernstein's 'laws' of movement is made in preparation for an evaluation of his account of the development of walking and running and comparison with some recent studies of the same problems. Than I shall endeavour to apply his concepts to findings of the last 15 years on infantile reaching and grasping, a form of movement which brings into being a rich, indeed unbounded, interrogation of the environment that begins well before the baby walks. Finally I shall attempt to derive, in the same spirit, some as yet speculative ideas on the genesis of expressive gestures by which the mover can engage the minds of other persons and transmit messages into their motor coordinations at the deepest levels. It would appear that humans have some implicit mastery of Bernstein's laws from the day they are born, and that they use this 'knowledge' not only to gain knowledge of what their bodies can do by acting on the world, but also to gain close communication with others, perhaps even becoming responsive to the mother's rhythms of displacement and patterning of somatic muscle activity before birth.

These are the laws of Bernstein's 'biodynamic structures' that make adaptive movement possible:

1.   Movements, while they are caused by changes in equilibria between muscle tensions, cannot be in one-to-one relationship to excitatory neural impulses or forces of muscular contraction.

2.   Events at the periphery of a moving member generate external, non-neurogenic or mechanical forces that may contribute substantially to the movement while it is happening (the 'peripheral cycle of interaction').

3.   Peripheral force vectors must be responded to accurately and smoothly with the aid of proprioceptive relay of their effects into the motor centres, if there is to be "adequate coordination and correspondence of the movement to the animal's intention".

4.   The regulation of movement in plastic response to sensory feedback requires a central structure that can perform accurate anticipatory tracking of peripheral stimuli, by changing responsiveness in the motor centres, or by a change in sensitivity of the receptors commanded by the centres. (This coordination cannot be reflexive, motor response following proprioceptive signal in a fixed manner with an irreducible delay. The time taken to integrate new information from receptors into a movement, at least 50 milli-

seconds and often as long as 250 milliseconds, is much longer than the duration of some large force changes in the system. Reflexive correction would come too late and it must be exceptional).

5. Well-coordinated movements have a regular, automatic, rhythmic or oscillatory structure (manifest in the small number of harmonic components of force curves), in relation to which events in all moving segments of the body are virtually interdependent. (Cooperative reciprocities of motion and support in linked segments and the smooth flow of forces down the kinematic system rely upon this 'orchestration' of the force momenta which is necessary to, and an expression of, the accurate anticipation of resultant mechanical events at the periphery by the centre).

6. Adjustments to a change in goal or tempo for a limb movement must involve generation of a new force program transmitted throughout the body, since change of movement in one segment alters the relationships between forces everywhere.

These laws define the characteristics of a complex dynamic organization of motor centres which exploit the peripheral mechanisms and respond to their signals.

An important corollary of predictive programming of movements by anticipatory recoding of proprioceptive response (Law 4) is that information obtained through exteroceptors about impending contacts with exterior objects must be immediately assimilated to the plan for movement that has been built up to take in data from mechanoreceptors. Surfaces against which locomotor thrusts are made and objects picked up are capable of adding large forces at the periphery. These effects must be taken into the calculation of the movement plan before they arrive. Mechanoreception verifies the immediate condition of the body. Exteroceptive assimilation may track the outside world's potential for assisting or destroying the movement, or for providing a reference to detect departure from a planned course. Thus efficient planning of movement requires perception of external events and resistant media. There will be a need for reciprocal adjustments and associations between all sensory modalities capable of transmitting information on the impending interactions between the moving body and the environment. For example, vision of the path ahead can provide unique data to forecast how and when mechanical perturbations are to be met when the feet touch the ground. Conversely proprioceptive readiness to monitor effects of catching or picking up an object will constitute a part of the description of that object's properties, added to information obtained by visual perception of its size, substance and location or velocity.

David Lee's concept of visual exproprioception explicates the direct motor coordinative function of vision and corrects a traditional bias towards thinking of vestibular and mechano-receptor channels as the only direct inputs for control of posture and locomotion (Lee, 1978, 1980). In lower vertebrates tactile, vestibular and lateral line systems have a dominant role for coordinating the tight automatisms of their body action as they swim through water or crawl on their bellies. Exteroceptive senses, especially vision, set a spatial frame around this, guiding head displacement (Harris, 1965; Trevarthen, 1968). In more active vertebrates, with more complex multiarticulated bodies, problems of motor coordination are greatly multiplied and direct visual input is necessary to guide their much more dynamic posture with, as Bernstein describes it, many more 'kinematic degrees of freedom'. Visual projections to their more developed neocerebellar 'computer' of motor coordinative programs undoubtedly contributes to this control (Glickstein & Gibson, 1976). Cetaceans (whales and dolphins) offer an extremely interesting special case shere sonic rather than visual guidance of high speed and extremely agile propulsion is associated with an enormous development of the cerebellum and parietal cerebral neocortex.

Bernstein considered neuro-anatomical interpretation of the control system required by his laws, and his most significant conclusion was that systems with different control functions can only be segregated spatially in the brain if they have the tightest intercommunication so that they may act for the most part at the same time and in a predetermined relationship, as do the efferent and afferent components of the peripheral motor system. Predetermined and controlled sequences of action in different hierarchically related parts of the peripheral motor system (trunk, limbs, distal appendages, head) with different relationship to specialized receptor structures, express an hierarchy of control systems or modes of action in the brain (Trevarthen, 1978). Their coordinated activity would require the existence of a superior level of representation that can determine their joint effects at the periphery in engagement with the environment. A common cerebral organization with respect to the spatial and temporal framework in which behaviour takes place is therefore necessary. I have elsewhere considered the ways in which inherent somatotopic patterning (body mapping) in major cerebral systems provides this integration during brain development (Trevarthen 1974a, 1979a, 1980a).

After explaining the advantages of locomotion for the study of universal principles of motor coordination, Bernstein shows that the regular beat of thrusts to keep the body above the ground as the feet exchange support (the

"struggle against the force of gravitation") is fully represented in vertical
component of forces in body and limb segments. The longitudinal (front-back)
component of the forces of leg swinging carries more information about the
local muscular activity that rotates foot, shin and thigh round the joints,
and about the reactive forces to which these rotations give rise. As the
weight of the body is transferred from one foot to the other, forward and
backward thrusts alternate in a fixed pattern. Other longitudinal force
waves reveal how the limb is transported when it is off the ground. In running
both feet are off the ground for most of the time. They move over a larger
space at higher velocity with each step than in walking, and thrust harder
and in a more horizontal resultant direction against the ground.

The alternating movements of a leg in walking are not driven by a
simple succession of forward and backward swings matched to opposite
movements in the other leg. There are many other "strikingly constant and
general" elements in the dynamics of each step which appear in unchanging
sequence in the longitudinal force curves and give it a "radically different
physiognomy form that which may be observed in the simple stepping reflex
of a decerebrate preparation". Bernstein concluded "The structural elements
of muscle action ... are of essential coordinational significance for the
locomotor act and ... they must consequently have a peculiar genesis,
history and basis in the central nervous system and elsewhere". Thus he
lays the foundation for discovery of the innate adaptive structures that
govern motor coordination.

Taking each segment of the limb in turn and examining the cycle of
forces about joints or at the centres of mass, attending even to minute
regularities and events separated by as little as one or two milliseconds,
it is possible to discern the place of origin of component events that drive
the surprisingly regular displacements. Bernstein explains how he distinguished
longitudinal accelerations and decelerations due to muscle contractions (e.g.
the primary ε and $n\beta$ waves) from reactive inertial forces. The identification
of the large α waves in the force momenta about the knee exemplifies this.
This wave is reflected as a backward (extensor) thrust on the thigh from
contraction of the extensors of the knee. As the shin and foot are thrown
forward, the thigh is forced back against concurrent flexor activity at the
hip. Immobilisation of the knee by a splint all but abolishes the effect.
Thus, except for a small proprioceptive component in skilled running, the
α wave proved to be purely mechanical.

Bernstein then describes how the attention of his "telescope" passed

from such large events ("stars of the first magnitude") to more informative
smaller features. Thus the succession of ζ waves, occupying about 200 msec,
which are seen at centres of gravity of the thigh and shin of the leg that
is flexing and moving forwards through the air while the body's weight is
being transferred to the foot recently planted on the ground, were identified
as 'reactively innervated' or responding to proprioceptive feedback. Presumably
this discharge of pulses is part of an active balancing which the body must
execute and the brain must record very precisely at this moment. One might
expect that events coordinating the two legs in coming to a standstill, in
moving over irregular and unstable footing and in changing direction would
be strongly represented at this phase of the locomotor program – but Bernstein
only makes passing reference to such variations in walking, stating that
the standard ζ waves are not displaced in distorted walking such as three-
part marching. The curves presented in Bernstein's Figure 27 for the skilled
running of the athlete Ladoumeg have a regular succession of small waves,
including the complex labelled ζ, of which Bernstein only says that they
are exactly repeated in the same dynamic instants of limb displacement
and they prove the existence of a highly efficient "correct response to
proprioception".

   I note that in this figure the longitudinal forces at the centres of
gravity of Ladoumeg's right and left legs while running have remarkably even
phases, but <u>different</u> frequencies of oscillation. Could there be different
proprioceptive governors for the two legs? Was the difference (right leg =
18.5 waves/sec; left = 16.7 waves/sec) maintained continuously underneath
the precise complementarity of major force waves in the two legs? Bernstein
gives no comment on this phenomenon though he numbers the phases on the
figure. Research by Grillner and Zangger (1979) with locomotion in spinal
cats on a split belt with the two halves moving at different rates shows
that the spinal locomotor system does indeed have separate left and right
generators which, however, can be coupled. It would be interesting to know
if right handed humans tend to have a slower system on the left side of the
spinal cord. Does their inherent lateral asymmetry extend to spinal centres?

   Bernstein's studies of walking and running in children demonstrate the
rather surprising fact that precise cerebral control of the forces arising
from movement is achieved on a time scale of decades comparable with the
learning of language and 'skills of culture'. The order in which features
of control are acquired casts light on the complex hierarchy of processes
by which the brain increases its repertoire of 'soft ware' or schemata, not

only for cognitive mastery of objects and actions, but also for control of
the body in action. The full potentialities of the innate neural systems
adapted to walking and running are achieved only after years of practice
as limbs grow and muscles gain in power. A significant correlate of this
development of agility and gymnastic skill in childhood is the increase
in size and complexity of structure in the cerebellum which has a postnatal
development comparable with that of the slow maturing 'uncommitted' cerebral
cortex (Yakovlev & Lecours, 1967; Jacobson, 1970).

The force curves of the limbs of infants show only the primitive pair
of impulses ε and n_{α} (later n_{β}) which produce an automatic pattern of
stepping. At this stage the vertical forces at the centre of gravity of
the head are "completely ordered and invariable from step to step, although
primitive in form ... Meanwhile, the movements of the head are extremely
chaotic, uneven and involved". Different children show similar force curves
but "extremely diverse and individual curves of displacement". This is
Bernstein's "innervationally primitive stage" in which highly irregular
patterns of displacement are produced by regular motor output, as in the
ataxia of a patient with loss of proprioceptive tracts (tabes dorsalis).
Early walking, far from being driven by stimuli, is comparatively incompetent
at responding to afference, like that of a deafferentiated patient.

At about two, new force elements appear, but they are weak signs and
they disappear when the child walks quickly. The whole inventory of
longitudinal force waves is only completed about five when the adult
"innervationally reactive" form of the wave complex appears. Then there is
what Bernstein describes as "an extremely interesting overemphasis of
structural details" between five and eight years and "this overabundance
energetically involutes between eight and ten years, but even by the age of
ten the process of formation of the adult structure has not been entirely
completed".

The first developments Bernstein attributes to maturation of proprioception,
the "slow and gradual appearance of the mechanisms of adequate response to
this signalling". In small children "the spontaneous effector impulses are
already developed while the innervationally-reactive impulses do not operate
in conjunction with them". In other words the plan for efficient assimilation
of proprioceptive input has not yet been formulated. A poor tracking of body
position is achieved, so the dynamic phases of force curves do not occur in
constant correspondence with positions of the body as they do in adult walking.
Thus in children under three unequal steps are obtained for constant values

of the immature ζ waves and to obtain steps of constant length variations
of ζ are required. In adults both stepping and the ζ waves are constant,
and Bernstein concludes "this means that even before the completion of the
main impulse ε, an exact regulation of the direct longitudinal forces on the
basis of proprioceptive signalling is necessary in carrying out steps of
constant metrical proportions. This preparatory regulation is not yet
developed in the child".

I have repeated these extracts from Bernstein's text to emphasize that
the most important contribution of this chapter is the definition it gives
to a strategy of behavioural development which involves formation in the
brain of a dynamic image of the moving body, and the achievement of precise
temporal and metrical prediction of reafferent feedback effects.

Figure 1 reproduces Bernstein's curves of acceleration of the knee for
a child of three years five months (A) and an adult (B) and puts them on
the same time scale. I have added the periods of support for the child which
are missing from Figure 28(b) in the translated paper. Two cycles are shown
for the child which illustrate the variation, for example, in ζ and γ waves.
These curves show numerous differences, but the most significant in relation
to the whole story of the development of walking are the appearance of a
period of double support, and two features of the transfer period. The
childish ζ, which Bernstein claims is essentially a mechanically reactive
curve, is replaced by the regular adult preprioceptively fed but preprogrammed
ζ, and there is added the large mechanical α wave which has a significant
role in the adult movement to assist extension. In other words the slower
and more powerful adult program tracks mechano-receptor feedback closely
and juggles the leg efficiently as a chain of penduli. Only part of the very
regular force profile of adult walking cycle is shown.

Bernstein outlines how running diverges from walking in the second and
third years of life. He suggests that this process works from the periphery
to the centre. As with walking, the program for running acquires accurate
central representation of peripheral events after the running form has been
created. This he calls the "secondary character of central divergency". It
could be described as learning how to cope with the motor problems created
by emergence of a new form of movement.

At this point Bernstein brings in a most interesting consideration of
the relationships between central control for proximal (i.e. near the trunk)
and distal components of the kinematic chain of the limb. He considers that
the earlier development of control for proximal segments follows from the

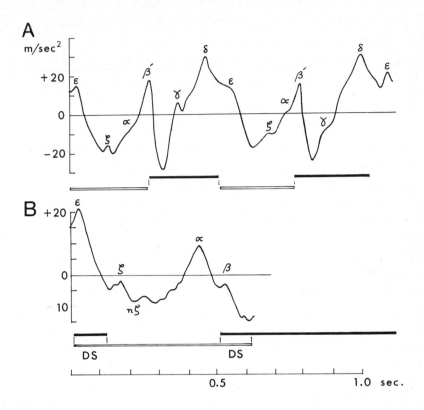

Fig. 1. Bernstein's longitudinal acceleration curves of the knee
in walking: for toddler (A), and adult (B). Double support
(DS) is absent for the child whose progression is half
running.

fact that effector impulses gain more ready expression, with less peripheral
interference in proximal segments. In contrast, to control the distal segments
"the effector impulse either must be very strong or must coincide exactly
with the moment when conditions in the distal system are particularly
favourable for its appearance"; and then he says, "it is possible that this
most opportune moment is a critical moment in the velocity of the limb when
the inertial resistance is least perceptible". In other words, there will be
a coordinative principle coupling placements or extension of the foot with a
certain place in the phasic activity of the thigh and shin. This analysis
applies to the placement of the feet in the substrate in agile walking and in

running, a process which is in the adult more elaborate and exhibiting "a greater deftness, a higher degree of coordinational technique" as required for control of distal parts. As we shall see it is also vital to an understanding of grasping, catching and manipulating objects in the hand.

Bernstein points out that although children do not achieve adult efficiency in walking or running until past the age of ten, already at three or four they have excellent coordination and equilibrium, in that they can hop, pedal a tricycle, dance, etc. We must assume that the system coordinating the posture in relation to gravity and the supporting environment is present before biodynamic control is mature.

Important new information on the standing and walking of infants has come in recent years. Lee and Aronson (1974) proved that from the onset of standing the motor system is responsive to information from the surrounding visual framework about surfaces and edges. Slight movement of the walls and ceiling of a room suspended around an infant who has just learned to stand causes an immediate fall. Evidently the child begins standing and walking in a visual frame that the brain takes to be a fixed reference; displacement of this frame easily overrides the vestibular and mechano-receptive (somesthetic and proprioceptive) channels. Forssberg has observed standing and walking in infants with the aid of myograms and the Selspot system which tracks by television the positions of blinking infra red marker lights attached to limbs and computes displacements, velocities and accelerations directly, generating 'stick' figures to show positions of limb segments. He and Nashner (1982) found that automatic and rapid adjustments of standing to tilts of the support surface (somesthetic sensitivity of the foot and ankle) and movement of the visual surround were like those observed by Nashner for adults, but more varied, from $1\frac{1}{2}$ years. Allowance must be made for the different dimensions of the body which put the child at a mechanical disadvantage. The infants also show automatic compensation for voluntary arm movements against an external load. Vestibular control could maintain an infant standing when support-surface information or visual inputs or both were eliminated (by unclamping the footplates or covering the eyes). Thus the basic control networks of the adult are functional, with about the same temporal efficiency, from the onset of standing. When somesthetic, vestibular and visual channels were put in conflict, however, children under $7\frac{1}{2}$ years could not adapt to different contexts in which one or other channel had become unreliable. Thus below this critical age they became very unstable with conflicting sensory conditions, shifting weighting at random between the three channels. The authors believe that the development is due to the maturation of higher level neural systems that perform an "integrative" function, governing varied combinations of the automatic postural activities. Presumably this development is necessary to the achievement of efficient voluntary activity.

In a study of infant walking, Forssberg and Wallberg (1980) found that the highly irregular stepping of a newborn held over a moving belt may at times exhibit a considerable degree of coordination, but the steps support only about one third of the body weight at maximum thrust, lead to large vertical excursions of the body and are organized for support on the toes or digitigrade walking as in quadrupeds, not the specialized heel and toe (plantigrade) stepping that enables a human adult to balance the body efficiently over two feet. The leg of the newborn is kicked forward in an extreme forward swing as in Prussian marching and the foot raised high and then lowered with extension at the ankle to a support phase that can neither hold the body up nor propel it forward.

Developmental psychologists seeking evidence for theories of how voluntary action develops have been intrigued that newborn innate walking generally disappears after six weeks, when a supported infant is more likely to crouch or push out against the surface with both legs together. This has been taken as an example of the development of cortical efferent pathways of 'voluntary' control inhibiting inborn 'reflexes'. But the patterns of neonatal stepping are not reflexive and in some infants they do not disappear during the first year, their maintenance being promoted by artificial exercise. Towards the end of the first year as the child begins to crawl and stand, stepping when the body is held to assist balance become less exaggerated in flexion and gradually more regular. It supports the body at full extension and pushes it forward with less vertical oscillation than in the newborn. The foot is now placed with the heel striking first.

Comparison of neonatal walking with locomotor patterns of spinal cats indicates that the human pattern (which may be elicited within minutes of birth) is produced in rudimentary form by autonomous activity of the spinal "locomotor generator". Effective walking is 'learned' as supra spinal control circuits mature and establish influence over spinal circuits, a process which starts about two months after birth. One important consequence is that early ankle extension is suppressed. This and other changes in the timing of muscle actions converts digitigrade (primitive) walking to plantigrade (human) bipedal walking. But free unassisted walking occurs well before this

matamorphosis is completed. Thus the control of equilibrium is achieved
before the most efficient form of stepping develops (Forssberg & Wallberg,
1980; Forssberg, 1982).

Putting these results in relation to Bernstein's findings, one can see
that effective proprioceptive management of plantigrade walking, with more
subtle and regular modulation of both support and swing through, continues
for some years after its inception. Modern analysis of the physiology of
standing and locomotion in cats indicates that in a widespread pattern of
developments in brain and stem and cortical tissues the cerebellum has a
central place in this management of the most efficient proprioceptive
assimilation (Forssberg, 1982).

We may conclude from the above studies that the fundamental neural
program for standing and walking on two feet is present in a newborn and
the spinal core of it is largely functional. Cerebral systems regulating
posture and balance by mechano-receptive and exproprioceptive feedback are
present in outline and they assist control of balance and posture from the
earliest stages of actual standing and walking. Calibration of more efficient
higher level controls takes a number of years, by a process which presumably
involves active growth and differentiation of dendrites and synapses and
maturation of axons in specific parts of the central nervous systems.
Children achieve agile walking and running and learn special forms of
progression in dancing, skiing and gymnastics by a process of selective
reinforcement or retention of the most adaptive combinations.

In the course of these developments the structural basis for change in
motor control is shown in both regressions in the overall efficiency of
movement and exuberant flowering of feedback systems in active, varying and
sometimes competitive interaction (Trevarthen, 1982). Every accurate
developmental study of how movements gain guidance by specific control
channels considered one at a time has revealed periods of sensitive and
insensitive response to stimuli and periods of conservative or cautious
exploitation of motor plans giving way to wasteful and experimental 'play'
with control before a higher level of efficiency in control is consolidated.
An example of change in sensitivity to feedback with maturation of a particular
form of action comes from recent research on locomotion artificially assisted
by means of wheeled 'crawlers' or 'walkers' before unaided crawling or
walking is possible. Infants show variation in sensitivity to a visual drop
(Rader, Bausano & Richards, 1980) and the evidence suggests that avoidance
of the deep side of a visual cliff may occur for crawling before it does

for walking; that is, the two forms of locomotion, quadripedal or bipedal
are open to this form of visual guidance at different stages in the first
year.

Now let us turn attention to the development of movements to reach and
grasp or manipulate objects. These activities follow a developmental plan
which has interesting points of resemblance to the maturation of walking.
Again complex innate motor program undergoes systematic modification as
sensory control processes are added. Even though the arm is a more complex
kinematic system, with much greater freedom of movement than the legs, and
dexterous use of the hands requires development of a much more elaborate
cerebral control of the distal segments than is required for placement of
the foot or clinging with the toes, object prehension attains a high level
of proficiency with elaborate direction from the cerebral cortex before
locomotion starts.

In 1967 and 1968 I made films at the Center for Cognitive Studies at
Harvard of the reactions of infants from 1 week to 6 months of age to small
objects that were suspended from a kind of fishing rod pivoted about the
infant's head. From this a small brown furry toy was dangled about eye level
and moved from side to side. I observed that not only were some babies one
or two weeks of age capable of orienting towards and tracking the object with
precisely coordinated rotations of head and eyes, even though their heads
frequently wobbled considerably; they were also emitting small arm and hand
movements towards the objects. Frame-by-frame analysis of films revealed
that while the latter movements were unpredictable in occurrence and extent,
they were certainly not random or reflex reactions. Observation of the
coordination of arm and hand movements with small displacements of the
object showed that they were definitely under some degree of visuo-spatial
control. Nothing in the literature had led me to expect these 'pre-reaching'
movements which I reported at a seminar at the Center. More detailed
descriptions made later from films made in Edinburgh, with the aid of drawings
made by projecting the film images on the underside of tracing paper, confirmed
that voluntary prehension develops in human beings out of a form of visually
age and directed towards an object moving slowly near the baby (Figure 2).

From the Harvard films of five subjects taken at weekly or biweekly
intervals over the first five months I determined that the rather fluid
total pattern of reach and grasp typical of newborns gave way to jerky,
erratically aimed and fractional movements of a much more forceful kind as
the infant became more robust in the second and third month. Ataxic swipes

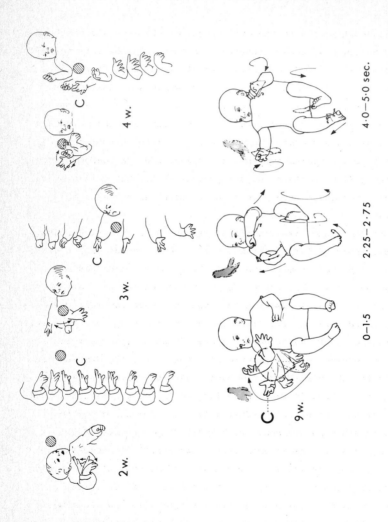

Fig. 2. Reach-and-grasp movements traced from films at 16 frames/second. Hand positions drawn at ¼ second intervals. Boy at 2, 3, 4 and 9 weeks.
<u>Top</u>: Newborn prereaching to a slowly displaced object varies from wrist extension to extension of the whole arm, but in all cases the fingers are maximally open at the climax of extension (C).
<u>Below</u>: At 2 months ataxic swipes are made without hand opening unless the infant is in a quiet state (left).

and grabs were then the commonest movements towards the toy (Trevarthen, 1974a, b; 1982). At the end of the fourth month a marked improvement in the steadiness and directedness of arm extensions occurred. Thereafter reaching and grasping followed the pattern of development described by other observers.

In previous work with split-brain animals I had seen that arm and hand movements of reaching to touch were under control of at least two complementary cerebral systems (Trevarthen, 1965, 1968b, 1975). Aimed arm extension, transporting the hand towards a visually located goal, could be directed by a system that was largely undivided after all the interhemispheric neocortical connections had been cut, but the mechanism for orientation and shaping of the fingers to make a discretely adapted touching or grasping movement was split into two parts, one serving each hand. Split-brain monkeys were able to catch rapidly moving objects efficiently with either hand when vision was restricted to one eye. This indicates that interception of the object was governed in them by an undivided or duplicate visumotor system different from the split one that controlled precise direction of dexterous manipulative movements - a result which gains interest in the light of von Hofsten's discovery, discussed below, that infants can catch objects efficiently before they have developed visually guided manipulation. I noted that while newborns were making integrated arm and hand movements of considerable delicacy in which proximal segments moved little, the 2- and 3-month olds were frequently responding to a suspended object, which they fixated and tracked avidly, with vigorous failing arm movements and clenched hands (Figure 3). Subsequently, as control of the extension of the upper arm improved so that a better aimed, slower and more regular reaching towards the object occurred, the hands again made guided grasping movements.

Studies by Kuypers and his colleagues (Kuypers, 1973) of the separate parallel motor systems of brain stem and spinal cord for musculature surrounding proximal and distal joints of the limbs led to a neat explanation of the effects of split-brain surgery on eye-hand coordination (Brinkman & Kuypers, 1973). It also offered the possibility of explaining developments in motor control during infancy in terms of successive waves of differentiation in a hierarchy of control systems. Proximal and distal segments of the forelimb, while designed to work concurrently in a cooperative manner, would be moved by systems with different types of reafferent sensory control and different phylogenetic histories. They could well have different epochs of maturation in the epigenesis of voluntary prehension, as indeed Kuypers had shown to be the case when he analyzed growth of cortico-spinal connections

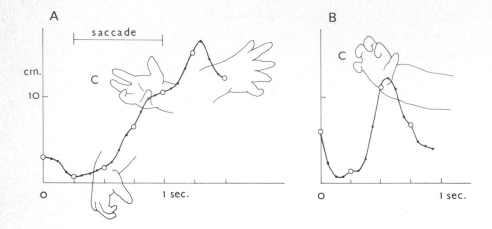

Fig. 3. Vertical displacements of wrist for 9-week-old shown in
        Figure 2, lower left and lower right. The slow reach, A,
        has a saccadic lift with slight deceleration at the
        midpoint. The hand is open at the brief climax (C).
        The swipe, B, is more accelerated and the hand is half-
        closed at the climax at which there is no arrest.

in young monkeys (Kuypers, 1962). The notion of assembly of a motor
coordinating system by formation of transcortical connections between reflex
arcs for different members and different special sense organs was replaced
by one of progressive incorporation of feedback control loops for successive
phases of action within an inherently programmed adaptive response system,
or, to use Coghill's terms, by individuation of local reactions within a
total pattern already given (Trevarthen, 1974a, 1978, 1979).

      Since newborns could aim a reaching movement to something of a size that
might be grasped it appeared that they could visually perceive the appropriate
'distal' object in the right part of the extracorporal space. I noted, however,
that a perfect aimed 'pre-reaching' movement, commonly but not always coupled
to a coordinated head and eyes orientation to the same locus on one side of
the baby, was often produced by a quiet alert newborn when no object was
present at that focal location. Therefore, although the form of movement was
preadapted to grasp an object, its evocation was not dependent upon perception
of a target. Its primary cause was a preformed neuronal network in which the
appropriate patterns of excitation and transmission could arise either

spontaneously or as a result of some unidentified extrafocal stimulation. (For example, the sound of movement of a person out of sight, or a change in the overall level of light).

In Figures 2, 3, 4 and 5 it may be seen that the patterning of pre-reaching with the baby seated upright is one which involves outward then inward rotation in the upper arm combined with weak extension or abduction then return, extension with supination then retraction with pronation in the forearm and extension then flexion of the wrist and fingers. When the infant was lying on its back, prereaching movements towards a suspended object appeared to be reprogrammed to take account of the changed pull of gravitation, which is evidence for rather complex postural controls. At the climax of the movement the forearm is balanced in a vertical position in both orientations of the trunk (Figure 4).

Patterns of finger extension and of apposition in flexion seem to vary widely in no obvious adaptation to the object's size and shape which is presumably poorly perceived, but frequently the hand shows signs of orienting with an outward or inward turning of the wrist. Therefore there was at least some organization of circuits in spinal motor centres for directing activity of the intricate muscles of forearm and hand that move the fingers. However, many hand movements appeared distorted by reflex grasping or avoidance responses. Both arm and hand were discoordinated when the infant was highly aroused or distressed, pre-reaching responses in orientation to a visual goal being clear only in reasonably calm and alert subjects.

Pre-reaching movements were too feeble and too stereotyped to achieve prehension with adequate guidance. They were also in prefunctional state with respect to body kinetics. Controlled arm extension, to allow progressive adjustment of grasp or prolonged handling of an object at a distance from the body or to track a displacing object and to transport an object once grasped, was beyong the newborn. The superordinate 'programs' for such accommodation of the movement developed in the next few months.

A preliminary kinetic analysis of pre-reaching movements exposes some interesting features of their genesis. Because the movement involves rotations uf upper arm and forearm about their long axes as well as extensions, retractions, abductions and adductions at shoulder and elbow, it can be only partly represented in one plane. Nevertheless vertical displacement of the wrist seen in the frontal plane gives a fair impression of the cycle which lasts about three seconds, reaching an apex in one second (Figure 5A). The movement oscillates and there is a preponderance

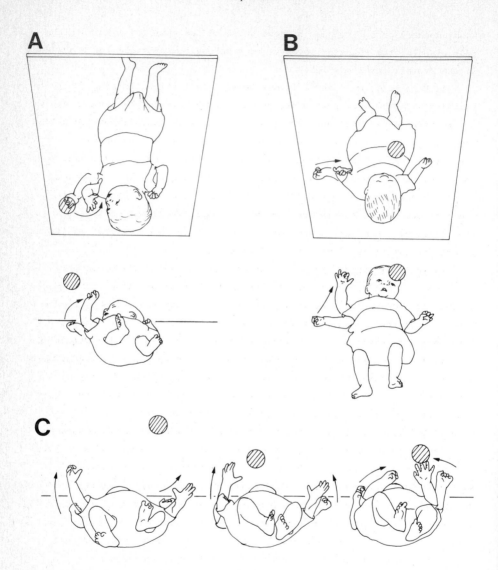

Fig. 4. Prereaching with different body positions, 2 to 3 weeks.
A, lying on back; B, in chair with back inclined 15° from
vertical. Mirror shows vertical downward views.
C, successive attempts of a prone newborn to reach for a
slowly displaced ball.

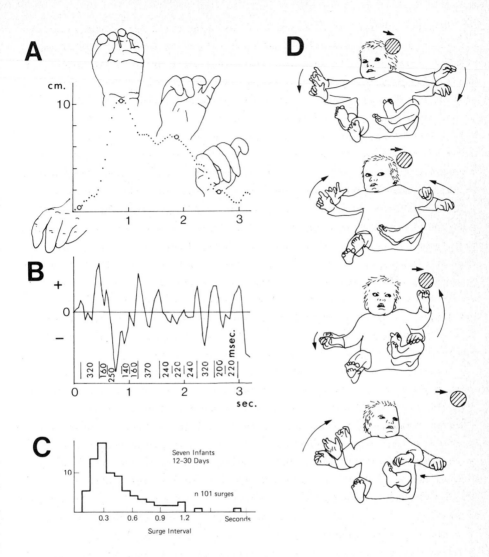

Fig. 5. Prereaching at 23 days after birth. Vertical displacement
of the center of the wrist (A); acceleration (B) showing
swinging or stepping. Hand part-open at climax of wrist
displacement. C: Frequency histogram of intervals between
lifts or wrist for 7 newborns shows a main period of
approximately 300 milliseconds.
D: Successive postures while infant tracks an object
moving slowly to her left.

of a regular stepping of motor activity at three lifts per second which is clearly revealed in an acceleration curve (Figure 5, B and C). The climax, when the wrist is at its apex of displacement and closest to the object, is usually achieved in two or three steps, and then the return to rest is slower. There is frequently a plateau or sustained elevation for about a second after the first drop from the climax.

Pre-reaching, since it does not involve guidance or redirection of movements during the cycle, can be described as 'ballistic' or 'open loop'. However, a succession of pre-reaching movements, possibly involving both hands, may show tracking in conjunction with whole body orientations (Figure 5D). Such oriented activities also involve the feet which move in quadripedal synchrony with the hands. The figures of hand and foot movements seem to be varied and complex, some resembling quadripedal walking, others more like climbing. It would be of interest to make an analysis of these movements in comparison with hand and foot placements of a person reaching while standing or walking, or a primate reaching to grasp while climbing and hanging on with the other limbs. I believe they show evidence of a very different organization from the crossed movements required when a standing quadruped extends a forelimb to touch an object on one side.

Opening of the hand and its aiming towards the target is tightly coordinated with the climax of wrist movement even in the earliest reaching (Figures 2 and 6). Thus the proximo-distal coordination essential to efficient reaching and grasping is provided for in the neural system that is formed before birth. Observations of Tryphena Humphrey suggest that this reach and grasp pattern is visible in movements of human fetuses at an age when it may be assumed that only spinal motor centres are functional (Humphrey, 1969). Humphrey (loc.cit) commented on the repetition of development of grasping movements, both fetal and postnatal stages showing a progress from closure of all fingers together without finger-thumb apposition to individual extension and retraction of index or little finger, and index-thumb apposition. Jeannerod's studies of adult movements to pick up objects show that the mature skill retains a temporal patterning of arm and hand movements which is independent of visual guidance (Jeannerod, 1982). This pattern is remarkably similar to the pre-reaching cycle illustrated in Figure 6.

When quiet, an infant of two- to three-months may perform a perfect and well-aimed reach and grasp, but the most common response is a jerky extension and retraction of the arm with considerable movement at the shoulder and

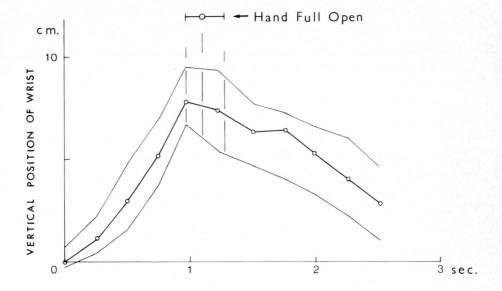

Fig. 6. Hand opening and arm extension in prereaching. Median
height and interquartile range of center of wrist, timed
from the start of displacement for 15 responses of 5
newborns. Maximum finger opening occurs at the climax
of lift.

little or no orientation of the hand which usually remains fisted. The baby
orients to objects and tracks them with improved oculomotor coordination,
but the arms are held stiffly out from the body and they make erratic and
poorly directed swipes. Both arms may make alternating jerks towards the
object with fingers in flexion (Figure 2 and 3). Thus the reach and grasp
pattern of pre-reaching is blocked or inhibited while the now visibly
growing musculature of the shoulder and limb is responding with strong
phasic contractions in which extensors and flexors are working in opposition.
At four months there occurs a rapid improvement in proximal muscular
coordination with a progressive diminution of the oscillations. By five
months most infants are capable of well-directed if ataxic reaching movements
in which the course of arm extension may be graded, redirected and stabilized
for several seconds to permit grasping of a suspended object. Objects resting
on a surface are not grasped so readily and reaching is less easily evoked

by them at this age.

James Alt and I carried out an experiment at Harvard calculated to test the theory of Piaget that eye-hand coordination is acquired by infants, after they have 'learned' to aim their arms in different directions and to orient their eyes, by the infant shifting gaze back and forth between the hand and the object. Alternation of gaze is supposed to allow 'mutual assimilation' of spatial schemata that are initially separate for oculomotor and reaching movements. This theory was supported by White Castle and Held (1964) who observed hand regard with institutionalized infants whose reaching was retarded in an impoverished environment that lacked opportunities for the babies to use spontaneous reaching and grasping.

Alt devised a lightweight screen that could be attached to a headband on a baby. With the head of the infant facing forwards, this screen completely blocked the view of the arm and hand in either peripheral or central vision. With infants 16 to 20 weeks of age reaching movements were directed towards an object suspended in front of the infant and in no case did the infant make an attempt to see the arm either before attempting the reach or in the course of its execution. Figure 7 traced from a film taken at 16 frames/second shows one such response. It may be seen that the vertical component of wrist displacement manifests ballistic propulsion with steps separated by about 250 msec which are clearly seen in the acceleration curve. There appears to be an excessive lift of the hand which is corrected at 1.7 seconds after the record starts. The correction may have followed entry of the hand into the visual field, but it seems too soon. An alternative hypothesis is that the infant deprived of some advantage of peripheral vision of the approaching hand has wandered slightly off course and made a correction on the basis of feedback from the limb and an accurate localization of the object from visual fixation. By measuring reaching movements of infants fitted with prisms, von Hofsten has shown that a subject of about this age is capable of accurately determining the distance of an object by convergence of gaze (von Hofsten, 1977). Presumably visual direction is estimated with equal accuracy.

Von Hofsten has recently made accurate measures of the transportations of the wrist and orientation of the hand that babies make to intercept an attractive object that passes in an horizontal arc at about chest level (von Hofsten, 1980). He discovered that catching movements were easily elicited and that they were surprisingly efficient even for objects moving at a velocity of 30cm/second with infants who are just beginning to perform controlled reaching (18 weeks of age). Response to faster moving objects

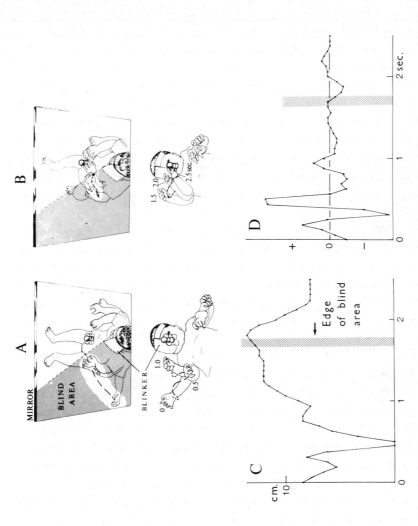

Fig. 7. Alt's experiment with screen preventing visual guidance of reaching arm. Subject 18 weeks. Center of wrist plotted from film at 16 frames/second. Possible visual correction of aim at last ½ second (B). Vertical displacement of wrist (C) and unsmoothed acceleration (D) show periodicity of lift, with correction for fall of arm at 0.5 seconds.

were quicker and more direct than those to slowly moving objects, the
movement showing clear anticipation - that is, the trajectory of the hand
was aimed ahead of the object from the start of the response, while the
object was still out of reach, to intercept it accurately. First reaches
were as accurate as those to subsequent presentations of the object and there
was no sign of alternation of gaze between the object and the hand. Von
Hofsten (1983) explains this performance by assuming that the infant makes
a direct internal representation of the vector of displacement of the object
from visual information, accurate for speed, direction and distance, and
combines this with a vector of arm extensions that would project the hand at
a definite rate towards the position of the object at the start of the reach.
The resultant of these two vectors is then the path along which the wrist
is actually carried. That is, the wrist is displaced both towards the object
and with it.

   Wrist displacement curves of von Hofsten's subjects confirm that there
is an improvement in the central program that responds to reafferent
(proprioceptive) information beyond four months. Initial reaches are ataxic
with an oscillation of approximately 3/second. Later the movement shows two
phases, an initial rapid extension lasting about $\frac{1}{2}$ second and then a varied
series of steps, more for a slower object, at about 4/second. Grasping and
holding of the object (which has a very low inertia) occurs more frequently
after six months in parallel with controlled reaching and these behaviours
develop earlier in females, males catching up after six months.

   Von Hofsten's observations of newborns (4-9 days of age) prove that
extensions of the arm can be directed towards a visually fixated object
whether there is a head rotation towards the object or not (von Hofsten,
1982). He confirmed that the hand moves in a succession of ballistic steps,
reaches a point closer to the object at the climax if the object is being
fixated and that it slows down at this point. He considers the movements
to be part of a coordinated exploratory impulse that provides the substrate
for later development of effective visuomotor coordination.

   A film study of grasping objects from a surface in Gesell's laboratory
by Halverson described improvement in orientation of the digits to obtain
a precisely measured grip between thumb and fingers and a change from placing
the whole palm over the object to orientation so that it came to lie between
index finger and thumb (Halverson, 1943). Delicate manipulation of small
objects under visual control occupies infants towards the end of the first
year. Reflex studies by Twitchell (1965) chart an increasing sensitivity in

the hand to contact with an object and differentiation of individual responses
by the fingers. Furthermore, touch-stimulated responses develop in
association with turning movements to correct for misreaching visually
perceived (visual groping). This use of the distal component of the inherent
reach-to-grasp program is refined after controlled arm extension has been
achieved about six months.

The evidence from accurate observations of how walking and reaching and
grasping develop which has been reviewed indicates that infants are born with
a considerable part of the neural structures that will coordinate these
functional patterns of muscle activity in adults. Responses newborns make to
stimuli appear to arise as modifications of movement sequences that they can
produce without stimulation. Developments in behaviour result, we find, from
the acquisition of more efficient preparation in the innate motor coordinative
structures for specific directions and magnitudes of stimulation. The process
is at least partly a learning how to perceive conditions for specific plans
for movement, and learning how to infer what conditions will be like in the
future. Some of the afferent contribution to motor control and to learned
improvement in control takes the form of inevitable reafference of feedback
from immediate consequences arising in the body itself. Other forms of
stimulation are dictated by events or objects outside the subject, who may
act with selective orientation, approach, withdrawal or avoidance with
respect to these events or objects. To accomplish such selective engagement
with exterior phenomena the subject must possess a representation of a spatial
field in which the locations of things may be specified with reference to the
body and its movements.

The coordinations that neonates make spontaneously between movements of
head and eyes, arms and hands, legs and feet when they orient to external
events that they see or hear indicate that a spatial field exists at birth
(Trevarthen, 1974b). However, a newborn infant can neither reach and grasp
an object nor walk. For both kinds of action there is a systematic improvement
in the uptake and prediction of information about the body itself (motor
learning), and improvement in the use of perception to gain a useful description
of the conditions, risks and opportunities for movement that are outside the
body. This latter kind of development includes what psychologists call
cognitive learning.

Although the products of cognitive development are mental representations
that may exist in absence of movement to describe reality outside the body,
the formation of these representations must be dependent upon biodynamic

principles that are built into the nervous system and visible in the immature
motor coordinations of infants. The anatomical and physiological specifications
of the innate structures for coordination of movements may be perceived in
the regular features of movements to which Bernstein's descriptive analysis
draws our attention.

In both walking and running we find an orchestrated sequence of
overlapping events at each joint such that, among other patterns, distal
segments execute their greatest movements at a time of reduced proximal
activity. The movements have a tendency to periodicity, being composed of
surges - accelerations followed by decelerations - that reflect well-timed
activity of antagonistic sets of muscles. Indeed the action may be described
as composed of a succession of saccades, like those that couple conjugate
rotations of the eyeballs, but with, in general, much lower maximum angular
velocity (Figures 3 and 5, C). Oculomotor saccades occupy about 50 milliseconds,
large displacements of the head or limbs take about 500 milliseconds (Figure
8). Major displacements are overlaid by small wavelets in the displacement
curves of limb segments that suggest a regulated periodicity of saccades
that serve to divide up or group episodes of engagement with sensory feedback.
We have not looked at the periodic movements used in visual, olfactory,
gustatory or tactual exploration, but we have seen periodicity in the output
that will produce intermittent proprioceptive effects in the body. The tempo
of this periodic output of motor activity in the course of complex behavioural
figures of movement does not appear to be imposed on a passive nervous system
by the inertial or pendular characteristics of the body and its parts, which
are under continuous restraint by the tonic contractions in antagonistic sets
of muscles. Saccadic periodicity expresses an intermittency in the central
motivating system, one form of neural coding of time for behaviour.

The coupling of action in proximal and distal segments and the linking of
special sensory systems (eyes, ears, hands, mouth) that use movement to
extract and select information for perception are expressed in the shared beat
of stepping of all the motor structures of the body. Further work is needed
to determine how this coordinative integrity arises in the system that
directs exploratory movements of different parts of the body and that couples
explorations to performances which utilize the environment more deliberately.
Available evidence would suggest that the anatomical structure for intermodal
sensory equivalence and for equivalence of alternative orienting movements
is functioning in newborns (Trevarthen, Murray & Hubley, 1981). Obviously
their capacity to make performatory actions is very limited.

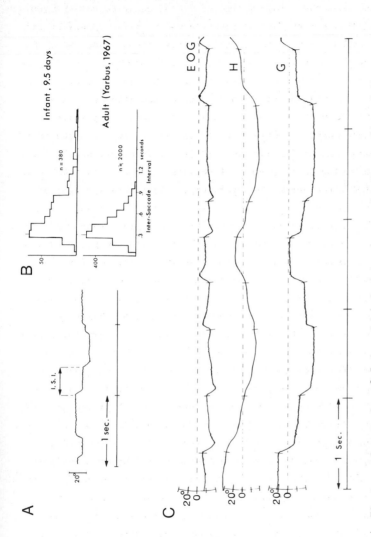

Fig. 8. A: Electrooculogram from 9.5 day old infant to show conjugate saccades of the eyes.
B: Histogram of intervals between saccades for same infant compared to that for adults
measured by Yarbus (1967).
C: Infant, 11 weeks, tracking ping-pong ball with illuminated bulb at center that is
oscillating in an arc concentric with infant's head. Tracking is saccadic. Eye rotations
(EOG) add to coincident steps of the head (H) producing steps of gaze (G). Note: Drifts in
gaze are an artifact reflecting mismatch in amplification of EOG and signal from potentiometer measuring head rotations. In reality back rotation of the eyes accurately compensate
head rotations.

Descriptive and experimental studies of the development of movements strongly support the idea that it is in the nature of motor coordination to 'explore' the mechanical periphery, to conduct a search for programs of activity that will exploit the potential of the body and of objects that come in contact with it, to generate forces that will contribute to adaptive actions and to efficiently subdue or avoid forces that might destroy coordination. Thus movements made by infants show up the strategy of the C.N.S. for achieving a more effective course of action; its caution, confidence, power and skill. These qualities of motivation appear in such features of the displacement curves as the number and acceleration of saccades, and the size of oscillations that arise from impulsive reactions of the muscles tightening or releasing to correct for errors of motor output (Bernstein's 'reactive' waves).

The scientific study of infant movements is just beginning and, so far, most attention has been given to their orienting movements and use of objects. Nevertheless, I believe enough has been described for us to entertain the following far-reaching hypothesis. I would propose that to understand the movements of infants fully we shall have to consider specialized forms of motivation that have evolved to show up steps of the planning for movement so other human beings can be affected. Certainly, expressive and communicative movements of adults capitalize on all the above described external signs of their brains' search for motor control, to generate messages about the intensity, confidence and curiosity behind what they are trying to do. Other subjects/agents, with appropriate perceptual and cognitive abilities, can respond to these messages. Thus is created the possibility of 'inter-subjective' engagement and cooperative action (Trevarthen, 1978, 1983b). There would seem to be a need for infants to possess at least the rudiments of this expressive and receptive ability, in order to obtain the human services they require from caretakers. They may also need to have it in order to develop more precise and effective forms of communication.

Figure 9 shows features of expressive manual gestures of young infants and their coordination with other expressive movements. These arm and hand movements have a close resemblance to those we saw in 'pre-reaching', but there are differences which appear to take account of the fact that such movements can have expressive value only if another person is playing attention to them.

Infants reach for, grasp and manipulate objects well before they crawl or walk. They gesticulate expressions of emotion and can regulate complex facial and vocal interactions with caretakers weeks before they manipulate

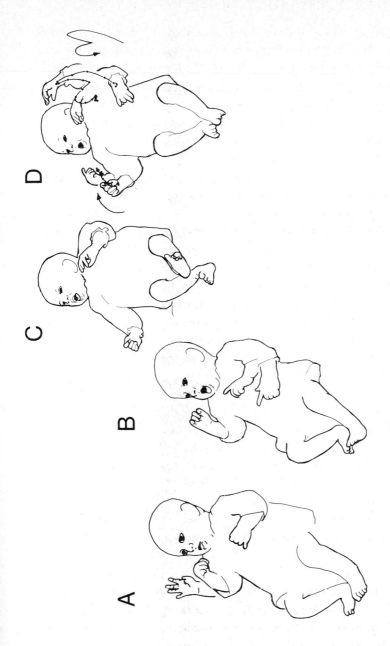

Fig. 9. Six-week-olds in face-to-face interaction with their mothers. Gestures accompany facial and vocal expression.
A: Infant waves right hand.
B: Two seconds later the right hand is closed and the baby extends and raises the left index finger, simultaneously opening mouth and extending tongue.
C: Infant raises left hand with fingers opposed and touches lower lip with tongue.
D: Same infant waves arms rhythmically while vocalising.

objects. Orienting and pre-reaching behaviours indicate that infants are
born with biodynamic structures that embody a certain 'knowledge' or
functional readiness for experience of objects, and the expressive
behaviours are evidence of innate readiness for human communication. The
order of development appears to be the reverse of that an empiricist would
assume. Infants do not learn either to take possession of objects or to
communicate by a process that builds links between sensory-motor arcs. Their
brains contain a representation of an external reality and the people in it.

It is generally accepted that very young infants are highly sensitive
to active stimuli - moving or changing visual effects, sounds of movement
including gently ringing bells and speech, stroking and patting, rocking,
etc. A baby is roused from sleep and calmed from agitation by human activity.
How do they detect this activity in such diverse sensory forms? Close
observation reveals that they attend particularly to events that specify
nearby movements of persons, and that they are highly sensitive to the
affective or motivational quality of behaviour. When briskly handled they
become still and withdrawn, if surprised by a sudden vigorous action they
cry, to gentle affectionate signs they attend quietly and with focalization.
Mothers ministering to young infants closely observe all such indications
of their state of alertness, contentment and interest. A mother coordinates
her stimulations to relate intimately to what the baby does. Mothers also
tend to employ repetitive movements grouped in clusters or bursts. The
tempo of their gestures, vocalizations and shifts of posture becomes slowed,
regular and accentuated (Figure 10A). The positive responses of the infants
to this behaviour indicates that their mothers are unconsciously providing
optimal communication. Microanalysis reveals that the movements of mother
and infant interact with timing precise to a fraction of a second (Figure
11B). The infant's movements are similar in tempo to those of the mother
(Figure 10A and C) and they may be very precisely reactive to and intercalated
with the utterances of the mothers (Figure 11B).

It is significant that the tempo and organization of adult communication
signals, especially those of baby talk, closely approaches the spontaneous
tempo and organization of infantile movements, structural features which
are discernible even when the infant is in a situation where there is no
possibility of pacing by an outside source. Some years ago I proposed that
this similarity of generative motor structure in infant and adult is
responsible for furnishing the infant with a detector of human movement
(Trevarthen, 1974c, 1978), a structure which resonates with the mother's

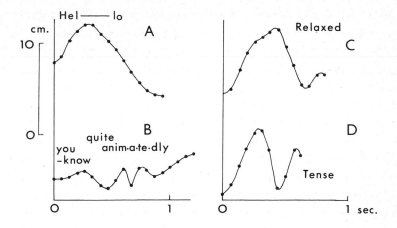

Fig. 10. Vertical displacements of tip of nose of mother coincide
with vocal emphasis.
A: Slow, regular displacement accompanying affectionate
speech to a two-month-old.
B: Staccato burst of nods while talking to an adult.

Arm movements (vertical displacements of wrist) express
level of motivation of her infant.
C: In animated, happy interaction with mother.
D: Angry trashing when ignored by mother, infant alternately
tense and withdrawn or protesting (From Tatam, 1974).

patterned activity. Condon and Sander showed that indeed newborns have a
high degree of self-synchrony between movements of parts of their bodies,
and they claimed evidence that a newborn could become synchronized with the
speech rhythms of an adult (Condon & Sander, 1974).

Other special features of human signals, such as the fundamental frequency
of the voice or the colour of light reflected from the face, and the peculiar
anatomy of expressive organs such as the face and hands must be preferentially
discriminated as well. How else would a newborn show selective awareness of
eyes, mouth and hands and their actions, and be able to imitate these actions
(Maratos, 1973; Meltzoff & Moore, 1977; Field et al., 1982)? Nevertheless,
the primary detector structure in the infant may be an 'ecphorator' for
movement, as Bernstein called it, which has a measure of time built into it
matching the time characteristics of the movements of an attentive and caring
adult partner. This neural basis for empathic response would underlie
imitation in both directions, and also turntaking and the more productive

complementary forms of action in the two partners that appear in game
playing and 'protoconversational' exchanges (Trevarthen, 1983a, b). In a
recent experimental test, Kuhl and Meltzoff (1983) showed that five month
olds could discriminate which movement of the mouth, seen in a pair of
silent moving displays of a face pronouncing two different syllables, matched
a speech sound presented on a loudspeaker. They also noted that the infants
vocalized in an imitative manner in alternation with the sounds, and that
the pattern of change of fundamental frequency in time of the infant sounds
closely resembled that of the sound made by the adult. Figure 11B shows
that already at six weeks, before voicing is controlled to produce pure
sounds, an infant makes vocalizations with a segmentation close to the
mother's utterances of baby talk. The mother modulates the pitch of her
vocalizations to match the infant's expressions (Figure 11A and C).

While newborns a few minutes old may exhibit orienting and affective
reactions that indicate a preference for human signals, a six-week-old
is capable of focalizing on a mother's face and vocalizing in interaction
with her (Figure 11). The improved orienting of the older baby guides the
mother to sharpen up the forms of her baby talk. Delicately regulated
engagements occur that depend on precise mutual tracking. If the engagements
are perturbed by interruption or tampering with the feedback of expressive
signals, the baby becomes distressed (Tatam, 1974; Murray, 1980, Trevarthen,
Hubley & Murray, 1981).

In recent years much has been learned about the fundamental basis for
human communication by detailed examination of the patterns of movement of
mothers and infants while they interact. But this is only the beginning of
an adequate analysis of the kinesics of mother-infant interaction. Well
controlled 'protoconversational' engagements occur before reaching is
effective. Indeed it appears as if the motor abilities related to expression
of feelings about other persons matures earliest, next to the essential
automatic activities of feeding, self-protection and crying for aid.
Expressive actions that regulate interpersonal contact mature at least as
quickly as the visual focalizing and tracking movements which undergo great
improvement in the second and third months (Trevarthen, Murray & Hubley,
1981; Trevarthen, 1983a).

Before infants reach, their interactions with their mothers become more
gamelike with an element of deliberate experimentation, positive and approach
behaviours being mixed with negative and avoidant or defiant behaviour
(Trevarthen, 1983a, b). A sense of humour emerges which is very sensitive

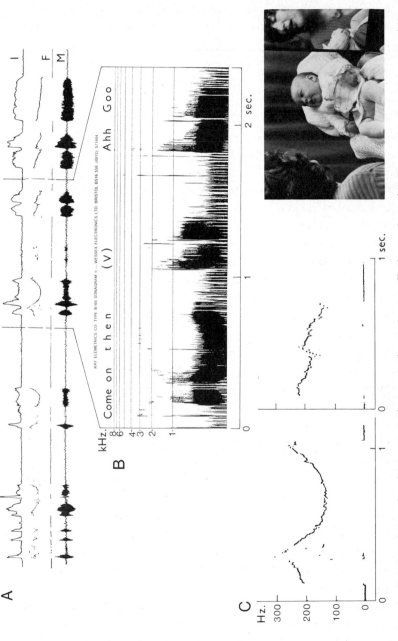

Fig. 11. A: Vocal interaction between mother and six-week-old. Mother makes three appeals for response with U-shaped intonation. After infant vocalizes a bi-syllable, V, she makes three imitative or sympathetic utterances with descending pitch. I= Sound intensity; F= Fundamental frequency; M= Microphone signal. B: Sonogram shows precise temporal intersynchrony of maternal and infant vocalizations. C: Enlarged plots of fundamental frequency for mother's utterances. Compare with head movements of Figure 10A. Photo shows infant at moment of vocalization, V.

to that special form of contingent and episodic activity from a partner
called 'teasing' (Figure 12). Here we have evidence that the inter-
subjective meachanisms that are empathizing with or mirroring and reacting
in reply to the signals of the partner undergo intrinsically regulated
development. The infant experiments with reafference from the human partner.
This important advance in communication occurs just before controlled arm
extension develops. That is, before the infant begins to manipulate objects
at four months of age (Trevarthen, 1983b). Play with objects develops later.

The expressive movements undergo rapid development in the second half
of the first year. The infant progresses from babbling to protolanguage and
may imitate a few words by one year. At the same time hand gestures become
more distinct from movements of prehension. Hands and voice may be used
by the baby to imitate a dancing or chanting game, such as 'clappa clappa
handies' (Trevarthen, 1983b). Facial mimicry is also characteristic of
humorous behaviour of infants over six months of age.

After nine months there is beginning to be an awareness in the infant
of the purposes behind the actions of others and of symbolic or conventional
forms of movement (Hubley & Trevarthen, 1979; Trevarthen, 1983b). Before the
end of the first year a deaf child of deaf mute parents may begin to learn
the arbitrary hand signs of American Sign Language (Bellugi, personal
communication). The gestures of pointing, waving and signing exhibit lateral
asymmetry from early in their development, which would appear to indicate
control from lateralized regions of the cerebral cortex, tissues which achieve
full maturity only years later (Trevarthen, 1983c). Obviously we have far
to go before we can describe the natural stages by which expressive behaviours
develop, but the outlines are already clear of an elaborate maturation before
language is mastered.

Now that we possess more detailed descriptions of what infants can do,
it is possible to put research into the development of coordinated behaviours
on a more secure factual basis. Previously the concept of conditioning, which
used a grossly oversimplified model of the cerebral mechanism for sensory-
motor coordination, was supposed to explain the acquisition of all forms of
adaptive response that required perception of external conditions. Social
patterns of behaviour, in particular, were thought to be entirely learned.
Although infants and children certainly do learn by imitation and this
learning influences the form of their expressive movements, the structural
foundations for the imitated movements cannot be learned. It is necessary
to assume an innate structure that at least partly matches the structure of

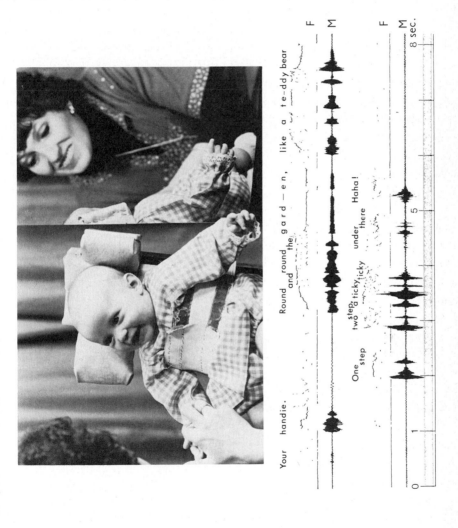

Your handie.   Round round gard—en, like a te—ddy bear and the.

One step two'a ticky ticky under Haha! step there

F
M

F
M
8 sec.

0   1   5

Fig. 12. Mother chants a nursery rhyme to an attentive 20-week-old, varying pitch and timing of her speech to control the emotion of her infant who collaborates enthusiastically.

els to explain both imitation and the more complex reciprocal
tary interactions which are characteristic of communication
between child and adult from immediately after birth.

By following the microdescriptive method of Bernstein and by applying
his kind of exact but imaginative theorizing all types of human activity
may reveal their natural coordinative principles. These principles are the
expression of structural features of neural systems that develop in the
brain of an unborn child and that gain in adaptive power by systematic,
directed exploitation of environmental conditions stage by stage through
childhood. Thus learning itself becomes an inseparable part of the maturation
of the 'biodynamic structures' that tie perception to action.

ACKNOWLEDGEMENTS

My research on split brain monkeys and human commissurotomy patients
was supported by the Frank P. Hixon Fund of the California Institute of
Technology and the U.S Public Health Service in Professor Roger Sperry's
laboratory.

The work on infants began under U.S Public Health Service support with
Professor Jerome Bruner at Harvard. Subsequent observations of the development
of reaching, made in collaboration with Penelope Hubley, was supported by the
Medical Research Council of the U.K, and studies of infant communication were
funded by the Social Science Research Council of the U.K and the Spencer
Foundation of Chicago.

I am indebted to Dr. David Lee and his colleagues for practical help and
much useful discussion in the preparation of this paper.

REFERENCES

Brinkman, J. & Kuypers, H.G.J.M. Cerebral control of contralateral and
ipsilateral arm, hand and finger movements in the split-brain rhesus
monkey. Brain, 1973, 96, 653-674.

Forssberg, H. Spinal locomotor functions and descending control. In, B.
Sjölund and A. Björhlund (Eds.), Brain Stem Control of Spinal Mechanisms,
Fernström Foundation Series, No. 1: New York, Oxford, 1982.

Forssberg, H. & Nashner, L.M. Ontogenetic development of postural control
in man: Adaptation to altered support and visual conditions during stance.
Journal of Neuroscience, 1982.

Forssberg, H. & Wallberg, H. Infant locomotion - a preliminary movement and
electromyographic study. In, K. Berg and B. Erikson (Eds.), International
Series on Sport Sciences, Vol. 10. Children and Exercise, IX. Baltimore:
University Park Press, 1980.

Glickstein, M. & Gibson, A. Visual cells in the pons of the brain.
Scientific American, 1976, 235, 90-98.

Grillner, S. & Zangger, P. On the central generation of locomotion in the
low spinal cat. Experimental Brain Research, 1979, 34, 241-262.

Halverson, H.M. The development of prehension in infants. In, R.G. Barker,
J.S. Kounin and H.F. Wright (Eds.), Child Behavior and Development.
New York: McGraw Hill, 1943.

Harris, A.J. Eye movements of the dogfish Squalis acanthias, L. Journal of
Experimental Biology, 1965, 43, 107-130.

Hubley, P. & Trevarthen, C. Sharing a task in infancy. In, I. Uzgiris (Ed.),
Social Interaction During Infancy, New Directions for Child Development,
1979, 4, 57-80.

Humphrey, T. Postnatal repetitions of human prenatal activity sequences with
some suggestions of their neuroanatomical basis. In, R.J. Robinson (Ed.),
Brain and Early Behaviour. London and New York: Academic Press, 1969.

Jacobson, M. Developmental Neurobiology. New York: Holt, 1970.

Jeannerod, M. Intersegmental coordination during reaching at natural visual
objects. In, J. Long and A. Baddeley, A. (Eds.), Attention and Performance,
IX, Hillsdale: Erlbaum, 1981.

Kuhl, P.K. & Meltzoff, A.N. The bimodal perception of speech in infancy.
Science, 1982, 218, 1138-1140.

Kuypers, H.G.J.M. Cortico-spinal connections: postnatal development in the
rhesus monkey. Science, 1962, 138, 678-680.

The anatomical organization of the descending pathways
ributions to motor control especially in primates. In,
(Ed.), New Developments in E.M.G. and Clinical Neurophysiology, Vol. 3. Basel: Karger, 1973.

Lee, D.N. The functions of vision. In, H.L. Pick and E. Saltzman (Eds.),
Psychological Modes of Perceiving and Processing Information. Hillsdale,
N.J.: Erlbaum, 1978.

Lee, D.N. The optic flow field: The foundation of vision. Philosophical
Transactions of the Royal Society, Series B, 1980, 290, 169-179.

Lee, D.N. & Aronson, E. Visual proprioceptive control of standing in human
infants. Perception and Psychophysics, 1974, 15, 529-532.

Meltzoff, A.N. & Moore, M.H. Imitation of facial and manual gestures by
human neonates. Science, 1977, 198, 75-78.

Rader, N., Bausano, M. & Richards, J.E. On the nature of visual-cliff-
avoidance response in human infants. Child Development, 1980, 51, 61-68.

Trevarthen, C. Functional interactions between the cerebral hemispheres of
the split-brain monkey. In, E.G. Ettlinger (Ed.), Functions of the Corpus
Callosum. Ciba Foundation Study Group, No. 20. London: Churchill, 1965,
24-40.

Trevarthen, C. Vision in fish: the origins of the visual frame for action
in vertebrates. In, D. Ingle (Ed.), The Central Nervous System and Fish
Behaviour. Chicago: Chicago University Press, 1968a, 61-94.

Trevarthen, C. Two mechanisms of vision in primates. Psychologische
Forschung, 1968b, 31, 299-377.

Trevarthen. C. Cerebral embryology and the split brain. In, M. Kinsbourne
and W.L. Smith (Eds.), Hemispheric Disconnection and Cerebral Function.
Springfield, Illinois: Charles C. Thomas, 1974a, 208-236.

Trevarthen, C. L'action dans l'espace et la perception de l'espace:
Méchanismes cérébraux de base. In, F. Bresson et al. (Eds.), De l'Espace
Corporel a l'Espace Écologique. Paris: Presses Universitaires de France,
1974b, 65-80.

Trevarthen, C. The psychobiology of speech development. In, E.H. Lenneberg
(Ed.), Language and Brain: Developmental Aspects (Neurosciences Research
Program Bulletin, 12). Cambridge, Mass: Neurosciences Research Program
1974c, 570-585.

Trevarthen, C. The role of midbrain visuo-motor centers in man. In, D. Ingle
and J. Sprague (Eds.), Sensorimotor Function of the Midbrain Tectum
(Neurosciences Research Program Bulletin, 13). Cambridge, Mass:
Neurosciences Research Program, 1975, 169-288.

Trevarthen, C. Modes of perceiving and modes of action. In, J.H. Pick (Ed.),
    Psychological Modes of Perceiving and Processing Information. Hillsdale,
    N.J.: Erlbaum, 1978, 99-136.

Trevarthen, C. Neuroembryology and the development of perception. In, F.
    Falkner and J.M. Tanner (Eds.), Human Growth: A comprehensive Treatise,
    Vol. III. New York: Plenum, 1979, 2-96.

Trevarthen, C. Neurological development and the growth of psychological
    functions. In, J. Sants (Ed.), Developmental Psychology and Society.
    London: MacMillans, 1980, 46-95.

Trevarthen, C. Basic patterns of psychogenetic change in infancy. In, T.
    Bever, (Ed.), Dips in Learning. Hillsdale, J.J.: Erlbaum, 1982.

Trevarthen, C. Emotions in infancy: Regulators of contacts and relationships
    with persons. In, K. Scherer and P. Ekman (Eds.), Approaches to Emotion,
    1983a (in press).

Trevarthen, C. Interpersonal abilities of infants as generators for
    transmissions of language and culture. In, A. Oliverio and M. Zapella
    (Eds.), The Behaviour of Human Infants. London and New York: Plenum,
    1983b.

Trevarthen, C. Cerebral mechanisms for language: Prenatal and postnatal
    development. In, U. Kirk (Ed.), Neuropsychology of Language, Reading and
    Spelling. New York: Academic Press, 1983c.

Twitchell, T.E. The automatic grasping responses of infants. Neuropsychologia,
    1965, 3, 247-259.

von Hofsten, C. Binocular convergence as a determinant of reaching behaviour
    in infancy. Perception, 1977, 6, 139-144.

von Hofsten, C. Predictive reaching for moving objects by human infants.
    Journal of Experimental Child Psychology, 1980, 30, 369-382.

von Hofsten, C. Eye-hand coordination in the newborn. Developmental Psychology,
    1982, 18, 450-461.

von Hofsten, C. Catching skills in infancy. Journal of Experimental Psychology:
    Human Perception and Performance, 1983, 9, 75-85.

White, B.L., Castle, P. & Held, R. Observations on the development of visually
    directed reaching. Child Development, 1964, 35, 349-364.

Yakovlev, P.I. & LeCours, A.R. The myelogenetic cycles of regional maturation
    of the brain. In, A. Minkowski (Ed.), Regional Development of the Brain
    in Early Life. Oxford: Blackwell, 1967.

CHAPTER IIIb

BIODYNAMICS OF LOCOMOTION, FORTY YEARS LATER

R.H. Rozendal

1.   INTRODUCTION.

Urging physiologists to study human movement in a new way, Bernstein inadvertently became — by postulating a coordinational reflex — one of the founders of cybernetics. This reflex is, metaphorically speaking, "not an arc but a closed circle with functional synapses at both ends of the arcs" (p. 216). More interesting, within the framework of this paper, is his departure from classical physiological views by postulating rather structuralistic concepts of movements "not as chains of details but structures which are differentiated into details" (p.179). In 1940, he considered one of the most important aspects of his approach to be his observational and descriptive work carried out with maximal refinement on the locomotor process as if it were a very complex morphological object. An object which reacts, evolves and involutes. After a thorough description, he had hoped to decipher the dynamics of locomotor acts by means of more or less complex mathemetical and physiological tools, which would permit the revealment of the underlying central nervous processes (p.176).

In setting this aim, he claimed that locomotor acts as such deserved investigation. Spontaneous or intentional movements, he maintained, comprise a peripheral and a central cycle of interaction corresponding with biomechanical and informational processes. His work stands as an important contribution to biophysical research on movement. Therefore, according to Bernstein the programme of this research had to be twofold. In conformity with this view this paper will contain biomechanical as well as cybernetical considerations, as is quite customary in modern biophysical studies of movement. Both approaches — the biomechanical and the neurophysiological — were needed at the same time, according to Bernstein, as a one-to-one correspondence does not exist between the neuronally induced forces and the resulting movements. "Movements are not completely determined by effector processes", (p. 213). This is formulated in biophysical language at the bottom of page 167, metaphorically illustrated in

Fig. 14 and discussed by him in Section 5 of Chapter III under the terms
functional non-univocality and indeterminacy.

In Section 3 of this paper this non-univocality will be discussed in
the light of 40 years of research. This discussion will not be limited - as
was Chapter III almost exclusively - to locomotion. Tentative conclusions
will be drawn concerning the reformulation of the task of the coordinating
nervous system in solving motor problems, starting from a biomechanical
analysis of the motor processes.

By such an analysis, Bernstein tried to explain the task of the
controlling (or coordinating) nervous system. By choosing locomotion, as an
automated movement for which, from ancient times, man has learned to bring
a lot of muscles into synergy, resulting in a movement of stable structure,
Bernstein sketched a new important line of research. Next to locomotion he
studied other skilled movements. Though he himself never used the word, the
concept of optimalization is implicit in the choice of the movements studied,
as well as in the more or less speculative considerations on motor coordination
in Section 5 of Chapter III (Bernstein, 1967). Many researchers have taken
the same classes of movements. Automated or - by training - highly skilled
movements are made by numerous subjects in order to give the researchers a
chance to "adopt constant criteria for the discrimination of the random from
the regular" (p. 171). Optimalized movements in sports and fast or ballistic
movements of the extremities, especially the upper one, are studied most
frequently next to walking and running.

General theories of walking and other forms of locomotion of idealized
animals also depend on optimalizational principles e.g., the transformation
of kinetic into potential energy or the storage and re-utilization of
potential energy in elastic tissues appear to be some of the mechanisms used
for optimalization of the energy cost of locomotion (Alexander, 1977; Cavagna,
1978).

Two points have to be made here. On the one hand it appears that the
concept of optimalization has played a unifying role in the development of
research on locomotion. It may be that the time has arrived for the various
approaches to be reconciled and an attempt will be made in this paper to do
so. On the other hand, such a reconciliation will be exclusively in the realm
of a mechanistic approach to the problem of human locomotion. This is an
inevitable corollary to the way in which the concept of optimalization has
been worked out in both biomechanical and work physiological research since
Bernstein's days.

In Section 4, amongst others, energetical optimalization of human
locomotion will be discussed. This Section will further be characterized by
a departure from one aspect Bernstein proposed to study: the neurophysiological
or cybernetic aspect. It will be dedicated to progress in the biomechanics
of locomotion in accordance with the preponderance Bernstein gave to the
biomechanical analysis of locomotion in his Chapter III.

If one is headed to discriminate between "the random and the regular",
to look at the generality and regularity and to the stabile and typical
hallmarks of the processes, as Bernstein has put it (p.165 and 166), the
finer mechanically reactive and especially the proprioceptive reactive (as
Bernstein calls them, p. 209) phenomena might well be overlooked. In later
cybernetical research, these phenomena and the reactions of the controlling
Nervous System in adjusting to them are the key to a comprehension of the
system. However, much of the biomechanical research on human locomotion has
been confined to defining the regular and has not been directed to reactive
details of the process. Only a few groups of researchers (e.g., Herman et
al., 1976 and Grillner, 1975, 1979, 1981) have tried to study neurophysiological
aspects of human locomotion. It is believed by the present author that a major
breakthrough is to be expected within short time, as indicated in Section 4.

With respect to other movements than human locomotion the two-fold
programme Bernstein proposed has been followed more directly. In his search
for fast neurophysiological processes responsible for optimalization on this
level, Bernstein postulated 'spontaneous pre-proprioceptive impulses' and
'reactive innervated impulses'. Furthermore he speculated on preparatory
organization of the motor periphery including the motor neuron pool. His
students have worked out this line of thought in a series of publications.
The optimalization principle on the neurophysiological level in these
publications is operationalized in the 'principle of least interaction' and
in the concept of 'synergy' (Gelfand et al., 1971). Preparatory organization
of the Central Nervous System as well as of the peripheral effectors is dealt
with (Gurfinkel et al., 1971a; Feldman, 1980 ab). In current biophysical
research, both play an important role.

Other lines of research dealing with neurophysiological problems are
concentrated on the role of $\alpha-\gamma$ coupling (Granit, 1970; Matthews, 1972; Stein,
1974) and on changes in the reflexes during movement (for recent symposia on
these topics, see Homma, 1976; Granit & Pompeiano, 1979). Here too, biophysical concepts enter: Houk (1979), taking the position that stiffness (the
ratio of force change to length change) will be the leading variable. On the

contrary Stein (1981) expressed "a hunch that with 10^{12} neurons and a considerable choice of motorneurons and peripheral receptors most if not all of the variables" (force, velocity, length, stiffness or viscosity) "can be used to control particular movements as required" (p. 211). The present essay will only deal with some of these approaches and only insofar as they are felt to be relevant for the present state of thinking on the problem of indeterminacy (or non-univocality) in Section 3. In this Section various attempts to analyze and explain the functional non-univocality from anatomical and neurophysiolocical sources are discussed. The possible biomechanical definition of the motor problem by recent modelling studies of human movement is sketched.

Bernstein's work up to 1940 gave rise to fruitful research and remainded valid in many respects notwithstanding new facts generated by people (often not aware of his work and that of his co-workers) up to this time. His contribution was remarkable, based as it was on methods lacking some modern tools now at our disposal. Foot reaction force measurement systems emerged in the years preceding his writing in 1940 (Asmussen, 1976), but he did not make use of it. Electromyography was used in human kinesiology only shortly after his 1940 writing (Inman et al., 1944). He had to content himself with rather primitive tools: from displacement time data differentiated twice, conclusions had to be drawn on forces, external or muscular. The question arises if we in our times do better? Other methodological questions,pertaining to generalization over various classes of movement, as well as on the validity of studies of walking on motor driven treadmills are discussed as well in Section 2.

This paper tries to react to some of the problems stated by Bernstein in 1940. Of necessity, it does not pretend to give a complete overview of the field of study and it lacks a thorough neurophysiological approach which lies outside the expertise of the author (1). In Section 5, the main stream of the essay is summarized.

2.   METHODOLOGICAL DEVELOPMENTS IN BIODYNAMICS OF LOCOMOTION.

2.1. Introduction.

Research on human locomotion has from its birth been connected to instrumentation. It will be sufficient to recall that Muybridge succeeded in inventing a way to the orderly use of multiple cameras. Marey invented the

movie film camera (Michaelis, 1955), which has led to a whole industry outside
the realm of science. By calculating the trajectories of falling balls from
the separate film frames, Braune and Fischer succeeded in a correct description
of the time histories of the events studied and recorded by hand driven film
cameras. Discussions about the correct use of the instruments and about new
instruments form an important part of the debate in the scientific forum.

Bernstein developed a system for registration of the movement in study
using photonics - as the modern glossary would describe it. He did not have
at his disposal a method for direct registration of (foot)-reaction forces.
He had to differentiate twice his photonic displacement time data in order
to get information on accelerations, and muscular and external (reactive)
forces. The question is, whether his procedure was reliable and moreover if
the procedures currently in use are more dependable? Bernstein did not have
electromyography - taken as a sign of neuromuscular activity - at his disposal.
The question arises to what extent the use of electromyography has succeeded
in throwing light on the problem of neural control of movement coordination
and regulation since it was introduced in human kinesiology in 1944?

Bernstein recommended the study of human locomotion as a subject matter
suitable for giving insight into the coordination and regulation of movement
in general. Lines of research have started since on other modes of locomotion,
other types or classes of movement. It is to be questioned if the generalizations
derived from any class of movement are valid for all classes of movement.
Information with respect to classes of movement pertaining to the involvement
of the Central Nervous System are hardly more than provisional at this time.
Generalization of the conclusions drawn from experiments on one class over
various classes of movements is indeed questionable.

The validity of conclusions on research on human movement from laboratory
experiments has been criticized, especially in the case where motor driven
treadmills were used to study human locomotion. These problems will be
discussed in the following subsections.

2.2. From guess to cost/profit analysis.

In biomechanics of human locomotion it is customary to differentiate
twice displacement time data (from film or opto-electronic registrations) in
order to extract information on accelerations and forces. This has a "very
dubious theoretical basis" (Cavanagh, 1976). In an introductory paper to the
session on "Instrumentation and Methodology" of the fifth International

Congress of Biomechanics Cavanagh (1976) stated:

> There are two basic questions that must be posed when
> displacement-time data from any source are to be used
> for subsequent numerical analysis. These are: 1) How
> fast should the sampling rate be? and 2) What techniques
> of smoothing and differentiation should be used?

He mentioned sampling rates found in the literature, varying from 16 frames
per second in a study of squats to 190 frames per second used by Bernstein
(2).

The rationale for the choice of sampling rates in registering the signal
digitally, or in AD conversion of an analogous signal and in differentiating
the signal is not always clearly stated in research reports. All signals are
contaminated by measurement noise, mostly stochastic and not to be discerned
from the signal proper in identical bandwidths. Reduction of this noise at
the source is indicative (Lees, 1980). This problem of measurement accuracy
remains difficult. Markers on the body for example may be a source of noise
as an effect of the combination of the presence of high frequency impact
situations and the existence of various time-histories of subcutaneous
tissues over which the markers are placed.

In all registrations and processing, the resolution is of importance for
accuracy. The resolution is the ratio of the dimensions of the total image
and the incremental steps Δx in amplitude (distances, angles). Small resolution
will result in low signal/noise ratio's. This will especially be the case if
the movement is slow with respect to the total image dimension, as the mean
noise will be constant and the signal will show lower increments or decrements
in time (e.g., the vertical displacements in Bernstein's Fig. 5).

The sample frequency is the inverse of the Δ_t steps at which the signal
is acquired. The desired minimal sample frequency is stated by the Shannon
sampling theorem, by defining the Nyquist frequency as the frequency which
is twice the highest frequency in the signal in which interest lies. When
interest is confined only to the characteristics of a process in the frequency
domain of signals of limited duration, a rule of thumb sampling frequency is
advised of five times the highest frequency of the signal (Cavanagh, 1976;
Lanshammar, 1982).

As all signals are contaminated by noise, and as the high frequencies
of the signal and noise do not contain valuable information, filtering of
the signal is recommended (Winter et al., 1974a; Lees, 1980), especially so,
as differentiation acts as a high pass filter and amplifies the high
frequencies (Lanshammar, 1982). This filtering has to be the first operation

when it is not certain that frequencies higher than half the sample frequency
do not occur in the signal. Otherwise the sampled signal will contain
irretrievable faults, known as aliasing errors. Frequencies higher than half
the sample frequency will be represented as lower frequencies in the sampled
signal and lead to completely false results in subsequent differentiations
(van Ingen Schenau, personal communication). Filtering will not, however,
separate noise from the signal in the frequency domain in which interest
lies.

In the time domain, various techniques of smoothing have been used in
order to prevent the effect of differentiation of noise (Hatze, 1981a; Lees,
1980; Pezzack & Winter, 1977; Soudan & Dierkx, 1977, etc.). Moreover, in
differentiating signals, which are stepwise quantified in amplitude and in
time sampled, quantification errors are introduced, as the converted signal
will have the form of a "staircase" instead of a "ramp". It is customary to
denote these errors as quantification noise. These errors are in most cases
not stochastic (Lanshammar, 1982). They may even be systematic, resulting
in apparent reproducible variations in the first or second derivatives. The
latter will become very misleading in higher frequencies, depending on the
original ratio of signal amplitude and the increment Δ_x. Thus the effects of
quantification noise will depend on the resolution. Quantification noise
will also result in unacceptable signal/noise ratios (Lanshammar, 1982).
Filtering and smoothing techniques have been used to overcome these
difficulties.

Although Bernstein was aware of the importance of choosing an adequate
sampling frequency, he apparently was not aware of the importance of
sufficient resolution to avoid systematic quantification noise. Comparison
of Bernstein's Fig. 22 with Figs. 1a en 1b will show differences in the
vertical force summated for both legs during double support in human walking.
This force was computed by Bernstein by differentiating twice displacement
time data and it was measured directly by Yamashita and Katoh (1976) (Fig.
1b). The latter two measurements show one large vertical peak very unlike
the "Vorderstosz" and "Hinterstosz" of Bernstein (3). The question then is
if we measure and compute better than Bernstein did in his time? This
question is addressed in what follows.

For a dependable choice of sample frequencies one has to know the highest
frequency of interest in the movement in study. Cavanagh (1976) stated that
such knowledge is scarce in the literature. Neilson (1972) studied - by means
of goniometry - with a sampling rate of 20 Hz the maximal frequency of fast

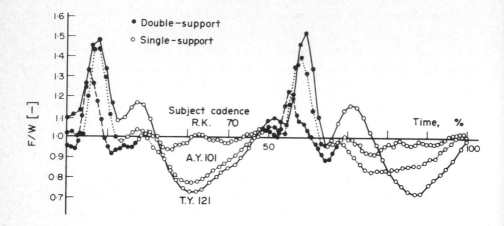

Fig. 1a. Vertical resultant forces in steady walking at different
cadences and different subjects. Reproduced from Yamashita,
T. and R. Katoh (1976) Fig. 4, Oxford, Pergamon Press, with
permission of the publishers.

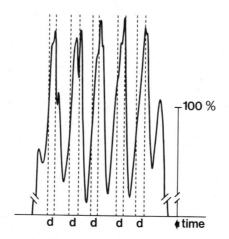

Fig. 1b. Vertical summated forces of a normal subject, registered by
the University of Technology of Twente, on a 5 m long double
force plate at the "Stadsmaten" Hospital, both in Enschede,
Netherlands; mean walking speed km/h (personal communication).

oscillating elbow movements. Depending on the inertial mass of the underarm
the movements occurred at a frequency of 4 - 6 Hz. Kinesthetic tracking
movements were slower and did not reach 2 Hz. The maximal frequency of the
signal was 5 Hz. The study of Gurfinkel et al. (1971b) mentioned maximal
Fourier analyzed frequencies of wrist oscillations of 7 Hz without, and 10 Hz
with, visual control. Njiokiktien (1970) as well as Thomas & Whitney (1959)
reported on fore-aft and left-right oscillations in standing. The oscillations
reported were 6 Hz and 15 Hz respectively. The maximal frequency of the
signal was not analyzed.

Winter et al. (1974a) reported that in walking registered with a TV-
system (60 Hz sampling frequency) 99.7 percent of the signal power of the
signal on vertical displacement of the toe marker was contained in the harmonics
below the 7th. This content was not speed dependent. They filtered their data
twice with a filter with a cut-off frequency of 7 Hz, which resulted in a
total cut-off at 4.5 Hz. Jacobs et al. (1972) analyzed vertical foot reaction
forces (sample frequency 54 per stride) and concluded that the 7th harmonic
and upwards contained only 10% of the fundamental harmonic (in walking this
is the first). They did not state the frequency (4).

Smidt et al. (1977) concluded on the basis of accelographic data of the
trunk (sample frequency 41 per stride) that most of the power was contained
in the lower harmonics up to the tenth. A speed dependency of the distribution
of the power over the even and odd harmonics was reported. Zarrugh and
Radcliffe (1979) in a study of human walking concluded that "at high
frequencies (above the fifteenth harmonic) the spectra resemble those of white
noise". They considered "seven to twelve harmonics good compromise between
information and noise for most gait variables, except ankle flexion which
requires at least 20 harmonics".

So far in studies of human walking, a sampling frequency of 50 Hz seems
quite reasonable. Capozzo et al. (1975) in stating the problem as a compromise
"between accuracy and cost of data acquisition in terms of man/time necessary
for the reading of the film", are of the opinion that even 20-30 frames per
second will be generally sufficient. Lanshammar (1982) concluded that, in
human walking, inclusion of the results of Zarrugh and Radcliffe (1979)
frequencies of 5 - 16 Hz should be analyzed. The upper limit would demand a
sampling frequency of 90 Hz for exceptional details. However, Simon et al.
(1981), in reaction to Pezzack et al. (1977), as well as Hatze and Venter
(1981) in reaction to Onyshko and Winter (1980) called attention to the fact
that in foot reaction force studies high frequency components occur at heel

strike in walking. Such frequencies appear in bare foot walking up to 75 Hz, and are liable to be dampened by shoewear to about 50 Hz (Simon et al., 1981). From the clinical viewpoint such impact waves will be of importance (Voloshin et al., 1981). In running, higher impact frequencies would be expected, but adequate shoewear may lessen the problem. Indeed Cavanagh and Lafortune (1980) measured peaks at heel strike in running with special shoewear, showing a rise time of 23 ms to 2.2 times body weight, resulting in frequencies of only about 10 Hz.

The conclusion must be, that the choice of the sampling frequency is dependent on the (details of the) movement in question. In human movement studies, sampling frequencies of 50 Hz will be sufficient in most cases (Lees, 1980). Filtering of data on a cut-off frequency based on the significant signal frequency, with a filter of known (and to be reported) characteristics is necessary (Pezzack et al., 1977). If the frequency of the motion in question is not known, a preliminary analysis is needed. The decisions on the cut-off frequency and sampling rate are arbitrary but may be reasonably founded and documented, on a cost/profit basis.

For the smoothing of amplitude-time data in order to reduce noise (including quantification noise) different techniques are advocated. Winter et al. (1974a) filtered their data twice with a 2nd order Butterworth filter having a cut-off frequency at 7 Hz. Moving average techniques were used by Smith (quoted by Lees, 1980). Pezzack et al. (1977) compared finite difference, Chebyshev least squares polynomials, and digital filtering followed by a first order finite difference technique, and found the latter procedure most promising for the analysis of a simple instrumented movement. Soudan & Dierkx (1979) used spline functions, while Hatze (1981) criticized such usage. In the use of cubic spline functions the smoothing factor has to be guessed by trial and error. In fact, when using spline functions, the shape of the derivatives is defined beforehand in deciding to fit the data with a known function. This should not be advised when one is interested in the actual shape of derivatives.

In the use of higher order polynomials or Fourier approximation, arbitrary decisions play also a role in the choice of the order of the approximation. Hatze (1981) proposed an algorithm which overcomes these difficulties. This algorithm appears to be much faster in terms of computation time than the cubic spline method. However, the method is only applicable if sufficient data points are available. This sufficient number depends on the character of the movement under study, meaning that if doubt

arises as to the smoothness of the movement, or if the smooth phases are of
a short duration, a large number of data points (from a high resolution data
acquisition system) is advised.

With the accumulation of a body of knowledge on the biodynamics of human
movement, such choices will be based more and more on rational cost/profit
analyses. In reporting, the pertinent data on the techniques used should be
given, in order to enable the reader to form an opinion about this choice.
By such means the study of the biodynamics of locomotion will at least
become of age. Workers will refrain from being content either with the
a posteriori reasonable looking outcomes of first and second order
derivatives, or with very time and money consuming procedures.

It is concluded that given the restricted resolution of most movement
registration systems, the calculation of the first and particularly of the
second order derivatives from sampled positions is still a problem as it was
in Bernstein's days. Only the time needed to analyse the subsequent frames
by the introduction of modern motion-analyzing equipment and opto-electronic
systems has since improved. Some of the latter systems have also very
satisfactory resolutions.

In choosing a method to acquire acceleration data direct measurement
of acceleration or forces should be considered. Smooth acceleration curves
derived by differentiating twice displacement time data are still to be
mistrusted. The smoothing and differentiating filters used may have had a too
low cut-off frequency. These frequencies should be reported.

Though Bernstein used presumably adequate shutter frequencies, he
apparently was not aware of the importance of adequate resolution in his
locomotion studies. So he presumably introduced systematic quantification
errors. Therefore the vast amount of facts Bernstein and his pupils Popova,
Saltzgeber and Spielberg accumulated, did not warrant the theory built on
it. Had they had electromyography at their disposal, their work would have
been easier while more directly carried out on muscular activity.Nevertheless,
Bernstein's genius in thinking about the various consequences on the neurophysiological level lead to a very successful theory: it has provoked many
followers to fruitful research and conclusions.

2.3. Kinesiological electromyography.

Bernstein was undoubtedly right in criticizing "the concept in elementary
textbooks that excitation of the flexor muscles results in flexion and that

stimulation of the <u>extensor</u> muscles results in extension of the joints they
control" (p. 174). This point of view was remarkable in an area without
electromyography (EMG) as a powerful tool in human kinesiological research.

Important moments in the development of this tool were its introduction
in human kinesiology in 1944 by Inman et al., the early attempts at
quantification (Inman et al., 1952) and, important for this discussion, the
paper of Ralston et al. (1976). In this latter paper as well as in other
papers quoted by Inman et al. (1981, p. 101), it was noted that a time lag
of about 30 ms exists between the onset of the EMG-signal and development
of force. This time lag is possibly caused by biomechanical processes
(stretching series elastic components) as well as phenomena of the excitation-
contraction coupling (5). As acceleration is not infinite a pure mechanical
cause of this time lag is present too. The lag between the end of the EMG-
signal and force production is ten times longer, due to the relaxation of
the chemical contractile machinery. Both time lags may hamper the validity
of the use of EMG as a tool in description of mechanical 'actual muscle
functions' (muscle functions within the mechanical context of the movement
in study).

The interplay of the muscle forces or moments and inertial or
gravitational moments is difficult to elucidate. In spite of this and of the
cautious remarks of Bernstein quoted above, researchers have tried to ascribe
'actual muscle functions' (in terms of moments or torque) to muscles electro-
myographically active during movements. In generalized human walking such
descriptions are beautifully illustrated by Inman et al. in their highly
instructive 1981 monograph.

For a good understanding of 'actual muscle functions' it is of importance
to know whether or not an active muscle shortens (concentric contraction)
lengthens (excentric contraction) or does not change its length. Better still,
estimations of the rate of change of muscle length should be related to
quantified and normalized EMG data (Grieve et al., 1978), even if it is
recognized that muscle length is not identical to muscle fibre length.

The orientation of muscle fibres will in many cases not be parallel to
the working line of the muscle. This will have a definite influence on possible
muscle function as revealed by the length-force relation (Woittiez et al.,
1983b). They showed that the length-force relation (often misnamed as length-
tension relation) depends on the architecture of the muscle in question.
Contrary to the theories of Benninghoff and Rollhäuser (1952) and of Gans &
Bock (1965) who thought that the angle between muscle fibres and tendons

might be decisive, the length of the muscle fibres relative to the muscle belly length appears to predict length-force relationships for muscles of different architecture of different species (rat, frog) very well (Woittiez et al., 1983a). Therefore, attempts towards quantification of muscle function in dynamic situations following the approach of Grieve et al. (1978) are recommended. They related EMG activity to length changes in the muscle in question and succeeded in stating qualitatively the muscle function.

Hof & van den Berg (1977, 1981a-d) succeeded in quantifying the EMG-force relationship in a dynamic situation. A linear relationship between force of the triceps surae muscle and EMG was established. The search for such relationships has not been as successful as it was in static conditions (e.g., Bigland & Lippold, 1954; Rau & Vredenbregt, 1973). This has hampered the use of EMG in explaining the force histories of movements. Operationally explored relationships are therefore of importance. In the study of Hof & van den Berg (1977, 1981a-d) a salient point was that the EMG signal was used as an input to their muscle model and not as a direct equivalent of the force output of the muscle. In the muscle model not only force, but also velocity was included by the incorporation of the Hill model (6).

Formulating muscular function, relative to the function of other structures delivering moments and forces about the joints as well, demands specific assumptions about the other structures. Quanbury et al. (1975), Robertson & Winter (1980), Winter et al. (1974b, 1976ab), Winter & Robertson (1978) computed power transmission by joint forces, muscles and other moments, between segments of the body in walking. Working with some crude assumptions (e.g., only movement in the saggittal plane was studied), they concluded that the joint forces are as important as the muscle forces. Correlation with EMG studies (like the one of Dubo et al., 1976) should render a better understanding of muscle function in walking. Such a study rendering views on muscle function in relation to other force and moment transmissions at the joint, is still awaited. The issue is, that at present it is not possible to ascribe un-equivocally force and moment transmission to the muscles and joint structures. Even if Pedotti (1977) was right in his statement that antagonistic muscle activity in walking is quite scarce, such activity appears to be of importance in many other movements (van Ingen Schenau et al., 1983), as well as in walking especially of bi-articular muscles in the thigh (Elftman, 1966). Modelling of joint motion and defining muscle function on the assumption of reciprocal activity of antagonistic muscles (Morrisson, 1970ab) may be proven to be an invalid procedure, as Lombard & Abbot (1907) foresaw (7).

From these examples it may be concluded that the understanding of the
biodynamics of human locomotion in terms of actual muscle functions as
revealed by EMG is as yet rather primitive. This is possibly the reason why
in human walking the EMG signal is scarcely used as a sign of the activity
of the nervous system in coordinating and regulating the movement as Bernstein
would have wished. Exceptions to this rule exist : the work of Herman et al.
(1976), Craig et al. (1976) and Cook & Cozzens (1976) to which reference will
be made in Section 4 and the work of Pedotti (1977) which has already been
mentioned.

In seemingly less complex motions, in human subjects, the use of EMG as
an estimate of neural activity has been abundant (e.g., Feldman, 1980ab;
Gurfinkel et al., 1971; Hallet et al., 1975; Wadman, 1979; Wadman et al.,
1979, 1980ab; as well as many studies of neurophysiological aspects of human
movement).

In the study of neural regulation of walking in cats and other animals
EMG has been used successfully (e.g., Grillner, 1975, 1979, 1981; Ivanova,
1973).

It is felt that in the near future other concepts of muscle function
than that of delivering of force or moments will become important. The thought
of Elftman (1966) about the role of biarticular muscles of the thigh as energy
savers in human walking is such a concept. These muscles appear to transmit
power from one segment to another and vice versa without a considerable change
in length. The work of Winter and his associates on power flow between body
segments in walking in conjunction with the method of Grieve et al. (1978)
relating EMG to length-changes in the muscle in question would render a
confirmation of the existence of such energy-saving mechanisms.

The stimulating thought of the existence of a "stretch-shortening cycle"
(Asmussen & Bonde-Petersen, 1974) in rather fast movements or in counter-
movements involves much debate and research (van Ingen Schenau et al., 1983).
Its possible importance in repetitive or cyclic movements was already stressed
by Elftman (1966). Both, the "stretch-shortening cycle" as well as the energy
conserving function of bi-articular muscles are involved in the explanations
of energetical optimalization of walking (Cavagna, 1978, see also sub-section
4.3.3).

Reciprocal innervation of monarticular antagonists might be another way
to save energy (Pedotti, 1977). In running and hopping storage of elastic
energy in muscles and in tendons also saves energy (Alexander, 1977, 1980;
Cavagna, 1978). Specialization of the muscle fibres into fast, slow and

various subtypes for different functional use is expected to be of importance
in the human subject as has been shown in various animals (Goldspink, 1977;
Pool,1980).

EMG studies will help in the future to elucidate such mechanical and
physiological processes. These processes form an important part of the degrees
of freedom, which Bernstein postulated to exist (see Section 3). It is felt
that much of the research on human kinesiological EMG has been used to better
define these degrees of freedom rather than to throw light on the regulative
activity of the Central Nervous System in coordinating human locomotion. It
is also felt that this has been a necessary condition for tackling the problems
of coordination, Bernstein tried to tackle with the indirect methods at his
disposal (8).

2.4. Generalization problems.

Bernstein thought that studying human locomotion and other highly skilled
movements in order to elucidate their coordination and regulation was imperative
because these movements are automated and "have generality". A large number of
subjects "have all mastered for example the act of walking incomparably better
than any of their individual professional skills" (p. 172).A large body of
knowledge on this automatic cyclic movement, walking and running has been
gathered since then.

Fast repetitive cyclic arm motions have also been studied (Feldman,
1980ab). Fast as well as slow arm movements have been the object of study by
many workers (e.g., van Dijk, 1979; Feldman, 1979, 1980ab; Wadman et al., 1980).
In some instances fast and slow movements have been compared with each other
(e.g., Hallet et al., 1975).

Standing, or posture, has been examined intensively by members of the
International Society of Posturography (Bles, 1977, 1978ab; Bonnet et al.,
1976; Gurfinkel, 1973ab, 1974, 1976, 1979abcd; Nashner & Woollacot, 1979).
Standing may be also considered as an automatic movement. Other quasi-static
movements, like aiming have been investigated (Gurfinkel et al., 1971). Most
of these studies have been undertaken with the ultimate goal Bernstein posed:
the elucidation of the role of the Central Nervous System in the coordination
and regulation of movement.

The rationale for the choice of these classes of movement appears to
lie in the contention that they are optimalized (e.g., by learning) and
therefore repeatable within narrow limits.

In biomechanics, most of the above-mentioned classes of movement have also been studied. Much research has been carried out into sport movements. Some of the research projects on sport movements have been successful in developing biomechanical models for each cycle of movement, in stating a general power balance for the particular sporting achievement as a whole and in defining efficiency terms on a biomechanical and work physiological level (van Ingen Schenau & Bakker, 1980; van Ingen Schenau, 1982; van Ingen Schenau & de Groot, 1983). The generality of these models is apparent from the fact that their essential elements are applicable to speed skating, cycling (van Ingen Schenau, 1981) as well as to swimming (Toussaint et al., 1983). Automated- learned- fast arm movements, automatic movements, like standing and walking as well as sportive movements, especially those of champions on national and international levels, will be optimalized. Subjects in the study of sport movements are willing and able to reach a fairly constant level of attainment allowing critical investigation of the model parameters (9).

Optimalization in the other direction, in order to instruct the performers how to perform better on the basis of the input of performance parameters in optimizing models has become a topic for research in recent years (Hatze, 1976, 1981b). This would imply that starting from biomechanics an insight can be reached into the coordination and regulation of such movements (see e.g., Hatze, 1980a).

Irrespective of the question whether the classes of movement in study are 'real life' or not, they are often denoted with terms like volitional, goal directed, intended, or, automatic, automated. Such terms imply or assume a varying but ill defined involvement of the Central Nervous System (CNS). It might even be said that a large part of the research programme is directed to solve the question of the nature of the involvement of the CNS, so for the time being these definitions have to be operational or provisional. In the theories of Bernstein's Russian associates and pupils, concepts have been formulated like synergies - being "those classes of movement which have similar kinematic characteristics, coinciding active muscle groups and conductive types of afferentation" (Gelfand et al., 1971, p. 331). The concept of synergy is related to the concept of least interaction at the level of the CNS, implying that on the basis of a small number of leading parameters and the determination of the basic afferentation necessary for the realisation of the movement, the task of the CNS is held to be quite simple.

Some of the synergies, like the one for walking might even be innate (Willemse, 1961; Andre-Thomas & Autgaarden, 1966; Bressan & Woollacot, 1982) needing only simple activating signals from higher centres as Grillner and associates (1975, 1979, 1981) and Shik et al. (1968) have shown for cats and dogs (Shik & Orlovsky, 1965). Such relatively simple explanations for the control of movements may also appear valid for human walking. But it is to be questioned if such explanations can be generalized to some or all other classes of movements studied?

Some examples will clarify this point. Firstly, in the author's department a series of experiments was undertaken to ascertain if the relative number of muscle spindles in a muscle would be correlated with the time of mastering single motor unit control. This appeared true (van Ravensberg et al., 1978). But learning motor unit control also appeared possible in muscles like mylohyoideus, for which it is reported, they do not contain muscle spindles (Kleppe et al., 1982). It was even shown that the recruitment order of single motor units could deviate from the size principle (Millner Brown et al., 1973; Bakker de et al., in press). In biceps brachii muscle, a multi-functional muscle (elbow flexion, supination of the forearm), single motor unit activity was registered in different tasks. Units with a high force threshold for flexion tended to show a low threshold for supination and vice versa (Ter Haar Romeny, et al., 1983). When high forces are asked for, both classes of motor units may be used. These facts strongly suggest that motor units are recruited selectively. The input of the motor neuron pool from higher centres differs for each task.

The second point relates to the sensory input. Sittig (personal communication) carried out experiments on slow arm motion. The subjects could not see the position of their arm. They could only see target lamps. In the starting position, indicated by a light, their biceps brachii tendon was subjected to vibration. As a consequence the arm drifted from this position. The subjects were unaware of this drift. They were asked to flex their arm in order to reach an end position indicated by a second lamp either under the condition of continuous vibration or without further vibration. In both conditions the end position was reached correctly. In performing these experiments as well as in carrying out single motor unit control tasks, the subjects do not know which information source they use in performing.

In the experiments in the author's laboratory on single motor unit control some subjects were not successful in learning the task while others were successful in a short time. Interestingly, trained musicians performed better than non-musicians (van Ravensberg, et al., 1978). In these experiments, too, subjects were not aware which information source they used. Apparently

the contention of Stein (1981) that a rather large number of control parameters
can be used by the CNS, is valid for the movements in these experiments. The
CNS appears to be more versatile than was thought. The use of control
parameters in question might possibly be trained as appeared the case for the
musicians.

Thus, in setting up experiments to disclose functions that will be
attributed to one of the sensory elements in muscle, it should be borne in
mind that other elements exist and may have a function. By choosing false or
prejudiced experimental designs the experimenter might succeed in either
begging the question or in harvesting irrelevant answers.

The results of the experiments mentioned in the preceding paragraphs
should not be generalized to other movements, studied in other experiments,
e.g., they do not imply that the size principle (Milner-Brown et al., 1973)
will not be valid. This principle will be valid in many circumstances as
well as in many classes of movement. The question arises: in which classes
of movement? Are the movements in the above mentioned experiments to be
classified volitional, intentional or conscious? Certainly, some of them have
a certain artificiality. Does the label artificial help any further? It seems
to the present author that as long as we do not know how to classify movements
in terms of involvement of the sensory and motor parts of the Nervous System,
some caution is required in generalizing from experiments on provisionally
classified movements to other classes of movement. Like Bernstein, in
choosing a certain class of movements, skilled or automated - whatever that
may say in terms of involvement of the Nervous System - many researchers tend
to generalize their findings to other classes of movement. As long as we do not
know how to classify movements in terms of involvement of the Nervous System,
such generalizations have to be considered with caution.

2.5. Validity of experiments on walking on motor driven treadmills.

The question posed in the preceding Section pertains to generalization.
In this Section a similar problem will be discussed: are the findings of
walking experiments performed under laboratory conditions on a motor driven
treadmill valid for free walking? This is a problem of ecological validity.

If walking on a motor driven treadmill is not ecologically valid, the
vast research efforts reviewed by Grillner (1975, 1979, 1981) on step
generators of automated walking movements would not be valid. Moreover, the
optimalization of energy expenditure in human walking studied by Molen et

al. (1972b) and Zarrugh et al. (1974) would not be valid, notwithstanding the firm grounds these researchers found in the work of Atzler and Herbst (1928) who eventually succeeded in inducing their subjects to walk overground, but in circles.

The problem is reviewed by van Ingen Schenau (1980) who appears to be the first to give a fundamental explanation of the biomechanics of treadmill walking. Using a reference frame (x-y-z coordinates) moving with the belt he demonstrated that a mechanical difference between overground and treadmill walking does not exist even if the treadmill is set at a slope. A rigorous, constant speed of the belt - not influenced by the variable inertia due to the movements of the subjects - is a necessary condition. Under this condition the Galilean invariance "indicates that the laws of Newtonian mechanics are identical in all reference frames which move with uniform speed with respect to one another". Van Ingen Schenau (1980) concludes:

> The only other possible cause for differences in treadmill
> and overground locomotion is the difference in visual and,
> to lesser extent, auditory information. The visual information
> will be particularly important in maintaining equilibrium and
> stability during locomotion. In overground locomotion the
> surroundings move with respect to the subject which is not the
> case in treadmill locomotion. This could cause a difference in
> regulation of the movement pattern resulting in differences in
> the kinematics and/or energy consumption. In studies concerning
> the regulation of human posture, the relative importance of
> visual information in this regulation has been shown (Bles et
> al., 1977; Brandt et al., 1976). The differences found will
> probably be diminished if the information from the surroundings
> during treadmill locomotion could be aligned with the information
> in overground locomotion. It would be interesting to develop
> an experimental set up in which the subjects get visual
> information comparable to that in overground locomotion. A
> treadmill can prove an extremely stressful environment for a
> subject. Experiments performed in our laboratory with 9 - 16
> year old boys showed that most of these children were rather
> frightened to walk on the treadmill used. This treadmill had a
> width of 1 m and was elevated 1 m above the surrounding floor.
> Nine out of ten subjects showed much longer double support
> phases when walking on this treadmill compared to overground
> walking (mean difference: 15%). This fear for walking on a
> treadmill will probably diminish when the treadmill is built
> in such a way that the belt seems an integral part of the
> floor.

We will end this Chapter in a prospective way. Walking on a motor-driven treadmill will constitute an expedient experimental set up. It will enable experimenters to study the influence of varying - by experimental manipulation - perceptive input. In this way human walking on a motor driven treadmill will

be used to study the biodynamics of human locomotion, with the Bernsteinian
goal: the elucidation of the regulation and coordination in motor acts, just
like the work of Grillner (1975, 1979, 1981) for cats. Two methodical
considerations are to be made. The motor driven treadmills used in such
studies are to be in conformity to the rigorous requirements van Ingen Schenau
(1980) stated. The registration of the movements has to be undertaken with
a data acquisition system of sufficient resolving power.

3.   FUNCTIONAL NON-UNIVOCALITY.

     As movements are - as Bernstein stressed - "non completely determined
by effector processes" (p.213), this indeterminacy or non-univocality has
been the central core in the argument for the need for (proprioceptive)
afferentation in Bernstein's theory. He postulated "more or less complicated
auxiliary systems which ensure constant and complete control by the centre"
(p. 213)(10).
     In this Section some of the many lines of research directed to elucidate
this non-univocality will be discussed. Bernstein (1940) stated:

>   The deeper the functional gap with the absence of
>   univocality between the centre and the periphery, the
>   more complex and unstable is the real relationship between
>   impulses and movements; the greater (in mathematical
>   language) are the number of degrees of freedom of the
>   motor periphery relative to the central effector, the
>   more complex and delicate must be the organizational
>   control to which we have referred. This organizational
>   control is motor coordination.
>   In this context the idea of coordination is in the
>   closest relationship to the idea of functional non-
>   univocality of the connections between the motor centre
>   and the periphery, between impulses and effects. The
>   more our knowledge of the forms and types of these non-
>   univocalities increases, the deeper becomes our
>   understanding of the coordination of movements.
>   At present a whole series of sources of this
>   indeterminacy are known (p. 105).

     He discerned anatomical, mechanical and (neuro-)physiological sources
of indeterminacy. On pages 105 and 106 examples have been cited by him. Some
of these sources would be formulated in contemporary language as non-
linearities of the functioning musculoskeletal system. For example the
length-force relation of muscles (Ramsey & Street, 1940; Ralston et al., 1947)
and the force velocity curve (Wilkie, 1950) are non-linear.

Some authors have tried to explain some non-linearities away by the assumption that lever arm values increase while according to the length-force relation, force decreases (Inman et al., 1981) resulting in quasi-linear torque values. Constant, or nearly constant lever arms, however, which are assumed to exist with respect to the extensors of the arms and legs by Inman et al. (1981) would lead to a problem of non-linearity for the controller which has to master the length-force relation as well as the force-velocity relation in effecting movements. Possibly, the problem for the controller in solving the motion problem, will be less in submaximal contractions. However, factual knowledge of length-force relations in non-isometric submaximal functioning of muscles is very scarce, and speculative considerations are abundant notwithstanding the elegant synthesis of Bahler et al. (1968).

The function of the control system itself, consisting of very non-linear devices - neurons - has been analyzed successfully in terms of linear system theory (van der Gon, 1983). Assuming parallel signal transmission and signal processing and a very simple processing device, van der Gon succeeded in modelling linear movement control by a system consisting of non-linear working units. Parallel transmission from higher centres has also been assumed in the theories of the descending α-γ co-activation (Merton, 1953). A second parallel signal-transmission originated from the various receptors in the motor system (11). The processing of both streams of impulses results in motor unit activation. Linearity is reached by the assumption of differences in size or input impedance of the motor neuron pool units, meaning the size principle (Milner Brown et al., 1973; Hatze, 1980a; Henneman, 1981). Van der Gon corroborates his theory by experiments of Vinken et al. (1983) and Ter Haar Romeny et al. (1983), carried out on simple arm movements.

The view of Houk (1975, 1979) on the functioning of muscle receptors in the signal processing might be appreciated as an endeavour to simplify muscle control. Parallel processing of Golgi tendon organ signals end muscle spindle signals could lead to the processing of quasi-linear muscle stiffness (force change over length change) in the regulation of simple movements like elbow flexion or extension. Parallel descending influences are hypothesized by Feldman (1974, 1976, 1980ab) in postulating a superposition of tonic and phasic co-activation of antagonistic muscle pairs. The first activation would lead to a pre-set stiffness of the effector system (invariant characteristic)(12).

The concept of invariant characteristics as well as manipulation of

sensory input were used by van Beekum (1979), Juta et al. (1979) and Vincken
(1982, 1983) in experiments on control of arm posture and movements. The
ecological validity (in the sense Gibson (1979) uses this concept) of such
experiments is strongly doubted by Reed (1982) in implying that such postures
and movements are highly "artificial". In most of such experiments, the
influence of gravity and of other sensory systems than the system the
experimenter wants to study, is excluded by the experimental design.
Conclusions drawn might not be valid for spontaneous movements, as in the
production of these movements the influence of gravity and many sensory
systems may play an important and decisive role in solving the motor problem
('spontaneous movements' and 'movement problem' are the terms Bernstein used).
Van der Gon (1983) remarked that modelling the nervous system while taking
in account all the existing differences between the elements of the system,
would ask for a model as complex as the system itself. "For that reason one
often starts with idealized elements with a kind of average properties". The
same holds true for the effector system and its motor and sensory elements.

In such relatively simple experimental designs, it was thought that at
least in the first 100 msec of fast movements open loop control exists: the
motor program as revealed by EMG will not be disturbed by suddenly blocking
the movement (Wadman et al., 1979, 1980ab). However, when the disturbance
consists of displacement of the target position (a light), very fast
modulation of the EMG takes place, suggesting a closed loop and the existence
of some kind of efference copy in the nervous system (Gielen et al., 1983).
Reed's (1982) opinion that "a functional movement is always under mixed
control" appears to be corroborated by these experiments on simple "artificial"
movements. Reed (1982) reformulated Bernstein's concept of functional non-
univocality:

> Bernstein suggests that the animal is in continual dis-
> equilibrium with its environment, requiring that it not
> react to stimuli, but rather that it act all the time and
> that it constantly evaluate its actions with respect to
> ever changing current conditions, while at the same time
> modulate its activities so as to meet its needs and goals
> within the environment (p. 108).

In fact, Reed's argument demands experimental designs on more complex and
ecological valid movements in which actively exploring perceptual systems
play an important role (13).

The Russian studies on the regulation of posture led to the conclusion
that another simplifying concept in motor control i.e. the use of the stretch

reflex is of no importance in the control of stance (14). It is in all
probability blocked in favour of a postural (reflex) control mechanism of a
superior kind (Eklund, 1973, quoted by Bonnet et al., 1976). In slow, whole
body sways, as well as in fast imposed disturbances the EMG activity of the
leg muscles appears not to be related to change in leg muscle length. A
central programme of postural fixation was postulated by Gurfinkel and his
co-workers. This programme would secure stability by regulating muscle function.
Short latency responses (45-55 msec) could not possibly result from receptors
in the foot. They suggested that these responses were mediated by afferentiation
from distant muscles and joints in the legs and the trunk. Gelfand et al.
(1971) proposed "the compensation of respirating disturbances of the erect
posture of man as an example of the organization of inter-articular interaction" (p. 373).

Indeed the coordination of posture as well as other movements is highly
complicated as Zalkind (1973) indicated:

> It is well established now, that performance of
> locomotor response is usually accompanied by changes
> in the activity of a lot of muscles, sometimes rather
> distant from the region of the main response (so
> called postural reaction)(p. 19).

If the various afferentations which have been proven to influence movement
tasks are taken into account (15) the chances for ambiguity of experimental
designs bearing on complex movements is apparent. Unequivocality will only
be brought about by rigorous experimental manipulations.

Gelfand et al. (1971) coined the concept 'functional synergy' defined
as:

> ...those classes of movements which have similar kinematic
> characteristics, coinciding active muscle groups and
> conductive types of afferentation (p. 331).

Cyclic locomotive synergies (walking, running, swimming, etc.), synergies of
throwing, blowing, jumping "and a certain (small) number of others" (p. 311)
have been discerned. When the concept of synergy for the explanation of the
regulation of all classes of movements is used, the existence of non-
univocality as defined by Bernstein is denied. This remains the case when
basic synergies are introduced which form "a dictionary of movements" (p. 332)
By using such concepts a one to one correspondence between CNS activity and
effector activity is assumed (16).

It seems to the present author, that in some movements synergies may
exist such as Nashner et al. (1979), Nashner and Woollacot (1979) claimed

for posture e.g. a sway and a suspensory synergy. Such synergies have to be
adaptive in character in order to enable the animal to react to various
disturbances. The adaptation will have a reflex-like character in one class
of movement - like standing - or in for example some details of a structured
movement in the Bernsteinian sense (p. 69) (Forssberg et al., 1975; Gurfinkel
& Latash, 1979a). In walking and running for example the adaptation to speed
will be under the influence of higher centers (Forssberg, 1983). In other
classes of movement these reactive adaptations may even have the character
of a conscious activity of higher CNS centers and may even be connected with
anticipation.

The principle of least interaction is another attempt to simplify the
task for the nervous system. This concept implies that on the basis of a small
number of leading effector parameters and the determination of the basic
afferentiation necessary for the realization of the movement, the higher levels
of the CNS are able to control movement in a simple way (Gelfand et al., 1971).
In this way these levels would be freed to be occupied by others tasks. If
this concept is to be successful, it must be applicable to those classes of
movement provisionally defined as 'automatic'.

Indeed, on the basis of experimental evidence, step generators at the
level of the spinal cord are postulated for automated movements such as
walking and running of cats. The generators, working with varying intensity,
produce variations predominantly in the stance phase of the limbs (the phase
in which the feet are in contact with the ground) or - better still - in the
extension phase (during which extensor muscles are active, a phase which is
slightly out of phase with the stance phase proper). These variations result
in a shorter duration and faster contractions of the muscles with the increase
of speed. The intensities of the generator's activities are regulated from
supraspinal structures (Grillner, 1975, 1979, 1981), but their intra-limb and
inter-limb coordinating functions appear to be organized at the spinal level
(Forssberg et al., 1980ab).

The integrated actions of muscles in the flexion phase and in the
extension phase could be regarded as two synergies. This idea is supported
from pathology; e.g., in hemiplegia where the extensor synergy has in most
cases a higher tone than the flexor synergy (Brunnström, 1970; Fugl-Meyer,
1980) in standing as well as in walking. This would indicate some similarity
between the generating neuronal subsystems. Such a similarity was also
proposed by Nashner (1979). In pathologic cases, e.g., hemiplegia, the
adaptive character of the synergy is decreased.

According to Kornhuber (1974) other non-automatic movements may be regulated as follows. In rapid movements cerebellar preprogramming regulates the spinal activity

> with regard to timing and duration of activity. The basal ganglia serve as a ramp generator for slow voluntary smooth movements of different speeds. For those movements that need sophisticated analysis of tactile objects, the output patterns of cerebellum and basal ganglia are further processed in the motor cortex (p. 267).

Even when it is granted that parts of these latter theories are speculative and at least rather imprecise in defining the classes of movement to which they pertain, it is nowadays possible to formulate the problem to be solved by these coordinating functions (generators, cerebellum, basal ganglia and cortex) at least on a theoretical level.

If it is supposed that the CNS has a certain "knowledge" of the peculiarities of the system it has to coordinate (i.e. the sensori-motor system) then a part of the non-univocalities would be explained away. Recent studies on non-linear properties of muscle activation show that the CNS seems to be capable of coping with the non-linearities of muscles by innervational impulses with varying time intervals (Stein et al., 1981). Energetically optimalized muscle contraction could be predicted by a relatively simple model. This was experimentally verified by Hatze & Buys, 1977 (cited by Hatze, 1980a). Hatze (1980a) proposed another "teleological adaptation operating in the neuromuscular control system". He modelled a logarithmic relation between the number of activated motor units and the relative cross-sectional areas occupied by these units. This model predicted the data of Milner Brown et al. (1973) on the recruitment order of motor units. Hatze concluded that in many non-maximal tetanic muscle contractions, a "principle of maximum grading sensitivity, the realization of which is the motor size unit law" (p. 34) can be postulated.

By such teleological reasoning it might be supposed - rightly - that the neuromuscular system is organized in such a way that the problems of non-univocality from both anatomical and (neuro)-physiological sources are solved. There still remains the problem of non-univocality from the mechanical sources enumerated by Bernstein on p. 214. The CNS, in coordinating movements has to solve these problems. On the basis of modern research it is now possible to formulate these problems very well. Computer programs of a multilinked model of hominoids consisting of 17 links exist (Hatze, 1977a, 1980b, 1981b). The model represents 42 three-dimensional degrees of freedom

roughly in conformity with the major determinants of human walking (Saunders
et al., 1953; Inman et al., 1981, see Fig. 2). Gravitational and inertial
moments are included. The model stimulates and optimizes movements. It is
able to analyze real life movements when fed with data from a Selspot movement
registration system. As the model also contains 46 muscle groups, it appears
possible to formulate the problem to be solved by the CNS in coordinating
movements, by muscle activation at least in the saggittal plane (17). As the
model contains general myo-cybernetic control sub-models, predicting motor
unit recruitment and stimulation rates (Hatze, 1977b, 1978) and accounting
for the non-linearities of the length-force and force-velocity characteristics
of muscle, the model should be able in the near future to pinpoint the task
of the neural controller in the optimal execution of movements such as walking,
jumping etc. In conclusion, by the use of the extensive models as developed
by Hatze it will be possible to formulate the complex task of the neural
control system with respect to the mechanical sources of non-univocality in
solving a motor problem.

These models have been developed using the principles of optimalized
actions of the CNS interacting with the non-linear peripheral musculoskeletal
system. These principles may only be valid for fully learned, automated or in
any way optimalized movements. In new movements, the non-linear feedback, to
which the CNS is fully accustomed is somehow manipulated by higher centres. The
CNS has a knowledge of the effector system and its relation to the environment
which largely surpasses our experimental descriptive and analytic understanding.

The existence of non-equivocality has a profound influence on the usage
of different experimental designs and on generalization of the conclusions so
derived.

4.   LOCOMOTION STUDIES.

4.1. Introduction.

Locomotion, especially human walking, has been studied since the work of
Braune & Fischer, Marey & Muybridge at the end of the 19th century. On the
West-European subcontinent, in the United Kingdom and the U.S.A. research on
this topic nearly came to a standstill in the early decades of this century.
The revitalization of research on human locomotion in the U.S.A. and especially
in California after World War II (Inman et al., 1981, preface) stemmed from

the urgent need of providing war-veterans with adequate protheses. Elsewhere in the U.S.A. researchers as Steindler & Drillis, exiled from pre-war Germany, had already transplanted the German interest in the functional anatomy of the muskolo-skeletal system (Fick, 1904-1911; Spalteholz, 1933; Braus, 1921; Benninghoff, 1938) to the U.S.A. (Steindler, 1935, 1955; Drillis, 1958). It is left to historians of science to place these developments in true perspective (18).

For such an historian it would appear that contrary to the trend elsewhere, in Russia an investigator - Bernstein - engaged in industrial ergonomic research, got an assignment to do an analysis of walking in order to solve some problems in the design of footbridges (see Bernstein, p. 171, footnote). He used photonic techniques. He concluded that the importance of the subject merited a special branch of physiology. This led to the monograph currently being reviewed. For the pupils of Bernstein, as well as for the numerous students of human locomotion elsewhere, the primary goals of the study were directed to specific applications of the knowledge gained by their work. These primary goals were surpassed by an ultimate goal developed in the publications contained in Bernstein's (1967) book. The ultimate goal of the developed programme was formulated by Bernstein in 1940 and earlier. It has been pursued by other workers as well, even while carrying out contract research directed to short term goals (e.g., the evaluation of presthetics and orthotics, Klopsteg & Wilson, 1954) or optimalization of sportive movements for coaching directives (e.g. de Groot et al., 1983). The scientific forum, in organizing itself in bodies such as the International Society of Biomechanics and its various branches, moved towards an independent research tradition aiming at high levels of generalizability. It is to be hoped that the scientific community will take the responsibility for this relative independency, as indeed did Bernstein.

In this Section attention is first paid to the phenomenalistic description of human gait and some issues in this type of work are taken up. Secondly the energetic optimalization of different modes of human walking is seen as a topic of much interest. Explanations for energetic optimalization are given. Walking and running are the two modes of human gait. It is well known that competition walking will cost more per metre distance traversed than running, so that in running other optimalizational principles must be assumed. The study of the transition of walking into running is recommended. General theories on stiff-legged (one linked) walks of idealized animals and man have been developed. An attempt is made to accommodate the knowledge on energy cost of human walking with such a theory.

Thirdly some attention is given to modelling of gait with n-linked models. Lastly some remarks are made on clinical applications.

4.2. Phenomenalistic description.

4.2.1. General overview

The important work on gait of the researchers in California over a period of 35 years has been reviewed recently by Inman et al. (1981). This beautifully produced book contains a well illustrated description of generalized human walking.

In generalized human walking seven major determinants or elements are considered by this group to be essential. The first three are pelvic rotation about a vertical axis, pelvic list (adduction in the hip joint of the stance leg) and flexion of the knee in stance. These elements result, amongst others, in a decrease in the vertical displacement of the body's center of mass (see Fig. 2).

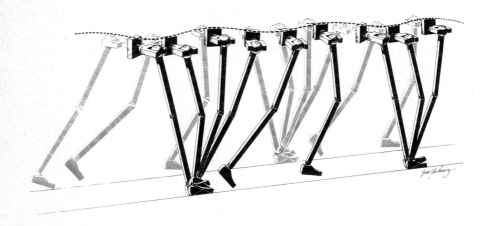

Fig. 2. Sinusoidal pathway of the center of mass under the influence of the major elements of walking (see text). Reproduced from Inman et al. (1981), Baltimore, Williams & Wilkins. The figure was published originally as illustration of Saunders J.B. de C.M., V.T. Inman and H.D. Eberhart (1953). The major determinants in normal and pathological gait, Journal of Bone and Joint Surgery 35A, 543, who gave also permission.

The ankle joint, of which the stiffness is regulated by flexor and extensor muscles, smoothes the path of the upper end of the leg. Supinatory and pronatory movements in the foot have a further, rather small, smoothing effect. Knee flexion in the first half of the stance phase and plantar flexion in the ankle, as well as knee flexion starting at the end of stance, also make a contribution to the smoothness of the pathway of the body's centre of mass. The movements in the joints mentioned are regulated by activity of muscles or by their compliance in active or passive states.

Lateral displacement of the body is related to the transverse distance of the feet when they are in contact with the floor. Rotations of the upper trunk segment, the shoulders, in counterphase with pelvic rotations, as well as the swing of the arms in counterphase to the swing of the lower limbs smoothes the forward accelerations of the centre of mass.

Most of the details, as well as the above-mentioned elements, of the complex walking process are dependent on the mean walking velocity. For that reason, a description of generalized walking will be preponderantly of didactic value. It renders no quantitative information. It gives an overview of "the general structure" but will not give information on "the finer details in which this structure is able to differentiate" in the meaning of Bernstein's views on locomotion. In order to analyze such details, laboratory experiments have been undertaken in which environmental variables are well under control and instrumentation is possible. The use of such an analytical approach poses the question of validity. It is well known that subjects are apt to alter their way of walking when they are conscious of being observed. Drillis (1958), Finley & Cody (1970) and Molen et al. (1972a) covertly observed walking pedestrians in order to obtain valid standards.

Differences in mean velocity, stride frequency as well as in step length in different locations occurred. A sex difference was noted: women taking more and smaller steps while maintaining lower speeds than men. The ratio step length/step frequency appeared to remain fairly constant for both sexes and over the range of speeds the subjects were found to walk. This ratio was different for both sexes.

Comparison of data of Molen et al. (1972a) with data from Du Chatinier et al. (1970), the latter pertaining to a constrained walk in which speed was imposed, showed that the subjects in this situation tended to a higher frequency resulting in a significant lower ratio. In contrast, Herman et al. (1976) reported, for a "preferred" walk under laboratory conditions, a lower frequency than the pedestrians covertly observed by Finley & Cody (1970).

The differences reported are quite small and will not contaminate general
theories.

Such differences may be of importance when one wants to study the finer
details which possibly occur in walking on motor driven treadmills (see sub-
section 2.5). Herman et al. (1976) pointed to the possibility that at very
low speeds a relatively longer time is spent in double support in order to
attain maximal stability. In constrained walks, according to Du Chatinier
et al. (1970) the same might be true. A higher step frequency resulting in
a longer total double support duration was observed in untrained adults
walking on a motor driven treadmill compared with track walking. Under both
these conditions, the step frequency appeared to be higher than in a covertly
observed outdoor walk (unpublished observation). The same was reported for
children by van Ingen Schenau (1980). However, such "artificialities" were
not seen after careful procedures during which, the subjects became accustomed
to the experimental conditions. Carefully designed instructions to subjects can
solve the problem of validity, as was confirmed by Herman et al. (1976).

Most authors working like Herman et al. (1976) with a range of speeds,
or like Murray (1967) and Murray et al. (1964, 1966, 1970) with clusters of
free and fast speeds, do find simple linear relations between the various
components such as stride frequency, step length, duration of stance and
swing phases on the one hand and walking speed on the other. Free chosen
speeds, as well as speeds imposed by instruction, as far as this is measured
by these variables, do not differ in structure (Herman et al. 1976). From
such data, it appears that at free speeds step length between subjects tends
to vary more than step frequency. In various speeds, the ratio step length/
step frequency remains fairly constant over a range of speeds of 0.7 - 2.0
meter per second (Herman et al., 1976). The same was found by Decan (1965)
after normalization for body height and by Inman et al. (1981). They concluded
however that body height could not be the only factor in deciding this spatio-
temporal dimension of walking (19).

Step length and step frequency vary linearly with speed, resulting in
an inverse relationship between speed and cycle duration. Stance time (i.e.
the duration of the stance phase) varies strongly and linearly with mean
walking velocity or cycle duration. Swing time varies also with speed but
considerably less so (Murray et al., 1966; Herman et al., 1976, see Fig. 3).

The above-mentioned relations have as a consequence that the double
support time shortens with higher speeds. The duration of the double support
time versus cycle time decreases exponentially with speed. At very low speeds

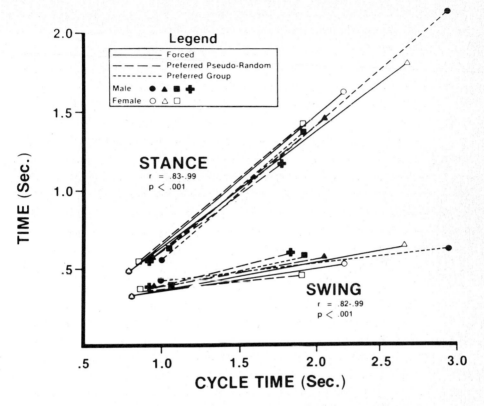

Fig. 3. Sample regression lines for the relationship between
stance and swing periods and cycle (= stride) time
period, during various instructed and preferred walks
in both sexes. Note that the time interval between
values of stance and swing times at any cycle time is
indicative of the double support period. Reproduced
from Herman et al. In: Herman, R.M., S. Grillner,
P.S.G. Stein & D.G. Stuart (1976) New York, Plenum
Publishing Corporation, with permission of authors
and publishers.

the double support time will take 50% of the cycle duration (20). At speeds
of about 2m/sec the duration of the double support phase will reach its
minimal value. Instead of walking, running without double support, may be
the choice of locomotion (Grillner et al., 1979).

Herman et al. (1976) noted further a strong covariance between times
of maximal joint excursions in both phases of gait and cycle time in walking
at normal speeds. Further analysis of the joint excursions suggested an
"unifying principle of joint coupling" (p. 34).

Herman et al. (1976) appear to have been the first and only researchers
who have statistically analyzed various details of the human walking process
over a wide range of speeds, including speeds like those seen in pathology
of walking. They correlated joint excursions, EMG data and temporal factors
of gait. The data were related to concepts of Bernstein and his coworkers as
well as to the work of Grillner and associates. It is felt that in the near
future the details of the research of Herman and associates will be of
importance, when the work of Grillner and associates is expanded to EMG of
human walking.

Herman and his associates related EMG to speed. At very low speeds the
EMG patterns varied very widely, whereas at preferred speeds the variability
of the magnitude and duration of the discharges of the muscles in study was
four to sixfold the variability of the magnitude and duration of joint
excursions. Nevertheless EMG bursts could be related to the time histories
of gait parameters. Any measure of EMG "intensity" increased with speed.

4.2.2. Problems in phenomenalistic descriptions of human gait

Three issues are of importance in the descriptive research on human
walking and running.

First, Inman et al. (1981) called attention to the fact that the
literature does not show good agreement on the relative duration of the double
support phase with respect to cycle duration. They cited studies of Contini
et al. (1964), Finley et al. (1975), Grieve & Gear (1966), Murray et al. (1966).
They commented that the accuracy of measurement and differences in measurement
procedures may be the cause of the disagreement (21). Drillis (1958) reported
a variation in the ratio of swing time/stance time of 0.5 to 0.8 with speed,
indicating a variation of 0.25 to 0.1 (22) for the ratio of double support
time versus stance time for the range of speeds studied. This would mean
that the ratio of double support time to cycle time is not invariant with
speed of walking. Thus, the contention that double support time decreases
exponentially with speed, is quite right (Herman et al., 1976, see Fig. 3).

The second issue, is a consequence of the first one: as the relationships
between stance, swing and double support periods and the cycle time vary
differently with speed, normalization of time-dependent data over speed may
be an unjustified procedure. In the double support phase the kinematic chain
of the legs and the pelvis is closed. A straightforward interpretation of
EMG data in connection with twice differentiated displacement-time data is
not possible without measurement of foot-reaction forces. Interpretation

of such data on the supposition that they pertain to swing phase, while in
reality double support existed, will lead to ambiguous results (23).

The third issue is related to the reasons why the results of many reports
on EMG during walking are not reviewed in this paper. It is quite customary
to relate EMG data to the timed phases of gait: stance, swing and double
support phase as percentages of gait cycle time. EMG data are utilized in
this way to explain muscle functions during gait in terms of forces,
generating accelerations etc.. Such research will not

> provide a more reliable comprehensive basis for a
> subsequent broad extension of investigation into the
> genesis and pathology of locomotion (Bernstein, p. 171).

Figure 4a   Figure 4b

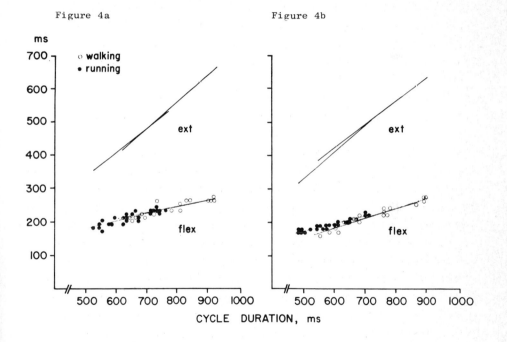

Fig. 4. Duration of the flexion and extension phases versus step
cycle duration. The lines for the flexion phases (flex)
are drawn for walking (open circles) and running (filled
circles) separately. For the extension phases only the
calculated lines are drawn. In A the general picture is
illustrated, in B one of two subjects out of 8 subjects
showing a significant difference (p < 0.05) between the
slopes for walking and running is illustrated. Reproduced
from Grillner, S., J. Halbertsma, J. Nilsson and A.
Thorstensson (1979), Amsterdam, Elsevier Biomedical Press,
with permission of authors and publishers.

Herman et al. (1976) clearly and explicitly carried out their research with this
goal in mind. Neural and biomechanical aspects of control were discussed
by these authors. They related EMG data to joint excursion data. Relating
EMG data to time factors of gait will not be the best choice of methods.
Grillner et al. (1979) stressed this issue. They described the relationship
of flexion phase and extension phase to cycle duration (and therefore speed)
in walking and running (see Fig. 4).

They defined flexion phase T_{FL} as the interval between the onset of
flexion in the knee joint (during stance phase) and the onset of the
subsequent extension (in mid or end of swing). T_{EXT} or extension phase was
defined as the rest of the cycle. The relationships of these phases to cycle
duration are linear. This can be expressed as $T_{FL} = aT_{EXT} + b$ in which a
varies from 0.14 to 0.34 and b from -0.02 to 16 sec. In 6 of the 8 subjects
the coefficients for walking and running did not differ significantly and
overlapped in the region of cycle durations found in the transition of
walking into running. In this region subjects are able to choose for one of
the two modes of gait.

It seems to the present author that the existence of rigid statistical
connections between EMG and time and space factors of gait - such as stance
and swing phase - is no proof of their existence as control elements. The
duration and the intensity of muscle contractions during flexion and
extension phases, as defined by Grillner and associates and not during the
stance and swing times, are better candidates. Observations of EMG in these
firstly named phases of human walking should be a critical experiment for
this issue. Such observations are to be expected within a short time
(Halbertsma, 1982, personal communication).

In a lot of the earlier work on human gait it was not known how to
relate effects (step length, frequency, stance time, swing time) to causes
(neuronal activity). Thus the description of these effects was only used as
a reference frame for the description of kinematic phenomena (as joint
excursions) or for the analysis of the mechanical functions of muscles. It
did not serve the goal Bernstein posed for such descriptions: analysis of
coordination and regulation of movement by neuronal activity.

4.3. Energetic optimalization of gait.

4.3.1. Introduction

Energy expenditure expressed in units per kg body mass per unit of

time is a measure of the physiological load on the body's cardio-respiratory
system. Energy cost expressed in units per kg body mass per unit of distance
traversed is a measure of energetic cost over profit.

In walking, the physiological load will not be a constraining factor.
Nevertheless the cost/profit ratio will be optimized. This mode of
locomotion can be maintained over long periods. In gait at higher speeds,
the rate of expenditure (per unit of time) will rise. Thus a mode of locomotion
should exist in which the cost per distance traversed will be such as to
postpone maximal use of all cardio-respiratory reserves: running.

The maximal speed attained in running is said to be 16 km/h in untrained
and 22 km/h in trained subjects. Running at moderate speeds can be kept up
for considerable times and distances. In competitional walking or race
walking the maximal speed is said to be 15 km/h. This mode of walking can
be kept up too for considerable times and distances. In both strategies –
running and competitional walking – the possibility exists that anaerobic
work will curtail the overt use of chemical energy. The latter is customarily
estimated from measurement of O_2-consumption, while the former is only to
be estimated by blood-gas analysis.

This Section will go into some aspects of energetic optimalization of
gait. Biomechanical and physiological mechanisms and processes are to be
explored. Next to the regulative and coordinational actions of the nervous
system these mechanisms and processes are believed to be decisive for the
optimal solutions of selection of speed, step frequency and length in walking.
In the selection of modes of gait at speeds far lower and higher than the
optimal speed, energetic aspects may also be decisive.

General theories on locomotion of animals (and men) also pertain to
optimalizational principles. At least two modes of gait, walking and running,
are discerned (next to galloping and jumping). They are in use by a wide
variety of terrestrial animals. The first one - walking - is characterized by
the use of legs which are thought to be rather stiff: a stiff-legged gait. In
running the flexion of knee and stiffle joint, counteracted by stretched
muscles or tendons, is characterized as a compliant mode of gait. Both modes
of gait are studied in terms of efficiency (Cavagna, 1978) and compared with
swimming and flying (Alexander & Goldspink, 1977). Rather low efficiencies
appear to exist in terrestrial stiff-legged walking modes. The efficiency
terms are formulated as a ratio between work done to reach potential and
energetic levels of energy of the body's centre of gravity of the total
potential and kinetic energy levels (Cavagna, 1978; Winter, 1979) on the one

hand and energy cost on the other hand.

Various energy saving mechanisms are proposed in the so called stiff-
legged walk of human beings. In the compliant running gait the very compliancy
is thought to lead to a lower energy cost.

Running differs from walking in the absence of a double support phase
in the former. This phenomenon is connected with the compliant and stiff
character of the contact with the ground in these modes of gait. Other modes
(hopping, galloping) will differ in another way in this respect. The general
theory of Alexander & Jayes (1978ab, 1980) and of Alexander (1980) tries to
correlate contact characteristics and potential and kinetic energy
characteristics of such modes of gait. In this Section an attempt will be
made to reconcile the various approaches to human gait.

4.3.2. Energy expenditure rate and cost of human gait

Energy expenditure expressed in units per kg body mass per unit of
time was shown by Ralston (1958) to depend on the speed of walking in a
quadratic fashion of format $\dot{E}=b+mv^2$, where $\dot{E}$ is the energy expenditure rate
(expressed as cal/min) per kilogram body weight, v is speed in m/min and b
and m are constants. The expression is valid for a range of speeds from
50m/min up to 100m/min.

Using weighted (24) data from various investigators Zarrugh et al.(1974)
and Inman et al. (1981) combined estimations for b and m:

$$\dot{E} = 32 + 0,0050v^2 \tag{1}$$

This equation is illustrated in Fig. 5 (lower dashed line).

As many of the implications and intricacies of such work have recently
been reviewed by Inman et al. (1981), it is not necessary to go into detail
here: differences in experimental conditions, in sex, the invalid convention
of some investigators in subtracting the expenditure in standing from that
in walking etc., will not be dealt with. Instead the focus will be on problems
of optimization.

Zarrugh et al. (1974) deduced from their own experimental data and data
from Molen et al. (1972) a general hyperbolic function which takes into
account the step frequency n in steps/min and the step length s in metres:

$$\dot{E}_w = \frac{\dot{E}_o}{(1 - \dfrac{s^2}{s_u^2}) \quad (1 - \dfrac{n^2}{n_u^2})} \tag{2}$$

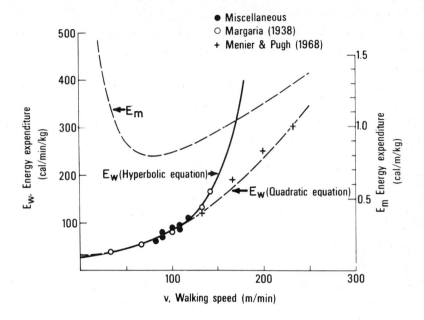

Fig. 5. Energy rate, bottom lines referring to the equations in
the text, and energy cost, top line, idem. Reproduced
from Inman, V.T., H.J. Ralston & F. Todd (1981) Baltimore,
The Williams and Wilkins Company, with permission of the
publishers.

where $\dot{E}_o = \dot{E}_w$ when $n=s=o$, n_u and s_u are upper limits of n (step frequency) and
s (step length) as $\dot{E}_w$ approaches infinity. The rationale for such an approach
was put forward by Molen et al. (1972b). In equating $\dot{E}$ with speed only, the
free choice of any combination of step frequency and step length at a given
velocity is not accounted for.

It was observed by Molen et al. (1972a) that walking pedestrians choose
such combinations of step length and frequency that a mean ratio of step
length/step frequency of 0.0070 results for males and 0.0060 for females. In
their study on energy expenditure in walking on a motor driven treadmill,
ratio's of 0.0072 and 0.0056 were found (Molen & Rozendal, 1967). From other
studies it was apparent that this ratio differed significantly between sexes
(Du Chatinier et al., 1970). It was thought that human subjects walking at
a range of speeds would choose an optimal combination of step length and
frequency, resulting in a minimal energy expenditure cost per unit task or

metre distance travelled. This appeared to be true as was graphically shown by Molen et al. (1972b) and mathemetically modelled by Zarrugh et al. (1974). (See Figs. 6 and 7).

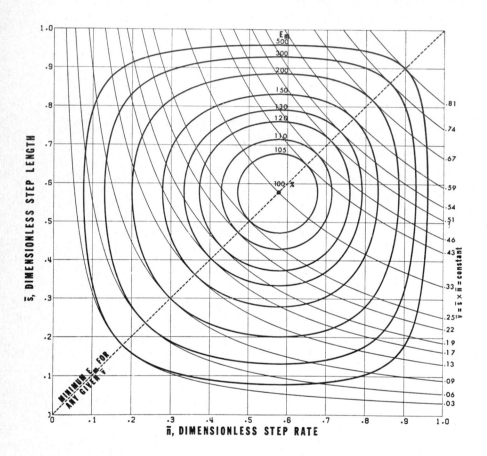

Fig. 6. General model of the dependence of the energy cost per metre in human walking, on the choice of step length and step frequency (here depicted in dimensionless formats). Hyperbolic functions of v̄ = s̄ x n̄ = constant. Ellipsoid functions denote percentages of energy cost per meter of the minimum (100%). Tangencies of both functions indicate combinations of s̄ and n̄, optimal with respect to energy cost. Reproduced from Zarrugh, M.Y., F.N. Todd & H.J. Ralston (1974) Berlin, Springer, with permission of the authors and publishers.

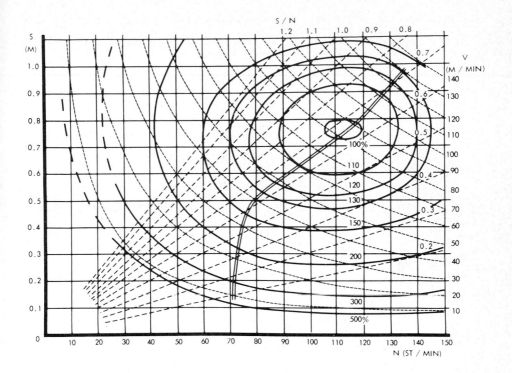

Fig. 7. Graphic representation of energy cost levels (ellipses)
expressed as in Fig. 6 in various combinations of s and
n as experimentally determined by Molen, N.H., R.H. Rozendal
and W. Boon (1972). Hyperbolae: levels of v. Optimal
combinations of s and n are depicted by a double line.

From this model it appears that an energetically optimal speed exists
between 4 and 6 km/h at which cost per metre is minimal. At higher and lower
speeds of walking the minimal cost is attained by specific combinations of
s and n. Over a range of speeds this ratio remains fairly constant. The
difference in this ratio between the sexes was shown to depend, at least
for a significant part on differences in leg length (Van Baak, 1979). At
very low speeds the ratio is lower too. Otherwise stated: lowering speed at
optimal cost levels will be reached by lowering step length while retaining
a fairly constant step frequency (Molen et al., 1972b). This latter detail
is not taken up in the model of Zarrugh et al. (1974).

Inman et al. (1981) in reviewing this work stated:

Equation (2) will be valid for all kinds of walking with
spontaneously chosen or intended combinations of step
frequency and step length. In natural walking, where the
subject adopts his own natural cadence for a particular
speed it can be shown that equation (2) reduces to:

$$\dot{E}_w = \frac{\dot{E}_o}{(1 - v/v_u)^2} \tag{3}$$

where v is speed and v_u is upper limit of v, equal to $n_u s_u$
(p. 66).

Equation (3) is illustrated in Fig. 5 (solid line).

$\dot{E}_o$ has an average value of 28 cal/min/kg and v_u = 240m/min, as was shown
experimentally by Ralston (1958) for $\dot{E}_o$, and as was mathematically deduced by
Zarrugh et al. (1974) from data of the authors, of Atzler and Herbst (1928)
and of Molen et al. (1972b) with regard to maximal speed. This latter figure
seems quite unrealistic for natural walking, since Inman et al. (1981) state
145 m/min as the top natural speed. A speed of 240 m/min will be reached in
race walking.

Up to 100 m/min, equations (2) and (3) predict virtually the same values
for energy expenditure rates. At speeds of 120 m/min the hyperbolic equation
(3) predicts higher expenditures than the quadratic (1). About this speed (of
2 m/sec) the subject has a choice. Heightening of s will change his walking
movement into a run, while heightening of n will result in competition walking
(race walking). Indeed, Hogberg (1952) found that in the course of a run at
between 10 and 12 km/h, increments in speed are predominantly caused by
lengthening of s.

Margaria (1963) and Menier & Pugh (1968) found that in speeds over 8 km/h
the energy rate in running is lower than that in race walking. Inman et al.
(1981) commented that to their surprise the quadratic equation (1) predicted
the energy cost of the competition walking Olympic subjects of Menier & Pugh
(1968) well within 10%. Data of Margaria (1938) on walking and running fitted
the hyperbolic function (3). The latter fact would suggest that running will
demand a higher expenditure rate than race walking at the same speed, a
suggestion which is quite contrary to naive expectancy. Indeed, Van Baak
(1979) confirmed that the energy rate in walking will be slightly higher than
that in running in the same subjects at the same speeds at 8 km/h and higher.

As the equations of Van Baak (1979) for walking and running were valid
for 4.2 up to 8.6 km/h and 7 - 16 km/h respectively, the range of common
speeds was not very extensive. Extrapolation of the quadratic equation of
Van Baak for walking renders over-estimations of the expenditure rates of

the Olympic competitional walkers analyzed by Menier & Pugh (1968). The
subjects of Van Baak (1979) were not trained. The issue of the training status
of subjects is of importance in the problem of the predictive power of energy
expenditure rate equations to (sub-)maximal speeds. In the transitional zone,
in which subjects can choose - irrespective of their special training - for
running or walking, cardio-respiratory functioning will not prove to be the
constraint. Do the models on energy cost per metre predict better?

The graphic model of Molen at al. (1972b) as well as the mathematical
model of Zarrugh et al. (1974) predict that either choice (for increasing
exclusively or mainly s or n) would give an increase of energy cost relative
to holding s/n constant. The only difference in what the two models would
predict is that this increase would be slightly larger in the case of Zarrugh's
model. Cavagna (1978) in a review of the work carried out by himself and his
associates, as well as Van Baak (1979) state that the cost per metre in running
remains fairly constant over a wide range of speeds, whereas in walking, in
the transitional range of speeds, the cost will rise steeply.

The conclusion must be, that models like those of Molen & Zerrugh do
not correctly predict the cost per distance traversed in running. Mechanisms
reducing the cost in running do however exist. At high speeds, Van Baak (1979)
showed that the cost diminished. This could possibly be related to anaerobic
work. At intermediate speeds, other mechanisms will, in later sections of
this essay, be proposed.

4.3.3. Biomechanical explanation of optimal speed in human walking

In walking, the external positive work of the muscles - as defined by
Cavagna (1978) - is quite small. The changes in potential and kinetic energy
of the body's centre of mass are 180° out of phase while opposite in direction.
It is assumed that muscles convert potential in kinetic energy and vice
versa. This mechanism is not possible in running as the kinetic and potential
energy changes are nearly in phase.

For walking Cavagna (1978) defined:

$$\text{percent recovery} = \frac{W_f + W_v - W_{ext}}{W_f + W_v} \times 100$$

where W_f is work brought about by the forward speed changes, W_v is work done
against gravity (potential and vertical kinetic energetic components) and
W_{ext} is the external work. This percentage recovery is maximal at the optimal
speed, when the external work as well as the cost per metre is minimal

(Cavagna et al., 1976). Cavagna (1978) offers the following explanation:

> The exchange between gravitational potential energy
> and kinetic energy take place in the best way at
> intermediate speeds of walking, leading to a reduction
> of the external work done per unit distance: this in
> turn leads to a reduction of the cost of walking per
> unit distance. Is this the only explanation for the
> minimum cost of walking at 4 - 5 km/h? As mentioned
> above, the metabolic energy expenditure in locomotion
> is not only the result of the mechanical energy changes
> of the centre of mass (W_{ext}) but also of the kinetic
> energy changes of the limbs relative to the centre of
> mass (W_{int}). The efficiency with which the muscles
> perform mechanical work done ($W_m = W_{ext} + W_{int}$) and the
> energy expended. This ratio was measured as a function
> of speed and attained a maximum at intermediate speeds
> of walking (Cavagna & Kaneko, 1977).

Thus a mechanical and a metabolic factor (greater efficiency of muscular
contraction) are introduced by Cavagna (1978).

Winter (1979) proposed a more rigorous definition of efficiency.
Internal work, in his definition, comprises all the changes in potential and
kinetic energy components. After computing the total energy of the body's
centre of mass, he compared this with the sum of the segment energies. He
expressed the differences as percentages of the sum of segment energies
approach. The differences between various test runs varied from + 3.2 to
- 41.7% with a mean of - 16% (± 10.6 SD). These differences do not appear
to be dependent on step frequency and consequently on speed of walking. The
refinement proposed by Winter (1979) will affect efficiencies as computed by
Cavagna & Kaneko (1977), but will not affect their conclusion with respect
to the dependency on speed of the efficiency.

Zarrugh (1981) pointed to the fact that the work rate of head, arms
and trunk (HAT) has a minimum at the speed and step frequency found in the
optimum. However, most explanatory remarks in the literature focus on
processes in the lower limbs.

For an explanation of the maximal efficiency at the optimal speed, as
well as for the choice of the constant ratio s/h at higher and lower speeds
pendulous (Herman et al., 1976) or quasipendulous (Grieve & Gear, 1966) motions
of the legs are proposed. In such pendulous movements the interchange of
potential and kinetic energy would not call for muscular intervention
(Cavagna, 1978) or only for a minimal muscular intervention. Elftman (1966)
proposed that the stretch shortening cycle in non-articular and even in bi-

articular muscles could save energy. Herman et al. (1976) as well as
Pedotti (1977) called attention to the fact that activation of antagonists
about most joints does not occur in walking.

Bernstein (1976, p. 106) believed that the functional non-univocality
resulted, in the multi-linked pendulous legs, in too many degrees of freedom,
which had to be mastered by neuro-muscular activity in a very complicated
way. More recent explanations of the energetic optimalization of walking
confirm such a belief.

4.3.4. The transition of walking into running

In the range of speeds at which transition of walking into running
customarily takes place, cardio-respiratory function is not decisive. This
transition has not as yet been studied very extensively.

It was experimentally studied by Grillner et al. (1979). They stated that
this transition occurred at about 2m/sec or 8 km/h, suggesting a rather wide
range of speeds. Herman et al. (1976) indicated that this transition has to
occur at the cycle duration in which stance and swing time (extrapolated)
would comprise the whole cycle time (25). According to these authors, cycle
frequency will then be 1.7 cycles (strides) per second ± 0.1 (s.d.). This
will result in 204 steps/min, seemingly an unrealistic value in reality to
be reached in competition walking.

Grillner et al. (1979) indicated stride cycle durations of 0.75 - 0.60
sec for the transitional zone between speeds of 1.8 and 4.0 m/sec (see Fig.
8). Walking with the latter velocity will be competition walking and will
reach the maximal speed Zarrug et al. (1974) predicted.

Alexander & Jayes (1978b) stated that at a velocity of 180 m/min the
change cannot be postponed except in race walking, while Inman et al. (1980)
stated a speed of 145 m/min as the upper limit of natural walking. At 150
m/min or 2.5 m/sec the subjects of Grillner et al. (1979) displayed a stride
cycle duration of about 0.75 sec. This would result in 1.33 cycles per second
or 159 steps per minute with a step length of 0.94 m and a step length/step
frequency ratio of about 0.0060.

In the transitional range of speeds, the flexion and extension phases,
as well as the cycle duration (and stride frequency) and consequently the
stride length are equal in walking and running at the same speeds. Support
phase duration falls in running, the cycle is completed with a floating phase.
Support length, an estimate of the distance traversed during support also
falls, while the floating phase accounts for a relatively longer distance

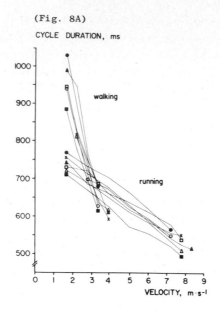

(Fig. 8A)

CYCLE DURATION, ms

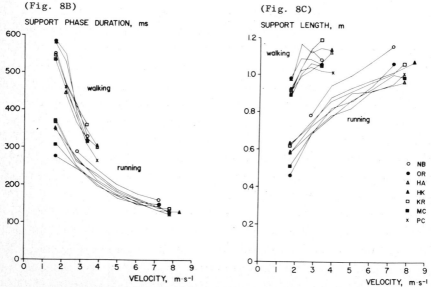

(Fig. 8B)

SUPPORT PHASE DURATION, ms

(Fig. 8C)

SUPPORT LENGTH, m

Fig. 8. Cycle duration, support phase duration and support length
(derived from support phase duration and v̄) versus velocity
of walking and running for different subjects. Each data point
is the mean of 10 successive measurements. Reproduced from
Grillner, S., J. Halbertsma, J. Nillson and A. Thorstensson
(1979) Amsterdam, Elsevier Biomedical Press, with permission
of the authors and publishers.

traversed. The amplitude of the knee flexion during the flexion phase is smaller in running than in walking at speeds below 2 m/sec. In running a range of speeds from 2m/sec to 8 m/sec the knee flexion amplitude increases strongly. At 8 m/sec the support length will attain the same maximal value of 1.1 m as is reached in race walking.

The cycle duration in race walking falls steeply, while the cycle duration in running does not. The implication is that, indeed, in running, different velocities are mainly reached by alterations in stride length and duration of the floating phase. In running, it is possible to reach shorter flexion and extension phases (Fig. 4) with higher amplitudes of knee flexion. Grillner et al. (1979) commented that lower torques in the hip joint would result from the higher amplitude of knee flexion. In running, the constraint of the maximal support length is also postponed to higher speeds. Lastly, in walking, the legs in the double support phase work against each other doing positive and negative work (Alexander & Jayes, 1978b). This will not be the case in running.

4.3.5. Energy cost and generalized theories on gait

As has been mentioned already, walking is characterized by Cavagna (1978) and by Alexander & Jayes (1978ab, 1980) as a stiff-legged walk. Apart from the two modes of gait - walking and running - numerous others may exist, especially in tetrapods (Hildebrand, 1976), but Alexander & Jayes (1978ab, 1980) maintain that a quadruped can be treated as two bipeds walking one behind the other. Notwithstanding the remarks of Grillner et al. (1979) that the amplitude of the step in quadrupeds is constrained by their very quadrupedy, the contention of Alexander and Jayes is taken for granted here, as well as their contention that only a few modes of gait exist if they are described in terms of time histories of the levels of potential and kinetic energies of the body's centre of mass with respect to the stride cycle.

In this respect human walking and running are different. In walking, the centre of gravity will rise upwards in midstance, when it passes over the rather extended leg, while in double support it will be at its lowest position. This has consequences for the level of potential energy. In one complete cycle (step from left through right mid-stance to left mid-stance) the centre of gravity will complete one sinusoid curve of which the frequency is dependent on mean velocity and the amplitude is dependent on the length of the legs. This is called by Alexander & Jayes (1978ab, 1980) a stiff-legged walk. In human running, the legs in stance phase bend considerably more and it is called a compliant walk. This compliancy is considered to be the cause

of the fact that the centre of gravity is lowest at mid-stance and highest
in the floating phase, resulting in a complete-stride trajectory which is in
opposition to that produced by walking.

In paragraph 4.3.3. it has been mentioned that, in walking, the level
of kinetic energy of the body's centre of mass is opposite to that of
potential energy. The total level of energy is flattened out. In running,
both levels add up (see Fig. 9a, I (a) and IV respectively). From an energetic
viewpoint both modes of walking are radically different in their demands on
the cardio-respiratory system.

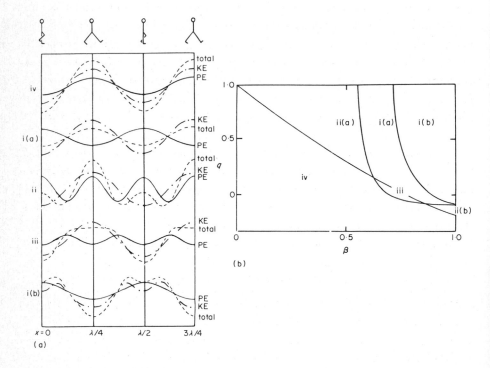

Fig. 9. a) Schematic graphs of total, kinetic and potential energy
levels (ordinate) against the stride as distance traversed
(abscissae) for a stiff-legged biped. b) A graph of q against
β, showing the values which give rise to each of the
possibilities illustrated in a). For explanation see text.
Reproduced from Alexander, R.M.N. & A.S. Jayes (1978) London,
The Zoological Society of London, with permission of the
authors and publishers.

Alexander & Jayes (1978ab, 1980) modelled these demands in relation to
β - q diagrams (see Fig. 9b). By q is meant the negative of the ratio of the

first and third arguments of the Fourier transformed vertical reaction forces.
This ratio is speed-dependent. In the fastest walking mode q would be 1.0 and
in running -0.33 (26). The definition of β is: the fraction of the duration
of the stride for which any particular foot is on the ground. As has already
been mentioned, the extreme value of β in walking is 0.5, lower values
resulting in running, without double support. In practice, at β values of
about 0.6 walking will transform into running. As the authors assume very low
fluctuations of speed within the stride, β approximately equals support length
(distance travelled during support) divided by stride length. By this assumption,
the model takes into account some of the effects of the major elements of
gait (Saunders et al., 1953) e.g. smoothing the curve of kinetic energy, while
the fluctuations of kinetic and potential energy in the vertical direction are
over-estimated by the assumption of stiff legs. This will result in an over-
estimation of the fluctuation of total potential energy in excess of the
assessment of Cavagna (1978).

In a further extension of the model Alexander (1980) commented that in
the model of Alexander & Jayes (1978) possibly another over-estimation of the
total work done had been introduced. They reasoned that in the double support
phase the legs were doing work against each other (positive and negative, both
demanding energy consumption). It has been argued by Cavagna (cited by
Alexander, 1980) that at the beginning of the double support phase the reaction
force on the forward leg is in line with the axes of the ankle, knee and hip
joints, not exerting any moment with respect to these joints.

> Since its length is (for the time being) constant and
> no moment is acting about any moving joint in it.

Cavagna concludes this leg is doing no work, positive or negative. Indeed
Winter (1979) showed that in human walking the level of energy in both legs is
rather low during double support, while lower still in the forward (stance)
leg. The energy level in the future swing leg rises steeply, to become maximal
in mid-swing.

The above mentioned refinement of the model of Alexander and coworkers
must affect the predicted energetic demands and, therefore, the $\beta - q$
conditions for reaching optimal levels of energetic demands, as it has been
shown (Alexander, 1980). However, the supposition of a stiff-legged walk will
over-estimate potential energy fluctuations. In the stance phase the knee
will be flexed, slightly with low and more clearly with higher speeds. Knee
flexion in stance is correlated with mean walking speed as well as with a
deeper valley between the two peaks of the vertical foot reaction forces in

human walking (van Ingen Schenau, personal communication). Alexander & Jayes
(1980) also showed the same dependence of q on mean walking speed. If this
dependence is indeed brought about by knee flexion in the stance leg, a
further refinement of the model is called for.

Nevertheless the model Alexander and his co-workers proposed appears to
be very powerful in predicting the energy demands in various modes of walking
of different animals as well as of humans. The model does not predict the
demands of running very well. According to the authors it was not developed
with this aim. Measurements of human walking on force plates confirmed the
assumptions about the speed dependency of q. Humans walking at various speeds
appeared to lie in zone Ia of Fig. 9b, while race walking at high values of
q and β > 0.5 will occur in zone IIa. Of this mode of walking, the authors
state that it is a mode most animals avoid with the significant exception of
athletes in races "in which the rules of the game override considerations of
economy and energy" (Alexander & Jayes, 1978a, p. 39).

They calculated the total positive work performed by idealized bipeds
per step, $\dot{E}$, defined as 32 $k/mg\lambda^2$, where k is a constant (for human walking
k is about 1.7) with the dimension of length, m is body mass, g is gravitational
acceleration and λ is stride length. As

$$k\mathbf{F}_{\mathbf{x}} = ut\mathbf{F}_{\mathbf{y}}$$

where u is mean velocity during the stride, F_x and F_y are the horizontal and
vertical sagittal forces, and t is time, in $\dot{E}$ the potential and kinetic energy
were represented. Levels of $\dot{E}$ were calculated for different speeds of walking:
72 m/min, 102 m/min and 163 m/min respectively (see Fig. 10a, 10b and 10c
respectively). At 72 m/min the minimal energy level is found at β = 0.6 and
q = 0.4. At 102 m/min it is found at nearly the same duty factor and q = 0.5,
meaning that the vertical reaction force has a deeper valley between the two
principal thrusts.

Both optima for these velocities lie within the 110% $\dot{E}_m$ zones of the
models of Molen et al. (1972b) and Zarrugh et al. (1974). At the competitional
walking speed of 163 m/min the minimal energy requirement would be reached
at a duty factor β of 0.6 and q values about 1.0. For this velocity the
models of Molen & Zarrugh and associates predict $\dot{E}_m$ at a level of 150% of
the absolute optimum. Alexander & Jayes show a value of total positive work
per step which is 1.5 times the values at the other two velocities (27).

Alexander (1980) corrected the above mentioned over-estimation of the
energetic demand (or power output, as it has been called by him) by calculating

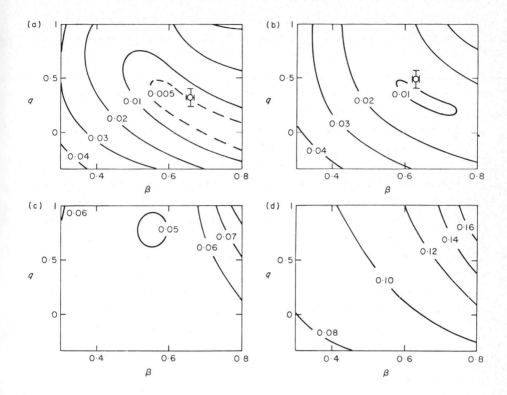

Fig. 10. Total positive work levels performed by the idealized biped, calculated from the model for about a) 72 m/min, b) 102 m/min and c) 163 m/min of human walking. Optima in dashed lines. Reproduced in adapted form, from Alexander, R.McN. and A.S. Jayes (1978) London, The Zoological Society of London, with permission of the authors and publisher.

the work of each leg separately. Graphs on speeds of about 50 m/min, 102 m/min, 204 m/min and 290 m/min were produced, showing energetic optima (see Fig. 11). The correction seems to result in a wider variation of the duty factor β and values for q over the range of speeds studied, in accordance with the data of Alexander & Jayes (1980) - with respect to the dependence of q on speed - and of Herman et al. (1976) on the dependence of stance, swing and double support duration on speed.

These facts indicate that the predictive power of this model of idealized gait modes of idealized animals seems rather rigorous. But if the finer details are considered, some issues need to be taken up (28).

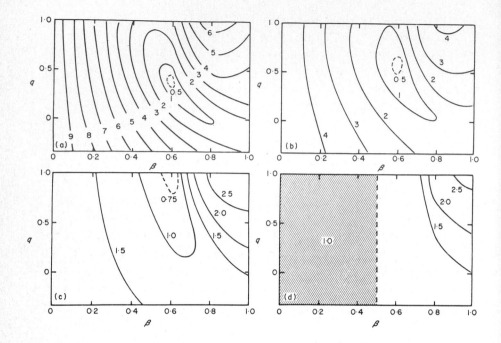

Fig. 11. Graphs of power output, based on energy demands and a
physiological efficiency term, and expressed as U/mg^2/fη),
where U is metabolic power, m is body mass, g is gravitational
acceleration, f is stride frequency and η is efficiency
expressed as 1/η units of metabolic energy. Note that the
values of work levels in these graphs must be multiplied by
16 gk/u^2 to obtain values comparable to those in Fig. 10. In
the multiplier mentioned, k is a constant and u is the mean
velocity during a stride. For human subjects the mean value
of k = 1.7 h, where h is hip height. The velocities are about
50 m/min (a), 102 m/min (b), 204 m/min and 289 m/min. The
latter speed will only be attained by running. Reproduced
from Alexander, R. McN. (1980), London, The Zoological
Society of London, with permission of the author and
publisher.

It has already been concluded that the models of Molen & Zarrugh and
associates do not predict the cost of running. Assuming the optimizational
principles of these models, Inman et al. (1981) calculated that Ė per stride
renders quite unrealistic optimal stride frequencies. Stride frequency is
related to the relative durations of time factors (swing, stance and double

support durations) and thus to the duty factor.

As Inman et al. (1981) showed that the energy rate of competition walkers was predicted very well by their compounded energy rate equation (1), the contention of Alexander and Jayes that competition walkers do not walk in an energetically optimal way needs to be refined.

The model of Alexander and Jayes possibly mis-estimates the required energy per step as the corrections proposed by Winter (1979) are not fully accounted for in the refinement Alexander (1980) proposed. The measurements of Alexander and Jayes (1978ab, 1980) on human subjects showed indeed that parameters of human walking had to be placed in the β-q diagram of Fig. 9b in the border zone between (Ia) and II(a).

Walking in zone II(a) results in variations in the total energy fluctuations depicted in Fig. 9a II. Comparison with Fig. 12 (taken from Winter, 1979) shows some interesting similarities. This calls for further refinement of the model of Alexander and Jayes, for example a two-linked model, with the possibility of knee-flexion during stance as a reaction to the impact at heel contact.

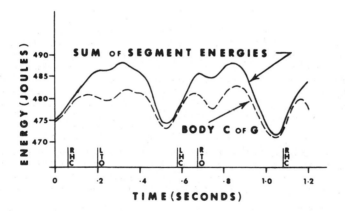

Fig. 12. Comparison of the results of two methods to calculate the total body energy during the walking stride. Dashed line: bodies centre of gravity approach is unable to detect the energy changes from reciprocal movements of different segments. Therefore the solid line resulting of the sum of segment energies approach will be higher during most of the walking cycle. Both approaches show peaks at double support and mid swing which do not resemble the total energy levels of Fig. 10aIa any better than those of Fig. 10a II. Reproduced from Winter, D.A. (1979) Rockville Pike: The American Physiological Society, with permission of the author and the publisher.

The calculations of Alexander and Jayes pertain essentially to energy demands, while the models of Molen and Zarrugh and associates pertain to energy consumption or cost. Cavagna (1978) showed that the efficiency - i.e. the relation between physical demand and physiological cost - varies with speed. Thus a straightforward correlation of the model of energy demand and energy cost at different speeds is not feasible. Future work, in which the energy demand is predicted according to the proposals of Winter (1979) and restating the efficiency terms, will be of value for the solution of these problems. Indeed, Alexander (1980) introduced an efficiency term. He indicated that work theories (energetic cost) and energy theories (energetic demand resulting from fluctuations in the various forms of mechanical energy) will only predict equal power requirements, if the work theories take into account "the possibility that different muscles in the same leg may do positive and negative work simultaneously". He further commented that in human walking the minima or optima might be "moved much by taking into account of leg mass". It must be concluded that future work will clarify these issues. In such work the work theories and energy theories will serve for each other as instruments for validation.

The model of Alexander and Jayes was not meant to and did not predict exactly the energy levels required by running. Alexander (1977) strongly advocated the storage of elastic energy as an energy saving mechanism in running. As in running, as well as in walking at moderate speeds, the cardio-respiratory functioning is not the constraint, studies on the cost per metre will be more instructive than studies of energy rates.

The transition of walking into running is governed by other constraints than the energy rate, it is dependent for example on leg length.

In general, research on human movement has been fostered and has flourished from studies on movements in extreme or constrained conditions such as sport activities. Race walking and the transition of walking into running are tasks many subjects are able to perform optimally. They are recommended for further study in order to reconciliate the work of the authors cited.

The format of this recommendation is felt to be completely Bernsteinian.

4.4. Modelling of gait

In the literature on walking and running, the reader is confronted with mathematical modelling of these processes. Such research is aimed at an understanding of the indeterminacy discussed in Section 3 of this essay as well as other aims. McGhee (1981), one of the leading investigators in this field, stated:

> While such models evidently represent a gross
> simplification of true biological complexity, many
> of the fundamental characteristics of human motion
> are nevertheless explainable by such an approach and
> there exists a substantial potential for further
> application of this methodology both in clinical
> medicine and in biomechanics of sports.

The methodology of modelling is at the present time dictated by the emerging theory of multi-jointed computer-controlled robotic systems. It is believed that from this connection new insights into neural control will be obtained. The models are n-linked rigid bodies with simple hinge joints or joints with three or six degrees of freedom. Torque generators act at each joint, representing muscles (intersegmental moments). Joint forces (inter-segmental forces) may be taken into account (Robertson & Winter, 1980). Next to the assumption of rigidity of the body segments, for some calculations additional assumptions have to be made (e.g. for the calculation of power flow fluctuations: pure rotation in joints, constant moment of inertia, absence of friction, and joint forces acting through the centre of rotation, were assumed by Quanbury et al., 1975). Generally, the admissibility of such assumptions and other simplifications, depends on the goals of the investigation in question. In Section 4.3 the power is shown of a very simple model in the hands of an ingenious investigator: Alexander used a quite simple model and by simplifying assumptions about the frequency domain of his measured data, succeeded in formulating a very general theory. By contrast, the work of Hatze cited in Section 3 of this paper is very complicated with respect both to the model proposed (17-linked) as well as to the mathematical procedures involved. His investigation is aimed amongst others at understanding optimalization in locomotion processes of individuals.

Other constraints appear more serious. For example, the complexity of the conventional mathematics applied to rigid body mechanics. Equations especially tailored for use with general computers may solve this problem (McGhee, 1981).

Models are used for motion analysis problems or conversely for motion simulation problems. The various methods (free body analysis), generalized coordinates and free body equations with hard constraints) were discussed recently by McGhee (1981). Applications by the same author to robot locomotion

are to be found in his article in Herman et al. (1976). A difficulty peculiar
to all modelling - and already mentioned by Bernstein (1967, p. 8 and
subsequent pages) - is the introduction of body parameters into the model.
Work on this problem is still needed and is in progress, as shown elsewhere
in this volume (Woltring, this volume).

Most work on gait appears to have been done on five to seven-linked
models. The interested reader will find numerous reports in the Journal of
Biomechanics as well as in Biofysika (Biophysics). The question of the choice
of the number of links will also depend on the goal of the study. A five
link-model, excluding the feet, but including HAT, will possibly be sufficient
for investigators interested in the general characteristics of energy states
of the body's centre of gravity. But, if a more detailed account of this
history is wanted, provision for the feet has to be made (Winter, 1979).
If interest lies in the exact measurement of step length, a massless pelvic
segment between the three-linked legs is needed (McGhee, 1981). HAT, and
one-linked arms are minimum requirements if interest lies in the time
histories of kinetic rotational and translational histories. This will result
in a nine- or ten-linked model.

Most of these models are two dimensional, medio-lateral movements, forces
and moments are assumed or proven to be of minor importance. It seems to the
present author that the validity of such simplifications requires to be
substantiated from more advanced work. This will be especially true for
applications on abnormal gaits in clinical practice. In future the work of
Aleshinsky and Zatsiorsky (1978), Orin et al. (1979) and others on three-
dimensional models will prove to be of utmost importance, as will the model
of Hatze (1977ab, 1978, 1980b and 1981b) mentioned in Section 3.

4.5. <u>Clinical applications</u>

A large number of investigations have been set up to evaluate such
movements as the gait of patients. Such evaluations should help in diagnosis
as well as in documentation of progress in therapy. It has been recommended
that gait or human movement laboratories would fulfil a role in rehabilitation
clinics and other centres, not unlike the role of laboratories in other
branches of medicine. In retrospect, it is contended by the present author,
that much of this work has been of tremendous value in so far as it was
carried out primarily with the goal of understanding human movement. The

monograph of Inman et al. (1980) will stand as a hallmark and proof of this contention.

A critical remark will be made here. Some of the complexly instrumented laboratories were developed with the intention of doing only clinical work. When the laboratory has been completed and instrumentation is in working order, one or more publications on the methods in use will be produced. These papers often illustrate a difference in one or more of the parameters measured between normal subjects and patients. The first group of subjects sometimes is hastily put together, while the latter group is inhomogeneous. In this way the "proven" difference is equivocal.

When the measured parameter cannot be interpreted in terms of functioning of the moving subject, such an approach will lead nowhere. Most measured parameters are interrelated in a complex way (e.g. see the discussion on double support duration in Section 4.2 of this paper) or are at least velocity-dependent. Velocity-dependent parameters will appear to be abnormal in most patients, while they are moving with (extreme) low velocities (see, for example, Jacobs et al. 1972). Again the work of Herman et al. (1976) has to be cited, as they tried to sample data of normal subjects walking at extremely low speeds - as seen in pathological states. Such work is regrettably scarce. If normative data are not available about the parameter used, detailed research on dependence of the parameter in question from for example velocity, step length, body characteristics etc., is indicated. This is a costly and cumbersome procedure, but it is a necessary one. Contini's (Contini et al., 1965, p. 430) remarks still hold:

> We still do not know enough about locomotion, particularly pathological locomotion. For the present, we suggest that, in providing an amputee with a prosthesis, his gait pattern should approach the "normal". We are not really sure, however, that the normal walking pattern for an amputee is the "normal" of the non-amputee which we try to achieve. We certainly do not know the normal walking patterns for those suffering from other motor disabilities. We have made some progress, but there is much research left for those who will follow.

5. CONCLUDING REMARKS

In Bernstein's days it was not possible to acquire high resolution displacement time data, nor did he have a system for direct measurement of forces or accelerations at his disposal. The facts upon which Bernstein

formulated his theory were insufficient: quantification noise of low
resolution displacement data, differentiated twice, leads to very misleading
results. Nevertheless his theory has been very successful and is still of
major importance today.

Resolution is still a problem. Filtering techniques are recommended to
cut-off unavoidable noise at frequencies higher than those in which interest
lies. In reporting, the characteristics of the filtering technique ought to
be mentioned. Filtering and smoothing techniques to lessen the unwanted
effects of processing of noise within the frequencies of interest are
recommended. The choise of these techniques, as well as of the sampling
frequency, can be rationalized on a cost/profit basis.

Kinesiological EMG has been used infrequently for the goals Bernstein
would have recommended: description and analysis of the neuronal regulation
of muscluar activity in walking. When the work of Grillner and associates
is extended to human walking and running a major breakthrough can be expected.

The use of motordriven treadmills in the study of walking and running
is, from a mechanical point of view, a valid approach, provided the velocity
of the band is not influenced by the varying load. However, the possibility
remains that e.g. visual information will influence some details of walking
and running. Research in the influence of sensory information on the
kinematics of these movements is recommended.

Generalisation from one provisionally defined class of movement to
another needs caution. This is the more so, as movements are not carried
out under conditions of a one to one relationship between neuronal activity
and effector processes. This indeterminacy or non-univocality is felt to be
the core of Bernstein's theory. Many sensory systems will be actively used
by the organism in order to keep itself informed about the ongoing
disequilibrium with the environment, on which it acts rather than reacts.

Experimental designs in which the information is diminished by
manipulation to only one or some of the sensory systems, will render simple
models. These models will render successful analyses, leading to linear
system control theories. On the other hand such theories will lack a firm
basis for generalization while not based on ecological valid experiments.
Alternatively, experiments designed to include the functioning of more
sensory systems and/or complex movements, are endangered by ambiguity of
explanation, due to functional non-univocality.

The mechanical sources of indeterminacy in the relationship between
the organism and its effector system on the one hand and the environment on

the other, are nowadays described with the help of complex models, including muscle control, for optimalized movements. Teleologically speaking the CNS "knows" the effects of the other sources of indeterminacy quite well and acts on the basis of this "knowledge". Its function is optimalized in this sense.

Bernstein's Russian colleagues proposed "synergies" and the "principle of least interaction" as working hypotheses for the explanation of non-univocality in the resolution of motor problems. It is concluded that the concept of synergy is in conflict with the Bernsteinean view on indeterminacy in a lot of classes of movements. Synergies are only to be postulated if they are adaptive in character. The principle of least interaction may be active in automated movements, like walking; in which generators at spinal levels are influenced by relatively simple descending signals. Within the effector processes, adaptive flexor and extensor synergies, known from pathology, may act. These may be concordant with synergies postulated for the maintenance of posture.

For other classes of movement, other controlling mechanisms from higher levels are postulated by neurophysiologists.

Human gait has been studied very extensively. Nevertheless, in simple descriptive and analytical studies problems existed which are nowadays capable of solution. The quite customary procedure of describing phenomena like EMG in the time course of normalized strides leads to ambiguous interpretations as the double support time varies exponentially and the stance and swing time vary directly (but differently) with speed.

Walking is optimalized energetically in terms of cost per distance traversed. In running, the cost per metre will be nearly constant for a large range of speeds and this cost will be lower in running than in competition walking.

The optimal cost at speeds of about 5 km/h in walking is tentatively explained on various levels: e.g. spatio-temporal factors, the stretch shortening cycle, the use of specialized muscle fibres. In running, storage of elastic energy is said to be another energy-saving mechanism.

However, human running, and the transition from walking into running has not been studied very well. As the study of human movement under various constraints (e.g. sport or optimalized movements) has been shown to be a successful approach this kind of study is to be recommended.

General theories on idealized biped locomotion leading to formulation of the energetic demands are to be reconciliated with the experimentally defined energetic cost. This reconciliation appears to be quite possible if the models of idealized animals become more complex: two- or n-linked models and/or refinement of the demands from kinetic energy are needed.

In general, modelling of gait has been rather successful especially if a sufficient number of links is incorporated into the model. Such modelling is not limited to walking, but pertains to all kinds of specialized movements, including those from sport.

Clinical application will benefit from studies of the factors which influence the variation of the generalized or idealized movements. In human walking, many parameters are speed dependent. Unless data on very low speeds have been gathered from normal subjects for comparison, measurement of a parameter of unknown significance is quite useless, as most patients walk with abnormally slow speeds. Parameters to be used to validate pathology, have to be explainable in terms of their functional significance.

Notes

(1) Recent reviews giving a more complete overview of the various parts
     of the programme Bernstein proposed are e.g. Alexander & Goldspink
     (1977), Gelfand et al. (1971), Getz (1980), Grillner (1975, 1979, 1981),
     Gydikov et al. (1973), Granit & Pompeiano (1979), Herman et al. (1976),
     Homma (1976), Inman et al. (1981), Schmitt & Worden (1974), Szentagothai
     & Arbib (1974) and Talbot & Humphrey (1979).

(2) It remains to the present author unclear which shutter frequency was
     used by Bernstein in his studies of walking and running. Though being
     aware of the importance of this point Bernstein nevertheless does not
     mention the exact data in the discussion of his results in Chapter III
     of his 1967 book. One of his co-workers, in a study of physiological
     tremor stated that a frequency of AD conversion of 50 Hz was adequate.
     In a footnote it was said that later on this rate was increased to
     125 Hz (Gurfinkel et al., 1971).

(3) As quantification errors are not random, a signal sampled with high
     shutter frequency after having been differentiated twice will show
     rather regular "accelerations".

(4) In walking with a stepcycle of about 0.6 sec (moderate speeds), the
     basic frequency will be 1.7 Hz. This would result in a highest frequency
     of importance of about 10 Hz.

(5) For a recent study using a calcium mediated activation model, coupled
     to a force generating model, simulated and experimentally confirmed,
     consult Wallinga-de Jonge et al. (1980, 1981).

(6) The Hill model states the force-velocity dependence (Hill, 1970).

(7) Lombards paradox states that two antagonistic bi-articular muscles,
     contracting at the same time will extend two joints, like the hip and
     knee joint, providing the moment arms on the extension sides surpass
     the moment arms on the flexion sides (Rasch & Burke, 1967).

(8) For a general discussion on EMG, the reader should consult Basmajian
     (1978). For an account of various methodological points of the use of
     EMG in kinesiology, especially quantification of the signal, reading
     of Grieve (1975) is recommended. Recently a report of the 'International
     Society for Electrophysiological Kinesiology Ad Hoc Committee on Units,
     Terms and Standards in the Reporting of EMG Research' became available.
     It may be requested from Dr. R. Lehr, School of Medicine, Southern
     Illinois University, Carbondale, Ill. 62901, U.S.A. Some of the
     recommendations of this report and further requirements of design and
     reporting EMG research in human kinesiology were discussed by Rozendal
     & Meijer (1982).

(9) Or, in Bernstein's words: formulating the regular in distinction from
     the random (see p.171).

(10) Modern views on Bernstein's thoughts (Reed, 1982) hold that as a
     consequence of this, descending (effector) pathways should not be
     called motoric, as they also control afferentiation. The latter should,
     in a similar manner, not be called "sensory". With respect to the
     first mentioned concept reference should be made to Wall (1967, 1978):
     descending pathways serving in gate control. This concept was more or
     less foreseen by Bernstein (1967, p. 219) in his remarks pertaining
     to effector pulses arriving but not passing through, as well as to
     "preparatory organization of the motor periphery in order to guarantee

optimal selection of conductivity".

Reed (1982) calls attention to the -explicitly speculative - paper of Wall (1970) in which it is suggested that the role of some movements is to gather information. The present author has for a long time cherished the thought that postural sway serves as a method of gaining information about one's own posture. But the possible existence of such mechanisms does not call for the abandoning of the concept of sensory input in analytical studies. Nor do Bernstein's views, as expressed in Chapter III of the 1967 book, corroborate Reed's (1982) view on this latter point. The α - γ co-activation, influencing the sensory input from the muscle spindles does not render the whole input non-sensory in character.

(11) These are not restricted to the muscle spindles (Houk, 1976, 1979) and possibly not to these and the Golgi tendo organs (see Section 2.4 of this essay) see further Stein (1981, p. 205) for some arguments against a one-parameter sensory input in the control of movement. For an example of a one-parameter approach, see Van Dijk (1978).

(12) Bernstein's (p. 219) remarks on tonus as a condition of readiness are to be understood as generalizations of this special case.

(13) Reed (1982) argues further that action systems, not motor systems would be the elements for such a study. This discussion will be left to other reactors with more competence in this area.

(14) Elner et al. (1972, 1976); Litvintsev (1973); Bonnet et al. (1976); Gurfinkel (1973); Gurfinkel et al. (1974, 1976, 1979abcd). This is not to say that in other movements or other experimental designs stretch-reflex mechanisms do not play a role (Gottlieb et al., 1970).

(15) E.g. the visual system in arm-hand movements (Herman et al., 1981); the visual system in standing (Gurfinkel et al., 1976), as well as various kineasthetic sources in standing (Gurfinkel et al., 1979abcd); the visual system in standing (Amblard & Cremieux, 1976; Berthoz et al., 1979; Galyan, 1978; Galoyan et al., 1976; Zikmund & Balla, 1973); the visual, vestibular and proprioceptive systems in standing (Kapteyn, 1973; Bles, 1979); the proprioceptive system of the trunk in standing (Gelfand et al., 1971).

(16) The quoted definition of synergies by Gelfand et al. (1971) is conflicting with the proposition of Bernstein (1967, p. 179) on the reactivity of live movements.

(17) The model as yet has to be extended for three-dimensional analysis (Hatze, 1981b).

(18) It is felt by the present author that between both World Wars in the United Kingdom mainly phisiologists were interested in the locomotor system. What would we do without the work of Hill, revisited by himself in 1970? (Hill, 1970).

(19) See also Van Baak (1979).

(20) E.g. Herman (1976) 0.9 cycles (strides)/sec.

(21) E.g. in a cycle of 0.7 sec, double support times of 50 ms or less were reported (Murray et al., 1966), suggesting that an accuracy of the measurement of 10 ms or less is desirable.

(22) It is to be noted that Herman et al. (1976) asked their subjects to walk at very slow speeds too, in conformity with speeds only seen in gross pathology, resulting in a variation of the double support time of 0.5 to 0.1.

(23) Onyshko & Winter (1980) introduced a constraint in their model in order
to draw conclusions about the joint forces and moments in the double
support phase, without measuring foot reaction forces.

(24) The weighting was according to numbers of subjects of investigations
of Bobbert, 1960; Corcoran & Brengelman, 1970; Cotes & Meade, 1960;
Molen & Rozendal, 1967 and Zarrugh et al., 1974, totalling up to 57
adult normal males and 29 normal adult females.

(25) This would theoretically occur at 0.5 cycle time (stride time) and 0.25
stance time and result in a duty factor β of 0.5. The duty factor β is
defined by McGhee (1968), as quoted by Alexander & Jayes (1978a). It
is the ratio of stance time to cycle time.

(26) Only 5 arguments of the Fourier series were studied for the vertical
and only three for the fore-aft forces.

(27) Note that comparison between cost per distance and rate per stride at
the same speed in walking and running is admissible: in Fig. 8a is
shown that at the same speeds in walking and running the cycle durations
are quite similar, meaning that stride lengths are also quite similar.

(28) First, some details pertaining to Fig. 10 are taken up. The speed of
72 m/min would result from 105 steps of 68 cm length. From 105 steps
or 52.5 cycles/min a cycle time of 1.12 sec and a stance time of 0.73
sec can be deduced (Fig. 3) resulting in β = 0.65. The speed of 102 m/min
would result from 122 steps of 82 cm length and β = 0.66.
$\dot{E}$ per meter would result in 1.5 times the optimum of Alexander &
Jayes at a speed of 72 m/min, and in 1.22 times this optimum at a speed
of 102 m/min. In the model of Molen et al. (1972) both speeds would
result in $\dot{E}$ per meter of 110% of the absolute optimum.
The speed of 163 m/min would be attained with about 150 steps of
110 cm length per minute. $\dot{E}$ per meter would be (0.9 x 1.5=) 1.35 times
the optimal values at the other two speeds. Indeed, 1.35 x 110% is about
150% the model of Molen et al. (1972) indicated.
In the hyperbolic equation (3) 57 cal/kg/min is predicted for the
lowest speed, 77.7 cal/kg/min for the speed of 102 m/min and 310 cal/kg/
min for the race walk. This would result in 0.19 cal/kg/step, 0.75 cal/
kg/step and about 2 cal/kg/step respectively. Per metre 0.8, 0.7 and
about 2 cal/kag respectively are predicted, 0.8 being the absolute
optimum (see Fig. 5, upper dashed line). The quadratic equation predicts,
for 163 m/min, an energy rate of 164 cal/kg/min, resulting in about 1.1
cal/kg/step and in about 1 cal/kg/m. This latter value appears too low,
while the earlier value, predicted from the hyperbolic equation (3),
namely 2 cal/kg/m, appears too high, if the models of Alexander & Jayes
(1978b) and of Molen et al. (1972) are invoked.
A further distinction is the above mentioned difference in the energy
rates per step predicted from the equations (2) and (3) for the speeds
of 72 and 102 m/min and the calculated energy fluctuations in the model
of Alexander & Jayes (1978). The latter predicts similar optima per
step at both speeds, as does the model of Molen et al. (1972) for cost
per metre, while Inman et al. (1981) predict different expenditures per
step for each of these speeds.
With respect to the data of Fig. 11c and 11b the quadratic equation
(1) predicts 44 cal/kg/min for 102 m/min and 240 cal/kg/min for 204 m/
min. The latter is about five times higher than the first. The hyperbolic
equation predicts for 204 m/min 200 cal/kg/min, which is less than three
times the predicted value for 102 m/min: 77.7 cal/kg/min.
The conclusion must be that further experimental studies have to

be carried out on the energy expenditure in race walking and running, on
the hypothesis that an energetic optimum for each speed will be found
to lie along a hyperbola going through the zone 0.01 in Fig. 11b and
the zone 0.05 in Fig. 11b. This would imply that even competition-
walkers will optimalize their mode of walking on the basis of energetic
demands as well as cardio-respiratory constraints. They will do this
by training, of course.

REFERENCES

Aleshinsky, S. Yu. & Zatsiorsky, V.M. Human locomotion in space analyzed
biomechanically through a multi-link chain model. Journal of Biomechanics,
1978, 11, 101-108.

Alexander, R. McN. 'Terrestial Locomotion'. In, R. McN. Alexander and G.
Goldspink (Eds.), Mechanics and energetics of animal locomotion. London:
Chapman and Hall, 1977.

Alexander, R. McN. Optimum walking techniques for quadrupeds and bipeds.
Journal of Zoology London, 1980, 192, 97-117.

Alexander, R. Mcn. & Goldspink, G. (Eds.), Mechanics and energetics of
animal locomotion. London: Chapman and Hall, 1977.

Alexander, R. McN. & Jayes, A.S. Vertical movements in walking and running.
Journal of Zoology London, 1978(a), 185, 27-40.

Alexander, d. McN. & Jayes, A.S. Optimum walking techniques for idealized
animals. Journal of Zoology London, 1978(b), 186, 61-81.

Alexander, R. McN. & Jayes, A.S. Fourier analysis of forces exerted in
walking and running. Journal of Biomechanics, 1980, 13, 383-390.

Amblard, B. & Cremieux, I. Rôle de l'information visuelle du mouvement dans
le maintien de l'equilibre postural chez l'homme. Agressologie, 1976,
17-C, 25-36.

André-Thomas & Autgaarden, S. (1966), cited by Bressan and Woollacot (1982).

Asmussen, E. Movement of man and study of man in motion: a scanning review
of the development of biomechanics. In, P.V. Komi (Ed.), Biomechanics
V-A. Baltimore: University Park Press, 1976.

Asmussen, E. & Bonde-Petersen, F. Apparent efficiency and storage of
elastic energy in human muscles. Acta Physiologica Scandinavia, 1974,
92, 537-545.

Asmussen, E. & Jørgensen, K. (Eds.), Biomechanics VI-a,b. Baltimore:
University Park Press, 1978.

Atzler, E. & Herbst, R. Arbeidsphysiologischen Studien III. Pflüger Archives
Gesammten Physiologie, 1928, 215, 292-328.

Baak, M.A. van. The physiological load during walking, cycling, running
and swimming, and the Cooper exercise programs. M.D. thesis. Catholic
University Nijmegen, Netherlands, 1979.

Bahler, A.S., Fales, T.J. & Zierler, K.L. The dynamic properties of mammalian
skeletal muscles. Journal of General Physiology, 1968, 51, 369-384.

Bakker, M. de, Bijlard, M., Krüse, F., Zantman, L., Wieringen, P.C.W. van
& Huijing, P.A. Single motor unit control and variation of recruitment

order of motor units. Electromyography and Clinical Neurophysiology, 1983, 23, 151-157.

Basmajian, J.V. Muscles alive. Their functions revealed by electromyography. Baltimore: Williams and Wilkins, 1978.

Beekum, W.T. van. The participation of muscle spindles in human position sense. Ph.D. Thesis. University of Utrecht, Netherlands, 1980.

Benninghof, A. Lehrbuch der Anatomie des Menschen 1: Allgemeine Anatomie und Bewegungsapparat. Berlin: Urban & Schwarzenberg, 1938.

Benninghof, A. & Rollhäuser, H. Zur inneren Mechanik des gefiederten Muskels. Pflügers Archiv, 1952, 254, 527-548.

Bernstein, N.A. The coordination and regulation of movements. Oxford: Pergamon Press, 1967.

Berthoz, A. Lacour, M., Soechting, J.F. & Vidal, P.P. 'The role of vision in the control of posture during linear motion'. In, R. Granit & O. Pompeiano (Eds.), Reflex control of posture and movement. Amsterdam: Elsevier/North Holland Biomedical Press, 1979.

Bigland, B. & Lippold, O.C.J. The relation between force, velocity and integrated electrical activity. Journal of Physiology, 1954, 123, 214-224.

Bles, W. Sensory interactions and human posture. Ph.D. Thesis. Free University, Amsterdam, Netherlands, 1979.

Bles, W., Kaptein, T.S. & Wit, G. de. Effects of visual-vestibular interaction on human posture. Advances in Oto-rhino-laryngology, 1977, 22, 111-118.

Bles, W. & Wit, G. de. La sensation de rotation et la marche circulaire. Agressologie, 1978, 19A, 29-30.

Bles, W., Brandt, Th., Kaptein, T.S. & Arnold, F. Le vestige de hauteur, un vestige de distance par une destabilisation visuelle. Agressologie, 1978(a), 19B, 63-64.

Bobbert, A.C. Energy expenditure in level and grade walking. Journal of Applied Physiology, 1960, 15, 1015-1021.

Bonnet, M., Gurfinkel, S., Lipshits, M.J. & Popov, K.E. Central programming of lower limbs muscular activity in the standing man. Agressologie, 1976, 17B, 35-42.

Brandt, Th., Wenzel, D. & Dickgans, J. Die entwicklung der vizuellen Stabilization des aufrechten Standes beim Kind: Ein Reifezeichen in der Kinderneurologie. Archive der Psychiatrie und Nervenkrankheiten, 1976, 223, 1-13.

Braus, H. Anatomie des Menschen. Berlin: Springer, 1921.

Bressan, E.S. & Wollacott, M.J. A prescriptive paradigm for sequencing instruction in physical education. Human Movement Science, 1982, 1, 155-175.

Brunnström, S. Movement therapy in hemiplegia. New York: Harper and Row, 1970.

Cappozzo, A., Leo, T. & Pedotti, A. A general computing method for the analysis of human locomotion. Journal of Biomechanics, 1975, 8, 307-320.

Cavagna, G.A. 'Aspects of efficiency and inefficiency of terrestial locomotion'. In, E. Asmussen and K. Jørgensen (Eds.), Biomechanics VI-A. Baltimore: University Park Press, 1978.

Cavagna, G.A. & Kaneko, M. Mechanical work and efficiency in level walking and running. Journal of Physiology, 1977, 268, 467-481.

Cavagna, G.A., Thijs, H. & Zamboni, A. The sources of external work in level walking and running. Journal of Physiology (London), 1976, 262, 639-657.

Cavanagh, P.R. Recent advances in instrumentation and methodology of biomechanical studies. In, P.V. Komi (Ed.), Biomechanics V-B. Baltimore: University Park Press, 1976.

Cavanagh, P.R. & Lafortune, M.A. Ground reaction forces in distance running. Journal of Biomechanics, 1980, 13, 397-406.

Cerquilini, S., Venerando, A. & Wartenweiler, J. (Eds.), Medicine and Sport 8, Biomechanics III. Basel: Karger, 1973.

Chatinier, K. du, Molen, N.H. & Rozendal, R.H. Step length, step frequency and temporal factors of the stride in normal human walking. Proceedings Koninklijke Nederlandse Academie voor Wetenschappen, 1970, C-73, 214-227.

Contini, R., Drillis, R.J., Gage, H. & Yatkausas, A. Functional evaluation and acceptability of the Henschke-Mauch 'Hydraulik' swing and stance control system. Report 1037-1, Washington D.C.: Department of Medicine and Surgery, Veteran Administration, 1964.

Contini, R., Gage, H. & Drillis, R.J. 'Human gait characteristics'. In, R.M. Kenedi (Ed.), Biomechanics. Oxford: Pergamon Press, 1964.

Cook, T. & Cozzens, B. 'Human solutions for locomotions: The initiation of Gait'. In, R.M. Herman, S. Grillner, P.S.G. Stein and D.G. Stuart (Eds.), Neural control of locomotion. New York: Plenum Press, 1976.

Decan, G.A. An analysis of the energy expenditure in level and grade walking. Ergonomics, 1965, 8, 31-47.

Desmedt, J.E. Motor unit types, recruitment and plasticity in health and disease. Basel: Karger, 1981.

Dijk, J.H.M. van. On the interaction between the central nervous system and the peripheral motor system. Biological Cybernetics, 1978, 30, 195-208.

Dijk, J.H.M. van. A theory on the control of arbitrary movements. Biological Cybernetics, 1979, 32, 187-199.

Drillis, R.J. Objective recording and biomechanics of pathological gait. Annals of the New York Academy of Science, 1958, 74, 86-109.

Dubo, H.I.C., Peat, M., Winter, D.A., Quanbury, A.D., Hobson, D.A., Steinke, T. & Reimer, G. Electromyographic temporal analysis of gait: normal human locomotion. Archives of Physical Medicine and Rehabilitation, 1976, 57, 415-420.

Elftman, H. Biomechanics of muscle. Journal of Bone and Joint Surgery, 1966, 48A, 363-377.

Elner, A.M., Popov, K.E. & Gurfinkel, V.S. Changes in stretch-reflex system concerned with the control of postural activity of human muscles. Agressologie, 1972, 13, 19-24.

Elner, A.M., Gurfinkel, V.S., Lipshits, M.I., Mamasakhlisoo, G.V. & Popov, K.E. Facilitation of stretch reflex by additional support during quiet stance. Agressologie, 1976, 17-A, 15-20.

Feldman, A.G. Change in the length of muscle as a consequence of a shift in equilibrium in the muscle-load system. Biofizika, 1974, 19, 534-538.

Feldman, A.G. Control of the postural length and strength of a muscle: advantages of a central co-activation of the α and static γ motoneurons. Biofizika, 1976, 21, 187-189.

Feldman, A.G. Superposition of motor programs. Neuroscience, 1979, 5, 81-95.

Feldman, A.G. Superposition of motor programs - I. Rhythmic forearm movements in a man. Neuroscience, 1980(a), 5, 81-90.

Feldman, A.G. Superposition of motor-programs - II. Rapid forearm flexion in man. Neuroscience, 1980(b), 5, 91-95.

Fick, R. Handbuch der Anatomie und Mechanik der Gelenke: unter Berücksichtigung der bewegende Muskeln. Jena: Fischer, 1904-1911.

Finley, F.R. & Cody, K.A. Locomotive characteristics of urban pedestrians. Archives of Physical Medicine and Rehabilitation, 1970, 51, 423-426.

Finley, F.R., Wirta, R.W., Craik, R., Bampton, S., Bolton, A.R. & Bryant, H. Fundamental study of human locomotion. In, Rehabilitation Service Administration, Rehabilitation Research and Training Center 8. Progress Report II, May 1, 1974 - April 30, 1975. Philadelphia: Temple University and Moss Rehabilitation Hospital, 1975.

Forssberg, H. 'Spinal locomotor functions and descending control'. In, B. Sjöland and A. Björklund (Eds.), Brain stem control of spinal mechanism. New York: Fernström Foundation Series I, in press.

Forssberg,H., Grillner, S. & Rossignol, S. Phase dependent reflex reversal during walking in chronic spinal cats. Brain Research, 1975, 85, 103-107.

Forssberg, H., Grillner, S. & Halbertsma, J. The locomotion of the low spinal cat I. Coordination within a handlimb. Acta Physiologica Scandinavica, 1980, 108, 269-281.

Forssberg, H., Grillner, S., Halbertsma, J. & Rossignol, S. The locomotion of the low spinal cat II. Interlimb coordination. Acta Physiologica Scandinavica, 1980, 283-295.

Fugl-Meyer, A.R. Post stroke hemiplegia. Assessment of physical properties. Scandinavian Journal of Rehabilitation Medicine, 1980, 7, 85-93.

Galoyan, V.R. Investigations of the torsional movements of the eyes. IV: passive movement of the body influence of reflexes of skeletal musculature, optokinetic torsional tracking. Biofizika, 1978, 23, 370-378.

Galoyan, V.R., Zenkin, G.M. & Petrov, A.P. Investigation of the torsional movements of human eyes I: some special aspects of the torsional movements on tilting the head towards the shoulder. Biofizika, 1976, 21, 570-577.

Gans, C. & Bock, W.J. The functional significance of muscle architecture - a theoretical analysis. Ergebnisse der Anatomie und der Entwicklungs- geschichte, 1965, 38, 115-152.

Gelfand, I.M. & Tsetlin, M.L. Models of the structural-functional organization of certain biological systems. Cambridge: MIT-Press, 1971.

Gelfand, I.M., Gurfinkel, V.S., Tsetlin, M.L. & Shil, M.L. 'Some problems in the analysis of movements'. In, J.M. Gelfand and M.L. Tsetlin (Eds.), Models of the structural-functional organization of certain biology systems. Cambridge: MIT-Press, 1971.

Getz, W.M. Mathematical modelling in biology and ecology. Lecture Notes in Biomathematics. Berlin: Springer, 1980.

Gibson, J.J. The ecological approach to visual perception. Boston: Houghton-Mifflin, 1979.

Gielen, C.C.A.M., van den Heuvel, P.J.M. & Gon, J.J. Denier van der.
Modification of muscle activation patterns during fast goal-directed
arm movements. Journal of Motor Behavior, in press.

Goldspink, G. 'Design of muscles in relation to locomotion'. In, R. McN.
Alexander and G. Goldspink (Eds.), Mechanics and energetics of animal
locomotion. London: Chapman and Hall, 1977.

Gon, J.J. Denier van der. Linear systems from non-linear neural elements.
Biological Cybernetics, in press.

Gottlieb, G.L., Agarwal, G.C. & Stark, L. Interactions between voluntary
and postural mechanisms of the human motor system. Journal of
Neurophysiology, 1970, 33, 365-380.

Granit, R. The basic of motor control. London: Academic Press, 1970.

Granit, R. & Pompeiano, O. (Eds.), Reflex control of posture and movement.
Progress in Brain Research 50, Amsterdam: Elsevier Scientific Publishing
Company, 1979.

Grieve, D.W. 'Electromyography'. In, D.W. Grieve, D.I. Muller, D. Mitchelsen,
J.P. Paul and A.J. Smith, Techniques for the analysis of human movement.
London: Lepus Books, 1975.

Grieve, D.W. & Gear, R.J. The relationship between length of stride, step
frequency, time of swing and speed of walking for children and adults.
Ergonomics, 1966, 5, 379-399.

Grieve, D.W., Pheasant, S. & Cavanagh, P.R. Prediction of gastrocnemius
length from knee and ankle joint posture. In, E. Asmussen and K.
Jørgensen (Eds.), Biomechanics VI-A. Baltimore: University Park Press,
1978.

Grillner, S. Locomotion in Vertebrates: central mechanisms and reflex
interaction. Physiological Reviews, 1975, 55-2, 247-304.

Grillner, S. 'Interaction between central and peripheral mechanisms in
control of locomotion'. In, R. Granit and O. Pompeiano (Eds.), Reflex
control of posture and movement. Amsterdam: Elsevier/North-Holland
Biomedical Press, 1979.

Grillner, S. Control of locomotion in bipeds. tetrapods and fish. In,
V.B. Brooks (Ed.), Handbook of Physiology Sec. I, 2 (Motor Control).
Bethesda: American Physiological Association, 1981.

Grillner, S., Halbertsma, J., Nilsson, J. & Thorstensson, A. The
adaption to speed in human locomotion. Brain Research, 1979, 165, 177-
182.

Groot, G. de, Hollander, A.P. & Huijing, P.A. Biomechanics and Medicine
   in Swimming. Champaign: Human Kinetics Publishers, 1983.

Gurfinkel, V.S. Muscle afferentation and postural control in man.
   Agressologie, 1973, 14-C, 1-8.

Gurfinkel, V.S. & Latash, M.L. Segmental postural mechanisms and reversal
   of muscle reflexes. Agressologie, 1979, 20-B, 145-146.

Gurfinkel, V.S., Lipshits, M.I. & Popov, K.E. Is the stretch reflex the
   main mechanism in the system of regulation of the vertical posture of
   man? Biofysics, 1974, 19, 761-766.

Gurfinkel,V.S., Lipshits, M.I., Latash, M.L. & Popov, K.E. An investigation
   of human postural regulation by lateral vibration of muscles.
   Agressologie, 1979, 20-B, 151-152.

Gurfinkel, V.S., Lipshits, M.I. & Popov, K.E. Kinesthetic thresholds in
   orthograde posture. Agressologie, 1979, 20-B, 133-134.

Gurfinkel, V.S., Lipshits, M.I. & K.E. Popov. On the origin of short
   latency muscle responses to postural disturbances. Agressologie, 1979,
   20-B, 151-152.

Gurfinkel, V.S., Lipshits, M.I., Mori, S. & Popov, K.E. Postural reactions
   to the controlled sinusoidal displacement of the supporting platform.
   Agressologie, 1976, 17, 71-76.

Gurfinkel, V.S., Kots, Ya, M., Krinsky, V.I., Tsetlin, M.L. & Shik, M.L.
   Concerning tuning before movement. In, I.M. Gelfand and M.L. Tsetlin
   (Eds.), Models of the structural-functional organization of certain
   biological systems. Cambridge: M.I.T. Press, 1971.

Gurfinkel, V.S., Sotnikova, L.E., Tereshkov, O.D., Fomin, S.V. & Shik, M.L.
   An analysis of physiological tremor by means of a general-purpose
   computer. In, I.M. Gelfand and M.L. Tsetlin (Eds.), Models of the
   structural-functional organization of certain biological systems.
   Cambridge: M.I.T. Press, 1971.

Gydikov, A.A., Tankov, N.T. & Kosarov, D.S. (Eds.), Motor control. New York:
   Plenum Press, 1973.

Haar Romeny, B.M. ter, Gon, J.J. Denier van der & Gielen, C.C.A.M. Changes
   in recruitment order of motor units in the human biceps muscle.
   Experimental Neurology, 1982, 78, 360-368.

Hallett, M., Shanani, B.T. & Young, R.R. EMG analysis of stereotyped
   voluntary movements in man. Journal of Neurology, Neurosurgery and
   Psychiatry, 1975, 38, 1154-1162.

Hatze, H. The complete optimization of a human motion. Mathematical
   Bio-sciences, 1976, 28, 99-135.

Hatze, H. A complete set of control equations for the human musculo-
    skeletal system. Journal of Biomechanics, 1977(a), 10, 799-805.

Hatze, H. A myocybernetic control model of skeletal muscle. Biological
    Cybernetics, 1977, 25, 103-119.

Hatze, H. A general myocybernetic control model of skeletal muscle.
    Biological Cybernetics, 1978, 28, 143-157.

Hatze, H. 'Optimal processes of neuromusculoskeletal control systems'.
    In, W.M. Getz (Ed.), Mathematical modelling in biology and ecology.
    Berlin: Springer-Verlag, 1980(a).

Hatze, H. A mathematical model for the computational determination of
    parameter values of anthropomorphic segments. Journal of Biomechanics,
    1980(b), 13, 833-843.

Hatze, H. The use of optimally regularized Fourier series for estimating
    higher-order derivatives of noisy biomechanical data. Journal of
    Biomechanics, 1981(a), 14, 13-18.

Hatze, H. A comprehensive model for human motion simulation and its
    application to the take-off phase of the long jump. Journal of
    Biomechanics, 1981(b), 14, 135-142.

Hatze, H. & Venter, A. Practical activation and retention of locomotion
    constraints in neuromuskuloskeletal control systems models. Journal of
    Biomechanics, 1981, 14, 839-876.

Henneman, E. Recruitment of motoneurons: The size principle. In, J.E.
    Desmedt (Ed.), Motor unit types, recruitment and plasticity in health
    and disease. Basel: S. Karger, 1981.

Herman, R.M., Grillner, S., Stein, P.S.G. & Stuart, D.G. Neural control
    of locomotion. New York: Plenum Press, 1976.

Herman, R. & Maulucci, R. Visually triggered eye-arm movements in man.
    Experimental Brain Research, 1981, 42, 392-398.

Herman, R., Wirta, R., Bampton, S. & Finley, F.R. Human solutions for
    locomotion: Single limb analysis. In, R.M. Herman, S. Grillner, P.S.G.
    Stein and D.G. Stuart (Eds.), Neural control of locomotion. New York:
    Plenum Press, 1976.

Hildebrand, M. 'Analysis of tetrapod gaits: General considerations and
    symmetrical gaits'. In, R.M. Herman, S. Grillner, P.S.G. Stein and
    D.G. Stuart (Eds.), Neurol control of locomotion. New York: Plenum
    Press, 1976.

Hill, A.V. First and last experiments in muscle mechanics. Cambridge:
    University Press, 1970.

Hof, A.L. & Berg, J.W. van den. Linearity between the weighted sum of the EMG's of human triceps surae and the total torque. Journal of Biomechanics, 1977, 10, 529-540.

Hof, A.L. & Berg, J.W. van den. EMG to force rpocessing: I, II, III and IV.

I   - An electrical analogue of the Hill muscle model.

II   - Estimation of parameters of the Hill muscle model for the human triceps surae by means of a calf ergometer.

III   - Estimation of model parameters for the human triceps surae muscle and assessment of accuracy by means of a torque plate.

IV   - Eccentric-concentric contractions on a spring-flywheel set-up.

Journal of Biomechanics, 1981(a-d), 14, 747-792.

Högberg, P. Length of stride, stride frequency, 'flight' period and maximum distance between the feet during running with different speeds. Arbeitsphysiologie, 1952, 14, 431-436.

Homma, S. (Ed.), Understanding of the stretch reflex. Progress in Brain research 44. Amsterdam: Elsevier Scientific Publishing Company, 1976.

Houk, J.C. Regulation of stiffness by skeletomotor reflexes. Annual Review of Physiology, 1976, 41, 99-114.

Houk, J.C. An assessment of stretch-reflex function. In, S. Homma (Ed.), Understanding of the stretch-reflex. Amsterdam: Elsevier Scientific Publishing Company, 1979.

Houk, J.C. & Rijmer, W.Z. 'Neural control of muscle length and tension'. In, V.B. Brooks (Ed.), Handbook of Physiology, sec. I, 2 (Motor Control). Bethesda: American Physiological Association, 1981.

Huiskes, R., Campen, D. van & Wijn, J. de (Eds.), Biomechanics: Principles and applications. The Hague: Martinus Nijhoff Publishers, 1982.

Ingen Schenau, G.J. van. Some fundamental aspects of the biomechanics of overground versus treadmill locomotion. Medicine and Science in Sport and Exercise, 1980, 12, 257-261.

Ingen Schenau, G.J. van. The influence of air friction in speed skating. Journal of Biomechanics, 1982, 15, 449-458.

Ingen Schenau, G.J. van & Groot, G. de. Some technical, physiological and anthropometrical aspects of speed skating. European Journal of Applied Physiology, 1983, 50, 343-354.

Ingen Schenau, G.J. van. A power balance applied to speed skating. Ph.D. Thesis. Free University, Amsterdam, Netherlands, 1981.

Ingen Schenau, G.J. van & Bakker, K. A biomechanical model of speed skating. Journal of Human Movement Studies, 1980, 6, 1-18.

Ingen Schenau, G.J. van, Boer, R.W. de, Bolier, T., Boon, K.L. &
    Vergroessen, I. Biomechanical aspects of the stretch shortening cycle
    in the vertical jump. Journal of Biomechanics (in press).

Inman, V.T., Ralston, H.J., Saunders, J.B. de C.M., Feinstein, B. &
    Wright, E.W. Relation of human electromyogram to muscular tension.
    Electromyography and Clinical Neurophysiology, 1952, 4, 187-194.

Inman, V.T., Saunders, J.B. de C.M. & Abbot, L.C. Observations on the
    functions of the shoulder joint. Journal of Bone and Joint Surgery,
    1944, 26, 1-30.

Inman, V.T., Ralston, H.J. & Todd, F. Human walking. London: Williams
    and Wilkins, 1981.

International Society for Electrophysiological Kinesiology. Report of the
    ad hoc committee on units, terms and standards in the Reporting of EMG
    Research. Carbondale, 1980.

Ivanova, S.N. Cortical control of muscular activity of the limbs in the
    course of walking. Agressologie, 1973, 14-A, 67-71.

Jacobs, N.A., Skorecki, J. & Charnley, J. Analysis of the vertical
    component of force in normal and pathological gait. Journal of
    Biomechanics, 1971, 5, 11-34.

Juta, A.J.A., Beekum, W.T. van & Gon, J.J. Denier van der. An attempt to
    quantify vibration induced movement sensation. Journal of Physiology,
    1979, 292, 18P.

Kaptein, T.S. Het staan van de mens. Ph.D. Thesis (Summary in English).
    Free University, Amsterdam, Netherlands, 1973.

Kenedi, R.M. Biomechanics and related bio-engineering topics. Oxford:
    Pergamon Press, 1965.

Kleppe, D., Groendijk, H.E., Huijing, P.A.J.B.M. & Wieringen, P.C.W. van.
    Single motor unit control in the human mm. abductor pollicis brevis and
    mylohyoideus in relation to the number of muscle spindles.
    Electromyography and Clinical Neurophysiology, 1982, 22, 21-25.

Klopsteg, P.E. & Wilson, P.D. (Eds.), Human limbs and their substitutes.
    New York: McGraw-Hill Book Cy., 1954.

Kornhuber, H.H. 'Cerebral cortex, cerebellum and basal ganglia: Introduction
    to their motor functions'. In, F.O. Schmitt and F.G. Worden (Eds.),
    The Neurosciences. Cambridge: M.I.T. Press, 1974.

Lanshammar, H. On precision limits for derivatives numerically calculated
    from noisy data. Journal of Biomechanics, 1982, 15, 459-470.

Lees, A. An optimised film analysis method based on finite difference
    techniques. Journal of Human Movement Studies, 1980, 6, 165-180.

Litvintsev, A.I. Mechanisms of man's vertical posture control. Agressologie, 1973, 14-B, 17-21.

Lombard, W.P. & Abbot, F.M. The mechanical effects produced by the contraction of individual muscles of the thigh in the frog. American Journal of Physiology, 1907, 20, 1-60.

Margaria, R. Positive and negative work performances and their efficiencies in human locomotion. Internationale Zeitschrift angewandter Physiologie, 1968, 25, 339-351.

Matthews, P.B.C. Mammalian muscle receptors and their central actions. London: Arnold, 1978.

McGhee, R.B. Mathematical models for dynamics and control of posture and gait. In, A. Morecki et al. (Eds.), Biomechanics VII-A. Baltimore: University Park Press, 1981.

Menier, D.R. & Pugh, L.G.C.E. The relation of oxygen intake and velocity of walking and running in competition walkers. Journal of Physiology, 1968, 197, 717-721.

Merton, P.A. 'Speculations on the servocontrol of movement'. In, G.E.W. Wolstenholme (Ed.), The spinal cord. London: Churchill, 1953.

Michaelis, R.M. Research films in biology, anthropology, psychology and medicine. New York: Academic Press, 1955.

Milner-Brown, H.S., Stein, R.B. & Yemm, R. The orderly recruitment of human motor units during voluntary contractions. Journal of Physiology, 1973, 230, 359-370.

Molen, N.H. & Rozendal, R.H. Energy expenditure in normal test subjects walking in a motor driven treadmill. Proceedings Koninklijke Nederlandse Academie van Wetenschappen, 1967, C-70, 192-200.

Molen, N.H., Rozendal, R.H. & Boon, W. Fundamental characteristics of human gait in relation to sex and location. Proceedings Koninklijke Nederlandse Academie van Wetenschappen, 1972, C-75, 215-223.

Molen, N.H., Rozendal, R.H. & Boon, W. Graphic representation of the relationship between oxygen consumption and characteristics of normal gait of the normal human male. Proceedings Koninklijke Nederlandse Academie van Wetenschappen, 1972, C-75, 305-314.

Morecki, A., Fidelus, K., Kedzior, K. & Wit, A. (Eds.). Biomechanics VII-a,b. Baltimore: University Park Press, 1981.

Morrison, J.B. The mechanics of the knee joint in relation to normal walking. Journal of Biomechanics, 1970, 3, 51-61.

Morrison, J.B. The mechanics of muscle function in locomotion. Journal of Biomechanics, 1970, 3, 431-451.

Murray, M.P. Gait as a total pattern of movement. American Journal of
    Physical Medicine, 1967, 46, 290-333.

Murray, M.P., Drought, A.B. & Kory, R.C. Walking pattern of normal men.
    The Journal of Bone and Joint Surgery, 1964, 46A, 335-360.

Murray, M.P., Kory, R.C., Clarkson, B.H. & Sepic, S.B. Comparison of
    free and fast speed walking patterns of normal men. American Journal
    of Physical Medicine, 1966, 45, 8-24.

Murray, M.P., Kory, R.C. & Sepic, S.B. Walking patterns of normal women.
    Archives of Physical Medicine and Rehabilitation, 1970, 70, 637-655.

Nashner, L.M. 'Organization and programming of motor activity during
    posture control'. In, R. Granit and V. Pompeiano (Eds.), Reflex control
    of posture and movement. Amsterdam: Elsevier-North Holland Biomedical
    Press, 1979.

Nashner, L. & Woollacott, M. 'The organization of rapid postural
    adjustments of standing humans: an experimental conceptual model'. In,
    R.E. Talbott and D.R. Humphrey (Eds.), Posture and movement. New York:
    Raven Press, 1979.

Neilson, P.D. Speed of response or bandwith of voluntary system controlling
    elbow position in intact man. Medican and Biological Engineering, 1972,
    10, 450-459.

Njiokiktjien, Ch. Statokinesimetrische registratie van het houdings-
    evenwicht. M.D. Thesis (Summary in English). Free University, Amsterdam,
    Netherlands, 1971.

Onyshko, S. & Winter, D.A. A mathematical model of the dynamics of human
    locomotion. Journal of Biomechanics, 1980, 13, 361-368.

Orin, D.E., McGhee, R.B., Vukobratovic, M. & Hartoch, G. Kinematic and
    kinetic analysis of open-chain linkages utilizing Newton-Euler methods.
    Mathematical Biosciences, 1979, 43, 107-130.

Pedotti, A. A study of motor coordination and neuromuscular activities
    in human locomotion. Biological Cybernetics, 1977, 26, 53-62.

Pool, C.W. An immune- and enzyme-histochemical determination of striated
    muscle fibre characteristics. D. Sc. Thesis. University of Amsterdam,
    Netherlands, 1980.

Pugh, L.G.C.E. The influence of wind resistance in running and walking
    and the mechanical efficiency of work against horizontal or vertical
    forces. Journal of Anatomy (London), 1970, 215, 225-276.

Quanbury, A.O., Winter, D.A. & Reimer, G.D. Instantaneous power and power
    flow in body segments during walking. Journal of Human Movement Studies,
    1975, 1, 59-67.

Ralston, H.J., Todd, F.N. & Inman, V.T. Comparison of electrical activity
and duration of tension in the human rectus femoris muscle.
Electromyography and Clinical Neurophysiology, 1976, 16, 277-286.

Ramsey, R.W. & Street, S.F. Isometric length tension diagram of isolated
muscle fibers in frog. Journal of Cellular and Comparative Physiology,
1940, 15, 11-34.

Rasch, P.J. & Burke, R.K. Kinesiology and applied anatomy. Philadelphia:
Lea & Febiger, 1967.

Ralston, H.J. Energy-speed relation and optimal speed during level walking.
Internationale Zeitschrift für angewandten Physiology, 1958, 17,
277-283.

Ralston, H.J., Inman, V.T., Shait, L.A. & Straffrath, M.D. Mechanics of
human isolated voluntary muscle. American Journal of Physiology, 1947,
151, 612-620.

Rau, G. & Vredenbregt, J. 'EMG-force relationship during voluntary static
contraction (m. biceps)'. In, S. Cerquilini, A. Venerando and J.
Wartenweiler (Eds.), Medicine and Sport 8: Biomechanics III. Basel:
Karger, 1973.

Ravensberg, C.D. van, Huijing, P.A.J.B.M., Rozendal, R.H. & Wieringen,
P.C.W. van. 'Single motor unit control: its dependence on the number
of muscle spindles'. In, E. Asmussen and K. Jørgensen (Eds.), Biomechanics
VI-A. Baltimore: University Park Press, 1978.

Reed, E.S. An outline of a theory of action systems. Journal of Motor
Behavior, 1982, 14, 98-134.

Robertson, D.G.E. & Winter, D.A. Mechanical energy generation absorption
and transfer amongst segments during walking. Journal of Biomechanics,
1980, 13, 845-854.

Rozendal, R.H. & Meyer, O.G. Human kinesiological electromyography: some
methodological problems. Human Movement Science, 1982, 1, 7-26.

Saunders, J.B. de C.M., Inman, V.T. & Eberhart, D.H. The major determinants
in normal and pathological gait. Journal of Bone and Joint Surgery,
1952, 38A, 543-558.

Schmitt, F.O. & Worden, F.C. (Eds.). The neurosciences, third study
program. Cambridge: MIT-Press, 1974.

Shik, M.L. & Orlovsky, G.N. Biophysics of complex systems and mathematical
models. Coordination of the limbs during running of the dog. Biofizika,
1965, 11, 1011-1047.

Simon, S.R., Paul, I.L., Mansour, J., Munro, M., Abernethy, P.J. & Radin, E.L. Peak dynamic force in human gait. Journal of Biomechanics, 1981, 14, 817-822.

Sjölund, B. & Björklund, A. (Eds.). Brainstem control of spinal mechanisms. New York: Fernström Foundation Series I, in press.

Smidt, G.L., Chiesa, G. & Pedotti, A. Accelerographic analysis of several types of walking. American Journal of Physical Medicine, 1977, 50, 285-300.

Soudan, K. & Dierkx, P. Calculation of derivatives and Fourier coefficients of human motion data, while using spline functions. Journal of Biomechanics, 1979, 12, 12, 21-26.

Spalteholz, W. Hand atlas of human anatomy. Philadelphia: Lippincott, 1933.

Stein, R.B. Peripheral control of movement. Physiological Reviews, 1974, 54, 215-243.

Stein, R.B. Nerve and muscle: membranes, cells and systems. New York: Plenum Press, 1980.

Stein, R.B., Parmigiani, F. & Oguztöreli, M.N. 'Linear and non-linear analysis of mammalian motor control'. In, W.M. Getz (Ed.), Mathematical modelling in biology and ecology. Berlin: Springer-Verlag, 1980.

Steindler, A. Mechanics of normal and pathological locomotion. Springfield Ill.: Thomas, 1935.

Steindler, A. Kinesiology of the human body. Springfield Ill.: Thomas, 1955.

Szentagothai, J. & Arbib, M.A. Conceptual models of neural organization. Cambridge: MIT-Press, 1975.

Talbot, R.E. & Humphrey, D.R. (Eds.), Posture and movement. New York: Raven Press, 1979.

Thomas, D.P. & Whitney, R.J. Postural movements during normal standing in man. Journal of Anatomy (London), 1959, 93, 524-539.

Toussaint, H.M., Helm, F.C.T. van de, Elzerman, J.R., Groot, G. de, Hollander, A.P. & Ingen Schenau, G.J. van. A power balance applied to swimming. In, G. de Groot, A.P. Hollander and P.A. Huijing (Eds.), Biomechanics and Medicine in swimming. Champaign: Human Kinetics Publishers, 1983.

Vinkcen, M.H., Gielen, C.G.A.M. & Gon, J.J. Denier van de. Intrinsic and afferent components in apparent muscle stiffness in man. Neurosciences, (in press).

Vincken, M.H., Gielen, C.G.A.M., Gon, J.J. Denier van der & Haar Romeny, B.M. ter. Afferent contributions to postural tasks. In, R. Huiskes,

D. van Campen and J. de Wijn (Eds.), Biomechanics: Principles and
    Applications. The Hague: Martinus Nijhoff, Publishers, 1982.

Voloshin, A., Wosk, J. & Brull, M. Force wave transmission through the
    human locomotor system. Journal of Biomechanical Engineering, 1981, 103,
    48-50.

Wadman, W.J. Control mechanisms of fast goal-directed arm movements.
    Ph.D. Thesis, University of Utrecht, Netherlands, 1979.

Wadman, W.J., Gon, J.J. Denier van der, Geuze, R.H. & Mol, C.R. Control
    of fast goal directed arm movements. Journal of Human Movement Studies,
    1979, 5, 3-17.

Wadman, W.J., Gon, J.J. Denier van der & Derksen, R.J.A. Muscle activation
    patterns for fast goal directed arm movements. Journal of Human Movement
    Studies, 1980, 6, 19-37.

Wadman, W.J., Boerhout, W. Gon, J.J. Denier van der. Responses of the arm
    movement control system to force impulses. Journal of Human Movement
    Studies, 1980, 6, 280-302.

Wall, P.D. The laminar organization of dorsal horn and effects of descending
    impulses. Journal of Physiology (London), 1967, 188, 403-423.

Wall, P.D. The sensory and motor role of impulses travelling in the dorsal
    columns towards cerebral cortex. Brain, 1970, 93, 505-524.

Wall, P.D. The gate control theory of pain mechanisms. A re-examination
    and re-statement. Brain, 1978, 101, 1-18.

Wallinga-de Jonge, W., Boom, H.B.K., Boon, K.L., Griep, P.A.M. & Lammarée,
    G.C. The force development of fast and slow skeletal muscle at different
    muscle lengths. American Journal of Physiology, 1980, 239 (Cell
    Physiology 8), C98-C104.

Wallinga-de Jonge, W., Boom, H.B.K., Meijink, R.J. & Vliet, G.H. van der.
    Calcium model for mammalian skeletal muscle. Medical and Biological
    Engineering and Computing, 1981, 19, 734-748.

Wilkie, D.V. The relation between force and velocity in human muscle.
    Journal of Physiology (London), 1950, 110, 249-280.

Willemse, J. De motoriek van de pasgeborene in de eerste levensuren.
    Utrecht: Erven J. Bijleveld, 1961.

Winter, D.A. A new definition of mechanical work done in human movement.
    Journal of Applied Physiology, 1979, 46, 79-83.

Winter, D.A., Sidwell, H.G. & Hobson, D.A. Measurement and reduction of
    noise in kinematics of locomotion. Journal of Biomechanics, 1974, 7,
    157-159.

Winter, D.A., Quanbury, A.O., Hobson, D.A., Sidwall, H.G., Reimer, G., Trenholm, B.G., Steinke, T. & Schlosser, H. Kinematics of normal locomotion- a statistical study based on TV data. Journal of Biomechanics, 1974, 7, 479-486.

Winter, D.A., Quanbury, A.O. & Reimer, G.D. Instantaneous energy and power flow in normal human gait. In, P.V. Komi (Ed.), Biomechanics V-A. Baltimore: University Park Press, 1976.

Winter, D.A., Quanbury, A.O. & Reimer, G.D. Analysis of instantaneous energy of normal gait. Journal of Biomechanics, 1976, 9, 253-257.

Winter, D.A. & Robertson, D.G.E. Joint torque and energy patterns in normal gait. Biological Cybernetics, 1978, 29, 137-142.

Woittiez, R.D., Huijing, P.A. & Rozendal, R.H. Influence of muscle architecture on the length-tension diagram: model and its verification. Pflügers Archiv (European Journal of Physiology), 1983, 397, 73-74.

Woittiez, R.D., Huijing, P.A. & Rozendal, R.H. Influence of muscle architecture on the length-tension diagram of mammalian muscle. Submitted to Pflügers Archiv, 1983.

Wolstenholme, G.E.W. (Ed.). The spinal cord. London: Churchill, 1953.

Yamashita, T. & Katoh, R. Moving pattern of point of application of vertical resultant force during level walking. Journal of Biomechanics, 1976, 9, 93-96.

Zalkind, M.S. On the unspecific components of human local motor reaction. Agressologie, 1973, 14-A, 19-25.

Zarrugh, M.Y. Power requirements and mechanical efficiency of treadmill walking. Journal of Biomechanics, 1981, 14, 157-165.

Zarrugh, M.Y. & Radcliffe, C.W. Computer generation of human gait kinematics. Journal of Biomechanics, 1979, 12, 99-111.

Zarrugh, M.Y., Todd, F.N. & Ralston, H.J. Optimization of energy expenditure during level walking. European Journal of Applied Physiology, 1974, 33, 293-306.

Zikmund, Vl. & Balla, J. The effect of directional optic stimuli on body gravity centre projection in standing man. Agressologie, 1973, 14-B, 71-77.

SECTION 4

CHAPTER IV

SOME EMERGENT PROBLEMS OF THE REGULATION OF MOTOR ACTS

N. Bernstein

(Published in Journal *Questions of Psychology*, No. 6, 1957).

The period of struggle towards the recognition of the biological importance, the reality and the generality of the principle of cyclical regulation of life processes is now behind us. As often happens during periods of scientific quarrying, glimpses of the new ideas and general forecasts may now be noted in the work of the older classical physiologists (Bell, Sechenov, Jackson), and of those nearer to our own epoch (Ukhtomskii, Wagner). The present author gave an account of the application of these concepts to the problem of the co-ordination of movements in a report in 1929 in which this principle was given a general mechanical foundation (15), and in 1935 he reduced it in general terms to differential equations (see Chapter II). The debate, in these initial stages, was conducted sharply, but now seems to be over. Now we are living through a period of the extensive development of this principle and of its elaboration and cultivation in heuristic models and in automatic processes in the most varied fields of practical application. Clearly, now is the time to look forward, to attempt to formulate some of the new problems which occur in this area, and to direct attention to some insufficiently illuminated and evaluated aspects of the circular principle of control. The most suitable data to be discussed are from the area of the physiology of motor acts.

I

The motor activity of organisms is of enormous biological significance - it is practically the only way in which the organism not only interacts with the surrounding environment, but also actively operates on this environment, altering it with respect to particular results. The theoretical lag observed in this area in comparison with the physiology of receptors or of internal processes is therefore very puzzling. So is the neglect which is obvious from the sections on movement in physiological textbooks which

vary up to now from zero to some few pages. It is necessary to indicate
briefly how great is the resulting loss sustained by physiology as a whole.

If movements are classified from the point of view of their biological significance to the organism making them, it is clear that on the
first level of significance we have acts which solve one or another
particular *motor problem* which the organism encounters. Leaving the analysis
of this expression aside for the moment, we may note that *meaningful*
problems which can be solved by motor action arise, as a rule, out of the
external environment. This at once draws a distinction between meaningful
actions and the range of independent movements which are not concerned with
overcoming external forces, or a large number of momentary single-phased
movements such as withdrawal of the paws. It is already apparent from this
that laboratory physiology which, with very minor exceptions excludes
from the experimental chamber all movements except reflexes to pain,
defensive reflexes (primarily the scratching reflex[*]), diminishes its
resources of explanation not only quantatively but also qualitatively, and
as we now see not only in relation to narrowly motor problems.

First, if in the case of relatively independent movements (pointing,
drawing lines in the air, etc.), some knowledge of mechanics and biomechanics
is necessary in order to demonstrate the incontrovertible necessity for
circular sensory regulation, for acts of movement which are concerned with
the surmounting of *external forces* this necessity is evident from the
outset. In all sorts of motor problems in locomotion (especially complicated
ones - running over uneven ground, jumping on to an elevation, swimming
through waves, and many other examples), in fighting with other animals, in
industrial processes carried on by human beings, the overcoming of
independent forces is always a prerequisite for solution. These forces are
consequently not foreseeable, and because of this they cannot be overcome
by any sort of stereotyped movements directed solely from within. A
careless consideration of these processes of active interaction with
independent surroundings (apparently the limitation of explanation to
"atomic movements" alone seemed quite justified to the atomist-mechanists
of the last century, who regarded a whole as the sum of its part and
nothing more) led to the situation that the principles of sensory-feedback

---

[*] The reaction designated as orientation reflex has only been included in
this category for terminological reasons, and as far as we know has never
been employed for the direct investigation of reflex action.

connections, which could have been examined and established for the case of
motor control a hundred years ago, remained obscure until the present.

For many years the concept of the open reflex *arc* has been a universal
guiding principle in physiology. We cannot exclude the possibility that in
such elementary processes as the salivation reflex, or in such abrupt
actions of secondary biological significance as withdrawal from a painful
stimulus, etc., the arc really does not form *a reflex ring* characteristic
for the scheme of the control process, partly because of the short duration
of the act, and partly because of its extreme simplicity. However, it is
both possible and probable that because of these characteristics of brief
duration and extreme simplicity the cyclical nature even of these processes
has so far escaped attention and record. (For the process of salivation this
is already almost beyond doubt). However this may be, it seems very likely
that a reflex visualized on the model of an *arc* is only a rudiment, or a
very special case, of a physiological reaction[*].

It remains to describe yet another loss which physiology has sustained
from the replacement of real acts of movement solving objective problems
as they arise, by fragments of movements of an almost artificial character.
This particular loss has so far not been sufficiently emphasized; it has
not merely impoverished our knowledge in the area of *receptor* physiology,
but contains the root of important methodological errors.

It must be noted that in the detection of *releaser signals* which are
incorporated in the operation of one or another reflex arc - the only role
in which they were studied by physiologists of classical schools - the
afferent systems, at least in the higher animals and in man, function in
essentially and qualitatively different ways than in the role of tracking
and corrective mechanisms which they play in the fulfilment of motor acts.
This difference becomes clear if, once again considering the matter from
the point of view of biological significance, we turn our attention to
those properties in the receptor organs which had to be developed by natural
selection. In order to act as a *signal-releasing system* the receptor must
necessarily have a high degree of sensitivity, that is thresholds which
are as low as possible, both for the detection of the absolute strength of
a signal, and for discrimination between signals. The most significant

---

[*] I would not even exclude the possibility that the first reflex in the
form of an arc appeared in the world in the same place as the first
"elementary sensation" - both of them in a laboratory experiment, or in
the minds of experimenters.

biologically are the *distance receptors*, smell, hearing (even of ultra-high
frequencies) and vision in various orders of rank for various types of
animals. In order to discriminate meaningful signals further from the
chaotic background of "noise" it is necessary to develop an entirely analytic
or *analysational* function for the corresponding apparatus in the central
nervous system. (It is quite natural that I.P. Pavlov, in greatly extending
our knowledge of the *signal-releasing* functions of the receptors, should have
termed them *analysers* only in his latest years complementing this with the
term synthesis). Finally, the most important mechanism in this signal-
releasing role, as Sechenov hypothesized in advance, has been clearly
revealed experimentally by investigators abroad (who were stimulated by the
practical problems of observation in war) to be the processes of active
systematic *search* ("scanning") or examination by telereceptors of every
diapason of function. This is an entirely active process, and the effector
side of the organism is here employed in a manner completely analogous to
that which is later explained to underly afferentation in the control of
movements. I must, however, note at once that this last process has nothing
in common with the processes of the evocation of organized effector acts
for the integral active perception of objects in the external world, as we
shall discuss later.

Once a meaningful motor act has been set in motion by any given
sensory signal, the demands of biological expediency on the afferent function
are quite different. It was these demands which led to the formation of the
processes of annular *sensory correction* during phylogenesis. We may consider
the formulation of the motor problem, and the perception of the object in
the external world with which it is concerned as having their necessary
prerequisites in *maximally full and objective* perception both of the object
and of each successive phase and detail of the corresponding movement which
is directed towards the solution of the particular problem. The first
attribute of the receptors which may be described in the context of this
role is that of completeness, or synthesis. This has been adequately
described and studied by both psychologists and neuro-physiologists under the
headings of sensory synthesis or the sensory fields. Among these fields we
have, for instance, the body scheme, the spatio-motor field, the synthesis
of objective or qualitative (topological) space and so on. The author has
attempted to give a thorough account of the roles of these fields in a book
on the structure of movements (23). It is here only necessary to recall
that: (1) in this functional area the synthesization of the operation of the

receptors is not manifest theoretically (as was the case above) but can be directly followed in the norm and in pathology and (2) for each of such sensory syntheses effecting the sequential direction of motor acts, the structural scheme of connections between the activities of various proprio-tango- and telereceptors has its own specific quantitative and qualitative properties.

In this case the confluence of elementary information flowing from the peripheral receptors to the central synthesizing apparatus is so deep and stable that it is in general practically impossible to distinguish by introspection. All, or almost all, types of receptors take part in the activity described above (possibly with the exception of taste alone), but to significantly different degrees. On the first level there is the general system of the proprioceptors in the narrow sense; further there is the co-function of all tango- and telereceptors, organized on the basis of all previous practical attempts in order to fulfil the role of functional proprioception. Other purely physiological aspects of the operation of the receptors in the circular function - parameters of adaptation, "comparison thresholds", periodicity of function, etc. - will be discussed in the second part of this chapter.

The second determining sign of the receptors as participants in the annular co-ordinational process - *objectivity* - is of such great significance that it will be necessary to deal with it more thoroughly.

It has been possible to analyse receptors in terms of an open arc only in their role as signals (releasers or inhibitors). It was this role which led to the use of the term *signal system* for the entire complex of organs of perception in the central nervous system. Where perceptual organs operate in this way, objective accurate information is not, in general, required of afferent function.

The reflex system will operate adequately if to each answering effector there is attached its own (a) constant and (b) correctly recognized releaser signal-code. The composition of this code may be entirely arbitrary, without introducing interference into the functional system if these two conditions alone are observed. This indifference on the part of the central nervous system to the meaningful content of a signal is not a strange, purely biological phenomenon but part of the very nature of the process of signal apprehension. This is shown by the conduction of signals, with perfect control of the necessary connecting and switching in remote-control apparatus. It is possible to construct two identical automata - aircraft-projectiles, motor boats, etc. - with identical motors, wheels, schemes and radio relays, etc., and to organize the situation without any structural differences so that in answer to the radio codes A, B, C, D, etc. the first system responds with the reactions 1, 2, 3, 4, and the second with the reactions 4, 2, 1, 3, or whatever is wanted.

The characteristics of operation of the receptor system are quite different, in respect of its control-co-ordination functioning, in the process of solution of a motor problem. Here the degree of *objective reality* of the information is a decisive prerequisite for the success or failure of the action to be performed. During the entire course of phylogenesis of living organisms natural selection inexorably sifted out those individuals in which the receptors controlling motor activity operated like a curved mirror. Over the course of ontogenesis each encounter of a particular individual with the surrounding environment, with conditions requiring the solution of a motor problem, results in a development (sometimes a very valuable one), in its nervous system of increasingly reliable and accurate *objective representations* of the external world, both in terms of the perception and comprehension involved in meeting the situation, and in terms of projecting and controlling the realization of the movements adequate to this situation. Each meaningful motor directive demands not an arbitrarily coded, but an objective, quantitatively and qualitatively reliable representation of the surrounding environment in the brain. Such an action is also an active implement for the correct cognition of the surrounding world. The achievement or failure of a solution to every active motor problem encountered during life leads to a progressive filtering and cross-indexing of the evidence in the sensory syntheses mentioned above and in their components[*]. This also leads to knowledge through action and *revision through practice* which is the cornerstone of the entire dialectical-materialistic theory of knowledge, and in the cases selected here serves as a sort of biological context for Lenin's theory of reflection[**].

_____

[*]   The indubitable fact of the existence in the human central nervous system of *some* qualitatively different sensory syntheses does not contradict the point made on the objectivity of the representation in the brain. The latter finds an adequate explanation in the physiology of the co-ordination of movements.

[**] "Domination over nature appearing in human practice is the result of objectively accurate representation in the head of the human being of the phenomena and processes of nature and this is evidence of the fact that this reflection (within the limits which practice demonstrates for us) is objective, absolute external truth". V.I. Lenin, *Materialism and Empiriocriticism*.

The comparison made in the last few pages between the two types of
theory of functioning of perceptual systems of the organism which are as
yet unequal in terms of their scientific pedigrees and in the extent to
which they have been worked out, allows us to illuminate some new aspects
of the mechanism of operation of classic signal processes of elicitation,
or of differential inhibition, of the reflex reaction.

A long time before telemechanics confirmed the essential principal of
conditionality† of releasing or switching codes, the same fact was established
for biological material by the famous discovery of I.P. Pavlov. The fact
that any perceptible stimulus may equally easily be converted into a
releaser signal for one or another organic reflex appears to be remarkably
universal in biological material. As subsequent studies by Pavlov's school
have shown (Speranskii, Bykov), in the entire complex of physiological
function, apparently down to the deepest least accessible processes such
as hormonal processes or the processes of cell metabolism, there is no
single process which may not be connected, and in principle by the same
method, to any releaser stimulus. This remarkable indifference of the nervous
system to the nature and content of releaser stimuli was noted by I.P. Pavlov
at the very beginning of his investigations into the range of phenomena
which he discovered. Even the term employed for the stimuli which he grafted
on to the trunks of the older organic reflexes - *conditioned* reflexes - is
evidence of this. The terminology suggested by V.M. Bekhterev, "combinational"
stimuli and reflexes, is less deep in relation to the internal significance
of the phenomena, but is nevertheless quite adequate to describe the system
of such mechanisms as have been explained up to the present time.

Two conditions are always necessary for the conversion of any given
supraliminal agent into a conditioned releasing stimulus for any given
organic reflex; (1) the coincidence or combination of this agent with the
realization of the given reflex within the limits of a short time interval
and (2) - an auxiliary condition - a given number of repetitions of this
conjunction. The former of these conditions directly relates the phenomenon
selected to the *cycle of association by contiguity*, as it were, characterized

---

† Conditionality in the plan under discussion does not *demand* objectivity
and does not contradict it. The comparison and delimitation of the signal-
releaser and corrective functions of the receptors undertaken in this
paper is probably sharper and more "either/or" than is the case in
physiological reality where, doubtless, both forms of function may be
superimposed upon each other from time to time and may interpenetrate.

by an indifference to the meaningful content of the associated items or
receptions. It is interesting to note that for the conversion of indifferent
stimuli into conditioned releasers their juxtaposition with the *effector* and
not with the *afferent* component of the natural reflex is necessary. This
last component is employed in the typical conditioning experiment only as a
means of establishing and working out the effector arc. This is proved, for
example, by the existence of so called conditioned reflexes of the second
order, when the indifferent stimulus possesses releaser properties for a
given reflex in spite of the fact that the effector part of the latter is
set into action, not by an unconditioned by by a conditioned stimulus of
the first order, which was earlier worked into the reflex. Another proof of
the above may be seen in the fact that in the methods employed in animal
training the reward which reinforces the unconditioned afferent impulses of
feeding in the animal is given *after* the correct performance of the ¬equired
activity in response to the corresponding conditioned command and is not,
in this case, the unconditioned releaser stimulus for the trained activity.
This detail, which has been underestimated in the past, attracts out
attention in the present context because it seems that the formation of
associative links in the brain between *afferent processes* and the *effector*
portion of the reflex can be explained only if this effector realization of
the reflex is reflected (again by means of ring feedback) in advance in the
central nervous system, and can there already undergo association with the
afferent processes of conditioned stimulation. We may find here yet another
confirmation of the fact that "return-afferent" or feedback acts exist as
direct components of the process in classical reflex arcs, and only escape
observation for the time being.

The second condition of formation of conditioned connections is that
termed auxiliary above. It would indeed be difficult to explain why a given
number of repeated associations is required otherwise than because of the
necessity for the experimental subject to discriminate the new reception
introduced from the whole chaos of external stimulation bombarding him. The
number of repetitions must be adequate to determine the *non-randomness* of
the juxtaposition in time of the intero- or proprioception of the realized
reflex with just one particular element out of the totality of extero-
reception. In this sense - in relation to the necessary and sufficient
number of repetitions - a stimulus which is indifferent in terms of its
meaningful content may prove more difficult to discriminate and require more
trials to attract the interest and attention ("orientational reaction") of

the subject. The older, naively materialistic conception of gradually "beaten" tracks or synaptic barriers in the central nervous system may already be considered to be relegated to the archives of science[*].

We must here mention a fact which remains obscure even in the light of new thinking in the physiology of regulation. The structure of almost all conditioned associations which have been set up is such that a new *conditioned afferent* signal is grafted on to an organic *unconditioned effector arc*. The variation, both in unconditioned effector processes and in the afferent "call-signs" which may be attached to them is almost infinite; but almost no single case is known in which we observe the *reverse* structure of a conditioned link, where a new conditioned reflex termination is attached to an unconditioned afferent arc. Cases of this reverse type were to some extent observed in the work of Eroofeeva at the beginning of this century, but I.P. Pavlov himself, in his "Lectures on the Operation of the Major Hemispheres", accompanied their description with a whole series of limitations and reservations. However this structural paradox may be explained in the future, it is clear that the inertia of actually existing effector semi-arcs makes it extremely difficult to employ their structural mechanism for the learning of unknown movements, for the establishment and learning of habits of movement and new skills, etc.

An examination of the question of signal codes and their conjoint roles in the aspect of regulatorary physiology may, it seems to us, throw a new light on the problem of the so-called *second signal system* (I.P. Pavlov). It is clear from the above analysis that the variability in possible conditioned signal codes is not in any way restricted, and that even speech phonemes, which do not in any way illustrate *in this respect* their role as members of any particular class, require, like all signal stimuli, only to be perceived and distinguished from each other.

Nobody has applied the concepts of a second signal system, or of architectonic fields homologous to Wernicke's field in man, to dogs, bears, sea-lions or cats; though all these animals may be trained to set up

---

[*] If any given indifferent reception is repeatedly coincident in time with some unconditioned process, for example interoreception of salivation, etc., then the so-called probability *a posteriori* that this coincidence is not accidental rises very rapidly, and after ten associations is already very little different from unity. For the formation of a connection it is, however, necessary that both the indifferent stimulus itself, and the fact of the constant coincidence of both stimuli attract attention, that is to say, stimulate the processes of the active reception by the subject.

linkages and differentiations in response to verbal signals (though they
are not even all higher mammals), as readily as to other forms of stimulation.
These phonemic signal codes, which are not in any way different from other
forms of codes, might have been the genetic embryos of phoneme signs in
primitive man - a type of rudimentary imperative from which verb forms
gradually evolved[*].

On the other hand, the *denominational* elements in speech out of which
human beings have formed the category of proper names never had, and logically
never could have a signal function in the sense described above. For this
reason the treatment of the second signal system as a system of verbal
representation of *things* (in general, the primary receptions of external
objects representing in this sense the aggregate of the elements of the
first signal system), which presents itself clearly in the list of names
employed by experimenters using the so-called speech-movement method, is
the result of a deep and mistaken confusion between two sharply distinct
physiological functions and speech categories. *Words as signals* do not form
any special type of system, and in the role of releaser phonemes are quite
accessible to many animals which are still very far indeed from the function
of speech. *Words and speech as reflections of the external world* in their
static (proper names) and dynamic action and interaction with the subject
(verbs, judgements) do indeed form a system which is attainable by, and
characteristic of man alone; but to call *speech* which has attained this
degree of meaningfulness and development a *signal system* is to confuse it
with one of its most inessential and rudimentary manifestations[**].

The idea of a second signal system is doubtless one of the consequences
of the methodological confusions described above, and due to the fact that
physiologists recognized only one signal-releaser role of the receptor
apparatus and undervalued its most important biological and social functions,

---

[*] I must here make the following points: firstly, I do not include in the
    above any attempt to define the *chronological order* in which verbs and
    nominative categories may have evolved in primitive man, and secondly,
    that I agree entirely with well known philologists as to the phenomenon
    of the *secondary* employment of nominative elements with an exhortatory
    signal meaning in primitive speech.

[**] We must add to the above that the construction of robot automata which
    are able to *understand* speech is a quite hopeless problem for modern
    technology. On the other hand, robots which can react differentially
    to a few different speech phoneme signs which are given to them may
    already be built without any difficulty in principle.

that is, the cognition of the surrounding world through action and the regulation of action within it. The sign of equality placed between the ideas of reception and signal obliged the investigators of this earlier period to refer even perceived words to the category of signals; meanwhile, it has not been possible to circumvent the striking independence of speech as a specific inherent form of *homo sapien's* symbolic representation of the perceptual world and of himself in it. The tolerance extended to atomism, as mentioned above, has allowed easy bypassing of the *structuring* of speech (which makes it not a collection of words, but an instrument of thought) and its treatment as a sum of speech signals mainly concrete-objective in content.

Russian physiology contrived to avoid another, much more important, gnosiological error perpetrated by many thinkers in the Western world. This is also entirely a result of considering only a single aspect of receptor function: from the fact that it is clearly possible to reconcile the perfect operation of reflex functions with the complete arbitrariness of their sensory codes it is very easy to slide from the position of the recognition of the symbolic nature of all reception in general, and of the conditionality of the picture of the world in the brain and the psyche, to the concept of the un-knowability of objective reality and similar idealistic conceptions which have been disproved by authentic science long ago.

II

We may now attempt to make our analysis of the mechanisms of motor co-ordination in the higher organisms more precise having two problems in view: (1) to extract from this analysis the maximum information available at the present time as to the general laws governing mechanisms of control; and (2) to attempt to discover what constitutes those motor peculiarities of the higher animals, and of man in particular, which sharply and quantitatively distinguish their operation and resources from all that we might expect from the techniques of automatic processes of the present day, and perhaps of the near future. In the present analysis we shall have to touch upon many points which have already been thoroughly analysed in their time (23, 29); in order to avoid irrelevant repetition I shall dwell on them as briefly as possible in the present report, merely pointing out logical lines of analysis, leaving the reader interested in a more detailed exposition to turn to the works referred to. It will here be best to attempt to complete and extend

the questions we have touched upon, which mainly concern the basic principal
mechanisms of co-ordination and control, touching in the process upon errors
which have now become apparent.

The first clear biomechanical distinction between the motor apparatus
in man and the higher animals and any artificial self-controlling devices,
as I have repeatedly emphasized, lies in the enormous number (which often
reaches three figures) of *degrees of freedom* which it can attain, both in
respect to the kinematics of the multiple linkages of its freely jointed
kinematic chains, and to the elasticity due to the resilience of their
connections - the muscles. Because of this there is no direct relationship
between the degree of activity of muscles, their tensions, their lengths,
or the speed of change in length. To explain how the control of a movement
is complicated by each additional degree of freedom we give the following
two examples.

A ship on the surface of the sea has three degrees of freedom (if we
ignore rocking movements) though, in practice, control of *one* degree of
freedom only - that of the direction or *course* is enough as on the surface
of the sea, if the ship deviates somewhat from its course it is not necessary
to return to the old *track* in order to establish its former direction, but
quite sufficient to follow a path parallel to it, a couple of cables to one
side or the other. This problem is easily and adequately solved by an
autopilot with a compass. Let us now, however, consider an automobile which
must travel along a *road of limited width* automatically dealing with all the
curves and bends which it encounters. Here the direction of the car depends
in practice upon *two degrees of freedom* of the car's mobility. This analysis
shows that irrespective of the means by which the machine receives information
on the course of the road (relative, for example, to the centre line),
whether this is perceived by photo-, electro- or mechanicoreceptors, etc.,
the block diagram of the apparatus which guides the car along a winding
road keeping it close to the centre line must incorporate: (1) a receptor of
the distance from the line, and its sign; (2) a receptor of the angle between
the axis of the machine and the line, and its sign; (3) a receptor of the
effective curvature of the road; (3) a summing and analysing comparator
system; and (5) a system of regulation to suppress incidental swing of the
machine to one or the other side of the course. This great increase in
complexity is a result of the problem of automatization with only one more
degree of freedom. As far as we know no automat of a similar type has yet
been constructed anywhere. It is useful to point out that the enormous

difficulties of construction are not in any way connected to problems of
signalling or to the construction of receptors of the types mentioned; the
technical knowledge for receptors of all these types exists at present.
The point of the difficulty lies in the organization of the *central
recording* of information originally obtained from photo-elements or magnetic
relays in the form of the nature, intensity, and succession of impulses
controlling the servomechanics of the steering apparatus.

I draw my second example, for comparison, from the field of normal
human motor co-ordination where all afferent organs function normally and the
only unusual conditions are those of the motor problem. Fasten-the handle
end of a ski-stick in front of the buckle of a subject's belt. Attach a weight
of 1-2 kg to the far end and on the right and left sides of the wheel attach
a length of rubber tubing long enough to allow the ends to be held in the
subject's left and right hands. Instruct the subject, turning the stick
point forwards, to stand before a vertical board on which a large circle,
square or other simple figure has been drawn, and to try, manipulating the
ski-stick only by pulling on the rubber tubing, to follow the contours of
the figure with the point of the ski-stick. The stick here represents one
segment of an extremity with two degrees of freedom; the tubing is
analogous to two antagonistic muscles introducing a further two degrees of
freedom into the system. This experiment (which is very useful for
demonstrations in an auditorium) makes clear to all who attempt it just how
difficult and complicated it is to control systems which require the co-
ordination of four degrees of freedom, even when under the control of a
human being in possession of his full complement of receptors, but without
motor practice with this task, who has been dealing with his bone-muscle
motor apparatus from the first weeks of his life.

The definition of co-ordination which I have given in previous accounts
still appears to me to be comprehensive and accurate: *The co-ordination of
a movement is the process of mastering redundant degrees of freedom of the
moving organ, in other words its conversion to a controllable system.* More
briefly, co-ordination is the *organization of the control* of the motor
apparatus. In the basic definition I have deliberately not discussed the
reinforcement, inhibition, etc., of the redundant degrees of freedom, but
their mastery. This is because (as extensive work on children, sportsmen,
and also hemiparetic subjects and amputees (9, 14, 21, 65) has shown)
fixation eliminating the redundant degrees of freedom mentioned above is
employed only as the most primitive and inconvenient method, and then only

at the beginning of the mastery of the motor skill, being later displaced
by more flexible, expedient and economic methods of overcoming this
redundancy through the *organization* of the process as a whole. The
importance of the role played by the organization of the control of
interactions, even in the simple case of the control of only two degrees of
freedom, is already apparent from our first example of the automatic control
of a car along a road. It follows, from the definition above, that co-
ordination cannot be regarded as some sort of independent activity – as a
particular act directed at the external world. It is better to regard it
as a means of ensuring responsiveness and flexibility of execution in the
motor system; it may be regarded as a type of *motor servo-mechanism*.

In studies on the structure of movements I have thoroughly considered
the reasons which emphasize the biodynamic necessity for the organization
of the mechanisms of motor co-ordination on the ring principle. I have also
described some aspects, revealed by observation, of those physiological
processes of interaction in control which effect the co-ordinational
guidance of a movement through the mediation of sensory syntheses of various
levels of structural complexity. We saw how important, among the
unpredictable and almost independent forces which must be perceived and
overcome, is the part played by *reactive forces* which occur together with
external forces, which are inevitably produced in movements of the multi-
linked kinematic chains of the motor organs, and which are complicated in
exponential progression by each additional link in a series of joints and
by each new degree of freedom of movement. We shall not discuss this purely
biodynamic side of the problem any further at this point (see Chapter III).

We now turn to a question which has been left obscure in the studies
above but which has become increasingly pressing in the context of
contemporary developments in physiological thought. If motor co-ordination
is a system of mechanisms ensuring the *control* of the motor apparatus and
permitting its rich and complex flexibility to be utilized to the full, what
can we say at the present time about the means and mechanisms of this *control*
of motor acts? How may the regularities we now observe in this control be
employed in the interests of applied cybernetics, and which aspects or
properties of these regularities can be isolated as most specific to the
nervous systems of the higher animals and of man, so that we may more
precisely illuminate the gap which still qualitatively divides (and clearly
will divide for some time to come) such processes as may be attained by
automata from those which are realized in the motor acts of the life

processes of highly developed organisms?

We must first briefly deal with some problems of terminology and attempt to systematize the principal types of self-regulating systems which are known at the present time (from here on we shall for brevity indicate this term by its first letters S.S.) and list the problems and topics in which we are interested.

All systems which are self-regulating for any given parameter, constant or variable, must incorporate the following elements as minimum requirements:

(1) *effector* (motor) activity, which is to be regulated along the given parameter;

(2) *a control element*, which conveys to the system in one way or another the *required value* of the parameter which is to be regulated;

(3) *a receptor* which perceives the *factual* course of the *value* of the parameter and signals it by some means to

(4) *a comparator device*, which perceives the discrepancy between the *factual* and *required* values with its magnitude and sign;

(5) *an apparatus* which encodes the data provided by the comparator device into correctional impulses which are transmitted by feedback linkages to

(6) *a regulator* which controls the function of the *effector* along the given parameter.

In this way the entire system displays a closed circle of interaction, the general scheme of which is given in Fig. 31. Between the elements which have been enumerated there are frequently included auxiliary devices of secondary importance such as amplifiers, relays, servomotors, etc.

The short terms used by German authors for values of the parameter to be regulated are very convenient and we also find it expedient to use them. The *required value* will in future be designated as Sw (from the German *Sollwert*), the *factual value as* Iw *(Istwert)*; the *discrepancy* between these which is perceived by element 4, or more exactly the excess or difference of Iw over Sw $(Iw - Sw)$, will be designated by the symbol Δw.

As an example given by Wiener (77) from an idea by his partner Rosenblueth the co-ordinational control of the act of seizing a visible object from a table top may be regarded as a constant process of estimation of the rate of diminution of that section of the path over which the hand must still travel to meet the object under consideration. We have every justification to designate the position of the object as Sw, the current position of the hand as Iw and the regularly diminishing distance between them as the variable Δw $(Iw - Sw)$. I must explain that both in the explanation above and henceforward, I shall regard the co-ordinational process in terms of *micro-intervals* of its track and of time, basing this treatment on data which have been accumulated over years of work by my colleagues and myself. For this reason I shall regard in this respect the *continuous planned path or process of movement of an organ* as the variable Sw and the factual variable coordinates of the latter as Iw. In the present context Δw will be the threshold values of deviations which are more or less

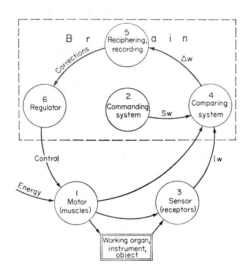

Fig. 31. The simplest possible block diagram of an apparatus
for the control of movements.

accurately corrected *during the course of the movement*, as an example of which we may take the deviations of lines drawn by hand with a pencil or the point of a planimeter from a ruled line which a subject is set to follow. Consequently, in our sense Δw is not a systematically diminishing macro-distance, but oscillates in value, increasing and diminishing with the attainment of small values of variable sign and direction.

The central command post of the entire S.S. ring system is naturally its control element 2. Depending on the character of the Sw given by this element all conceivable types of S.S. may be divided into two large classes: S.S. with fixed constant values of Sw (so-called stabilizing systems) and S.S. with values of Sw which vary for one reason or other (tracking systems). The law of the course of the change of the given Sw may be called the *program* of the functioning of the S.S. Changes between successive stages in the realization of a program may be stepwise or continuous, and may, in various cases, be functions of time, of the path of action, of the working-point of the motor effector or of some intermediate resultant stage of operation, etc. In the most complex and flexible systems even the programs may be interchangeable.

Stabilizing systems are most primitive in their function and least interesting from our point of view although their analogues may be found in the operation of reflex-ring regulation among physiological systems. There are numerous examples of such systems in technology, beginning with Watt's centrifugal speed stabilizer for steam engines. A biological example is the pressure-receptor system of stabilization of arterial pressure which has been subjected to a thorough experimental examination from this point of view by Wagner (75). The motor apparatus of the organism, in all its functions and in principle of an S.S. system of the tracking type with a continuous program of changes for successive regulations of Sw in each case.

All elements of the most simple scheme of circular control incorporated in our list and in our plan (see Fig. 31) must also necessarily occur in organic regulational systems in one form or another, most especially in systems of motor control. Our knowledge of these structural elements in the living motor apparatus is very uneven. We still know nothing whatever of the physiological properties, or even the neural substrates, of elements 5 and 6. The moving elements of 1, the motor effectors of our movements - the skeletal muscles - belong, on the other hand, to a category of objects which have been investigated by physiologists and biophysicists very thoroughly and in great detail. The operation of element 3 of the schema - the receptor complex - has been thoroughly studied, but only from one point of view - as was shown in the first part of this report - and the aspect of its operation now under consideration still provides a great number of topics for investigation. I shall attempt to discuss here what can at present be said, both factually and hypothetically (with ordered degrees of probability), about the physiological structure of elements, 2, 4 and 3 of the scheme for the control of motor acts; I shall also incidentally discuss as they arise problems which we have already encountered, though we are still very far from being able to solve them. It will be appropriate to begin this review with the "command point" of the scheme - with the control element 2.

Every intelligent purposeful movement is made as an answer to a motor problem, and is determined - directly or indirectly - by the situation as a whole. Inasmuch as a motor act by the individual (an animal or human being)

incorporates a solution to this problem, there is a basis of some program or
other which will be realized by the control element. What is it that
represents such a program of control for a movement, and by what is this
program controlled in its turn?

In the monograph on the structure of movements (23) I discussed in
detail *how* sensory corrections arise and *how* they affect the course of a
movement. The topic raised here concerns a different problem which was
almost ignored by the book referred to; *what it is precisely* that is
corrected, and *what* controls the process and the basis of such corrections.

Observation of the simplest movements, such as those in the category
of isolated movements (drawing straight lines through the air, indicating
a point, etc.), may give the impression that the guiding principle
underlying the program of changes in Sw, by means of which corrections to
the movements are realized, is the geometrical form of such movements: the
observation of linearity if it is necessary to describe a straight line,
the observation of direction when indicating a particular point, etc. In
coming to this conclusion, however, we fall into the error of mistaking
the particular for the general. In the forms of movement described above
it is indeed true that correction is effected by means of a geometrical
image, but only because this is precisely the point of the problem. In the
second of the examples which we have given (i.e. that of pointing), the
geometrical guiding element of the movement has shrunk to a single point in
the visual field. It is quite sufficient to be acquainted with cyclogrametric
records of the movements of pointing with a finger at an object, carried out
with optimal skill and accuracy, to become convinced that N successive
gestures by the same subject are made through N non-coincident trajectories
which only gather, as at a focus, in the vicinity of the same required
point which is being indicated[*]. This means that the geometrical principle
of correction is restricted, as far as possible, to the determination of the
minimum extent of a movement which is absolutely necessary, and gives way in
the remaining parts of the movement to some other guiding principles. The
reliability and speed of their courses and their faultless coincidence on
the target provides evidence that such principles are certainly incorporated
in each micro-element of the gesture of pointing. (Compare this movement
with one of a patient with ataxia!).

The error of mistaking the particular for the general becomes obvious

_____
[*] Cf., also, Fig. 21.

as soon as we turn from movements which are geometrical in respect to their
goal to motor acts of another type. If we consider relatively simple
specialized motor acts which are repeated many times and so become, as the
term is, automatized, we may be sure that the attainment of their motor
goal (locomotion in sport, industrial processes, etc.) is adequately
achieved much earlier than the automatization of the movement and its
stabilization to a significant degree of geometrical consistency. In many
cases the goal of the movement is attained at the very first attempt. It
follows that the kinematic motor composition of an act is by no means a
universal invariant which guarantees the success of the action to be
fulfilled. If we turn from the simplest and most repetitive actions to more
complex purposeful movements, which are frequently multiphasic and
conditioned by the need to overcome variable external conditions and
resistances, such broad variations in the motor composition of movements
become a universal rule.

    If the program of a motor act is discussed, as a whole, in macro-
scopic terms we cannot discover any other determining factor than the image
or representation of the result of the action (final or intermediate) in
terms of which this action is directed and which leads towards the
comprehension of the corresponding motor problem. In particular, how and by
what physiological means the image of the envisaged or required effect of
the movement may function as a guiding principle of the motor structure of
an act, and as a program for the direction of the effector element, is a
problem to which there are as yet no signs of any concrete or determinate
answers. Whatever forms of the motor activity of higher organisms we
consider, from elementary movements to multiphasic industrial processes,
writing, articulation, etc., analysis suggests no other guiding constant
than the form and sense of the motor problem and the dominance of the
required result of its solution, which determine, from step to step, now
the fixation and now the reconstruction of the course of the program as well
as the realization of the sensory correction.

    The fact that I have referred, as the characteristic guiding principle
of the motor act, to the understanding or the representation of the result
of an action (which is a topic for psychological investigation), and that
I have emphasized that we do not yet understand the physiological mechanisms
at its basis, does not mean that we can never understand the essentials of
these mechanisms, or that we must not give them our attention. We are already
in a position to consider the undivided psychophysiological unity of the

processes of the planning and co-ordination of movements, and to apply a
determinate terminology to the psychological aspects of the necessary control
factor, while as physiologists - lagging behind psychology in the forefront
of the study of movements (as we said above) - we are unable to analyse the
physiological aspects to these processes. However, *ignoramus* does not
signify *ignorabimus*; and the very title of the present chapter emphasizes
that its purposes were rather to raise and formulate unsolved subsidiary
questions than to answer those already propounded.

In Chapter 8 of the book referred to in ref. 23 there was a thorough
discussion of how, and under the operation of what causes, the motor
structure of movements which are repeatedly carried out may be formed and
stabilized during the development of so-called motor habits through practice.
As a brief extract we may here emphasize that even in the case of such
uniformly repetitive acts the variability in the motor picture and in the
range of initial conditions may at first be very great, and a more or less
fixed program develops depending on the extent to which a motion is
practised, and by no means at the first attempt. The process of practice
towards the achievement of new motor habits essentially consists in the
gradual success of a search for optimal motor solutions to the appropriate
problems. Because of this, practice, when properly undertaken, does not
consist in repeating the *means of solution* of a motor problem time after
time, but in the *process of solving* this problem again and again by
techniques which we changed and perfected from repetition to repetition. It
is already apparent here that, in many cases, "practice is a particular type
of repetition without repetition" and that motor training, if this position
is ignored, is merely mechanical repetition by rote, a method which has been
discredited in pedagogy for some time[*].

It is possible to be a little more concrete in one's statements in
regard to the *microstructure* of the control of continuously flowing motor
processes. In whatever form the general guiding directives of the anticipated
solution are decoded into the concrete, detailed Sw elements of direction,

---

[*] In exercises in sports and gymnastics, the motor structure (referred to as
style) is incorporated as an integral part in the meaningful aspect of
the given problem. For this reason it is one of the primary objects of
the trainer to achieve as determinate a formulation and as rapid a
stabilization of the motor structure as is possible for his pupil, but
this does not in any way contradict the position maintained above as to
the correct definition of practice.

forces, velocities, etc., of each limitingly small (more exactly, threshold value) section of the movement, it is beyond dispute that in the subordinate sections of the effector complex there exists a corresponding version of Sw broken up into details in this way. It must be observed that the impingement of each current proprioception (in the broad or in the functional sense of the expression) upon successive momentary directing values of Sw provides at least three different types of information, all equally important for control. Firstly, one or another degree of discrepancy between Iw and Sw (Δw) determines, on passage through the ring system, the necessary correctional impulses; this part of the process will be more thoroughly studied in discussions of the "comparator element" (No. 4 in our list). Secondly, the information which is provided by the receptors as to the particular point of succession attained by the realization of the motor act incorporates the excitatory impulse for the transfer or switching of Sw to the next micro-element of the program in the train; this aspect of function is mainly reminiscent of what Anokhin (4, 5) has termed sanctional afferentation. There is, finally, a third side to the process of reception - apparently one of those phenomena which may be adapted to perceptual models only with extreme difficulty. In every act of movement related to the overcoming of independent and variable external forces the organism continually encounters complications which are irregular, and in most cases unpredictable, which disrupt the course of the movement from paths which are set up in advance by programs. It is impossible, or at least extremely difficult, to master these by means of correctional impulses integrated with the initial program of the movement, whatever this may be. In these cases the receptor information acts as the stimulus for the adaptive restructuring of the program itself "in progress". These may range from minor purely technical alterations in the trajectories of the movement to other adjacent paths, to qualitative reorganizations of programs which involve changes in the very nomenclature of successive elements and stages of the motor act, and eventually amount to the adoption of new strategies of solution. Such terminations and reconstructions of programs as a result of receptor information occur much more often than one would expect, because they often involve only the lower levels of co-ordination and do not draw on the assistance of conscious attention (anyone who has walked, if only once in his life, on a surface that is not as level as a parquet floor will agree with this).

In the monograph on the structure of movements (23) it has been

thoroughly demonstrated how numerous are the forms and ranges of
correctional processes which, in the organization and mastery of a motor act,
may be found to be distributed between interacting background levels of co-
ordinational control. As was said in this book, what we describe as the
automatization of a motor act is the constantly maintained transmission of
numerous technical (background) corrections to the lower co-ordinational
systems, the sensory syntheses of which are most adequately organized for
corrections of the given type and quality. The general law, to which we
know of practically no exception, that all component processes in control
corrections disappear from the field of consciousness, besides being
related to the guiding level connected to the very sense of the motor task,
also provides us with evidence of the apportionment of correction in terms
of levels which we call automatization. It is useful to emphasize at this
point that in higher organisms (and in man in particular) there exists a
rich and multisided sensorily equipped hierarchical system of co-ordinational
levels involved in circular control both for the realization and for the
momentary meaningful restructuring of various motor programs. This is clearly
a consequence of the enormous number of degrees of freedom of the motor
apparatus referred to earlier (which can only be controlled by a system as
complex as we find here). This is also the underlying biological mechanism
which permitted organisms having such a powerful central apparatus for
motor control to develop their organs of movement during phylogenesis without
being limited by the number of kinematic and dynamic degrees of freedom
involved.

We must now turn to element 4 of the scheme given in Fig. 31. This
element - the comparator device (as we have conditionally termed it) - is
simultaneously a most interesting and puzzling physiological object,
although the time is already quite ripe to begin its systematical
investigation.

The ring principle of regulation is necessary in any mechanism which
undertakes a comparison of the current values of Iw and Sw, just as it is
in all artificially constructed S.S. Some such systems transmit an
estimate of their mutual discrepancy (Δw) to the subsequent stages of the
regulating systems. This (Δw) is basic to the process of transmission of
effector correctional impulses to the periphery. If there were no such
functional system in the brain it would be impossible, acting on the basis
of the Iw receptions alone, to provide for any sort of independently acting
correction. Here we at once encounter a completely distinct process, by

means of which we compare and perceive not differences between two
simultaneous or successive receptions, (as, for example, in the case of
measurements of the thresholds of differentiation for any given receptor),
but between *current perceptions*, and the representation, in some form or
other, of the *internally controlled element* in the nervous system (we do
not yet precisely know whether this is a representation, an engram, etc.).
The value of Δw is obtained as a result of this comparison. Because of this
process we may discuss a separate threshold, the comparison threshold, as
we may term it; in the most elementary cases this threshold is obvious, and
easily accessible to measurement. So, for example, we have the threshold
of the visual-vestibular correctional reaction at the beginning of the tilt
of a bicycle from the vertical; the threshold which characterizes the
beginning of the corrective movement of a pencil on a deviation from an
imaginary straight line which has to be drawn between two points on a sheet
of paper; the threshold for the control of the voice which may be obtained
from the voice oscillograms of students learning to sing and attempting to
hold the voice to a note of determined frequency, etc. More interesting and
typical features of the process under discussion wil be given below.

One of the most important elements of control over the motor processes
is the reception of currently occurring variations in Iw for *velocity*. The
tachometry of artificial S.S. may be carried out on various principles which,
however, always make use of some physical value directly measured by a
particular apparatus, and directly related to velocity. (As an example we
have the amount of friction on an armature of a spring controlled by the
intensity of a magnetic field, etc.). It is essential for our purpose to
recognize that receptors which are directly and immediately sensitive to
changes in velocity do not exist in the organisms which we are considering.
This problem, however, is solved in the central nervous system in some
quite special manner, and clearly either by the same sort of comparator
mechanism, or by an extremely close homolog to it, the reception of the
momentary position of a moving organ being compared *with the trace* of the
same reception of the momentary position at a preceding interval of time
Δt. The value of Δt may be estimated (for the purposes of an orientational
approach) as being of the order of 0.07-0.12 sec, as I shall try to
demonstrate below.

If we consider the course of synthetic receptor processes of the most
various types, then the phenomenon of *fresh traces* (as we have conditionally
termed it), to which we have referred above, appears to be remarkably

universal and of fundamental significance. In the visual perception of
movements it would be impossible to perceive *not only the velocity but also*
the direction of a given movement if the process of perception were not
based on ceaseless *comparison* of current receptions with the fresh traces of
immediately preceding ones. When we perceive a melody or a word aurally, we
do not merely register the separate successive elements – the sounds – but
also the time course of a melodic line, or the time picture of the phonemes
together with their tempo. We can discriminate qualitatively between rising
and falling sequences of tones, between the phoneme *Va* and the phoneme *Av*,
etc. If I perceive, with my eyes closed, that a line is being traced with
a pointer on my skin, I do not perceive merely the location, but also the
direction of succession and the *velocity* of the movement of the pointer as
two qualitatively distinct *properties*. These are perceived as being in some
way primary. They appear to be primary or primitive to such an extent that
they are in all respects qualitatively similar to raw sensations. These
traces retain their active form only for a minute fraction of a second, so
that fresh traces are sharply distinct from the usual phenomena of *memory*
– which is the means of long term retention of centrally coded phenomena.

   In a large number of cases the control of a movement requires the
continuous perception not only of current *values* of this difference (Δw)
but also of the *velocities* with which these differences increase or diminish.
As Wagner (75) has correctly observed, often (for example in cases of small
but rapidly increasing values of Iw), control is exercised precisely by
means of perception of the velocity of change of Δw, because it is useful
to react sensitively to the very beginning of the development of an adverse
deviation even earlier than the absolute threshold value of this deviation
may be recognized and responded to. The indisputable fact that our sensory
synthesis can also respond differentially to various rates of change of Δw
is evidence that in the process of comparison under discussion the phenomenon
of fresh traces must operate. The process of comparison is not, in this case,
that of Iw and Sw, but of the fresh trace of their difference (Δw) occurring
a fraction of a second earlier in time with a current value perceived at a
given moment. In mathematical terms this is the process of the perception of
the derivative $d(\Delta w)/dt$.

   There is no doubt that the processes of perception of velocities and
directions, the processes of comparison of Iw and Δw with their fresh traces
for all dimensions of reception, etc., cannot in fact proceed *continuously*,
but most rather do so in terms of differential intervals of time dt, there

being some lower limit to the interval of time Δt which we may consequently regard as a threshold value. At the basis of these processes we find values of a particular type of thresholds, thresholds for *time*, which are clearly in very close physiological relationship both to the thresholds characterizing the speed of the psychomotor reaction and to physiological parameters such as lability, refractoriness, constants of adaptation, etc., which are clearly in need of immediate and intensive investigation. There is no doubt that psychologists specializing in the organs of sensation will already be in a position to criticize and to add material which is important to the argument in favour of the idea of fresh traces given above for the elucidation of the present problems[*].

I should like to put forward the following notes towards a working hypothesis. In the thirties of the present century, M.N. Livanov had already found that the amplitudes of the peaks of the β waves on electro-encephalograms vary considerably in magnitude from the peaks and troughs of the α waves, appearing, as it were, to be modulated by the latter. This fact may be taken as evidence of some sort of periodicity in the variations of excitability of the *cortical elements observed in the α rhythm*. Gray-Walter (47) noted that the lower threshold limit for the fusion frequency for flashes, cinema pictures, etc., in the ocular apparatus closely coincides with the frequency of the α rhythm, and even varies in parallel to the latter in individuals. It also does not seem to be a coincidence that the lower limit of the fusion frequency for hearing at which the specific sensory properties of a *sound* can be discriminated lies at about the same range of frequencies. There are, moreover, some unpublished orientational investigations by V.S. Gurfinkel on holding and movement in the unloaded hand (cf., also, (46)) and also a series of cyclogrametric observations by L.B. Chkhaidze on the rhythms of the acceleration impulses in the foot of a cyclist[**]. In both these cases the alternation of correctional impulses

---

[*] In particular there arises the natural problem of the relationship which the mechanism of fresh traces bears to psychological mechanisms in the more general problems of engrammatization and of memory. Recent data suggest with ever increasing persuasiveness the paramount importance of the complex and many-sided nature of the biological processes organizing the reception and transmission of information. Further investigation shows how distinct are the phenomena of fresh traces from other earlier investigated forms of the function of retention of impressions, and of what the anatomic-physiological substrates of such impressions, etc., may be.

[**] I must express my debt to V.S. Gurfinkel and L.V. Chkhaidze for these personal communications.

is in complete mutual synchrony, and falls within the limits of the same
frequency band as the α rhythm, i.e. 8-14 c/s. Is there no reason to suppose
that this frequency marks the appearance of rhythmic oscillations in the
excitability of all, or of the main alements of the reflex S.S. of our
motor apparatus, in which a mutual synchronization through rhythm is
doubtless necessary? We might also see in this light the ordering of the
sensory and co-ordinational processes in terms of threshold values of the
intervals of time Δt separating the moments of greatest refractoriness from
the moments of maximal lability during which a momentary impression Iw is
held in the form of a fresh trace until a subsequent rise of excitability.
The distribution of the α rhythm over the entire surface of the cortex, its
particular dominance in the receptor zones, and their synchronism with it
over the whole of this range may also be taken as evidence in favour of this
hypothesis. We may then describe the α rhythm as the pacemaker mechanism
which gives to co-ordinational processes their determinate time parameter
- their type of Sw of time, and intervals of Δt - as a regulating internal
physiological pendulum appearing in these processes, such as that which
British physiologists describe as a pacemaker. It must naturally be
emphasized that whether this pacemaker is related to the α rhythm or not it
has great physiological importance. There is an urgent need for quantitative
investigation and for the determination of its relationships with such
psychophysiological indicators as simple reaction time, the personal equation,
etc.

It remains for me breifly to describe one more characteristic of the
co-ordinational process which is closely related to the phenomenon of fresh
traces and to the parameter Δt.

Situations are encountered in the processes of motor control in which
great, sometimes decisive, importance attaches to correction of an advance
or anticipatory character. This is particularly the case where, during the
course of any given segment of a movement, retrospective control becomes
practically impossible. There is a whole class of such motor acts (so-called
ballistic movements) whose existence is only made possible by means of this
type of anticipation: throwing at a target (throwing stones, spears, all
possible ball games, etc.) jumping across a ditch or a high obstacle, a
sweeping blow with a heavy hammer, etc. We must also note the existence of
analogous anticipation in a number of similar motor acts, where it
necessarily co-exists with corrections of a usual type; these are *movements
which forestall others*, similar to those made by hounds following a wild

animal and making rushes which are directed, not towards the momentarily
visibly position of the quarry, but across, towards an anticipated or extrapolated point of intersection with its trajectory. There are many examples
of this sort of thing - cathing a moving object with one's hand, passing a
ball to a running team-mate, interposing a racket across the path of a
moving ball or spheroid as in the game of table-tennis, and many others.
Mittelstaedt (58) proposes that these two types of correction be distinguished
from each other, and that they should be regarded as two equally important
classes which he terms *Regelung* and *Steuerung*. Another category is more
important in the present context.

The existence of correction of the anticipatory type, and the fact that
we encounter it much more frequently than appears at first sight, directs
our attention to the importance of anticipation in realizing any type of
goal-directed motor act. Programming, as has been demonstrated above, is
determined by the apprehension of motor problems as they arise, and
represents an anticipation both of the result which is determined by its
solution, and of such motor techniques as are necessary for its attainment
(the latter if only in the most general terms). Many psychophysiological
processes are entirely based on a similar "sight into the future". These
have been termed "sets" and only in recent years has the term come to attain
its full significance. Just as an analysis of the operation of the "setting
or commanding complex" 3 reveals an hierarchical range (of levels of operation)
beginning with the organization of the program of the motor act as a whole,
and extending down to the level of the most detailed "micro-Sw" from moment
to moment, or from Δt to Δt, we cannot now avoid the conclusion that in
order to guarantee the completion of the micro-elements of the program and
to undertake the direction of the motor process the successively emitted
Sw must always *precede the actual movements*, preceding them if only by the
threshold interval of time Δt. This is, however, enough to ensure that the
equilibrium destroyed in this way (between the attained Iw and the future
intended Sw) guarantees the dynamics of striving towards the end result.
So, speaking semi-figuratively, the current micro-regulation of movements
shuttles constantly between the present moment t and the limits of the
interval from $t - \Delta t$ ("fresh traces") to $t + \Delta t$ (the anticipatory Sw).

I have brought together in these pages a number of problems related to
the regulation of the life activity of the higher organisms, prompted by
the analysis of motor acts. In the following chapter, I shall consider
critically such current or imminent problems as the function of the coding

organs, the interdependence between discrete and wave-like processes in
the central nervous system, and, finally, some new prospects in the
direction of the application of mathematics to the physiology of the
activity of the nervous system.

REFERENCES

4. Anokhin, P.K. Particular features of the afferent apparatus of conditioned reflexes. Journal Questions of Psychology, No. 6 (in Russian), 1955.

5. Anokhin, P.K. The role of the orientation and search reaction in the formation of a conditioned reflex. Orientation Reflex (in Russian), 1958.

9. Bernstein, N.A. A biomechanical norm for the stroke. Research of the Central Institute of Labour, Moscow 1, 2 (in Russian), 1924.

14. Bernstein, N.A. & Popova, T.S. Untersuchung der Biodynamik des Klavieranschlags. Arbeitsphysiologie, 1929, 1, 5.

15. Bernstein, N.A. Clinical Ways of Modern Biomechanics. Collection of papers of the Institute for Medical Improvement, Kazan, 1929.

21. Bernstein, N.A. et al. Studies of the Biodynamics of Walking, Running and Jumping (in Russian), Moscow, 1940.

23. Bernstein, N.A. On the Construction of Movements. Monograph (in Russian), Moscow, 1947.

29. Bernstein, N.A. Current problems in the theoretical physiology of activity. Problems of Cybernetics, 1961, 6.

46. Gelfand, I.M. & Tsetlin, M.L. The principal of non-local search in systems of automatic optimization, Report of the Academy of Sciences of the U.S.S.R., 1961, 137 (in Russian).

47. Gray-Walter, W. The living brain. London: Duckworth, 1953.

58. Mittelstaedt, H. Regelung und Steuerung bei der Orientierung der Lebewesen. Regelungstechnik, 1954, 2.

65. Salzgeber, O.A. Biodynamics of the locomotion of amputation. Works of the Central Institute of Prostheses, 1948, 1, (in Russian).

75. Wagner, R. Probleme und Beispiele biologischer Regelung. Stuttgart: Thieme, 1954.

77. Wiener, N. Cybernetics, or control and communication in the animal and the machine. New York: Wiley, 1948.

CHAPTER IVα

AN ECOLOGICAL APPROACH TO PERCEPTION AND ACTION

M.T. Turvey, P.N. Kugler

1.0 INTRODUCTION

In his chapter on "Some emergent problems of the regulation of motor acts" Bernstein identifies four major problems:

(1) If perceiving were not a matter of being accurately aware of the objective facts of the environment and of one's actions, then the reliable control of activity would not be possible. However, the orthodox theory of receptor processes implies an arbitrary relation between these processes and the circumstances - environment and action - to which they nominally refer. This theory is inadequate to explain the everyday achievements of animal activity. What is needed is a theory that accounts for how perceiving keeps an animal in contact with the reality that bears on the successful conduct of its actions.

(2) Patently, animal activity is an instance of self-regulation, but what kind of self-regulation? Is it of the type conventionally expressed by self-regulating artifacts or do the regularities of animal activity follow from principles that are, as yet, unique to natural systems?

(3) Neither the geometry nor the kinematics of movement can serve, in the general case, as the determinant of the composition of an act. An action is what it is by virtue of its intention, that is, the motor problem (a needed change in the relation of the animal and its environment) toward which the action is directed as a solution. How are we to understand an intention as (a) the principle guiding the overall formation of an act and (b) the influence dominating the selection of its details?

(4) Clearly the control of activity is more than a retrospective matter. In the most general of cases, control must be prospective. For example, in basketball, one exerts forces against the ground of a specific magnitude so as to cause the hands to be at a specific height at a specific time to intercept a thrown ball. What is the basis of this anticipatory capability

that makes possible the realization of any goal-directed activity?

Problems (1) and (4) are discussed in Section 2.0 and problems (2) and (3) are discussed in Section 3.0.

2.0 ON THE OBJECTIVITY AND ACCURACY OF PERCEIVING

For any animal, activity takes place with respect to surfaces. For terrestrial animals, the most important surface is the ground. The ground is not even. Neither is it geometrically and materially uniform from place to place. There are gradual and sharp changes in the ground level. There are cracks and gaps. Liquid and solid areas are interspersed. Further, the ground surface is cluttered with closed, substantial surfaces. Some of these are attached, others are movable and some move under their own power. The clutter varies greatly in size. But for any terrestrial animal there are always closed, substantial surfaces both smaller and larger than its size. Some of the ground's clutter are barriers to locomotion but invariably there are gaps large enough to permit passage and barriers small enough to be hurdled or climbed. Locomoting from place to place, finding paths through the clutter, is necessary given the uneven distribution of the resources on which the persistence of the animal depends.

As Bernstein remarks, the meaningful problems that activity solves arise out of the layout of surfaces surrounding the animal, the environment. A few such meaningful problems are depicted in Figure 1. Awareness of the "problems" and awareness of the activities that do or do not solve them is the role of perceiving. It is obvious to Bernstein that perceiving (both the layout of surfaces and activities with respect to the layout) must be "objective" and "accurate". If perceiving fell short of these requirements - if it were, on the contrary, "subjective" and "inaccurate" - then meaningful, adaptive activity would not be possible. Bernstein writes (p.346): "We may consider the formulation of the motor problem, and the perception of the object in the external world with which it is concerned as having their necessary prerequisites in maximally full and objective perception both of the object and of each successive phase and detail of the corresponding movement which is directed towards the solution of the particular problem". What Bernstein says seems straightforward enough: perceiving must keep an animal in contact with its surroundings and with its behavior. It will be argued, however,

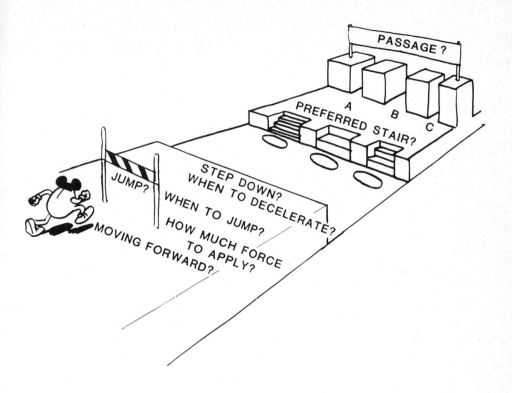

Fig. 1. A small sample of the meaningful problems that the surrounding
layout of surfaces poses for a locomoting animal.

that a number of fairly radical steps have to be taken to insure that the
theory of perception that we develop as scientists can live up to the natural
demands placed on perception by normal activity in cluttered surroundings.

Clearly, Bernstein believes that the role of "afferentation" in the
guidance of activity is the significant role, even though afferentation as a
trigger of reflexes has a better scientific pedigree and is better understood
by physiologists. The triggering role of afference assumed prominence because
of the tendency to focus research on artificial movements - discrete responses
made to momentary and punctate stimuli - rather than on activities resolving

environmentally defined problems. Bernstein considered this triggering role
of afference, developed as it was in the context of the reflex arc, to be
overvalued and pointed out two unwelcome consequences of this overvaluation.

First, it established a bias to equate receptor processes in general
with signals that release or inhibit reactions. Bernstein reminds us that
this equation leads to the unacceptable interpretation of the receptor
processes accompanying linguistic events as just triggers - the so-called
second-signalling system. Closer to the present concerns, he points out
that the emphasis on the afferent triggering of reactions obscured the fact
that afference modulates ongoing movements. Bernstein saw a distinction
between the traditional physiology of reaction and the physiology he wished
to promote - a physiology of activity (Gelfand, Gurfinkel, Fomin & Tsetlin,
1971; Reed, 1982a). In this respect (and others) he was of kindred spirit
with Gibson (1966, 1979, 1982) in rejecting the classical view of action as
(merely) responses triggered by signals emanating from either outside the
body or inside the brain. However, it should be noted that Bernstein labored
under a major terminological manifestation of the classical view, namely,
the correspondencies of the terms "sensory" and "afferent", "motor" and
"efferent". This was unfortunate given that he rejected the conceptual
identity that these correspondences implied.

As Gibson (1966, 1979, 1982) and Reed (1982a) have ably argued, the
psychological concepts of sensory and motor cannot be equated, respectively,
with the anatomical structures termed afferent and efferent. The anatomical
definition of sensory system (as receptor elements, cortex, and the afferent
pathways that mediate them) fails to accommodate the adjusting, optimizing
steering and symmetricalizing of sense organs - that is, their purposive
activity (Gibson, 1966). Bernstein recognized this inadequacy. In referring
to the systematic searching by sense organs, he wrote (p.346): "This is an
entirely active process, and the effector side of the organism is here
employed in a manner completely analogous to that which is later explained
to underlie afferentation in the control of movements". The anatomical
definition of motor system (as cortex, motoneurons, and the efferent pathways
that mediate them) fails to accommodate the dynamic responsiveness of effector
organs to changes in the external force field brought about by changes in
the orientation of effectors to the surround and to the body - that is, their
contextual sensitivity (Turvey, Shaw & Mace, 1978). More than anybody before
him, Bernstein sought to substitute the analysis of action in terms of
efferent commands from cortex to motoneurons by an analysis of action as the

selective use of information about the environment and about one's movements
to selectively modulate one's movements with respect to the environment
(cf. Gibson, 1979).

Second, the tradition of regarding afferents as triggering signals
enforced, in Bernstein's view, a general attitude toward afference as
arbitrarily related to the environmental conditions that cause it. All that
is required for the successful initiation of a reflex is afferentation that
is constant and recognizable by the effector apparatus. The proximal cause
of a reaction need bear no necessary relation to the distal cause. As
Bernstein sees it, this idea of an arbitrary connection between afferent
states of affairs and environmental states of affairs is pernicious. If the
afferent (or sensory) codes are arbitrary (as is claimed by Müller's Doctrine
of Specific Nerve Energies and its successors) and if what the animal
perceives is based on these codes, then what is there to guarantee that the
animal's perception is objective and accurate? The depth of Bernstein's concern
is expressed in this quotation (p. 359): "...from the fact that it is clearly
possible to reconcile the perfect operation of reflex functions with the
complete arbitrariness of their sensory codes it is very easy to slide from
the position of the recognition of the symbolic nature of all reception in
general, and of the conditionality of the picture of the world in the brain
and the psyche, to the concept of unknowability of objective reality and
similar idealistic conceptions..."

2.1 THE CARTESIAN PROGRAM

The orthodox and very popular representational/computational approach
to mind (see Chomsky, 1980; Fodor, 1975; Pylyshyn, 1980) is consistent with
the arbitrary coding theme that Bernstein believes (incorrectly, as we will
claim below) to be rooted in the reflex philosophy and methodology. The
representational/computational view abides by a "formality condition" - the
explicit understanding that mental operations are formal, symbol manipulations
performed on formal, symbol structures (Fodor, 1980). To a computer (and, by
analogy, to a brain) it is immaterial whether its internal codes refer to
this or that fact; how the signals are formatted and how they relate
consistently among themselves by rule are what matters, not their meaningful
content. We raise the spectre of the formality condition for two reasons.
One reason is that Bernstein, despite his dislike of this condition in the

guise that was familiar to him, invokes a mechanism for the control of
activity that is continuous with the representational/computational thesis
and, therefore, with the formality condition. Bernstein suggests that an
ordered sequence of set points - representations of required values - governs
the flow of afference and efference within the acting animal. The ordered
sequence is a program prescribing the general form of the activity; it is a
representation of the activity for the effector organs (cf. Cummins, 1977;
Shaw, Turvey & Mace, 1982).

The other reason is that the formality condition is clearly tied to
the historical tradition that began with the Cartesian Doctrine of Corporeal
Ideas. It is this tradition that encourages the arbitrary coding interpretation
of afference, not the reflex arc methodology which is itself a restatement
of the Cartesian doctrine (Reed, 1982b). Descartes' doctrine, stated very
generally, is that all awarenesses are awarenesses of states of the body or,
as we would be more prone to say today, states of the brain. In contemporary
thought, it is said that direct access to environmental and behavioral states
of affairs is limited to the physical (or bodily) outputs of transducers
which are linked not to the environmental and behavioral states but to the
basic energy variables (e.g., intensity and wavelengths of light) (e.g.,
Boynton, 1975; Fodor & Pylyshyn, 1981). The question that this
doctrine poses has been at the base of almost all theories in psychology,
viz.: How can the environment be known objectively and accurately and acted
upon successfully when the ideas one has about such things are based on
awarenesses merely of brain states? Descartes had an answer to the subsidiary
question of how primary objective qualities might be derived from secondary
subjective qualities and it has been a persistent ingredient in almost all
subsequent theorizing. He assumed an act of understanding that passed
judgment on what environmental things might have caused the brain state; in
his best known example, he assumed a rule-governed, quasi-mathematical process
of inference from the states of the eye muscles and the visual nerves to the
distance of an environmental object.

We can now focus sharply on the full implications of Bernstein's innocent
claim that the coordination of an animal and its environment must be based on
objective and accurate facts. Because of the pervasiveness of the Cartesian
doctrine in physiology, psychology and cognitive science (see Reed, 1982b;
Shaw, Turvey & Mace, 1982), it is generally accepted that an animal's
awareness of its activities and of the surface layout to which they refer is
not direct but mediated. Descartes had proposed rules, inferences and judgments

to get to these objective facts of activity and environment from the directly
given, subjective brain states. To Descartes' list of cognitive or epistemic
mediators, later theorists have added representations, schemas, programs,
models, organizing principles, meanings, concepts and the like. Whether
dressed in its traditional or modern garb, the Cartesian program for
explaining how felicitous activity is achieved in a cluttered environment
faces a profound predicament. There is nothing in this explanation to
guarantee that the proposed inferential operations performed on the brain
states will yield conclusions that are objective and accurate rather than
fatuous. In responding to John Locke's version of the Cartesian program,
Berkeley thought a guarantee was unwarranted and emphasized the phenomenalism
(that there are only phenomenal objects such as ideas) implicit in the
Cartesian program. Hume thought a guarantee was unlikely to be forthcoming
and emphasized the skepticism (that there may well be an environment and
activities oriented to it, but no one can be sure of their existence) implicit
in the Cartesian program. It is to thoughts such as those expressed by
Berkeley and Hume that Bernstein refers when he remarks on "...the concept of
unknowability of objective reality and similar idealistic conceptions..."
Bernstein (p. 353) goes on to say (too cavalierly, in our opinion) that such
thoughts "...have been disproved by authentic science long ago." As
scientists committed to an objective reality, we must claim that it is
knowable by animals, more or less. However, a scientific account of perception
that is consistent with this realist posture has been thwarted, in our view,
by the almost universal acceptance of the Cartesian program. As long as the
Cartesian program is the accepted strategy for explaining the coordination
of an animal and its environment - as long as the awareness of surface layout
and action is claimed to be cognitively mediated - then the thoughts of
Berkeley and Hume cannot be dismissed cavalierly and the predicament
identified above remains firmly entrenched in psychological and physiological
theory.

Accurate, objective conclusions might be assured if the inferential
operations (and the various cognitive entities such as representations, etc.)
were tightly constrained by reality. But the Cartesian program denies an
animal direct contact with reality; to reiterate, only brain states are
directly contactable. The problem for the Cartesian program, therefore, is
how to get the reality that bears on the felicitous control of activity into
the mind or nervous system of the animal. There are several responses to
this problem. The most popular response is that a model of reality is

constructed by a process of justifying inferences in the course of either
evolution or ontogeny, or both (Bernstein advances a solution of this type).
We will briefly summarize some of the reasons that render this response
(scientifically) unacceptable (see Shaw, Turvey & Mace, 1982; Turvey, Shaw,
Reed & Mace, 1981, for a fuller discussion).

All forms of non-demonstrative inference proposed by inductive
logicians - enumerative inference, eliminative inference, and abductive
inference - can be expressed as a confirmatory relation between evidence
and hypothesis. The conditions of adequacy for confirmation vary among the
forms of inference (see Smokler, 1968) but this is immaterial to the points
we wish to make, viz., that the very notion of inference requires (1) the
ability to project relevant hypotheses and (2) the availability of predicates
in which to frame evidence statements and hypotheses. To clarify, the notion
of a basic set of hypotheses is explicit in eliminative and abductive inference
and implied in enumerative inference. For example, one version of abduction
(Hanson, 1958, p. 72) goes as follows:

> Some surprising phenomenon P is observed.
>
> P would be explicable as a matter of course if H were true.
>
> Hence, there is reason to think that H is true.

If a model of reality were derived from inference, then it would have to be
supposed that appropriate hypotheses - hypotheses that were generalizations
about environmental states of affairs - were already at the disposal of the
animal. What is their origin? Surely the answer cannot be "inference" for
that would precipitate a vicious regress. But if the answer is not "inference"
then the only option for the Cartesian program is that the origin of the
hypotheses is both extra-physical and extra-conceptual. These are mutually
exclusive categories.

The same conclusion follows from the point about the availability of
two kinds of predicates, those for framing evidence statements and those for
framing hypotheses. The predicates in an evidence statement stand for energy
variables and, by argument, have their origin in physical processes. But for
any form of inference there must be available, concurrently, predicates in
which to couch hypotheses and these must be predicates that stand for
environmental properties (such as an obstacle to locomotion). The origin of
these environment-referential predicates cannot be inferential otherwise the
argument is regressive; and it cannot be physical (law-based) because that
option is denied the Cartesian program, by definition.

The general conclusion to be drawn is that a reliance on inference takes

out a loan of intelligence that science can never repay: The Cartesian
program is not a scientifically tractable program and, a fortiori, is a
program for perception that science would be ill-advised to pursue.

2.2　GIBSON'S ECOLOGICAL PROGRAM

We believe that the Cartesian program must be abandoned if a scientifically
acceptable account is to be provided of the perceptual objectivity that
Bernstein regards as the sine qua non of action. To ease the break with
tradition, it may help to remember that Descartes built his perceptual theory
around thought, not action. Gibson's (1979) is an approach to perceiving
that takes the control of activity as its central concern. In this approach
the Cartesian doctrine of corporeal ideas is rejected together with the many
perplexities that it entails. Rather than founding perceptual theory on brain
states that are related tenuously to the environments and activities of
animals, Gibson founds perceptual theory on structured energy distributions
that are lawfully related to the environments and actions of animals. Rather
than asking how accurate objective inferences from brain states to the facts
of environments and actions are made, Gibson asks how information specific
to the facts of environments and actions is detected. Rather than assuming
that the conventional variables of physics provide the only legitimate basis
for describing the environment, Gibson advances the idea that the environment
can be legitimately described in terms that are referential of the activity
capabilities of animals.

It will not be possible for us to do complete justice to Gibson's
perceptual theory in these pages (see Gibson, 1979; Michaels & Carello, 1981;
Reed & Jones, 1982; Turvey et al., 1981; Turvey & Carello, 1981). We will
restrict ourselves, therefore, to those Gibsonian concepts that we take to
be most central to the control of activity - the concepts of information and
affordance. And we will restrict ourselves to the perceptual system of
greatest relevance - the visual perceptual system.

Information is optical structure generated in a lawful way by
environmental structure (for example, surface layout) and by the movements
of the animal, both the movements of its body parts relative to its body and
the movements of its body as a unit relative to the environment. This
optical structure does not resemble the sources that generate it, but is
specific to those sources in the sense that it is nomically (lawfully)
dependent on them. The claim is that there are laws at the ecological scale

that relate optical structure to properties of the environment and action (Gibson, 1979; Turvey et al., 1981).

This treatment of information and the notion of ecological laws rests on an optical analysis that departs from the classical geometric ray optics and the more contemporary physical optics. Though some have argued to the contrary (e.g., Boynton, 1975; Johansson, 1970), neither of these analyses is sufficient to capture the richness of light's structure subsequent to multiple reflections from surfaces of varying inclination and substance and undergoing various types of change. Gibson's push has been for a theory of optics that can do justice to ambient light as a basis for the control of activity. Given that activity is at the ecological scale of animals and their environments, Gibson termed the sought-after optical theory ecological optics. The limitations of conventional optical analyses recognized by Gibson (1961, 1979) are echoed by illumination engineers (e.g., Gershun, 1939; Moon, 1961; Moon & Spencer, 1981) whose goals are much more modest than Gibson's. In the subsection that follows we consider the activity-relevant questions raised by Figure 1 in terms of Gibson's ecological optics.

2.2.1 HOW DOES THE ANIMAL KNOW THAT IT IS MOVING FORWARD?

Forward rectilinear motion of a point of observation relative to the surroundings will lawfully generate an expanding optical flow pattern globally defined over the entire optic array to the point of observation. (A locally defined expansion pattern, kinematically discontinuous at its borders with the optical structure in the large, would be lawfully determined by a part of the surround moving relative to the point of observation. In natural circumstances there can be no ambiguity, contrary to the standard claim (von Holst & Mittelstaedt, 1950) about what is moving – the animal or part of its environment (Turvey, 1979). As noted above, the lawfulness of optical structure at the ecological scale is the basis for its functioning as information for the control of activity: If A lawfully generates B, then B specifies A. Lishman and Lee (1973) have shown that humans walking voluntarily forward will report that they are walking backwards when exposed to the global optical transformation that is lawfully generated by backward locomotion (and which, therefore, specifies that the walker is moving backward). Further, when flying insects are exposed to global optical transformations that are the lawful consequences of forces that produce rotation, vertical displacement, and yaw, they respond with the appropriate counteracting forces (Srinivasan, 1977); Turvey & Remez, 1979).

2.2.2 <u>HOW DOES THE ANIMAL KNOW FROM WHERE TO JUMP (TO ACCOMMODATE AN</u>
<u>UPCOMING BARRIER) AND HOW DOES IT KNOW WHETHER ITS DECELERATION IS</u>
<u>ADEQUATE (TO ACCOMMODATE ITS LOCOMOTION TO AN UPCOMING BRINK IN THE</u>
<u>GROUND)</u>?

The answers to both of these questions depend, in the Gibsonian
perspective, on information about the imminence of contact (with barrier or
brink). Lee (1974, 1976, 1980) and others (e.g., Koenderink & Van Doorn,
1981) have identified an optical variable, symbolized as $T(t)$ by Lee (1976),
that is equal to the inverse of the rate of dilation of a bounded region of
optical structure. $T(t)$ is lawfully generated by the approach at constant
velocity of a point of observation to a substantial surface in the frontal
plane, or vice versa; it specifies the time at which the point of observation
will make contact with the surface.

Obviously, the existence of an optical variable specifying time-to-
contact bears directly on the question posed by Bernstein (Question (4)
above) of how control can be prospective. Any answer to the question of
prospective control is constrained by the requirements that (1) causes
precede effects and (2) causes be actual rather than possible states of
affairs. An event at a later time cannot cause an action at an earlier time
and only actual events can be causal. In the Cartesian program, the bases
of prospective control are representations; actual mental states existing
in the present (rather than future, possible states of the animal-environment
system) are the causes of activity. The logical format of these representations
in the case of controlled collisions must be that of a counter-factual,
roughly of the form "if I don't change what I am doing and the conditions
continue to be as they are, then X is likely to occur". The basis of
prospective control in the Gibsonian program is exemplified by the time-to-
contact variable, viz., <u>there is information in the present optical structure</u>
(e.g., the value of $T(t)$ at t_i) <u>specific to what will occur if the present</u>
<u>conditions continue</u> (e.g., collision at time t_j). To draw the contrast
sharply, in the Gibsonian program the basis for prospective control is
sought in laws at the ecological scale (that relate present optical
properties to upcoming properties of the animal-environment system); in the
Cartesian program the basis is sought in inferential processes (that relate
the semantically neutral outputs of transducers to a counter-factual
representation). Reiterating the arguments raised above, the Cartesian
solution to the problem of prospective control begs the interesting

questions; for example, how does the animal construct just that counter-
factual representation that is right for the current situation?

    Let us look at an example of the use of the time-to-contact variable.
The gannet, a large seabird that feeds on fish, hovers about thirty meters
above the water. On sighting a prey, it dives down first with its wings
partly spread for steering and then with its wings folded so that it enters
the water vigorously but cleanly. It may hit the water at speeds approaching
25 ms^{-1} (or 55 miles h^{-1}). The action problem for the gannet is to retract
its wings soon enough to avoid fracturing them but not so soon as to hinder
the accuracy of its dive. Given that the gannet dives from varying heights,
at varying initial speeds, and in varying wind conditions, how does it
properly control its entry? Lee (1980) and Lee and Reddish (1981) have
concluded that wing retraction is initiated when the time-to-contact
variable reaches a certain margin value. (Because the animal is accelerating
in the dive, the same margin value of $T(t)$ will be associated with different
actual times-to-contact. The birds are seen to fold their wings a longer
time before contact the higher the starting point of the dive).

    There is reason to believe that the time-to-contact variable is the
basis of prospective control in a number of related circumstances. Data on
the kinematics of catching a ball (Sharp & Whiting, 1974, 1975), hitting a
baseball (Hubbard & Seng, 1954), infants' reaching for a moving object (Van
Hofsten & Lindhagen, 1979; Van Hofsten, 1983), stepping down (Friedman,
Wannstedt & Herman, 1976) and falling on one's hands against an inclined
board (Dietz & Noth, 1978) are amenable to such an analysis (see Fitch,
Tuller & Turvey, 1982; Fitch & Turvey, 1978; Lee, 1980). The last situation
is depicted in Figure 2. The triceps brachii muscles are shown to tense in
preparation for an upcoming collision in which the arms must absorb the
momentum. With the eyes closed, the electromyographic index of the initiation
of muscle tension is tied to the start of falling; with the eyes open and
with different falling distances the index occurs at varying times after the
start of falling but at an approximately constant time prior to contact.

    We should remark that the fact of a simple, single optical property
specifying the imminence of contact has implications for another of
Bernstein's concerns, namely, how an animal can adjust its behavior to the
velocity of things. Bernstein pursues a conventional argument that velocity
is arrived at by a process of comparing the present location of a thing
with the memory trace of an immediately preceding location and dividing the
deduced distance traveled by an internally determined estimate of elapsed

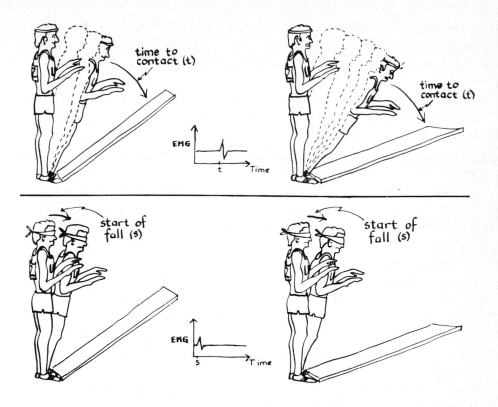

Fig. 2. With the eyes open and with different falling distances the
initiation of tension in the triceps brachii muscles occurs
at varying times after the start of falling but at an
approximately constant time prior to contact (Above). With the
eyes closed initiation of muscle tension is tied to the start
of falling (Below). (From Fitch, H.L., Turvey, M.T. & Tuller,
B. The Bernstein perspective: III. Tuning of coordinative
structures with special reference to perception. In, J.A.S.
Kelso (Ed.), <u>Human motor behavior</u>. Hillsdale, N.J.: Erlbaum,
1982).

time. The inadequacies of this kind of explanation have been discussed in
detail (Gibson, 1979; Turvey, 1977). Here we wish to comment only on the
questionable strategy of analyzing higher-order activity-relevant variables
in terms of the putatively more basic variables of displacement and time.
Inertial guidance systems are based on Newton's laws of inertia and gravity.
These systems detect accelerative forces. They determine velocity and
distance indirectly through the single and double integration, respectively,
of the accelerative forces. In like fashion, adherents to the Gibsonian
program (Lee, 1980; Runeson, 1977; Turvey & Shaw, 1978) argue that the
imminence of collision is not inferred from a preliminary determination of
speed of approach and distance from surface; rather, the basis for an
animal's knowing when a surface will be contacted is the detection of $T(t)$
as such. The point is that to understand how perception controls activity
we must be willing (i) to question the primary reality status of the basic
variables of physics; (ii) to look for variables (observables, quantities)
at the ecological scale that uniquely specify the relation of
animal to environment; and (iii) to consider hard- or soft-molded processes
that detect these ecological variables (rather than knowledge-based
procedures that construct representations of them from conventional physical
variables).

So, how does the animal know from where to leap? The answer, to be
blunt, is that it does not need to know the proper place; rather, it needs
to know the proper time. The former depends on the speed, the latter does
not. Evidently, as anticipated, the successful leaping of a barrier depends
on the time-to-contact variable. It also depends on body-scaled information,
but we will have more to say about that below. And how does the animal know
whether it is braking sufficiently? An animal's deceleration is adequate
if and only if the distance it will take the animal to stop is less than or
equal to its current distance from the brink (Lee, 1980). Adequacy of braking
is specified by whether the rate of change of $T(t)$ equals or exceeds a
critical value (Lee, 1976; 1980). A related observation is that flies begin
to decelerate prior to contact with a surface at a critical value of $T(t)^{-1}$
(Wagner, 1982).

2.2.3 HOW DOES THE ANIMAL KNOW THAT THE BARRIER IS JUMPABLE AND THAT THE BRINK IS A STEP-DOWN PLACE (RATHER THAN A FALLING-OFF PLACE)?

Knowing that something is in the class of jumpable objects and that

some other thing is in the class of step-down places would be treated in the
Cartesian program as the imposition of subjective, meaningful categories on
an objective, meaningless surround. Conventionally, it would be said that
the animal has concepts of such things and debate would focus on how such
mental entities could be established. Careful analysis would reveal that,
given the departure point of the Cartesian program, empirical contributions
to such concepts would have to be secondary to the rational contribution
(Fodor, 1975). In sharp contrast, the Gibsonian program seeks to uncover a
natural, lawful basis for knowing what activity (or activities) a situation
offers. Consider a brink in the surface that happens to be a step-down place
for a given animal rather than a place where it would have to jump down or
climb down or steer away from. To begin with, the property of the brink as
a step-down place for the animal cannot be captured in the scales and
stardard units of physics. These scales and units are intended to be "fully
objective", that is, observer- or user-independent. They are <u>extrinsic</u>
measures, in that the standards on which they are based are divorced from
and external to the situations to which they are applied. To capture a step-
down place for a given animal requires <u>intrinsic</u> measures, those whose
standards are to be found in the situation of animal and brink. In Figure 3

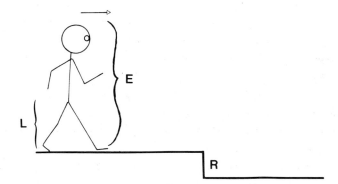

Fig. 3. Approaching a brink of a surface. E is eye height, L is leg
length and R is the surface separation.

the separation of surfaces (R) must somehow be expressed in units of the
animal. Leg length is obviously significant but scaling surface magnitudes
in terms of the unit 'eye-height' is probably a better move (cf. Lee, 1974,
1980). A lawful allometric relation (Huxley, 1932; Gunther,
1975; Rosen, 1968) is to be expected between eye height (E) and leg length
(L): $L = aE^{b}$, where a and b are constants. (Eye height will, of course, vary

with the animal's posture but our intent here is to convey the style of the
analysis rather than its full detail). If the separation of surfaces (R)
at a brink is below some critical number, nE (or is less than or within a
tolerance range nE + S), then the separation is a step-down place; above
this critical number (or range) it is a place that requires some locomotory
strategy other than stepping down. Noting that E is unity, there is a
dimensionless quantity that marks the boundary between the activities
stepping down vs. jumping down, for example - that a brink offers an animal.
Now the question becomes whether or not there is an optical property specific
to this dimensionless quantity.

First, a point of observation moving toward a brink in a surface (where
one surface partially occludes another) will lawfully generate an optical
flow pattern in which there is a discontinuity, viz., a horizontal contour
above which optical structure magnifies and gains and below which optical
structure magnifies but does not gain. The non-gain and gain of structure
are specific, respectively, to the occluding surface currently supporting
the animal and the occluded surface to which it is heading. Second, from
Figure 4 (after Warren, 1982) it can be seen that the separation (R) of
the occluding and occluded surfaces can be expressed in units of the height
of the point of observation E and in terms of the ratio of the rate of

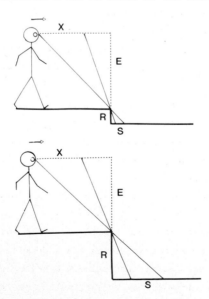

Fig. 4. In approaching a brink of a surface the ratio of (dX/dt)/(dS/dt)
        depends on the surface separation R relative to the eye height E.

displacement of the point of observation (dx/dt) to the rate of gain of
structure (ds/dt). Letting $t_1 - t_0$ be the time of a step (x), for the same
stepping rate the gain of structure (s) is greater the greater the separation
of surfaces (R). Although the example is crudely developed, it makes an in
principle argument that there will be a dimensionless quantity of optical
flow, such as (dx/dt)/(ds/dt), which is specific to the vertical separation
of surfaces at a brink, scaled in units of the observer. A critical value
or range of this optical flow property will specify the boundary between
places the animal can step down from - those that can be accommodated by
limb extension - and places requiring a different manoeuver.

Dimensionless numbers play a significant role in many branches of
physics. The commonly used numbers, referred to as principal π-numbers by
Schuring (1980) (of which the Reynolds, Raleigh, Mach, Prandtl, and Froude
are prime examples), are built from laws. Thus, the Reynolds number which
applies to fluids, is built from Newton's law of inertia and the law for
shear stress of a Nowtonian fluid. The two laws are cast as dimensionless
ratios or numbers (e.g., $\pi = F/ma$), and these two numbers in ratio give the
Reynolds number. At a critical value of the Reynolds number, the inertial
forces (favoring turbulence) dominate the viscous forces (favoring laminar
flow) and there is a shift from the one kind of flow to the other. Generally
speaking, the major dimensionless numbers in physics mark off, at critical
values, a change in the relation of forces from a balance between them to a
dominance by one of them and, thereby, mark off distinct physical states.
In like fashion, it seems that the dimensionless numbers built from purely
optical variables mark off, at critical values, distinct states. They are not
physical states associated with distinct forms of energy absorption, however,
but specificational states (see Kugler, Turvey, Carello & Shaw, in press).
Thus, in the example just given, the dimensionless quantity (dx/dt)/(ds/dt)
specifies step-downable when it is below a critical value and non-step-
downable when it is above that critical value.

We wish to underscore with two well developed examples the potential
significance of dimensionless quantities to law-based explanations of the
control of activity. When $dT(t)/dt \geq -0.5$, it specifies that the point of
observation will stop prior to contact with an upcoming substantial surface
if current conditions persist, whereas when $dT(t)/dt < -0.5$ it specifies
that there will be a collision between the point of observation and the
surface if the current conditions persist. This critical value of the rate
of change of the time-to-contact variable is an invariant optical quantity:

Whether the animal is approaching a surface or being approached by a surface, the quantity -0.5 marks off two distinct specificational states concerning the collisional consequences of the animal's current activity.

The second example returns the focus of this subsection to the perception of the kind of activity that an arrangement of surfaces affords an animal. Warren (1982) investigated the perception of stairways that varied in riser heights in terms of two questions: (1) Could a person perceive whether a stairway was climbable in the normal fashion (a question of the critical riser height)? and (2) Could a person perceive how costly, in metabolic terms, a stairway would be to climb (a question of the optimal riser height)? A preliminary analysis of the biomechanics of stepping up revealed that the riser height (R) beyond which normal stair climbing would be impossible was a constant proportion of leg length (L), viz., .88L, or R/L (a dimensionless quantity) = .88. Subjects, who differed markedly in height (1.63m vs. 1.93m), saw photographs of stairways with risers that ranged between .51m and 1.02m and were asked to judge the climbableness of each stairway. Although the riser height that distinguished the stairways judged to be climbable from the stairways judged to be nonclimbable differed between the two groups of subjects when measured in meters, it did not differ when measured in leg length. For both groups of subjects R/L = .88, that is, the critical riser value that had been determined from biomechanical considerations. With respect to the optimal riser height, the metabolic cost of climbing at 50 steps/min on an adjustable, motor-driven stairmill was evaluated at riser heights varying from .13m to .25m for short (1.63m) and tall (1.93m) subjects. The minimum energy expenditure per vertical meter (cal/kg-m), indicating optimal riser height, occurred at a riser height of R = .26L. In two visual tasks, a forced choice task and a rating task, the stairways were pitted against each other in pairs. The tasks revealed that the preferred riser height (the stairway that was seen to be the one that could be climbed most comfortably) differed between the two groups of subjects when measured in meters but it did not differ when measured in leg length. The preferred or optimal value for both groups was .25L in the forced choice task and .24L in the rating task, very close to the optimal value of .26L determined by metabolic measurement.

2.2.4 AFFORDANCES

In Gibson's (1979) terminology, step-down places, falling-off places,

climbable-places, collide-withable surfaces, travel-throughable openings
and so on (Figure 1) are affordances. That is to say, they are properties
of the environment taken with reference to the animal. An affordance is an
invariant arrangement of surface/substance properties that permits a given
animal a particular activity. It is a real property - one might even say a
physical property - but one that is defined at the ecological scale of
animals and their niches. By the laws of ecological optics, the light
structured by an affordance will be specific to the affordance - as the
above examples suggest. The optical property specific to an affordance is like
the time-to-contact property: It is not decomposable into optical variables
of a putatively more basic type. Consequently, it is claimed, the perceiving
of an affordance is based on detecting the optical property that specifies
the affordance. In the Gibsonian program, perceiving an affordance is not
mediated by computational/representational processes. It is said to be direct,
and understanding how this can be - understanding the physical processes at
the ecological scale that make possible the direct perception of the reality
that bears on the control of activity - is what the Gibsonian program is
fundamentally about (Section 3.2).

3.0   PRINCIPLES OF SELF-REGULATION

It is fair to say that working under the Cartesian program one is inclined
to explain regularity (of activity) by reference to intelligent regulators.
In the Cartesian view of things, it is an act of the intellect that interprets
the outputs of sensory transducers and puts them to use with respect to
externally oriented desires. Intelligence in its various manifestations (e.g.,
judging, comprehending, decision making, comparing, projecting and evaluating
hypotheses, recognizing, reconsidering, commanding, and so on) is at the core
of the Cartesian explanation of the control and coordination of movement.
For Descartes himself the intellect was equated with the soul - or as Ryle
(1949) liked to say, disdainfully, "the ghost in the machine".

The contemporary student of movement who chides all 'little man in the
brain' explanations of control may, however, be firm in his belief that the
concepts he borrows from cybernetics and formal machine theory are acceptable
explanatory tools. Personally, we think such convictions are suspect. Concepts
such as set-points, programs, and so on are superficially attractive in that
they refer to material things that perform the role historically ascribed to

homonculi. Under closer scrutiny, such concepts are revealed to be the
products of an intelligent act performed by a being with foreknowledge of
the regularity to be achieved. The concepts of cybernetics and formal machine
theory are seductive because they facilitate the simulation of 'regularities'
but they are not, we believe, in the best interests of explanatory science.
First, these concepts necessarily assume intelligence and rationality -
assumptions that were, after all, the reason for science's original and
persistent displeasure with Descartes' homunculus. Second, their promise is
limited, at best, to describing and, perhaps, to predicting regularities.
But explaining, in the sense of identifying the lawful basis for behavior,
is ineffably beyond their reach.

At one time, Bernstein was enthusiastic about the relevance of
cybernetical and formal machine analogues to the physiology of activity. He
later became much more circumspect with regard to their appropriateness.
Cybernetical notions figure prominently in his discussion of "Some Emergent
Problems of the Regulation of Motor Acts" (as we will underscore in the
subsections that follow). But in later chapters he questions the propriety
of cybernetics for biology and physiology and intimates that "the "honeymoon"
between these two sciences" (p. 542) may be over (also pp.546 - 547). In
Section 3.1 we critically evaluate the cybernetical treatment of Bernstein's
regulatory notion of circular causality and in Section 3.2 we outline the
physical conditions for that principle. Our belief, consonant with Bernstein's
later impressions, is that the physiology of activity would fare better
married to a physics that addresses the ecological scale and its natural
regularities than to a formal theory of the regulation of artifacts.

3.1   THE RING PRINCIPLE (CYBERNETICALLY INTERPRETED)

Bernstein is convinced, and properly so, that self-regulation is
based on circular causality - the "ring principle" as he terms it. He
embraces the familiar interpretation of this principle, the one advanced
by cybernetics: a referent signal or set point mediates signals fed forward
to and fed back from a device or process (generically referred to as 'the
plant'). For the conduct of an activity a single referent - and, a fortiori,
a single ring - will rarely be sufficient. Bernstein assumes an ordered
sequence of referent signals. Insofar as a referent signal must predate
the afferent and efferent flow that it mediates, so the order of the
referent signals must largely be ascribed prefatory to the activity. In

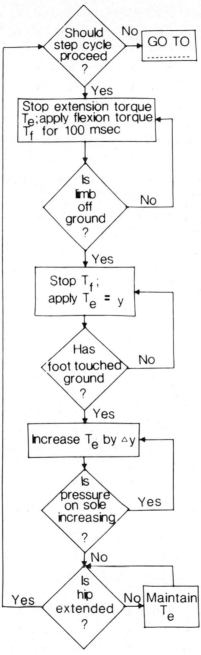

Fig. 5. A program formulation of a locomotory step cycle (Adapted from MacKay, W.A. The motor program: Back to the computer. <u>Trends in Neuroscience,</u> 1980, 3, 97-100).

brief, Bernstein's proposal for self-regulation is the popular notion of a
program. MacKay (1980) identifies the kinds of detail one might expect to
find in a program for a step cycle of locomotion (Figure 5).

In addition to identifying (1) the general a priori prescriptive nature
of the program, this example illustrates nicely that a program is (2) an
orderly sequence of preferred quantities, (3) an orderly sequence of commands
(to the skeletomuscular machinery that realizes these quantities), and (4) an
orderly sequence of symbol strings (the representational format for the
quantities and the commands). It also illustrates a more profound feature
of the program conception: (5) that rate-dependent processes - the irreversible
thermodynamics and the mechanics of the skeletomuscular system - are coupled
to and constrained by rate-independent structures - the symbol strings.

The centrality of the ring principle to self-regulation cannot be
doubted. (The reciprocity of locomotion and global optical transformations
described in Section 2.0 is one example of the principle's ubiquitous
application). What can be doubted is whether the properties identified in
(1) through (5) above are necessarily entailed by the principle.

3.1.2 THE CONCEPT OF THE REFERENT SIGNAL

The sollwerts (required values, set points) that have been used
frequently to 'explain' the stabilities of vegetative processes (thermoregulation
respiration, feeding, drinking, etc.) are more fictitious than real (e.g.,
Friedman & Stricker, 1976; Iberall, Weinberg & Schindler, 1971; Mitchell,
Snellen & Atkins, 1970; Werner, 1977). The observed stable quantities of
vegetative processes (e.g., human body temperature of 37 degrees centigrade)
are not prescribed values or goals playing a causal role. They are, more
accurately, resultant quantities, indexing a stable relation between independent
processes (force systems) defined over the same state variables (Iberall, 1978;
Kugler, Kelso & Turvey, 1980, 1982; Yates, 1982b). As we like to put it, these
so-called sollwerts are not a priori prescriptions for the system but a
posteriori facts of the system's processes.

The experiments of Zavelishin and Tenenbaum (1968) are illuminating in
this regard. They focussed on two respiratory variables - the resistance r
of the air to inspiration and the duration d of inspiration. The function f
relating d to r was identified. A function F relating r to d was imposed
(Figure 6). Circular causality was thereby established.

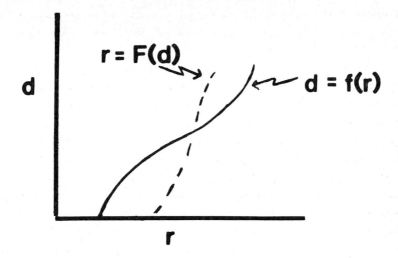

Fig. 6. Circular causality defined over the respiratory variables r
(resistance to inspiration) and d (duration of inspiration).

The value of d at which the respiratory system settled down was that value
mutual to the two functions. If F was chosen to intersect f at more than one
value of d then the system would settle at one of the mutual points or
oscillate between them depending on the actual details. Figures similar to
Figure 6 are to be seen in Mitchell et al. (1970) and Werner (1978) with
reference to temperature regulation, and in Guyton (1981) and Yates (1982a)
with reference to the pressure-flow relationships for blood circulation.

Each of the aforementioned instances of the ring principle or circular
causality involves two distinct pathways of influence between two variables,
x and y. The system in question must satisfy two independent causal laws,
one linking x to y and one linking y to x. The real equivalent of the point
of intersection of the two functions in the x by y coordinate space is the
equilibrium operating point of the system - the only point that satisfies
both causal laws. The equilibrium point is not frozen; it can be shifted by
changing the system parameters (see Guyton, 1981; Mitchell et al., 1970;
Werner, 1977; Zavelishin & Tenenbaum, 1968). In sum, each of these instances
of circular causality exemplifies a stable equilibrium state that is achieved
without the processes of measuring the istwert of the bounded variable,
comparing it to the sollwert, and amplifying the difference to bring about
an action that reduces this difference. The processes of measurement, feedback

amplification, and comparison that Bernstein takes to be the minimal
requirements of self-regulation are not to be found.

3.1.3 INTENSIONAL DESCRIPTIONS AND TELEOLOGICAL EXPLANATION

How general is an interpretation of self-regulation that does not
implicate the conventional, intelligence-based, mediating mechanism of
cybernetics? Intuitively, a notion such as a referent signal or program,
and the related processes of feedback and the like seem to be called for
whenever we construct a description of a system (S) such as:

'S prefers (wants, desires, seeks, etc.) G,'

where G can be the value of a property of S, a property of a thing in S's
environment, an orientation of S to the layout of the environment, and so on.
A statement of the above kind is called an intensional context or description.
Basically, it involves borrowing the property of one thing, G, to build a
property of another thing, S, viz. 'prefers G'. What is the status of the
borrowed property G?

Orthodoxy invariably interprets intensional description as license to
ascribe concepts: To predicate of S the property 'prefers (wants, desires,
seeks, etc.) G' is to ascribe to S the concept of G. Similarly, in matters
of perception, to say that 'S can perceive step-down places' (Section 2.2.3)
is to say, by the orthodox interpretation, that S has a concept of step-down
places. What is it about intensional description that invites conceptual
ascription? Why should the convenience of describing a property of a thing
S in terms of a thing G be translated into the claim that S possesses or
embodies in some form the thing G? Empirical considerations reveal that the
intensional context 'biological system S prefers a body temperature of 37
degrees centigrade' does not mean that the end-state of 37 degrees is
encoded in the system's central nervous system and, relatedly, does not
identify a relation between S and a central nervous system representation
of the quantity 37 degrees centigrade. The lesson of this example is twofold:
First, intensional description does not mandate conceptual ascription; and
second, intensional may simply be a way of referring indirectly to lawful
processes. It seems, therefore, that intensional description will invite
conceptual ascription to the degree that a lawful basis for a given
regularity is unexplored or indiscernible (Turvey et al., 1981).

Let us turn away from vegetative processes, such as temperature
regulation, to the more general case. Consider the following example of a

goal-directed activity, to be designated L. A swiftly flying bird suddenly changes its posture, spreads its wings, flaps them briefly, glides, flaps its wings a little more, and alights gently on a branch. A teleological description (Woodfield, 1976) of L reads:

'S did B in order to do G',

where S refers to the bird, B to the behavior and G to the goal of alighting on the branch with a minimal transfer of momentum to the bird's interior (Kugler, Turvey, Carello & Shaw, in press). This teleological description of L can be expanded (after Woodfield, 1976) to make the implied internal conditions transparent, albeit in "mentalese" (Fodor, 1975):

'S did B because S (i) wanted to do G and (ii) believed that B would lead to G'.

Now we have a teleological explanation of L.

It is very important to distinguish a ring principle (or circular causality) explanation of L from a teleological explanation of L. The ring principle takes G for granted and explains how S gets to G. By definition, a ring principle explanation consists not so much of a single sentence of the type 'S did B (at a particular time, in a particular way, etc.) because ...' but consists, rather, of a set of sentences describing cycles of acting-perceiving-change (in the animal-environment relation). The ring principle explanation of L would be in terms of the reciprocity of the bird's approach and optical flow, with particular emphasis on the decelerative forces supplied by the bird with respect to maintaining the optical flow property $dT(t)/dt$ within the range specifying a "soft" contact (see Section 2.2.2). The teleological explanation of L also takes G for granted, but it explains why S does B. Thus, the two explanations are complementary (Woodfield, 1976). If the processes governed by the ring principle are viewed as dynamical, then the states of S ('wanted', 'believed') are tantamount to field boundary conditions on dynamical processes. The form of these particular boundary conditions is that of non-holonomic constraints (about which more will be said below).

Clearly, the intention (i) in the teleological explanation of L above is Bernstein's 'image of achievement' (Pribram, 1971) that constrains the variations in the content of the belief (ii) until G is done. Recall that, for Bernstein, where actions are planned they are planned in terms of biological consequences (that is, in terms of how an activity will change the animal-environment relation) and not in terms of the pattern of bodily

movement (Problem 3 of the introduction). But can the state picked out by the
phrase 'wanted to do G' be interpreted as an 'image' in the sense of an
actually existing mental or neural representation of G? Woodfield (1976)
cautions thusly:

> It is tempting to think of a goal as a concrete future event,
> and to think of the present desire as involving a conception
> of that future event, with the conception of the goal being
> in some sense logically or ontologically derivative from the
> goal itself. But this is the wrong way round. A goal just is
> the intentional object of the relevant kind of conception
> (p. 205).

Let us see what a Gibsonian analysis of G looks like. The goal G in the
goal-directed activity L involves two aspects: one, a surface X that can
support S and two, a soft, feet-first collision with X. The former aspect
defines an affordance, and under the Gibsonian program an affordance is
optically specified. That is, the light structured by a branch is specific
to the support property of that surface layout vis-a-vis the bird's
proportions. The latter aspect, that of the soft collision, is specified by
$dT(t)/dt \geq -0.5$. The two aspects of the intention 'wanted to do G' in L might
be interpreted in the Gibsonian program as follows: 'wanted to do G' is a
matter of having detected information that continuously specified a surface
of support and having detected information that continuously specified the
intensity of an up-coming collision with that surface, on the occasion of a
certain metabolic condition of S.

One should be circumspect about the generalizability of an analysis of
the preceding type. Intentionality is a large issue and the reader's favorite
example of intentional behavior is probably much more elaborate than L.
However, states of affairs such as L are common; they comprise the larger
part of an animal's daily directed activities. And insofar as the Gibsonian
program can anchor teleological explanations of goal-directed activities such
as L in natural laws at the ecological scale, it promises a natural basis for
intentionality. Be that as it may, the comparison between the Cartesian and
Gibsonian programs on the subject of intentional objects (the goals of goal-
directed activities) is sharply drawn. Under the Cartesian program, intentional
objects are represented in an internal medium; under the Gibsonian program,
intentional objects are lawfully specified by structured energy distributions
(Turvey et al., 1981).

3.1.4 COMMANDS AS INFORMATION IN THE INDICATIONAL SENSE

Any disquiet with the concepts of internally encoded required values
or intentional objects as representations, extends to the concept of 'commands'.
Is circular causality in general, and the perception-action ring in particular,
mediated by commands? Although it has been a commonplace to say that the brain
commands the body, this way of talking has been subject to little scrutiny.
As Reed (1981) has observed, there is an entire theory of action wrapped up
in the notion of central nervous system commands and much conceptual effort
will be required to unravel it. We will give some hints of what is involved.
To anticipate, issues raised in the preceding subsections will make a repeat
appearance but in a subtly different form.

The control of activity is founded on information, as both Bernstein and
Gibson have sought to understand. "Commands" are a kind of information which
can be termed <u>indicational</u> because their role is to indicate an action to be
performed (Reed, 1981), much as a stop sign on the highway indicates the
action of arresting the forward motion of a car and a directional sign on
the highway indicates which turn to make. Indicational information is incomplete.
To be commanded to stop one's car is not to be told the details of how to do
so. Obviously, the informational basis for controlling activity is not exhausted
by information in the indicational sense. To stop the car requires information
about when to begin decelerating and information about when the deceleration
is sufficient and so forth. This sense of information was discussed in Section
2.2 and in the immediately preceding section. Consonant with the terminology
of these earlier sections, we will refer to this sense of information as
<u>specificational</u>. The important point to be made is that an indicated act
cannot be performed without information in the specificational sense. On
generalizing, this point reads: <u>The indicational sense of information is</u>
<u>always predicated on the specificational sense of information.</u>

Holding this dependency in abeyance for the present, let us focus on
the commonalities between commands - as sources of information in the
indicational sense- and rules. Neither commands nor rules can determine an
action, both commands and rules can be violated or ignored, both commands
and rules can enter into conflict (creating demands for impossible outcomes),
and both commands and rules require an explicit act of comprehension for
their functioning (Reed, 1981). For these reasons, a lawful determinate
account of the control and coordination of activity cannot be founded on the
notion of commands or information in the indicational sense. A further

undesirable feature is that the criticisms that apply to a body-states or
sensation-based theory of perception (see Section 2.0) apply to a command-
based theory of action: There is no rational explanation of the genesis of
the knowledge that forms and interprets commands. A command-based theory of
action looks like another unrepayable loan of intelligence.

The lawful basis of optical structure relevant to activity's control
was labored in Section 2.2 in order to make the notion of specification
transparent. Where information in the indicational sense is close to the
concept of rule, information in the specificational sense is cognate with
law. Laws are determinate, non-negotiable (they can never be violated or
ignored), harmonious (they can never give rise to impossibilities), and they
do not depend on explicit knowledge for their functioning. In the cybernetical
interpretation, the ring-principle is mediated by indicators (commands). But
it is apparent that this need not be so, for the same reason that mediation
by referent signals need not be so. It is an unmediated, law-based interpretation
of the ring principle (rather than a mediated, rule-based interpretation)
that is the focus of the Gibsonian program (see Section 3.2). A lawful account
of the control and coordination of activity cannot be founded on information
in the indicational sense but it could be founded on information in the
specificational sense.

3.1.5 <u>SYMBOLIC AND DYNAMICAL MODES</u>

The contrast of indicational information and specificational information
parallels that of discrete symbol strings and continuous dynamical processes
or, equivalently, rate-independent structures and rate-dependent processes.
These contrasts are said by Pattee (1973, 1977, 1979) to identify a
Complementarity Principle that is the hallmark of living systems. Living
systems are seen to execute in two modes, the symbolic and the dynamic, which
are incompatible and irreducible. Consequently, understanding biological,
physiological and psychological phenomena is said by Pattee to rest with the
elaboration of this complementarity. The computational/representational
approach to these phenomena that is championed by the Cartesian program is
flawed - in Pattee's view - because it attempts to explain only through the
discrete symbolic mode. Similarly, in his view, an approach that seeks to
explain such phenomena using only (sic) the laws of dynamics will also
prove inadequate. By Pattee's reasoning, both modes must be given full

recognition; the phenomena in question are the result of the coordination between the two modes. Stated more sharply, complementarity is advanced as a principle that calls for simultaneous use of formally incompatible descriptive modes in the explanation of the characteristic phenomena of living systems (Pattee, 1982).

There is, however, an asymmetry between the two modes that has to be appreciated. Nature uses the symbolic mode - nonholonomic (nonintegrable) constraints - sparingly. Dynamics are used to the fullest, wherever and whenever, to achieve characteristic biological effects. Symbol strings are used, now and then, to direct dynamical processes and to keep down their complexity - in other words, to trim the dynamical degrees of freedom. In Figure 5, which depicts a prototypical program formulation of activity, the opposite strategy is at work. Very many nonholonomic constraints are exploited to achieve ('to explain') the kinetic and kinematic regularities of a locomotory step cycle. The question of how the dynamics - properly construed for the biological scale in terms of the conjunction of statistical mechanics and irreversible thermodynamics (Iberall, 1977; Prigogine, 1980; Soodak & Iberall, 1978) - might fashion the phenomenon is not addressed, nor is the question of how the symbol strings interface with the dynamics. Pattee's analysis is an important one for those students of movement who would pursue the Cartesian program with its emphasis on the symbolic mode: Only in the working out of the physics of a regularity can one identify the nature and type of symbol strings (nonholonomic constraints) needed to complete the explanation. To begin with the symbolic mode, and to adhere strictly to it, invites an account that will be plagued by arbitrariness (as, surely, is the account of a step-cycle represented by Figure 5). To begin with the dynamical mode, and to pursue it earnestly, promises an account that will be principled.

There is, however, a deep problem with Pattee's Complementarity Principle. For Pattee, the discrete symbol strings function as information in the indicational sense. The proposed complementarity, therefore, is one of indicational information and dynamics. The problem with endorsing a view of indicational information and dynamics as formally incompatible is that it rules out any explanation of the origin of indicational information. We and others have recorded our disquiet with the Complementarity Principle for just this reason (Carello et al., 1983; Kugler, Kelso & Turvey, 1982). One suspects that for the consistency of physical theory, information in the indicational sense should be lawfully derivable from dynamics (or information in the specificational sense).

3.2   <u>THE RING PRINCIPLE (PHYSICALLY INTERPRETED)</u>

    In this final section we provide an overview of the physical foundations
of Bernstein's ring principle. Whereas the cybernetical interpretation of
the ring principle is consistent with the Cartesian program, the interpretation
evolving in physical biology is consistent with the Gibsonian program.

3.2.1 <u>OPEN SYSTEMS AND THE ROLE OF CAUSAL DYNAMICS</u>

    According to classical physics, living systems are continuously
struggling against the laws of physics. Within the last few decades, however,
it has become increasingly apparent that those physical systems that are
open to the flow of energy and matter into and out of their operational
components behave in a manner which suggests the behavior of living things
and suggests a dramatically different view of <u>causal dynamics</u> (see Yates,
1982a,b, for a review). Whereas the behavior of an isolated physical system is
strictly determined by the system's initial and boundary conditions, systems
open to the flow of energy and matter can evolve internal constraints which
'free' the system's dynamics from its initial conditions. The arising of
the new internal constraints serves to limit the trajectories of the
internal components, thereby reducing the system's internal degrees of
freedom. As these constraints arise, new spatio/temporal orderings are created
and the system derives new ways of doing business with its surroundings
(that is, new ways of transacting energy).
    While living systems can be viewed as following from the laws of
physics, one distinguishing characteristic that emerges in systems of this
order of complexity is the ability to internally time-delay energy flows.
This is accomplished through the maintenance of internal potentials from
which the system can periodically draw energy so as to produce a generalized
external work cycle. This self-contained source of potential energy (usually
in chemical form) allows the system to be characterized as self-sustaining.
The ability to be self-sustaining means that the system's behavior is no
longer governed strictly by minimum energy trajectories or external work
cycles defined on external gradient fields. The possibility now arises that

a self-sustained system can temporarily depart from the constraints defined
by the external potential minimums. Departures from and returns to minimum
regions defined in the external potential field require some form of
sensitivity to the gradients; and this, in turn, requires some form of
self-sustaining system. The ability to selectively discriminate low order
potential gradients (Frohlich, 1974; Volkenstein & Chernavskii, 1978) and
the ability to form an autonomous, persistent self-sustaining system
(Iberall, 1973, 1977) are fundamental characteristics of living systems.

3.2.2 DETERMINANT TRAJECTORIES IN PARTICLE/FIELD SYSTEMS

Particle physics (classical, quantum and relativistic) studies the
trajectories of particles to infer the dispositions of potential fields.
The assumption underlying the above strategy is that variations in the
observed force field are strictly a function of the particle's position in
the field. The above assumption rests on two requirements: (i) that external
potentials remain constant (in both space and time), and (ii) that the
particle has no internal means for introducing or absorbing forces (which
could contribute to a trajectory's departing from the minimum regions defined
by the external potential field). Particles satisfying these two requirements
have their trajectories completely determined by the form of the external
potential field: The minimum regions identify geometrical singularities in
a topological field. The particle system is completely determined by and
causally dependent on the topological form of the external potential field.

3.2.3 SELF-SERVING SYSTEMS AND CIRCULAR CAUSALITY

If, however, the particle system of interest has an internal means for
generating and dissipating forces of a magnitude comparable to the external
forces - that is, the system is self-serving - then the behavior of the
particle need not be completely determined by the topological form of the
external potential field. The particle has available internal potentials that
can generate and absorb forces that, when combined with the forces generated
by the external potential field, can yield equilibrium states that are not
strictly defined by the topological singularities of the external potential
field. The behavior of this class of particle system can be said to be

nondeterminant with respect to its relationship with the external potential
field (cf. Kugler, Kelso & Turvey, 1982; Kugler, Turvey & Shaw, 1982).
While the particle's equilibrium states are no longer determinately
specified by the state of the external potential field, the particle is still,
nonetheless, causally coupled to the forces generated by the external
potential field. That is to say, changes in the forces
generated by the external potential field will require compensatory changes
in the particle's internally generated forces if an equilibrium state is to
be maintained invariant - the external and internal force systems are
causally linked in a circular causality with respect to invariant equilibrium
states.

The physical concept of circular causality (cf. Iberall, 1977) is meant
to identify the lawful nature of the coupling that links the exterior
potential field (and its associated force field) with the interior potential
field (and its associated force field). Self-serving systems and their
associated equilibrium states are lawfully coupled to the external potential
field through circular causality; they are systems whose interior potential
fields play an active role in fashioning final equilibrium states.

Self-serving particle systems are characterized by low energy couplings
that relate the particle's position to its external field. The low energy
coupling is defined relative to the external work cycle generated by the
particle. The coupling defines a ratio of the forces generated by the external
work cycle in proportion to the forces generated by the external potential
field. A dimensionless number can be used to qualitatively distinguish the
nature of the coupling:

$$Pi = \frac{(\text{forces generated by the external work cycle})}{(\text{forces generated by the external potential field})}$$

$$Pi \leq 1 = \text{high energy coupling}$$

$$Pi > 1 = \text{low energy coupling.}$$

A high energy coupling (Pi $\leq$ 1) defines a coupling in which the particle's
external work cycle is insufficient to resist the external
field's potential gradients. If, however, an external work cycle is generated
that resists the external field's potential gradients (Pi > 1), and contributes
actively in the organization of equilibrium states, then the coupling can be
considered to be of a low energy nature. The low energy coupling realized by
a self-serving system forms a lawful basis from which a generalized theory
of information can be derived.

3.2.4 INFORMATION AND THE ECOLOGICAL APPROACH TO PERCEPTION AND ACTION

Central to the Gibsonian program is the claim that information must refer to physical states of affairs that are specific and meaningful to the control and coordination requirements of activity (Turvey & Carello, 1981).

Following Gibson (1950, 1966, 1979) the above requirements for information are to be found in the qualitative properties captured in the structured patterns of energy distributions coupling an animal to its environment (see Section 2.2). These patterns (1) carry, in their topological form, properties that are specific to components of change and components of persistence in the animal-environment relation; (2) are meaningful (i.e. they define gradient values) with respect to the animal's internal potentials; and (3) are lawfully determined by the environment and by the animal's movements relative to the environment. According to the Gibsonian program, information is a physical variable that defines a coupling that is specific and meaningful with respect to the changing geometry of the econiche (defined by the animal/ environment qua particle/field system totality). The energy patterns coupling the animal (internal potential field) and environment (external potential field) are continuously scaled to the changing parameters and dimensionality of the system (cf. Kugler et al., 1980). The information carried in the evolving geometry of structured energy distribution is information about the animal dynamics (internal potential layout) relative to the environmental dynamics (external potential layout). This concept of information is consistent with Thom's view of information as geometric form (cf. Kugler, Kelso & Turvey, 1982):

> ...any geometric form whatsoever can be the carrier of information, and in the set of geometric forms carrying information of the same type the topological complexity of the form is the qualitative scalar of the information (Thom, 1975, p. 145).

Information as a geometry of form (defined over potential fields) arises as an a posteriori fact of the system. The information can be carried in the form of geometric manifolds which are created, sustained and dissolved within a large variety of physical flow fields. The flow fields can be assembled out of mechanical, chemical or electro-magnetic constraints.

3.2.5 ON THE DETERMINANT NATURE OF INFORMATION AND THE NON-DETERMINANT NATURE OF BEHAVIOR

The goal of physics for the twentieth century has been to understand the nature of the energy states exhibited by particles at all scales of magnitude. The foundation of physics rests on the commitment (explicit or implicit) to natural laws, that is, the commitment to a natural continuity is energy states reducible to symmetry statements (equations) defined on conservations. The strategy for defining natural laws rests on the identification of trajectories assumed by particles. While this strategy has valid application for simple particle systems (non-self-serving systems), its application toward explicating the natural laws governing the energy states of self-serving systems must be seriously questioned. The behavior of a self-serving system is <u>not</u> strictly determined by the energy states of the external potential fields. As noted, the energy states of the internal potential field play an active role in the determination of the observed trajectory. While the behavior (observed trajectory) of a self-serving system has a nondeterminant status, the informational states defining the low energy coupling that relates the external potential field to the internal potential field has a determinant status. The information states are invariant (i.e., stable and reproducible) in the strictest sense of lawful determinism. A physical analysis of the behavior (observed trajectories) of self-serving systems must entail an inquiry into the low energy informational states that lawfully couple an animal (complex self-serving particle) to its environment (external potential field). (For an example of a physical analysis of the role of low energy couplings, see Kugler, Turvey, Carello & Shaw, in press). <u>It can be argued that the goal of a physics befitting Bernstein's physiology of activity is that of identifying the laws that create, sustain and dissolve low energy informational states.</u>

ACKNOWLEDGEMENTS

The preparation of this paper was supported in part by ONR Contract N00014-83-C-0083 awarded to the Haskins Laboratories. The authors wish to thank Robert Shaw and Claudia Carello for their artistic contributions to this paper.

REFERENCES

Bernstein, N.A. The coordination and regulation of movements. London: Pergamon Press, 1967.

Boynton, R. The visual system: Environmental information. In, E.C. Carterette and M.P. Friedman (Eds.), Handbook of perception Vol. III. New York: Academic Press, 1975.

Chomsky, N. Rules and representations. The Behavioral and Brain Sciences, 1980, 3, 1-62.

Cummins, R. Programs in the explanation of behavior. Philosophy of Science, 1977, 44, 269-287.

Dietz, V. & Noth. J. Pre-innervation and stretch responses of triceps bracchii in man falling with and without visual control. Brain Research, 1978, 142, 576-579.

Fitch, H. & Turvey, M.T. On the control of activity: Some remarks from an ecological point of view. In, D. Landers and R. Christina (Eds.), Psychology of motor behavior and sports. Urbana, Ill.: Human Kinetics, 1978.

Fitch, H.L., Turvey, M.T. & Tuller, B. The Bernstein perspective: III. Tuning of coordinative structures with special reference to perception. In, J.A.S. Kelso (Ed.), Human motor behavior. Hillsdale, N.J.: Erlbaum, in press.

Fodor, J.A. The language of thought. New York: Thomas Y. Crowell, 1975.

Fodor, J.A. Methodological solipsism considered as a research strategy in cognitive psychology. Behavioral and Brain Science, 1980, 3, 63-109.

Fodor, J.A. & Pylyshyn, Z. How direct is visual perception? Some reflections on Gibson's 'Ecological Approach'. Cognition, 1981, 9, 139-196.

Freedman, W., Wannstedt, G. & Herman, R. EMG patterns and forces developed during step-down. American Journal of Physical Medicine, 1976, 5, 275-290.

Friedman, M.I. & Stricker, E.M. The physiological psychology of hunger: A physiological perspective. Psychological Review, 1976, 86, 409-431.

Frohlich, H. Collective phenomena of biological systems. In, H. Haken (Ed.), Cooperative effects: Progress in synergetics. Amsterdam: North Holland, 1974.

Gelfand, I.M., Gurfinkel, V.S., Fomin, S.V. & Tsetlin, M.L. (Eds.), Models of the structural-functional organization of certain biological systems. Cambridge, Mass.: MIT Press, 1971.

Gershun, A. The light field. Journal of Mathematics and Physics, 1939, 18, 51-151.

Gibson, J.J. The perception of the visual world. Boston: Houghton-Mifflin, 1950.

Gibson, J.J. Ecological optics. Vision Research, 1961, 1, 253-262.

Gibson, J.J. The senses considered as perceptual systems. Boston, Mass.: Houghton-Mifflin, 1966.

Gibson, J.J. The ecological approach to visual perception. Boston: Houghton-Mifflin, 1979.

Gibson, J.J. Notes on action. In, E. Reed and R. Jones (Eds.), Reasons for realism: Selected essays of James J. Gibson. Hillsdale, N.J.: Erlbaum, 1982.

Gunther, B. Dimensional analysis and theory of biological similarity. Physiological Review, 1975, 55, 659-699.

Guyton, A.C. Textbook of medical physiology. Philadelphia: W.B. Saunders, 1981.

Hanson, N.R. Patterns of discovery. Cambridge, U.K.: Cambridge University Press, 1958.

Hofsten, C. von. Catching skills in infancy. Journal of Experimental Psychology: Human Perception and Performance, 1983, 9, 75-85.

Hofsten, C. von & Lindhagen, K. Observations on the development of reaching for moving objects. Journal of Experimental Child Psychology, 1979, 28, 158-173.

Holst, E. von & Mittelstädt, H. Das reafferenzprinzip. Naturwiss, 1950, 37, 464-476.

Hubbard, A.W. & Seng, C.N. Visual movements of batters. Research Quarterly, 1954, 25, 42-57.

Huxley, J. Problems of relative growth. London: Metheun, 1932.

Iberall, A.S. Toward a general science of viable systems. New York: McGraw-Hill, 1972.

Iberall, A.S. A field and circuit thermodynamics for integrative physiology: I. Introduction to general notions. American Journal of Physiology/Regulatory, Integrative & Comparative Physiology, 1977, 2, R171-R180.

Iberall, A.S. A field and circuit thermodynamics for integrative physiology: III. Keeping the books - a general experimental method. American Journal of Physiology/Regulatory, Integrative & Comparative Physiology, 1978, 3, R85-R97.

Iberall, A.S., Weinberg, M. & Schindler, A. General dynamics of the physical-chemical systems in mammals. NASA Contractor Report 1806, June 1971.

Johansson, G. A letter to Gibson. Scandinavian Journal of Psychology, 1970, 11, 67-74.

Koenderink, J.J. & van Doorn, A.J. Exterospecific component of the motion parallax field. Journal of the Optical Society of America, 1981, 71, 953-957.

Kugler, P.N., Kelso, J.A.S. & Turvey, M.T. On the concept of coordinative structures as dissipative structures: I. Theoretical lines of convergence. In, G.E. Stelmach & J. Requin (Eds.), Tutorials in motor behavior. New York: North-Holland Publishing Co., 1980, 1-47.

Kugler, P.N., Kelso, J.A.S. & Turvey, M.T. On the control and coordination of naturally developing systems. In, J.A.S. Kelso and J.E. Clark (Eds.), The development of movement control and coordination. Chichester: John Wiley, 1982.

Kugler, P.N., Turvey, M.T., Carello, C. & Shaw, R. The physics of controlled collisions: A reverie about locomotion. In, W.H. Warren, Jr. and R. Shaw (Eds.), Persistence and change: Proceedings of the first international conference on event perception. Hillsdale, N.J.: Erlbaum, 1984.

Kugler, P.N., Turvey, M.T. & Shaw, R.E. Is the "cognitive impenetrability condition" invalidated by contemporary physics? The Behavioral and Brain Sciences, 1982, 2, 303-306.

Lee, D.N. Visual information during locomotion. In, R. McLeod and H. Pick (Eds.), Perception: Essays in honor of J.J. Gibson. Ithaca, N.Y.: Cornell University Press, 1974.

Lee, D.N. & Reddish, P.E. Plummeting gannets: A paradigm of ecological optics. Nature, 1981, 293, 293-294.

Lee, D.H. A theory of visual control of braking based on information about time-to-collision. Perception, 1976, 5, 437-459.

Lishman, R. & Lee, D.N. The autonomy of visual kinaesthesis. Perception, 1973, 2, 287-294.

MacKay, W.A. The motor program: Back to the computer. Trends in Neuroscience, 1980, 3, 97-100.

Michaels, C.F. & Carello, C. Direct perception. New York: Prentice-Hall, 1981.

Mitchell, D., Snellen, J.W. & Atkins, A.R. Thermoregulation during fever: Change of set-point or change of gain. Pflügers Arch, 1970, 321, 293-302.

Moon, P. Scientific basis of illuminating engineering. New York: Dover, 1961.

Moon, P. & Spencer, D.E. The photic field. Cambridge, Mass.: MIT Press,
    1981.

Pattee, H.H. Physical problems of the origin of natural controls. In,
    A. Locker (Ed.), Biogenesis, evolution, homeostasis. Heidelberg:
    Springer-Verlag, 1973, 41-49.

Pattee, H.H. Dynamic and linguistic modes of complex systems. International
    Journal of General Systems, 1977, 3, 259-266.

Pattee, H.H. The complementarity principle and the origin of macromolecular
    information. Biosystems, 1979, 11, 217-226.

Pattee, H.H. The need for complementarity in models of cognitive behavior -
    A response to Carol Fowler and Michael Turvey. In, W. Weimer & D. Palermo
    (Eds.), Cognition and the symbolic processes Vol. 2. Hillsdale, N.J.:
    Erlbaum, 1982.

Pribram, K.H. Languages of the brain. Englewood Cliffs, N.J.: Prentice-
    Hall, 1971.

Prigogine, I. From being to becoming: Time and complexity in the physical
    sciences. San Francisco: W.H. Freeman & Co., 1980.

Pylyshyn, Z.W. Computation and cognition: Issues in the foundations of
    cognitive science. The Behavioral and Brain Sciences, 1980, 3, 111-169.

Reed, E.S. Indirect action. Unpublished manuscript, Center for Research in
    Human Learning, University of Minnesota, November 1981.

Reed, E.S. An outline of a theory of action systems. Journal of Motor
    Behavior, 1982a, 14, 98-134 (a).

Reed, E.S. The corporeal idea hypothesis and the origin of experimental
    psychology. Review of Metaphysics, 1982b, 35, 731-752 (b).

Reed, E. & Jones, R. Reasons for realism: Selected essays of James J.
    Gibson. Hillsdale, N.J.: Erlbaum, 1982.

Rosen, R. Optimality principles in biology. New York: Plenum Press, 1967.

Runeson, S. On the possibility of "smart" perceptual mechanisms. Scandinavian
    Journal of Psychology, 1977, 18, 172-179.

Ryle, G. The concept of mind. London: Hutchinson, 1949.

Schuring, D.J. Scale models in engineering. New York: Pergamon Press, 1980.

Sharp, R.H. & Whiting, H.T.A. Exposure and occluded duration effects in
    ball-catching skill. Journal of Motor Behavior, 1974, 6, 139-147.

Sharp, R.H. & Whiting, H.T.A. Information-processing and eye movement in
    a ball-catching skill. Journal of Movement Studies, 1975, 1, 124-131.

Shaw, R.E., Turvey, M.T. & Mace, W. Ecological psychology: The consequences
    of a commitment to realism. In, W. Weimer & D. Palermo (Eds.), Cognition
    and the symbolic processes (II). Hillsdale, N.J.: Erlbaum, 1982.

Smokler, H.E. Conflicting conceptions of confirmation. Journal of
Philosophy, 1968, 115, 300-312.

Soodak, H. & Iberall, A.S. Homeokinetics: A physical science for complex
systems. Science, 1978, 201, 579-582.

Srinivasan, M.V. A visually-evoked roll response in the housefly: Open-loop
and closed-loop studies. Journal of Comparative Physiology, 1977, 119,
1-14.

Thom, R. Structural stability and morphogenesis. In, D.H. Fowler (Trans.).
Reading, Mass.: Benjamin, Inc., 1975.

Turvey, M.T. Contrasting orientations to the theory of visual information
processing. Psychological Review, 1977, 84, 67-88.

Turvey, M.T. The thesis of efference-mediation of vision cannot be
rationalized. The Behavioral and Brain Sciences, 1979, 2, 81-83.

Turvey, M.T. & Carello, C. Cognition: The view from ecological realism.
Cognition, 1981, 10, 313-321.

Turvey, M.T. & Remez, R. Visual control of locomotion in animals: An
overview. In, Proceedings of Conference on Interrelations among the
communicative senses. NSF publication, 1979.

Turvey, M.T. & Shaw, R.E. The primacy of perceiving: An ecological
reformulation of perception for understanding memory. In, L.G. Nilsson
(Ed.), Perspectives on memory research: Essays in honor of Uppsala
University's 500th anniversary. Hillsdale, N.J.: Erlbaum, 1979.

Turvey, M.T., Shaw, R.E. & Mace, W. Issues in the theory of action: Degrees
of freedom, coordinative structures and coalitions. In, J. Requin (Ed.),
Attention and performance VII. Hillsdale, N.J.: Erlbaum, 1978.

Turvey, M.T., Shaw, R.E., Reed, E.S. & Mace, W.M. Ecological laws of
perceiving and acting: In reply to Fodor and Pylyshyn (1981). Cognition,
1981, 9, 237-304.

Volkenstein, M.V. & Chernavskii, D.S. Information and biology. Journal of
Social and Biological Structures, 1978, 1, 95-108.

Wagner, H. Flow-field variables trigger landing in flies. Nature, 1982,
297, 147-148.

Warren, W. A biodynamic basis for perception and action in bipedal climbing.
Ph.D. dissertation, University of Connecticut, 1982.

Werner, J. Mathematical treatment of structure and function of the human
thermoregulatory system. Biological Cynernetics, 1977, 25, 93-101.

Woodfield, A. Teleology. Cambridge, U.K.: Cambridge University Press, 1976.

Yates, F.E. Outline of a physical theory of physiological systems. Canadian
Journal of Physiology and Pharmacology, 1982, 60, 217-248(a).

Yates, F.E. Systems analysis of hormone action: Principles and strategies.
    In, R.F. Goldberger (Ed.), Biological regulation and development, Vol. III
    - Hormone action. New York: Plenum, 1982(b).

Zavelishin, N.V. & Tenenbaum, L.A. Control processes in the respiratory
    system. Automation and Remote Control, 1968, 9, 1456-1470.

Human Motor Actions — Bernstein Reassessed
H.T.A. Whiting (editor)
© Elsevier Science Publishers B.V. (North-Holland), 1984

CHAPTER IVb

SOME COMPUTATIONAL SOLUTIONS TO BERNSTEIN'S PROBLEMS

G. Hinton

INTRODUCTION

Bernstein's great strength was his appreciation of the immense complexity of the apparently simple task of motor control. He lived at a time when movements were seen as "responses", and their structure was generally regarded as a minor matter, of much less interest than their variable relationship to the "stimuli" that elicited them. Against this background, he insisted on analyzing the difficulties inherent in real motor acts. He understood the profound problems caused by reactive forces, surplus degrees of freedom, the unpredictability of external forces, and the need to use sensory feedback to modulate the effects of central commands. One may quibble with some of his solutions, but his understanding of the major problems was far ahead of his time.

In this commentary, I shall focus on three issues that were of major concern to Bernstein. First, what can we infer about the code that the brain uses to communicate with the periphery, and what does that tell us about how the computation is organized? Second, if the brain knew just what movements it wanted the body to make, could it figure out what to tell the muscles in order to make it happen? Third, how is it possible to coordinate a system with so many degrees of freedom that interact in such complex ways? How does the brain make sensible choices among the myriad possibilities for movement that the body offers?

Experiments on people, animals, and robots, and a better understanding of the computational problems have led to interesting theoretical advances in the last few years. I shall concentrate on explaining some of these developments and showing how they provide solutions to some of Bernstein's problems. To simplify matters, I assume a particular task - rapid reaching movements to a visually specified point without visual feedback from the movement. This task is complex enough to contain many of the problems that

interested Bernstein but simple enough to be tractable. I shall have little
further to say about the many important problems that the task avoids. These
include:

1. *Impedance control*: By setting the stiffness of the muscles
   appropriately, it is possible to control the mechanical response of
   the body to externally applied forces (Benati et. al., 1980b; Hogan,
   1980).

2. *Manipulation planning*: Skilled manipulation involves figuring out
   what forces, impulses, or movements to apply to objects and how to
   use the arms and fingers to do it (Mason, 1981; Lozano-Perez, 1979).

3. *Dynamic refinement of motor plans*: Planning is just one component
   of manipulation. Another crucial aspect is the use of tactile feedback
   to dynamically refine under-specified aspects of the plan as it is
   being performed. Bernstein emphasises that this type of close
   integration of movements and feedback is a central feature of motor
   control.

4. *Locomotion*: The maintenance of dynamic balance while walking or
   running is an area where rapid progress is currently being made in
   the computational theory (Raibert & Sutherland, 1983).

1.   THE EQUIVOCAL EFFECTS OF CENTRAL COMMANDS

   Suppose you want your finger to trace out a geometrical form in space.
To do this you must activate the muscles in your arm so that they generate
the necessary torques at the joints (though this may not be the best way
to think about it). As Bernstein points out, generating the right torques
is harder than it seems for several reasons:

   1. The force exerted by a muscle depends not only on its level of
activation, but also on its current length and the rate at which it is
changing. So neural impulses to the muscles cannot unequivocally specify the
forces to be exerted.

   2. The magnitude and axis of the torque created by a given force in a
muscle depends on the geometrical configuration of the muscle about the
joint, and this varies as the joint angle changes.

3. It is hard to know what torques *should* be exerted to achieve a desired effect on a joint angle. The effect of a torque depends on the angular inertia about the joint, and in a moving chain of linkages like the arm, the angular inertia about each joint depends on the angles and *angular velocities* of all the joints. Also torques applied at one joint produce angular accelerations at *other* joints.

4. Even if the torques could be computed centrally and applied unequivocally by the muscles, the problem would still not be solved because small variations in the static or dynamic configuration of the body cause the same torques to produce different effects, and the central apparatus cannot know what the exact state of the body will be when its torque signals arrive there.

Between them, these arguments are certainly compelling evidence against the idea that the central apparatus simply sends out the right force signals to the muscles. They suggest that some more subtle code is used and that some peripheral computation is involved. This is an important discovery. Bernstein, however, seems to draw a further conclusion which is not justified and which hinges on a false assumption and a mathematical error. He appears to believe that the central apparatus is not concerned with torques and that it somehow deals with a different kind of representation that only gets turned into torques at the periphery. I think he would have been firmly opposed to the idea that the required torques are computed centrally and are then encoded in some other form for transmission to the muscles. I also think that this may be what actually happens.

Bernstein's false assumption is never explicitly stated, but is clearly evident in his discussion of the six properties required of every self-regulating system. He assumes that the detection of error and the corrective feedback signal are both neural events. He does not seem to have realized that the complex properties of muscles, which make them respond equivocally to neural impulses, are not a *problem* that makes motor control more difficult but an evolutionary adaptation that makes motor control easier. These special properties allow muscles themselves to act as very fast, negative feedback devices without any neural detection of the error (as will be explained in the next section).

Naturally, neural feedback is very important in real motor acts and the existence of other types of feedback does not mean that we can ignore the complex problem of how neural feedback is integrated into the action. However, physical feedback effects must be properly understood before it is

possible to analyze the role played by neural feedback loops in real motor
acts, even if these neural loops are very fast (Adams, 1976). I therefore
describe in some detail how the physical properties of muscles can be used
to simplify motor control.

I shall show that muscles can provide almost instantaneous feedback
effects *provided* that the signals sent to the muscles use an indirect
encoding of the required forces. Thus the fact that the signals do not
directly encode torques (or rather the muscular forces needed to generate
them) may not be because the forces are too hard to compute or because
evolution could not produce muscles that responded unequivocally to force
signals, but because the centrally computed forces need to be encoded in a
special way to cash in on a neat trick for getting instant feedback.

When this trick was first discovered it was initially interpreted as a
way of avoiding force computations altogether. The feedback provided by the
muscles was seen as a way of moving the limbs around without any explicit
force computations, but there is now convincing evidence against this
interpretation (Hogan, 1982; Bizzi, Accornero, Chapple and Hogan, 1982), and
it seems probable that the properties of muscles allow them to produce a
very rapid feedback effect, but the forces still need to be precomputed.
In general, it is always better to combine a precomputed feedforward component
with a feedback loop than to rely on feedback alone. Feedback can only
produce forces when there are errors, so big forces require big errors (Horn,
1978). By using feedforward to generate some of the required force, the
errors can be reduced to those needed to produce the difference between the
precomputed force and the force that is actually needed.

Bernstein's mathematical error is his claim that reactive interactions
make the computation of torques exponentially hard. This claim underpins his
view that the central apparatus does not explicitly compute torques. He is
just plain wrong about the difficulty of the computation. It is not trivial,
but it is now known to be quite easy. It has linear rather than exponential
complexity. (This is discussed in more detail in section 2). Bernstein can
hardly be faulted for his mistake. The easy way to do the computation has
only been discovered in the last few years, and even this algorithm is quite
complex when compared with the kinds of computation people were willing to
attribute to the brain before we had modern computers.

Bernstein's overestimation of the difficulties created by reactive
interactions, and his failure to realize *why* the signals to muscles did not
directly represent forces appear to have led him to reject the idea of a full

internal model of the dynamics of the body, and I think this was a serious mistake.

WHY LENGTH-TENSION FUNCTIONS MAKE GOOD CONTROL SIGNALS

Although it is intellectually easier to imagine that central signals specify forces or torques, it is actually much easier to control a system by sending out signals that specify *functions*. The α-motoneuron inputs to a muscle specify not a force, but a function that relates the length and the rate of change of length of the muscle to its tension, and hence to the force and torque that it generates (Asratyan and Feldman, 1965). From a design standpoint, the use of "length-tension" functions seems like an unnecessarily roundabout way of getting the muscles to generate the right forces. Why didn't we just evolve muscles that unequivocally generate a required force when told to do so?

To understand why it is better to specify length-tension functions than forces, consider the following simple problem: Suppose we have a system with just one joint, and we wish to change the joint angle according to some internal schedule which specifies what the joint angle should be at each instant. If there is an internal model of the dynamics of the physical system, it is possible to compute what torque is required at each moment in order to follow the required trajectory. If there is a torque motor at the joint, all we need to do is to tell it the computed torque. This open-loop scheme is simple but it is not robust. If the internal model is imperfect in any way, the computed torques will not be quite right, and the joint angle will diverge from its desired value. We could add a mechanism that sensed these deviations and modified the torque signals appropriately, but this mechanism would be subject to delays due to the slowness of neural transmission.

Now consider the alternative scheme using "angle-torque" functions. The internal model is used to compute the required torque, as before, but then a further computation takes place. The required torque and the desired joint angle are used to select an angle-torque function which will yield that torque at that angle. Then this function is sent down to an angle-torque motor which combines the angle-torque function with the current joint angle to generate the actual torque. Clearly, if the internal model is correct, this scheme will generate the internally computed torque. But why bother to turn the torque into a function and then convert it back again in the motor? The reason is that this scheme makes the system robust against errors in the internal model.

Suppose the internal model underestimates the physical mass that is being moved. In the simple open-loop scheme, the torque motor will always generate torques that are too small. In the angle-torque scheme, the internally computed torques will also be too small, but when these are combined with the current angle to select an appropriate angle-torque function, the *desired* value of the angle will be used. When the function is turned back into a torque by the angle-torque motor, the *actual* angle is used. So the torque actually generated differs from the computed torque, and it differs in an interesting way. If the physical system lags behind the internal model, the angle-torque function will generate a larger actual torque than was intended. So by using angle-torque functions we get an automatic feedback effect. The discrepancy between the internally desired joint angle and the actual joint angle gets converted into an increment in the actual torque. If the angle-torque function is linear, the mathematics is easy. The torque, τ, can be expressed as:

$$\tau = s(\alpha - \alpha_0) \tag{1}$$

where α_0 is the angle at which this function would yield zero torque, α is the joint angle, and s is the stiffness. (The equation assumes that angles are measured in the opposite direction to torques). The two parameters which can be varied to generate the different functions within this class are α_0 and s. At any particular moment, they must be chosen to yield a particular function which gives the appropriate torque at the appropriate angle. In other words, the function must be selected so that:

$$\tau_c = s(\alpha_c - \alpha_0)$$

where τ_c is the internally computed torque and α_c is the internal specification of the required angle. The *actual* torque generated is given by:

$$\tau_a = s(\alpha_a - \alpha_0) \tag{2a}$$

$$= s(\alpha_c - \alpha_0) - s(\alpha_c - \alpha_a)$$

$$= \tau_c - s.e \tag{2b}$$

where α_a is the actual angle and e is the difference between the actual and intended angles. Thus, by encoding the required torques into angle-torque functions we get an automatic negative feedback term in addition to the computed torque. Moreover, this feedback term does not require any neural sensing of the positional error. It is just a property of the way the angle-torque motor behaves. If the functions are non-linear, the mathematics is more complex, but the actual torque can still be characterized as the computed torque plus a negative feedback term that depends on the positional error.

In equation 1 there are two quite different parameters, α_0 and s which determine an angle-torque function. At first sight this seems redundant, because a single free parameter, α_0, would allow a function to be chosen that would satisfy equation 1 (i.e. would generate the desired torque at the desired angle). However, equation 2 shows why it is advantageous to be able to vary s as well as α_0 when choosing an angle-torque function. The value of stiffness, s, determines the size of the feedback term for any given positional error. If the internal model is fairly accurate, the discrepancy between τ_a and τ_c will be small and so the positional error, e, will not need to grow very big before the feedback term s.e is sufficient to compensate for the difference between τ_a and τ_c. If the internal model is inaccurate a larger value of s.e will be needed. If s was a constant, a bigger feedback term would require a bigger error to generate it. If, however, the internal model is *known* to be inaccurate a larger value of s can be used so that the necessary feedback is generated without requiring large positional errors. This use of high stiffness to overcome the inadequacies of a poor internal model fits in well with Bernstein's observation that when first performing a new task people's movements are very stiff but that they later become more relaxed as they master the task.

Even if there is no reliable information about the inaccuracy of the internal model it is still possible to dynamically optimize the stiffness parameter so that the errors are kept within reasonable bounds with as little stiffness as possible. Houk (1979) has suggested that neural detection of the error in position may be used to control the stiffness. This rather indirect type of feedback has a major advantage over the more conventional idea of using the neurally detected error to directly generate a corrective force. Neural detection and transmission are slow, and by the time an error has been detected and fed back as a correction, the system may have changed enough so that the original error is no longer what needs to be corrected. Indeed, the current error may be in the opposite direction so that the correction only makes things worse (this is the classic cause of oscillations in systems with delayed feedback). By modulating the stiffness of the angle-torque function and leaving the actual feedback to the muscles themselves, these problems are avoided because the feedback is all in the physics so there is very little delay.

There are no angle-torque motors in the body, but by using two or more opposing muscles about each joint, it is easy to implement angle-torque functions provided the muscles exhibit the linear equivalent - length-tension functions. In the simplest case, the relationship between the length-tension functions of two opposing muscles and the angle-torque function they implement is easy to state. Simple length-tension functions have the form:

$$t = s(l - r)$$

where t is the tension, s is the stiffness, l is the length and r is the resting length. If the leverage of the muscle about the joint remains constant, this can be rewritten in angular terms as:

$$\tau = s(\alpha - \rho)$$

where α is the joint angle for which the muscle has lengt l and ρ is the angle for which it has its resting length. The net torque generated by two opposing muscles is therefore:

$$\tau_{net} = \tau_1 - \tau_2$$
$$= s_1(\alpha - \rho_1) + s_2(\alpha - \rho_2)$$
$$= (s_1 + s_2)(\alpha - (s_1\rho_1 + s_2\rho_2)/(s_1 + s_2))$$

This has the same form as equation 2a with s equal to the sum of s_1 and s_2 and α_0 equal to the weighted average of ρ_1 and ρ_2, using s_1 and s_2 as weighting coefficients.

More complex cases in which there are many muscles acting about a joint, non-linear length-tension functions, and varying leverages of a muscle about a joint are trickier, but they retain an important modularity. The required length-tension functions can be computed from the required angle-torque function, and so this function is all that needs to be communicated. Decisions about how to implement it can be made locally.

A further complication is created by the fact that many muscles act about two different joints. This means that the length of the muscle and hence the torque it exerts at any given level of innervation depends on both joint angles. This allows the torque exerted at one joint to be contingent upon the current angle of a neighboring joint, and Hogan (1980) has shown how this property can be very useful for giving the body the right motor impedances.

VISCOSITY PROVIDES A VELOCITY FEEDBACK TERM

The idea that the physics can be used to provide feedback effects is not restricted to positional feedback terms. In many circumstances, it is also helpful to have negative feedback that is determined by the difference between the desired and actual *velocities*.

So far, we have ignored the fact that the force generated by a muscle depends on its rate of contraction. Again, this initially seems to be a complicating factor but actually makes control easier by providing a velocity feedback term. The simple one-joint model illustrates this effect if there is viscosity at the joint (or in the motor). If the internal model of the dynamics of the system includes an accurate representation of this viscosity, it is possible to allow for it in selecting the appropriate angle-torque function. The computed torque then has two components, one to accelerate the system and one to overcome viscous drag. The angle-torque function must be selected to provide the sum of these two torques. Now, suppose the physical system is actually going more slowly than the internal model. There will be less viscous drag than predicted, and so some of the torque that was destined to overcome viscous drag will actually be left over and will go into accelerating the system. This gives a velocity feedback effect. The discrepancy between the actual angular velocity and the intended one gets turned into a torque that reduces this discrepancy. Moreover, no neural comparison of the intended and actual velocity is required. The feedback is generated by the physics.

In the body, there is little viscosity at the joints themselves, but the viscosity in the muscles gives an equivalent effect. From a design standpoint, the viscosity of muscles initially looks like a mistake and one is tempted to see it as a regretable imperfection of the biological hardware. It is true that it consumes energy and it is true that it slightly complicates internal models of the dynamics, but the almost instantaneous velocity feedback term that it provides may make it worth while.

2. COMPUTING TORQUES

An important ingredient of Bernstein's argument for the necessity of co-ordinative structures is his claim that computing torques is extremely difficult because of the reactive forces. This helps support his view that higher levels of the motor system are not directly concerned with torques. The idea is that higher levels use some other code, and the reactive forces

are dealt with lower down in the system. This might be feasible if reactive
interactions are handled by local feedback mechanisms, but if feedforward
components are involved then they are much harder to compute locally because
they necessarily involve non-local reactive interactions. Bernstein himself
points out the importance of feedforward control towards the end of chapter
4, but he gives no hint as to how it is to be achieved.

    Bernstein claims that reactive interactions between different joints in
a chain of segments have exponential complexity. In other words, for each
extra mechanical degree of freedom, the magnitude of the computation required
to figure out the reactive forces is *multiplied* by a constant factor. If this
factor is large the problem rapidly becomes intractable. Actually, far from
being exponential, the problem is linear. For each new degree of mechanical
freedom, a constant amount is *added* to the computation. Bernstein can hardly
be blamed for not realizing this, since it was only recently discovered. Over
the last few years the complexity of the best known algorithm has fallen
from order (N^4) (Uicker, 1965) to order(N)(Luh, Walker and Paul, 1980).
This makes it far more plausible that the brain could actually compute the
torques required to follow a desired trajectory.

    The mathematics used in computing the torques is fairly complicated
(Luh et. al., 1980), but the physics underlying it is relatively straightforward. We first convert all the information about the desired trajectory
into a single global non-accelerating frame of reference. Then we simply
solve the equations of motion for each segment in turn starting with the
most distal one. The desired linear and angular accelerations of this segment
relative to the global frame are known and they allow us to compute the
forces and torques acting at the joint between this segment and the penultimate
one. Once these forces and torques are known, we can solve for the unknown
forces and torques at the proximal end of the penultimate segment, and so on.

    Luh et. al. work with the general case in which sliding joints are
allowed as well as rotating ones. If there are only rotational joints, we
can further simplify their method by only solving for the torques. Even
though the joints are moving through space, at any instant a joint is at a
point in space and the angular momentum of the whole of the system distal
to the joint about that point in space can only be affected by the torque
applied at the joint and by externally applied or gravitational torques.
If these latter are known, the torque applied at the joint can be determined
from the rate of change of angular momentum of the distal system about the
point where the joint now is. Linear forces acting through the joint cannot

affect the angular momentum about it, and neither can torques acting at other joints. The rate of change of angular momentum is simply the sum of the rates of change for each of the segments that is distal to the joint. This means that it is possible to solve for the torque at one joint without first solving for the torques at all more distal joints.

CAN THE BRAIN DO ARITHMETIC

The discovery of an algorithm of linear complexity for computing torques is an important advance for robotics, but it is not necessarily relevant to the issue of whether the brain can do the computation. Computers do arithmetic very well. They represent numbers precisely enough so that the progressive accumulation of rounding errors during a long computation does not swamp the answer, and they perform each operation so fast that they can perform long sequences in a fraction of a second. Brains seems to work quite differently (Von Neumann, 1958). They have neither the speed nor the accuracy for the kind of computation discussed above. But they do have billions of processors each connected to thousands of others. If the computation can be decomposed into many pieces that can be performed in parallel, and if each piece has little sequential depth, both the speed and the accuracy problems can be solved. It may be possible to decompose the torque computation into separate pieces that can be performed in parallel for each joint, at the cost of a certain amount of duplication. It would be necessary, for example, to perform separate additions, at each joint, of the rates of change of angular momentum of the distal segments. This inevitably involves adding together the same numbers several different times, and increases the computational complexity from order(N) to order(N^2). However, the increased number of operations is not large, and may well be worth the time saved by the parallelism. The brain has lots of processors, but not much time. Benati et. al. (1980a) present a way of decomposing a similar computation into pieces each of which can be done in parallel by a hardware module that might correspond to a group of neurons.

It is important to remember that the internal computation of the torques does not need to be nearly as accurate as performance measures might suggest. If angle-torque functions are used, the "instant feedback" effect will take care of minor errors. Even rather inaccurate feedforward computations of the torques yield much better performance than feedback alone, so a sloppy internal model of the dynamics is much better than none at all.

A RECONSIDERATION OF THE EQUIVOCAL EFFECTS OF CENTRAL COMMANDS

Given the preceding discussion of the merits of angle-torque functions and the feasibility of computing torques ahead of time, it is easy to see the flaws in the arguments that suggested that torques are not computed centrally. The equivocal response of muscles to neural signals is just right for implementing angle-torque functions, and the optimal choice of these functions requires precomputation of the required torques. The need for feedback is satisfied by the physics of the system, but this does not mean that the torque computations are left entirely to the periphery, because the advantages of feedforward control over pure feedback require precomputation of torques. Finally, the idea that reactive interactions lead to exponential complexity in the computation of the torques is a plausible conclusion, but it is false.

The use of angle-torque functions is a particular example of a much more general principle. If a central controller does not know the precise state of the system it is controlling, or the precise forces that will be encountered, it can either wait for sensory feedback before it sends down commands for action, or it can send down contingency plans and leave the periphery to decide which contingency applies. Angle-torque functions are just contingency plans that have a very compact form. Even though he does not seem to have realized that muscles themselves can decode contingency plans, Bernstein was well aware of the advantages of the contingency plan approach as a way of organizing the interactions between different levels of control in the motor system.

3.   THE DEGREES OF FREEDOM PROBLEM

Bernstein, was committed to achieving a mechanistic understanding of human motor control and he realized that the kinds of mechanism available at the time were totally inadequate. He was therefore forced (in the true spirit of articial intelligence) to speculate about possible mechanisms that might be adequate for the task. Unfortunately, he did not have computers to simulate these mechanisms and so they remained vague in many respects.

Bernstein decided that the existence of surplus degrees of freedom in the motor system posed a major problem for any theory of motor control. There are more joints in the human body than seem to be necessary for any one task, and each joint is typically affected by more muscles than seem to be necessary. This creates two kinds of problem. First, it is hard to decide exactly what to do because there are more degrees of freedom in the way the body moves than there are constraints in a typical "motor problem" so the motor problem cannot uniquely specify its solution. Second, even if we could decide exactly what to do with each joint and each muscle, there are still so many of them to be coordinated that the task is liable to swamp any "central executive", especially if modifications are required to cope with un-predictable external forces or the effects of errors in the internal model.

Bernstein proposed that the motor system handles these complexities by using hierarchical coordinative structures. He does not give a very clear statement of the idea anywhere in this book, but it appears to be an example of a way of handling complexity that should be familiar to all computer programmers. Instead of trying to bridge the gap between the "motor problem" and the neural impulses to the muscles in a single span, the gap is progressively narrowed by using a hierarchy of schemas. At the highest level there are schemas that translate the motor problem into terms that are more suitable for the next level down, and so on all the way down to the muscles. At each level, the schemas mediate between the task requirements passed down by the higher level schemas, and the possibilities that are made available by the lower level schemas, given the current state of the motor apparatus. The main advantage of the hierarchical approach is that the higher levels do not need to be concerned with low-level details. The myriad degrees of freedom provided by the individual muscles do not need to be explicitly considered, much as a general does not need to explicitly consider each soldier's actions in planning a battle.

The idea of hierarchical coordinative structures is very attractive, but it is under-specified and there are several different ways to make it more precise. One interpretation is in terms of a qualitative hierarchy in which each level deals with a different type of entity. Examples of possible types are hand-positions, joint-angles, torques, and muscle activations. A different interpretation of coordinative structures is discussed and criticized later.

A FOUR-LEVEL HIERARCHY

Hierarchical decomposition is an excellent way to deal with complexity when the task can be naturally divided into a number of levels, and decisions can be made at one level with little or no consideration of the level below. Saltzman (1979) has discussed possible levels at length, and makes finer distinctions than the ones which follow. Four good candidates for natural levels in motor control are:

1. *The level of the motor problem*. The planning activities that govern
deliberate behavior may give rise to a sequence of relatively well-specified
and self-contained motor problems such as "reach out to object A" or "grasp
object A". This would allow the planning routines to ignore the details of
the movements (though they would have to be sure that they were feasible).

2. *The level of movements of the body*. It may be possible, in solving
a given motor problem, to decide how the body should move without explicitly
considering the torques required to implement the movements. Similarly,
decisions can be made about how the end-effectors should respond to external
forces (Mason 1981) without considering the angle-torque functions at the
joints that are needed to implement the desired motor impedance of the end
effectors.

3. *The level of torques*. The torques required to cause a desired
movement can be computed without explicitly considering how the muscles are
going to implement these torques. Similarly, the angle-torque functions
required to implement the desired impedances of the end-effectors can be
computed without considering how these functions are to be implemented.

4. *The level of muscle innervation*. This is the bottom level of the
hierarchy, and motor control is considerably simplified if the required
muscle properties are only computed after the required torques or angle-
torque functions have been decided.

In this modular decomposition, as in most modular schemes, there are
various intrusions of lower level constraints on higher level modules.
Certain movements, for example, are impossible because the muscles are not
strong enough. More importantly, the efficiency or accuracy of certain
movements depends on the magnitude or rate of change of magnitude of the
muscle forces required for the movement. So the choice of a good movement
appears to depend on considerations that are two levels down in the hierarchy.
However, the modularity of the levels can probably be saved by incorporating,
at each level, heuristics for making choices that will be easy of efficient
to implement at the next level down. The heuristics contain *implicit* knowledge
about the level below, but they are phrased in the terms of the level they
are at, and are thus easy and fast to apply at this level. A concrete example
of such heuristics is given below.

In chapter 4, Bernstein argues against the idea that a motor problem
like reaching to a particular point in space is solved by computing a spatial
trajectory. If he is right, the separation between levels 2 and 3 above may

well be wrong, but this argument appears to be flawed. It rests on the observation that there is considerable variation in the trajectory used from trial to trial, but very little variation in the endpoint. This observation certainly rules out any model in which the knowledge of where to reach is encoded as a spatial trajectory, but is does not rule out models in which the spatial trajectory is computed afresh on each trial. Minor variations in the rules used for forming the trajectory could easily give rise to a family of slightly different trajectories that all had the same endpoint. (Slight variations in the coefficients in the model of reaching described below would have just this effect).

Minor variations in the spatial trajectory from trial to trial, would be very helpful in discovering a trajectory that not only solved the problem, but did so with the least effort or greatest accuracy. They would allow changes in the trajectory formation rules to be correlated with measures of performance like energy expenditure, jerk, or accuracy. In this way it would be possible to progressively improve the trajectory formation rules so that they gave rise to trajectories that had good dynamic properties, even though the formation rules did not mention torques or forces explicitly. This is an example of the idea of using heuristics at one level that *implicitly* contain knowledge about lower-level considerations such as torques and forces.

The idea of qualitatively different levels is only one of the ways in which hierarchical structure can be applied to motor control, and although Bernstein clearly distinguished some of these qualitative levels, his notion of coordinative structures seems to have been far richer. Several people, influenced by Bernstein, have proposed a view of coordinative structures which emphasizes the role of higher level schemas in constraining the possibilities at the next level down (Greene, 1972; Turvey, Shaw, and Mace, 1978).

Underlying this view is the belief that surplus degrees of freedom make motor control *harder*, and that they therefore need to be removed by imposing extra constraints. This may be true if control is performed by a sequential central executive with limited resources, but there are parallel, distributed forms of computation which are not hampered by surplus degrees of freedom. Indeed, if the right kind of computation is used, extra degrees of freedom make motor control *easier*. The next section briefly described an iterative distributed computation that coordinates many degrees of freedom in satisfying two goals simultaneously. A simplified task has been used to illustrate the style of computation, but the same style would work for more complex, three-dimensional tasks with more degrees of freedom.

4.   A DISTRIBUTED PROGRAM THAT REACHES AND BALANCES

Consider a two-dimensional puppet composed of six segments as shown in
Figure 1. The foot always remains fixed and is regarded as the proximal end
of the puppet. The joints can all move between limits that are roughly
appropriate for a person, and each segment has a roughly appropriate mass.
Given a starting configuration and a desired position for the distal end of
the lower arm (the tip), the task is to compute a set of joint angles that
puts the tip at the goal position, puts the center of gravity vertically
above the foot, and is as similar as possible to the initial configuration.

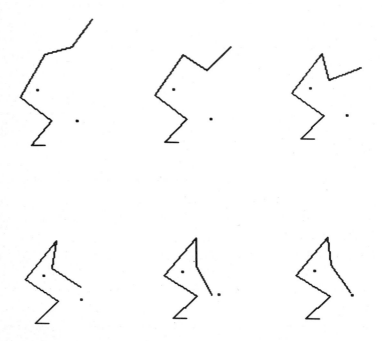

Fig. 1. This shows a sequence of configurations generated by the iterative
        algorithm. One of the black dots represents the center of gravity
        of the whole stick-figure, and the other represents the goal to
        be reached. The configuration is shown on every second iteration.
        The reason for the overshoot is that in addition to the computed
        joint increment, half of the previous increment is also added. This
        smoothes out oscillations and thus allows bigger co-efficients to
        be used without causing divergent oscillations. Extra processors
        which control several joints at once were used in this example.
        These extra processors are described later in the text.

REACHING ALONE

To begin with, let us ignore balance and just consider the problem of getting the tip to the goal. A simple physical analogy suggests a way of organizing the computation. Suppose we took a real pin-jointed puppet and connected the tip to the goal with a rubber band. The tip would move towards the goal and the surplus degrees of freedom would not cause any difficulties. Moreover, the method would work perfectly well if some of the joint angles were temporarily frozen.

It is relatively easy to *approximately* simulate the physics using a distributed computation in which there is one processor for each joint. The rubber band (the "desire vector") generates a torque about each joint that is given by:

$$T_j = d.r_j$$

where d is the magnitude of the desire vector and r_j is the perpendicular distance from the j'th joint to the line along which the desire vector acts. The joint angle is then incremented by a small amount that is proportional to the torque. To ensure that light segments move more easily than heavy ones, the increment, ΔA_j, is also proportional to the moment of inertia, I_j, of the distal portion of the system about the j'th joint:

$$\Delta A_j = k_r.T_j.I_j \tag{3}$$

where k_r is a constant that determines the size of the increments used in the reaching computation.

On each iteration, three types of computation occur in sequence:

1. The processor for each joint computes a new joint angle. To do this it must have access to the global desire vector, the line along which the vector acts, the position of the joint in space, and the moment of inertia of the distal portion of the system. The new joint angles can all be computed in parallel.

2. Given the new joint angles, the new positions of the joints in space can be computed by starting at the foot and following the chain of segment-lengths and joint-angles. Once the position of the tip is known the new desire vector can be computed.

3. Given the new joint positions, the new centers of gravity and hence the new angular inertias of the distal portions about each joint can be computed by starting at the tip and adding in the segments one at a time.

Provided k_r is sufficiently small, the combined effect on the desire vector of all the separate joint increments will be approximately the same as the sum of the effects of each increment by itself. All of the interactions (i.e. cases in which changes in one joint angle alter the way in which the desire vector is affected by changes in another joint angle) are mediated by the process of updating the positions of the joints in space, because the angle at one joint determines the positions of more distal joints and hence it determines the magnitude of the torque exerted by the desire vector about those joints. (The torque is a measure of the amount the desire vector would be changed by incrementing the joint angle).

This simulation glosses over all the complexities of the dynamics of a real physical system. It is actually a faithful simulation of a bizarre system in which inertial forces are negligible compared with viscous ones, but the viscosity at a joint is always set equal to the angular inertia about that joint.

BALANCING ALONE

If we ignore the reaching problem and just try to find a balanced configuration in which the center of gravity of the whole system is above the foot, a very similar computational scheme can be used. Instead of a global desire vector, there is a global measure of the extent to which the system is out of balance. This is simply the horizontal distance of the center of gravity from a vertical line through the center of the foot. Each joint angle can be incremented, in parallel, so as to reduce this quantity and then the new joint positions and new centers of gravity can be computed just as in the reaching algorithm.

Each joint controls the position of the center of gravity of the segments that are distal to it. The extent to which an angular increment to the j'th joint restores balance is determined by the mass, M_j, of the distal portion and also by the horizontal distance that its center of gravity moves. The horizontal distance moved is proportional to the vertical distance, V_j, between the joint and the center of gravity. So to help restore balance, the angular increment at the j'th joint is given by:

$$\Delta A_j = k_b . V_j . M_j / I_j \tag{4}$$

where k_b is a constant and I_j is its moment of inertia of the distal portion about the j'th joint.

COMBINING REACHING WITH BALANCING

To find a configuration that satisfies both the reaching and balancing goals simultaneously, the increments required for reaching and the increments required for balancing can simply be added together on each iteration. The relative values of k_r and k_b determine the relative importance of satisfying the two goals. If these values are set appropriately, joints near the foot are primarily influenced by the balancing goal because they control a large distal mass (M_j in equation 4), whereas joints near the tip are mainly affected by the reaching goal. Figure 1 shows a typical sequence of configurations generated by this simple parallel algorithm.

INADEQUACIES OF THE MODEL

There are many criticisms of this simple computational model:

1. It gets stuck at local optimum, and so it can fail to find a suitable final configuration even though one exists. This is an important limitation of this kind of iterative parallel computation and it suggests that any computation of this type would need to be combined with more qualitative, schematic knowledge which could specify, very approximately, which region should be searched in the space of possible configurations. The use of schematic knowledge resembles table look-up, but it differs because the iterative computation used to compute the precise details of the final configuration is more powerful than simple linear interpolation between table entries.

2. It does not take obstacles into consideration. Obstacle avoidance requires an understanding of the space occupied by the body, and it also requires a more global view of the trajectory. The kind of myopic computation in which the current configuration is gradually changed into the desired one cannot deal with obstacles properly because it cannot see far enough into the future to avoid cul de sacs. An altogether different style of parallel computation may be required to avoid obstacles.

3. It is not parallel enough. Steps 2 and 3 in the computation seem to be inherently sequential. Actually, at the cost of some extra computation, they can be made parallel. If, for example, the orientations of the segments relative to the global frame of reference are stored and updated at the same time as the joint angles, it is possible to compute the new position of a joint in space simply by adding together the vectors for all the more proximal segments. This addition can be performed in parallel. The extra cost is that the same vectors get added several different times in computing the positions of different joints, and when a joint processor decides to update its joint angle it must also increment the global orientations of all the segments distal to it. This destroys the purely local communication structure in which each joint-processor only communicates with the processors for adjacent joints.

4. It takes a large number of iterations in certain situations. A simple
example is shown in Figure 2a. The problem is that the line of action of the
desire vector passes almost exactly through the shoulder and elbow joint. This
means that the torques about these joints are very small so the joint angles
are only changed very slightly on each iteration. It is obvious to us that the
way to reach the goal is to shorten the arm by flexing it, but there is no
explicit representation of the length of the arm in the parallel computation
and so this insight cannot be incorporated. The next section shows how the
introduction of higher order variables that coordinate the activities of
several neighboring joints can overcome this problem and can dramatically
reduce the number of iterations required.

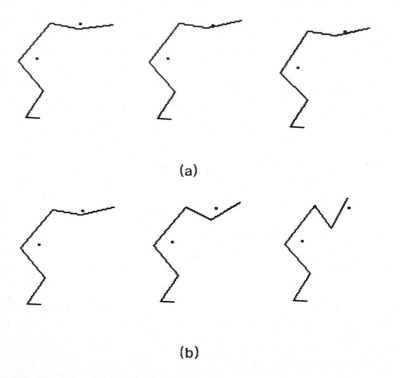

(a)

(b)

Fig. 2. (a) shows how the simple iterative algorithm fails when the line
         of action of the "desire" vector passes close to the joints that
         need to be changed. The configuration is shown on every third
         iteration. (b) shows how the behaviour is improved by adding a
         synergy that controls the shoulder and elbow angles together
         and is invoked when the desire vector aligns with the direction
         from the tip to the shoulder. The configuration is shown after
         every iteration, so a single iteration with the synergy produces
         more progress than six iterations without it.

SYNERGIES

Changes in the angle of the elbow change the length of the arm ,but they also have side effects. They make the hand move along a circular arc centered on the elbow, and they change the hand's orientation in space. To make the hand move in a straight line away from the shoulder that cancel out the side-effects of the changes at the elbow. If the upper and lower arm segments are the same length, this can be done by increasing the elbow angle by 2α and decreasing the shoulder and wrist angles by α.

In cases like the one shown in Figure 2a, the iterative computation can discover the need for compensating changes at the shoulder. It first changes the elbow angle, and this changes the line of action of the desire vector so that it no longer passes directly through the shoulder. The desire vector then generates a torque about the shoulder which causes a change that compensates for the side-effect of the change in the elbow. However, this method of generating side-effects and then figuring out how to get rid of them is not nearly as efficient as avoiding unwanted side-effects by using "synergies" - combinations of changes whose side effects cancel.

Synergies are easy to incorporate within the parallel iterative framework. In addition to the processors for the individual joints, we simply add a processor for each synergy. This processor knows about the combined effect of a number of changes, and it is invoked whenever that effect is desired. When it is invoked it attempts to change the joints it controls in the appropriate way. Since a given joint may be under the control of several synergies as well as having its own processor, some principled way of combining different influences is required. As with the coordination of reaching and balancing, the correct combination rule is simply to add together the changes requested by the various synergies and by the joint processor itself.

Figure 2b shows how reaching is improved by adding a synergy that controls arm length by coordinating changes at the shoulder and elbow. The synergy is invoked by the degree of alignment between the desire vector and the vector from the shoulder to the distal end of the arm. If the angle between these two vectors is ϕ, the changes requested by the synergy on the current iteration are:

$$\Delta A_{elbow} = 2.k_s.\cos(\phi).I$$
$$\Delta A_{shoulder} = -k_s.\cos(\phi).I$$

where k_s is a constant that determines the relative importance of synergies as compared with the primitive changes computed by the individual joint processors, and I is the effective inertia.

ADDING NEW SYNERGIES

The simple additive rule for combining the changes requested by the
various synergies makes it very easy to add new ones. They can just be
thrown into the pool of existing synergies. Provided each synergy has its
own processor, and provided the basic joint processors can perform the
necessary additions of the requested increments in parallel, additional
synergies do not increase the time required per iteration.

THE FUNCTION OF SYNERGIES

The use of higher order synergies to speed up a parallel iterative
search is quite different from the use of higher order schemas to eliminate
surplus degrees of freedom by imposing constraints on lower level variables.
In the parallel iterative scheme, there may well be a hierarchy of synergies,
each influencing the values of lower level ones, but every synergy in the
hierarchy has access to the global goals (e.g. the desire vector and the
measure of imbalance). Because surplus degrees of freedom do not present a
problem to the parallel computation, there is no need to place each lower
order variable strictly under the control of a single higher order one. All
the processors for all the different levels of variable can compute in
parallel, and every synergy can be activated to the extent that it helps
reduce the difference between the current state of the system and the desired
final state.

5.   THE ROLE OF FEEDBACK IN MODEL-BUILDING

In the preceding sections I have described some computational advances
that help to solve some of the problems that Bernstein raised. This final
section contains meta-level comments on the role of feedback in model-
building and on a new source of potential feedback for theories of human
motor control.

At the start of chapter 4 there is a long discussion of feedback from
historical and philosophical perspectives. Bernstein points out (as Gibson
did in the field of perception) that most of the interesting issues in motor
control were ignored for many years because of the laboratory study of
artificially simple situations. This is a familiar modern view which is
probably as uncontroversial now as it was radical at the time. His
philosophical views, however, are more questionable.

Bernstein correctly points out that internal symbolic representations can be objectively correct, and that they do not require the implicit internal observer assumed by idealists (see Dennett, 1978, pp 89-108 for an excellent recent discussion of this issue). Bernstein also points out that the development of a valid internal model is aided by two-way interactions with the domain being modelled. This is a point of great practical significance, but Bernstein tries to elevate the point to a philosophical principle that feedback of the effects of actions is *essential* for objective knowledge. This is a far more dubious propositionel. If it is true astronomers are out of luck.

Returning to the practical significance of feedback, recent technological developments have created the potential for a new source of feedback about the adequacy of theories of motor control. Progress in robotics clearly yields insights that supplement the experimental data on biological motor control, but there is always the worry that many problems in robotics may be the result of using conventional digital computers and may have little relevance to biological computation. The fundamental differences between the architecture of a general purpose computer and the architecture of the brain have led some people to suspect that computation may work in very different ways in these two types of machine (Von Neumann, 1958; Hinton & Anderson, 1981). Even though general purpose computers can be made to simulate any other kind of computer, there is still the suspicion that the sensible way to do a particular computational task in a conventional computer may be quite unlike the sensible way to do it in the brain.

Until recently, computers were very expensive to design and very expensive to build. This meant that they had to be general purpose, because the cost of designing and building dedicated hardware for a specific task was prohibitive. It was much more cost-effective to use a general purpose computer which was tailored to a specific task by its program. Now, however, very large scale integration makes computers cheap to build, and advanced computer aided design makes it relatively easy to design novel hardware structures. This opens up the possibility of tailoring the hardware to specific tasks, and thus avoiding the sequential bottleneck that is imposed by insisting on the architecture of a general purpose machine. It is now possible to design and produce a chip with hundreds of simple processors all computing in parallel and all communicating directly with specific other processors. The sequential execution of stored instructions is no longer necessary, and it may be possible, using dedicated hardware, to perform computational tasks hundreds or thousands of times faster by making good

use of the parallelism (Mead and Lewicki, 1982). There is just one snag.
There are very few good ideas about how to organize parallel computations
using a hard-wired network of local processors each of which is much simpler
than a general purpose computer. Perhaps this will be an area where theories
of human motor coordination can suggest practical hardware designs, and
where experience with these designs can provide useful feedback.

ACKNOWLEDGEMENTS

    I thank Peter Greene for helpful comments on the manuscript. Many people
helped me formulate the ideas presented here. They include Paul Smolensky,
Don Norman, Dave Rumelhart and Don Gentner in the skills group at the
University of California, San Diego; Tim Shallice and Alan Wing of the
Applied Psychology Unit in Cambridge; and Marc Raibert and Scott Fahlman
at Carnegie-Mellon University.

REFERENCES

Adams, J.A. Issues for a closed loop theory of motor learning. In, G.E.
    Stelmach (Ed.), Motor Control: Issues and Trends. New York: Academic
    Press, 1976.

Asratyan, D.G. & Feldman, A.G. Functional tuning of the nervous system
    with control of movement or maintenence of a steady posture. 1.
    Mechanographic analysis of the work of the joint on execution of a
    postural task. Biophysics, 1965, 10, 925-935.

Benati, M., Gaglio, S., Morasso, P., Tagliasco, V. & Zaccaria Z.
    Anthropomorphic Robotics. 1. Representing Mechanical Complexity.
    Biological Cybernetics, 1980, 38, 125-140.

Benati, M., Gaglio, S., Morasso, Pl, Tagliasco, V. & Zaccaria, R.
    Anthropomorphic Robotics, 2. Analysis of manipulator dynamics and
    the output motor impedance. Biological Cybernetics, 1980, 38, 141-150.

Bizzi, E., Accornero, N., Chapple, W. & Hogan, N. Arm trajectory formation
    in monkeys. Experimental Brain Research, 1982, 40, 139-143.

Dennett, D.O. Brainstorms: Philosophical essays on mind and psychology.
    New York: Bradford Books, 1978.

Greene, P.H. Problems of organization of motor systems. In, R. Rosen and
    F.M. Snell (Eds.), Progress in theoretical biology, Volume 2. New York:
    Academic Press, 1972.

Hinton, G.E. & Anderson, J.A. Parallel models of associative memory.
    Hillsdale, NJ: Erlbaum, 1981.

Hogan, N. Mechanical impedance control in assistive devices and manipulators.
    In, Proceedings of the Joint Automatic Control Conference, Volume 1.
    San Francisco, 1980.

Hogan, N. Control and coordination of voluntary arm movements. In, Proceedings
    of the American Control Conference. Arlington, Virginia, 1982.

Horn, B.K.P. What is delaying the manipulator revolution? Working paper 161.
    Cambridge, MA: Artificial Intelligence Laboratory, MIT, 1978.

Houk, J.C. Regulation of stiffness by skeletometer reflexes. Annual Review
    of Physiology, 1979, 41, 99-114.

Lozano-Perez, T. A language for automatic mechanical assembly. In, P.H.
    Winston and R.H. Brown (Eds.), Artificial Intelligence: An MIT
    Perspective, Volume 2. Cambridge MA: MIT press, 1979.

Luh, J.Y.S., Walker, M.W. & Paul, R.P.C. On-line computational scheme for
    mechanical manipulators. ASME Journal of Dynamic Systems, Measurement,
    and Control, 1980, 102, 69-76.

Mason, M.T. Compliance and force control for computer controlled
    manipulators. IEEE Transactions on Systems, Man, and Cybernetics SMC-11,
    1981.

Mead, C.A. & Lewicki, G. Sillicon Compilers and Foundries will Usher in
    User-designed VLSI. Electronics, 1982, August 11, 107-111.

Polit, A. & Bizzi, E. Characteristics of motor programs underlying arm
    movements in monkeys. Journal of Neurophysiology, 1978, 42, 183-194.

Raibert, M.H. & Sutherland, I. Machines that walk. Scientific American,
    1983, January, 44-53.

Saltzman, E. Levels of sensorimotor representation. Journal of
    Mathematical Psychology, 1979, 20, 91-163.

Turvey, M.T., Shaw, R.E. & Mace, W. Issues in the theory of action: Degrees
    of freedom, Coordinative structures and coalitions. In, J. Requin (Ed.),
    Attention and Performance VII. Hillsdale, N.J.: Lawrence Erlbaum
    Associates, 1978.

Uicker, J.J. On the dynamic analysis of spatial linkages using 4x4 matrices.
    Ph.D. Thesis, Northwestern University, 1965.

Von Neumann, J. The computer and the brain. New Haven: Yale University
    Press, 1958.

SECTION 5

CHAPTER V

TRENDS AND PROBLEMS IN THE STUDY OF INVESTIGATION OF PHYSIOLOGY OF ACTIVITY

N. Bernstein

(Published in *Questions of Philosophy*, No. 6, 1961)

New concepts and problems which have arisen out of the development of cybernetics have powerfully seized the attention of physiologists. The overwhelming majority of these problems appearing in our physiological journals indicate a desire to establish a *rapprochement* between the current state of cybernetic theory and the attitudes and achievements of classical Russian physiology. This forces us to consider the history of the subject intently and thoughtfully. It seems, however, that the uninterrupted development of strictly materialistic concepts and points of view which are our heritage from native physiologists of the schools of Sechenov, Pavlov, Vvedenskii, Ukhtomskii and others depends on their further integration into the contemporary body of biological science. It is now more important to look ahead, and to attempt to discern, though perhaps only in the most general terms, *problems* (though still remote from a solution) deriving from the new facts and concepts, and some new *directions* which still need to be carefully considered, but which, it seems, may allow us to attain the discovery of new and wide horizons. We may justifiably relate the study of the *physiology of activity* to these new directions of investigation.

I

The classical physiology of the last hundred years is characterized by two sharply defined features. The first of these is the study of the operation of the organism under quiescent inactive conditions. Such conditions were artificially secured wherever possible by decortication, by anaesthetization of the animal, or by fixing it in a stand under conditions of maximal isolation from the external world. This analytical approach to the study of quiescent conditions derived from the attempt to study every organ and every elementary process in isolation, attempting to exclude side effects or mutual interactions. In general terms this approach corresponded

to the predominance of mechanistic atomism in the natural science of that
era. The absolutism of that point of view led to the conviction that the
whole is always the sum of its parts and no more than this, that the
organism is a collection of cells, that all behaviour is a chain of
reflexes, and that a sufficient acquaintance with the individual bricks
would be enough for the comprehension of the edifice constructed from them.

The second characteristic feature consisted of the concept that the
organism exists in a state of continuous equilibrium with the universe
surrounding it, and that this rigid equilibrium is maintained by means of
appropriate reactions, unrelated to each other, and made to each successive
stimulus impinging on the organism from the surrounding environment. The
whole existence and behaviour of the organism was visualized as a
continuous chain of reactions on the stimulus:response model (nowadays we
would talk of input and output). The standard of the classical materialistic
physiologists was the *reflex arc*, and their central aim was the analysis of
regularities in *reactions* considered as rigidly determined input-output
relationships.

The general technico-economical conditions maintaining after the First
World War sharpened interest in the *working* condition of the organism. New
branches of applied physiology arose - the physiology of movements (here,
and from this point on, we shall use this term to indicate goal-directed
motor acts and not insignificant fragments of movements such as the
withdrawal of a paw because of pain, or the knee-jerk reflex). If this
department of physiology has not been given sufficient weight and attention
in the pages of the older physiology of rest and equilibrium, its pre-
eminent importance now began to be apparent. In fact movements are almost
the only expressions of the life activity of the organism. Movements are
the means by which it does not simply passively interact with the
environment, but actively *acts upon it* in whatever way is necessary.
Sechenov had already indicated the general significance of movements in his
remarkable book *Cerebral Reflexes* one hundred years ago. If we add that time
has since revealed the integral nature of the participation of movements in
all acts of sensory perception, in the education of the sense organs during
early childhood, in the active development of an objectively consistent
world image in the brain by means of the regulation of perceptual *synthesis*
through practice, it is easy to understand the displacement of the centre
of gravity of interest which is becoming increasingly felt in contemporary
physiology.

The progressive growth in the complexity and power of technical devices has demonstrated very clearly that problems of control and regulation form an independent area of study - a study which is in no way less complex, important or comprehensive than that of the energies which are subordinated to these controls. The problem of the rider has begun to overshadow the problem of the horse.

Analogously in physiology, beginning with a study of the energetics of the operating (working) condition of the organism (gas exchange, the control of secondary systems which do not directly participate in external work - breathing, circulation, sweating, etc.) interest has gradually begun to centre on the more comprehensive problems of the regulation and central control of the activity of living organisms.

II

For further discussion it is necessary to pause briefly on one particularly important feature of the control of motor acts which has been established with complete objective reliability for both animals and men[*]. This is the fact that the relationship between the *result* - for example, the movement of a limb or of one of its joints - and such commands as are delivered to the musculature from the brain through the *effector nerves* is very complex and non-univocal[†]. This absence of univocality is a result of the fact that muscles are elastic belts (imagine the connecting rod of a steam engine replaced by rubber, or by a spiral spring) and the effects of their action on the organ which is moved depends essentially on the position and the particular velocity of that organ at the beginning of the

---

[*] For a bibliography enabling the reader to become better acquainted with experimental and clinical data see the author's paper "Immanent problems in the theoretical physiology of activity" in the textbook *Problems of Cybernetics*, publ. 1961, and the journal *Voprosi Psikologii*, No. 6, p. 70, 1957.

[†] The indicated relationship between muscular excitation and the resulting movements is very different from the picture which was confidently described by physiologists of the last century (Bekhterev, Munk, etc.). It then seemed natural to treat the motor area of the cortex as a sort of keyboard on which somebody's hand, in sovereign control, described the program for a given motor stereotype. The pressing (excitation) of one of these cell buttons always brought about a given degree of flexion at a given joint, the pressing of a second brought about extension, etc.

muscular activity. This absence of univocality is further explained by the
fact that, as in any physical multijointed pendulum, involved and complex
involuntary forces (*reactive forces*) arise in a moving limb. The lack of
one-to-one correspondence between messages to the limbs and the actions
produced at particular junctures is finally also due to the fact that any
meaningful movements overcome external forces which are quite beyond the
control of the participant (gravity, friction, the opposition of an
adversary, etc.) and which cannot be predicted by him. It is clear that
organisms, whose only channels of operation upon the surrounding world are
commands given to their muscles, may achieve controlled movements serving
a particular purpose only by means of continuous monitoring and control
achieved by the participation of the sense organs. The physiology of the
remarkable and varied signalling equipment with which the organism is
equipped, located in the muscles themselves, in the joints, and in the
observation post of the body - the head incorporating the distance
receptors of vision, hearing and smell - is now well understood. This
apparatus provides for perfectly accurate and continuous *circular control*
(i.e. feedback control) and revision (i.e. correction) of movements, even
of movements comprising such complicated multiple-jointed structures as
our limbs, and effected by the non-rigid muscles which drive them[*].

It is possible that these complex dynamic features of motor acts
which have just been described are the reasons for yet another characteristic
feature appearing most clearly in habitual movements; that is, the remarkable
structurality and completeness of a motor act, which makes it impossible to
treat it as an arbitrary collection of successive reflex elements (see
Chapters II and III). We will not dwell on this feature at present. It is
more important to turn to another set of characteristics of goal-directed
movements which are still very far from clear, and which still require
careful investigation. The analysis of the peculiarities of this group of
properties allows us to find a bridge between the *physiology of reactions*,

---

[*] Here we have a typical case of *control by means of negative feedback*, a
device which is widely used in simple forms in modern technical devices.
We may incidentally note that this principle of negative feedback control
has been observed by physiologists in recent years to operate in the most
various forms of control exerted by the organism - the pupilliary reflex,
regulation of blood pressure, of the heart-beat, of chemical equilibrium,
etc. It is now beyond any doubt that the most general and prevalent form
of organization in live organisms is not the reflex *arc*, but the reflex
ring.

with which psychophysiologists have been exclusively concerned for some time, and *the physiology of activity*.

III

What is the standard invariable determinant of this involved structurality of motor acts which we have just discussed? We cannot suppose *effector commands* to be such a standard determinant. These commands are emitted into a system involving at least two types of independent forces (reactive and external forces), they act upon the organ through a non-rigid musculature, and they must also vary between very wide limits in order to accommodate to signals coming from the sense organs. These afferent (incoming) signals also cannot act as standard determinants, because signals giving the degree of match or mismatch between movement and effect can only be as variable as the cues which provide them, and, more importantly, the information which they contain is a description of "what is" and not of "what must be done". The brain mechanisms by which the signals giving the progress of a movement, are coded and deciphered, and the degree of mismatch between emitted commands and the operation of the required muscle at the required time, also cannot be considered for this role, because they are necessarily just as variable and non-standard as the codes which they transform.

All our long experience in the study of motor activity, of motor habits and of clinical disorganization has demonstrated with great clarity that the standard determinant both for the programming of motor activity and its effection and correction by feedback connections can only be the formation and representation of a *motor problem* by the brain in one way or another. The analysis of this concept, and of the wide circle of relationships and facts which it entails, will be the particular business to which the remainder of this chapter is devoted.

If we do not, for the present, avoid simple commonplace terminology, then the sequence of the arousal and realization of any action of the class of so-called voluntary movements may be represented in the form of successive stages.

1. Perception, and the necessary evaluation of the *situation* and of its bearing on the individual caught up in it.

2. The individual determines in what way it is necessary to alter this situation; what, by means of his activity, the situation *must become* instead

of *what it is*. The motor problem has already appeared at this stage. It is
not difficult to guess that this motor problem must contain more information
than is included in the bare perception of the situation, some of which is
at least partially not present in the latter. Animals in a herd, or people
in a crowd, may be confronted with the same situation, but the motor
behaviour of each individual will be different. Examples of this may be
readily found.

3. The individual must next determine *what* must be done and

4. *How* it must be done, and what are the available resources.

These two micro-stages already represent a program of the solution of
the problem, and after these there follows the process of its actual
solution in terms of motor activity. It is scarcely necessary to emphasize
that the control and evaluation of successive moments of the actual activity,
the variability of the situation itself, with the fact that it is, generally
speaking, possible to program only rather roughly movements which have some
duration in time, all explain the adaptational variability of programs and
of acts, permitting changes ranging from small corrections to widespread
alterations in strategy.

It would be false to suppose that the micro-stages in the transition
from the situation to the act which have been described above are found
only in highly organized nervous systems. The same stages must also
necessarily be found in such primitive acts as, for example, the pursuit of
live prey by predatory fish. In this case we also have a situation which is
perceived in the necessary form and measure, and a motor problem with a
program for its solution. The precise way in which either of these aspects
of the process is coded in the nervous system of a predatory fish is quite
unknown to us, but it is beyond doubt that neither consciousness nor a
particularly high level of nervous organization is necessary for them to
take place.

Concerning the topic of the higher information content of the problem
in comparison with the actual perceived situation, we must add the following.
From the point of view of the dependence of the actions of an organism on
the stimuli which provoke them, or on the input in general, we may draw up an
imaginary series in which we may rank all actions (confining ourselves here
to the actions of human beings) according to their degree of dependence on
such activating stimuli. At one end of the series we have movements which
can be fully explained in terms of the stimuli which activate them. Among
these we have all the so-called unconditioned or innate reflexes. We may

also include all reflexes conditioned during life experience which are nevertheless dependent on the activating stimulus - reactions of the general class of *conditioned reflexes* found in humans and animals alike.

We may place next in our rank order, movements for which the stimulus or signal continues to play the role of an activator, but which have a meaningful content that is increasingly independent of the stimulus. For motor acts of this class the activating signal increasingly takes on the features of a trigger signal, analogous to the pressing of a button which sets in motion the whole complex process of firing a rocket, or to the interjections "hep" or "arch" after which follow sequences of activity which are very little related in significance to these interjections. Finally, at the other end of the series, we find acts for which the activating or triggering signal does not play a decisive role, and in which it may be entirely absent. These are actions for which the program, and also the initiative, are entirely determined within the individual, and which, with greater accuracy, may be described as the operations to which the term "voluntary movements" may properly be applied. It is not difficult to see that a progression along our scale coincides with the gradual shift from passive acts, to acts having an ever-increasing degree of active involvement[*].

IV

Now we shall see what can be said at present about the necessary concomitants of every act of translation of the perceived situation into a motor action - of the phenomenon which would be called "looking forward" in Chinese, and which in more scientific terms may be called *extrapolation to the future*. Indeed, planning a motor act (irrespective of the way in which it may be coded in the nervous system) necessarily involves the recognition in some form of the pattern of what must be, but is not yet, the case. In a similar way to that in which the brain forms an *image* of the real *external world* - an image of the factual situation at a given

---

[*] Conditoned reflexes must be referred, not to the intermediate class, but to the first of the types described here, as in the case of established and differentiated conditioned reflexes a stimulus fulfils not only a *releaser* function, but also acts in an informational way, completely determining whether it will be followed by an appropriate act, by differential inhibition, or by an act of another type, etc.

moment, and of situations which have been exprienced in the *past* of which
we have impressions in our memory - it must possess to some degree the
capacity to form a representation of (or, what is the essence of the
matter, to plan in advance) situations which are as yet unrealized, and
which the biological requirements of the organism impel it to realize.
Only such an explanatory image of the necessary future can serve as a basis
for the formulation of problems and the programming of their solutions.
It is certain that this image of the future is qualitatively very different
from images of either past or present reality but, as the ensuing discussion
will show, the possibility of its existence in some coded form in the
brain (which need not in the least involve subjective consciousness), both
in animals and in men, does not admit anything which is methodologically
undesirable.

In a number of cases similar to the illustration provided and, it is
possible, in experimental situations also, this "looking into the future"
which we are discussing is accessible both to introspective observation
and to chronometric measurement. We have, in the first place, cases where
the program for meeting the motor problem is formulated as a physical code
which is accessible to the sense organs. A musician playing by sight or
any one of us reading a text aloud, advances his gaze some interval ahead
of the notes or words sounded at any given moment. This is to say that
both acoustic and psychomotor images of what is to be realized by motor
means within a second, or fraction of a second, must be present in the brain
all the while. It is possible, in this connection, to carry out an
illustrative experiment on oneself. Try, without hurrying, to declaim to
yourself (in the same way as reading to yourself silently) any piece of
poetry which you know well by heart. Mentally listening to yourself doing
this, you will clearly perceive that two texts pass before the inner ear:
one text in the tempo of the mental declamation, sometimes accompanied by
lip movements which are often intense enough to be perceived, and a second
which runs ahead, easily outstripping the first text, as if you are preceded,
stanza by stanza, by some internal prompter. I have no doubt but that
psychologists can suggest many more successful and fruitful types of
demonstration for this phenomenon.

There is one very idiosyncratic group of phenomena, which have been
observed on more than one occasion, indicating that the image of the
future discussed here is not only limited to effects on the course of the
programming of motor acts but may in certain cases possess a great

physiological reality, as if this foreshadowing of the future already gave
it an existence in the present. I have in mind sources of the *emotion of
fear*, an experience which can be aroused solely on the basis of a clear
image of the imminent future in the brain. In both ancient and contemporary
scientific literature we encounter a whole series of descriptions of *death
from fear* - so severe may be the autonomic-vegetative shock which is produced
by this coded image. In literature we encounter examples of this in Gogel
(*Vyi*) and Edgar Allen Poe (*The Fall of the House of Usher*).

In order to approach an experimental investigation of those principles
by which the image of the future, in the widest sense of this term, may be
coded in the brain - that is to say, the nervous processes serving as the
basic guiding compass of the organism in all its behavioural manifestations -
and its essential difference from the image of the present and immediate
past, we must begin with a small theoretical discussion.

Let all elements of a given set E (of any number of dimensions) be
related in terms of a determinate law to the elements of a second set J so
that each element of the second set will be brought into correspondence
with one or more elements of the first, and vice versa. We will refer to
the set E in this case as the *primary image*, to the set J as its *reflection*,
and to the principle or law of connection as the *law of reflection, or
projection of E on J*. The elements of the primary set may (all or partly)
be time functions. The elements of the set J would then be functions of
time in the same way, and with them, the set J as a whole. Even the laws
of reflection may be functions of time, and in this case the reflection J
will be doubly variable in time for both these reasons. As physical
examples of systems of the type described we may take the optical image
on the retina of a human being watching the movements in a street from a
motor car. The continuously occurring changes in this image will be due
both to the motions of the objects in the street, and to the changes in
the law of optical projection on the retina of the eye because of the
motion of the latter.

It is difficult for anyone who is not mathematically sophisticated
to visualize the enormous number of possible laws of reflection amongst
which we may search for the true law or laws of the formation of the image
of the real external world in the brain. Meanwhile, repeated lack of
information on theories, because of which the enormous number of such laws
are naively reduced, has already frequently led both physiologists and
clinicians to erroneous conceptions, sometimes to harmless errors, but often

very far astray from a correct comprehension of the essence of the matter.

A characteristic example of such a discarded misunderstanding, is the problem of how we see objects in the external world the right way up in spite of the inversion of the visual field on the retina. This question attracted serious attention, and several hypotheses were put forward to describe a reinverting mechanism. The error in these explanations of the mechanism responsible for reinversion lay in the assumption of the separate existence of "percept" and "observer" in the brain. The former was in some way supposed to be reproduced element for element from the evidence available in the optical projection on the retina. The latter in some way perceived or saw this image, in a similar way to that of the subject seeing the external world. From this, it was a small step to postulate that this observer had his own visual area.

The error which has just been described has now already been exposed, and it has been mentioned only because it is instructive. Another important error is still alive and we must consider it.

V

The genesis of the concept of one-to-one correspondence between the cell network of the cerebral cortex and the elements of the perceptual fields of the organs of sensation - vision, hearing, touch, muscle and joint receptors (proprioception) - is not difficult to determine. An enormous amount of material gathered from the experimental physiology and pathology of the brain from 1870 onwards (the date of the first discoveries in this area) indicated beyond doubt that not only was it the case that each type of sensation has its own corresponding separate *zone*, but that within these zones there was some sort of precise correspondence with the elements of the peripheral territory of a given sense organ. This correspondence was more or less highly differentiated depending on the particular zone involved. Among these projection areas of the cortex the most detailed appeared to be those subserving touch and proprioception, in which it was actually possible to trace a sort of cartographical projection (accurate, however, in very general features only) of the sensitive surface of the entire body.

The dynamic variability of the information from the sense organs, changing from moment to moment as it reached the primary projection areas of the cortex described above, forced investigators to postulate the existence of secondary zones alongside them which would subserve the functions of retention (memory) of sense impressions transmitted by the primary projection areas. It was assumed that these secondary zones had the same point-to-point projection characteristics as the former.

In order to turn now to the analysis of the error of atomism which is inherent in these postulates, which clearly was in great part a result of inadequate information in the field of projection theory, and which was discussed above, we must again make a small digression.

It is not difficult to demonstrate by means of two or three extremely simple visual examples that there may indeed exist pairs of sets such as project fully upon each other, but that while each of them is easily and completely divisible into its component elements, a relationship in terms of projecting elements, such as described above for the projection of the type E on J, leads to an obvious absurdity.

A blueprint for a machine is made up of a thousand lines. In order to make this machine the craftsmen must carry out a thousand operations. Does this mean that the matching of every line demands a separate operation?

I make a statement containing 1000 words. My opponent entirely refutes my case, also in 1000 words. Does it follow from this that each of the words which he uses refutes one of the words in my statement?

Or finally, 1000 people read a book of 1000 pages. May we understand from this that the first reader reads page 1, the second page 2, and the hundredth page 100?

The technique of *reductio ad absurdum* is often a very useful device for the detection of an erroneous line of thinking.

Armed with the preceding examples let us turn again to the discussion of the basic position of the theory of the secondary fields, after which we may attempt an approach to a theoretical generalization of what has been said above.

What do we feel, touch or perceive with each of our organs of sensation? Things, objects. What are the elements of the multitude of environments which we encounter? Objects. What must be the elements for a cerebral projection of the type E on J in the corresponding cortical systems and in their cells? It is clear that it must be objects which figure here, both as separate reflections by the brain of the elements of the external world and as the stimulus signals for reactions to it.

If the erroneous nature of discussions of the brain image in these terms is not already clear enough from what has been said, we may proceed further along these lines.

A type of brain function which is the monopoly of man alone is articulate *speech*. We already have a collection of representations of the external world in the form of the first signal system. But words are the names of objects, so that it is necessary to add yet another projection in terms of elements arising out of this signal system, and we will obtain a second signal system, so to say, a projection of a projection, in which every object signal, image element of the first system will have its corresponding name in the second. Clearly, atomism has a very powerful hold upon the imagination if there still exists such an interpretation of the second signal system as reduces speech, the inexhaustibly powerful tool of thought, which no less than the hand makes a man a man, to the level of a dictionary of terms for concrete objects in the nominative case singular. Neither space, nor the aims of this statement, allow us to develop the theme we have touched upon. We shall accordingly limit ourselves to two or three questions. (1) In the second signal system what exactly are the signals for which such elements as "again", "twice", "y function", "without", "indeed" and "or" stand? (2) How and where in the atomistic second signal projection system are such signal words as "you think, he does not think, we will think, you would think, they will not think" incorporated into its structure? (3) Is it perhaps better not to discuss at all such verbal signals as "wave function", "quaternion", "antinomy", "transfinite"?[*]

An example of the same category of erroneous connections between two sets which are indisputably divisible in their elements, and also indisputably related to each other, is found at the boundary between psychiatry and neurosurgery. That is, the theory of psychomorphologism (now exposed as an error, and discarded) which classified and subdivided elementary psychic functions and the symptoms of their deterioration in

---

[*] The most convincing example of the inconsistency of the second signal system theory arises out of a practical problem. It must be pointed out that it has been quite impossible so far to use the results of many years' attempts to delineate the second signal system as algorithms for machine translation, whereas a true physiological theory of speech and language ought to play a leading role. A comprehensive analysis of the essence of this argument and the reasons for it are given in L. Uspenskii's *Word about words*, Ch. 6, p. 283, Molodaya Gvardia, 1960. Also in O. Kulagin's paper "On the operators describing the algorithm of translation" in the textbook *Problems of Cybernetics*, 2nd. edn., p. 289, 1959.

relation to their connection with determinate locations in the brain. In this case also we can trace the confusion to the same error, which, in reference to the first of the examples of absurdities which we provided, we may term the error of the "blue print and the machine".

VI

Now, to turn from illustration to generalization: let us suppose that there are connections between the elements of the set E, which in one way or another join these elements into subsets by determinate laws, or even that we ourselves impose such ordering laws on the set as divide it up into families or subsystems of elements. The simplest example of an operation of this sort is the relation of a system of coordinates to a plane or a spherical surface. It is possible to give many examples of such sets in which an ordering of this type is not imposed from without, but exists within the set itself, and it is only necessary that the system should be observable and describable.

Let us now suppose that the elements of a given set M are related, not to separate elements of E (as was the case in the projection of E on J in terms of sub-elements), but to whole subsystems of its elements - representing their systematic ordering. In cases of this type we will describe the set M as *a model* of the set E, and the principle of the given ordering and relationships as *the operator of modelling*.

It is not necessary to emphasize how varied the forms and principles of modelling may be. In some cases, to every function of the families making up the set of the first order E there corresponds a determinate in M (termed in the functional). In other cases the operator of modelling determines an ordering or a grouping of functions of the primary set, in series, either continuous or discrete, so that such a series answers in M a certain type of a "function of functions". The very forms of selection of representative functions from the first set may be qualitatively very different from each other. The representation in the model may include exhaustively all the endless multiplicity of systemal functions which cover the first representation, or they may select discretely among them (for example, selecting only integer numbers as values for their parameters, etc.). This may also relate to each element or any constellation of elements in the model - discrete function axes of the first representation E - incorporating probability determinations of the strips of territory

along them, etc. It is now necessary for us to formulate some basic
points emerging from all that has been said so far, and which directly
bear on our theme.

In the first place, describing this widening of the limits of the
principle of representation, we may affirm with confidence that in the
brain a *representation* (or representations) of the world is *constructed
along the principles of a model*. The brain does not receive an impression
of the external world in the form of a passive inventory of elements, and
does not employ such primitive means of subdividing the world into
elements as first come to mind (phrases for words, and plans for drawings),
but applies to them such operators as most accurately model the world,
casting the models in the most consistent, exact and comprehensive forms.
This process, or act, of mentally modelling the world is, under all
circumstances, undertaken *actively*. In reality if the principles of
analysis, systematization and reflection of the set by the system are
applied to the primary image by the brain itself, this process of the
formation and use of operators is active by its very nature. And if the
regularities in the internal ordering of the set E are inherent, then it
is only possible to note them, recognize their significance, and employ
them in the capacity of operator principles by means of active observation
and investigation.

Something more may be said about the general characteristics and
properties of active operational modelling of the external world.

Imposing on the first representation E one or other systematic
regularity, or formulating a regularity which is already observed in
the first representation, the brain brings some degree of additional
information to the task, and by this means the information we obtain from
the first representation is quantitatively extremely economized, but enriched
in its meaningful content. It is possible to compare this additional
information introduced from within to an enzyme, a small quantity of which,
secreted by the organism, produces the optimal conditions for the digestion
of a large quantity of a food.

It becomes clear in passing that the arguments hypothesizing an
internal isomorphic representation of the sensory periphery (the retinae,
skin, etc.) are false in principles, and cannot be accepted as circumstantial
evidence for the existence of the observer in the brain whom we described
above. The consequent duality of the observer and the percept, which alone
of all schemes requires this detailed isomorphism, becomes superfluous and

unnecessary from the point of view of active operational modelling. A
model does not contemplate anything which confronts it from without, but
is a coalescent indivisible unity of processes and mechanisms transforming
received information, which constantly changes without losing its continuity,
or unity, and directs the course of the active behaviour of the organism.

The phenomenon of looking into the future which has already been
mentioned as the basis for every motor problem (or, as we may now say, for
every *model of the future*) forces us to recognize that in the brain there
exist two unitary opposed categories or forms of modelling the perceptual
world: the model of the past-present, or what has happened and is happening,
and the model of the future. The latter proceeds directly from the former,
and is organized in it. These are necessarily distinct from each other,
chiefly because the first type of model is single-valued and categorical,
while the latter can only operate by means of extrapolation to some or
other *degree of confidence* or probability*.

Problems related to the model of the present lie beyond the scope of
this paper. Many psychological investigations have already been undertaken
along these lines. We shall limit ourselves to a single example which may
incidentally indicate the great practical importance of explanations of
the nature of operators and operational models of the objects of the
perceptual world. This example concerns the processes underlying the
perception of *configurations*.

The visual image of a circle has five degrees of freedom (or represents

---

* It is interesting to note that the two aspects of models of the
surrounding world co-existing in the central nervous system are very
clearly connected localizationally to different parts of the hemispheres.
The neurosurgical clinic brings evidence of the contrasting forms of
disturbances resulting from the lesions in the posterior and the anterior
parts of the cerebral cortex. Lesions of the lower parietal fields,
surrounded with the primary and the secondary zones of principal categories
of reception (vision, hearing, touch), bring with them all sorts of
disturbance in the simultaneous perception, in the ordering of objects
and movements *in space*, briefly, in the structural synthesis of sensory
information which are all the essential features of a model of factually
existing reality. On the other hand, in the clinics it is demonstrated
that with prefrontal and frontal lesions there are various types of loss
in the planning and programming of active behaviour, in ordering the links
of the chain of a motor act *in time*, in the chief premise of every form
of activity, the so-called orientation reaction - that is to say the
orientational prognosis of surrounding events and changes. All these forms
of nervous activity indisputably belong to the domain of modelling of
the future in the sense discussed above.

a five dimensional continuum) in terms of the multiplicity of its optical
projections on the retinae. A triangle has six degrees of freedom, while
the projection of the letter H has twelve, and the projections of some of
the other letters of the alphabet have even more. This does not, however,
prevent the operator processes in the brain (although their structure is
quite unknown to us) from correlating the enormous variety of such optical
projections and (we may suppose) of cortical projections, with a single
meaningful code of symbols. There can be no doubt that when it is possible
in the future to build a machine modelling this process which will
recognize *letters* irrespective of their sizes of type faces, it will surely
operate not by means of passive *scanning* (as do present experimental
examples), but solely in terms of the cerebral principles of operator
modelling, when these are understood.

VII

That important form of cerebral modelling which was only recognized
by investigators after the arousal of interest in the physiology of
activity – that is, *the modelling of the future* to which we now turn – is
logically possible only by means of *extrapolation* from whatever the brain
is able to select from the current situation, from the fresh traces (see
Chapter IV) of immediately preceding perceptions, from the entire previous
experience of the individual, and finally from those active trials and
assays belonging to the class of actions which have so far been summarized
briefly as orientational reactions and whose fundamental significance
has certainly been underestimated.

The complex of nervous processes which makes up a model of the future
is so unclear and enigmatic that very little can be said about it. Apart
from the indisputable statement that such a complex exists, and plays a
most important directional role in the active perception of the surrounding
world, as has been described above, we may make the following observations.

In sharp distinction to the model of the present the model of the
future has *a probabilistic* character. The anticipation or expectancy of
the possible outcome towards which the current situation is moving is only
possible by means of extrapolation and never, generally speaking, can be
brought to a categorical result. At any phase of this process the brain is
only in a position to survey a sort of table of probabilities for possible
outcomes.

Outcomes	A	B	$C\ldots$	$M\ldots$	X	Y	
Probabilities	P_A	P_B	$P_C\cdots$	$P_M\cdots$	P_X	P_Y	$\left.\vphantom{\begin{matrix}a\\b\end{matrix}}\right\}\ \Sigma_\rho = 1$
Motor problem	0	0	$0\ldots$	1	0	0	

It is hardly necessary to make the point that, in the interests of analysis, we have restricted ourselves to a very simplified schematization.

Meanwhile, the motor problem which the individual determined for himself is formulated as a cetegorically unique outcome of the current situation, whatever its *a priori* probability may or may not be in the table (even if it is equal to zero). In this way the organism's activity is directed against the probabilistic model of the future, and the determination of problems that arise is the dynamic struggle of the individual to raise the probability P_M of the desired outcome until it reaches unity, or becomes an accomplished fact. This struggle implies the reduction of the probabilities of all other outcomes to zero. It is clear that this struggle must result in the lowering of the entropy of the system involving the individual and his immediate environment, that is to say, this must always be a process endowed with *negative entropy*.

The struggle described above takes place in a complex field of conditions with a multiplicity of variables. In the first place, the extent to which the brain is able to make successful extrapolations, and its estimation of perspective and of possible outcomes must necessarily be very approximate. (It is, however, probably no more approximate in relation to the requirements of a given living creature, in the case of extremely elementary organisms, than in the case of creatures with very highly developed brains). The coarseness of the possible extrapolation must necessarily increase with the interval of time, Δt, over which the organism attempts to exercise foresight. In the second place, the success of the extrapolation also depends on the term which the subject sets for its completion. If conditions are rapidly changing, and the organism is involved in time trouble, it may be obliged to limit itself to primary, coarsely exploratory techniques and responses, since it does not have sufficient time for more accurate ones. However, even when caught up in the toils of a threatening situation, where time is important, the selection of strategies of behaviour always involves a choice between responses which may be rapidly effected, though these may also be less accurate, and slower responses which have been more reliably evaluated. Thirdly, and finally, the field of conditions encountered by the organism is itself variable in time, and is both dependent on, and independent of, the activity of the individual, so that the organism is, in fact, constantly involved in a sort of conflict situation with the environment. It is already apparent from the foregoing that the evolution of Theory of Games is of great importance to the physiology of activity.

Among the related questions which require the combined attention of physiologists and mathematicians is the problem of the forms of extrapolation which are employed by the nervous systems of organisms of high and low development, and the particular mechanisms which they employ to achieve this guidance. Considering the lower, purely biomechanical, types of regulation which antecede a particular action by a minimal period of time, we apparently encounter extrapolation of the same type as that incorporated in a Taylor series with the use of two primary derivatives as information, that is, data from the joint and muscle signalling systems. (This is sometimes described as gradient extrapolation). Considering more complex and meaningful types of plans for movements, such as may require reprogramming during their course, the higher co-ordinational brain systems and the synthetic processes involved will be found to include forms of probabilistic extrapolation among their equipment, and these will doubtless include just such methods of active sampling as have been formulated and described in the contemporary mathematics of estimation as methods of non-local search (46). It is necessary to emphasize the decisive difference in principle between the appearance in the physiology of activity, of extrapolational search which has been described above, and the concept of trial and error described by the behaviourists. The latter indicates a sequence of attempts, each of which is unrelated to preceding ones, and is, like them, made at random. In this case it is only the external form which is active, the sum of trials being essentially treated as a passive statistical computation of successes and failures. Figuratively, we may say that each trial of this sort gives information of the type "this is not the way", but gives no information as to where or how to do "what is necessary". It is no accident that this principle is easy to imitate in machine models. On the other hand active non-local search, which is apparently a real component of orientational behaviour, after the first couple of attempts are either made at random or else directed in some approximate way by elementary mechanisms working on the principle of gradient extrapolation, results in the deduction of how and where the next step must be taken. In this way each attempt renders more accurate a progress towards the optimum means by which the maximum amount of the most useful information can be obtained.

VIII

What is known at present in experimental physiology about the manifestations and effects of this model of the future, and by what experimental techniques may these best be described in the light of exact modern knowledge? Let us turn again to the consideration of concrete examples of movements.

Among the multiplicity of functions of the central nervous system involved in the control of motor acts, the first to be explained are the processes by which movements are corrected while they are in progress. This is achieved by a system of feedback connections served by the numerous informational sources available to the body. The mediation of this uninterrupted system of correction is a most important biomechanical premise for the production of any purposeful motor act: the mastery of the enormous number of degrees of freedom possessed by our motor organs, and their conversion by these means into a directed system. This function may be regarded as the technical aspect of *motor co-ordination*.

During the course of the co-ordinational process (considered in micro-intervals both of time and of the path of the movement) one characteristic peculiarity of all excitable organs plays a decisive role. All such organs possess *finite* and also *variable* values of *thresholds of arousal*. The absolute values of these thresholds are remakably varied for different organs, and for each particular organ they may further vary between wide limits, depending on overall physiological conditions.

This is a circumstance which has very important consequences for the control of motor acts. The central brain systems organizing and co-ordinating motor acts, primed by the wealth of information from sensory sources, are enabled to do more than correct such disagreements as may arise between intended and actual movements *post factum*. Proceeding with a determinate program of operation, the central nervous system can, and indeed does, achieve *anticipatory adaptations* in terms of the tuning in advance of the arousal of all the sensory and motor elements which are employed.

These interesting but still barely investigated examples of regulation *ante factum* outstrip, as it were, movements by micro-intervals of time, and are closely bound up with the mechanisms of anticipation and extrapolation which have been discussed above. They have been described under various experimental conditions, and by various investigators, now as neuromuscular *tonus*, now as physiological *sets* and, in recent years, as functions of the reticular formation of the brain, although a growing amount of evidence suggests that we are here concerned with the same wide range of interrelated factors. In terms of contemporary electrophysiological techniques these processes of anticipatory adaptation can only be observed with some difficulty and as disconnected manifestations. It is naturally most convenient to observe them *before the beginning* of a movement, when the weak bioelectrical manifestations of tonic commands are not masked by the far more powerful potentials accompanying muscular activity. These tonic impulses, which precede the beginning of a movement, are the neuromuscular concomitants of *sets*. Improvements in the techniques of recording bio-electrical phenomena in nerves and muscles will make it possible to study these processes of set (switching processes in Lapicque's metaphor) during the course of the entire motor act.

The most interesting problems in this area, which have only just begun to be considered, are naturally related to the central nervous regulation of processes which involve set. Some of the problems encountered in this area bring us once again, and in an unexpected way, to the central problem of the cerebral representation of reality and of the types of coding which the brain imposes on its evidence. We approach this topic a little indirectly.

Physiologists have distinguished for some time between two very different forms of arousal process which exist concurrently in the neural and muscular substrate. One of these forms, which appears to be more recent in terms of evolutionary history (it may properly be called neokinetic), is manifested as a rhythmic sequence of bursts of excitatory impulses (sometimes called peaks, or spikes) following the all-or-none law. (That is to say, they have the same height, whatever may be the strength of the supraliminal stimulus impinging for the given variable degree of their excitability). These impulses travel at considerable speeds (of the order of tens of meters per second), and are transmitted without damping along nerve fibres. Because these impulses are transmitted over the entire course of the reflex ring through fibres enclosed in isolating myelinated envelopes with dielectric

properties, the neural impulse codes running along adjacent fibres in a
nerve do not suffer from mutual interference or leakage. This allows us to
regard them as a *"channelized"* form of nervous process.

A second manifestation of nervous activity in neurons and muscular
units, which is much more ancient in terms of its appearance during
phylogenesis (it may be called palaeokinetic) has retained, in man and the
higher mammals, the monopoly of the control of the smooth musculature in
internal organs, and has also taken over the role of the tonic transmission
of adaptational impulses to sense organs and effector apparatus, as discussed
previously. These impulses differ sharply from neokinetic phenomena. Firstly,
they are dosable, that is, they do not obey the all-or-none law; secondly,
they have two types or signs of significance - or, in other words, they
may promote either excitation or inhibition. Thirdly, their activity is
not explosive - that is, instead of discrete peaks occurring at millisecond
intervals they exhibit slow waves of various forms and heights. Finally,
their most typical property lies in the fact that the dielectric coverings
of the fibres *do not constitute obstacles* for their passage, so that they,
or at least their major components, are able to spread *across the fibres*.
For these reasons it is more correct to regard this form of nervous
activity as being of *wave form* in distinction to the channelized form of
neokinetic impulses. This latter property does not have much practical
scope within the comparatively narrow peripheral nerve fibres. However,
in the main brain mass itself we may say with some certainty that it is
precisely these processes, penetrating considerable masses of brain tissue,
and even the carapace of the skull, which are nowadays accessible to
electroencephalographical investigation, being frequently called, in loose
terms, *cortical bioelectrical currents*.

It is important to bear in mind that the neokinetic chains of impulses
in the cortical neurons, being channelized and rigidly isolated from each
other, cannot escape from their channels and appear on electroencephalograms
(E.E.G. records). It is again unnecessary to make the point that
encephalograms are quite unrelated, either in terms of their frequency or
their overall form to chains of impulses of the all-or-none variety such as
are observed in nerve fibres, and that they do not also represent the result
of the superimposition of patterns of such activity upon each other. A whole
range of clinical observations, particularly of cases of abnormal E.E.G.s
accompanying pathological conditions, leaves little doubt that wave-form
processes in the cortex play a certain important role in the regulation of

channelized impulses. It is more than probable that this regulational
activity is bound up with the function of the *reticular formation* of the
brain, as we remarked earlier. We shall not consider this aspect of the
problem any further - it is currently under extensive and successful
investigation by experimentalists and clinicians. We may now choose another
line of approach to the problem.

IX

During the last 200 years the history of the science of brain function
has undergone wide oscillations between two opposing points of view as to
the relationship of these functions to the substrate of the brain. After the
work of Flourens and his contemporaries in the first half of the 19th
century, the final triumph of the anti-localizational point of view appeared
to be assured - that is to say, there was a wide recognition of the wave
type of brain processes, acting on an undifferentiated substrate. The
discovery of the projection zones of the cortex (in about 1870) swung the
pendulum sharply in the opposite direction. In particular, the accumulation
of an ever-increasing amount of information about the primary projection
areas led to the intensive development of all the theories of cellular
centrism with which we have been earlier concerned in this chapter. The
cortex began to be regarded as a highly differentiated receptacle solely
for channelized processes taking place in neural conductors (axons) with
corresponding cortical cells acting as trigger-buttons for actions in the
motor sphere, and as storage receptacles for the acquisition of experience
of the environment in the perceptual areas.

The narrowness of these concepts was so clear that even within the
memory of the living generation of scientists, in the thirties of this
century, the "extreme left" of antilocalization again raised its head (the
schools of Lashley, Paul Weiss, et al.), attempting to demonstrate the
concept of mass action of the cortical cells and to shift the centre of
gravity of the study of nervous processes towards a search for specificity
among the codes of impulses transmitted along the nerves in the brain mass
itself.

There is now no reason to decide the question in terms of either of
these extreme cases - to put the problem on an either/or basis. Although the
enormous mass of data now available provides solid arguments in favour of
both points of view, it would be useless to bring them to discussion, or to

seek for reconciling solutions. It is time that the following was clearly understood.

The high degree of differentiation of the cortical substrate, particularly in the higher animals, is now beyond question. However, just because of this great conglomeration of active excitable neural elements packed in electrolytic substance, there exist all the nessecary conditions for the development of wave processes acting transversely to neural paths, and involving the interaction of very large numbers of these elements. It would further be difficult to deny that the greater the degree of morphological localizational differentiation and subdivision of the cortical substrate, the more favourable are the conditions for an intensive development upon it of nonlocalized wave processes. Any electrician who is concerned with alternating currents and fields will confirm that it is a real problem to protect, by means of shielding, the function of the aggregate apparatus from the effects of mutual inductance and capacitance between its components. This must naturally apply in a far greater degree to the extremely complex living ensemble within a fluid electrolytic mass, where properties and charges vary both as functions of time and of the co-ordinates of each of their points.

It would be incorrect to visualize wave processes in the cortex as macroscopic fronts which are comparable in extent with the size of the entire skull. On the contrary, in correspondence with the microscopic non-homogeneities of the brain mass, its variable electrical parameters, and the momentarily altering pattern of its potentials, one must regard these processes as having a very delicate lace-like spatial and temporal structure. Such fluctuations in potential which can be recorded through the skull as the E.E.G. are naturally no more than a fused "hubbub".

It is hard to doubt that the wave processes which are composed of innumerable transverse interactions between the neurons and conductive pathways of the brain are not dominated in some way by the tonic regulationary activity of the reticular formation, and possibly also of the cerebellum and of the cellular centres of the brain stem. In these areas there is certainly infinitely more to be learnt than has been investigated.

The whole of this discussion points to the necessity for the consideration by physiologists of the study of central-nervous processes as an indivisible synthesis of channelized and wave-form components, and this once again, and for the last time, brings us to the problem of models of brain action, and to the question of the separation of the observer and the percept.

Cellular centrists have always diligently avoided the problem as to what exactly may be said about the cells of secondary projection areas in respect to the content with which they are supposed to be entrusted. What (besides the indeterminate chronic excitation postulated by the conditioned reflex school) is imprinted upon a cell which must store for months and years the images of chairs and lamps, and hypotenuses, or the terms for these things? If these contents are represented by the brain in the form of corresponding codes, then what determines the selection of an appropriate non-occupied storage cell for this code, and in what form is it retained?

The problem of the form taken by informational codes employed by the brain, and of their storage in the mechanisms composing memory, is still far from a solution. It is, however, necessary to approach it in terms of the most modern concept.

The falsity of the view of the opposition of the observer and the percept in the brain has already been emphasized. Instead of the passive expectation of information by an observer we now visualize active operators co-operating in synthetic and dynamic ways to capture information, and the modelling of preformulated and anticipatory actions. We now also expect to encounter, in place of stationary cells which select, and in some way store, microscopic atoms of a representation of the world, dynamically synthetic neural processes which are simultaneously multiply channelized and wave-like in form, and which we have hardly begun to consider in this way. There now appears to be more evidence for the view that the distinction between the cells of the brain (supposed initially to be empty and undifferentiated from each other), and the externally introduced and alien meaningful content, is just as inaccurate as the distinctions drawn between the internal observer and percept.

If every active process of perception and action is represented in the brain by the formation of a corresponding operator, then the most probable form which the latter may take is the formation of a determinate kind of contour, resulting in a new path for the circulation of both channelized and wave-form processes - a contour, the existence and characteristics of which are not determined by the nature of some hypothetical content of the cells, synapses, interstitial tissues, etc., but by the very dynamic form of its organization and connections. To put the matter as briefly and schematically as possible, we may say that the meaningful content and adequacy of a given portion of the model of the environment does not lie in what is or is not contained in it, but is no other than this operator, in the sense in which this term has been defined here.

The present account of the directions and problems confronting physiology does not pretend to fulfil the functions of a program, and so is not an exhaustive survey of the problems which exist in this area. The problems of the *affective motivation* of voluntary actions and of the physiological relationship between affective activity and its conscious intellectual forms has also been entirely neglected. Further, it has also not been possible to include details of processes in which negative entropy is clearly expressed, such as in the development and growth of organisms, beginning at the stage of the impregnation of the ovum and the coding or modelling within it of the *future* organism which will grow out of it. We have neglected the cardinal problems of structuring, expressed in terms of the qualitative and quantitative interaction between schemas and (metrical) forms in the processes of growth and activity. Nevertheless if, within the range of problems on which this account touches, we may provoke ideas, crucial objections or counterarguments which are important for future investigation, the purpose of this account will have been fulfilled.

REFERENCES

46. Gelfand, I.M. & Tsetlin, M.L. The principal of non-local search in
    systems of automatic optimization, Report of the Academy of Sciences
    of the U.S.S.R., 1961, 137 (in Russian).

Human Motor Actions — Bernstein Reassessed
H.T.A. Whiting (editor)
© Elsevier Science Publishers B.V. (North-Holland), 1984

CHAPTER Va

BERNSTEIN's PURPOSEFUL BRAIN

J. Requin, A. Semjen, M. Bonnet

INTRODUCTION

Having been invited to play somewhat the role of a referee for a scientific book which was alaborated, written and transmitted to the scientific community in exceptional conditions, we think it indispensable to specify the context of Bernstein's activity as well as the context in which his work became familiar to us. This gives the present volume a very unusual character, namely the significance of a rehabilitation. This context explains in particular the form of our contribution which will constantly reflect the difficulties to make comments on the chapter of a book published 15 years ago, in which were collected articles written between 1934 and 1961. The issue of this book suddenly made available to Western scientific workers a volume, the outcome of which remains ambiguous. Bernstein's work rapidly became a sort of bible for those who considered him as a "laboratory genius", to quote Phillips and Porter (1977), who anticipated the necessity of a renewal in the approach to voluntary motricity. For many others, the value of the book lies only in the fact that it reveals the conceptions and critical considerations of a researcher who was certainly creative and undoubtedly a victim of historical vicissitudes that scientific exchanges may sometimes undergo. To them, the exhumation of Bernstein's writings no longer has the power of modifying profoundly the development of studies devoted to the elaboration and control of movements, which have known a considerable expansion in the last two decades.

A first element of this context stems from what could be called the marginal character of the work of Bernstein (who, on several grounds, appears to have been an independent scientist). Let us mention first the troubles he had with the directivism of the scientific establishment of his country which emerge on several occasions in the course of his book in an explicit controversial form: his discussion of the dominant ideology of classical reflexologism and associationism not only resulted in excluding him from

experimental research but also in distancing him from his scientific
environment for many years. On the other hand, there are good reasons to
believe that Bernstein, especially in the last years of his life, received
only limited information on the development of Western studies concerning
the fields in which he was interested. In particular, if one takes into
account the variety of questions dealt with, which often go far beyond the
organization and control of motricity and concern very general problems of
epistemology, one is struck by significant lacunae in his bibliographical
references. However, for a number of questions, the effects of these
omissions are attenuated or even masked by Bernstein's penetrating
intuitions. Finally, while Bernstein probably only had partial information
about the views and works of Western physiologists and psychologists, these
scientists were also totally ignorant of Bernstein's work until the
translation of his collected articles was published, and even today his
importance is not recognized by all. In a way, Bernstein's marganilization
continues, thus favoring controversy duly amplified by the diversity of
opinion concerning the value with which his work should be credited some
twenty years later. As an illustration, in the Handbook of Physiology issued
recently, neither Keele's (1981) contribution nor Granit's article (1981)[*]
refer to Bernstein. This can be considered as clearly revealing partiality
by those who see themselves as his natural disciples and who contributed to
the rehabilitation of this work. Nevertheless those who think Bernstein's
work not very decisive and no longer interesting will consider this lack of
reference as a simple omission. They will underevaluate this work all the
more as they feel bitter for having ignored it for so long and not having
benefitted from it earlier.

A second element of the context which runs counter to the usual role of
a referee is due to the very form of the book "The Coordination and Regulation
of Movements". It does not offer a structured synthesis of Bernstein's view
on the different physiological and psychological problems involved in the
organization of motor activity. It is rather a conglomerate of articles, each
of them intended to be self-sufficient. Articles are presented in the order
of their publication, their selection being made on the basis of the topic
dealt with, namely the control of movement. However, the book is far from
being devoted to this one question and Bernstein is often led to put forward

------

[*] Granit's article, however, was devoted to a history of conceptions in the
domain of the control of motricity.

more general considerations about, for instance, the philosophy of biological
sciences. Let us note that the many readers who knew Bernstein indirectly
will be surprised when going back to the origins of a work known mainly for
nourishing contemporary debates on the elaboration and control of movement.
Beyond the "biomechanician", which remains the label most generally linked
to Bernstein, they will discover not only the physiologist and the
psychologist but also the pertinacious, often aggressive epistemologist who
occasionally criticizes his immediate or distant circle. Such a juxtaposition
of texts, while bringing some light on the evolution of the author's views
regarding a number of problems, also underlines, through the redundancies
of a discursive reasoning, Bernstein's main preoccupations and reveals the
unavoidable internal contradictions of a train of thought which was sustained
for 30 years. In this sense, Bernstein's writings do have something in common
with the bible in which, as it is known, when exerting the art of using
quotations one may find an adequate support for whatever limited point of
view one chooses. Consequently, it was not only impossible but hazardous to
restrict critical comments solely to one article without taking into account
the previous or subsequent ones.

The last and probably the most important element of the context within
which a new reading of Bernstein's writings is made nowadays, is evidently
the whole set of exegeses, developments and comments to which his work gave
rise. From this point of view, the systematic analysis that the Science
Quotation Index provides is quite interesting. In effect it reveals that
there are very few references to "Coordination and Regulation of Movements".
These references can be classified into two constrasted categories, which is
a good indication of the attitudes which contribute to the perpetuation of
what we called Bernstein's marginality. The first category, the most
important, refers with some exception to Haskins Laboratories' studies which
played a decisive role in the circulation of Bernstein's view. Haskins'
scientists, amply using paraphrases and quotations, presented, summarized or
developed Bernstein's ideas within the framework of a new formulation of the
problems raised by the organization and control of motor activity. It should
be noted that it is at times difficult to draw the dividing line between what
should be attributed to the influence of Bernstein's views and what
constitutes the original, indisputable contribution of these authors.
Finally, the amplification of Bernstein's views, within the perspective of
an innovative thesis, naturally goes together with a will to disassociate
from conceptions of motor control considered to be classical and outdated.

This amplification leads inevitably to a selected or truncated exploitation
of Bernstein's views and arguments, which is facilitated - as already
underscored - by the very content and form of the book. Consequently, it is
now quite impossible to ignore the controversy which was unintentionally
provoked by Bernstein. The second group of references to Bernstein's work is
characterized by extremely general allusions to his views. They would not
deserve any comment if they did not attest to the fact that it is nowadays
well thought of, if not prudent, to quote him - which is easy in many cases,
given the extent of Bernstein's views. Consequently, when making comments,
it seems difficult not to adopt one of the two asymmetric alternatives:
either to follow those who, since they became the disciples of a prophet,
both contributing to the circulation of his ideas and proselytizing, can
only be laudatory, or to maintain a distance which may conceal potential
criticism as well as ignorance or lack of interest. This is why we thought
that a real reintegration of Bernstein into the dynamics of the views and
studies on the organization of movement could not be done without a critical
evaluation of his work, a scientific requirement which probably comes rather
late but which is one of the reasons for the present book.

The content of the chapter entitled "Trends and problems in the study
of investigation of physiology of activity" seems to be characterized by
three main themes. Our comments written within the above-mentioned perspective
will concentrate on these. They are devoted in the first place to Bernstein's
epistemological concerns, which are still relevant. They justify the basic
idea that in the relationships between the environment and an organism the
former does not always have the initiative. An organism acts through its
motor activity, i.e. it intervenes upon the environment and constructs a
perceptual synthesis which allows for a consistent image of the world. Such
a view implies a radical criticism of atomism directed against the use of
the reflex arc as a unit of analysis in the domain of motricity and, in the
domain of perception, against the principle of an accurate and amorphous
image leading to an insoluble antagonism between the "percept" and the
"internal" observer. The world representation, as a source of information
and a target for action, follows the principle of a dynamic modelling which
cannot be separated from the activity of the organism.

The second main theme concerns the problems raised by the planning and
execution of movement. In this chapter, emphasis is placed upon the
necessary implication that Bernstein discovered in the "structurality" and
"completeness" of motor acts. A lesser emphasis is given to the principles

of organization and the modes of functioning of a sensorimotor system, which integrates motor commands and information derived from afference and reafference. Bernstein stresses the role of primum movens assigned to an organisatory entity (what he calls "the motor problem") which gives biologically meaningful motor activities their adaptive finality. Taking into account the criticisms addressed to the theories of motor control, for which the concepts of program and programming are crucial, we shall emphasize the view that Bernstein's work cannot be used as an argument to solve the conflict between "peripheralists" and "centralists" since it is concerned with what may be centrally processed, once the state of the periphery has been evaluated.

Finally we shall expand upon one aspect of Bernstein's views which seems to have been somewhat disregarded by his exegetes, namely the role of the representation of the future in the planning and execution of a motor act. This representation is at the origin of permanent anticipatory activities which range from the probabilistic image of what must be and/or will be realized in the environment, to the functional preparation of sensory and motor elements which will be involved in action. Even though less elaborated than the views concerning the circularity of movement regulation, these references to expectancy as an important dimension of motor control nevertheless complement Bernstein's considerations devoted to the application of concepts of cybernetics to the control of voluntary motricity.

I. BERNSTEIN AS A PRECURSOR OF COGNITIVE NEUROBIOLOGY

Bernstein was well aware that Russian physiology could benefit from contemporary developments in biological sciences, especially from the application of the cybernetic model to living systems. This concern for ideological openness, as well as his own ideas on the theoretical foundations of a physiology of activity, led him to adopt a critical attitude concerning the systems of explanation advanced by orthodox Pavlovian reflexology. He claimed that it was not possible to base a theory of the elaboration and control of biologically and behaviorally significant motor acts on the sole principles of a sequential chaining or a hierarchical series of elementary reflex pathways, which would restrict the organism to respond passively and stereotypically to the unceasing appeals of the environment. The only function of such a chaining would be to maintain a stable equilibrium between the organism and the environment. We would like to emphasize that

Bernstein's critical argumentation and presentation of an alternative theory - in which the decisive notion of the active intervention on the environment replaces the notion of a passive interaction - refers to an oversimplified view of the concept of reflex; such an oversimplification was no longer supported by the data on the functional characteristics of reflex reactions which were available to Bernstein, and are still less supported by the results obtained in most recent studies on reflex activity.

It is extremely surprising that Bernstein was content to consider that movements triggered by reflex activity were "fully explained in terms of the stimuli which activate them", given that even Sechenov, as early as the end of the last century, had mentioned that the spatial and temporal characteristics of a reflex reaction in the spinalized frog depended not only on the parameters of the stimulus but also on the initial joint configuration of the stimulated limb. The tendency to systematically underestimate the factors of variability of the most elementary reactions - especially factors of central origin - reflects a general conception in which reflexes receive a trivial functional interpretation which barely acknowledges their evident biological finality in the restoration of the equilibrium that a stimulating agent imperils. For example, it is because the motor reaction tends to develop toward a compensation of the load imposed upon the muscle, without truly compensating it, that the role of the stretch reflex in movement regulation was at first accepted, before gradually being questioned. At this point, it is worthwhile to note Granit's position in 1972. With good reason, he was impressed by the power of the structural organization of the myotatic reflex which is not only converged by the fastest sensory fibers of the neural system (which are strongly and monosynaptically connected with spinal motoneurons), but also benefits from a specialized servomechanism, the gamma system, which ensures it a permanent efficiency. On these grounds, Granit admitted the principle that the control of voluntary movement was submitted to the progressive stabilization of a chaining of reflex responses. "Even those movements which we regard as voluntary are largely automatic (then reflex in nature). Most of them intrude upon consciousness only at the moment when they are triggered off into action". The perturbing effect caused by any attempt of consciously controlling the execution of an automatic motor sequence was interpreted within this perspective. Even if the view that motor spinal organization would exert a sort of leadership is challenged, the contribution of this organization to the processes underlying the execution of movement can no

Real life examples reflect the intruding into consciousness

longer be reduced to the sole function of load compensation, an interpretation that was facilitated by the experimental conditions in which the stretch reflex was investigated.

Analogous uncertainty dominates the interpretation of long latency electromyographic responses triggered by muscular overload. Even though the problems raised by the nature of these responses - are they reflex, as claimed by Evarts (1973), or voluntary? - and by the level at which their pathways loop - is it transcortical or not? - are controversial issues (cf. Wiesendanger, 1978; Bonnet and Requin, 1982), it was suggested and admitted that they had the functional meaning of compensatory responses. Such an interpretation is more and more often disputed (cf. for instance Bizzi, Dev, Morasso and Polit, 1978) and more cautious proposals are being advanced. It is now suggested that long latency electromyographic responses would reflect the intervention of pathways that continuously convey sensory feedback to central structures, so as to adapt motor control to the peripheral conditions of movement execution (Conrad and Meyer-Lohman, 1980). This hypothesis, if supported by experimental data, would probably have been attractive to Bernstein and led him to reconsider his own position, especially his underevaluation of reflex chaining in the elaboration of motor activities that are behaviorally meaningful. Let us add, within this perspective, that while there are several experimental arguments in favor of a preeminence of central programming in such an automatic activity as stabilization of standing posture (Bonnet, Gurfinkel, Lipshits and Popov, 1976), cortico-spinal commands were considered by Bernstein's followers as playing a double role: on one hand, responsibility for the activation or interruption of the automatic program and, on the other hand, control of motoneurons and interneurons including the oligosynaptic reflex pathways (Gurfinkel & Schik, 1973).

It should be pointed out that Bernstein's more or less explicit scepticism concerning investigations conducted within the reflexologic approach is partly based on the fact that the problems raised by the functional meaning of reflex reactions in motor activity regulation were not well differentiated from the methodological interest that such reactions present for the study of the characteristics of supraspinal processes. In spite of Paillard's (1955) princeps work, where he clearly distinguished the two perspectives and showed how they could be exploited, there still remains some confusion. It should be underlined that studies devoted to proprioceptive reflexes and, in more recent years, to long latency electromyographic

responses are justified in part by the functional role of these reflexes in
motor control (even though this role, while important, still remains unclear).
The main justification lies in the fact that methods of reflexology provide
a powerful tool for the investigation of the functions of the central neural
system of awake and active subjects (cf. Bonnet, Requin and Semjen, 1981).
Let us add that the very principle on which these methods are based consists
in the analysis of controlled factors regulating the reactivity of reflex
pathways, thus taking advantage of a fundamental characteristic of reflexes,
namely their variability. This characteristic is totally opposed to the
notion of rigidity that Bernstein used as an argument in his criticism of
the conception of reflex activity as a functional module underlying motor
organization.

  In short, Bernstein was indisputably ahead of his time in denouncing
the inadequacies of an atomist and mechanistic physiology, which claimed the
possibility of adopting an approach based on the sole principle that the
whole is the sum of the parts to analyze the processes controlling and
regulating the activity of the whole organism and , a fortiori, the action of
the individual. It should be stressed that Bernstein's perspective became,
with a few exceptions, a source of innovation for Western research in
physiology, both because it emphasized the conceptual and methodological
autonomy of the "physiology of activity" and because it anticipated the
increasing interest that studies in this field would elicit. ("The problem
of the rider has begun to overshadow the problem of the horse"). Bernstein's
originality may be evaluated by reference to the fact that it is only
recently that some of the most famous neurophysiologists admitted the limits
of the classical approach. For the first time, in 1973, before the publication
of a book with a suggestive title (The Purposive Brain, 1978), Granit
expressed doubts as to the universal power of the strict analytic approach
adopted in studies devoted to the control of motor activity. Because such
an approach neglects the "teleological" questions raised, on the one hand,
by the nature of the goals that the organism tries to reach using motor
systems and, on the other hand, by the processes which enable motor systems
to respond to variations in the demands of the environment, it can produce
only a corpus of knowledge consisting of an "amorphous conglomerate of well-
documented facts". A similar remark might be directed toward Mountcastle who
began by applying this analytical neurophysiology to the cortical mapping
of sensory projections and later on, when it became possible to investigate
unanaesthetized and active animals, contributed to the introduction of

concepts derived from psychological studies (e.g. the concept of attention), using an experimental strategy combining the concepts and methods of neurobiology and psychology. It does not seem superfluous to insist on the present relevance of Bernstein's message, since it is still true that every technological or methodological advance in the field of neuroscience regularly cause the reappearance of the reductionist temptation. Scientists who promote these new sophisticated tools have a tendency to consider themselves equipped for a "direct" approach of the processes underlying complex behavior, and thus able to avoid the theoretical elaborations and the study of concepts which characterize the evolution of the scientific approach embraced by those for whom the central concern was the investigation of behavior. As Neisser (1967) wrote in a book published the same year as Bernstein's volume: "Psychology should not be viewed as just something to do until electrophysiology comes around to solve the problems".

However, we think that Bernstein's disciples sometimes went far beyond their precursor's conception, especially when developing the idea that a molecular investigation of movement, reduced to a fragment of activity isolated from the behavioral context, should be replaced with a molar approach to action, the motor expression of which being inseparable from the goals pursued. One may have two purposes in mind when saying that the distance between experimental paradigms used in laboratory conditions and the conditions in "real" life is so large that the heuristic value of the data obtained in laboratory is of little interest for the comprehension of the control of movement in "natural" conditions (for instance, Kelso, 1981). This position may constitute a reasonable warning against the dangers that the artificiality of certain experimental paradigms presents, i.e. against the risks of overgeneralizing conclusions to conditions which are very different from the ones in which experimental data were collected. This position may also be understood as an agnostic attitude toward every experimental investigation conducted in laboratory conditions; this raises a serious epistemological problem since it leads to a rejection of any reductive approach. Most certainly, Bernstein did not share this view, as testified by his concern for making the study of the "physiology of activity" benefit from a multidisciplinary approach. Neither is such an attitude consistent with the concerns of the Haskins' group: the reductive approach is constant in their work, as exemplified by their legitimate interest in modelling, borrowing concepts from physics and mathematics. However, this position is adopted by some authors, as illustrated by the astonishing conclusions of Reed (1982) who proposed to "integrate" Bernstein's physiology of activity and Gibson's ecological psychology into a theory of action. "There is no place in the theory for S-R analysis (...). S-R psychology and S-CNS-R psychophysiology are both to be rejected. Cognitive theories, with their Pandora's boxes of intervening variables can no longer be accepted". One may easily assume that Bernstein would have been reluctant to publish his book, not wanting such a disintegration to appear one day as the logical outcome of his critical - though certainly not destructive - analysis. This analysis was conducted with the resources of a subtle reasoning, trained to dialectic, within the perspective of promoting a new expansion in the conceptualization of motor control and in the paradigms used for its experimental study.

The abusive exploitation of Bernstein's explicit antireductionist positions in order to promote syncretic views based, in particular, on a systematic ecologism would lead to an underestimation of the modernism of a creative train of thought. Bernstein's conceptions seem to be the result of a universal evolution of ideas in behavioral science which were, for a long time, smothered by coercive mechanistic conceptions: Russian reflexologism or Anglo-Saxon behaviorism pretended to provide these disciplines with a "scientific" structure, proposing to them as a unique model the approach used in the physical sciences, and thus refusing them any conceptual or theoretical originality or methodological autonomy. Bernstein's ideas, as well as the conceptions of some of his Western contemporaries (e.g. Hebb, 1949; Wallon, 1942), announced both the resurgence of neo-mentalism, which enriched the cognitivist trend of contemporary psychology, and the spectacular recentering of biological sciences on the problems raised by the active organism. Bernstein's views contributed to the creation of conditions propitious to the suppression of separations between disciplines; their vitality, already evident but mainly potential, is now expressed in the dynamics of the concept of cognitive neurosciences (cf. Posner, 1982; Requin, 1982).

II. BERNSTEIN AS THE PROMOTOR OF A DYNAMIC PHYSIOLOGY OF ACTION

For about the last 10 years an important trend of thought, particularly well illustrated by the work of Kelso, Turvey and their colleagues, contributed not only to popularize Bernstein's ideas, but also to develop them within the perspective of a renewal, if not a reformulation, of the problems raised by the organization and control of motor activity. Before

we propose some comments on this dimension of Bernstein's work, not
distinguishing his own contribution from what his disciples attributed him
and from their own further developments, we shall attempt to show that the
perspectives he opened are indissolubly, but probably improperly, linked to
an often radical questioning of motor control theories in which programming
is a central concept.

1. The fallacious controversy on motor program

We find rather excessive the criticism addressed to theories which
assume that a central executor is in charge of translating the schedule
implied in an action project into a pattern of commands directed to
peripheral executants.

In the first place, they crystallize on a narrow, oversimplified,
conception of motor program which those who have exploited the fecundity
of this concept for the comprehension of movement organization cannot accept.
It is unfortunate that Keele's (1968) lapidary formulation - which was not
intended to summarize in an exhaustive definition how a motor program is
constructed, structured and executed, but rather to outline his conception -
became the privileged target of pertinacious criticisms. We consider the
formulation he proposed in 1968: "a set of muscles commands that are
structured before a movement sequence begins and that allows the entire
sequence to be carried out uninfluenced by peripheral feedback" as a summary
of the methodological principles on which are based experiments that consider
the concept of program as necessary for interpreting the data, mainly the
demonstration that movements can be executed in the absence of sensory
control, either because an experimental procedure prevents that type of
feedback, or because the movement is executed within a time course such that
feedback of peripheral origin cannot yet modulate the central command.
Keele, however, does not claim that in most cases motor activity develops
in such conditions, as testified by a later formulation (Keele, 1973): "If[*]
neither visual nor kinesthetic feedback is needed for the execution of
patterns of movement, then[*] the movement patterns must be represented
centrally in the brain". Since the logic of this proposal could bot be disputed
it did not invite oversimplified criticisms.

In the second place, through a constant but often imprecise reference
to Bernstein, the ideas developed in the volume "Coordination and Regulation

---

[*] Underlined by the authors.

of Movements" are presented as foreshadowing and justifying the entire
reformulation of the problem of motor control; this reformulation is set
out as an original synthesis of two radically antithetical conceptions
underlying the "peripheralist" and "centralist" theories of movement. A good
illustration of such a dichotomic view is provided by a recent critical
review by Reed (1982) who writes: "At the same time that Lashley and other
Western scientists were showing the limitations of the peripheralist theory,
the Soviet physiologist N. Bernstein was demonstrating[*] that the central
program theory was also untenable".

Any attempt to submit to an evaluation both the validity of these
criticisms and the arguments they find in Bernstein's conceptions
necessitates, beforehand, the softening of the extreme expressions which
tend to abusively radicalize if not completely forge the above mentioned
oppositions.

Let us consider for instance the status of the motor program which is
referred to by its belittlers not only under the lable of concept but also
of theory. The peripheralist theory, in which movement is considered as a
reaction triggered by a stimulus bringing into play either a prewired
circuit or a gradually built associative chaining, is contrasted either with
the concept of motor program, thus creating an asymmetrical opposition
between levels that are not equivalent from the formal point of view, or
with a theory of motor programming assuming that the sole intervention of
an omnipotent central executive gives a comprehensive account of movement
organization; as a result, this theory is improperly considered as exclusively
and radically centralist. As far as we know, Keele is the only one to have
mentioned, probably unwisely, a "theory" of motor programming and, besided,
the considerations presented in his paper do not allow one to think that
to him motor program is more than a concept, though certainly a basic one
in a theory of motor control.

Similarly, due to a constant metaphoric assimilation to a simplified
version of computer programs, the concept of motor program was gradually
reduced by its decriers to a rigid set of commands, a conception which
strongly diverges from the view - advanced regularly for more than 50 years -
that a central representation of action contributes in some way or another
to the structuring of the outputs responsible for movement execution. It
should be noted that the concepts of "Bewegungsentwurf" (Wacholder, 1927)

---

[*] Underlined by the authors.

"scheme of action" (Del Bianco, 1947), "motor scheme" (Head, 1920), "kinetic formula" (Liepmann, 1900), "action plan" (Miller, Galanter and Pribram, 1960), all variants of the same basic idea that was to be developed in various modern theories of motor programming, do not allow so easily for simplistic "anticentralist" criticism, perhaps because they are more "vague" and do not suggest so strongly neurobiological models, as underlined by Gallistel (1981), but mostly because they did not become spoiled by the reductive metaphor of computer program. This metaphor results in a grotesque point of view and, furthermore, in an artificial homogenization of conceptions in which the concept of motor programming is not given the same status, which opens the way for extreme oversimplifications (e.g. Reed, see above, p. 470).

A thorough critical analysis of the concept of motor program cannot be limited to the restrictive points of view adopted by scientists who are considered to be in Lashley's (1917) tradition - such as Keele (1968) and, to a lesser degree, Schmidt (1975). In effect, such restrictive positions imply either that the operationality of this concept is restricted to the very few motor activities in which there is no sensory feedback, or that the spatial and temporal characteristics of movement are exclusively determined by a "context free" central executive, in Kelso's view (1981). A detailed critical analysis should also consider theories of motor control in which the central and peripheral origin of motor command though well differentiated are closely integrated. This critical analysis would include for instance the conceptions in which feedback and feedforward mechanisms are the source of the adaptive flexibility of control functions exerted by different hierarchized levels of the neural organization (cf. for example Brooks, 1979), as well as conceptions in which the concept of program is enlarged so as to include either the elements of response elicited by sensory feedback (cf. for example Sternberg, Monsell, Knoll and Wright, 1978) or postural adjustments accompanying and/or anticipating movement and taking into account actual and/or predictable context elements (cf. Gahery and Massion, 1981). Finally, even the partisans of an extreme peripheralist conception, in which information transmitted by closed loops is given an almost exclusive role in motor elaboration, cannot totally discard the notion of program: "I must point out that a very limited idea of a motor program is necessary for any theory of movement because a movement must be started and feedback does not occur until a fraction of a second later" (Adams, 1976).

The objection that conceptions reducing the role of the central program

of action reveal the explicit or implicit influence of Bernstein's ideas
cannot be rejected; we would like to emphasize however that such an objection
simply acknowledges the integrative process underlying the advance of any
scientific approach. It should be noted, however, that at the time when
Western scientists ignored or underestimated Bernstein's conceptions, the
notion of hierarchization in the organization of motor control systems, of
permanent remodelling of the central command by the reafferences from
movement execution and of anticipation of the changes in the context where
the action is to take place were already considered as necessary and not
mutually exclusive elements of a synthetic theory emphasizing the adaptive
flexibility of systems responsible for movement elaboration and execution
(Paillard, 1960).

We believe that Bernstein's conceptions arose in this context where,
at the same time, the deciphering of the functional organization of motor
systems progressed rapidly and where the fecundity of applying the principles
of cybernetics to the regulation of the activity of living systems became
quite apparent. In our opinion, it is within the light of this context that
Bernstein's book should be read.

In the article published in "Questions of Philosophy" in 1961, Bernstein
uses more than twelve times the concepts of program and programming, not from
a critical point of view, but in order to specify a stage in the chronological
analysis of the operations underlying motor acts; this prefigures the later
widespread recourse to serial models referring to processing stages on, in
information processing theories that was to be observed from 1969 under
Steinberg's influence (cf. for example, Requin, 1980a, b; Sanders, 1977,
1980; Shaffer, 1980; Theios, 1975) as well as in the study of functional
organization of motor systems by neurobiologists following Allen and Tsukahara
(1974) (cf. for example, Brooks, 1975; Kornhuber, 1974; Paillard, 1982; Thach,
1975). Bernstein outlines a rather broad definition of the concept of program,
incorporating "what has to be done" and "how it should be done", which does
not leave any uncertainty about his interest for this concept. Even though
this definition is immediately tempered, according to the principles of the
art of dialectic to which Bernstein was well trained, by underlying the
necessity of a large adaptive variability of the program which has to take
into account considerable strategic modifications, it would be fallacious
to conclude that Bernstein abandoned the concept of motor program. From this
point of view, no lines revealing Bernstein's recognition of the necessity
to admit a central determination of action are more illustrative than the

passages where he proposes a taxonomy of motor activities as a function of
their dependency on the stimuli that may trigger them, and locates at one
end of a continuum, unconditional reflexes, and at the other end, voluntary
activities in which stimuli would play no role: "These are actions for which
the program and also the initiative, are entirely determined within the
individual...". Let us note that this quotation, if taken out of context,
could elicit criticisms quite analogous to the ones addressed to conceptions
as excessively centralist.

Such a point of view would clearly be partial, since it would neglect
what the decriers of the notion of motor program underscore and consider as
Bernstein's main contribution, namely his considerations on the necessary
properties of a system of control: such a system, in order to ensure the
adaptation of a motor act to its goal implies an invariant determinant, hence
a system of reference, despite the multiple internal and external sources
of variability that may complicate or disturb its functioning. However it
should also be emphasized that the analysis on which this conception is
based – which was to be often paraphrased and/or developed later on (cf.
for example, Turvey, Shaw and Mace, 1978; Kugler, Kelso and Turvey, 1980;
Kelso, Holt, Kugler and Turvey, 1980; Kelso, 1981) – led Bernstein to a
conclusion that could be abusively used as an argument to close the pseudo-
debate between centralists and peripheralists, since Bernstein rejects the
possibility that the pattern of muscular commands as well as sensory feedback
might be invariant determinants of motor control activity (p.445). Thus, we
disagree with Turvey et al. (1978) who wrote: "Indeed, for Bernstein, the
decisive factor in coordinated activity is not the efferent impulses but
the complex system of afferentation...".

To us, it is much more important to stress that Bernstein's adhesion
to a conception which would explain the problem of motor control would be
explained in terms of sensory afferentation rather than in terms of motor
efferentation. The contributions he made, most probably not intentionally,
to promote this view, are at times expressed in somewhat vague formulations,
and consequently easily distorted; these formulations are far removed from
the central idea that the guideline of an action control system is not to be
found either in the motor output or in the sensory input, but beyond that,
in the elaboration of a motor problem or of an action representation. It
is for instance very surprising to read (p.444) that "gravity", "friction",
and "the opposition of an adversary" are the origin of unpredictable forces,
a very questionable view that is totally in contradiction with the thesis

that Bernstein clearly considers as crucial for a theory of action and which
he presents in a detailed way: the importance of modelling the future, the
source of a permanent anticipatory activity of the organism the aim of which
is, precisely, to master what the future holds for the active individual.

2. Autocratic centralization vs democratic distribution of motor control

       An essential premise in Bernstein's conception concerning the
organization of the motor control system is based on the observation of a
non-univocal relationship between the pattern of corticospinal commands and
motor output. This relationship is expressed in the variability observed in
the details of the execution of movements which have an identical purpose.
This non-univocal relationship is interpreted, on the one hand, as a
consequence of the more or less predictable variations of the environment in
which the action is executed and, on the other hand, as a consequence of the
complexity of a biomechanical effector device composed of several relatively
independent elements with compliant connections. This absence of univocity
suggests that the organization of the motor control system is incompatible
with the notion of a unique central process, entirely responsible for the
details of the pattern of neuromuscular commands, and having at its disposal
periodically - and not continuously - updated information about the
peripheral conditions in which these commands are executed. Control
decentralization and "regulation circularity" thus constitute for Bernstein
the two basic concepts enabling the elaboration of a coherent theory of
action.

       It should be noted that at roughly the same time, some Western authors
also put forward ideas concerning the hierarchization of motor control
systems. In 1960, Paillard wrote: "the spatial and temporal pattern of
impulses required for a purposeful movement (...) is progressively built
up by the spread of central commands through the lower structures (...), is
remodelled at each way station of the executive system in accordance with
the modulating influences which converge from the peripheral sensory
mechanisms". Before analyzing experimental data supporting Bernstein's
thesis and its implications, it is interesting to ask why the micro-
differences, all things being kept equal, observed in the repetition of a
globally identical movement, would be related to the variability of the
conditions in which the transduction of a univocal command is realized by
the biomechanical instrument of execution, rather than to the variations of
the pattern of neuromuscular commands, once it is admitted that mastering the

complexity is not an insurmountable problem for a unique or multiple controller. The idea that a new program needs to be elaborated each time there is an attempt to give an adequate response to the same motor problem was advanced by Welford (1974) for interpreting the gradual decrease with practice in the amount of imperfections of a goal-directed movement. A subject, when confronted with a new task, would first generate an approximate solution to the problem that must be solved, and later would actively modify this solution, thus avoiding the stabilization of the initial programming error. The movement variability would not then reflect random variations - random because unpredictable - in the conditions in which the biomechanical executant is prompted, but rather controlled fluctuations of the central command that attempts to optimize its effects. These adaptive fluctuations would reflect the diversity of strategies of actions available to motor control systems. This would explain that an identical goal-directed movement may result from very different patterns of electromyographic activity. This observation is precisely the second argument on which is grounded the view that the relationship between the neuromuscular command and the motor output is non-univocal. Thus, we do not think that the interpretation of a univocal relationship involving solely, fluctuations of the pattern of centrospinal commands might be so readily excluded.

In the first place, a major problem posed to motor control systems is the mastery of the variability of the context in which action will take place. This variability is a function of the initial joint configuration, of the reactive forces linked to the involvement of a limb and of the external forces that may interfere with those which will be called into play by moving one or several segments of the body. Without disputing the relevance of Bernstein's analysis of these factors of variability, we find it hard to conceive of variability as a truly original argument in favor of the indispensable role of the information conveyed by the complex system of sensory afferentation in the control of movement elaboration and execution. Paillard's (1960) review of the organization of skilled movements suggests, undoubtedly, that from this standpoint Bernstein belonged to the trend of thought and research initiated by Exner, expanded by Sherrington and Walcholder and later by Rusch, Gellhorn and many others. This school of thought considered the concept of sensorimotor integration to be the basic concept of any theory of motor control. "Even at the level at which relational impulses originate, the modulating action of sensory messages at every moment keeps the activity of central structures in harmony with the varying

positions of the body parts in movement and with the state of the ever-
changing external field of action" (Paillard, 1960). Such a formulation
summarizes, without ambiguity, what the penetrating vision of almost half
a century's work and theoretical developments in this area of research had
allowed, by the fifties, to be considered as well-established facts.

The many studies which, since then, contributed to enrich our knowledge
of the structural and functional organization of proprioceptive afferentation
systems, and which today constitute the necessary basis for the elaboration
of models of movement coordination, support the notion of a central executor
monitoring the multiple variability factors of the intrinsic and extrinsic
conditions in which motor activity occurs. It is above all a system
constituted by neuromuscular spindles and their gamma motoneurons:

> In addition to conveying information about the body state
> mechanical parameters, they provide a picture of the peripheral
> reception of the central control. Because spindle responses to
> gamma motoneurons depend upon the kinetic state of the muscle,
> proprioceptive efferents thus make it possible to evaluate the
> correlation between parameters of motor control and conditions
> under which the latter are executed (Bonnet, Requin and Semjen,
> 1981).

The accuracy of the link between the command and the peripheral effect seems
ensured by the specificity of muscular receptors for length and tension. This
specificity permits a distinct coding of the active forces produced by the
command, and of the passive forces coming from the environment (cf. for
instance, Miles and Evarts, 1979).

Concerning the absence of linearity in the functioning of proprioceptive
receptors and of muscles, it does not necessarily constitute, as Bernstein
suggested, an insurmountable obstacle to the control of effectors. On one
hand, there is evidence of the existence of filtering mechanisms intervening
at the level of sensory relay neurons and participating in the command of
the movement itself (Coquery, 1972). These data suggest that the central
processor monitors and modulates anticipated sensory effects. On the other
hand, by initiating a phasic contraction by action potentials "en doublet"
in order to reach instantly a high level of tension, the central control
system uses the typical non-linear relationship between the activation
frequency of motor units and the tension level in order to improve its
efficiency (Burke, Rudomin and Zajac, 1970; Gurfinkel and Levik, 1973).

In the second place, it is now classical, within that perspective, to
advance as an argument the difficulty of the task that a possible unique
central executor would have to carry out. This executor would have to

determine the "optimal" solution among the many configurations of possible muscular activations when monitoring the execution of a spatially oriented movement mobilizing a plurijoint mechanical set which, consequently, involves a rather high level of degrees of freedom. It is of course necessary to inquire into the meaning of the notion of optimal solution, which only makes sense if referring to some variable in relation to which the optimum could be located.

A first formal approach which consists in conceiving of this problem in terms of biomechanics, i.e. borrowing concepts from physics, seems to us of limited relevance when considering an organism actively engaged in a behavioral sequence. As noted by Hollerbach (1982), pointing movements, executed most often with a roughly rectilinear trajectory, minimize neither energy consumption nor displacement duration, contrary to what would be the case if the problem posed in terms of control of a biomechanical system was given a rational solution. Within this perspective, it is necessary to specify the constraints which minimize this "optimal" solution. One may think that they are not limited to the physical constraints, mentioned by Hollerbach on the basis of the models provided by robotics, but rather that they involve constraints imposed by the biological and behavioral meaning of action, including its ontogenetic, socio-cultural, and possibly aesthetic determinants which participate in what Bernstein called "structurality" and "completeness" of motor acts. However, as already observed, a relative constancy of spatio-temporal movement parameters may be accompanied by a high variability in the pattern of underlying muscular activations, and there is also a high diversity in the strategies adopted by different individuals confronted with the same problem. These observations provide different arguments - if one does not consider only elementary acts of very limited meaning from the behavioral standpoint - favoring the view that, on the contrary, there does not exist an "optimal" solution to the control of action but rather a set of solutions, probably "equivalent" because of the multiplicity of points of view from which their "advantages" and "disadvantages" may be evaluated. It seems to us that the size of the set of solutions and motives for strategic choices this plurality makes necessary is beyond the scope of an analysis which makes sole use of the concepts derived from a theory of the control of a biomechanical system. Such an analysis is far removed from a theory of action within which Bernstein wished to integrate the behavioral and ecological meanings of the motor act.

In this sense, Gel'fand and Tsetlin's (1962) analysis - which underlines

the difficulty, if not the impossibility, given the available techniques
of computation, of rapidly determining this biomechanical "optimal" solution
- besides the fact that it prejudges the capacity of the neural machine,
which possibly is far superior to the logical and technological resources
at our disposal- appears to be an objection of limited bearing to the
hypothesis of a unique central monitor. The neural system probably works
less according to the formal principles of a mathematician trying to find
the solution of an equation with several unknowns than according to the more
pragmatic style of a computer scientist who is content with one solution
among the range of possible solutions. To conclude, it is not certain that
the analogy with robotics whose "relevance to the analysis of the brain
remains speculative" (Arbib, 1981) is more fertile in the domain of motor
control than was and still is the metaphor of the computer. Bernstein was
aware of this when he wrote in his book's conclusions: "...We are becoming
increasingly committed to the importance of studying the principal
differences between living systems and artificial systems".

A second formal approach likely to provide relevant critical arguments
against the unicity and omnipotence of a central executor is based on the
application of the theory of complex systems to the functional organization
of living systems interacting with their environment. It consists in
questioning the principles of organization enabling the realization of the
best management of a system whose complexity lies in the structural
differentiation of interconnected subsets presenting a certain degree of
functional specialization for processing afferent and efferent information,
this management being conceived of in terms of economy of means and/or
efficiency of decision and control processes. It should be stressed that
this type of analysis does not lead to clear cut solutions either. Arbib
(1972), for instance, when comparing, within this perspective, the merits
of a centralized control system versus a hierarchical control system, noted
that the economy of means, defined in terms of storing and duration of
programming, attained in the second case was compensated for by the greater
efficiency, defined in terms of accuracy and adaptability, obtained in the
first case. It does not seem to us that the choice is simple when, once the
principle of a decentralization of control exerted by relatively autonomous
subsystems is admitted, one inquires into the respective merits of a
hierarchical organization or a heterarchical organization. In a hierarchical
organization the preservation of a distinction between actors and instruments,
implying that the flow of information within the system is unidirectional,

seems to be an obstacle to plasticity but a guarantee for the conservation, at least temporarily, of action identity. In contrast, in a heterarchical organization the functional pluripotentiality of subsystems implies a reciprocity in exchanges of information permitting a "free dominance" which, while ensuring a total flexibility of the control system, risks to lead to an anarchic disintegration of behavior.

Irrespective of the outcome of the debates on these problems of formalization, it is not at all clear to us that, in this domain, the metaphor of the computer is without promise, as noted by MacKay (1980) in a different context. Oscillators and "coordinative structures" may probably be assimilated by analogy to the subroutines of a computer program when the function of this program is to control a complex process for which a certain number of parameters remain unspecified, hence, unpredictable to a certain extent. It is the case, for example, of a program devised for an on-line experiment on the acquisition and control of sensorimotor behavior in animals (Schematically, the computer-animal is a sort of ecosystem in which the activity of the animal-prey constitutes a source of variability that the computer-predator intends to constrain within the limits of the goal, its strategies of intervention being necessarily continuously adapted). Such a program involves a set of subroutines, relatively autonomous and adapted functionally to specified sequences of activity, their interconnections defined within the main program, such that a routine calls another as soon as the animal's behavior changes and does not remain within the control capacity of the first subroutine. These programs are based on a modular conception of systems and are conceived of as a catalogue from which are extracted certain subsystems that are put together to fulfil a function, that become disconnected and are then restructured in order to reach another goal. It should be noted that models of this type have already been proposed to account for the ontogenetic development in the learning of motor skills (cf, for example, Fitts, 1964; Bruner, 1971).

To conclude, we do not deny the theoretical interest of the sophisticated speculations to which a formal approach to degrees of freedom may lead (From this point of view the heuristic value of the ideas put forward by Bernstein is unquestionable). It appears necessary to inquire, however, at least in the present circumstances, into the operationality of these formalizations as possible guidelines for experimental research in the field of motor control. Our intuition, possibly erroneous, that they leave unexplained an entire body of experimental data which are perhaps abusively

considered as well-established, constitutes an obstacle to an unreserved
adhesion. To take only one example, what is their compatibility with the
experimental data obtained in the theoretical context of the neural system
considered as a channel of limited information processing capacity, which
implies, if not the concept of a unique central monitor, at least the concept
of a hierarchical organization of control systems? In other words, where
would be the "bottleneck" in a system which would function according to
the principles of a heterarchical coalition of "coordinative structures".

     To us, the most important implication of Bernstein's ideas, and the
most original in its historical context, is not the door he would have
opened to conceptions of the functional organization of control systems
based on an information and execution division of labor between relatively
independent and specialized subsets coordinated according to a hierarchical
or a heterarchical mode. We consider Bernstein's most important contribution
to reside in his emphasis - that has, in our opinion, been underestimated
and that we find preminotory - to set out the invariant frame of reference
of the organization of action within an elaborated model of the future which
reduces uncertainty and takes into account the variability of the context
as well as the potential multiplicity of strategies of action. Let us note,
moreover, that if one did not wish to remain confined in the artificial
controversy concerning "centralism vs peripheralism", it would be possible,
in playing the devil's advocate, to find a strong argument in favor of a
decidedly centralist position in the many passages Bernstein devoted to the
role of an internalized and anticipatory representation of action. However,
as underlined in our introduction, Bernstein's epistemological and historico-
critical concerns appear to us as bearing on a quite different level.

III. BERNSTEIN AS THE THEORETICIAN OF AN ANTICIPATORY ORGANIZING ACTIVITY

     One of the main merits of Bernstein's contribution is to have envisioned
the problems raised by movement coordination and regulation within the more
general perspective of the activity of higher living organisms, human beings
in particular, who do not simply interact with their environment but, on the
contrary, take the initiative to act upon it, using all the means they
believe necessary. Bernstein's insistent concern for meaningful goal-directed
motor acts, his questioning of the use of insignificant fragments of movement
as units of analysis, such as the knee jerk reflex, reflect epistemological,
if not philosophical considerations which, in the more limited field of
physiology and psychology, could lead him only to challenge S-R models.

These models are totally backward oriented, as noted by Poulton (1950) who
pointed to the fact that "expectations about the near future" are the
essential determinants of an individual's behavior. Bernstein opposes the
narrow image of an organism mainly confined in procedures aiming at
maintaining its initial equilibrium, to the image of an organism which
anticipates its future, which somehow constructs it and whose behavior is
consequently determined as much by what must be as by what has been.

It is this orientation toward the future, the representation of the
"necessary future", that causes the emergence of the motor problem, whose
apprehension and solution enable the organism to go from the actual state
of affairs to the desired one. The solution of a motor problem is nothing
else, indeed, than the undertaking of a program which both anticipates the
result of an action and the means that the action mobilizes. This notion of
motor problem is at the core of Bernstein's thought on the elaboration and
structuration of motor acts. It does not seem, however, to have aroused all
the interest it deserves. In a first series of remarks we shall attempt to
determine the function played by this notion in a model of motor act
organization, as well as to appreciate its more general relevance to the
physiology and psychology of activity.

The occurrence of a motor problem in a given situation is but one of
the expressions of organism's orientation toward the future. In the motor
problem and in the program for its solution, the "image of the future" is
represented under very general features. It must be admitted though, that in
the actual solution of the problem in terms of motor activity, the image of
the future is expressed in a detailed way as the outcome of a permanent
anticipatory activity. This activity relies both on the predictable
properties of the ever changing surroundings in which the motor act is
accomplished, and consequent effects of the motor act on the environment
and on the organism itself. Reading Bernstein's writings does not leave any
doubt about the importance he gives to the diverse forms of anticipation,
prediction, extrapolation and preparation activities in the organization and
accomplishment of a goal-directed motor act. From this standpoint, the
chapter that we comment on is particularly illustrative. It is striking,
however, that these different forms of anticipatory activities are often
loosely-defined or, at least, very unequally elaborated. In a second series
of remarks, we shall attempt to make explicit the function of anticipatory
activities in Bernstein's theory and to confront the often implicit
potentialities of this theory with the developments that the notions of

anticipation and preparation have undergone in recent years.

1. <u>The formulation of the motor problem and its solution: an act of</u>
   <u>intelligence.</u>

How are voluntary movements triggered and how is their internal
cohesion ensured? It is not possible to sketch the evolution of ideas
concerning these questions since, in order to do so, one should have to
go back at least to W. James and to what he said of the anticipated image
of movement. Let us note, however, that at the time of the publication of
Bernstein's first work, the German physiologist Wachholder underlined that
a voluntary movement in unfolded into its slightest details as a function
of a "subjective" event, the planning of a movement (Bewegungsentwurf),
and that it continues until the attainment of the best correspondence
between what was projected and what was actually done (Wachholder, 1927).

In his search for a factor which could account for "the homogeneity
of a movement and its unity in terms of the interrelations of its parts in
space and time", Bernstein envisioned in his earlier writings the existence
of "guiding" or "directional engrams", i.e. the existence of a motor image
which would correspond to the planned movement in its real factual form, as
well as the contribution of more general engrams representing classes of
responses taken as "topological classes". The organizing entity that Bernstein
proposes in the present article, as well as in "Some emergent problems of
the regulation of motor acts" which was published 4 years before, is less
precise, less "structural" but, in its generality, involves very interesting
implications. The problem considered goes beyond the simple question of the
image of movement and anticipation of the result: "the standard determinant
both for the programming of motor activity and its effection and correction
by feedback connections can only be the formation and representation of a
motor problem by the brain in one way or another". If the questions of a
problem and its solution are to be discussed separately, goal and means
must be differentiated, at least under a very general form. The solution
implies either the selection of the most appropriate means among the already
existing means, or a novel (and original) combination of these means, or else
the elaboration of entirely new means. If the regulation of motor-activities
is conceived of as depending on problem solving types of processes, it becomes
possible to consider motor activities in a broader perspective of active and
adaptive exchanges between an organism and its environment. Such exchanges

result not only in a transformation of the environment, but also (and in some cases mainly) in the transformation of the organism, since it acquires, in the course of its activity, a better and more reliable knowledge of the surrounding world as well as of its own possibilities. In turn, this knowledge provides the means of a new "adaptation". If the word intelligence is a shortcut which links knowledge and adaptation, the reference to "the motor problem" and its solution places the motor act in the class of intelligent behavior or, more exactly, underlines what renders the motor act a manifestation of intelligence.

"The conception (...) that we defend involves, as an evident epistemological consequence, the statement that the external world is not "given" with already prefixed structures and that the object, while existing independently of the subject, constitutes only a limit, in the mathematical sense, toward which are tending approximations of the subject who is trying to interpret it through steps of increasing objectivity; there then exists a proper activity on the part of the subject (...) which can be detected in the contribution he makes over and above the information extracted from the object". When one bears in mind Bernstein's statement that every meaningful motor act command supposes a qualitatively and quantitatively reliable representation of the environment and that every corresponding action constitutes "an active implement for the correct cognition of the surrounding world", and when one also bears in mind the way he opposes a purely "formal" activity to a directed search activity, - the former being characteristic of a behavioristic description of behavior in terms of trials and errors, the latter implying that any attempt to a solution, whether successful or not, gives a defined orientation to further attempts of solution, through processes of stochastic extrapolation -, one might think that the above quotation comes from Bernstein's writings. As a matter of fact, this is extracted from a study by Piaget (1960) and illustrates, in a way that we hope is convincing, convergences, or at least common preoccupations in the "physiology of activity" that Bernstein wished to promote, and in Piaget's conception of operational intelligence. However, to establish a parallelism between these authors would have but a restricted interest if it were not to improve our understanding of movement coordination and regulation. We think it very likely that the confrontation of Bernstein's and Piaget's ideas could arouse some suggestions which would constitute guidelines for further investigations, particularly in the field of motor skills acquisition.

     To formulate a motor problem consists, among other things, in
discerning the constraints which, within the whole situation, hinder the
achievement of the desired objective. Once these constraints have been
detected and understood, they orient the selection of the means to be used.
Insofar as a motor problem is referred to, these means necessarily imply a
particular mobilization of the motor system, in other words they imply a
particular form of coordination and control. The question is whether the
particular form required for solving the problem is already available, which
would imply a selection among already existing means or a combination of
these means. If such is not the case, the problem is no longer the achievement
of a goal conceived of in terms of changes within the environment, but rather
the elaboration of the means necessary for the achievement of this goal, i.e.
the elaboration of a novel and appropriate form of coordination and control.
In this case, and only in this case, the solution of the problem does not
differentiate from the acquisition of a motor skill. It seems that this
double interpretation of the motor problem and its solution hardly attracted
Bernstein's attention. However he noted that: "the process of practice towards
the achievement of new motor habits essentially consists in the gradual
success of search for optimal motor solutions to the appropriate problem".
This very idea was paraphrased by Fowler and Turvey (1978): "In this
perspective, learning a skill involves discovering an optimal self-organization".

     The question is then to know what exactly is "discovered" and how the
result of this discovery is stored. In effect, one of the most surprising
properties of acquired motor skills lies in their resistance to forgetting,
which distinguishes them from most "arbitrary" acquisitions obtained by
conditioning or association which, per se, are temporary. It is on this issue
of how acquisitions are preserved that we share Piaget's (1960) concern when
he states: "It is remarkable that current theories of learning mostly
emphasized acquisition and partially neglected the problem of the stability
of retention, as if it were not a problem. They do indeed pose a problem and
this is why the intervention of a factor of equilibration seems indispensable,
and this factor probably does not obey the laws of learning in a strict sense.
Furthermore, as soon as one invokes regulatory mechanisms leading to
equilibrium, some new acquisitions may depend only on them and not on
experience" (Piaget, 1960). Let us recall that Piaget refers essentially to
the structures of operational intelligence, in which equilibrium is ensured
by operations' reversibility. Contrary to endogenous rhythms which ensure
equilibrium through an oscillatory process between two extremes, and to

regulations which ensure equilibrium through corrective changes triggered
by negative feedback, reversibility ensures equilibrium by accompanying
every change by a simultaneous correlative process, which ensures virtual
or actual compensation of certain effects that may result from this change
(cf. Berlyne, 1960). Thus, the acquired structure of operations would be
"reinforced" and hence preserved, insofar as the organization of compensatory
processes goes, toward a more and more stable equilibrium.

What are the common elements in Piaget's and Bernstein's ideas concerning
the process by which the organism overcomes "the internal physiological
indeterminacy of the periphery", i.e. the coordination process? It would
certainly be difficult to find in Bernstein's works explicit references to
equilibration processes and to equilibrium structures in Piaget's sense. But
we believe, and this requires further investigation, that several elements
in Bernstein's theoretical elaboration refer to such functions. Let us note,
firstly, the decisive role given to (directed) active search for the maximal
amount of useful information, this searching behavior being under the control
of stochastic processes which participate in orientation behavior, in
Bernstein's as well as in Berlyne's (1960) views. It also should be noted
that this active search for information is directed, in the first place,
toward "essential variables" which define the structure of coordinations. In
other terms, they could be the "organizational invariant" which, instead of
being, as Fowler and Turvey (1978) said,"an information about something
which preserves its specificity over relevant transformation",could well then
be an equilibrium structure with a set of intrinsic compensations between
operations and functions. This remark is very important since, depending
upon which solution is adopted, the genesis of motor "forms" and "formulae"
- in other words the genesis of invariants of which Bernstein underlined the
"topological" character - can be explained by gestaltist laws of perceptual
organization, or by functions (operations) implying a certain degree of
reversibility. Let us finally recall the diversity of anticipation and
extrapolation forms that Bernstein considers as possible sources of "ante
factum" regulation, as opposed to feedback regulations. It is this multiform
anticipatory activity, expressing a more and more reliable and thorough
knowledge of the possible consequences of a motor act for the environment
and for the organism itself, that enables it to reach "a degree of coordination
at which the organism is not only unafraid of reactive phenomena in a system
with many degrees of freedom, but is able to structure its movements so as
to utilize entirely the reactive phenomena which arise". Evaluating the

possibilities and utilizing the consequences of the action is certainly an
intelligent act, and it is based, according to us, on the gradual discovery
of a structure of relationship, within which simultaneous correlative
processes of compensation, hence of equilibrium, certainly play a decisive
role.

2. The images of the future

   To Bernstein, the problem of action is the problem of the objective
and subjective requirements with which the organism will be confronted. It
is therefore entirely dependent upon and tributary to the image of the
future constituted by the organism. The image of the future can only be
probabilistic, since it originates in an extrapolation whose reliability
depends on the temporal span that anticipation encompasses. It also depends
on the degree of stability of the context within which it is elaborated,
and on the time available for its elaboration. Therefore, the actualization
of the future is a conflictual process, a struggle against the obstacles
- be they anticipated or not - the action encounters, a fight whose finality
is to increase the probability of the desired outcome up to the unit and to
nullify the value of other equally probable but undesired issues. This
struggle for the accomplishment of an anticipated future may be conceived
of as a process reducing the entropy of the system which embraces the
individual and his immediate environment and, consequently, it may be
assimilated, as it was by Bernstein, to processes of "programmed morphogenesis"
through which the individual constructs himself, in spite of the obstacles,
according to a predetermined model. "And so, what in a particular case of
motor functions in organism appears to be (1) the modelling of future
requirements in terms of a problem of action, and (2) the realization of an
integrated program of this action by the conquest of external obstacles and
by active struggle for the result, turns out to be a manifestation of the
general principle of activity running through the whole of biology".

   One may wonder whether this dialectic view of the foreseeable and the
unforeseeable is the result of Bernstein's apprehension of the structural
properties of the meaningful motor act (meaningful insofar as it refers to
an image of the future) or whether, on the contrary, this view oriented his
scientific approach. One may also ask to what point the analogy between
morphogenesis and self-realization of an intended motor act may be pursued.
It seems to us that the limits would rapidly be reached: the genetic program
does not need an image of the future for its functioning, whereas the image

of the future cannot ensure the realization of the desired state of affairs
directly. Nevertheless, given that the anticipation of the future is
normative, it inevitably leads into a program which maintains directionality
of action as a result of the "motor problem". It could then seem that the
two extremes of the dialectic conflict which presides over the action,
namely the conflict between the foreseeable and the unforeseeable, would be
replaced by the command coming from the "central" program and the information
feedback by the "peripheral" sensory device, respectively. This superficial
and, in the last analysis, erroneous view is induced by Bernstein's reiterated
remarks concerning the unforeseeable character of independent external forces
which act upon the organism and the unpredictable nature of reactive forces
which arise in the course of movement execution "in the multi-linked
biokenetic chains of the motor organs".

What is the precise scope of these remarks? It is hard to conceive of
an organism realizing its "program of the future" if it were reduced to
receiving and processing unexpected and bizarre information about an
environment lacking in any consistency and/or predictibility. In Bernstein's
view, the complete mastery of coordination consists in a judicial utilization
of reactive forces, i.e. the introduction of the necessary impulse at the
proper time. Such a "skill" certainly could not be exerted without the
permanent and powerful intervention of the processes of anticipation of
the spatio-temporal characteristics of events. The circular and uninterrupted
flow of information between the "periphery" and the "center", whose importance
was stressed by Bernstein, is the immediate condition as well as the
consequence and the subsequent expression of coordination. It expresses the
functioning of a system of foreseeable relations, which is projected both
on the external and internal events elicited by the action, and on the
events which, while independent of the action, accompany it and serve as
potential cues. At this stage of exercise and practice (apparently, Bernstein
did not like the term "learning") the informational load of centripetal
messages which flow within the system is less heavy, insofar as these
messages are known in advance and expected. Their local regulation and
"sanctional" afferentation functions (Bernstein borrowed the term "sanctional"
from Anokhin) are certainly more important than their function of informing
about a totally unexpected event.

In these conditions, there is not one image of the future but rather
several images, all extracted "from whatever the brain is able to select
from the current situation, from the fresh traces of immediately preceding

perceptions, from the entire previous experience of the individual, and
finally from those active trials and essays belonging to the class of (...)
orientational reactions". They cooperate in different ways to direct the
action toward its final accomplishment through the preparatory activities
that they elicit. However, while the image of the action's general goal
throws light on the whole action and is located at a strategic level, other
images of the future which anticipate "intermediary" events are located at
a tactical level.

The reader is entitled to ask whether the analysis of intermediary
anticipations that we have proposed is simply a paraphrase of Bernstein's
more or less implicit ideas or, on the contrary, if we projected on
Bernstein's writings some essential elements of a new trend of thought; a
trend which, fed with an ever increasing number of experimental data in the
field of perceptual and motor activities as well as in the domain of
cognition, has insisted unceasingly on the decisive importance of anticipatory
activities in actions (cf., for instance, Pew, 1974; Requin, 1980a). This
question may be answered by saying that the context of contemporary works
constitutes evidently a factor of sensitization to Bernstein's approach of
anticipation. Furthermore, we would like to say that even though Bernstein
did not give the various forms of anticipatory activities a definite status,
he was well aware of the importance of these activities for a general theory
of action.

In the remainder of this chapter, we shall attempt to show, with the
help of some examples, how the different forms of anticipation are referred
to in Bernstein's writings, and to outline their importance for, and their
function in, the theory of action. In order to simplify, we shall follow
Poulton's (1950, 1952) categorization in which he distinguished three types
of anticipation concerning the receptor, perceptual and effector processes.

Receptor anticipation intervenes when, using a suitable mode for
presenting the signals, the subject receives useful information prior to the
time at which it will be used. Whether partial or exhaustive, this prior
information enables the execution of preparatory cognitive or motor adjustments
which may thus facilitate action efficiency and fluidity (Requin, 1980a).
Bernstein gives the example of reading aloud: the eye is searching for new
information while the previous word is being uttered. This example also
shows the lack of a clear frontier between receptor anticipation, considered
as being the less sophisticated, and perceptual anticipation which would
participate in more complex functions. In effect, the coordination of verbal

responses, of text coding and of the control of ocular motricity is extremely complex and the anticipation, in other words the more precocious reception of patterns of visual stimuli, is an activity inscribed within the frame of more general processes of anticipation and prediction.

Perceptual anticipation intervenes when the subject employs his capacity to learn the predictable characteristics of signals. On the basis of this knowledge, his anticipation of temporal and spatial events enables him to set up preparatory adaptations before the occurrence of the events. As a result, perceptual, cognitive and motor preparations permit partial compensation of the inertia of systems brought into play. Works devoted to the study of reaction times as a function of situational entropy (uncertainty concerning the events, their time of occurrence and their sequential dependence) investigate these anticipation and preparation problems to differing degrees and in different manners (cf. Requin, 1980a, b). Perceptual anticipation seems particularly important with respect to behavioral activities in which sensorimotor activity is not discrete but, on the contrary, continuous. In such cases, the detection of stable configurations within the input, and of the regularity of changes in the error signal (i.e. the detection of higher order derivatives of this signal), constitutes the very condition of an "ante factum" control capable of compensating the delays inherent in control systems which react to the error made. Bernstein pointed to the significance of this predictive activity for the regulation of rapid (ballistic) movements as well as tracking movements and, more generally, for all conditions where it is more important to prevent an error than to correct it.

Preventing error does not depend solely on the organism's capacity to anticipate changes in the environment, but also on its capacity to produce the most appropriate movements, i.e. on its capacity to anticipate their effects accurately. This type of anticipation, termed effector anticipation, is based on the information available to the subject concerning "the transmission properties of the muscle system, the limbs and any external devices being controlled" (Pew, 1974). This conception is very similar to Bernstein's view that one of the basic problems of coordination is the adaptation of active forces to the dynamic properties of the control system. In Bernstein's description of the functioning of the control process, the micro-instructions prescribing the direction, strength, velocity, etc... of infinitesimal segments of a movement are presented as prediction and anticipation activities. In this model, the triggering and pursuit of movement are ensured by the desequilibrium created between the momentary state

and the desired state of affairs by the emission of these normative
instructions. However, it is likely, and from a logical standpoint it seems
necessary, that movement anticipation, in terms of instructions concerning
its execution, should be accompanied by anticipation of the consequent
sensory effects, not simply of the planned movement, but also of that
particular movement which has the highest probability of achieving the goal
of the action (Adams, 1971; Schmidt, 1975; Semjen, 1977). The anticipated
sensory image of the movement that is the most appropriate to the goal is
the only one that may serve as a reference against which sensory information
generated by the executed movement can be compared for efficient interpretation.

The last aspect of Bernstein's ideas on anticipation processes concerns
"the anticipatory adaptations in terms of tuning in advance of the arousal
of all the sensory and motor elements which are employed". These anticipations
do not really constitute a separate class of events but rather simply
correspond to preparatory adjustments. We suggested that these anticipatory
adjustments depend on other forms of anticipation concerning the requirements
and regularities of the situation with which the organism is confronted. In
a different article, Bernstein mentioned the role of "the preparatory
organization of the motor periphery". The appropriateness of Bernstein's
views is confirmed by the many studies providing evidence of preparatory
organization, specific to a particular context, of not only peripheral but
also central regulation loops (cf. Bonnet, Requin and Semjen, 1982;
Wiesendanger, 1978). However, the explanatory value of the mechanisms proposed
by Bernstein (neuromuscular tonus, physiological sets, reticular formation)
seems to us rather limited by virtue of the poor level of specificity of
these mechanisms.

The essence of preparatory adjustments so far mentioned is that they
are latent; they become overt only when an appropriate stimulation questions
underlying neuronal circuits. On the contrary, postural adjustments constitute
overt forms of adaptation and one of their functions, according to Bernstein,
is to anticipate the dynamic and static forces to which the body is submitted
when executing a movement. Many current studies confirm this intuition and
specify the feedforward mechanisms intervening in that particular form of
preparation (Gahery and Massion, 1981).

In conclusion, what elements of this analysis of the "images of the
future" can be retained? At the heart of Bernstein's theoretical elaborations
on motor coordination and regulation, these images "anticipated", in our
opinion, certain essential aspects of current preoccupations in the behavioral

neurosciences. Bernstein certainly does not have the monopoly on invention and utilization of the notions of anticipation, expectation or preparation in a theory of "voluntary" movements (cf. for instance, Paillard, 1959). Even so, in 1960, one year before the publication of Bernstein's writings on this question, it was possible to present a synthesis of learning theories (Mowrer, 1960) by referring mainly to Tolman for introducing the concepts of expectation and anticipation. This remark is not at all intended to criticize Mowrer's review, it simply permits appreciation of what constituted Bernstein's originality in his time.

REFERENCES

Adams, J.A. A closed-loop theory of motor learning. Journal of Motor
    Behavior, 1971, 3, 111-149.

Adams, J.A. Issues for a closed-loop theory of motor learning. In, G.E.
    Stelmach (Ed.), Motor control : issues and trends, New York: Academic
    Press, 1976.

Allen, G.I. & Tsukahara, N. Cerebro-cerebellar communication system.
    Physiological Review, 1974, 54, 957-1006.

Arbib, M.A. The metaphorical brain : An introduction to cybernetics as
    artificial intelligence and brain theory. New York: Wiley, 1972.

Arbib, M.A. Perceptual structures and distributed motor control. In, V.B.
    Brooks (Ed.), Handbook of Physiology, section 1 : The nervous system.
    vol. II : Motor control, part 2. Bethesda: American Physiological Society,
    1981.

Berlyne, D.E. Les équivalences psychologiques et les notions quantitatives.
    In, D.E. Berlyne and J. Piaget (Eds.), Thèorie du comportement et
    opérations. Paris : P.U.F., 1960.

Bizzi, E., Dev, P., Morasso, P. & Polit, A. Effect of load disturbances
    during centrally initiated movements. Journal of Neurophysiology, 1978,
    41, 542-556.

Bonnet, M., Gurfinkel, V.S., Lipshits, M.I. & Popov, K.E. Central programming
    of lower limb muscular activity in the standing man. Agressologie, 1976,
    17B, 35-42.

Bonnet, M. & Requin, J. Long-loop and spinal reflexes in man during
    preparation for intended directional hand movements. Journal of Neuro-
    sciences, 1982, 2, 90-96.

Bonnet, M., Requin, J. & Semjen, A. Human reflexology and motor preparation.
    In, D. Miller (Ed.), Exercise and Sport Sciences Reviews, vol. 9,
    Philadelphia : Franklin Institute Press, 1981.

Brooks, V.B. Roles of cerebellum and basal ganglia in initiation and control
    of movements. Canadian Journal of Neurological Sciences, 1975, 2, 265-277.

Brooks, V.B. Motor programs revisited. In, R.E. Talbott and D.R. Humphrey
    (Eds.), Posture and movement. New-York: Raven Press, 1979.

Bruner, J.S. The growth and structure of skill. In, K.J. Connolly (Ed.),
    Motor skills in infancy. New-York : Academic Press, 1971.

Burke, R.E., Rudomin, P. & Zajac, F.E. Catch property in single mammalian
    motor units. Science, 1970, 168, 122-124.

Conrad, B. & Meyer-Lohmann, J. The long-loop transcortical load compensating reflex. Trends in Neurosciences, 1980, 3, 269-272.

Coquery, J.M. Fonctions motrices et contrôle des messages sensoriels d'origine somatique. Journal de Physiologie, 1972, 64, 533-560.

Evarts, E.V. Motor cortex reflexes associated with learned movements. Science, 1973, 179, 501-503.

Fitts, P.M. Perceptual-motor skill learning. In, A.W. Melton (Ed.), Categories of human learning. New-York : Academic Press, 1964.

Fowler, C. & Turvey, M. Skill acquisition : an event approach with special reference to searching for the optimum of a function of several variables. In, G.E. Stelmach (Ed.), Information processing in motor control and learning. New-York : Academic Press, 1978.

Gahéry, Y. & Massion, J. Co-ordination between posture and movement. Trends in Neurosciences, 1981, 4, 199-202.

Gallistel, C.R. Precis of Gallistel's, the organization of action : a new synthesis. The Behavioral and Brain Sciences, 1981, 4, 609-650.

Gelfand, I.M. & Tsetlin, M.L. Some methods of control for complex systems. Russian Mathematical Surveys, 1962, 17, 95-116.

Granit, R. Constant errors in the execution and appreciation of movement. Brain, 1972, 95, 649-660.

Granit, R. Demand and accomplishment in voluntary movement. In, R.B. Stein, K.G. Pearson, R.S. Smith and J.B. Redford (Eds.), Control of posture and locomotion. Advances in Behavioral Biology, vol. 7. New-York : Plenum Press, 1973.

Granit, R. The purposive brain. Cambridge : M.I.T. Press, 1977.

Granit, R. Comments on history of motor control. In, V.B. Brooks (Ed.), Handbook of Physiology, section 1 : The nervous system. vol. II : Motor control, part 1. Bethesda: American Physiological Society, 1981.

Gurfinkel, V.S. & Levik, Y.S. Dependence of muscle contraction on the succession of stimulating impulses. Biophizika (Moscow), 1973, 18, 116-121.

Gurfinkel, V.S. & Schik, M.L. The control of posture and locomotion. In, A.A. Gydikov, N. Tankov and D. Kosarov (Eds.), Motor control. New-York : Plenum Press, 1973.

Head, H. Studies in neurology. 2. London : Frowde, Hodder & Stoughton, 1920.

Hebb, D.O. The organization of behavior. New-York : Wiley, 1949.

Hollerbach, J.M. Computers, brains and the control of movement. Trends in Neurosciences, 1982, 5, 189-192.

Keele, S.W. Movement control in skilled motor performance. Psychological
    Bulletin, 1968, 70, 387-403.

Keele, S.W. Attention and human performance. Pacific Palisades : Goodyear
    Publishing, 1973.

Keele, S.W. Behavioral analysis of movement. In, V.B. Brooks (Ed.),
    Handbook of Physiology, section 1 : The nervous system. vol. II :
    Motor control, part 2. Bethesda : American Physiological Society, 1981.

Kelso, J.A.S. Contrasting perspectives on order and regulation in movement.
    In, J. Long and A. Baddeley (Eds.), Attention and Performance IX.
    Hillsdale, N.J. : Erlbaum, 1981.

Kelso, J.A.S., Holt, K.G., Kugler, P.N. & Turvey, M.T. On the concept of
    coordinative structures as dissipative structures. II : Empirical lines
    of convergency. In, G.E. Stelmach and J. Requin (Eds.), Tutorials in
    motor behavior. Amsterdam : North-Holland, 1980.

Kornhuber, H.H. Cerebral cortex, cerebellum and basal ganglia : an
    introduction to their motor functions. In, F.O. Schmitt and G. Worden
    (Eds.), The Neurosciences, third study program. Cambridge : M.I.T. Press,
    1974.

Kugler, P.M., Kelso, J.A.S. & Turvey, M.T. On the concept of coordinative
    structures as dissipative structures. II : Theoretical line. In, G.E.
    Stelmach and J. Requin (Eds.), Tutorials in motor behavior. Amsterdam :
    North-Holland, 1980.

Lashley, K.S. The accuracy of movement in the absence of excitation from
    the moving organ. American Journal of Physiology, 1917, 43, 169-194.

Liepman, H. Das Krankheitsbild der Apraxia ("motorischen Asymbolie") auf
    grund eines Falles von einseitiger Apraxie. Monatschrift für Psychiatrie
    und Neurologie, 1900, 8, 15-44 ; 102-132 ; 188-197.

MacKay, W.A. The motor program : back to the computer. Trends in Neuro-
    sciences, 1980, 3, 97-100.

Miles, F.A. & Evarts, E.V. Concepts of motor organization. Annual Review
    of Psychology, 1979, 30, 327-362.

Miller, G.A., Galanter, E. & Pribram, K.H. Plans and the structure of
    behavior. New-York : Holt, Rinehart and Winston, 1960.

Mountcastle, V.B. The world around us : neural command functions for
    selective attention. Neural Sciences Research Bulletin, 1976, 16,
    suppl. n° 2.

Mowrer, O.H. Learning theory and behavior. New-York : John Wiley & Sons,
    Inc., 1960.

Neisser, U. Cognitive psychology. New-York : Appleton Century Crofts, 1967.

Paillard, J. Réflexes et régulations d'origine proprioceptive. Etude
    neuro-physiologique et psychophysiologique. Paris : Arnette, 1955.

Paillard, J. The patterning of skilled movements. In, J. Field, H.W. Magoun,
    and V.E. Hall (Eds.), Handbook of Physiology, section 1 : Neurophysiology.
    vol. 3. Washington : American Physiological Society, 1960.

Paillard, J. Les attitudes dans la motricité. In, Les Attitudes. Paris :
    P.U.F., 1961.

Paillard, J. Apraxia and the neurophysiology of motor control. Philosophical
    Transaction, Royal Society of London, 1982, B 298, 111-134.

Pew, R.W. Human perceptual-motor performance. In, H.B. Kantowitz (Ed.),
    Human information processing : Tutorials in performance and cognition.
    Hillsdale N.J., Erlbaum, 1974.

Phillips, C.G. & Porter, R. Corticospinal neurones : their role in movement.
    London : Academic Press, 1977.

Piaget, J. La portée psychologique et épistémologique des essais néo-hulliens
    de D. Berlyne. In, D.E. Berlyne and J. Piaget (Eds.), Théorie de
    comportement et opérations. Paris : P.U.F., 1960.

Posner, M.I., Pea, R. & Volpe, B. Cognitive neuroscience : toward a science
    of synthesis. In, J. Mehler, S. Wlaker and A. Garrett (Eds.),
    Perspectives on mental representation. Hillsdale, N.J., Erlbaum, 1982.

Poulton, E.C. Perceptual anticipation and reaction time. Quarterly Journal
    of Experimental Psychology, 1950, 2, 99-112.

Poulton, E.C. Perceptual anticipation in tracking with two-pointer and
    one-pointer displays. British Journal of Psychology. General Section,
    1952, 43, 222-229.

Reed, E.S. An outline of a theory of action systems. Journal of Motor
    Behavior, 1982, 14, 98-134.

Requin, J. Toward a psychobiology of preparation for action. In, G.E.
    Stelmach and J. Requin (Eds.), Tutorials in motor behavior. Amsterdam :
    North-Holland, 1980a.

Requin, J. La préparation à l'activité motrice : vers une convergence des
    problématiques psychologique et neurophysiologique. In, J. Requin (Ed.),
    Anticipation et Comportement. Paris : Editions du C.N.R.S., 1980b.

Requin, J. The meaning of an experiment combining cognitive and neurobiological
    approaches. In, J. Mehler, S. Walker and A. Garrett (Eds.), Perspectives
    on mental representation. Hillsdale, N.J. : Erlbaum, 1982.

Sanders, A.F. Structural and functional aspects of the reaction process.
    In, S. Dornic (Ed.), Attention and performance VI. Hillsdale, N.J. :
    Erlbaum, 1977.

Sanders, A.F. Stage analysis of reaction processes. In, G.E. Stelmach and
    J. Requin (Eds.), Tutorials in motor behavior. Amsterdam : North-Holland,
    1980.

Schmidt, R.A. A schema theory of discrete motor skill learning. Psychological
    Review, 1975, 82, 225-260.

Semjen, A. From motor learning to sensorimotor skill acquisition. Journal
    of Human Movement Studies, 1977, 3, 182-191.

Shaffer, L.H. Analysing piano performances : A study of concert pianists.
    In, G.E. Stelmach and J. Requin (Eds.), Tutorials in motor behavior.
    Amsterdam : North-Holland, 1980.

Sternberg, S. The discovery of processing stages : extensions of Donder's
    method. In, W.G. Koster (Ed.), Attention and Performance II. Amsterdam :
    North-Holland, 1969.

Sternberg, S., Monsell, S., Knoll, R. & Wright, C. The latency and duration
    of rapid movement sequences : comparisons of speech and type-writing.
    In, G.E. Stelmach (Ed.), Information processing in motor control and
    learning. New-York : Academic Press, 1978.

Thach, W.T. Timing of activity in cerebellar dentate nucleus and cerebral
    motor cortex during prompt volitional movement. Brain Research, 1975,
    88, 233-241.

Theios, J. The components of response latency in simple human information
    processing tasks. In, P. Rabbitt and S. Dornic (Eds.), Attention and
    Performance V. London : Academic Press, 1975.

Turvey, M.T., Shaw, R. & Mace, W. Issues in a theory of action : degrees
    of freedom, coordinative structures and coalitions. In, J. Requin (Ed.),
    Attention and Performance VII. Hillsdale, N.J. : Erlbaum, 1978.

Wachholder, K. Willkürliche Haltung und Bewegung. Ergebnisse der Physiologie,
    1928, 26, 568-775.

Wallon, H. De l'acte à la pensée. Paris : Flammarion, 1942.

Welford, A.T. On the sequencing of action. Brain Research, 1974, 71, 381-392.

Wiesendanger, M. Comments on the problem of transcortical reflexes. Journal
    de Physiologie, 1978, 74, 325-330.

Human Motor Actions — Bernstein Reassessed
H.T.A. Whiting (editor)
© Elsevier Science Publishers B.V. (North-Holland), 1984

CHAPTER Vb

TOWARDS A HOLISTIC CONCEPTION OF MOVEMENT CONTROL

L. Pickenhain

> Yes, we shall question all, again and again. And we shall
> not proceed with seven-league boots, but at a snail's pace.
> And what we find to-day, we shall erase from the board
> to-morrow, and we shall only write it down again, if we
> have found it once more. And what we wish to find, and do
> find, that shall we look at with particular suspicion...
> But if every other assumption than this one has been
> banished from our hands, then no more mercy to those who
> have not studied, but still speak about (Bertolt Brecht,
> The Life of Gallilei).

Bernstein started his scientific work with diligent and exact
experimental investigations into the coordination of movement in healty
humans both under working conditions and during different types of locomotion.
Later on, he extended this study to subjects with lesions in the central
motor system. Summarizing and generalizing the results of these
investigations, he developed a new and comprehensive conception of the
principles and mechanism of human motion. This completely new and prospective
idea was in contradiction to some officially accepted dogmatic interpretations
of Pavlov's ideas which in the Soviet Union prevailed in the forties and
fifties. Academically, Bernstein was viciously attacked - especially during
the Scientific Session on Problems of the Physiological Theory of Pavlov in
1950 in Moscow - and was accused of propagating idealistic and vitalistic
positions. He - like Anokhin and many other scientists - was relegated from
his laboratory and had to leave Moscow for some years. After Stalin's death
(1953) he was able to return, but he never again had the possibility to
participate in experimental investigations. Instead, he intensified his
efforts to create a holistic conception of movement control in animals and
humans. On the basis of the extensive experimental results of himself and of
his pupils, together with an appreciation of the latest results and hypotheses
from physiology and mathematics, he was able to develop fascinating, future-
oriented ideas about the principles and mechanisms of programming and control
of movements which consequently led him to postulate a physiology of activity.

Bernstein's paper 'Trends and problems in the study and investigation
of the physiology of activity', written at that time, has not lost any of
its fascination during the twenty years that have passed. Moreover, many of
the assumptions underlying his theoretical framework for what he called the
'science of movement' have been confirmed by new research data and many of
his critical remarks are equally valid today. His predictions and ideas
about the discovery of new and wider horizons have turned out to be true.
But, these horizons have become somewhat more precisely specified in some
of the topic areas, and new questions have arisen on the lines of his
prognostic thinking. In what follows, an attempt will be made to indicate
the state of knowledge with respect to some of the questions he raises and
- as he did - to accentuate especially those questions about human motor
activity which seem most important for further developments.

In particular, the following issues will be addressed:

I.   The model of the structure of motor acts and the determinants of
their central control.

II.   The reflection of the image of the real external world and the
modelling of the future in the brain.

III. The programming of movements and the hierarchical complexity of
their control - localized in numerous centres and systems of the brain.

IV.   Some philosophical implications of Bernstein's views, especially
regarding the activity of the organism as the leading life-developing
principle in physiology.

I.

Evaluating and summarizing his immense experimental material on the
coordination of movement during the performance of working acts, locomotion
and other activities, Bernstein very soon concluded that the organization
and control of movement cannot be understood as a chain of reflexes based
on the conception of the simple reflex arc. In an article (not included in
the present collection), he emphasised:

> The reflex is not the element of action, but the reflex
> itself is an elementary action (Bernstein, 1965).

The performance of purposeful movements requires continuous information
from, and evaluation of the effect of movement, both as an instrument of

reinforcement and for making the necessary corrections. From the beginning of the thirties Bernstein used what he termed the reflex ring to operationalise this experimentally based fact.

This statement parallels propositions formulated by Anokhin (1975) arising from his experimental work between 1932 and 1934 on the mutual connections between the activity of the central and peripheral parts of the nervous system. Both authors recognized the significance of recurrent afferentation for understanding the biological phenomenon of regulation and for which, Wiener (1948) later coined the term Cybernetics. In 1978, Anokhin, in his paper 'Theory of the functional system as a starting point for the construction of physiological cybernetics', refers to the work of Bernstein. He writes:

> During the last years N.A. Bernstein has elaborated this physiological architecture of behaviour acts very clearly (Anokhin, 1978).

Bernstein several times mentions the conformity between his idea of the reflex ring and the principal assumptions of Anokhin on the architecture of the functional system.

If Anokhin's model of the general architecture of the functional system (Fig. 1) is compared with the block diagram of an apparatus for the control

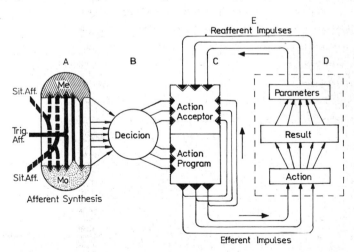

Fig. 1. General architecture of the functional system of behaviour according to Anokhin. A - afference synthesis: Sit. Aff. - afferences from the situation; Trig. Aff. - triggering afference; B - stage of decision; C - formation of the acceptor of the results of action and formulation of the efferent action program; D-E - analysis of the results of action and formulation of the reafferent impulses for the comparison of the preprogrammed and the real results; Me - memory; Mo - motivation (changed from Anokhin, 1978).

of movements designed by Bernstein (Fig. 2), the coincidence of the principal
ideas on the participating elements is obvious. Both have the same circuit
of efferent and afferent impulses (Anokhin calls them 'reafferent' - a term
not acknowledged by Bernstein), the same comparator system (Bernstein:
comparing system; Anokhin: acceptor of the results of action), and the same
decision system for central control (Bernstein: commanding system; Anokhin:
decision as effect of the actual afferent synthesis). Similar ideas on the
continuous control of motion by comparing the motor command (feed forward)
with the afferent feedback signals concerning the performed motor acts were
developed in 1950 by Sperry on the basis of experiments with fish and by
Von Holst and Mittelstaedt (1950) on the basis of experiments with insects.
Independent of one another they postulated the existence of a trace of the
motor command persisting for some time in the central nervous system and
being compared with the afferent signals arising from the movements. This
temporary trace was named 'corollary discharge' by Sperry (1950) and
'efference copy' by Von Holst and Mittelstaedt (1950). Until now, the
intrinsic physiological nature of this short duration persistent trace has
not been clarified, and it may be that its structure and mechanism are
completely different in distinct situations, i.e. it may be more a principle
than a determinate mechanism. Newer discussions about the role of efference
copy ('effecence as a feedforward process') are more speculative than
elucidative (Schmidt, 1976).

Bernstein does not discuss the possible intrinsic mechanism of the
'comparing system'. He thinks the most important question to be: 'What is
the standard invariable determinant of this involved structurality of motor
acts?' The answer to this question plays - as he asserts - the key-role in
the complicated control system for goal-directed purposeful movements:

> ...the standard determinant both for the programming
> of motor activity and its effection and correction by
> feedback connections can only be the formation and
> representation of a motor problem by the brain in one
> way or another.

The greatest part of the relevant article (Chapter V) deals with the
analysis of this statement and the search for the type of mechanisms which
might be participating in the organism's solution of such a problem.

It is instructive that Anokhin (1968), independently, comes to the same
conclusion. He stresses the necessity to regard the results of action as an
independent physiological category. While the scientist is more interested
in the 'reflectory action', for the acting animal or human subject the most
important information is the result of his action. The prediction and control

of the results of action play the leading role in all purposeful behavioural
acts.

Astonishingly, the leading role of the results of action is not to be
found in the schema of Anokhin (Fig. 1) nor in the block diagram of
Bernstein (Fig. 2). In the motor response schema of Schmidt (1976) the
'desired outcome' also plays a leading role in the formation of the correct
'motor response schema'; but 'knowledge of results' is not connected with
the 'desired outcome', and therefore the real dynamics between the planned
program and the information on the real outcome which again influences the
desired outcome is not shown. A similar block diagram is given by Batuev
and Tairov (1978). Later (Fig. 3) a schema is presented in which this
backward influence of the outcome on the formulation of the desired goal is
considered.

This principal assumption that the formation and representation of the
motor problem in the brain plays the deciding role in the performance and
control of goal-directed motor acts raises some important questions concerning
the type and mechanisms of reflection of the actual and the future situation
of the surrounding world, the relation between the actual and the future
model of the external world within the brain, and the plasticity of the motor
coordination during the execution of the planned program to reach the desired
goal. In addition, the way in which Bernstein and Anokhin treat the problem,
taking the goal as the deciding element, raises both methodological and
philosophical questions. In particular, a clear answer needs to be found to
the question: Must this approach be considered as a teleological (vitalistic)
one or not?

II.

The reflection of the real surrounding world within the central nervous
system is one of the preconditions for building up movement programs which
are determined to reach any external goal and to satisfy any important need
of the organism. Neurophysiology has collected an immense experimental
material related to this question. Stimulating any receptor organ one can
find nerve cells or sets of nerve cells in the cerebral cortex as well as in
distinct subcortical structures which are activated (or inhibited). The so-
called primary, secondary and tertiary projection areas in the cerebral
cortex illustrate the results of such investigations. In every textbook of

physiology can be found the well-known homunculus for the representation
of sensory and motor afferents in the post- and pre-Sylvian areas. Very
precise study has been carried out on projections within the visual system.
While it can be shown that there are distinct topographical projections from
the retina to the geniculate body and from there to the cortical regions –
as Bernstein indeed postulated – these projections never show a one-to-one
correspondence. Instead it is found that the projecting pathways work as
analysers for special features of the incoming visual information. Thus, in
the primary projection area of the visual cortex can be found special
neuronal networks for the representation of orientation, binocularity, depth,
colour, and movement of visual stimuli. Starting with the retina and
proceeding via the ascending pathways, it can be shown that the projecting
visual system progressively extracts more and more abstract and general
features of the visual information.

The experimental investigations of the last two decades have confirmed
the assumption made by Bernstein that the projection of sensory information
in the brain does not display a one-to-one correspondence between the elements
of the perceptual fields or the organs of sensation and the cell network in
the cerebral cortex. But the danger of atomism, about which Bernstein gives
warning, arises again at the level of generalization. Thus, Gross, Rossa-
Miranda and Bender (1972) believe that they have found cells in the monkey's
cortex that respond only when the animal sees a monkey's hand. They do not
even respond to a human hand. Such hypothetical cells for recognizing
complicated features have been called 'gnostic neurones'. It is clear that
this is a complete misinterpretation which does not take into consideration
the very intricate function of the brain as a system (Young, 1978).

The question is even more difficult if the projections to the secondary
and tertiary cortical fields and the multiple intervening connections
between the different areas of the cortex and between the two hemispheres
are considered. Obviously, in these complex areas of higher order there is
not only a coding of intermodal influences, but also integrated neuronal
circuits which are able – within the systemic organization – to organize and
control special elements of complex motor behaviour. The most convincing
study in this field is the investigation of the neurones of area 7 in monkeys
by Mountcastle and his co-workers (Mountcastle, 1975; Lynch, Mountcastle,
Talbot & Yin, 1977). They trained monkeys to execute tasks requiring the
fixation of stationary visual targets, the tracking of slow moving targets
and the making of saccadic movements to foveate those which suddenly jumped

from one locus to another within the field of view. During these tasks they found, in area 7, different classes of cells with visuomotor neurones, in both a special and conditional sense: visual fixation neurones, visual tracking neurones and a great number of cells whose properties in the behavioural task used could not be specified precisely. Mountcastle does not try to give an atomistic interpretation of these results; rather, he supposes that there exists within the parietal lobe a neuronal mechanism for directing visual attention (only within the distance which can be reached by the monkey), for the fixation of gaze on objects of interest (the task must be highly motivating), for maintaining visual grasp of the object if it moves slowly, and for loosening fixation and initiating rapid saccadic movements towards new objects of interest presented within the visual field. He expresses the idea that in area 7 can be seen a command operation linked to certain motivational states and combined with a continually updated central representation of the relations between the body, head and eyes, and surrounding space. But such experiments, as subtle and interesting as they are, cannot yet answer the question put by Bernstein, according to which mathematical law the external world is represented in the brain and becomes the basis for goal-directed future behaviour. Most people would agree that this representation (or representations) must be 'constructed along the principles of a model', and that in no sense can the representation be isomorphic. So far no one has been able to demonstrate operator principles of this process. In this connection, the demand of Bernstein that these operator principles must ensure, under all circumstances, an active mental modelling of the world is very important.

During the last few years a completely new idea which attacks this very intricate set of questions was proposed by a scientist - Edelman (1979) - who earned his merits in a field seemingly far from neurophysiology, immunology, for which he was awarded a Nobel laureate. He suggests a selective theory of brain function in which the unit of selection is a neuronal group (Mountcastle, 1979). Such neuronal groups containing up to 10.000 neurones are formed during embryogenesis and during epigenetic development. Within each neuronal group intrinsic connections exist and can involve a variety of modes of interaction within a local circuit, including synaptic and all modes of non-synaptic interactions. These intrinsic connections - he assumes - have great variability from group to group. Among the groups, extrinsic connections exist, which are also specified by gene programming and synaptic selection. Neuronal groups of different structures and connectivity form primary repertoires (one repertoire comprising up to 10^6 cell groups) which can respond to or recognize a particular signal pattern. This many-to-one response implies that each repertoire is degenerate. By degeneracy Edelman means that, given a particular threshold condition, there must be more than one way of satisfactorily recognizing a given input signal. This implies the presence of multiple neuronal groups with different structures capable of carrying out the same function more or less well. Therefore, degenerate groups are iso-functional, but non-isomorphic. The polling of such <u>degenerate primary repertoires</u> by signals leads to associative recognition. Moreover, repetition of signals interacting with selected neuronal groups results in the emergence of secondary repertoires of groups with a higher likelihood of response.

Based on these principal assumptions, Edelman considers a hierarchy of responses that, in its later stage, will be non-linear because of the presence of feedback and feedforward loops with their associated alterations of temporal patterns and response times. In the hierarchy:

$$S \rightarrow R \rightarrow (R \text{ of } R)_n, \; n = 1, 2, 3, \ldots$$

S represents transduced sensory input from the environment, R represents cortical cellular groups that can act as 'recognizers' of the input, and (R of R) represents groups of neurons in the association cortex, or in temporal, frontal, or prefrontal cortex, that act as 'recognizers of recognizers'. Thus, by the selection of certain subgroups, altering their properties as a result of experienced input and altering also the probability of future selection of these groups over their neighbours, a secondary repertoire as a collection of different high-order neuronal groups is produced Following this line of reasoning, the central nervous system can recognize modes of itself selectively and in a nonlinear and degenerate fashion. By this means, Edelman shows how degenerate selection and cell-group signalling in a re-entrant fashion could provide the necessary conditions for the explanation of consciousness at the cellular level.

In general, this type of modelling, the representation of the external (and internal) world within the brain, answers the principal arguments raised by Bernstein. It has the advantage of an associative system with successive recognitions across different levels of hierarchical nesting in a non-linear way. The system of group-degenerate selection shows all features of a distributive property, and it treats subjective phenomena like consciousness in a monistic manner as a process occurring in certain defined

gross areas, for example the two cortical hemispheres, the thalamo-cortical
radiations, and the limbic and reticular systems. It also explains the
increasing plasticity at every succeeding hierarchical level of the brain.
But - as Edelman (1979) states -, the described scientific theory:

> ...proposes a particular set of mechanisms to account
> for higher brain function, and it must stand or fall
> on their verifiability.

Nevertheless, it sets forth a principle of brain functioning which opens the
way for future research into the intrinsic operator for modelling.

III.

Bernstein assumes that the basic mechanism by which the central nervous
system controls, simultaneously, the large number of degrees of freedom of
the multijointed, musculoskeletal system, must be a modelling of the future,
and the programming of movement must be dependent on rules that permit
original and creative motor solutions to problems such as reaching for
objects in a structured space. During the last two decades, complex electrophysiological methods in combination with lesions and cooling experiments
have been used to tackle this intricate question. Special attention has been
directed towards the classification of different types of movement, as
Bernstein had already done, to the hierarchical structuring of the initiation
and control of different movement programs, and to the different types of
feedback control.

Now-adays it is widely accepted that motor programming at different
levels of the central nervous system is a basic principle of all active
behaviour of animals and humans. Locomotion is one example of an action that
has been extensively studied for this purpose. In higher animals and humans
there are inborn local circuits in the spinal cord subserving the generation
of the necessary agonistic and antagonistic impulse patterns for simple, more
or less rigid locomotory acts. At higher levels of the central nervous system
local circuits provide more complex programs, the execution of which is
realized by using the simpler programs at deeper levels of organization in
a more and more differentiated way. This 'multiplex hierarchical complexity,
localized in the numerous centres and systems of the brain' ensures high
redundancy and the possibility of learning by feedback, command and control
flexibility, and command specialization and plasticity (Herman, Grillner,

Stein & Stuart, 1976).

    This is not a simple 'top-down' hierarchy, but a system that is
distributed in space and time:

>   Spatial distribution consists of parallel transmission
>   on many kinds of information; somesthesia and kinesthesia
>   ascending to the cerebellum as well as to the cerebrum.
>   Temporal distribution results from unceasing activity
>   in all afferent and efferent parts of the sensorimotor
>   apparatus. Movements thus evolve in multiple ascending
>   and descending loops whose activities are distributed
>   in time and space (Brooks & Thach, 1981).

On the highest level of motor coordination this task is distributed in a
very intricate and flexible manner between sensorimotor cortex, basal
ganglia and cerebellum. The complex organization of motor programs is
provided by these three main structures of the central motor system in such
a way that the adequate type of movement can be performed at the necessary
time with the necessary force and velocity (one including the other) to reach
the intended goal in external space (Bizzi, Accornero, Chapple & Hogan, 1981;
Miles & Evarts, 1979).

    The actual existence of complex central motor programs completely
sufficient to reach any goal, if learned in an orderly manner is confirmed
by much experimental data. Thus, ballistic movements can be performed in
the correct (learned) fashion, if all afferent control signals are excluded
(Lamarre, Spidalieri, Busby & Lund, 1980). The cerebellum plays a special
role in programming and controlling the execution and stopping of relatively
simple ballistic movements (Kornhuber, 1971, 1974). The command for a
ballistic movement occurs in the cerebral association cortex and passes
through the cerebellum via the pons and returns to the motor cortex via the
thalamus. Cooling the involved cerebellar parts of this cortico-cerebellar-
cortical loop only delays, but does not exclude their exact execution.
Cortico-cortical connections provide an alternative pathway for the initiation
of ballistic movements, although after a longer delay. Fast and slow intended
movements, on the other hand, which need continuous feedback control, are
programmed through the special participation of cortico-striatal loops (De
Long & Georgopoulos, 1981; Garibian & Gambarian, 1982); but cerebellar
circuits are also included in this control mechanism (Miller & Brooks, 1982).
It can be concluded that the brain has many operational motor programs at its
disposal, at the level of the cortico-cerebellar and cortico-striatal loops
including some thalamic structures. This gives the possibility to select
the appropriate program according to previous experience in a very flexible

way and to change the selection, if required by the actual environmental
or internal (need) situation. Thus, the movement activity can be changed
in time and space according to the goal that should be reached.

The choice of an adequate motor pattern is mostly determined by the
influence of the association cortex on the previously mentioned motor
systems. This part of the cortex receives and integrates the information
coming from internal and external feedback which, in parrallel, also goes
to the cerebellum. But, whereas the cerebellar circuit has only a self-
sustaining control of simple programs such as ballistic movements and, in
addition, helps to realize the higher intent, what is still under discussion
is:

> ...how the necessary codes and commands are transferred
> from association cortex to the machinery of movement
> (Brooks & Thach, 1981).

In a well trained situation the task-relevant triggering signal determines
at any level which preprogrammed movement pattern at which level of sub-
programs will be initiated. On the other hand, feedback may order major
program changes when the program is grossly inappropriate, and higher levels
of programming must be included to prepare a more adequate program. But,
feedback may also be used to monitor small errors and enhance modest
corrections at deeper levels. In other cases, it may aid in coordinating
one movement system with another, as when raising a limb requires background
postural adjustments (Keele, 1981).

Thus, modern brain research has confirmed the assumption of Bernstein
that the central nervous system has a 'highly homeostatic hierarchical
system of coordination of motor function in all its complexity' at its
disposal. This system can be used to realise those purposeful motor acts,
necessary from moment to moment, to reach intended goals. The fundamental
condition for this to take place, must be the:

> ...modelling of the future by means of extrapolation
> from whatever the brain is able to select from the
> current situation, from the fresh traces of the
> immediately preceding perceptions, and finally from
> those active trials and assays ... as orientational
> reactions whose fundamental significance has certainly
> been underestimated (Bernstein, 1967).

The parts of the brain which provide this leading role are the frontal
lobes in continuous direct and indirect connection with the association
cortex. The pre-frontal cortex is the substrate for cognitive operations
of short-term memory and preparatory set that allow the appropriate choice,

timing, and use of the necessary motor programs. Because it is continuously
updating the model of the future in a probabilistic way, it appears
indispensable for the protection of purposive behaviour from competing drives
and for inhibiting the execution of untimely acts. It realizes these tasks
by efferents to the striatal-cortical-cerebellar loops on the one side and by
way of efferents to the limbic system and the diencephalon on the other side
(Fuster, 1981). How this 'probabilistic extrapolation of the future' as the
fundament for adequate choice and correction of the actual motor programs is
realized in detail, remains open to question. But, the demands Bernstein has
formulated for the basic mechanisms of this process, remain valid for future
research. The approach proposed by Mountcastle (1979) and Edelman (1979) may be
a high-road to disclose substantial mechanisms of this process in the brain.

Electrophysiological study of slow potential shifting in the human scalp
records during the preparation of voluntary movements confirms the assumption
of pre-programming preparation at the highest levels of the brain. About 800
msec before the execution of a voluntary movement a negative shift of the
cortical potential bilaterally can be observed which extends far into the
pre-central and parietal areas. This potential has been called Bereitschafts-
potential (readiness potential)(Deecke, Scheid & Kornhuber, 1982). The amplitude
of this potential is interestingly enough, connected with the probability of
feedback guessed by the subject (Hink, Kohler, Deecke & Kornhuber, 1982).
Ninety milliseconds before the start of a movement, the potential displays a
pre-motor positive shift which is also bilateral and extensive. At least, 50
msec before a movement the negative, so-called motor potential, appears and
is only present in the motor cortex contralateral to the moving part of the
body; it is immediately followed by the EMG response of the involved muscles
preceding their contraction. These slow potential changes, especially over
the associative and frontal areas of both sides of the cortex, may be
interpreted as a sign of the probabilistic adjustment of the modelling of
the future and the selection of the most adequate triggering signals. The
same is valid for the so-called negative contingent variation, a widely
extended cortical negativity, which depends upon the contingency between
some event and an expected, task-relevant stimulus such as a feedback signal
(Walter, Cooper, Aldridge, McCallum & Winter, 1964).

Bernstein's assumption that in the central nervous system channelized
processes ('impulse activity ...transmitted without damping along nerve
fibres') and slower wave-like activity which is 'spread across the fibres'
are operating together is confirmed by more recent investigations (Schmitt,
Dev & Smith, 1976). It must be extended by the (at that time unknown) fact that

there are triadic and other complex configurations of synaptic contacts, and substance exchange between nerve (and glial) cells through specialized channel structures (gap junctions, tight junctions). This must be especially effective within the local circuits of neuronal groups suggested by Edelman (1979) and others. The neurones within these groups are so densely arranged that every form of information exchange through channelized electric currents and electrotonic influences as well as through mutual substance exchange must be possible. The intra-neuronal and inter-neuronal transport of various types of substances suggests that the biochemical and bioelectrical parameters are functionally interwoven.

Also, Bernstein's statement that:

> ...proceeding with a determinate program of operation,
> the central nervous system ... achieves anticipatory
> adaptations in terms of the tuning in advance of the
> arousal of all the sensory and motor elements which
> are employed,

is completely confirmed by numerous experiments. This anticipatory adaptation, can be demonstrated at all levels of the motor system, from the highest goal-programming level at the frontal-associative cortical areas (see above) to the pre-innervation of agonistic and antagonistic motor units at the spinal level (Koc, 1975). The central movement program comprises all preparatory innervations that are necessary for the exact execution of the impending movement. They are acquired on a probabilistic base as result of learning and training and are ready to be changed on the same basis if they are not appropriate for the given task in the respective situation. In addition, the central motor pre-programming includes commands to the different vegetative functions which provide the necessary prerequisite to the planned motor action. This is clearly seen in the preparatory activation of metabolic, cardiovascular, and respiratory functions immediately before any intended performance.

This strong inter-connection between the motor commands and the commands to the vegetative systems may be used in special cases to disclose some preparatory and executive features of the model. For instance, this is possible by having subjects mentally perform a well-trained motor program and simultaneously recording the changes in some peripheral parameters. This may be illustrated by the example, shown in Fig. 2. A well-trained swimmer sits quietly in a chair. In front of his nostrils a thermosensitive sensor is attached by means of which his breathing may be recorded continuously. The subject is asked mentally to perform swimming over a given distance in a

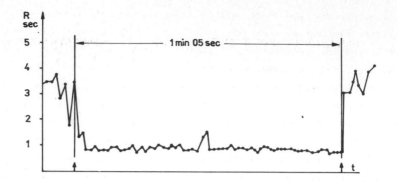

Fig. 2. Acceleration of the respiration frequency during mentally
(ideomotorly) swimming a given distance in a predetermined
time. R - duration of the consecutive breathing movements in
sec; vertical arrows and lines - start and end of the
ideomotor "swimming movements" (from Pickenhain & Beyer, 1979).

predetermined time. As is well known, there exists a strong correlation
between the swimming movements of the arms and the respiration rate. This
means that in a well trained subject the commands for the rhythmic
respiration movements are integrated constituents of the complex central
motor program. Therefore, the whole subjective performance of the mental
swimming can be followed by looking at the respiration curve. At the first
vertical line (Fig. 2) the subject announces, by pressing a button, that he
is starting his mental swimming. The respiration curve indicates a strong
acceleration which coincides with the frequency of the mentally executed
arm movements. In the middle of the distance, the moment of the turn (a
short deceleration of breathing) can be seen, and in the second half of the
distance the subject evidently performs mental swimming with the same time
program as in the first half. If the subject mentally reaches the goal, the
respiration rate goes back to its original value; this the subject indicates
by again pressing the button (the second vertical line) (Pickenhain, 1976,
1977).

        This phenomenon is only observable, if the subject imagines the
performance of the swimming movements very vividly and 'as really doing it'.
By this way, the efferent impulses of the complex motor program of swimming
reach all parts of the central nervous system which serve as subprogram
effectors of the whole process of realization. The real movements of the
extremities are inhibited by the given instruction to sit quietly and not to
move. But, the EMG record may indicate a sub-threshold innervation of the

involved muscles (the so-called ideomotor or Carpenter effect). Thus, can
be shown, how precisely the subject is able to reproduce his trained motor
program mentally and how well he executes his ideo-motor training program
(Pickenhain & Beyer, 1979).

Ideomotor training is now widely used in the practice of sports and in
the applied work physiology. The learning effect which can be observed is
difficult to explain by the assumptions of the classic principle of feedback
reinforcement. Because signals from the movement result are lacking, it must
be supposed that internal feedback signals at the different sub-program levels
involved are responsible (Fig. 3). The necessary pre-condition consists of
the involvement of as many lower levels of the central nervous system as
possible in the mental reproduction of the leading motor program. This supplies
the higher centres with the necessary reinforcing feedback information. The
occurrence of respiration changes in the respective case (Fig. 2) is an
obvious indication of the participation of lower levels, as is the evidence
of sub-threshold EMG in other cases.

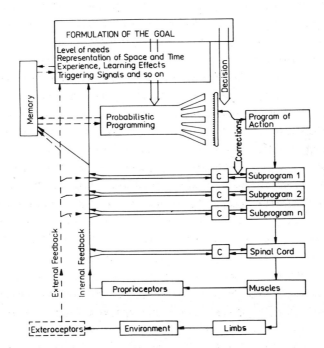

Fig. 3. Scheme of the goal-directed programming and decision mechanisms with
the external and internal feedback pathways and their correction
influences (C) at multiple hierarchival levels. Continuous lines -
obligatory information pathways; interrupted lines - facultative
information pathways (changed from Pickenhain, 1977).

The question as to the manner in which time is represented in the brain
is difficult to answer. It is a crucial question for Bernstein's idea of the
modelling of the future by means of extrapolation leading to a probabilistic
image of the future external world. He recognizes this difficulty when he
states:

> ...that in the brain there exist two unitary opposed
> categories of forms of modelling the perceptual world:
> the model of the past-present, or what happened and
> is happening, and the model of the future. The latter
> proceeds directly from the former, and is organized in
> it. These are necessarily distinct from each other,
> chiefly because the first type of model is single-valued
> and categorical, while the latter can only operate by
> means of extrapolation to some or other degree of
> confidence or probability.

It must be added that this question is even more intricate, because in
biological subjects neither space nor time have a linear structure. There
are many observations which show very clearly that the biological structure
of time is not congruent with that of physical time. There is no simple
continuity from future through present to past. Rather, there exists an
asymmetry and - as observations of brain-injured patients have shown -
possibly a difference in central representation (as a very variable function),
the future being more connected to the left and the past to the right
hemisphere (Bragina & Dobrochotova, 1981). If this is correct, it would have
serious consequences for the processes which are participating in the
probabilistic modelling of the future and their transition, by the decision
in the present, to the 'single-valued and categorical' experience of the
past. The origin of the model of the present-past resulting from the
probabilistic model of the future is up to now completely unclear and
urgently needs further research and elucidation.

                                IV.

The philosophical background of Bernstein's work was acrimoniously
disputed. Therefore, some remarks on his methodological position seems
necessary.

Firstly, his monistic conception of the mind-brain problem is completely
obvious. Without special discussion he treats the psychic processes as
functions of the highest levels of brain structure, and he uses psychological

and neurophysiological terms without any mutual exclusiveness. He considers modelling of the future equally as a mental as well as a biological phenomenon. The leading factor of all purposeful motor acts - the desired goal - is the expression of the needs of the organism as well as an idea the organism wishes to realize. In these terms there is no argument by which he might be accused of adopting an idealistic (or vitalistic) position about the mind-body problem. His position is much nearer to the conception of emergent materialism proposed by Bunge (1980).

Secondly, Bernstein has severely criticized the oversimplification of the findings of Pavlov by some of his pupils and followers. He did this especially in two papers which are not included in this collection (Bernstein, 1975): 'New trends in the development of the physiology and biology of activity' (published 1963) and 'On the road to a biology of activity' (published 1965). Acknowledging the immense merits of Pavlov at the beginning of this century in the discovery and investigation of the conditioned reflex, Bernstein at the same time opposes the exaggeration implicit in talking about a 'slave reflex' or a 'reflex of liberty'. He also contradicts the extension of the conditioned reflex conception to all mental processes and the dogmatism of some of Pavlov's followers who 'have distorted the reputation of this excellent scientist known all over the world'. On the other side, Bernstein really developed the reflex conception by adding the afferent feedback mechanism ('closing the reflex ring') and so connecting it with the concept of cybernetics.

Bernstein's reduction to absurdity of the idea of the second signal system as a scientific term which could explain the existence of words, verbal thinking, and articulate speech in humans has to be accepted. Whereas the first signal system is a collection of representations of the directly perceived objects and events in the external world, the second signal system should be a:

> ...projection of the projection, in which every object
> signal, image element of the first system, will have
> its corresponding name in the second.

This would presuppose a two-fold one-to-one projection which is not yet valid for the first system alone (see above) and which never can explain the nature of language, this 'inexhaustibly powerful tool of thought'. Pavlov expressed the idea of the second signal system during the last years of his life in a more symbolic manner to demonstrate the new quality of the human higher nervous activity. He never did support it by any experiments, and his followers also were not very successful in this direction. Therefore, this term may maintain its significance for symbolic demonstration and didactic purposes, but cannot be fundamental for scientific work.

Thirdly, Bernstein was accused of propagating vitalistic and teleological opinions, because he assumed that the modelling of the future requirements of the individual, a model of that which is not yet, but which must be the case, determines the motor actions of the present, i.e. the goal guides the on-going behaviour. This assumption does not fit in with ideas about linear causal connections between all natural events. But, as has been shown by other authors, the idea of linear causal connections is not sufficient to explain the real events in the world of living organisms. Therefore, the term teleonomy was created (Pittendrigh, 1958). This term is intentionally opposed to the term teleology which tries to interpret biological regulatory mechanisms in an unscientific, idealistic way. Teleonomic connections comprise complexes of causal connections which, uniting necessity and chance, are interwoven into a closed (cyclic) process, thus determining the goal-directed and purposeful behaviour of organismic systems. Already in 1961 the term teleonomy was successfully used by many biologists during the Cold Spring Harbor Symposium. Monod (1970) used it in his analysis of 'Change and Necessity' to characterize:

> ...objects that are equipped with a plan which they
> represent by their structure and which they realize
> by their performance.

This means, that a new philosophical approach and terminology are necessary to explain the inherent laws of closed biological systems which are both self-regulating and goal-directed. This is a complete confirmation of Bernstein's conception of modelling the future requirements, and on the other hand, Bernstein's arguments are important contributions to support the idea of teleonomy.

Fourthly, Bernstein repeatedly stresses the importance of extrapolation as a means which the brain uses to select the adequate solution to the probabilistic possibilities of future modelling. It is very interesting that the Soviet biologist Krushinskii (1962, 1977) during his experimental study of the behaviour of different kinds of animals (birds, mammals) has found extra-polation behaviour to be an essential and very important constituent of the complex behaviour of animals. In conclusion, he states that the extra-polation behaviour and the modelling of future events are leading factors for the different purposeful motor acts of animals and must be interpreted

as elementary reasoning (Krushinskii, 1977). His experimental data are
important confirmations of the theoretical implications of Bernstein's idea.

Fifthly, up to now, the conception of a homeostatic balance between
organism and environment is widely acknowledged. But, scientists who follow
this line do not realize the real consequences of this idea. Bernstein (1963)
- in a paper not included in this collection - points to the fact that such:

> ...homeostatic balance would sentence every individual
> to be entirely dependent on the environment and on its
> changes; a program-regulated morphogenesis with the
> preservation of constant species features would be
> completely impossible.

By this, Bernstein does not deny homeostatic partial mechanisms, but he
refuses to acknowledge that the homeostatic principle plays the leading
role in directing the behaviour of the organism. Life is by no means a:

> ...homeostatic balance with the environment, as the
> thinker of the classical period of mechanics assumed,
> but the overcoming of the environment. In this connection,
> the goal of the organism is not to maintain homeostasis,
> but the further development in the direction of the species-
> specific self-sustaining and developing programs (Bernstein,
> 1963, 1975).

Again, can be seen that in Bernstein's opinion the deciding and leading
element in the behavioural architecture of movements is the desired goal the
realization of which is pre-programmed in the model of the future. This
leads back to his assumption that the formulation and execution of the model
of the future is by its very nature an active process. This active process
starts with the representation of the world in the brain which is only
reached by active exploratory and checking processes and which is followed
by the active performance (or active inhibition) of motor acts that are
adequate (or inadequate) to reach the desired goal. This includes a temporary
disturbance of the homeostatic balance between the organism and its
environment which is re-established if the desired goal is reached.

Therefore, the activity of the organism is a particular category in
itself which ensures the existence of the organism and of the species.
Comparing the probabilistic model of the future with the desired and
necessary goal, the organism's activity represents the dynamic struggle of
the individual and raises the probability of the desired outcome, until it
becomes an accomplished fact. This means realization of the genetic program
by continuous battle during epigenetic development in a changing world.
Bernstein postulates that this fact must be the topic of a special discipline

- the Physiology of Activity. He outlines some essential principles of this special direction of research. But, during the twenty five years which have passed since this postulate was first stated, no one has taken over this difficult task, although many scattered results in nearly all life science disciplines have underlined its great importance. The realization of this postulate remains open for future research.

REFERENCES

Anokhin, P.K. Biology and Neurophysiology of the Conditioned Reflex. Moscow:
    Medicina (in Russian), 1968.

Anokhin, P.K. Essays of Physiology of Functional Systems. Moscow: Medicina
    (in Russian), 1975.

Anokhin, P.K. Beiträge zur allgemeinen Theorie des funktionellen Systems.
    In, Brain and Behaviour Research, Monograph Series, Vol. 8. Jena:
    G. Fischer (in German), 1978.

Batuev, A.S. & Tairov, O.P. Brain and organization of movement: Conceptional
    models. Leningrad: Nauka (in Russian), 1978.

Bernstein, N.A. New trends in the development of the physiology and biology
    of activity. Philosophical Questions of the Physiology of Higher Nervous
    Activity and of Psychology. Moscow: Nauka (in Russian), 1963.

Bernstein, N.A. On the road to a biology of activity. Voprosy filosofii
    (Moscow), 1975, 19, 65-78 (in Russian).

Bernstein, N.A. Bewegungsphysiologie. L. Pickenhain and G. Schnabel (Eds.),
    German edition. Leipzig: J.A. Barth, 1975.

Bizzi, E., Accornero, N., Chapple, W. & Hogan, N. Central and peripheral
    mechanisms in motor control. In, R.A. Thompson (Ed.), New Perspectives
    in Cerebral Localization. New York: Raven Press, 1981.

Bragina, N.N. & Dobrochotova, T.A. Functional asymmetries of human beings.
    Moscow: Medicina (in Russian), 1981. (German translation by L. Pickenhain,
    1983. Leipzig: G. Thieme).

Brooks, V.B. & Thach, W.T. Cerebellar control of posture and movement. In,
    V.B. Brooks (Ed.), Handbook of Physiology. Section 1 : The Nervous System.
    Vol. II: Motor Control, Part 2. Baltimore: American Physiological Society,
    1981.

Bunge, M. The Mind-Body Problem: a psychobiological approach. Oxford:
    Pergamon Press, 1980.

Deecke, L., Scheid, P. & Kornhuber, H.H. Distribution of readiness potential,
    pre-motion positivity and motor potential of the human cerebral cortex,
    preceding voluntary finger movements. Experimental Brain Research, 1969,
    7, 158-168.

DeLong, M.R. & Georgopoulos, A.P. Motor functions of the basal ganglia. In,
    V.B. Brooks (Ed.), Handbook of Physiology. Section 1 : The Nervous System.
    Vol. II: Motor Control, Part 2. Baltimore: American Physiological Society,
    1981.

Edelman, G.M. Group selection and phasic reentrant signalling: a theory of
    higher brain function. In, F.O. Schmitt and F.G. Worden (Eds.), The
    Neurosciences. Fourth Study Program. Cambridge, Mass.: MIT Press, 1979.

Fuster, J.M. Prefrontal cortex in motor control. In, V.B. Brooks (Ed.),
    Handbook of Physiology. Section 1 : The Nervous System. Vol. II: Motor
    Control, Part 2. Baltimore: American Physiological Society, 1981.

Garibian, A.A. & Gambarian, L.S. Behaviour and Basal Ganglia. Erevan: Academy
    of Sciences of the Armenian SSR, 1982.

Gross, C.G., Rossa-Miranda, C.E. & Bender, D.B. Visual properties of neurons
    in inferotemporal cortex of the macaque. Journal of Neurophysiology,
    1972, 35, 96-111.

Herman, R.M., Grillner, S., Stein, P.S.G. & Stuart, D.G.(Eds.), Neural Control
    of Locomotion. New York: Plenum Press, 1976.

Hink, R.F., Kohler, H., Deecke, L. & Kornhuber, H.H. Risk-taking and the
    human Bereitschaftspotential. Electroencephalography and Clinical
    Neurophysiology, 1982, 53, 361-373.

Keele, S.W. Behavioral analysis of movement. In, V.B. Brooks (Ed.), Handbook
    of Physiology. Section 1: The Nervous System. Vol. II: Motor Control,
    Part 2. Baltimore: American Physiological Society, 1981.

Koc, J.M. The Organization of Voluntary Movement: Neurophysiological
    Mechanisms. Moscow: Nauka (in Russian), 1975.

Kornhuber, H.H. Motor functions of the cerebellum and basal ganglia: the
    cerebello-cortical (ballistic) clock, the cerebello-nuclear hold
    regulator, and the basal ganglia ramp (voluntary speed smooth movement)
    generator. Kybernetik, 1971, 8, 157-162.

Kornhuber, H.H. Cerebral cortex, cerebellum, and basal ganglia: an
    introduction to their motor functions. In, F.O. Schmitt and F.G. Worden
    (Eds.), The Neurosciences. Third Study Program. Cambridge, Mass.: MIT
    Press, 1974.

Krushinskii, L.V. Animal Behavior. Its normal and abnormal development.
    New York: Consultants Bureau, 1962.

Krushinskii, L.V. Biological bases of reasoning activity: Evolutionary and
    physiological-genetic aspects of behavior. Moscow: University Press
    (in Russian), 1977.

Lamarre, Y., Spidalieri, G., Busby, L. & Lund, J.P. Programming of initiation
    and execution of ballistic arm movements in the monkey. In, H.H. Kornhuber
    and L. Deecke (Eds.), Motivation, Motor and Sensory Processes of the Brain.
    Progress in Brain Research, Vol. 54. Amsterdam: Elsevier/North-Holland
    Biomedical Press, 1980.

Lynch, J.C., Mountcastle, V.B., Talbot, W.H. & Yin, T.C.T. Parietal lobe
    mechanisms for directed visual attention. Journal of Neurophysiology,
    1977, 40, 362-389.

Miles, F.A. & Evarts, E.V. Concepts of motor organization. Annual Review of
    Psychology, 1979, 30, 327-362.

Miller, A.D. & Brooks, V.B. Parallel pathways for movement initiation in
    monkeys. Experimental Brain Research, 1982, 45, 328-332.

Monod, J. Le hasard et la nécessité. Paris: Editions du Seuil, 1970.

Mountcastle, V.B. The world around us : neural command functions for selective
    attention. Neurosciences Research Program Bulletin (Supplement), 1976, 14,
    1-47.

Mountcastle, V.B. An organizing principle for cerebral function: the unit
    module and the distributed system. In, F.O. Schmitt and F.G. Worden (Eds.),
    The Neurosciences. Fourth Study Program. Cambridge, Mass.: MIT Press,
    1979.

Pickenhain, L. Die Bedeutung innerer Rückkopplungskreise für den Lernvorgang
    (gezeigt am Beispiel des motorischen Lernens). Zeitschrift für Psycholo-
    gie (Leipzig), 1976, 184, 551-561.

Pickenhain, L. Das Verhalten. In, D. Biesold and H. Matthies (Eds.),
    Neurobiologie, 1977, 693-733.

Pickenhain, L. & Beyer, L. Beziehungen zwischen den hierarchisch organisierten
    Rückmeldekreisen und der Ergebnisrückmeldung als wesentlicher Faktor für
    die Ausbildung innerer Modelle von Arbeitshandlungen. In, F. Klix and
    K.P. Timpe (Eds.), Arbeits- und Ingenieurpsychologie und Intensivierung.
    Berlin: Deutscher Verlag der Wissenschaften, 1979.

Pittendrigh, C.S. In, A. Roe and G.G. Simpson (Eds.), Behavior and evolution.
    New Haven: Yale University Press, 1958.

Schmidt, R.A. The schema as a solution to some persistent problems in motor
    learning theory. In, G.E. Stelmach (Ed.), Motor control: Issues and
    trends. New York: Academic Press, 1976.

Schmitt, F.O., Dev, P. & Smith, B.H. Electrotonic processing of information
    by brain cells. Science, 1976, 193, 114-120.

Sperry, R.W. Neural basis of the spontaneous optokinetic response produced
    by visual inversion. Journal of Comparative and Physiological Psychology,
    1950, 43, 482-489.

von Holst, E. & Mittelstaedt, H. Das Reafferenzprinzip. Naturwissenschaften,
    1950, 37, 464-476.

Walter, W.G., Cooper, R., Aldridge, V.J., McCallum, W.C. & Winter, A.L.
    Contingent negative variation: an electric sign of sensorimotor
    association and expectancy in the human brain. Nature, 1964, 203,
    380-384.

Wiener, N. Cybernetics of Control and Communication in the Animal and
    the Machine. New York: Wiley, 1948.

Young, J.Z. Programs of the Brain. Oxford: University Press, 1978.

SECTION 6

CHAPTER VI

TRENDS IN PHYSIOLOGY AND THEIR RELATION TO CYBERNETICS

N. Bernstein

(Published in *Questions of Philosophy*, No. 8, 1962)

The introduction and development of new methods in industry have acted as a spur to the new trends in physiology with which we are concerned in this article, and to the formulation of the general problems which led, after a series of attempts, to the establishment of cybernetics as a science. If, when we think of cybernetics, we have in mind not the doctrine of Wiener, Shannon, Ashby, etc., but a general science which is concerned with the regulation of complex systems in conjunction with information and communication (and it is this which we shall consider from now on), it will be seen that a considerable number of the problems confronting modern physiologists are closely related to the more general ones for which cybernetics was first intended.

As the amount of heavy physical labour steadily decreases in everyday work, applied biology, starting with the energetics of work, biomechanics, protection and hygienics of work, etc. has begun to turn its attention to problems concerning intellectualized work in man-machine complexes, rationalization of control and communication, distribution of function etc., and it is precisely in elucidating such problems that the methods and concepts of cybernetics have turned out to be particularly valuable. An important area in modern applied psychophysiology is undoubtedly the study of work under conditions where very high demands are made on the subject's attention, adaptability and will, etc. (astronautics, high-speed flight, work at high attitudes, underwater or underground).

There are some recent offshoots of theoretical physiology which deserve mention and consideration here. The first one - the physiology of regulation - was established at about the same time as cybernetics and was to a certain extent its forerunner; the second - the physiology of activity - is emerging and developing, opening up a wide range of problems which have not been realized before.

In increasing our knowledge of the principle behind the cyclic

regulation of the life processes we have discovered more and more about
activity which is bound up indissolubly with that principle. The active
form and structure of all the processes of reception and of central
processing of information is no longer a matter of doubt, not to mention
the phenomena and forms of activity - in the strictest sense of the word -
namely, motor functions (where the prevalence and significance of the cyclic
principle of regulation and correction have been described repeatedly).
Nowadays Sechenov's thesis has been fully vindicated. He declared that we
"listen rather than hear, and look rather than see". All our main peripheral
receptors are equipped with efferent innervation and a muscular system on
which depend functions of optimal adjustment (in a very broad sense), and
also the countless phenomena of search, guidance, haptic tracking, etc.;
here, also, are included all types of verification through practical
experience of both concrete receptions and the entire system of sense organs,
cross-checking, and the synthesization of evidence obtained from the various
receptors in the organizational system of the sensory receptors; finally,
selection of the necessary minimum of information and rejection of
superfluous noise are active processes.

The significance of active forms of operation has been felt most
strongly perhaps in the central cortex processes which deal with the
construction of a dynamic image of the external world inside the brain.
Whereas ideas concerning cellular centrism have been essentially inseparable
from an assumption of the passive nature of the brain's intake and
registration of sensory information, performed by primordial cells intended
for this purpose, modern psychophysiological thinking tends to regard the
cognitive processes as active simulations differing in principle from the
mechanistic element-to-element relation. The selection of the principle by
which perceptible sets of numbers are put into order is an active one, and
so is the internal classification of separable subsets and the regulation
of the haptic in the widest sense of the term, that is, regulation of the
processes of active reception that were mentioned above (see, also, Chapter
V).

The source of the principle of activity in living organisms, however,
lies much further back than has yet been stated, and from this principle
attains the significance of a significant general biological factor.
Research into the subject should proceed from an analysis of motor functions.

Motor functions comprise a basic group of processes by which the
organism not merely reacts to its environment but ever acts on the latter.

This fact allows the following conclusions to be drawn.

Each significant act is a solution (or an attempt at one) of a specific problem of action. But the problem of action, in other words the effect which the organism is striving to achieve, is something which is not yet, but which is due to be brought about. The problem of action, thus, is the reflection or model of future requirements (somehow coded in the brain); and a vitally useful or significant action cannot be either programmed or accomplished if the brain has not created a prerequisite directive in the form of the future requirements that we have just mentioned.

From this it would seem that we are looking at two connected processes. One is a probabilistic estimation based on the current situation - a kind of extrapolation ahead over a period of time; both neurophysiologists and those engaged in clinical studies are already gathering empirical data and observations which throw light on these processes.* Together with this probabilistic extrapolation of the course of surrounding events (it would be a course under conditions of non-interference), there is the programming of action which is intended to fulfil the future requirements. This (simple or chain) programming of action already resembles a kind of extrapolation between the actually existing situation and what the latter has to become in the interests of the subject. We shall not delay over the fact that programming and accomplishment of action usually both take place under conditions of vital pressure, that is, an inner conflict between urgency and accuracy of estimation; nor over the fact (completely obvious) that the practical accomplishment of action takes place necessarily as a struggle or active surmounting of variable external obstacles, whatever form these may take (insuperable external opposition, opposition from an enemy, surprise, etc.). It is interesting to note here that acknowledgement of the reality of a model coded in the brain, or of an extrapolation of future probabilities, and of a reflection of problems of action in the brain as a formula of future requirements, allow a strictly materialistic interpretation to be given to the concepts of singleness of purpose, expediency, etc.

Facts which are nowadays established, such as the coded reflections of informational material, whether original or recombined by the brain, were still completely unknown when scientific physiology was in its early

---

* The so-called orientational reactions are a category of responses made by the actual reception to a divergence from or disagreement with the current probabilistic estimation (a low probability response).

period of development. Therefore most ideas such as the problem or aim of
action answering to the requirements of the organism, i.e. a coded program
aimed at producing the best possible conditions of existence for the
organism, etc., were regarded as inherently part of psychology - a highly
developed branch of science capable of formulating for itself the routine
problems and aims of action. Scientists holding materialistic views were
faced with a choice of two alternatives; either to admit the presence of a
psychic force and consciousness in the earth worm and the tree - this of
course was rejected as being absurd - or to believe that not one of the
classes of motion discussed could be applied to the vast majority of
organisms. The only ones who felt at ease in this sphere were the adherents
of vitalism whose unsupported hypotheses enabled them to proceed as far as
they desired in the direction of finalism.

It is precisely the discovery that an organism can construct and
combine material codes that reflect all the countless forms of activity and
extrapolation of the future, from tropisms up to the most complex forms of
directed reaction to environment, that enables us to speak now of singleness
of purpose and endeavour, etc., in the action of any organisms, ranging
perhaps from Protista upwards, without the slightest risk of our slipping
into finalism. The empirical data now supplied by comparative physiology
testifies to an unsuspected variety in the material substrates of regulating
codes and in the actual coding forms and principles themselves, among which
the psychological codes of the human brain are seen as only one of the
individual forms (although the most highly developed one).

It would be appropriate to add the following to this brief discussion
of the problem of the simulation and programming of actions designed to
bring about the optimal future state.

The physiologists of the classical period, by sticking to the idea
of the reflex arc and confining their attention strictly to response
processes, were able, with only slight schematization, to represent the
effector processes of the organism as strictly (and in the majority of
cases unequivocally) determinate signals arriving through an afferent semi-
arc. Now, when we are forced by the facts to regard all phenomena pertaining
to the organism's interaction with the world, and its even more active
influence upon it, as being cyclic processes based on the principle of a
reflector circuit, our evaluation of the existing correlations undergoes
a fundamental change. Unlike the processes that supposedly take place along
an open arc, the closed-circuit (ring) process may just as easily be started

from any point on the ring; and as a result the processes of interaction
termed (in the old sense) reactive (i.e. those originating from the afferent
semi-ring) and those termed spontaneous (i.e. originating from the effector
semi-ring) are both here combined into a single general class. In many
respects it is precisely this latter subclass which includes the most vitally
significant phenomena of activity. Meanwhile, in all such cases the organism
not only reacts to the situation or to some particular singificant element
discernible in it but also encounters a situation which, being dynamically
variable, forces it to make a probabilistic forecast and then a choice.
To use a metaphor, we might say that the organism is constantly playing a
game with its environment, a game where the rules are not defined and the
moves planned by the opponent are not known. It is this peculiarity of real
relationships - the evaluation of situations by the organism is probably no
less sensitive than its choice of action - that distinguishes the living
organism from a reactive machine no matter how sensitive and complex the
latter may be. Reactive mechanisms play an important role as technical
components in the adjustable regulation of action, but never as direct
determinants of action and behaviour. It is very easy, perhaps for just this
reason, to construct a reactive model capable of forming both unconditioned
and conditioned reflexes (see, for example, the models of G. Walter, etc.),
but to build a model which carries out (or improves) a choice of optimal
behaviour under conditions of purely probabilistic information about the
opponent's moves entails difficulties which up to now have not been
successfully solved.

Recent research has led to re-formulations of the concepts of organism,
which are in many respects different from the formulations of the classical
period - in which the organism was treated as a reactively equilibrating or
self-regulating system. An organism must be considered to be an organization
possessing two determining features.

Firstly, it is an organization which preserves its own (systemic)
identity in spite of the continuous flow of energy and substrate matter
passing through it. Despite the fact that not a single individual atom in
the organism is retained in the cell structure for longer than a certain
and (with few exceptions) comparatively brief space of time, the organism
remains the same now as it was previously and its present life activity
is determined by its previous life (and, of course, not only previous).

Secondly, the organism is continually changing in a set direction
at all stages of its existence. The fact that thousands of examples

belonging to the same animal or plant type develop into species that are
identical in all their basic determining features (in spite of the often
enormous differences in living conditions between the various individuals)
is ample proof of this directional trend in ontogenetic evolution. As regards
the embryogenetic stage, we know today the carriers of heriditary traits,
their chemical structure and code alphabet, by means of which the organism
possesses from the moment of fertilization of the ovum a coded model of its
future development and a coded program of the consecutive stages in this
development.

It should be clearly realized that the chromosome "mastercopy", i.e.
the determining factor in the future of a species, is unquestionably
material, in the sense that as regards the genus as a whole and the
immediate ancestors of the species in particular, it springs from the past
and is determined by it (as we are not competent in the field we shall not
go into the question of the possible origin of mutations). But the most
significant and striking fact lies not in this totally incomprehensible
programming of the future by ancestors for their immediate offspring, but
in the dynamic source (eventually also coded somehow, probably, and possessing
its own somatic substrate carrier in the cell), which generates in the species
an active, anti-entropic, overwhelming urge to realize the model. This
movement towards structurization, that is to say, towards lower probability
of the images which are being created, involves large metabolic expenditure
of valuable energy, as does any anti-entropic process. This liberality
displayed by the organism in the face of all obstacles, whether great or
small, in order to realize its programmed morphogenesis is a most impressive
phenomenon.

We have a close analogy (in miniature) to this supposed conflict
between the future (for the immediate species) and the past (for the genus
as a whole) in the case which we considered above, where the modelling of
future requirements was seen as the formulation of a problem of action.
The result that a living being requires for a given action is in the
future; but, of course, the forecast, and program, and even the co-ordinating
technique of this action, are based on past experience accumulated by the
individual and by the genus, only recombined actively anew.

Let us now return to our main theme after this digression. The above-
mentioned identity in all the essential features of morphogenetic
development, seen against a background of variable conditions and
independently of their variability, tells us that the organism actively

overcomes possible or unavoidable external obstacles, which might prevent it from accomplishing its program of morphogenesis. Experimental data concerning damage and partial amputation to which, for example, the buds of the extremities have been subjected in embryogenesis, and which did not prevent them from growing into complete extremities; the facts of anatomical and also functional regeneration; the mass of clinical material that testifies to the struggle made by the organism and its functional system to overcome pathogenetic factors - all this data supports the view that both the organism as a whole and, very possibly, each of its cells struggle actively for survival, development and reproduction. The life process is not a balancing with the environment,[*] but a conquest of the latter, aimed not at preserving the status quo or homeostasis, but at an advance towards fulfilment of the developmental and self-preservational program of the genus.

And so, what in a particular case of motor functions in organisms appears to be (1) the modelling of future requirements in terms of a problem of action, and (2) the realization of an integrated program of this action by the conquest of external obstacles and by an active struggle for the result, turns out to be a manifestation of the general principle of activity running through the whole of biology. The principle emerges in the forms we have discussed and in the processes of development both of animals and of plants and in all features of their struggle for existence.

A very interesting problem, and one which seems relevant to the entire domain of biology, now arises. It is connected closely with the theoretical principles of biological model-making and also with the directional evolution of the individual. This question and its ramifications call for comprehensive study.

We shall begin by drawing a number of parallels between processes that are, externally, highly unlike, with the intention of formulating their common characteristics.

On an oak or a maple there are several thousand leaves, no two of which will be found to be exactly alike; in fact all their metrical features vary over a wide range. Nevertheless, we can confidently say that

---

[*] Such a balancing would mean that every species is completely dependent on its environment and the changes therein, with the result that we could not hold the theory of a programmed morphogenesis and the retention of persistent features of the genus.

each leaf belongs either to an oak or a maple, because of certain
characteristics which we have to call essential whether we like it or not,
in spite of the difficulty of formulating them mathematically.

A person carries out repeated habitual movements (the best examples
of these are the movements performed during writing, since they leave
behind them obvious documentation). He may write out dozens of pages, write
his signature a hundred times, write with a pen on paper or with chalk
in large letters on a blackboard; he may write (as we have shown in
experiments) using various limbs, or his mouth; and in all this we shall
not be able to find two outlines that are exactly the same. Yet, one
individual handwriting is retained in all these different examples. The
trajectories of separate cycles in chronocyclograms made for all kinds of
cyclic habitual movements corroborate this fact. Our perceptions, without
the support of any exact formulation, have created concepts similar to
handwriting, such as gait, touch (on the piano), pitch of voice,
pronunciation or accent, etc. The same demarcation is applicable in all
these cases, viz. fundamental affinity, that is, congruence in some of the
characteristics, and absence of congruence and also rankability in variation
ranges according to other (usually metrical) characteristics.

We may also cite here (we will list without giving any details) the
recognition of outlines, especially of letters, of all sizes and type
faces, etc. (it is curious that this can be done with equal ease for white
letters on a black background, and with black on a white one); recognition
of a person by sight with six degrees of freedom for variation of his
image on the retina (and even with rejection of any mimetic variations);
the ability of each one of us, right from infancy, to recognize a "dog" or
"cat" in a definite instance of these animals, and so on. Some of the last
examples relate to what psychologists have called for a long time
correlation; but this term still does not explain either the mechanism of
this process (which we have also attributed to cerebral model-making), or,
more important, the principles by which the brain is directed while the
attributes of the object are being separated into contrasting groups. Even
less clear as yet is the obvious analogy of psychological processes of
correlation during perception with habitual movements and the results of
morphogenesis, that is, the very clearly different relationship between an
organism, in all the cases we have compared, and attributes or characteristics
of category.

It would seem that there are far-reaching perspectives ahead for the application and development of I.M. Gelfand and M.L. Tsetlin's mathemetical idea (Some methods of regulating complex systems, *Advances in Mathematical Sciences* 17, 1 (103) 1962, p. 3), which consists in applying to the problems which here concern us, a class of functions of a large number of variables, designated by these two authors as "well-organized functions". A function is well organized if (1) its arguments can be separated into essential and non-essential variables and if (2) all the arguments retain firmly their attachment to one or other sub-class. The non-essential variables may cause abrupt changes and discontinuities in the function, sharp graduations in value, etc.; at the same time (and this explains their name) they do not exert any determining influence on the course of the function as a whole or over large ranges or on the location of its extremes, etc. The marked variance from the non-essential variables may interfere with, and conceal the influence of, the essential ones over narrow ranges, but in the end the form and course of the function are determined mainly by the latter. Apparently an argument's appurtenance to one or the other subclass is not so much determined by its basic, underlying, concrete, physico-chemical (or other) process, as by the actual form of functional link which the argument has with the function.

It appears both tempting and reasonable to make use of this class of functions, by representing each aspect of the development and active life of a living organism by such a function of many variables, where each sub-class of variable is directly superimposed on the behaviour of the corresponding essential or non-essential characteristics, as subdivided above. Then, with reference to the morphogenesis of say a leaf, a flower, etc., we may say that the traits which determine the species, and which are clearly coded in the chromosomes, are seen as the result of essential (in the Gelfand-Tsetlin sense) variables, whereas the material characteristics, each producing variational ranges, are seen as the result of non-essential variables. The same would apply to the co-ordination of movements, for example, to cyclic habitual acts such as writing. We have already discussed above a classification of the characteristics of such acts. The fact that a completely similar organization of determining characteristics occurs during acts of perception, first of all in form perception and then also in kinds of acts of correlation, indicated that the nature of these remarkable functions is inherent even in active brain model-making, during processes of perception and reflection of the environment.

The first attempts at using these functions to depict mechanisms of

active life are already presenting important and promising new information
about their characteristics in addition to what is already known. It has
already been observed how differently an organism behaves under the influence
of its surroundings with reference to essential and non-essential variables.
As regards the latter type, it is reactive and, so to speak, yieldingly
adaptable: if one leaf on a tree receives more food than another, then that
leaf grows more vigorously than the other one; and if it is placed in better
illumination it accumulates a higher concentration of chlorophyll, and so on.
But essential characteristics of structure and shape such as those which
determine the plan of the flower, or negative geotropism (i.e. the tendency
to preserve the vertical direction of the trunk or stem under all conditions),
are only relinquished by an organism if it is subjected to very violent
interference, and that usually after a longer period than anticipated
(regeneration serves as an example). Thus the function, that is the
organism, may be said to be reactive as far as its non-essential variables
are concerned, but highly non-reactive, or active, with regard to its
essential ones.

    Structural analysis of motor acts and of their co-ordination reveals
exactly the same picture. As was shown by our research, the co-ordinational
regulation of each complete cognitive motor act is constructed on a kind
of multiple hierarchical system of circuits of regulation and adjustment.
The need for this multiplicity of stages is due to the very great number
of degrees of freedom in our multiconnected organs of movement, and by the
enormous number of muscular units which actively co-operate to guarantee
a posture or to perform a required body movement. In addition to this,
there are also the attendant facts of muscular elasticity, complex reactive
dynamics of the organs of movement, and, of course, the entire combination
of those independent and, for that reason, unforeseeable external forces
of resistance; the expedient conquest of these is the very essence of most
of our arbitrary motor acts. In the co-ordinational regulation of movement,
numerous types and grades of circuital corrections are distributed between
the level systems of the brain, on the one hand, according to the
composition and quality of the sensory syntheses inherent in them, and
clearly, on the other hand, according to the relative importance and
significance in the cognitive relation of any other corrections aimed at
fully realizing a program of movement (see the author's book *The Construction
of Motions* and also his paper in the symposium *Problems of Cybernetics*, No.
6).

In the context of the present discussion, some importance attaches to the fact that the apparatus for regulating movements displays two different types of co-ordinational tactic: when secondary technical disagreements or hindrances are encountered it operates reactively and accommodatingly without fearing any variational tendencies; but when aspects of regulation that are essential to the program are involved, this apparatus struggles for the required results actively, whatever might happen, overcoming obstacles and, if necessary, reprogramming during operation, etc.

There is now another problem which, although it is at present very topical and is closely related to the subject of the Gelfand-Tsetlin well-organized functions, can be mentioned here only in passing. It concerns the interrelations between the concept of biological systems and the concept or class of discrete number. The traits, arguments, correctional functions, etc., belonging to the non-essential type are obviously continuous, and form variational series correspondingly. What is the situation, then, regarding essential variables? In particular, is the question "to what extent does the apparatus we are dealing with 'know' how to count?" admissible in relation to hereditarily transmitted traits coded in the chromosomes?

This question is raised today in a wide variety of works. Judging, for instance, from the data provided by anatomy and comparative anatomy, this assured counting extends approximately to two to the sixth power (number of teeth, vertebrae, cyto-architectonic fields of the brain, elements of the collateral line of a fish, etc.). After this there begins the idea of "many", and of course it is impossible that in a gene apparatus there should be a code, for example, of the number of hairs on the head, or the number of cells in the cortex of the brain.

Undoubtedly, the border regions of the mumerical series offer, in the main, the greatest interest and significance. The cyto- and myelo-architectonic fields of the human brain cortex are calculated and standard; but how far does this calculation extend, and at what moment does randomization start in the number of cells and in the plan of their synaptic interrelationships? Are the numbers of glomerules in the kidney, of islets of Langerhans, Pacinian corpuscles, muscular units in a muscle, calculated or chance? How does the apparatus of hereditary transmission behave when it comes to numbers of the order of hundreds, that is to say, where is the limit of its informational capacity?

The following is of some importance in the light of the topic we are

discussing. The informational capacity of the gene apparatus is clearly
not imposed on it from outside, but expresses the evolutionarily determined
need of the animal, plant, cell, etc., in question. Therefore, an analysis
of the mentioned boundary relationships and regions of transition from the
necessary to the haphazard is at the same time an analysis of the
distribution between essential and non-essential arguments, which corresponds
to the evolutionarily determined requirement of the organism. At the same
time this is an analysis of where and how the organism demarcates the
boundary between active and reactive processes, between number and
multiplicity (calculated or continuous), between areas for applying the
theory of well organized functions and those for applying the theory of
casual processes.

In conclusion, another must be made to consider a fundamentally
significant problem.

Right from the beginnings of scientific cybernetics, when there first
appeared a parallel between the urgent basic problems of physiology and the
problems which established cybernetics as a separate science in its own
right, a rewarding exchange started between the two sciences with regard to
practical data, theoretical formulations and correlations. The entire period
from the publication of Wiener's work right up to the present day is full
of the search for and use of analogies between living and artificial
systems - analogies which, on the one hand, have aided physiologists in
working out system interrelationships in the organism, and have, on the
other hand, provided technologists with valuable new ideas on the
construction of automatic systems.

It is difficult to say whether or not the "honeymoon" between these
two sciences is over, and with it their common quest for and use of
analogies and other similarities; but problems that suggest an opposite
line of development have been increasingly coming to the fore in recent
scientific literature: is there, after all, a fundamental difference in
principle between living and non-living systems, and if there is, where
does the "watershed" forming the boundary between them lie?

We are naturally not concerned here with differences in the materials
out of which systems are made, or even with quantitive differences which
would make it impossible for modern technology to imitate the 15 billion
cells of the brain. Quite clearly, also, the difference we are concerned
with has to be formulated in accordance with the principle of the unity of
nature, whose laws control both living and non-living matter alike.

However, before the above concept of biological activity may be advanced as a working hypothesis, a reply must be made, if only in very general terms, to the question of whether one can talk about any deep-seated specificity of life processes without at the same time surrendering strict mathematical rigour, and without slipping into a form, albeit disguised, of vitalism.

As early as the 18th century, when militant mechanistic materialism firmly defined its scientific positions, natural science was faced with a choice which appeared unavoidable at that time (and also for a long time afterwards). On the one hand, the contrast between the phenomena of life activity and the then-known processes of inanimate nature was so striking that some explanation was demanded. On the other hand, the store of knowledge concerning deepseated physico-chemical processes, biophysical and biochemical principles on the molecular level, was still very small. The result was that many scientists, finding that their physico-chemical knowledge did not offer them an adequate means of explaining the specificity of life, put forward the notion of a non-material life force by way of explanation; this was completely satisfactory for the ones who readily entertained notions on all sorts of non-material factors and entities, and who consequently joined the idealist camp. The materialists, however, could generally do nothing but repudiate all research into vital specificity which could not be supported by the physics or chemistry of the day. This notion has been preserved even up to the present day. Meanwhile, during the more recent past, a great deal of fresh information has been collected and this has permitted a close enquiry into the nature of many processes, primarily those that take place on the cell and molecular levels, in a manner that was inconceivable in the last century. Indeed, these new discoveries have made it possible now to raise the problem of reviewing the traditional opinion outlined above. It is neither within the scope of the present paper nor the author's competence to undertake any detailed elucidation of the problem, but at least some indication as to its nature should be given here.

First of all, in the past only the most rudimentary information was available concerning the process of catalysis. Nowadays, however, the increase of knowledge concerning these processes reveals an ever wider area of operation and a hitherto unknown range of functions. For instance, there is the role played by enzymes in the regulated synthesis of high-molecular compounds; the reduplication of these compounds; the enormous

variety and peculiarity of chemo-autotrophic micro-organisms; with their
assistance, processes which would require enormous temperatures and
pressures, etc., under laboratory conditions take place intensively.
Nothing was known in the last century about stochastic processes (unless
one counts the kinetic theory of gases and solutions); nor was anything
known about anti-entropic processes in open systems, or under what
conditions they took place and how they could be regulated, whereas every
year now sees an increasingly rich fund of knowledge being amassed on this
subject. Biological codes and their role in structurization and self-
organization have already been mentioned above.

We will not prolong this enumeration; its aim has been merely to show
that the extensive increases in factual knowledge up to the present will
no doubt provide an impetus for scientific research to apply the newly
discovered principles of biochemistry, biophysics and the new branches of
mathematics to an unconditionally materialistic account of the phenomena
of life, and this without prejudice to the dialectical principle of the
transition from quantity to quality and without any risk of falling into
idealism.

It is now necessary, whilst holding firmly and strictly to the
principle of the unity of nature and its laws, to indicate and study the
differences between living and articifial systems. It will be some time,
perhaps, before the nature of this difference is formulated, but it seems
reasonable to suppose that the features and character of physiological
activity that we have been discussing here might at some later date form
an essential part of this unknown characteristic. In any case, what has
been said in this paper may facilitate the task of future exploration
of the subject and indicate in some way how the problem of surmounting the
division between the biological and technical sciences may be approached.

Human Motor Actions — Bernstein Reassessed
H.T.A. Whiting (editor)
© Elsevier Science Publishers B.V. (North-Holland), 1984

CHAPTER VIa

FROM SYNERGIES AND EMBRYOS TO MOTOR SCHEMAS

M.A. Arbib

In this paper, we try to place Bernstein's "Trends in Physiology and
their Relation to Cybernetics" in the perspective of two decades of research
since its publication in Questions of Philosophy in 1962. It was reprinted
in English translation as the last chapter of The Co-Ordination and Regulation
of Movements in 1967, and stands in contrast to the other five chapters in
that its emphasis is not primarily on the physiology of movement. Nor,
surprisingly, does it have much to say about the discipline of cybernetics.
Rather, in words taken from the last two paragraphs, its aim is to provide
an impetus for "an unconditionally materialistic account of the phenomena of
life, and this without prejudice to the dialectical principle of the transition
from quantity to quality and without any risk of falling into idealism".
Nonetheless, he asserts that it is "now necessary, whilst holding firmly and
strictly to the principle of the unity of nature and its laws, to indicate
and study the differences between living and artificial systems". The core of
his paper is to draw parallels between embryology and the physiology of
activity in arguing that self-directed activity is the distinguishing mark of
living things. While my ignorance of dialectical principles precludes my
offering an analysis of the extent to which this view is grounded in Marxist-
Leninist philosophy, I can offer a brief survey of research in theoretical
biology which addresses issues in embryology and in the physiology of
activity, and then state my own opinions on the status of Bernstein's
philosophical position.

A Brief Historical Perspective

Western cybernetics traces its roots to Maxwell's (1868) mathematical
study of feedback, "On Governors", and Bernard's (1878) study of feedback
systems in physiology, the mechanisms underlying what Cannon (1939) would call

homeostasis. By contrast, as Bernstein implies, the Russians developed a
separate tradition of the study of the physiology of regulation, which may
be traced back to Sechenov's (1863) study of "Reflexes of the Brain". Western
readers wishing a perspective on that tradition would do well to read the
chapters on "Russian Contributions to an Understanding of the Central Nervous
System and Behavior - A Pictorial Survey", "The Nineteenth Century Background
of the Russian Neurophysiologists, and Sechenov" and on "Pavlov" in the
volume edited by Brazier (1959). Clearly, Pavlov was the shaping figure of
20th century Soviet physiology, but too many scientists have taken his work
on the conditioned reflex to downplay what Bernstein calls "Sechenov's
thesis", namely "the active form of all the processes of reception and of
central processing of information". To see that the study of reflexes is
not incompatible with Sechenov's thesis we may turn to Sokolov's (1975)
study of neuronal mechanisms of the orienting reflex, in which habituation
is posited to depend on the organism's active formation of a model against
which new stimuli may be matched for an estimate of their novelty. The
Western reader may round out his appreciation of this distinctly Soviet view
of physiology and neurology by reading not only Bernstein's work, but that
of Vygotsky (1934) on thought and language, and of Anokhin (1935) on problems
of center and periphery in the physiology of nervous activity. In addressing
the neuropsychological problem of predicting lesion sites in the brain from
symptom-complexes and vice versa, Luria (1973) explicitly bases his idea of
"functional system" on the work of Anokhin, Bernstein and Vygotsky, asserting
that the fundamental task of neuropsychology is to ascertain "which groups
of concertedly working zones are responsible for the performance of complex
mental activity (and) what contribution is made by each of these zones to
the complex functional system". (I have developed this view within the
perspective of Artificial Intelligence and Brain Theory in Arbib (1982)).

    To trace the process whereby the term "cybernetics" became accepted in
the Soviet Union, it may be of interest to quote the following from a survey
of Soviet cybernetics:

        Before about 1955, cybernetics was anathema to the
    Soviets, even though many Russian scientists made contributions
    to what in the West was called cybernetics.
    ... Articles appeared which labelled cybernetics a 'bourgeois
    pseudoscience', 'the philosophy of the captains of a rotten
    ship'; one article was paranoid enough to suggest that cybernetics
    was a deliberate mystification devised by the capitalists to
    mislead Soviet scientists!
    ...
        In 1956, the Twentieth Congress of the CPSU not only heard

Krushchev denounce Stalin, but also heard that 'automation
of machines and operations must be extended to the automation
of factory departments and technological processes and to the
construction of fully automatic plants'. The Soviet Government
formed the Ministry of Automation. ...

   Starting in 1959, the Academy of Sciences held a series
of discussions on philosophical problems of cybernetics, which
were published in 1961 under the same title. The general line
of these papers was:

1. Cybernetics is the science of control, and will help build
   socialism.
2. Cybernetics is a science with a well-defined problem area,
   and must not be considered a philosophy. It cannot compete
   with material dialectics.
3. Bourgeois cyberneticians gloss over the vital distinctions
   between man, machine, and society. To understand the brain
   of man is the task of Pavlovian research on higher nervous
   activity. To understand society we need Marxism-Leninism.
4. Thought is an attribute of man alone, as a result of his
   social history. It is thus unquestionable dogma that machines
   cannot think. In fact, the question is considered highly
   improper, and attempts to define thought in a form suitable
   for discussion are not encouraged.

Kolmogorov, however, stated in an interview that he believes
thinking machines, which are operationally indistinguishable
from humans, will be created by cybernetics. ...
   In 1961, the Twenty-Second Congress of the CPSU emphasized
that cybernetics, computers, and control systems must be
introduced on a large scale in industry, research, designing,
planning, accounting, statistics, and management. (Arbib, 1966,
pp. 196-198).

In 1962 came the publication of Bernstein's paper under review here.
With this background, we may turn to an explicit introduction to Bernstein's
central concept of synergy in his physiology of activity. We then study
schema theory, theoretical embryology and Piaget's views on their relationship,
before returning to the broad philosophical questions of Bernstein's paper.

From Synergies to Motor Schemas

Bernstein asserts that:

   classical physiologists stuck to the idea of the reflex
   arc to represent the effector processes of the organism
   as strictly determinate signals arriving through an
   afferent semi-arc. But cyclical processes may start
   anywhere, and so reactive and spontaneous processes
   are combined into a single general class. The organism
   not only reacts to the situation but, encountering a

situation which is dynamically variable, must make a
probabilistic forecast and then a choice. The evaluation
of situations by the organism is no less sensitive than
its choice of action.

In fact, Bernstein's work says rather little about the "evaluation of
situations", and we shall sketch the theory of schema-assemblages in the next
section to remedy this deficiency. For the present, however, we shall contrast
two approaches to the 'units of control' employed by the brain in controlling
movement. Both are called synergies. The first, due to Sherrington, posits
a reflex unit above that of the motor unit; while the second, due to Bernstein,
suggests that a restricted number of programs may underlie most of our
behavior.

To understand Sherrington's views we must start with the notion of a
reflex. Two familiar examples: In the knee-jerk reflex, the tap of the
physician's hammer stretches a tendon, this is sensed by a sensor (proprioceptor)
which activates a motor neuron which contracts the extensor muscle (which had
'appeared' to be too long) so that the foot kicks out. In the scratch reflex,
an irritant localized to part of the skin activates receptors which in turn
activate motor neurons which control muscles to bring a foot or hand to the
irritated skin and rub back and forth. In each case, we have a reflex-loop
which mediates direct stimulus-response behavior: from external world via
receptors to the spinal cord where motor neurons respond by controlling muscles
to yield movement in the external world. Now consider the scratch-reflex more
carefully. We may see it as made up of two components. The rubbing component
needs the limb movement to ensure that it contacts the (right place on the)
skin, the limb movement is tuned into contact by feedback from the rubbing
movement. The two reflex actions 'synergize' or work together. More generally:

> The executant musculature ... provides a reflex means of
> supporting or reinforcing the co-operation of flexors
> with flexors, extensors with extensors, etc. The
> proprioceptors of reaching muscles operate reflexly upon
> other muscles of near functional relation to themselves.
> Active contraction (including active stretch) and passive
> stretch in the reach muscles are stimuli for reflexes
> influencing other muscles, and the reflex influence so
> exerted is on some muscles excitatory and on others
> inhibitory; it is largely reciprocally distributed,
> knitting synergists together. (Creed et al., 1932, p. 129).

Thus, for Sherrington, the synergy is an anatomically based reflex
linkage of a group of muscles.

The Bernstein school is informed by notions of control theory. The brain

is to generate control signals which will cause all the muscles to contract
with just the right timing to bring about some desired behavior. But there
are so many muscles, they suggest, that to independently control every muscle
to its optimum would be a computationally unmanageable problem. They thus see
the crucial problem in the 'design' of a brain which controls movement to be
that of reducing the number of 'degrees of freedom', i.e. the number of
independent parameters which must be controlled*:

> In order for the higher levels of the central nervous
> system to effectively solve the task of organizing motor
> acts within a required time, it is necessary that the
> number of controlled parameters be not too large, and the
> afferentation, requiring analysis, not too great. (This
> is achieved) by the so-called synergies. ... Each synergy
> is associated with certain peculiar connections imposed on
> some muscle groups, as subdivision of all the participant
> muscles into a small number of related groups. Due to this
> fact, to perform motion it is sufficient to control a small
> number of independent parameters, even though the number
> of muscles participating in the movement may be large.

So far, the general framework is consonant with the Sherrington synergies.
But these are restricted to stimulus-response patterns. Bernstein had a more
general concern with dynamic patterns changing over time during some motor
act:

> (A) complex synergy is involved in walking. ...'The
> biodynamic tissue' of live movements (appears) to be
> full of an enormous number of regular and stable
> details. ... (In old people) the synergy existing in
> normal walking between the action of the arms and legs
> is destroyed.

However, this was too global a view of synergy, and later work of the
Moscow school came to view synergies as the functional building blocks from
which most motions can be composed:

> Although synergies are few in number, they make it
> possible to encompass almost all the diversity of
> arbitrary motions. One can separate relatively simple
> synergies of pose control (synergy of stabilization),
> cyclic locomotive synergies (walking, running, swimming,
> etc.), synergies of throwing, striking, jumping, and a
> certain (small) number of others. (Gel'fand et al.,
> 1973, p. 162).

---

* The next two quotations are from Bernstein's paper "Biodynamics of
  Locomotion" in the present volume. He does not appear to use the term
  'synergy' in other papers in this collection.

One thus comes to see a synergy in general as a program for controlling
some distinctive motor performance extended in space and time, built upon
synergies of coordinated reflexes as substrate.

The concept of synergy has much in common with that of schema as within
the motor skills literature, e.g. in the work of Schmidt (1975, 1976). Schmidt'
schemas seem suited to the performance of a single motion in the laboratory
or in sports (e.g. swinging a bat) rather than to a complex manipulation or
to goal-oriented performance in a dynamic environment. Each such schema is
broken into two parts: The recall schema seems akin to feedforward, being
responsible for the complete control of a rapid movement, even though
environmental feedback may later signal errors. The recognition schema is
responsible for the evaluation of response-produced feedback that makes
possible the generation of error information about the movement. It thus
seems to combine on-line feedback and identification procedures which may
operate even after a movement is completed to better tune the schema for its
next activation. We shall use the term motor schema for such a unit for the
control of skilled movement, and use it as a synonym for synergy in the sense
of Bernstein. We may compare this with Piaget's (1971, p. 7) notion of an
action schema as "whatever, in an action, can ... be transposed, generalized,
or differentiated from one situation to another, in other words, whatever
there is in common between various repetitions or superpositions of the same
action".

When we move to catch a ball, we must interpret our view of the ball's
movement to estimate its future trajectory. Our attempt to catch the ball
incorporates this anticipation of the ball's movement in determining our own
movement. As the ball gets closer, or exhibits spin, we may find the ball
departing from the expected trajectory, and we must adjust our movements
accordingly. In this example, we think of the visual system as providing
inputs to a controller (our brain) which must generate control signals to
cause some system (our musculature) to behave in some desired way (to catch
the ball). Feedforward anticipates the relation between system and environment
to determine a course of action; feedback monitors discrepancies which can be
used to refine the actions. In describing the control of muscle Fel'dman
(1966) notes that, for a mass-spring system, the control neurons must maintain
a specific level of firing to hold a limb in a desired position - there is a
functional relation between a desired output (e.g. muscle length) and a
necessary input and a necessary input (e.g. maintained tension). In this case,
the feed-forward would be co-activated with the feedback system, so that

feedforward sets and maintains the control level specified by the functional
relationship, while feedback compensates for minor departures therefrom.

It is important to note that feedback can only be used effectively if
the controller is 'in the right ballpark' in its model of the controlled system.
However, in the real world the exact values of the parameters describing a
system are seldom available to the controller, and may actually change (compare
short-term loading effects on muscles and longer-term aging effects and weight
changes). To adapt to such changes, the feedback loop must be argumented by
an identification algorithm. The job of this algorithm is to monitor the output
of the controlled system continually and to compare it with the output that
would be expected on the basis of the current estimated state, the current
estimated parameters, and the current control signals. On the basis of these
data, the identification algorithm can identify more and more accurate
estimates of the parameters that define the controlled system, and these
updated parameters can then be supplied to the controller as the basis for
its state estimation and control computations. The identification algorithm
can only do its job if the controller is of the right general class and
system parameters do not change too quickly. It is unlikely that a controller
adapted for guiding the arm during ball-catching will be able, simply as a
result of parameter-adjustment, to properly control the legs in the performance
of a waltz. Thus an adaptive control system (controller + identification
procedure) is not to be thought of as a model of the brain; rather each such
control system is a model of a brain 'unit' which can be activated when
appropriate. We may think of it as a motor schema or synergy. An important
problem in analyzing human movement is that of the coordinated phasing in
and out of the brain's manifold motor schemas.

Perception and the Schema-Assemblage

Having now viewed Bernstein's synergies as motor schemas, we now sketch
a theory of assemblages of perceptual schemas, and their integration with
planning in the action-perception cycle (Arbib, 1981), in addressing the
problem of "evaluations of situations" that, we have suggested, has been
relatively neglected within Bernstein's own work. To relate this theory to
one's everyday activity, consider that, in walking down the street with a
friend, one simultaneously engages in at least five movement processes:
walking (including maintaining posture); breathing; talking; gesticulating;

and scanning the shop windows and passers-by. But each of these processes
involves the co-operation of multiple processes: for example, stepping is
determined inter alia by high-level route-selection processes ("turn left
at the town hall"), visual feedback about the location of obstacles, and
tactile feedback from the soles of the feet. And each of these in turn
requires activity in a neural network linking an array of receptors with
an array of motor neurons.

These behaviors involve not only 'externally-directed' movement, but
also a variety of 'exploratory' movements that help update an 'internal
model of the world' (here we may see such Western writers as Craik (1943),
Minsky (1961), and Gregory (1969) making their contribution to Sechenov's
thesis). In a new situation, we can recognize that familiar things are in
new relationships, and use our knowledge of those individual things and
our perception of those relationships to guide our behavior on that occasion.
It thus seems reasonable to posit that the 'internal model of the world' must
be built of units which correspond, roughly, to "domains of interaction" -
a phrase carefully chosen to include objects in the usual sense, but to
include many other things besides, from some attention-riveting detail of an
object all the way up to some sophisticated domain of social or linguistic
interaction for purposeful beings. We shall use the word schema to correspond
to the unit of knowledge - the internal representation of a domain of
interaction - within the brain.

The intelligent organism does not so much respond to stimuli as it
selects information which will help it achieve current goals - though a well-
designed or evolved system will certainly need to take appropriate account
of unexpected changes in its environment. To a first approximation, then,
planning is the process whereby the system combines an array of relevant
knowledge to determine a course of action suited to current goals. In its
fullest subtlety, planning can involve the refinement of knowledge structures
and goal structures, as well as action per se. While an animal may perceive
many aspects of its environment, only a few of these can at any time become
the primary locus of interaction. In general, our thesis is that perception
of an object (at least at the pre-verbal level) involves gaining access to
routines for interaction with it, but does not necessarily involve execution
of even one of these sub-routines. Our image for the control of the ensuing
behavior is context-dependent interpretation (Arbib, 1972a) in that new
inputs (e.g. coming upon an unexpected obstacle) can alter the elaboration
of the high-level structures into lower-level tests and actions which in turn

call upon the interaction of motor and sensory systems. We study programs
which are part of the internal state of the system prior to action, and which
can flexibly guide that action in terms of internal goals or drives and
external circumstances. As Bernstein asserts, "problem of action ... is the
reflection of the model of future requirements (somehow coded in the brain);
and a vitally useful or significant action cannot be either programmed or
accomplished if the brain has not created a prerequisite directive ..."

To better appreciate the intimate relation between perception and
action, consider the perceptual cycle (Neisser, 1976). The subject actively
explores the visual world, for example, by moving eyes, head or body (or
manipulating the environment). Exploration is directed by anticipatory schemas,
which Neisser defines as plans for perceptual action as well as readiness
for particular kinds of optical structure. The information thus picked up
modifies the perceiver's anticipations of certain kinds of information which
- thus modified - direct further exploration and become ready for more
information. For example, to tell whether or not any coffee is left in a cup
we may reach out and tilt the cup to make the interior visible, and keep
tilting the cup further and further as we fail to see any coffee until we
either see the coffee at last or conclude that the cup is empty. We here see
Sechenov's thesis in the form that one cannot understand perception unless
it is embedded within the organism's on-going interaction with its environment.
For as the organism moves in a complex environment - making, executing, and
updating plans as it does so - it must stay tuned to its spatial relationship
with its immediate environment, anticipating facets of the environment before
they come into view. The information gathered during ego-motion must be
systematically related to a cognitive map (Tolman, 1948; Lieblich and Arbib,
1982), which is not so much a mental picture of the environment as an active,
information-seeking structure.

The "co-ordinated structures" of Gibson (1977) and the action-perception
cycle remind the neuroscientist to eschew too Sherringtonian a view of a
brain responding to an environment via a chain of reflexes. The "co-ordinated
control programs" of Arbib (1981) remind us that this mutuality of organism-
environment interaction must be embedded within a regnant plan of action which
the organism brings to bear upon the pattern of interaction. To this context,
we add that that portion of the environment which provides the current focus
for the animal's interaction is part of a larger whole. Because of this, we
may view the animal's 'internal model of the world' as being, functionally,
a schema-assemblage - the assemblage being made up of a spatially-tagged array

of parametrized schema instantiations. Let us unpack this mouthful. The
spatial relationship between objects can be crucial, and so we speak of a
spatially-tagged array. If we speak of a chair-schema, for example, as the
internal representation of a chair and our possibilities for interaction
with it, then the internal representation of a scene with three chairs may
well involve three instantiations of the chair-schema, and each of these
must be individually parametrized by pertinent characteristics (affordances)
specific to the chair that it represents.

This notion of a schema as but a unit within an assemblage is the author's.
Another root of the use of 'schema' in current psychology is found in the work
of Piaget. The Piagetian schema is the internal representation of some
generalized class of situations, enabling the organism to act in a coordinated
fashion over a whole range of analogous situations. Reviewing this approach to
the genesis and development of knowledge, Piaget (1971) relates his schemas to
the innate releasing mechanisms of the ethologists and thus, via Lorenz
(1941), to the schemas of Kant (1787).

Parallels with Embryology

About a third of the way through his article, Bernstein shifts emphasis
from the physiology of activity to embryology, likening the regulatory
properties of the embryo to the self-directed activity of the mature organism.
In his extended analysis of the organism's growth, Bernstein suggests that the
"life process is not a balancing with the environment, but a conquest of the
latter, aimed not at preserving the status quo or homeostasis, but at an
advance towards fulfilment of the development and self-preservational program
of the genus". One is reminded of Waddington's (1957, 1968) introduction of
the concept of "homeorhesis" in contrast to "homeostasis". Whereas, in
homeostasis, organismic variables are regulated to fall within a certain
physiologically acceptable range, in homeorhesis there is a stabilized flow
rather than a stabilized state. Waddington views development as following a
'chreod', a canalized trajectory which acts as an attractor for nearby
trajectories. However, he does allow that chreods may branch. Away from a
branch, development is highly regulated; near a branch, external factors can
control bifurcation, the switching to one branch or another. These notions
received one mathematical form at the hands of Rene Thom (1975) in his theory
of structural stability and morphogenesis. Thom, in what is known as

catastrophe theory, seeks to give an abstract mathematical theory of
bifurcations by looking at systems which belong to a parametrically-defined
family of systems. A system of the family is structurally stable when small
changes in parameter values do not change its qualitative behavior (i.e., the
numerical description of its trajectories may change, but the overall pattern
of its stabilities and instabilities remains unchanged). Only for an
exceptional submanifold of the parameter space do the corresponding systems
exhibit structural instability - this submanifold constitutes what Thom calls
a catastrophe. Slight changes in a system characterized by these parameters
can yield 'catastrophic' changes such as those exhibited at certain critical
stages in morphogenesis. Thom gives an abstract topological characterization
of a set of "elementary" catastrophes, and a number of theorists share his
view that these topological invariants capture what is essential in
morphogenetic processes. We see here a strikingly different approach to the
issue of essential vs. non-essential variables from that, due to Gel'fand
and Tsetlin (1962), discussed by Bernstein. While many workers do share Thom's
views, others hold that applied mathematics offers less topological methods
of handling nonlinearities and bifurcations which offer more detailed
insights into biological processes.

Zeeman (1974) has used catastrophe theory to prove that when differentiation
of a mass of cells occurs, forming two types of cells, then the boundary that
forms between these cell types always moves from its initial position before
stabilizing in its final position in the tissue. Ransom (1981, p. 62-65)
offers an informal discussion of this theorem, and discusses the attempt by
Cooke and Zeeman (1976) to apply it to explain the formation of the repeated
pattern of vertebrate somites. It is beyond the scope of this article to
survey the literature on cybernetic approaches to embryology - the reader may
turn to Arbib (1972b) and Ransom (1981) for comprehensive reviews of
automaton-theoretic and computational approaches to developmental biology;
to the papers by Ede, Wolpert, Wilby, Bryant and Cooke in the volume edited
by Ede et al. (1977) for a view of how modelling concepts have affected work
on vertebrate limb and somite morphogenesis; and to the papers by Hope,
Hammond and Gaze (1976), Willshaw and von der Malsburg (1979), and Overton
and Arbib (1982) for a range of models of regulatory processes in the
development of connections in the brain. Instead, we use the rest of the
section to address certain questions raised by Bernstein by noting Piaget's
concern for parallels between cognitive activity and embryology.

Piaget's studies of the cognitive development of the child were part of

a broader philosophical concern to construct a 'genetic epistemology', a
concern rooted in the embryological studies of his boyhood. In his Biology
and Knowledge* (translated from the French of 1967), Piaget (1971) offers an
essay on the parallels between organic regulations and cognitive processes.
The most widely cited author in this volume is Waddington (Lamarck is second!)
and, although Piaget does not cite Bernstein, his analysis of schemas and
epigenesis make his text central to any discussion of the issues Bernstein
raised in the paper under discussion here. The parallelism of active roles
in embryology and in cognition is well-expressed in the following quotation:

> In genetic terms, the genome is in no sense the product
> of environmental influences but is an organized system,
> supplying 'responses' to environmental tensions
> (Dobzhansky and Waddington) and containing its own norms
> of reaction. In terms of embryology, however, epigenetic
> development implies a series of exchanges with some
> internal control imposing choices on the materials used...
> In neurological terms the nervous system is not subjected
> to some constraining influence from the stimuli but shows
> spontaneous action, reacting only to stimuli which sensitize
> it - that is, it assimilated them actively into schemata
> established before it made its response (Piaget, 1971,
> p. 31-32).

Note, however, that Piaget not only analyzes how stimuli are assimilated
to pre-existent schemas. He also provides a theory of the process of
accommodation whereby new schemas are formed from the old. Thus, although
Piaget does seem to share Bernstein's notion that the organism has a "coded
program of the successive stages in (its) development" (see Brainerd (1978)
for a critique of the stage concept in cognitive development), he would not
go so far as to assert that "the organism is continually changing in a *set*
direction (my italics)". In addition to assimilation, Piaget posits a process
of accommodation whereby the animal modifies its schemas to accord with an
external world situation. Piaget thus sees adaptation as an equilibrium between
the two functions of assimilation and accommodation, which he views as
indissociable. He sees these processes of adaptation occurring first in
embryology, and again playing an essential part in the cognitive domain.
But he extends to intellectual growth a power which goes beyond the
embryological:

> From the point of view of organization, intelligence
> succeeds in making structures that are both more stable
> and more highly differentiated, for although it would

---

* I thank my students Donald House and Francisco Cervantes for their
thoughtful schema-theoretic reviews of this volume.

be possible to conceive of the mathematization of
all biological structures, all mathematical structures
could not be realized in the organic plane (Piaget,
1971, p. 213).

Philosophical Conclusions

Bernstein has stressed the material basis for embryonic development
and for psychological processes, contra claims for vitalism or the postulation
of mind as a separate substance, respectively. It seems that no reputable
embryologist believes in vitalism any more - which is not to deny that the
exact mechanisms whereby genes interact with cytoplasm in guiding development
still hold many mysteries for scientists to resolve. But scientists do not
doubt that the resolution will involve the explication of mechanisms, rather
than resort to some elan vital. By contrast, some eminent neuroscientists
still espouse a mind-body dualism, even though the majority are in some sense
materialists. To conclude this essay, then, I briefly recall the dualist
position of Sir John Eccles, the Australian Nobel Laureate in neurophysiology,
and indicate why I do not find his case convincing.

Eccles follows Popper in distinguishing three "Worlds": World 1 comprises
physical objects and states (including brain and body); World 2 comprises
states of consciousness (mind and soul); while World 3, comprising the
knowledge accumulated by society (social reality) elevates Cartesian dualism
to a Popperian trialism. Eccles seems to misread Popper by locating records
of intellectual efforts in World 3 - these records are clearly in World 1,
and Popper is speaking more strongly, regarding theoretical systems and
social systems as having a reality of their own apart from any embodiment.
Thus Eccles and Popper see the physical, the mental, and the social as three
separate substances.

Eccles addresses the question of their interaction. Where Sherrington,
in Man on his Nature, had been a dualist - mind talks to brain, and vice
versa - Eccles has to have World 2 interact with World 3 as well as World 1.
Interestingly, he eschews the sort of direct communication between World 3
and World 2 that one might associate with such terms as "collective unconscious"
and "racial memory", and has World 3 embody itself in books and artefacts which
can then be sensed as is any other part of World 1 by the perceptual systems
of the brain, themselves part of World 1. He then posits a specialized portion
of the brain, the liaison brain which communicates with World 2, the mind.

Note that each mind is cut off from every other mind save to the extent that they communicate through their liaison brains, and thus through World 1.

Eccles then calls on the data on split brains. It is well known that 98% of people have the left hemisphere as the dominant hemisphere - it has the ability to use complex speech, whereas the right hemisphere has at best limited use of concrete words. When the corpus callosum, the massive fiber tract linking the two hemispheres, is severed, each half-brain can independently guide motor behavior, but only the left hemisphere can talk about what it is doing. This leads to two hypotheses: either the left brain alone has consciousness and personality, with the right brain providing additional computing power when the corpus callosum is intact (so that the functions of the right brain can then enter consciousness and affect personality via its modulation of the left brain); or both brains embody conscious personalities (which usually reach consensus via the corpus callosum when it is intact), but only the left brain can articulate this consciousness. Eccles opts, without further argument, for the first view, and then goes much further. He rejects the possibility that consciousness and personality could be functions of the left brain <u>qua</u> physical structure; rather he asserts that we have consciousness and personality as a separate entity in World 2, the mind, but that is is only the specialized structures of the left hemisphere that enable the mind to communicate with the brain. Unfortunately, this explains nothing. If the mind is separate from the brain, what tasks does it perform that the brain cannot? Eccles would answer that it makes those free decisions that constitute free will. I would argue that, in fact, our brains are sufficiently complex to make those "free" decisions. But even if Eccles is right, how does the World 2 mind make such decisions? Brain Theory offers potential mechanisms, Mind Theory does not - unless we postulate schemas in World 2 in communion with their neural embodiments, but somehow able to work independently of them. Eccles states that:

> I believe that my genetic coding is not responsible for
> my uniqueness as an experiencing being. ... Nor do my
> postnatal experiences and education provide a satisfactory
> explanation of the self that I experience. It is a
> necessary but not sufficient condition. ... We go through
> life living with this mysterious experience of ourselves
> as experiencing beings. I believe that we have to accept
> what I call a personalist philosophy - that central to
> our experienced existence is our personal uniqueness.
> (Eccles, 1977, p. 227).

Thus where we would argue that to the extent that we are more than our

accumulated genetic and individual experience it is because of the people and
physical world that surround us, Eccles explicity postulates a "something
extra" - our uniqueness cannot be embodied in World 1, but requires the
separate stuff of World 2. He makes this very explicit:

> I think that for my personal life as a conscious
> self, the brain is necessary, but it is not sufficient.
> In liaison with the brain events in World 1, there is
> the World 2 of my conscious experience, including a
> personal self at the core of my being. Throughout our
> lifetime this personal self has continuity despite
> the failure of liaison with the brain in states of
> unconsciousness such as dreamless sleep, anesthesia,
> coma. The brain states are then unsuitable for liaison,
> but the self can achieve in dreams a partial liaison
> (Ibid, p. 227).

But if the World 2 self "continues to be" while there is no liaison
with the brain, why does it not have "things to tell us" when contact is
re-established. Certainly, we sometimes "solve a problem in our sleep", but
what evidence is there that this is the work of a disembodied mind reporting
directly to consciousness rather than the fruit of the subconscious dynamics
of the brain? The point I am making is not that we can prove Eccles wrong,
but rather that there is no "this far can the brain go, and no farther"
argument to prove him right. Thus we can hardly agree with Eccles that "there
is *evidence* (my italics) that the self in World 2 has an autonomous existence,
bridging gaps of unconsciousness when the brain fails to be in a state of
liaison".

One final comment. If the above material argues for a fully materialist
embryology and psychology, it does not augur well for Bernstein's aim to
define the underline between living and artificial systems. As we come to
develop cybernetic theories of the self-directedness that now distinguishes
living systems, so will we come to build artificial systems that share this
characteristic in increasing measure.

REFERENCES

Anokhin, P.I. Problems of Centre and Periphery in the Physiology of Nervous
    Activity. Gorki : Gosizdat (in Russian), 1935.

Arbib, M.A. A partial survey of cybernetics in Eastern Europe and the
    Soviet Union. Behavioral Science, 1966, 11, 193-216.

Arbib, M.A. The metaphorical brain : An introduction to cybernetics as
    artificial intelligence and brain theory. New York : Wiley Interscience,
    1972(a).

Arbib, M.A. Automata theory in the context of theoretical embryology.
    In, R. Rosen (Ed.), Foundations of mathematical biology, Vol. II,
    New York : Academic Press, 1972(b).

Arbib, M.A. Perceptual structures and distributed motor control. In, V.B.
    Brooks (Ed.), Handbook of physiology - The nervous system II. Motor
    control, Bethesda, MD : American Physiological Society, 1981.

Arbib, M. Perceptual-motor processes and the neural basis of language.
    In, M.A. Arbib, D. Caplan and J.C. Marshall (Eds.), Neural models of
    language processes, New York : Academic Press, 1982.

Bernard, C. Lecons sur les phenomenes de la vie. Paris: Brailliere, 1878.

Brainerd, C.J. The stage question in cognitive-development theory. The
    Behavioral and Brain Sciences, 1978, 1, 173-213.

Brazier, M.A.B. The central nervous system and behavior, transactions of
    the first conference. New York : Josiah Macy, Jr. Foundation, 1959.

Cannon, W.B. The Wisdom of the Body. London: Norton, 1939.

Cooke, J. & Zeeman, E.C. A clock and wavefront model for control of the
    number of repeated structures during animal morphogenesis. Journal of
    Theoretical Biology, 1976, 58, 455-476.

Craik, K.J.W. The Nature of Explanation . Cambridge:University Press, 1943.

Creed, R.S., Denny-Brown, D., Eccles, J.C., Liddell, E.G.T. & Sherrington,
    C.S. Reflex Activity of the Spinal Cord. Oxford : University Press, 1932.

Eccles, J.C. The Understanding of the Brain, 2nd. Ed. New York : McGraw-
    Hill, 1977.

Ede, D.A., Hinchliffe, J.R. & Balls, M. (Eds.), Vertebrate Limb and Somite
    Morphogenesis. Cambridge University Press, 1977.

Fel'dman, A.G. Functional tuning of the nervous system with control of
    movement or maintenance of a steady posture --II. Controllable
    parameters of the muscles. Biophysics, 1966, 11, 565-578 (Translated
    from Biofizika, 1966, 11, 498-508).

Gel'fand, I.M., Gurfinkel, V.S., Shik, M.L. & Tsetlin, M.L. Certain
    problems in the investigation of movement. In: Automata Theory and
    Modeling of Biological Systems (translated by M.L. Tsetlin). New York :
    Academic Press, 1973.

Gregory, R.L. On how so little information controls so much behavior. In,
    C.H. Waddington (Ed.), Towards a Theoretical Biology, 2: Sketches.
    Edinburgh : University Press, 1969.

Hope, R.A., Hammond, B.J. & Gaze, R.M. The arrow model of retino-tectal
    specificity and map formation in the goldfish visual system. Proceedings
    of the Royal Society London, 1976, B 194, 447-466.

Kant, I. Kritik der reinen Vernunft. Riga : Johann Friedrich Hartknoch,
    1787. (English translation by N.K. Smith. Critique of Pure Reason.
    London : MacMillan, 1929).

Lieblich, I. & Arbib, M.A. Multiple representations of space underlying
    behavior. Behavioral and Brain Sciences 2, 1982, 627-659.

Lorenz, K. Kants Lehre vom Apriorischen im Lichte der gegenwartigen Biologie.
    Blatter fur Deutsche Philosophie, 1941, 15, 94-125.

Luria, A.R. The Working Brain. Harmondsworth : Penguin Books, 1973.

MacKay, D.M. Cerebral organization and the conscious control of action.
    In, J.C. Eccles (Ed.), Brain and Conscious Experience. Hamburg :
    Springer-Verlag, 1966.

Maxwell, J.C. On governors. Proceedings of the Royal Society London, 1868,
    16, 270-283.

Minsky, M.L. Steps toward artificial intelligence. Proceedings of the IRE,
    1961, 49, 8-30.

Neisser, U. Cognition and reality : principles and implications of cognitive
    psychology. San Francisco : Freeman, 1976.

Overton, K.J. & Arbib, M.A. The extended branch-arrow model of the formation
    of retino-tectal connections. Biological Cybernetics, 1982, 45, 157-175.

Piaget, J. Biology and knowledge : An essay on the relations between organic
    regulations and cognitive processes. Edinburgh : University Press, 1971.

Popper, K. & Eccles, J.C. The Self and its Brain. New York : Springer
    International, 1977.

Ransom, R. Computers and embryos : Models in developmental biology. New
    York : Wiley, 1981.

Schmidt, R.A. A schema theory of discrete motor skill learning.
    Psychological Review, 1975, 82, 225-260.

Schmidt, R.A. The schema as a solution to some persistent problems in motor
    learning theory. In, G.E. Stelmach (Ed.), Motor control : issues and
    trends. New York : Academic Press, 1976.

Sechenov, I. Reflexes of the Brain (1863) (English Translation by S. Belsky).
    Cambridge, Mass. : MIT Press, 1965.

Sherrington, C.S. Man on his nature. Cambridge : University Press, 1940.

Sokolov, E.N. The neuronal mechanisms of the orienting reflex. In, E.N.
    Sokolov and O.S. Vinogradova (Eds.), Neuronal mechanisms of the
    orienting reflex. Hillsdale, N.J. : Lawrence Erlbaum Associates, 1975.

Thom, R. Structural stability and morphogenesis. Reading, Mass. : W.A.
    Benjamin, (Translated from the French Edition of 1972 by D.H. Fowler),
    1975.

Vygotsky, L.S. Thought and language (translated from the Russian original
    of 1934). Cambridge, Mass. : The MIT Press, 1962.

Waddington, C.H. The strategy of the genes. London : Allen and Unwin, 1957.

Waddington, C.H. The basic ideas of biology. In, C.H. Waddington (Ed.),
    Towards a Theoretical Biology 1 : Prolegomena. Edinburgh : University
    press, 1968.

Willshaw, D.J. & van der Malsburg, C. A marker induction mechanism for
    the establishment of ordered neural mappings : its application to the
    retinotectal problem. Philosophical Transactions of the Royal Society
    London, 1979, B 187, 203-243.

Zeeman, E.C. Primary and secondary waves in developmental biology. Lectures
    on Mathematics in the Life Sciences, 1974, 7, 69-161 (Providence, R.I. :
    American Mathematical Society).

Human Motor Actions — Bernstein Reassessed
H.T.A. Whiting (editor)
© Elsevier Science Publishers B.V. (North-Holland), 1984

CHAPTER VIb

CONTROL THEORY AND CYBERNETIC ASPECTS OF MOTOR SYSTEMS

G.C. Agarwal and G.L. Gottlieb

This philosophical essay by Bernstein was a culmination of his long research work and was published in 1962, just a few years before his death. This was also the time when control engineers started considering the information aspects of a system and the concepts of adaptive and learning systems were being developed.

At the outset of the essay, Bernstein draws a distinction between the cybernetics of Wiener, Shannon and Ashby and the cybernetic concepts he proceeds to apply to physiology. The basis of this distinction is not entirely clear but is perhaps based upon the relative complexity of physiological systems when compared to classical engineering systems. This issue is not addressed again until the last paragraph of the paper when he proposes that "It is now necessary ... to indicate and study the differences between living and artificial systems" (p. 546). Whether this distinction exists seems unclear and whether we have enough understanding of living systems to make that determination is even more uncertain. This issue, like the issue of rigid materialism discussed below, seems just beyond determination by scientific methods at our current level of ignorance.

In the preceding paper Arbib has reviewed the historical development of the artificial intelligence field in the Soviet Union as it related to the biological problems. He has also extensively reviewed the concept of motor synergies and development of motor schemas. Our discussion on these topics will be limited to supplement Arbib's paper with an orientation based on modern control theory. Before going into the control theory and cybernetic aspects of motor systems, we wish to comment on two themes which are interwoven throughout the body of this paper: the unity of nature and its materialistic laws governing the phenomena of life. He means this with a vengeance.

Unity of Nature and Materialisric Laws

Most scientists would probably accept the notion that the domain of

science is the material world. To the extent that some consider this an
incomplete description of our personal world of experience, there is room
for other "worlds" which do not contradict the material one. The distinction
between mind and brain is one issue of this sort that has been addressed by
such notable scientists as Sperry and Eccles (see Arbib). Bernstein, we
believe, would disagree and insist upon "a strictly materialistic
interpretation to be given to the concepts of singleness of purpose,
expediency, etc." (p. 533) in the action of any organism.

What is the character of the natural laws governing living systems?
Bernstein tells us that "An organism must ... possess two determining
features. Firstly, it ... preserves its own (systemic) identity ... Secondly,
the organism is continually changing in a set direction at all stages of
its existence." (p. 535) "the organism as a whole and, very possibly, each
of its cells struggle actively for survival, development and reproduction.
The life process is not a balancing with the environment, but a conquest of
the latter, aimed not at preserving the status quo or homeostasis, but at
an advance towards fulfilment of the developmental and self-preservational
program of the genus" (p. 537).

Furthermore, Bernstein goes on to state that "we are forced by the
facts to regard all phenomena pertaining to an organism's interaction with
the world ... as being cyclic processes ...; and as a result the processes
of interaction termed (in the old sense) reactive ... and those termed
spontaneous ... are both here combined into a single general class" (p.534).

Problems of Motor Functions

Having stated these very general principles, applicable to all living
systems from single cells on up to human beings, Bernstein returns to the
themes of previous essays (e.g. Chapters 4 and 5) concerning the problems
of motor functions. These involve the same cyclic issues of action and
reaction: a) a tuned perception of the state of the organism in its
interactions with the environment; b) the definition of future requirements
based upon extrapolation from the present state; c) a programming of the
action intended to fulfil these requirements; and d) the execution of the
action which alters the state of the organism and its consequent perceptions.

This addresses experimental problems which remain at issue today in
the field of motor control. What sorts of programs are generated and how can
they be related to future requirements (e.g. simply moving a joint from one
state to another)? Do programs incorporate peripheral input only in their

generation or during their execution. What are the operational rules that
govern this and where does it happen?

Bernstein suggests that our understanding of these problems might be
aided by Gelfand and Tsetlin's ideas on "well organized functions". Well
organized functions have arguments which can be separated into two classes,
termed essential and non-essential (Gelfand et al., 1971).

Non-essential variables can produce abrupt but limited variation in a
function such that two different realizations of the same function (e.g. the
shape of an oak leaf or a person's signature) may differ yet be recognizably
related to each other. Motor acts are yielding and reflexive regarding those
features that are non-essential.

Essential variables are dealt with in a more active, vigorous way. The
organism will seek to preserve them in every member of a class. Structural
examples easily come to mind such as all individuals having two arms although
between individuals their lengths will differ. The former is an essential and
the latter a non-essential variable.

We can find an analogous concept in the current search for invariant
properties of movement. This notion that we can find elements in a diverse
set of movements that remain the same has been and continues to be studied
by many diverse groups (Asatryan & Fel'dman, 1965; Fel'dman & Latash, 1982;
Bizzi et al., 1976, 1982; Soechting & Lacquaniti, 1982). The existence of
such invariant (or essential) properties would enormously simplify the task
of programming movements, at least as we now understand it.

Application of Engineering Methodology

In applying engineering tools to study the mechanism of human movements,
one is faced with a serious methodological problem. The analytical tools have
been developed to study cause-and-effect (or input-output) types of
relationships one finds in engineering systems. Bernstein had noted that
"Motor functions comprise a basic group of processes by which the organism
not merely reacts to its environment but even acts on the latter" (p. 532).
The implication was that the motor system was acting on a probabilistic
extrapolation of the course of events (which would have occurred under
conditions of non-interference) using some "common sense" simulation of the
environment and anticipating future input-outputs of the system. The field
of artificial intelligence is presently unable to define systematic rules
to develop models of "common sense". At a recent meeting McCarthy of
Stanford University noted that "much of the ordinary common sense ability

to predict the consequences of actions requires going beyond the rules
present in expert systems" (Kolata, 1982). Although considerable progress
has been made in the last 20 years in applying control engineering and
cybernetics concepts to motor control problems, some very fundamental
questions about the functional organization and hierarchical information and
control structures have yet to be answered.

The study of the motor system requires applications of four disciplines;
namely biological control theory, neural modelling, artificial intelligence,
and cognitive psychology (Arbib, 1982).

Biological control theory deals with the application of control theory
techniques such as linear modelling and stability analysis applied to study
problems such as the stretch reflex and tremor. Merton's hypotheses of motor
control via the gamma loop (1953) - the follow-up servo hypothesis - was
based on simple concepts of feedback control theory. This example also points
to a very significant problem of identification in feedback systems when
access to signals at various points in the system is very limited. Merton's
original hypothesis was modified to the concept of alpha-gamma linkage by
Granit (1955) emphasizing co-activation of alpha and gamma motoneurons and
later on to servo-assisted motor control by Matthews (1972).

In Merton's hypothesis, the length of the muscle is assumed to be the
controlled variable by a follow-up servo. Over the last 30 years, the question
of what muscle variable(s) the nervous system controls in limb movements has
been discussed repeatedly. In a recent article Stein (1982) has reviewed
the arguments for and against the control of force, length, stiffness,
velocity and/or viscosity. He concluded that different physical variables
may be controlled depending on the type of limb movement required. Other
possibilities also exist such as energy consumption or minimum response time
which are frequently the design criteria for man-made systems.

On the output side of a muscle, there are two state-variables, length
and tension, which are always linked by the external load and the internal
electro-mechanical events in the muscle. The nervous system can only regulate
the firing rates and the number of active motor units. This results in
externally measurable force between limb and load which acts to move the limb
and load through some trajectory in space and time. All intermediate variables
are, in a sense, controlled in that the nervous system can affect and to
some degree determine their future behavior.

In dealing with the central nervous system, we are faced with an
enormous problem of the interacting nuclei with cerebrum and cerebellum as

two dominant centers. Eccles (1973) has emphasized the role of the cerebellum
in the control of movements. For example, he writes "Let us now try to
visualize what would be happening in the cerebro-cerebellar circuits during
some skilled action, for example, a golf stroke. In the first place we will
assume a loop time of the cerebro-cerebellar circuit of a fiftieth of a
second, so that a motor command to start the stroke will result in a "wise"
comment from the cerebellum to modify the pyramidal tract (PT) discharge in
accord with its learnt performance. The modified (PT) discharge is reported
to the cerebellum and this in turn evokes a further corrective comment from
the cerebellum. Thus there is this continuous on-going cerebellar modification
of PT discharge. These hypotheses of the manner of cerebellar action in the
control of movement provide great challenges for future research" (Eccles,
1973, p. 131). Eccles emphasized the concept of evolving movements and their
continuous monitoring and control by multiple feedback loops through various
levels of central nervous system (Figure 4-15, p. 132, Eccles, 1973).

The development of neural models to elucidate some of these concepts of
cerebellar control of movements has been a difficult task. Several efforts
have been made along these lines by Marr (1969), Albus (1971), Boylls (1976)
and others. However, as Eccles pointed out there are good reasons to believe
that the cerebellum functions as a special type of computer but there is not
sufficient "hard data" as a basis for computer modelling.

Neurophysiological techniques of single cell recording and using
correlation techniques, have made significant progress in tracing relevant
connections. However, this frequently does not lead us to establish a
cause-and-effect relationship in complex structures. Much remains to be done
in developing techniques in the field of artificial intelligence to study
such problems.

One clinical approach to study the function of a neural unit has been
to observe the system performance by surgical removal of the region. As
Granit (1977) pointed out this may not provide a final answer, because often
it will merely tell us what the brain can do despite the loss instead of
telling us what the lost portion did.

Motor Programs

Psychologists, artificial intelligence experts and researchers from the
field of robotics in recent years have been focusing attention on the concept
of the motor program (Mackay, 1980; Hollerbach, 1982). As Mackay points out,
the motor theory has been split between two schools of thought; peripheralist

and centralist. The peripheral hypothesis of motor control was pioneered by Sherrington and it essentially sought to explain all movement in terms of chains of reflexes, i.e., the control loops which are directly linked to sensory events at the periphery. The centralist dogma arose from the patterning of motor output within the CNS without the need of sensory information.

Considering the structure of the motor system one would think that neither approach is likely to be entirely correct. The truth lies somewhere in between the two concepts. It is quite possible that in certain experimental situations the peripheral or the central control hypothesis may be the dominant mechanism. For example, although Graham Brown and Karl Lashley demonstrated evidence of controlled motor output in the absence of sensory input this does not necessarily imply that sensory input does not play any role in an intact system.

Keele (1968) defined the concept of motor program as "a set of muscle commands that are structured before a movement sequence begins, and that allows the entire sequence to be carried out uninfluenced by peripheral feedback". Certain ballistic movements may seem preprogrammed but even in those cases the peripheral feedbacks contribute to load compensation as well as to modulate the central command to effectively use the most recent peripheral states of the system (Gottlieb & Agarwal, 1981; Gottlieb et al., 1983).

One final comment:

It seems then that the fundamental questions raised by Bernstein in 1962 remain equally fundamental and equally unanswered 20 years later. We may optimistically suggest that they will provide many individuals with a way to pass the time for the next 20 years.

ACKNOWLEDGEMENTS

This work was supported by National Science Foundation grant IESE 82-12067 and National Institutes of Health grant NS-12877.

REFERENCES

Albus, J.S. A theory of cerebellar function. Mathematical Biosciences, 1971, 10, 25-61.

Arbib, M.A. Perceptual structures and distributed motor control. In, V.B. Brooks (Ed.), Handbook of physiology - The nervous system II. Motor control. Bethesda, MD : American Physiological Society, 1981.

Asatryan D.S. & Fel'dman, A.G. Functional tuning of nervous system with control of movement or maintenance of a steady posture. I. Mechanographic analysis of the work of the joint on execution of a postural task. Biofizika, 1965, 10, 837-846. (English translation Biophysics, 925-935).

Bernstein, N.A. Trends in physiology and their relation to cybernetics. Questions of Philosophy, 1962, 8. Reprinted as Chapter 6 in the Co-ordination and Regulation of Movements. Oxford: Pergamon Press, 1967.

Bizzi, E., Polit, A. & Morasso, P. Mechanism underlying achievement of final head position. Journal of Neurophysiology, 1976, 39, 435-444.

Bizzi, E., Chapple, W. & Hogan, N. Mechanical properties of muscles: Implications for motor control. Trends in Neuroscience, 1982, 5, 395-398.

Boylls, C.C. Jr. The function of the cerebellum and its related nuclei as embedded in a general paradigm for motor control. Ph.D. Thesis, Stanford University, 1976.

Eccles, J.C. The Understanding of the Brain. New York: McGraw-Hill, 1973.

Fel'dman, A.G. & Latash, M.L. Interaction of afferent and efferent signals underlying joint position sense: Empirical and theoretical approaches. Journal of Motor Behavior, 1982, 14, 174-193.

Gelfand, I.M., Gurfinkel, V.S., Fomin, S.V. & Tsetlin, M.L. (Eds.), Models of the Structural-Functional Organization of Certain Biological Systems. M.I.T. Press, 1971.

Gottlieb, G.L., Agarwal, G.C. & Jaeger, R.J. Response to sudden torques about ankle in man: V. Effects of peripheral ischemia. Journal of Neurophysiology, 1983, 50, 297-312.

Granit, R. Receptors and Sensory Perception. Yale: University Press, 1955.

Granit, R. The Purposive Brain. M.I.T. Press, 1977.

Hollerbach, J.M. Computers, brains and the control of movement. Trends in Neuroscience, 1982, 5, 189-192.

Keele, S.W. Movement control in skilled motor performance. Psychological Bulletin, 1968, 70, 387-403.

Kolata, G. How can computers get common sense? (a conference report). Science, 1982, 217, 1237-1238.

Mackay, W.A. The motor program: back to the computer. Trends in Neuroscience,
    1980, 3, 97-100.

Marr, D. A theory of cerebellar cortex. Journal of Physiology (London), 1969,
    202, 437-470.

Matthews, P.B.C. Mammalian Muscle Receptors and Their Central Actions.
    Baltimore: Williams & Wilkins, 1972.

Merton, P.A. Speculations on the servo-control of movement. In, J. Malcolm
    and J.A.B. Gray (Eds.), The Spinal Cord. Boston: Brown & Company, 1953.

Soechting, J.F. & Lacquaniti, F. Invariant characteristics of a pointing
    movement in man. Journal of Neuroscience, 1981, 1, 710-720.

Stein, R.N. What muscle variable(s) does the nervous system control in limb
    movements? Behavioral & Brain Sciences, 1982, 5, 535-577.

REFERENCES FROM ORIGINAL TEXT OF BERNSTEIN

1. Adrian, E.D. The mechanism of nervous action. Oxford: University Press, 1932.

2. Anokhin, P.K. The problems of the centre and the periphery in the physiology of neural activity, Collection of papers, Gorkij (in Russian), 1935.

3. Anokhin, P.K. Nodal questions in the study of superior nervous activity, Problems of the superior nervous act (in Russian), 1949.

4. Anokhin, P.K. Particular features of the afferent apparatus of conditioned reflexes. Journal Questions of Psychology, No. 6 (in Russian), 1955.

5. Anokhin, P.K. The role of the orientation and search reaction in the formation of a conditioned reflex. Orientation Reflex (in Russian), 1958.

6. Ashby, W.R. An introduction to cybernetics. London: Chapman & Hall, 1956.

7. Basler, A. Neue Untersuchungen über die beim Gehen nach abwärts wirkende Kraft, Arbeitsphysiologie 8, 1935.

8. Bernstein, N.A. Studies of the biomechanics of the stroke by means of photo-registration, Research of the Central Institute of Labour, Moscow 1 (in Russian), 1923.

9. Bernstein, N.A. A biomechanical norm for the stroke. Research of the Central Institute of Labour, Moscow 1,2 (in Russian), 1924.

10. Bernstein, N.A. The origin of species in technics (to the railway centenary). Journal Iskra, 1925, No. 9 (in Russian).

11. Bernstein, N.A. General Biomechanics, Monograph (in Russian), 1926.

12. Bernstein, N.A. Die kymocyclographische Methode der Bewegungs-Untersuchung. Handbuch der Biologischen Arbeitsmethoden, Vol. 5, Pt. 5a, Abderhalden, 1927.

13. Bernstein, N.A. Studies of the biomechanics of walking and running, Questions of the Dynamics of Bridges. Research of the Scientific Committee of the People's Comissariate of Transport, No. 63 (in Russian), 1927.

14. Bernstein, N.A. & Popova, T.S. Untersuchung der Biodynamik des Klavieranschlags. Arbeitsphysiologie, 1929, 1, 5.

15. Bernstein, N.A. Clinical Ways of Modern Biomechanics. Collection of papers of the Institute for Medical Improvement, Kazan, 1929.

16. Bernstein, N.A. Analyse der Körperbewegungen und Stellungen im Raum mittels Spiegel-Stereoaufnahmen. Arbeitsphysiologie, 1930, 3, 3.

17. Bernstein, N.A. & Dement'ev, E. Ein Zeit-Okular zu der Zeitlupe.
    Arbeitsphysiologie, 1933, 6, 4.

18. Bernstein, N.A., Mogilanskaia, Z. & Popova, T. Technics of Motion-Study
    (in Russian), Moscow, 1934.

19. Bernstein, N.A. et al. Studies of the Biodynamics of Locomotions (Normal
    Gait, Load and Fatigue). Institute of Experimental Medicine, Moscow
    (in Russian), 1935.

20. Bernstein, N.A. Modern data on the structure of the neuro-motor process.
    To the Musician-Pedagogue (in Russian), Moscow, 1939.

21. Bernstein, N.A. et al. Studies of the Biodynamics of Walking, Running
    and Jumping (in Russian), Moscow, 1940.

22. Bernstein, N.A. Current questions in modern neurophysiology. Physiology
    Journal U.S.S.R., 1945, 31, 5-6 (in Russian).

23. Bernstein, N.A. On the Construction of Movements. Monograph (in Russian)
    Moscow, 1947.

24. Bernstein, N.A. Fundamental biomechanical regularities of start-movements.
    Theory and Practice of Physical Culture (in Russian), Moscow, 1947.

25. Bernstein, N.A. An account of the theory of the construction of prostheses
    for lower limbs. Works of Moscow Scientific Institute for Prostheses,
    1948, 1 (in Russian).

26. Bernstein, N.A. & Salzgeber, O.A. Analysis of some three-dimensional
    movements of the arm and propositions basic to the construction of
    a working prosthesis, Works of Moscow Scientific Institute of
    Prostheses, 1948, 1 (in Russian).

27. Bernstein, N.A. & Buravtzeva, G.R. Coordination disturbances and
    restitution of the biodynamics of gait after brain damage. Thesis,
    7th Session of the Institute of Neurology, Moscow, Academy of Medical
    Sciences (in Russian), 1954.

28. Bernstein, N.A. Modelling as a means of study of neuromotor processes.
    Report of the Academy of Pedagogic Sciences, No. 2, 1952.

29. Bernstein, N.A. Current problems in the theoretical physiology of
    activity. Problems of Cybernetics, 1961, 6.

30. Bethe, A. & Fischer, R. Die Plastizität der Nervensysteme. Handbuch
    der normale und pathologische Physiologie, 1927, 10.

31. Braus, H. Anatomie des Menschen. Volume 1. Berlin, 1921.

32. Borowski, V.M. On transposition and abstraction in rats. Reflexes,
    Instincts and Habits, Volume 1 (in Russian). Moscow, 1935.

33. Brillouin, L. Science and Information Theory. New York, 1956.

34. Buytendijk, F. Allgemeine Theorie der menschlichen Haltung und Bewegung. Berlin, 1956.

35. Contini, R. & Drillis, R. Biomechanics. Applied Mechanical Reviews, 1954.

36. Drillis, R. Chronocyclographische Arbeitsstudien-Nagel Einschlagen. Psychophysiologische Arbeit, Riga, 1930.

37. Drillis, R. Untersuchungen über den Hammerschlag. Neue Psychologische Studien, 1933, 9, 2, München.

38. Drillis, R. Objective recording and biomechanics of pathological gait. Annals of the New York Academy of Sciences, 1958, 74, 1.

39. Drillis, R. The use of gliding cyclograms in the biomechanical analysis of movements. Human Factors 1, 2. Oxford: Pergamon Press, 1959.

40. Eberhart, H.D., Inman, V.T. et al. Fundamental studies of human locomotion and other information relating to design of artificial limbs. Subcontractor's Report to Committee on Artificial Limbs, National Research Council, 1947.

41. Eberhart, H.D. & Inman, V.T. An evaluation of experimental procedures used in a fundamental study of human locomotion. Annals of the New York Academy of Sciences, 1951, 51, 1213-1228.

42. Fischer, O. Der Gang des Menschen, Volume 1. Leipzig, 1895.

43. Fischer, O. Methodik der speziellen Bewegungslehre. Handbuch der physiologischen Methodik, Vol. 2, Pt. 1. Leipzig: Tigerstedt, 1911.

44. Foerster, O. Die Physiologie und Pathologie der Koordination. Zeitblad f. die ges. Neurol. Psychiatrie, 41, 11-12.

45. French, J. The reticular formation. Handbook of Physiology, Vol. 2. American Physiological Society, 1960.

46. Gelfand, I.M. & Tsetlin, M.L. The principal of non-local search in systems of automatic optimization, Report of the Academy of Sciences of the U.S.S.R., 1961, 137 (in Russian).

47. Gray-Walter, W. The living brain. London: Duckworth, 1953.

48. Gurevitch, M.J. Psychomotorics (in Russian). Moscow, 1930.

49. Gurfinkel, V.S. The dealy in the afferent feedback and the coordination of movements. Works of the Moscow Scientific Institute of Prostheses (in Russian), Moscow, 1958.

50. Gurjanov, E.V. Habit and Action. Scientific Papers, Moscow University, 1945, 90 (in Russian).

51. Krushinski, L.V. Studies on the extrapolation reflexes in animals, Problems of Cybernetics, 1959, 2.

52. Lewy, F. Die Lehre vom Tonus und der Bewegung. Berlin, 1923.

53. Luria, A.R. The disturbances of movements accompanying brain motor system affections. Scientific Papers of the Chair of Psychology of the Moscow University (in Russian), 1945.

54. Luria, A.R. Contribution to the question of forming of voluntary movements in the child. Report of the Pedagogic Academy, 1957, 1 (in Russian), Moscow.

55. Magnus, R. Die Körperstellung. Berlin, 1924.

56. Marey, E.J. La machine animale, locomotion terrestre et aèrienne. Paris, 1837.

57. Marey, E.J. La locomotion animale. Traité de physiologie biologique, Volume 1. Paris, 1901.

58. Mittelstaedt, H. Regelung und Steuerung bei der Orientierung der Lebewesen. Regelungstechnik, 1954, 2.

59. Monacow, C. Die Localisation im Grosshirn. Wiesbaden, 1914.

60. Moreinis, J.S. The study of the assymetry of movements in walking on a prosthesis. Works of the Central Institute of Prosthesis, Moscow, (in Russian), 1958.

61. Muybridge, E. The Human Figure in Motion. London: Chapman & Hall, 1901.

62. Penfield, W. Mechanisms of voluntary movement. Brain, 1954, 77.

63. Pribram, K. The intrinsic systems of the forebrain. Handbook of Physiology, Vol. 2. American Physiological Society, 1960.

64. Ponomarev, J.A. The psychology of creative thinking. Academy of Pedagogic Science, Moscow, Monograph (in Russian), 1960.

65. Salzgeber, O.A. Biodynamics of the locomotion of amputation. Works of the Central Institute of Prostheses, 1948, 1 (in Russian).

66. Setchenov, J.M. A sketch of the working movements of man. St. Petersburg (in Russian), 1901.

67. Sherrington, C. The integrative action of the nervous system. London, 1911.

68. Sommerhoff, G. Analytical Biology. Oxford: University Press, 1950.

69. Spielberg, P.J. Einfluss der Ermüdung ab den Gang. Arbeitsphysiologie, 1934, 7, 6.

70. Spielberg, P.J. Die Änderungen der Bewegungskoordinationen im Gange während des Arbeitstages. Arbeitsphysiologie, 1935, 8, 6.

71. Steinhausen, W. Mechanik des menschlichen Körpers (Ruhelagen, Gehen, Laufen, Springen), Handbuch der normale und pathologische Physiologie, 1930, 15, 1.

72. Strasser, E. Über die Grundbewegungen der aktiven Lokomotion. Halle, 1880.

73. Uchtomski, A.A. Lability - a condition for the synchronism and coordination of nervous acts. Works of the Physiological Institute of the Leningrad University, 1936, 17 (in Russian).

74. Uchtomski, A.A. The physiology of the motor apparatus. Selected of Papers, 1952 (Vol. 3 (in Russian), 1927).

75. Wagner, R. Probleme und Beispiele biologischer Regelung. Stuttgart: Thieme, 1954.

76. Weber, W. & Weber, E. Mechanik der menschlichen Gehwerkzeuge (1836), Berlin, 1894.

77. Wiener, N. Cybernetics, or control and communication in the animal and the machine. New York: Wiley, 1948.

78. Wiener, N. The human use of human beings. New York, 1954.

79. Zaporozhets, A.V. Development of voluntary movements. In, A. Simon (Ed.), Psychology in the Soviet Union, London, 1957.

80. Bernstein, N.A. The analysis of aperiodic sums of oscillations with variable spectra by the method of pondered grids. Biophysics (in Russian), 1962.

81. Drillis, R. The influence of ageing on the kinematics of gait. Geriatric Amputee, Publication 919, National Academy of Science, National Research Council, U.S.A.

82. Fidelus, K. Some biomechanical problems of coordination of movements in the light of investigations of functional currents in muscles. Wychowanie Fyzyczne i Sport, 1961, 5, 537 (in Polish).

83. Fidelus, K. Biomechaniczna Analiza Postawy. Wychowanie Fizyczne i Sport, 1961, 5, 155.

84. Keidel, W. Grenzen der Übertragbarkeit der Regelungslehre auf biologische Probleme, Naturwissenschaft, 1961, 48, 264.

85. Pribram, K. A review of theory in physiolocal psychology, Annual Review of Psychology, 1960.

86. Stanley-Jones, D. and K. The kybernetics of natural systems - a study of patterns of control. Oxford: Pergamon Press, 1960.

87. Chkhaidze, L. To the problem on the connection between the muscular tension and the resulting movement. Biophysics, 1961, 6, 363 (in Russian).

88. Wagner, R. Über Geschichte, Problematik und Bedeutung biologischer Regelung, Münch. med. Wochenschr. 1961, 103, 711.

AUTHOR INDEX

A

SUBJECT INDEX